THE SOCCER BOOK

THE SOCCER BOOK

THE TEAMS · THE RULES · THE LEAGUES · THE TACTICS

DK

 Penguin Random House

Writers David Goldblatt, Johnny Acton
Senior Editor Conor Kilgallon
Senior Art Editor Michael Duffy
Editors Bob Bridle, Chris Hawkes, Chris Stone
Designers Katie Eke, Brian Flynn,
Phil Gamble, Jillian Burr
Editorial Assistant Rory Thomas
Researcher Neil Mason
Illustrators Phil Gamble, Mike Garland,
Mark Walker
Production Editor Tony Phipps
Production Controller Imogen Boase
Managing Editor Stephanie Farrow
Managing Art Editor Lee Griffiths
Publisher Jonathan Metcalf
Art Director Bryn Walls
Produced with assistance from
Cooling Brown

REVISED EDITION
**Revised, project managed, and art directed
for DK by Dynamo Limited.**
Design Project Manager Andrew Fishleigh
Editorial Project Manager Emma McGuinness

DK DELHI
Art Editor Debjyoti Mukherjee
Editor Ekta Chadha
DTP Designer Jaypal Chauhan
Senior DTP Designer Harish Aggarwal
Senior Jackets Coordinator
Priyanka Sharma Saddi
Picture Researcher Sumedha Chopra
Pre-production Manager Balwant Singh
Senior Managing Editor Rohan Sinha
Managing Art Editor Sudakshina Basu
Creative Head Malavika Talukder

DK LONDON
Senior Art Editor Helen Spencer

Editor Daniel Byrne
Senior US Editor Megan Douglass
Production Editor Jacqueline Street-Elkayam
Senior Production Controller Rachel Ng
Jacket Designer Akiko Kato
Jacket Design Development Manager
Sophia MTT
Managing Editor Gareth Jones
Senior Managing Art Editor Lee Griffiths
Art Director Karen Self
Design Director Phil Ormerod
Associate Publishing Director Liz Wheeler
Publishing Director Jonathan Metcalf

This American Edition, 2023
First American Edition, 2009
Published in the United States by DK Publishing,
a division of Penguin Random House LLC
1745 Broadway, 20th Floor, New York, NY 10019

Dorling Kindersley Limited
24 25 26 27 10 9 8 7 6 5 4 3 2
002– 335613–Jun/2023

A catalog record for this book is available from the
Library of Congress.
ISBN: 978-0-7440-8078-0

DK books are available at special discounts
when purchased in bulk for sales promotions,
premiums, fund-raising, or educational use.

For details, contact: DK Publishing Special Markets,
1745 Broadway, 20th Floor, New York, NY 10019
SpecialSales@dk.com

Printed and bound in Slovakia

www.dk.com

CONTENTS

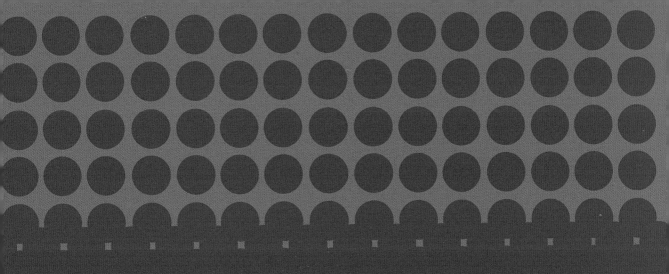

5. PLANET SOCCER

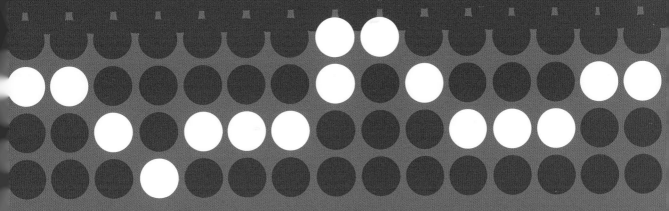

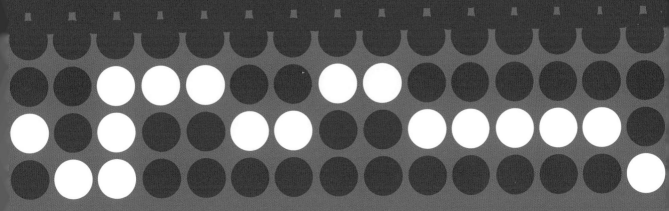

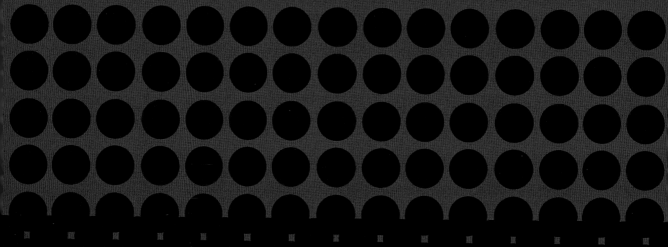

INTRODUCTION

Soccer is the most popular sport in the world. From Greenland to the Andes, people just can't seem to resist kicking a leather ball around or watching others doing the same. The figures are staggering. Approximately 250 million people play the game regularly. If players made up a nation, it would be the fifth most populous on earth. Meanwhile, it has been estimated that the global television audience for past World Cups has been nearly half of the total human population.

You could almost say that soccer is the universal language. If you found yourself in the middle of a strange country with no knowledge of the local tongue, you would still be able to strike up a conversation by using a few hand gestures accompanied by the names of some prominent players. Place one hand at chest level while saying "Pelé" then raise it with the word "Maradona," and you'll quickly start making friends.

Soccer brings people together and gives them a sense of identity. It is a never-ending soap opera that provides a timeline to our lives and a source of endless debate. All aspects of human existence are here: heroes and villains, love and loathing, power, politics, and money. Like life itself, the game provides moments of sublime beauty and others of crushing disappointment.

The Soccer Book celebrates this amazing diversity in full, from the relative merits of zonal and man marking to the most amusing bleacher chants. Within its pages, you will learn how to bend the ball like Beckham, meet the dog who found the World Cup hidden in a suburban garden, and discover how a Madagascan league game could possibly have finished 149–0. The one thing this book cannot do is provide an ultimate explanation of why people are so fascinated by soccer. Still, there's no harm in looking at some of the theories.

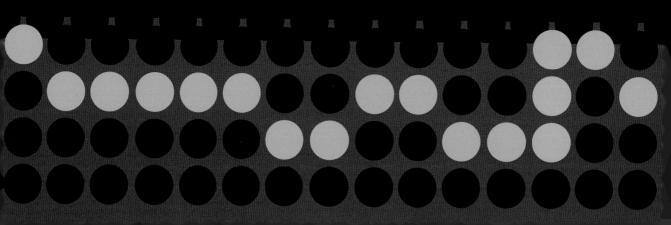

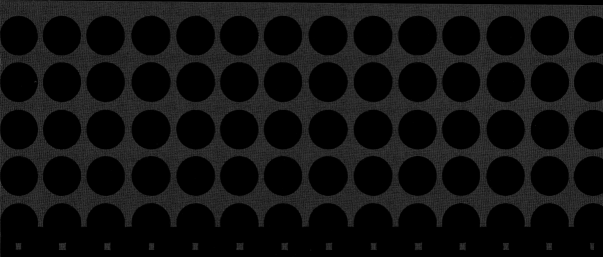

Some have claimed that the game is a surrogate for hunting—on which, of course, our ancestors depended for their survival. According to this view, a goal is equivalent to a kill, which would certainly explain the sense of importance surrounding the game. Another possibility is that soccer is a kind of ritualized warfare. After all, the sport is couched in military language (such as campaigns, tactics, and captains), and it may be no accident that its modern popularity with both players and spectators coincided with a period in which many young people were spared the rigors of combat in actual battles.

Both of these theories have their merits, but perhaps another, simpler explanation needs to be added. Our history can be seen as the story of an increasing split between our physical selves and our minds. Soccer works the other way around. By uniting the brain with the parts of the body at the opposite extremity (the feet), it temporarily heals the split. When we play the game or identify with others who are doing so, we become whole again. And, of course, it is not just men who feel this way. The women's game is extremely popular—for every reference to a "he" in this book, a "she" can and should just as easily be substituted.

Maybe even this overcomplicates things. We planned to write this book without using soccer's most famous and clichéd quotation, but in the end we might as well admit defeat. "Some people believe football [soccer] is a matter of life and death," the great Liverpool manager Bill Shankly once said. "I am very disappointed with that attitude. I can assure you it is much, much more important than that." No one has better captured the irrational depth of passion

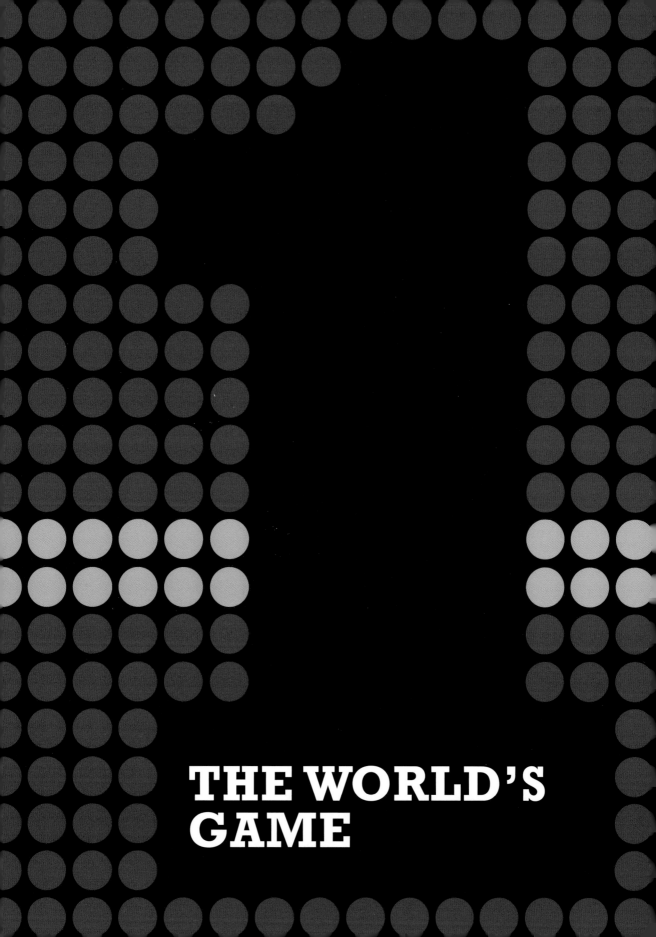

THE WORLD'S
GAME

ANCIENT BALL GAMES

Humanity has been kicking spherical objects for as long as both been around, but more formal games with balls date from at least 3,500 to 4,000 years ago, when ball games were played in Egypt and elsewhere. As with most good ideas, a lot of people had the same thought in different parts of the world, and each of them created their own distinct ancient ball game.

KEMARI
The game was enormously popular in Japan between the 10th and 16th centuries.

HISTORIC RELATIONS

Of all the ancient ball games, *cuju*, from China, in its oldest form, was the closest to modern soccer, with two teams moving a ball toward a fixed goal. But it was in Mesoamerica that a ball game acquired the kind of importance that soccer has today. For 3,000 years, the "ball game," as it was known, was a pastime, a spectator sport, a passion, and a ritual. Soccer as we know it today descends from the variety of riotous folk-soccer games played in medieval England.

THE WORLD'S FIRST MASS-APPEAL BALL GAME

Although the exact rules of the Mesoamerican ball game are not known, the sport's widespread popularity is not in doubt: ball courts have been found as far north as Arizona in the United States and as far south as Nicaragua in Central America. The main aim appears to have been to keep the solid rubber ball in play. The game was an integral part of society—it is thought that children played the game recreationally.

SOCCER FOR THE MASSES

English folk soccer, also known as "mob football," involved huge numbers of people (often the population of a village divided into two sides, based on who lived where) and few, if any, rules. Games were usually linked to special events in the calendar, such as saints' days. The sport was not universally popular, though: English Kings Edward II, Henry V, Edward IV, Henry VII, and Henry VIII all issued edicts against the over-rowdy game.

A ROUND BALL AND A SQUARE WALL. JUST LIKE THE YIN AND YANG

LI YU (50–136 CE) ON THE CHINESE GAME OF *CUJU*

EVOLUTION OF THE MODERN GAME

From Central America to the Roman Empire, history is littered with various types of ball game.

1500 BCE The first rubber ball is made in Mesoamerica

1200 BCE The first major Olmec ball courts emerge in Mesoamerica

350 BCE First written evidence of *harpastum* in Roman Empire

c. 200 BCE *Cuju* first formalized in the Han Dynasty, China

| 1500 BCE | 1250 BCE | 1000 BCE | 750 BCE | 500 BCE | 250 BCE | 0 |

SOCCER'S ORIGINS

The origins of soccer can be found in every corner of the world. Civilizations throughout history have all invented games that are played with balls, and every one of them can be considered as an ancient forerunner to the modern game.

CURIOUS DISCOVERIES

During the 1930s, Costa Rican banana plantation workers started to uncover enormous stone spheres hidden in the jungle. They weighed up to 16 tons (14 tonnes) and date to between 200 BCE and 1500 CE. No one knows their purpose, but they attest to the human fascination with spherical objects.

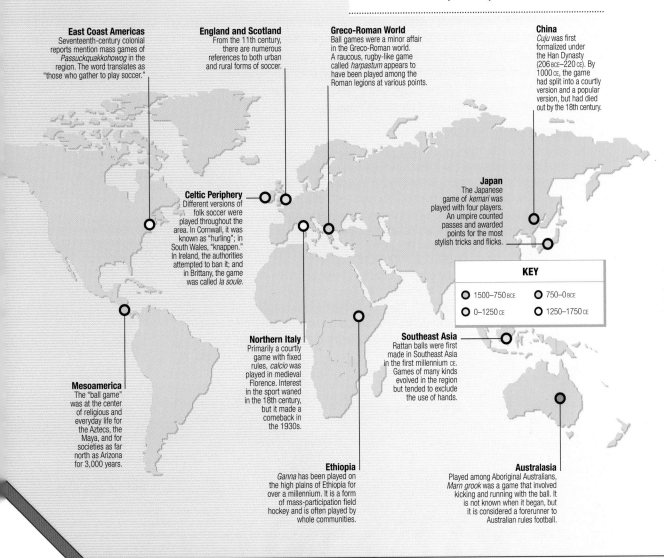

East Coast Americas
Seventeenth-century colonial reports mention mass games of *Passuckquakkohowog* in the region. The word translates as "those who gather to play soccer."

England and Scotland
From the 11th century, there are numerous references to both urban and rural forms of soccer.

Greco-Roman World
Ball games were a minor affair in the Greco-Roman world. A raucous, rugby-like game called *harpastum* appears to have been played among the Roman legions at various points.

China
Cuju was first formalized under the Han Dynasty (206 BCE–220 CE). By 1000 CE, the game had split into a courtly version and a popular version, but had died out by the 18th century.

Celtic Periphery
Different versions of folk soccer were played throughout the area. In Cornwall, it was known as "hurling"; in South Wales, "knappen." In Ireland, the authorities attempted to ban it; and in Brittany, the game was called *la soule*.

Japan
The Japanese game of *kemari* was played with four players. An umpire counted passes and awarded points for the most stylish tricks and flicks.

KEY
- 1500–750 BCE
- 750–0 BCE
- 0–1250 CE
- 1250–1750 CE

Northern Italy
Primarily a courtly game with fixed rules, *calcio* was played in medieval Florence. Interest in the sport waned in the 18th century, but it made a comeback in the 1930s.

Southeast Asia
Rattan balls were first made in Southeast Asia in the first millennium CE. Games of many kinds evolved in the region but tended to exclude the use of hands.

Mesoamerica
The "ball game" was at the center of religious and everyday life for the Aztecs, the Maya, and for societies as far north as Arizona for 3,000 years.

Ethiopia
Ganna has been played on the high plains of Ethiopia for over a millennium. It is a form of mass-participation field hockey and is often played by whole communities.

Australasia
Played among Aboriginal Australians, *Marn grook* was a game that involved kicking and running with the ball. It is not known when it began, but it is considered a forerunner to Australian rules football.

1100 First reports of *la soule* in France and street soccer in London

1750s First attempts to formalize *sepan tawak* in Malaysia

600 Evidence of *kemari* played in imperial court in Kyoto, Japan

800 Evidence of ball games played in southern Britain

1650 Puritans attempt to ban soccer after the English Civil War

1580 First rules of *calcio* published in Italy

250 CE   500 CE   750 CE   1000 CE   1250 CE   1500 CE   1750 CE

FROM FOLK TO ASSOCIATION

Soccer was transformed from a dying folk ritual in the British countryside to the world's most popular and commercialized sport in just a century. It was nurtured in England's elite universities and private schools before bursting out into the cities of Victorian Britain. Along the way, the game acquired field markings, 11 players per side, and a set of rules.

FOLK SOCCER

By the early 19th century, folk soccer was dying. Increasingly, the authorities feared the drunken mob and the impact their games would have on property and land. In 1835, the new Highways Act gave magistrates the power to ban street soccer, which they did. By the 1860s, the game had been taken into the private schools, where it underwent a transformation and emerged as what we now call "association soccer."

THE PRIVATE SCHOOLS AND SOCCER

Reformers in private schools in the early 19th century resolved to create muscular Christian gentlemen fit in mind and body to run the British Empire—and what better way to enforce this than through regular playing of soccer. Aside from physical activity, this new breed of schoolmaster hoped to teach their charges discipline, teamwork, fair play, and courage.

THE ETON FIELD GAME
A cross between soccer and rugby, the rules for this traditional game were documented for the first time in 1815.

YEAR	SOCCER FIRSTS
1857	The first dedicated soccer club, Sheffield FC, is established.
1870	Specified goalkeepers are used for the first time.
1872	First FA Cup final; first international.
1873	Players could be sent off for a serious offense for the first time.
1877	Match length fixed at 90 minutes.
1878	Referees use whistles for the first time.
1880	Crowds pay an admission fee to watch matches for the first time.
1882	Crossbars for goalposts are introduced.
1887	The center mark and center circle are first used.
1888	The first season of the Football League is played in England.
1895	The first official women's game is played.
1898	Linesmen introduced for first time.
1909	Goalkeepers first required to wear a different colored uniform.

PRIVATE SCHOOL GAMES

Played since the mid-18th century, the Eton Field Game has no offside rule and is closer to rugby than soccer (see left). Harrow Football, played with a large flat-bottomed ball, saw the first use of the defensive wall for free kicks. Winchester Football, a 6-, 10-, or 15-a-side game played on a long, narrow field, places an emphasis on kicking.

MAKING OF THE MODERN GAME

1846
Cambridge Rules drawn up at Cambridge University

1863
FA founded; FA rules first published

1872
First official international, England vs. Scotland, ends 0–0 in Glasgow; the first FA Cup final sees Wanderers beat Royal Engineers 1–0

1840   1850   1860   1870   1880

ESTABLISHING THE RULES

In November 1863, members of 12 London clubs met to agree on an accepted set of rules. They decided that there would be no carrying of the ball with the hands and no hacking (kicking an opponent's shins). Those who disagreed created rugby union; those who agreed wrote the rules of association soccer and created its governing body, the Football Association (FA).

1863 RULES

Field: maximum dimensions of 200 x 100 yards (180 x 90 m); goalposts should be 8 yards (7.32 m) apart, with no tape or crossbar.

Coin toss determines ends; kick off to be taken from center mark.

Teams change ends after every goal.

Goal scored if the ball is kicked between the two posts (at whatever height).

Throw-ins to be taken by player who first touches the ball after it has gone out of play; from the restart, the ball is not in play until it has touched the ground.

When a player kicks the ball, any teammate who is in front of the player is offside.

No running with the ball in the hands.

No hands to throw or pass the ball.

No tripping, hacking, or holding.

THE SPREAD OF SOCCER

As the first generation of players left the private schools and elite universities, they took soccer into the world with them. Once the rules had been set down, the game quickly spread to the middle and working classes. Throughout the 1880s, fierce competition between clubs saw under-the-counter payments to the best players. Through gritted teeth, the FA legalized professionalism in 1885.

THE EARLY SOCCER MAP

Association soccer grew out of traditional folk soccer (games of which are still played in some locations today) and evolved further in English private schools and universities.

CLUBS INVOLVED IN THE FORMATION OF THE ENGLISH FA IN 1863

Barnes
Blackheath (later withdrew)
Blackheath School
Charterhouse
Crusaders
Crystal Palace
Forest
Kensington School
No Names of Kilburn
Percival House
Surbiton
The War Office

KEY
- Major private schools
- Surviving folk-soccer venues
- Major universities

Scone
Duns
Alnwick
Sedgefield
Workington

Haxey
Ashbourne
Atherstone
Sutton Coldfield
Rugby
Cambridge
Oxford
Aldenham
Cheltenham
Harrow
Marlborough
Eton
Westminster
Winchester
Charterhouse
Corfe Castle

WILLIAM McGREGOR
A director at Aston Villa FC, the Scot is regarded as the founder of the Football League—the first organized soccer league in the world—in 1888.

1883
Blackburn Olympic beat Old Etonians in the FA Cup final—the first working-class team to win it

1885
FA legalizes professionalism in English soccer

1888
Football League created: Preston North End are the first champions

1892
Second Division created

1880
1890
1900

THE GLOBAL GAME

In just over a century, the professional game reached nearly every country and culture in the world. Soccer was traveling almost as soon as it was invented, through the many tentacles and connections of the formal British Empire (to South Africa, for example) and the huge network of British traders, sailors, miners, merchants, bankers, and teachers who traveled the globe in search of business in the late 19th century.

THE GREAT ENTERTAINER

Soccer's mass appeal can be explained because it is one of the simplest, most flexible games ever invented. It can be played on a variety of surfaces, by many different body types, and requires several skills rather than one. It needs almost no equipment, can be played without referees, and is an extraordinary and unpredictable game to watch. It demands a unique combination of individual skills and teamwork, and goals scored are both rare and special. Above all, anyone can beat anyone else.

CHARLES MILLER

The son of a rich coffee merchant, Charles William Miller (left) is considered the father of soccer in Brazil. Sent off to school in England in 1884 (aged 10), he returned to São Paulo in 1894 bringing with him two soccer balls and a set of rules. The following year, he arranged a soccer match between gas, bank, and railroad workers in the city. It was the first-ever organized soccer match played in Brazil.

EARLY SOCCER HOT SPOTS

In the late 19th and early 20th centuries, soccer took off in key cities, ports, and coastal regions around the world. These became beachheads from which the game would steadily expand to reach the provincial cities, countryside, and peripheries of every nation in the world.

Eastern United States
Despite the already established popularity of other sports in the United States in the 1880s and 1890s, new waves of working-class British immigrants established a thriving soccer culture in the years before World War I.

Mexico City
Soccer's popularity exploded in Mexico City at the turn of the 20th century as British expatriates formed clubs all over the city. The first league was contested in 1903.

Rio de Janeiro-São Paulo (Brazil)
Brazil's two biggest cities were the first home of soccer in the country. Men such as Charles Miller (see left) were important figures in soccer's development in the region.

Rio Plata
With more than 40,000 Britons in Buenos Aires in the 1870s and more in Montevideo, soccer established itself quickly on the Rio Plata. Buenos Aires had established a city league by 1891, and Montevideo followed a year later.

MAKING OF THE MODERN GAME

1900
First Olympic soccer tournament in Paris—Great Britain wins the gold medal

1904
Fédération Internationale de Football Association (FIFA) is established in Paris

1920s
Soccer becomes the sport of the working class all over Europe

1930
The first World Cup is played in Montevideo, Uruguay—the hosts become first world champions

MID-1930s
Shift to professionalism in continental Europe and Latin America

1900   1910   1920   1930   1940   1950

SOCCER ... IS DIRECTED AT PEOPLE WITH **ADVANCED CULTIVATED IDEAS**

SPECTATOR AT AN EARLY SOCCER MATCH, c. 1903

DIVISION AMONG THE RANKS

Not everyone was in favor of the game spreading to foreign parts. F. W. Campbell of Blackheath resigned from the infant FA when the practice of hacking was outlawed. "If you do away with [it], I will be bound to bring over a lot of Frenchmen who would beat you with a week's practice," he warned.

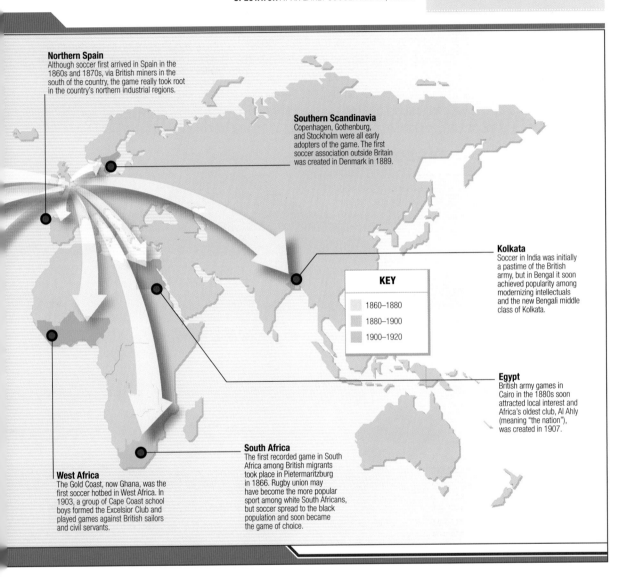

Northern Spain
Although soccer first arrived in Spain in the 1860s and 1870s, via British miners in the south of the country, the game really took root in the country's northern industrial regions.

Southern Scandinavia
Copenhagen, Gothenburg, and Stockholm were all early adopters of the game. The first soccer association outside Britain was created in Denmark in 1889.

Kolkata
Soccer in India was initially a pastime of the British army, but in Bengal it soon achieved popularity among modernizing intellectuals and the new Bengali middle class of Kolkata.

KEY

	1860–1880
	1880–1900
	1900–1920

Egypt
British army games in Cairo in the 1880s soon attracted local interest and Africa's oldest club, Al Ahly (meaning "the nation"), was created in 1907.

South Africa
The first recorded game in South Africa among British migrants took place in Pietermaritzburg in 1866. Rugby union may have become the more popular sport among white South Africans, but soccer spread to the black population and soon became the game of choice.

West Africa
The Gold Coast, now Ghana, was the first soccer hotbed in West Africa. In 1903, a group of Cape Coast school boys formed the Excelsior Club and played games against British sailors and civil servants.

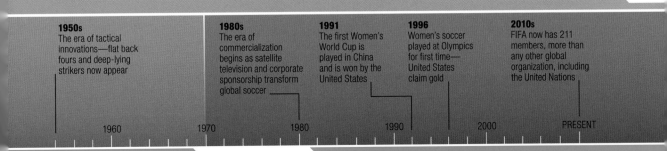

1950s
The era of tactical innovations—flat back fours and deep-lying strikers now appear

1980s
The era of commercialization begins as satellite television and corporate sponsorship transform global soccer

1991
The first Women's World Cup is played in China and is won by the United States

1996
Women's soccer played at Olympics for first time— United States claim gold

2010s
FIFA now has 211 members, more than any other global organization, including the United Nations

1960   1970   1980   1990   2000   PRESENT

THE WORLD'S GAME

INTO THE 20TH CENTURY

It was only at the turn of the 20th century that soccer fields began to take on their modern form and not until the 1920s that the rules finally settled down. The game achieved immediate and widespread popularity and was soon transformed into the biggest mass-entertainment sport in Victorian Britain. It did not take long before the rules and innovations spread around the world and formed the basis of what we now know as a global game.

THE EVOLUTION OF THE SOCCER FIELD

The FA's first rule book in 1863 contained no field markings. In fact, it took until 1882 for the sidelines and goal lines to become compulsory. By then, the size of the field had shrunk, and a steady series of rule changes and innovations turned the blank, muddy fields of the 1860s into the modern markings that are used all over the world today.

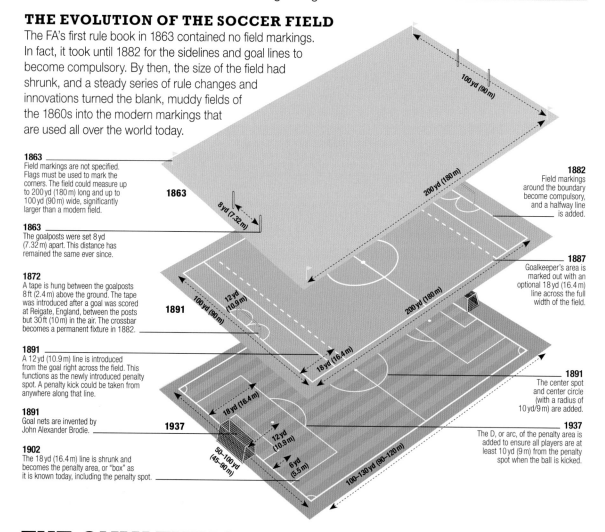

1863
Field markings are not specified. Flags must be used to mark the corners. The field could measure up to 200 yd (180 m) long and up to 100 yd (90 m) wide, significantly larger than a modern field.

1863
The goalposts were set 8 yd (7.32 m) apart. This distance has remained the same ever since.

1872
A tape is hung between the goalposts 8 ft (2.4 m) above the ground. The tape was introduced after a goal was scored at Reigate, England, between the posts but 30 ft (10 m) in the air. The crossbar becomes a permanent fixture in 1882.

1891
A 12 yd (10.9 m) line is introduced from the goal right across the field. This functions as the newly introduced penalty spot. A penalty kick could be taken from anywhere along that line.

1891
Goal nets are invented by John Alexander Brodie.

1902
The 18 yd (16.4 m) line is shrunk and becomes the penalty area, or "box" as it is known today, including the penalty spot.

1882
Field markings around the boundary become compulsory, and a halfway line is added.

1887
Goalkeeper's area is marked out with an optional 18 yd (16.4 m) line across the full width of the field.

1891
The center spot and center circle (with a radius of 10 yd/9 m) are added.

1937
The D, or arc, of the penalty area is added to ensure all players are at least 10 yd (9 m) from the penalty spot when the ball is kicked.

THE ONLY THING THAT HASN'T CHANGED IS ... THE SHAPE OF THE BALL

FORMER MANCHESTER UNITED AND SCOTLAND FORWARD **DENIS LAW**

HISTORY OF THE OFFSIDE RULE

Soccer had been plagued by the offside issue from its very earliest private school forms—the perennial problem of how to stop players from hanging around the goal. The offside rule (see pp.66–67) was designed to prevent thi s and has undergone subtle revisions since its inception in 1863.

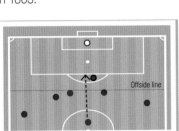

1863 A player is offside unless three players of the opposing side are in front.

● Attacking team
● Defensive team
● Offside player
- - Pass

1925 A player is offside unless two opponents are in front of the player when the ball is received.

● Attacking team
● Defensive team
● Offside player
- - Pass

1990 A player is onside if level with—rather than just behind—the second-to-last opponent.

● Attacking team
● Defensive team
● Offside player
- - Pass

HOW SOCCER BECAME A SPECTATOR SPORT

Crowds had gathered to watch kickabouts since the 1850s, but in Victorian Britain, the crowds began to boom in the 1870s and 1880s. The working week was getting shorter, wages were increasing, and, as professionalism arrived in 1885, the quality of play and the size of stadiums began to grow. Large numbers of fans from the north of England began to make FA Cup Final day in London a day-out pilgrimage, and in just 30 years, attendance at the match had grown more than 50-fold. This was mirrored around the world where soccer fever quickly caught on.

RISE IN POPULARITY

FA Cup final attendances 1872–1901

1872	1892	1897	1901
2,000	**25,000**	**65,891**	**114,815**

TOP 5: DERBIES

Derbies are the big, tension-filled games between two local rivals—usually from the same city. The term is derived from either the folk-soccer game played in Ashbourne, Derbyshire, or from the often chaotic games of street soccer played in the city of Derby.

GALATASARAY vs. FENERBAHÇE
Istanbul's biggest derby pits Galatasaray, from the European side of the city, against Fenerbahçe, the biggest team on the Asian side of the Bosphorus. The geographical divide is heightened by a social one: Galatasaray grew out of one of the most elite schools in the city, while Fener has always been the people's club.

RIVER PLATE vs. BOCA JUNIORS
El Superclásico is the biggest derby in Buenos Aires, a city full of intense local rivalries. It pitches the upmarket, uptown River Plate against the low-down, downtown Boca. The rivalry is as much about style as social origins.

OLYMPIACOS vs. PANATHINAIKOS
Known in Greece as the "Derby of the Eternal Enemies," the game pits Olympiacos (from the working-class port zone of Piraeus) against Panathinaikos (from the well-heeled central districts of Athens). The result often determines the outcome of the Greek league.

PARTIZAN vs. RED STAR
The two clubs were founded within six months and one-third of a mile (500 m) of each other in central Belgrade. Partizan was the team of the Yugoslav army; Red Star the team of the police and Communist party. The game has become even more intense since the breakup of Yugoslavia in 1992.

CELTIC vs. RANGERS
The "Old Firm" play out the oldest derby in the world. Passions are always high but have been regularly inflamed by the state of community relations in Glasgow between Protestants and Catholics, and especially by the political conflicts that took place in Ireland.

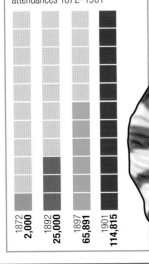

MO JOHNSTON
The striker (who played for Celtic between 1984 and 1987) defied tradition in 1989 when he turned down a chance to rejoin his former team and signed for the club's arch-rivals, Rangers.

FUTSAL (FUTEBOL DE SALÃO)

Futsal is FIFA's official form of indoor five-a-side soccer. Invented in Uruguay—and perfected in Brazil—in the first half of the 20th century, it uses a small, heavy ball that ensures a frenetic, high-speed game in which touch, control, and love of the ball are the keys to success. It is the fastest-growing variant of soccer in the world.

FUTEBOL DE SALÃO

Juan Carlos Ceriani, who worked at Uruguay's Montevideo YMCA in the 1930s, was the first person to think systematically about playing soccer on a basketball court—which every YMCA possessed, since it had invented basketball in the first place. However, because a standard soccer ball was too large and bouncy for the game to be played on the polished, hardwood floors, something smaller and more controllable was required before the game could really take off.

MAKING ITS MARK

The new ball was perfected, and the first rules of what was then called *futebol de salão* ("drawing-room soccer") were created at Brazil's São Paulo YMCA in 1936. The ball was weighted with a mixture of cork, horsehair, and sawdust and then reduced in size. In Brazil, the game's first nickname was "sport of the heavy ball," though in the end the compressed futsal—an abbreviation of *futebol de salão*—won out.

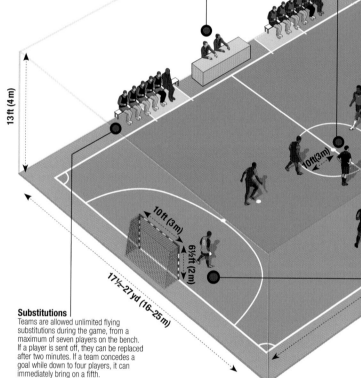

Timekeeper and third referee
A timekeeper and a third referee sit outside the playing area on the same side of the field as the substitute zone. The timekeeper monitors time; the third referee keeps a record of a team's number of fouls.

Officials
Futsal is played with two referees on the field. The first referee has the final say; the second referee assists.

13 ft (4 m)

10 ft (3 m)

10 ft (3 m)

6½ ft (2 m)

17½–27 yd (16–25 m)

Substitutions
Teams are allowed unlimited flying substitutions during the game, from a maximum of seven players on the bench. If a player is sent off, they can be replaced after two minutes. If a team concedes a goal while down to four players, it can immediately bring on a fifth.

THE RULES

1. Size 3 or 4 ball with reduced bounce (see pp.76–77).

2. Five players.

3. Unlimited flying substitutions.

4. Smaller-sized goal: 10 x 6½ ft (3 x 2 m).

5. Ball kicked into play.

6. Referee and an assistant plus a third referee and a timekeeper.

7. Running clock.

8. Twenty-four-minute halves.

9. One time-out per team per half.

10. No offsides.

11. Goalkeeper throws ball back into play.

12. Four-second rule to put ball back into play.

13. Five-foul limit.

14. Defending team not allowed to form a wall for free kicks.

15. Player sent off can be substituted after two minutes.

16. Corners taken from corner arc.

17. No slide tackles are allowed.

THE SKILLS

BALL TOUCHES

A statistical study comparing futsal to indoor-arena soccer with walls showed that players are 210 percent more likely to touch the ball in futsal.

BALL CONTROL

Playing in such a limited space and under constant pressure, futsal demands improved ball-control skills and a calm temperament.

SPEEDY PLAY

With fewer stoppages than in the 11-a-side game, the four-second restart rule, and smaller spaces to cover, players must learn to play and think faster; there is nowhere to hide on a futsal court.

SUPPORT PLAY

Without a wall to bounce the ball off, players must make supporting runs when their teammates have the ball.

GETTING ORGANIZED

Rules were not codified in Brazil until the 1980s, and until that time bizarre variants of the game existed across the country (see below). In 1988, FIFA took co-responsibility for the sport, alongside the International Futsal Federation, and the first FIFA Futsal World Cup (won by Brazil) was held in the Netherlands the following year.

EQUIPMENT

A major factor in futsal's increasing popularity is that it does not require much equipment to play, simply a specialized indoor ball (with a reduced bounce) and rubber-soled, non-marking sneakers.

25–26 in (63.5–66 cm) circumference

Rubber soles
Molded soles aid a player's control and movement during a match.

The goal
The goalposts must be 10 ft (3 m) apart, and the lower edge of the crossbar must be 6½ ft (2 m) above the ground. The lower part of the net is attached to the goal frame's curved tubing, creating a depth of 31½ in (80 cm) at the top and 3½ ft (1 m) at the bottom.

Five fouls and the second penalty spot
Teams are allowed five fouls that result in free kicks. If a player commits a team's sixth foul, the free kick becomes a penalty taken from the second penalty spot.

Ceilings
Many futsal arenas are indoors, and the ceiling must be at least 13 ft (4 m) high. If a player kicks the ball and it hits the ceiling, then play is restarted with a kick-in for the opposing side.

Kick-in
If a ball crosses the touchline or goal line, it is kicked back into play. Players must be 16½ ft (5 m) away from the ball when it is kicked back into play.

Indirect free kicks
Goalkeepers concede a free kick if they control a back pass from one of their own players with their hands or if they control the ball for more than four seconds in their own half.

6 m) radius

3 ft (10 m)

27–46 yd (25–42 m)

THE BALL

Only a size 3 ball with a circumference of 23–24 in (58.5–61 cm) or a size 4 ball with a circumference of 25–26 in (63.5–66 cm) can be used (see pp.76–77).

SHOES

The only types of footwear permitted in futsal are canvas or soft-leather sneakers with soles made of rubber or a similar material.

BIZARRE BEGINNINGS

Unusual rules existed in the early days of futsal in Brazil. In some states, players who had a hand on the floor could not play the ball. Consequently, players would fall in absurd ways to keep their hands off the floor, resulting in a huge increase in fractures.

FALCÃO

Alessandro Rosa Vieira, better known as Falcão, was one of the world's leading futsal players. He appeared at five FIFA Futsal World Cups and scored 400 goals for his country.

IN FUTSAL YOU NEED TO **THINK AND PLAY QUICK,** SO IT IS EASIER FOR YOU WHEN YOU PLAY OUTDOOR SOCCER

PELÉ

BEACH SOCCER

People have been playing with a ball on the beach for many years, but it wasn't until the 1920s, in Rio de Janeiro, that the game acquired informal rules and new, evolving styles of play. Mayor Henrique Dodsworth tried to ban the game from the beaches at that time but received a petition containing 50,000 signatures complaining about his proposed actions. The rules were formalized in 1992 in an attempt to make it suitable for television.

MADE FOR TV

Beach soccer, in its new version, was designed for television. The three periods, 12 minutes in length, provide perfectly timed, regular advertising breaks without the need to introduce time-outs. The creation of temporary, closed mini-stadiums removed the problems of overcrowding and spectator intrusion. The main appeal, however, is that beach soccer delivers relentless shots on goals and high-scoring games.

THE FIELD

The playing surface must be level, composed of sand, and free of any stones, pebbles, or any other objects that could cause injury to players. In international competitions, the sand used must be fine (rather than coarse) and at least 15¾ in (40 cm) deep.

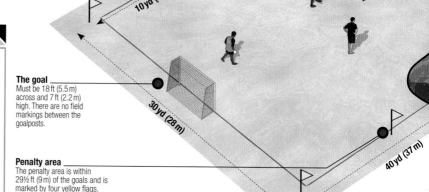

Officials
Beach soccer has two referees on the field and one off it who is charged with keeping the team benches under control.

Halfway line
Two red flags on opposite sides of the field represent the halfway line.

10 yd (9 m)

30 yd (28 m)

40 yd (37 m)

The goal
Must be 18 ft (5.5 m) across and 7 ft (2.2 m) high. There are no field markings between the goalposts.

Penalty area
The penalty area is within 29½ ft (9 m) of the goals and is marked by four yellow flags.

THE RULES

1. Five-a-side.

2. Unlimited substitutions.

3. No shoes allowed.

4. Coin toss determines choice of ends.

5. Goalkeepers must throw the ball back into play rather than kick it.

6. There are three periods of 12 minutes with a three-minute break between each period.

7. No draw. In the event of a tie, three minutes of overtime is followed by sudden-death penalties.

8. No offside rule.

9. Defenders are not allowed to form a wall for free kicks; all defending players must be at least 16 ft (5 m) away when the kick is taken.

10. No kicking sand in anyone's face.

11. Free kicks to be taken by the person who was fouled.

12. Balls that cross sidelines can be put back into play either as a throw-in or a kick-in.

13. Yellow card awarded for serious fouls.

14. Blue card awarded after second yellow-card offense. Recipient is suspended for two minutes and cannot be replaced.

15. Red card awarded for very serious fouls or for a third yellow-card offense. A team can replace dismissed player after two minutes.

OLD HABITS DIE HARD

Some traditions from the 11-a-side game carry over to beach soccer. At the 2006 Beach Soccer World Cup, held in Rio de Janeiro, Brazil, Uruguay came back from 1–0 down to beat Argentina 2–1 and knock them out of the competition. The game, already fractious, descended into a vast melee of players and officials fighting after the Uruguayans celebrated their second goal.

ON SAND YOU CAN NEVER BE SURE OF ANYTHING

ERIC CANTONA

EQUIPMENT

In keeping with its informal nature, the emphasis in beach soccer has always been on keeping the game and equipment simple and cheap. Players wear neither shoes nor socks, field markings are minimal, and no walls or sideboards are allowed around the field.

30 Average time in seconds between every shot on goal in a beach soccer match

14 Number of Beach Soccer World Championship titles won by Brazil up to 2019—the most won by any nation

17 Goals scored by Italy's Gabriele Gori at the 2017 World Championship. With 16 goals, he was also the top scorer at the 2019 event

ERIC CANTONA
Eric Cantona (above) was one among the many professional soccer stars to have moved from the 11-a-side game to beach soccer. After retiring from Manchester United in 1997, Cantona was a key figure in building the French national beach soccer team.

soccadelic BEACH SOCCER

Beach ball
The ball's soft polyurethane (PU) cover is forgiving on a player's bare feet.

27–28 in (68.5–71 cm) circumference

BALL
The ball is the same size as those used in the 11-a-side game, with a circumference between 27–28 in (68.5–71 cm), but beach soccer balls are much lighter.

Shin protection
A high-density shield provides durable protection for the shins.

SHIN GUARDS
Players may wear adapted shin guards for protection: ankle supports, giving support to a player's ankles, are also permitted.

SKILLS

Sand is a very difficult surface on which to run and over which to pass a ball. On the other hand, it is much better to fall on than either grass or concrete. Given this, and the small, intense space and time in which the game is played, beach soccer uses all the skills of 11-a-side soccer but favors some over others.

TOUCH

Touch is everything in any version of soccer, but in beach soccer, players needs to practice the kind of touch and control that enables them to pluck the ball out of the air, because that's where it will be a lot of the time.

KEEP IT UP

The ball is harder to control and slower to move in the sand, so a player tries to keep the ball in the air and not on the ground. Chips and flicks are much more effective than long, slide-rule passes along the ground.

VOLLEYING

With small goals and crowded penalty areas, a shot needs to be accurate and fast if a player wants to score. Anyone who can volley a pass, or flick the ball up and volley it themselves, is going to do well.

HEADING

With so many balls coming in the air, a player has to use his head, not just for scoring but as another form of passing.

ACCELERATION

The sand saps much of the power from players' legs and can prevent them from accelerating away from opponents. If players can develop both the strength and balance to overcome this, they will have a real edge over their opponents.

OVERHEAD KICK

A rare but spectacular feature of the 11-a-side game, the overhead kick is commonplace in beach soccer.

INDOOR/STREET SOCCER

Indoor soccer takes a number of different forms, but what distinguishes these forms from the official indoor variant—futsal (see pp.22–23)—is that they use walls and boards instead of touchlines. The ball can be played directly off the wall, which eliminates the need for throw-ins, goal kicks, and corners, and so produces a very fast-paced game.

INDOOR SOCCER

In Britain, the main form of indoor soccer is five-a-side, which is played both informally and in organized leagues around the country. In the United States and in Spain, the game is usually played with six players. All the different leagues in the world play slightly different rules and versions of the game, but they have many similar features.

The team
Five or six players, one of whom is the goalkeeper. Substitutes are permitted

Walls
Walls or boards—at least 6 ft (1.8 m) high in the US version of the game—surround the field

The ball
For games that are played on hardwood, the ball is generally covered with suede

The crease
Some versions of indoor soccer enforce a special zone inside the goalkeeper's box called the "crease." No player may shoot from inside the crease unless the player was already in possession of the ball when entering it. If a defender enters the crease, a penalty is awarded to the opposition.

The pitch
Most indoor soccer is played on artificial turf. The game can also be played on hardwood basketball courts

30 yd (27.4 m)
8 yd (7.3 m)
5 yd (4.6 m)
50 yd (45.7 m)

MASTERS SOCCER

Masters soccer is an indoor competition open to retired professional players over the age of 35, who play in six-a-side teams representing their old clubs. The field is 66 x 33 yd (60 x 30 m), there is no offside, and the games consist of two 8-minute halves. The format was particularly popular in the UK up until 2011, when the last tournament was played. There is also an international version of the Masters tournament, which was won by the Netherlands in 2006.

INDOOR SOCCER RULES

Indoor soccer rules vary around the world, but these are among the most commonly found ones.

1. Most professional indoor soccer games play four quarters of 15 minutes, with overtime for draws. Amateur leagues tend to play two 25-minute halves with no overtime.

2. If the ball flies over the walls or touches the ceiling, play is stopped and the opposing team is awarded a free kick at the point of the infringement.

3. Standard contact rules as used in the 11-a-side game.

4. There is no offside in indoor soccer.

5. No headers allowed.

6. The ball is not allowed to go above head height. If it does, the opposition is awarded a free kick at the point of the infringement.

7. Some versions of the game rule that the ball may not cross three lines without touching the ground. The lines are evenly spaced along the length of the field, one of them being the exact center.

INDOOR LEAGUES

BELGIUM: Belgian Indoor Board Football League

SPAIN: Campeonato Nacional de Liga de Fútbol Indoor

UNITED STATES AND MEXICO: National Indoor Soccer League

UNITED STATES, CANADA, AND MEXICO: Major Arena Soccer League

The Major Arena Soccer League offers an elite level of indoor soccer, with thousands regularly watching in the stadiums. It features men's and women's teams.

STREET SOCCER

Soccer has always been a game of the city, and where there is no grass, the street has served as a field. Coats function as goalposts, a goalmouth is chalked on a wall, and rules are invented as a match progresses. Generations of players have honed their ball skills in these tight, crowded spaces.

STREET SOCCER RULES AND VARIANTS

Street soccer is played with the minimum of rules and accommodates any number of players. No one plays offside because there are no officials and there are no time limits unless agreed. When team numbers are uneven, rules evolve or are invented to deal with the situation.

TAKING SOCCER OFF THE STREETS

One explanation often put forward for the supposed decline in standards in English soccer is the gradual disappearance of street soccer. Local regulations, the installation of speed bumps, and a general increase in intolerance have all taken their toll on this traditional form of the game.

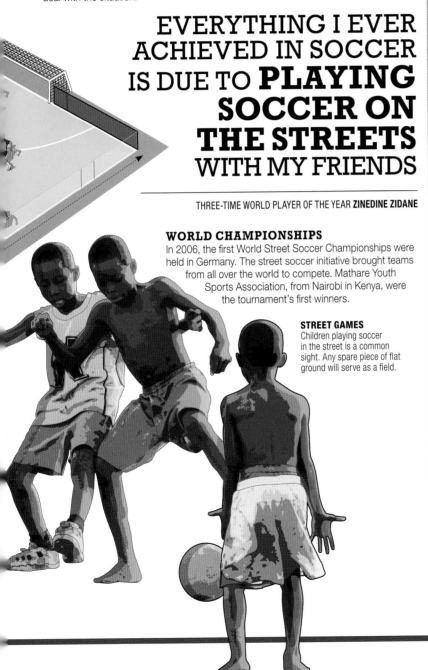

EVERYTHING I EVER ACHIEVED IN SOCCER IS DUE TO **PLAYING SOCCER ON THE STREETS** WITH MY FRIENDS

THREE-TIME WORLD PLAYER OF THE YEAR **ZINEDINE ZIDANE**

WORLD CHAMPIONSHIPS

In 2006, the first World Street Soccer Championships were held in Germany. The street soccer initiative brought teams from all over the world to compete. Mathare Youth Sports Association, from Nairobi in Kenya, were the tournament's first winners.

STREET GAMES

Children playing soccer in the street is a common sight. Any spare piece of flat ground will serve as a field.

STREET VARIATIONS

CUBBIES

Also known as "Wembley Doubles." One player goes in the game's only goal. Any number of other players must try to score and stop other players from doing so.

60 SECONDS

Played with one goalkeeper and at least two other players. The goalkeeper kicks the ball out, and then others have to cooperate to score with a volley within 60 seconds.

21

One player goes in goal; three or more others try to score goals from volleys or headers. Points are awarded for the manner in which goals are scored.

FOUR NETS

The game is played with multiple goals and multiple teams, often four. Teams have to score a set number of goals into one of the opposing team's nets.

GOL PARA MI

A three-player game in which a goal is set up against a fence or wall. One player starts as goalkeeper but can't use his hands. Shots have to be at waist height or below.

MUNICH

Played one on one. Players have two touches to score in their opponent's goal from within their own half. Players may not enter their own penalty area or their opponent's half.

THREE AND IN

A game played with any number of players, one of whom is the goalkeeper. When an outfield player scores three goals, the player changes positions with the goalkeeper.

HEADERS AND VOLLEYS

A game played with a minimum of three players, one of whom is the goalkeeper. Players can only score goals with either a header or a volley.

POINTS

The goalkeeper awards points out of five for each goal scored, typically five for an outstanding attempt, such as an overhead kick. The first player to score 20 points wins.

TEN SHOTS

A two-player game. Each player takes turns to take 10 shots against the other player, who goes in goal. The winner is the player who scores the most goals out of 10.

SHOOTIES

A game played with a minimum of two players. Each player is allowed only in his own half and is allowed only one touch of the ball before shooting.

FREESTYLE SOCCER

Freestyle soccer is essentially juggling with a ball in as creative a fashion as possible. As in the real game, any part of the body can be used except the hands and arms. At the highest level, freestyle is like a cross between break dancing and gymnastics, with a sprinkling of martial arts and a soccer ball thrown into the mix. Originally a street art, freestyle soccer is rapidly becoming a legitimate sport in its own right.

FREESTYLE SOCCER'S ORIGINS

People have been juggling with balls without using their hands for millennia. During Japan's Heian Period (794–1185 CE), for instance, a ritualized form of the game, called *kemari* (see p.15), was extremely popular at the Japanese imperial court. Since then, almost all children have tried to develop clever solo tricks to impress their friends. Freestyle in its modern form, however, owes its popularity to two things: the advertising industry and video sharing on the Internet. Both have propelled the sport into the limelight and are a constant source of inspiration and fun.

UNOFFICIAL WORLD CHAMPIONSHIPS

The sport is now recognized by an international governing body, the World Freestyle Football Association (WFFA), and a world tour competition takes place each year, with events taking place on different continents. Previously unheard-of players, such as Mr. Woo (see far right), John Farnworth, Nam "the Man," and Arnaud Garnier, have shot to prominence as freestyle soccer players and have gone on to feature in a number of television advertisements.

YOU NEED TO HAVE A STRONG WILL, PUT IN THE TIME AND THE EFFORT, AND REMEMBER ... THERE ARE **NO SHORTCUTS**

MR. WOO

US PRESIDENT PLAYS *KEMARI*

During a state visit to Japan in 1992, George Bush, Sr. noticed a game of *kemari* in progress at the old Imperial Palace in Kyoto. He decided to join in, despite not being dressed in the required traditional costume. When he further violated the game's etiquette by heading the ball, the president of Japan, Hirotada Kohno, joined the American president to ensure that any ensuing embarrassment would be diffused.

IMPRESSING THE JUDGES
Style and an impressive array of tricks mark a stand-out freestyle soccer performance.

THE JUDGES' BRIEF

MARKS OUT OF 10

According to the WFFA, established in 2005, performers should be given marks out of 10 in the following categories:

1. Control: demonstrating and maintaining ball control using various parts of the body.
2. Transitions: moving fluidly from one trick to the next.
3. Use of both feet.
4. Use of entire body, except hands.
5. Combinations: including consistently completing the same move twice or more.
6. Sticks: stalling the ball on different parts of the body.
7. Variety of tricks.
8. Level of difficulty.
9. Creativity: originality and imagination shown in performance, using crowd reaction as a guide.
10. Blotto: pushing the envelope of the sport to new levels.

IN THE HANDS OF THE GODS

Freestyle soccer hit the silver screen in 2007 with the release of *In the Hands of the Gods*. The much-acclaimed documentary follows five British freestylers from varied backgrounds as they attempt to use their skills to raise enough money to track down their idol, Diego Maradona—the player considered by many to be the father of the freestyle soccer movement. In a journey that changes their lives forever, the five finally track down the Argentine star at his home in Buenos Aires.

8:32 Duration in hours and minutes of Tomas Lundman's record for head-juggling a ball, set on February 27, 2004

644 Year of first written reference to *kemari*, the ancient Japanese ancestor of freestyle soccer

MR. WOO
One of the stars of freestyle soccer, Woo Hee-young has appeared in numerous advertisements and holds several world records.

MADE FOR TV

For several years, a leading sports equipment manufacturer has had a policy of using top soccer players in its advertisements. The one that really catapulted freestyle soccer into public consciousness featured the Brazil squad for the 1998 World Cup performing tricks around an airport. Players subsequently filmed doing incredible things with soccer balls have included Ronaldinho, Lionel Messi, Wayne Rooney, and Cristiano Ronaldo.

FEMALE FREESTYLERS

In the 21st century, there has been a surge in skillful female players displaying their solo tricks and talent. The World Freestyle Football Federation introduced their first female-only competition in 2011. Freestyle artists like Kathy Vije, Melody Donchet, and Kitti Szász have wowed crowds and arenas.

MAJOR FREESTYLE TOURNAMENTS

Rules may not have been standardized, and the sport may lack an official world championship, but there have been several important freestyle soccer events over the years.

MASTERS OF THE GAME I

An organization called "Masters of the Game" held a tournament at the Amsterdam Arena, Netherlands, in 2003. It was won by South Korea's Mr. Woo (above).

MASTERS OF THE GAME II

The second Masters of the Game world championship was held in 2006 and was won by the UK's John Farnworth.

KOMBALL KONTEST

The Komball Kontest held in France in 2008 introduced a new format for freestyle competitions. Sixteen participants performed individually in front of three judges, with the best eight progressing to a knockout phase. Ireland's Nam "the Man" Ngueyen was crowned European soccer freestyle champion.

RED BULL STREET STYLE

Created in 2008, the Red Bull Street Style world finals were held in São Paulo, Brazil. A panel judged the participants on technique, style, ball control, and their ability to synchronize their movements with background music.

PARALYMPIC SOCCER

Paralympic soccer describes variants of association soccer that have been adapted for people with disabilities. Games played by the deaf have perhaps the longest history. Two versions, played by the visually impaired and those with cerebral palsy, have become paralympic sports. Amputee soccer has grown hugely, especially in Africa, whereas in the richer nations of the global north, power wheelchair soccer has prospered.

FIRST WORLD CROWN

Spain hosted and won the first Blind Futsal World Cup in 2005, beating France 1–0 in the final. Seven teams—all from Europe—competed, and the biggest win went to Italy, who beat Russia 5–0 to take fifth place.

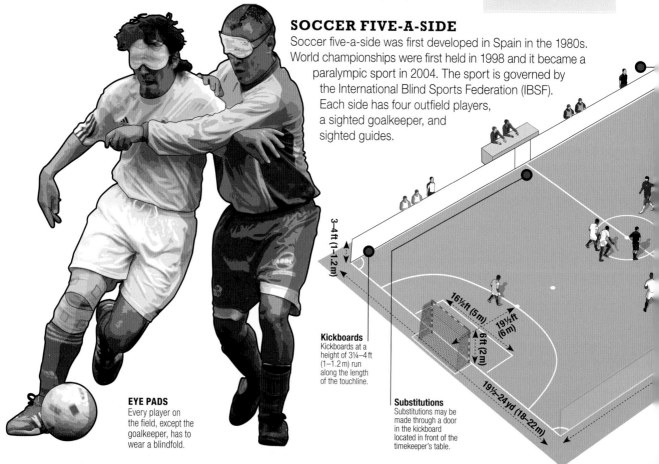

SOCCER FIVE-A-SIDE

Soccer five-a-side was first developed in Spain in the 1980s. World championships were first held in 1998 and it became a paralympic sport in 2004. The sport is governed by the International Blind Sports Federation (IBSF). Each side has four outfield players, a sighted goalkeeper, and sighted guides.

EYE PADS
Every player on the field, except the goalkeeper, has to wear a blindfold.

Kickboards
Kickboards at a height of 3¼–4 ft (1–1.2 m) run along the length of the touchline.

Substitutions
Substitutions may be made through a door in the kickboard located in front of the timekeeper's table.

3–4 ft (1–1.2 m)

16½ ft (5 m)

19½ ft (6 m)

6 ft (2 m)

19½–24 yd (18–22 m)

THE RULES

1. Field is surrounded by boards.

2. Two 25-minute halves.

3. Teams are allowed to use sighted goalkeepers and guides.

4. The four outfield players must wear blindfolds.

5. No offside.

6. Unlimited substitutions.

7. A player who has committed five fouls during a match may take no further part in the game.

8. A player who is sent off may be replaced after a period of five minutes.

9. Teams are allowed one time-out (of one minute) per half.

10. Teams must field at least two B2 category players (see right) at all times.

ELIGIBILITY

B1 Totally or almost blind.

B2 Partially sighted—able to recognize the shape of a hand up to visual acuity of 2/60.

B3 Able to recognize the shape of a hand up to visual acuity from between 2/60 and 6/60.

SEVEN-A-SIDE SOCCER

This version of soccer is designed for players with cerebral palsy and other neurological disorders, especially those resulting from a stroke and other kinds of brain injury. The Cerebral Palsy International Sports and Recreation Association governs the sport. International competitions began in 1978, and it became an Olympic sport in 1984.

DEAF SOCCER

Deaf soccer is played to standard FIFA rules and has grown out of the organized communities of deaf people all over the world. Scotland boasts the oldest deaf soccer club in the world, Glasgow Deaf Athletic Football Club, which was founded in 1871. Leagues and cup competitions for deaf people have been running for many years all over the world.

THE RULES

1. Field: 41½–46 yd (38–42 m) by 19½–24 yd (18–22 m).
2. Ball rolled into play from throw-ins with one hand.
3. Two 30-minute halves.
4. At least one C5 or C6 player (see below) at all times.
5. No more than two C8 players (see below) at the same time.

ELIGIBILITY

C5 Athletes with difficulties when walking or running but not when standing or kicking a ball.
C6 Athletes with control and coordination problems of upper limbs.
C7 Athletes with hemiplegia (i.e., suffering from paralysis on one side of the body).
C8 Minimally disabled athletes.

Officials
Matches are officiated by three officials (two on opposite sides of the field and one who oversees substitutions) and a timekeeper.

DEAF AND PROFESSIONAL

Deafness is only a minor hurdle for a player, and several deaf players have gone on to enjoy a successful career in the professional game. Former deaf players include Cliff Bastin (Arsenal and England) and Rodney Marsh (Fulham, QPR, Manchester City, and England).

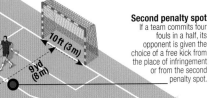

Second penalty spot
If a team commits four fouls in a half, its opponent is given the choice of a free kick from the place of infringement or from the second penalty spot.

10 ft (3 m)
9 yd (8 m)

The ball
The ball has a circumference of 23½–24½ in (60–62 cm), with a pressure of 0.4–0.6 atmospheres. It also contains a sound system.

41½–46 yd (38–42 m)

Guides' areas
The field is split into three imaginary zones, each of which is controlled by one of the team's guides.

OTHER VERSIONS

Ingenuity and imagination mean that the loss of a limb or being restricted to a wheelchair are not barriers when it comes to playing soccer. Confirming the all-inclusive spirit of the game, soccer for amputees and wheelchair soccer are becoming more popular year after year.

WHEELCHAIR SOCCER

Wheelchair soccer is played on a standard five-a-side field. Players may use any wheelchair, but most use battery-powered ones. The sport was first created in France in the 1970s, while a similar version emerged in North America in the 1980s. In 2005, the International Federation of Power Football Associations was created.

SOCCER FOR AMPUTEES

Officially, an amputee is someone who is "abbreviated" at least at the wrist or ankle. Outfielders may have two hands but only one foot. Goalkeepers may have two legs, but only one hand. The game is played without prostheses and always on metal crutches. A player's crutches may touch the ball incidentally, but they can't be used to pass or shoot.

WHEELCHAIR SOCCER
Most wheelchairs can be adapted to protect the player's feet with plates or bumpers that are used to strike the ball.

BECAUSE OF [SOCCER], PEOPLE RECOGNIZE US IN A POSITIVE WAY. MOST OF ALL, I JUST FEEL HAPPY WHEN I AM PLAYING

JIMMY HARRISON
FIRST CAPTAIN OF LIBERIA'S NATIONAL TEAM, 2006

GRASSROOTS SOCCER

Soccer has to be played before it can be watched or followed. At the base of every healthy soccer culture is a vigorous network of clubs, players, and coaches who do it for the love of the game. In the developed world, the challenge is to get players away from their game consoles, phones, and tablets and out onto the field. In the developing world, players are plentiful—it's fields and equipment that are in short supply.

THE SOCCER HIERARCHY

International soccer and professional club soccer are at the tip of an enormous hierarchy of playing, organizing, and coaching that makes a soccer culture. Without a huge base of youth and recreational soccer, the professional game can't hope to recruit the playing and administrative talent of the next generation, or secure a wide base of fans and enthusiasts.

INTERNATIONAL SOCCER									
	ELITE CLUB SOCCER								
		PROFESSIONAL CLUB SOCCER							
			SEMI-PROFESSIONAL SOCCER						
				ORGANIZED AMATEUR SOCCER					
					UNORGANIZED AMATEUR SOCCER				
						ORGANIZED SOCCER			
							UNORGANIZED SOCCER		
								ARMCHAIR FANS	

> ## GRASSROOTS SOCCER IS FOR ALL AGES, GENDERS, SIZES, SHAPES, LEVELS OF SKILL, NATIONALITIES, FAITHS, RACES ...
> ## EVERYONE!
>
> **JÜRGEN KLINSMANN**
> FORMER GERMAN SOCCER PLAYER AND MANAGER

PARENTAL INFLUENCE

Grassroots soccer would struggle without the efforts of the legions of parents (often the moms) who routinely ferry their children to and from the practice field—the so-called "soccer moms."

HACKNEY MARSHES

Hackney Marshes is an area of wetland in East London and is considered the San Siro of grassroots soccer. Matches have been played there since the 19th century, and the area contains more than 80 soccer fields.

SOCCER CRAZY

Youth soccer can be plagued by overly competitive and demanding parents who rage on the touchline screaming at opponents and abusing referees—sometimes before the game has even started. Incidents occur around the world and include a father who drove his car onto the field in protest at a referee's decision and refused to back it off unless the decision was reversed.

PLAYERS OF TOMORROW

Youth soccer has proved hugely successful in recent years, and that success is dependent on a whole army of parents, coaches, and caregivers.

WORLD GRASSROOTS CUPS

The two biggest grassroots youth tournaments in world soccer are the Norway Cup and the Swedish Gothia Cup. The Norway Cup was started in 1974, and in recent years more than 1,500 youth teams from over 40 nations have competed. The Gothia Cup, held in Gothenburg, Sweden, is very similar. It started in 1975, and more than a million young players from 149 countries have participated in it. In 2015 a record 1,754 teams attended.

SUPER TOURNAMENT

With world stars such as David Beckham, Paul Scholes, and Sergio Busquets making appearances as teenagers, the SupercupNI has been a showcase for young talent since it started in 1983. Originally called the Milk Cup, the tournament is held every year in Northern Ireland, and top teams from around the world regularly send junior players to take part. The competitive games and the prestige of winning gives these talented young players the chance to shine on a big stage.

GLOBAL INITIATIVE

Launched in 2002, streetfootballworld is a global nongovernmental organization that networks the world's grassroots soccer projects. Connecting leagues, teams, and players on six continents, streetfootballworld channels money and expertise to soccer projects that are linked to social development, education, and environmental programs. The first Street Football World Championship was held in Germany in 2006.

WAYNE ROONEY

The legendary England goal scorer's career started on the streets and playing fields of his native Liverpool. He made his debut with Everton at 16.

11,000,000

The estimated number of people playing soccer in England

2006

The year of the inaugural Street Football World Championship, in Berlin, Germany, in which 24 teams competed

605

Percentage increase in the number of registered female players in the UEFA (European) confederation since 1985

FEEDING THE GRASSROOTS

A healthy grassroots structure sends a constant stream of new playing and coaching talent to the elite game, and sustains the interest and enthusiasm of its future fan base. UEFA, the group responsible for developing and looking after the sport in Europe, released details of its support for the grassroots game from 2020 onward. Some of the key initiatives include the Football in Schools, Grassroots club development, and Together WePlayStrong campaigns. In the wake of the COVID-19 pandemic, UEFA remains committed to attracting and retaining players at a youth level for the good of the game in the long run. Together WePlayStrong has a powerful message across social media and is designed to encourage girls to take up, and continue playing, soccer and to promote women's competitions.

WATCHING THE GAME

Soccer is nothing without its crowds. For well over a century, they have paid the players' wages, filled the stadiums with atmosphere, and served as both a chorus and commentary on the game. Nothing is sadder than a match played behind closed doors to empty stands. Crowds have changed in many ways over the years, but the energy and passion they bring has not diminished.

MUSICAL INSTRUMENTS

Music has played a major part in creating a charged atmosphere in stadiums for many years. Rapid Vienna had its own fans' orchestra in the 1920s, African stadiums pulsate to the beat of drums, and the England team is followed by a brass band who hammer out the theme tune to *The Great Escape*.

FOLLOWING THE TEAM
Rosettes and rattles were the way to show support for a team in the early 1920s.

SOCCER FAN HISTORY

Vast crowds first started to gather in Britain's industrial cities in the mid-1880s and the first "break club"—drinking parties of fans going to away games—was created in Glasgow. The crowds that came to the grounds found their home on the terraces, which became a natural breeding ground for communal banter. Later, chanting and singing started, creating a cauldron of noise, although modern all-seat stadia can be less raucous, albeit safer for spectators.

WHEN **THE CROWD SURGES**, A MAN CAN BE **LIFTED OFF THE GROUND** ... AS IF BY SOME SOFT-SIDE CRANE

ARTHUR HOPCRAFT DESCRIBING A SCENE ON THE KOP AT ANFIELD IN THE 1960s BEFORE ALL-SEATER STADIUMS ARRIVED, IN HIS BOOK *THE FOOTBALL MAN: PEOPLE AND PASSIONS IN SOCCER*

THE CHANGING FACE OF SOCCER

What was once akin to a mass gathering at a factory gate has become more like a day out at a shopping mall. Following the mass introduction of all-seater stadiums after the Hillsborough disaster in 1989, it is no longer possible to stand through a game at many top league matches around the world. Some things don't change, though: the ubiquitous poor-quality halftime snack still remains many fans' food of choice.

OLD STADIUMS

SEATS: Most standing on concrete bleachers

CROWD CONTROL: No monitoring and few police

CONDITIONS: Most fans exposed to all weather; few facilities such as bathrooms at the stadiums

FOOD: Generally bad and almost universally unhealthy

ADVERTISEMENTS: Hand-painted billboards

CLASS: Overwhelmingly working class

GENDER: Almost 100 percent men

MUSIC: No music, no announcements, and no PA system

MODERN STADIUMS

SEATS: All-seater grounds; some clubs are thinking of reintroducing some standing terracing

CROWD CONTROL: Highly organized by ushers; widespread use of CCTV cameras

CONDITIONS: Most fans under roofs; many more facilities and corporate hospitality

FOOD: Variable, often traditional

ADVERTISEMENTS: Video screens and advertising hoardings

CLASS: Diverse mix of class and background

GENDER: 15–20 percent women

MUSIC: Relentless advertising, cheesy announcements, and loud music

ATTENDANCES

As more countries create professional leagues and the popularity of the game continues to grow, global attendances at soccer matches are steadily rising. The best-attended leagues are in Europe—the Premier League in England, the Bundesliga in Germany, and La Liga in Spain. All attract more than 11 million fans a season. In recent years, the Championship—England's second-level league—has become the fourth most attended league in the world, ahead of Serie A in Italy and Ligue 1 in France.

TICKET PRICES

In the early days of professional soccer in Europe and Latin America, ticket prices were kept low—on par with a trip to the musical hall or to the movies. With an overwhelmingly working-class clientele, there was no sense in pricing customers out of the market—though stopping them from jumping the turnstiles or climbing over walls to get into the stadium was far trickier.

80,841
Average attendance at Borussia Dortmund matches in the 2018–2019 season

40,867
Highest average attendance in Europe—at Germany's Bundesliga in the 2019–2020 season

10.8
Total attendance (in millions) at England's Championship during the 2018–2019 season— the best-attended second-tier league in the world

TICKET PRICE EXPLOSION

In the early years of soccer, tickets for matches were priced to attract working-class fans. In more recent years, however, ticket prices have skyrocketed. The graphic below shows the meteoric rise in FA Cup final ticket prices (in dollars) from the 1930s to the present day.

- 1930: **$0.29**
- 1970: **$0.81**
- 1990: **$9.62**
- 2016: **$67.50**
- 2019: **$62–200**

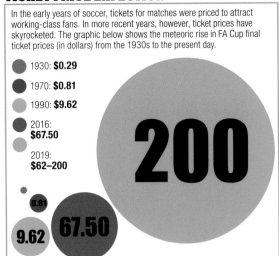

SOCCER AS A CARNIVAL

Sometimes the crowd can be the best thing about soccer. Fans have been making a carnival of the game for more than a century. Homemade rosettes, hats, and banners started appearing in the 1920s. Pioneered by fans of the Danish national team, face paint arrived in the 1980s, while fans of the Dutch national team have filled stadiums with their unbroken banks of orange shirts for a number of years.

MODERN FANS
Replica shirts, baseball caps, and team scarves are a must for the modern soccer supporter.

THE MEXICAN WAVE
The origins of the Mexican wave, produced by fans standing and sitting in order around the stadium, is disputed. Some say Frank Zappa started it at a rock festival in 1969; others say it started at ice hockey rinks—but it reached a global public at the 1986 World Cup in Mexico.

FAN CULTURE

Following the game in between matches has always been important. Indeed, soccer magazines were on sale even before the game turned professional in the 1880s. Fans today can follow soccer in innumerable ways—through radio, TV, smartphone, Internet coverage, newspapers, magazines, and an ever-growing number of books. In addition, there are fantasy soccer leagues, betting, computer games, board games, and a mountain of other soccer-themed memorabilia.

BRAZIL'S #1 FAN

Claudio Ribeiro, better known as "Cotton Bud," became Brazil's #1 fan in the 1970s. At Brazil World Cup games, cameras liked to hover on his huge afro and energetic dancing. He attended World Cup finals and claimed never to leave the country with a valid ticket, but always managed to find his way into the stadiums.

NEWSPAPERS

Despite the rise of the Internet, some soccer cultures still require their daily fix in print. In Italy, one of the bestselling newspapers— *Gazzetta dello Sport* (with an average daily circulation of more than 150,000 copies)—is devoted to sports and in particular soccer. Italy is not alone: Portugal has three dailies focused on soccer, Spain has four, and Greece, incredibly, had nine at one time.

THE NATURAL STATE OF THE SOCCER FAN IS ... BITTER DISAPPOINTMENT

AUTHOR AND ARSENAL FAN **NICK HORNBY**

CIRCULATION OF SPORTS NEWSPAPERS

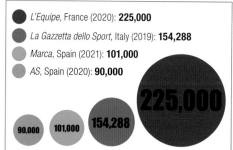

- *L'Equipe*, France (2020): **225,000**
- *La Gazzetta dello Sport*, Italy (2019): **154,288**
- *Marca*, Spain (2021): **101,000**
- *AS*, Spain (2020): **90,000**

225,000
154,288
101,000
90,000

RADIO

The BBC in the UK aired the first live radio broadcast of a soccer match in 1927, between Arsenal and Sheffield United. Fans loved being able to follow the action as it happened, and the idea quickly spread around the world, making commentators cult heroes as they revealed their respective countries' passion for the game. Radio still broadcasts games, and post-match radio phone-ins allow fans to air their views.

ARY BARROSO

Ary Barroso was the leading soccer commentator on Brazilian radio in the 1940s and '50s. Moonlighting from his day job as one of the country's great composers, his accounts of games would be accompanied by him playing the harmonica and hysterical partisan support for his club Flamengo. He was the first to report live from the field, interviewing players before, during, and after games.

FANZINES

In the 1970s and '80s, a new generation of soccer fans and writers emerged. Taking their cue from the do-it-yourself ethos of punk rock, they began to make their own magazines and to say things that official club publications and the traditional press could not.

FOLLOWING THE GAME

ELECTRONIC	PRINT MEDIA		MERCHANDISE		GAMES	
Club websites	Newspapers	Yearbooks	Club credit cards	Mugs/glasses	Table foosball	Soccer pools
Television	Fanzines	Trivia books	Club shirts	T-Shirts	Subbuteo	Spot the ball
Videos	Club magazines		Bed linen	Bags/backpacks	Computer games	Fantasy soccer
DVDs	Books		Pajamas	Posters	Board games	
Cellphone text alerts	Encyclopedias		Towels	Calenders		
Soccer-related music	Biographies		Baby clothes	Mouse pads		
Social media	Autobiographies		Club scarves	Soft toys		
Podcasts						

TELEVISION

Although experiments began before World War II, matches were not televised live until the 1950s—parts of the 1954 World Cup were broadcast live across Europe. Resistance among traditionalists was fierce—they feared that no one would come to games if it could be seen live on television, but their fears were largely unfounded.

TV VIEWERS FOR TOURNAMENT FINALS

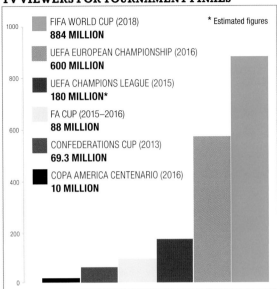

* Estimated figures

FIFA WORLD CUP (2018)
884 MILLION

UEFA EUROPEAN CHAMPIONSHIP (2016)
600 MILLION

UEFA CHAMPIONS LEAGUE (2015)
180 MILLION*

FA CUP (2015–2016)
88 MILLION

CONFEDERATIONS CUP (2013)
69.3 MILLION

COPA AMERICA CENTENARIO (2016)
10 MILLION

FULL-TIME PASSION
Following a favorite team has become a 24-hour-a-day pastime for many soccer fans.

THE MEMORABILIA INDUSTRY

Although fans have been collecting soccer memorabilia for a long time, it is only since the 1980s that prices for old programs, shirts, medals, and balls have begun to climb. Soccer programs have certainly proved to be a good investment.

SOCIAL MEDIA

The Internet and social media give fans and supporter groups a chance to express their passion and opinions about the teams, tournaments, and players that they support. Social media can be a power for good and promote all areas of the game. Unfortunately, though, online abuse can also become a problem.

VIRTUAL SOCCER

Console and computer games have enabled fans to simulate the sport and compete with friends online. Since the release of its first edition in 1993, the official FIFA series has sold more than 300 million copies worldwide, making it the bestselling sports video game series in the world. More recently, fantasy soccer, a parallel online soccer universe in which fans can create imaginary teams from real league players, has also become popular.

139,900 The price paid (in dollars) at auction for Geoff Hurst's 1966 England World Cup Final shirt

728,500 The price paid (in dollars) at auction for the oldest surviving FA Cup, dating from 1896 when Sheffield Wednesday beat Wolverhampton Wanderers at the Crystal Palace

7,000,000 The price paid (in British pounds) at auction for Diego Maradona's 1986 World Cup Final shirt—when he scored twice against England

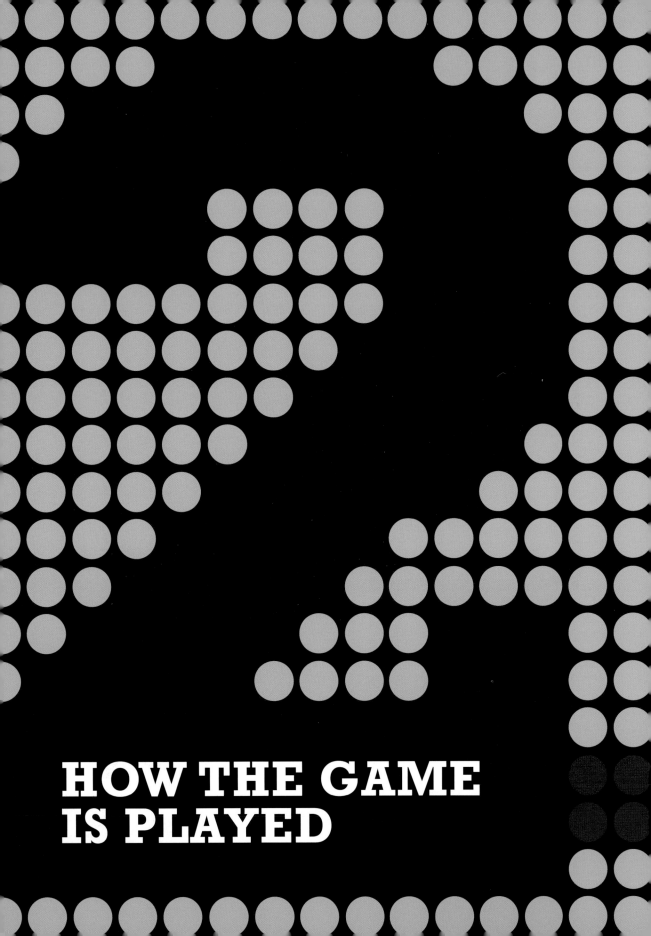

HOW THE GAME
IS PLAYED

THE FIELD

Professional soccer is played on a flat grass or artificial turf field, the markings of which must be in a set position. However, the overall area of the field may vary. The playing area must be rectangular—the length of the sideline must be greater than the length of the goal line.

PLAYING SURFACE

Outside of the professional game, soccer can be played on any flat surface—such as sand, hard-packed mud, or synthetic materials—but natural turf is the most desirable. However, turf needs people to maintain it, using tractors, rollers, forks, and sprinklers. But whatever the surface, anyone can play social soccer: all that is needed are two teams, a ball, two goals, and an even surface.

THE FIELD OF PLAY

The outer extremes of the field are delineated by the sidelines and goal lines: if the ball wholly crosses the sideline, it is out of play; if the ball crosses the goal line between the goalposts, a goal is scored. If part of the ball is on the line, it is still in play.

Penalty spot
The penalty spot is located 12 yd (11 m) from the goal line. Penalty kicks are taken from here.

Goal area
Also known as the 6-yard box, goal kicks are taken from anywhere inside this area.

Technical area
Both teams have a technical area that extends 3 ft (1 m) on either side of the dugout. One person at a time is allowed to shout instructions from here.

Penalty area
Also known as the 18-yard box, the goalkeeper can handle the ball anywhere inside this area. Fouls committed in this area result in a penalty kick.

Field diagram labels: 18 yd (16.5 m); 10 yd (9.15 m); 10 yd (9.15 m); 12 yd (11 m); 6 yd (5.5 m); 6 yd (5.5 m); 100–130 yd (90–120 m); 50–100 yd (45–90 m); 10 yd (9.15 m); 4¾ in (12 cm)

SIZE MATTERS

Barcelona's Nou Camp stadium has one of the largest fields in the world. It measures 115 yd x 78 yd (105 m x 72 m). Opened in 1957, the stadium can hold nearly 99,000.

FIELD DIMENSIONS

The Laws of the Game published by FIFA (see pp.62–63) state that the position of the field markings within the playing area is unchangeable. There is, however, a degree of flexibility regarding the overall dimensions of the field. The permitted range of field sizes varies depending on whether matches are being played in domestic or international competitions (see right). The line markings must be 4¾in (12 cm) in width.

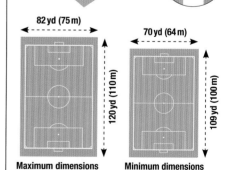

100 yd (90 m) — **131 yd (120 m)**
Maximum dimensions

49 yd (45 m) — **98 yd (90 m)**
Minimum dimensions

DOMESTIC GAMES
For domestic games, the overall size of the field can range between the measurements shown above, as long as the field does not become square.

82 yd (75 m) — **120 yd (110 m)**
Maximum dimensions

70 yd (64 m) — **109 yd (100 m)**
Minimum dimensions

INTERNATIONAL GAMES
For international games, the dimensions of the field can vary within allowed parameters, although the range is narrower than it is for domestic matches.

24,428

The weight in tons (22,161 metric tons) of stone, gravel, sand, and soil that is used to create a typical professional soccer field

23

The distance in miles (37 km) of undersoil heating pipes at Manchester United's Old Trafford stadium

1

The number of time capsules buried at Wembley Stadium

528

The distance in yards (0.6 km) of white lines on a typical playing surface

1

The optimum length in inches (25 mm) of the blades of grass

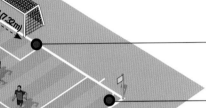

Goal
A goal is placed in the center of each goal line and must be 8 yd (7.32 m) long.

Goal line
When the ball crosses this line, a goal kick or corner is awarded, depending on which team kicked it out of play.

Corner arc
Corner kicks are taken from the corner arc, which has a radius of 1 yd (1 m).

Center mark and circle
A game begins, or recommences after a goal or following halftime, from the center mark. Opposing players must not encroach inside the center circle until the kickoff has taken place.

Halfway line
This line divides the playing area into two equal halves.

Sideline
If the ball wholly crosses this line, a throw-in is awarded to whichever team did not put the ball out of play.

IMPERFECT FIELD?

English team Yeovil Town's former field at Huish was famous in the game for its alarmingly sloping field. There was a difference in height of approximately 6 ft (1.8 m) from one side to the other. The site of the old field, which is located in the center of the town, is now home to a supermarket.

TOP 5: MOST UNUSUAL FIELDS

Every field is unique, but the following are among the most unusual in the world.

ESTADIO HERNANDO SILES

Bolivia's national stadium is 2⅓ miles (3.6 km) above sea level. In May 2007, following complaints that competing at this altitude left many players gasping for breath, FIFA banned the playing of international matches more than 1¾ miles (2.75 km) above sea level. After protests from affected nations, FIFA backed down.

THE FLOAT AT MARINA BAY

Having decided to demolish Singapore's National Stadium, the island state's authorities chose to build a giant floating field anchored in Marina Bay. The first competitive matches were played on the platform in February 2009.

ADIDAS FOOTBALL PARK

In 2001, a field was opened on the roof of the Tokyu Toyoko department store in Tokyo's Shibuya district. Approximately 500 teams have since registered to play futsal there—130 ft (40 m) above the space-strapped metropolis.

MOUNT SAJAMA

In 2001, two 20-minute halves of soccer were played on the flat summit of South America's second highest mountain— 4 miles (6.5 km) above sea level.

GRYTVIKEN

The world's most southerly permanent soccer field is located at Grytviken on the island of South Georgia in the South Atlantic Ocean (latitude 54.3 degrees south). The island is still used by British Antarctic Survey staff.

PLAYING SURFACES

According to the Laws of the Game (see pp.62–63), official matches may be played on either natural or synthetic surfaces. Artificial fields must meet the requirements set out by FIFA, and the surface must be green.

NATURAL PLAYING SURFACES

Grass is the most natural form of playing surface. At the highest level, grass fields are regularly watered and forked to improve drainage and get air to the roots. Typically, fields will be re-turfed at least once a season to maintain high standards. Many feature undersoil heating to prevent frost damage.

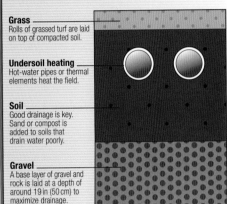

Grass
Rolls of grassed turf are laid on top of compacted soil.

Undersoil heating
Hot-water pipes or thermal elements heat the field.

Soil
Good drainage is key. Sand or compost is added to soils that drain water poorly.

Gravel
A base layer of gravel and rock is laid at a depth of around 19 in (50 cm) to maximize drainage.

ARTIFICIAL PLAYING SURFACES

Artificial, or synthetic, surfaces have existed since 1965 when AstroTurf™ was used in the Astrodome in Houston, Texas. In soccer, the surface was initially popular in the 1980s, before falling out of favor. In recent years, FIFA has expressed renewed interest in artificial fields following technological advances, and artificial grass is now "woven" into real grass to make the pitches more durable.

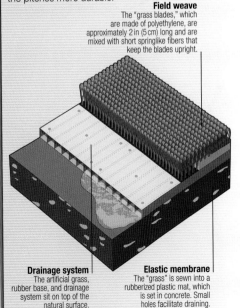

Field weave
The "grass blades," which are made of polyethylene, are approximately 2 in (5 cm) long and are mixed with short springlike fibers that keep the blades upright.

Drainage system
The artificial grass, rubber base, and drainage system sit on top of the natural surface.

Elastic membrane
The "grass" is sewn into a rubberized plastic mat, which is set in concrete. Small holes facilitate draining.

HOW THE GAME IS PLAYED

DEFENDERS

Defenders are responsible for preventing the attacking team from scoring and for winning back possession of the ball so that a counterattack can be mounted. While every player on the field must contribute to these two tasks, responsibility lies most heavily with the defenders. They can be categorized as either "central" (see opposite) or "wide" (see p.44).

THE DEFENDER'S ROLE

In addition to taking individual initiative when required, defenders must work with their teammates, using a variety of skills and tactics. Defenders force the attacking team to make mistakes by marking opponents closely, intercepting their passes, and gaining possession of the ball. Defensive strategies may involve "zonal defending" or "man-to-man marking" (see pp.90–93).

SKILLS REQUIRED

The defender must be a highly skilled player who is able to bring the ball out of defense in a controlled way before making accurate passes to teammates who are better placed to set up attacking moves. An ability to accurately anticipate threats is important, as is possessing the necessary levels of concentration to focus on the task at hand. Courage and excellent technical ability combine in the defender to produce a player willing to make last-ditch tackles in front of the goalmouth. Strength and precision will also enable the player to deal effectively with one-on-one attacks wherever they happen to occur on the field.

Defensive pressure
The player being marked is under constant pressure from the defending player.

MARKING
When a defender closely shadows the movements of an attacker, this is known as marking. The defender may be able to intercept the ball, or an attacker may be dissuaded from passing to a marked teammate.

Quick work
Defenders need fast reflexes to intercept well.

INTERCEPTING
When a defender intercepts an attacker's pass, this is often the result of the pressure applied by the defending team as a whole, through persistent marking and closing down the available space.

THE ULTIMATE PRICE

When defenders make mistakes, a goal often results. One such mistake was made by Andrés Escobar, a defender for Colombia in the 1994 World Cup. His own goal, which helped knock his team out of the tournament, cost him his life—he was gunned down on his return to Colombia.

ROBERTO AYALA
Ayala was regarded as one of the best central defenders in the game. He played 115 games for Argentina, with 63 of those as captain.

Battle for possession
The defender launches a feet-first slide toward the ball; they must tackle the ball and not the player.

TACKLING
Using the feet to take the ball away from a player is known as tackling. The sliding tackle (above) can be highly effective, but the defender's timing must be perfect, and there is a risk of conceding a foul.

FIELD PERFORMANCE

Defenders must be able to "read" the game well. On average, they make more interceptions per game than any other player:

Interceptions made by a player per game—**15**

Interceptions made by a defender per game—**20**

15   **20**

CENTRAL DEFENDERS

The role of the central defender, which includes the positions center back and sweeper (see below), requires constant alertness and great physical strength. The ability to anticipate danger before it materializes—and take effective preventative action—is often fundamental to a team's success.

CENTER BACK

The center back—sometimes known as center half (see box, p.45)—is a team's last line of defense. Success or failure often rests on the player's ability to tackle effectively and win the ball. A center back is ideally tall and strong, with the ability to win the ball in the air. A good center back has clever positional sense, and is fearless and decisive when making tackles and interceptions.

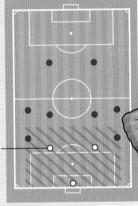

On patrol
The center backs are responsible for patrolling the area in front of the goalmouth.

RIO FERDINAND
The former England center back had great passing ability as well as the skills needed to bring the ball out of defense.

CENTER BACK'S DOMAIN
Playing in a central position, a team typically places two center backs in front of the goalkeeper. They mark the most advanced attacking forwards, aiming to bring the ball away from the penalty area.

[SOCCER] IS GENERAL, DEFENDING IS ...
SPECIFIC

RICARDO CARVALHO
PORTUGUESE DEFENDER, 2003–2016

THE SWEEPER

As the name suggests, the role of the sweeper is to "sweep up" the ball if the attacking team breaks through the defensive line. Unlike their other colleagues in defense, the sweeper does not mark a specific attacker. Instead, they remain "fluid" and free to roam around the goalmouth, closing down any gaps in defense. An ability to anticipate play is especially important, as the sweeper must predict attacks from any quarter.

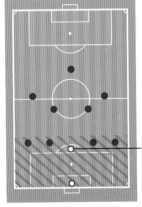

Roaming
The sweeper roams laterally in front of the goal but can advance upfield.

THE SWEEPER'S DOMAIN
The sweeper is usually positioned behind the center backs. As they have no marking duties, they may travel a long way forward when their team is in possession.

GAETANO SCIREA

A real gentleman of soccer, Gaetano Scirea was one of the greatest defenders in the history of the game. A World Cup winner with Italy in 1982, the Juventus player was famed for his grace, style, and sportsmanship. He was equally adept at initiating attacks and snuffing out danger and won every available soccer honor.

WIDE DEFENDERS

The standard four-man defense consists of two center backs (see p.43) in the middle of the field and two fullbacks to the side. Attack-minded backs, or wing-backs, will regularly advance a long way down the flanks. All wide defenders are expected to prevent the opposing team from launching attacks down the flanks and to join in with their own team's attacks.

FULLBACK

The main responsibility of the fullback is to stay wide and prevent the attacking team from developing attacks down the flanks. Backs must be quick and will usually mark a designated forward. They should also join in with attacking play.

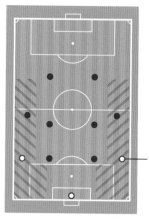

Forward run
One of the fullbacks may decide to advance up the field during attacks.

FULLBACK'S DOMAIN

The fullback operates on either the right- or left-hand side of the field and defends the flanks. When one fullback goes on a forward run, the other "tucks in" to support the central defenders.

OLYMPIC PERFORMANCE

One of the world's fastest players is diminutive Iranian right back Hossein Kaebi. He claims to be able to run 330 ft (100 m) in less than 10 seconds, which, if true, would make him a contender for an Olympic medal.

PUTTING THE BOOT IN

The England and Leeds United center half Jack Charlton was introduced to the tougher side of the game from the start. At his 1953 debut, he asked his manager, Raich Carter, what tactics he should use. Carter replied: "See how fast their center forward can limp."

WINGBACK

The wingback is a cross between the fullback (see left) and the winger (see p.55). Defending like a fullback, preventing attackers from reaching the goal line, when charging forward, the wingback plays like a winger to take part in attacks.

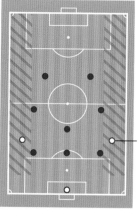

Upfield
The wingback has an attacking role and ranges up the field.

WINGBACK'S DOMAIN

The wingback operates on either the right- or left-hand side of the field but further upfield than the fullback. They are responsible for both defending and attacking along the flanks.

CAFU

Brazilian soccer teams have a long tradition of using wingbacks. Cafu (aka Marcos Evangelista de Moraes) was a prime example. Famous for his overlapping runs, he is one of a select group of players to have appeared in four World Cup tournaments.

TOP 5: OWN GOALS

The first official own goal was scored by Gersham Cox of Aston Villa in 1888. Since then, countless balls have been knocked into the wrong net by a succession of shame-faced players. The following are five of the most notorious own goals.

GARY MABBUT

Although Gary Mabbut had already scored a defining goal for Tottenham Hotspur against Coventry in the 1987 Cup Final, he left his "best" attempt at goal to last. Having taken the game into extra time, he placed a ball over the head of his own keeper and handed the cup to Coventry.

DELFI GELI

In the 2001 UEFA Cup Final, tiny Spanish team Alaves came from behind three times to level the score against Liverpool. With 117 minutes gone, Alaves player Delfi Geli tried to clear a cross but instead scored a match-winning, golden goal for Liverpool.

STAN VAN DEN BUYS

The hapless van den Buys holds the unique record in professional soccer of having scored the most own goals in a single game. Playing for Belgian team Germinal Ekeren in 1995, he put three balls past his own goalkeeper, handing a 3–2 victory to Anderlecht.

BARBADOS VS. GRENADA

Barbados was 2–0 up against Grenada in the 1994 Shell Caribbean Cup and needed a two-goal advantage to qualify. When Grenada scored a late goal, Barbados exploited a rule stating that the match must go to extra time in the event of a tie by equalizing with an own goal.

MADAGASCAR CHAMPIONSHIP

During the 2002 Madagascar Championship, reigning champions Stade Olympique protested against a questionable penalty decision by scoring an own goal from the kickoff—and repeated the process for 90 minutes. The final score was Stade Olympique 0, AS Adema 149.

THE "BACK FOUR"

The members of a standard four-man defense are known as the "back four." This unit consists of two fullbacks (see left) and two central defenders (see p.43) or two fullbacks, one central defender, and one sweeper (see p.43). The back four must work together as a coordinated unit. For example, a "flat" formation provides defensive cover across the whole width of the field.

BACK FOUR AS A UNIT

Good attacking invariably begins with a solid defense. A strong back four should be well organized, committed, and focused. The unit must contain a mix of talented players who are able to work together to throw off the attacking team. At the highest level of the game, the pressure to perform effectively can be immense—especially given that an attacker who outwits the back four will almost certainly score.

CARLES PUYOL

Influential defender Carles Puyol won the European Championship with Spain in 2008 and the World Cup two years later.

1 The number of clubs Franco Baresi played for during his 20-year career (AC Milan)

−3 Jamie Carragher's net goal total for Liverpool (four goals, seven own goals)

108 The number of games ASEC Abidjan went unbeaten between 1989 and 1994

15 The number of goals conceded by Chelsea's defense during the 2004–2005 Premiership season

MISLEADING POSITION NAMES

In the early 20th century, when the standard formation was 2-3-5, the two players at the back were known as "fullbacks" and the three players in front were called "half-backs" or "halves." As tactics grew more cautious over time, the central of the three halves was moved back into defense, pushing the fullbacks out to the sides. Although the name doesn't make much sense today, center backs are often still called "center halves."

DEFENDERS RECEIVE ... LESS ATTENTION FROM FANS THAN GOAL SCORERS. WE ARE MORE IN **THE ENGINE ROOM**

PAOLO MALDINI, ITALIAN INTERNATIONAL, 1988–2002

STAR DEFENDERS

BEST BACK FOURS

Successful teams are invariably built on solid defenses. The following back fours provided the greatest defensive support in the history of the game.

BRAZIL (1958)

While center backs Hilderaldo Bellini and Orlando and fullbacks Nilton Santos and Djalma Santos may not have invented the phenomenon of the "back four," they were the first to perfect it. This formidable unit helped propel Brazil to victory at the 1958 World Cup.

LEEDS UNITED (1960s–1970s)

Jack Charlton, Norman Hunter, Terry Cooper, and Paul Reaney didn't exactly have a delicate touch when it came to tackling, but they were highly effective. The Leeds team of the late 1960s and early '70s owed much of its success to this hard-as-nails back four.

AC MILAN (1980s–1990s)

Sweeper Franco Baresi, center back Alessandro Costacurta, and fullbacks Mauro Tassotti and Paolo Maldini formed one of the greatest back fours of all time at AC Milan during the 1980s and '90s. They helped AC Milan claim three European Cup titles.

AFC AJAX (1995)

Center backs Frank Rijkaard and Danny Blind and fullbacks Frank de Boer and Michael Reizeger oozed talent. They were the Amsterdam team's formidable back four in the Champions League winning side of 1995.

MIDFIELDERS

As the name implies, midfielders play in the middle of the field between the defenders (see pp.42–45) and the forwards (see pp.50–53). Depending on the formation being used (see pp.86–89), there can be two to five midfielders in a team. Their precise roles will vary accordingly, but they can usually be categorized as either "central" or "wide."

THE MIDFIELDER'S ROLE

The midfielder has an all-around view of the game, and their role is to both anticipate and exploit as many attacking opportunities as possible. They must be actively involved in both defense and attack, which involves gaining and retaining possession of the ball, feeding it to the forwards, and making attempts at goal themselves.

SKILLS REQUIRED

The midfielder must have excellent fitness as they are required to cover the whole field, alternating between defense and attack as play dictates. Above all, they need to be a good all-arounder. To fulfill their defensive duties, they need to be an excellent tackler who is able to win aerial battles in the center of the field. Meanwhile, the attacking aspects of the role require them to be equally adept at tackling, passing, dribbling, and shooting. In addition to possessing excellent technical ability, a good midfielder needs creativity and vision. Setting up goal-scoring opportunities is a major part of the midfielder's job, and, without these attributes, they are unlikely to do so very often.

Timing
A well-timed sliding tackle is an effective way to gain the ball.

TACKLING
As part of their defensive duties, midfielders must be accomplished tacklers. Much of the technique in tackling comes from pressuring the opponent before seizing the ball.

Types of pass
The midfielder must be equally at home making both short and long passes.

PASSING
Midfielders pass the ball more than any other players on the field. Top-class performers may make 50 or more passes during a match, with a success rate above 80 percent.

Moving up
Dribbling is the main way for a wide midfielder to move upfield.

DRIBBLING
The wide midfielders in particular need good dribbling skills in order to get themselves into positions from which they can deliver effective crosses into the opponent's penalty area.

MAGNUS FORCE

The technique behind adding curve to a shot (as perfected by midfielder David Beckham) has its roots in science. In 1853, a German physicist named Heinrich Magnus showed (with his Magnus Theory) how a ball kicked to the right of center will spin in a counterclockwise direction and curl to the left.

LIAM BRADY

Former Irish midfielder Liam Brady—who played for Arsenal, Juventus, and Republic of Ireland in the 1970s and '80s—had great technical ability.

AVERAGE DISTANCE COVERED PER MATCH

● Midfielders—**7½** miles (12 km)
● Forwards—**7** miles (11.25 km)
● Defenders—**6¼** miles (10 km)

6¼   **7**   **7½**

CENTRAL MIDFIELDER—BOX-TO-BOX

The central midfielder, as typified by the box-to-box midfielder, is the hardest-working player on the field. They must work to create and exploit attacking possibilities—such as identifying and passing the ball to forwards who are running into space—while also ensuring that they meet their defensive responsibilities. Technical skills such as dribbling and passing must become second nature so that they can distribute the ball effectively to teammates. When they are not setting up offensive attacks or engineering plays, they drop back into defense to pressurize the attacking team.

ARCHETYPAL MIDFIELDER

The box-to-box player is the archetypal midfielder. They are actively involved in every part of the game, running from one penalty area to the other in an attempt to dominate play. They typically have incredible stamina and impeccable technical ability. The mold for the role was set by the great Alfred Di Stefano of Argentina and Real Madrid in the 1950s. Later exponents were Rubén Baraja, Bryan Robson, and Steven Gerrard.

BOX-TO-BOX PLAYER'S DOMAIN

The box-to-box midfielder must cover nearly all of the field. When on the offensive, they race up to the opposition's penalty area; when defending, they race back to their own penalty area.

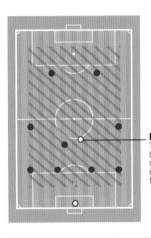

End to end
The box-to-box midfielder races from one end of the field to the other.

BRYAN ROBSON
As one of Manchester United's most well-known midfielders, Bryan Robson remains the longest-serving captain in the club's history (1982–1994).

CENTRAL MIDFIELDER—HOLDING

Primarily a defensive role, the holding midfielder is stationed in front of the back four (see p.45). They are responsible for repelling attacking players who have made it through the midfield.

Defense
The holding midfielder is responsible for preventing the attacking team from reaching the defenders.

HOLDING MIDFIELDER'S DOMAIN

The holding midfielder operates further back down the field than the box-to-box midfielder. They "hold back" attacking players by intercepting passes with hard tackling and shrewd positioning.

WHY PUT ANOTHER LAYER OF GOLD PAINT ON THE BENTLEY WHEN YOU ARE LOSING THE ENTIRE ENGINE?

ZINEDINE ZIDANE
ON DAVID BECKHAM REPLACING CLAUDE MAKÉLÉLÉ AT REAL MADRID, 2003

N'GOLO KANTE
Kanté first rose to prominence at Leicester City, where he won the Premier League in 2016. He then moved to Chelsea and picked up another title along with the Champions League and Europa League. At the 2018 World Cup, his energy, tackling, positioning, and passing make him the ultimate holding midfielder.

CENTRAL MIDFIELDER—PLAYMAKER

The playmaker is a midfielder who is responsible for setting up attacking plays for the forwards (see pp.50–53), usually from a central position. To do this effectively, they must have great passing ability and vision. A playmaker can be described as either "advanced" or "withdrawn" (see below).

ADVANCED PLAYMAKERS

Advanced playmakers make themselves available for passes and can turn defensive moves into attacking ones by using short, incisive passes. They usually have very little time in which to make decisions and very little space in which to make passes.

WITHDRAWN PLAYMAKERS

Withdrawn playmakers usually play alongside a holding midfielder (see p.47). While the holding midfielder concentrates on defensive duties, the withdrawn playmaker takes advantage of this support to launch long, decisive passes.

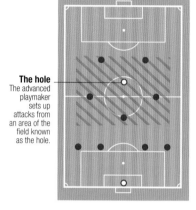

The hole
The advanced playmaker sets up attacks from an area of the field known as the hole.

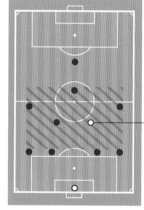

Defensive
The withdrawn playmaker sets up attacks from further down the field.

ADVANCED PLAYMAKER'S DOMAIN
The advanced playmaker plays in the "hole"— an area between midfield and the opposing line of defense. In occupying this position, it is hard for the defensive team to mark them.

WITHDRAWN PLAYMAKER'S DOMAIN
Despite being relatively deep-lying, the withdrawn playmaker must set up attacks. They make long balls through the middle (into the path of a running center forward, for example) or to a wide player.

CESC FÀBREGAS
The skilled and mobile Spanish midfielder Cesc Fàbregas typified the role of the advanced playmaker. These players' skills display vision, creativity, and a great passing range.

KAKÁ
Kaká of Brazil mastered the role of the attacking midfielder. His skill secured his place as one of the highest-paid players in the world.

CENTRAL MIDFIELDER— ATTACKING

Midfielders with particularly attacking instincts are often deployed relatively far upfield. Known as attacking central midfielders, these players often produce excellent shots, contribute several goals during a season, and have the potential to be a team's star player. The attacking central midfielder must have great vision and technical ability, including faultless passing and shooting skills.

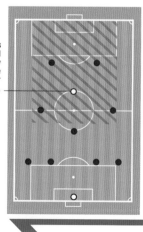

Great shooters
Attacking central midfielders usually play upfield and are renowned for their shooting ability.

ATTACKING CENTRAL MIDFIELDER'S DOMAIN
With a talent for bursting into the attacking team's penalty area at exactly the right moment (either with or without the ball), attacking central midfielders are positioned in an advanced position. They often form the front point of a four-man diamond in a 4-4-2 formation (see p.88).

WIDE MIDFIELDERS

The wide midfield players are attacking midfielders. However, in contrast to the attacking central midfielder (see left), this player focuses on one particular side of the field. The extent to which wide midfielders are restricted to patrolling the touchline varies. They are often required to be relatively flexible in their movements, for example, rather than just sticking to the flanks.

TRADITIONAL WINGERS

Prior to the mid-1960s, wingers were attacking players who rarely helped with defense. Stationed toward the touchline, they stretched the attacking team's defense and provided an outlet for their own defenders. Their main duty was to take the ball past the attacking team's fullback and deliver crosses into the penalty area. England's Stanley Matthews (1915–2000) was one of the all-time greats.

MODERN WIDE MIDFIELDER

In recent years, the role of wide midfielder has become very fluid. This is the result of increasing tactical sophistication, as well as a desire to confuse the opposition. The rise of the wingback (see p.45) also means that the modern winger must provide defensive cover when the wingback is upfield.

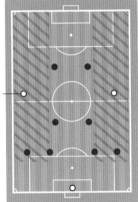

In attack
The modern wide midfielder stays wide to stretch the attacking team's defense.

MODERN WIDE MIDFIELDER'S DOMAIN
Active in both defense and offense, the modern wide midfielder provides defensive cover by tracking back and moving in toward the middle to help maintain a tight defensive unit.

SOMETHING DEEP IN MY CHARACTER ALLOWS ME TO TAKE THE HITS AND GET ON WITH **TRYING TO WIN**

LIONEL MESSI
ARGENTINA AND PARIS SAINT-GERMAIN

LIONEL **MESSI**

Argentina's Lionel Messi, who has a sublime left foot, great close-ball control, and enviable shooting ability, is most effective when playing in a forward right position. This allows him to "cut in" with his stronger foot before shooting, passing to an overlapping defender, or running with the ball. His skill is particularly impressive given that he was diagnosed with growth hormone deficiency when he was just 11 years old.

TOP FIVE "NEW MARADONAS"

Exceptionally talented players (usually midfielders or forwards) are often favorably compared to Argentina's Diego Maradona. The following global players have been associated with the legendary midfielder.

GHEORGHE HAGI

An erratic but undoubtedly brilliant playmaker, Romania's greatest player was a star of Spanish, Italian, and Turkish soccer. The defining moment for the "Maradona of the Carpathians" came with his goal against Colombia in the 1994 World Cup.

SAEED OWAIRAN

Already a national hero for taking Saudi Arabia to its first World Cup Finals in 1994, Owairan proceeded to dribble the ball for 70 yd (64 m) against Belgium before scoring and taking the team into the knock-out phases. It earned him the nickname "Maradona of the Arabs."

AHMED EL-KASS

El-Kass was a goal-scoring midfielder who was constantly on the lookout for attacking opportunities. The "Maradona of the Nile" led the Egyptian national team to the 1990 World Cup Finals.

GEORGI KINKLADZE

The "Maradona of the Caucuses" moved to Manchester City in 1995, where he displayed such brilliance as an attacking playmaker—with exceptional dribbling skills—that fans voted him one of Manchester City's top three cult heroes of all time.

MIRKO VUČINIĆ

Montenegro's "Maradona of the Balkans" (a title previously claimed by Albania's Edvin Murati) was a star in Italy's Serie A. Following a five-month ban for abusing a referee, the newly matured playmaker showed a flair that Maradona himself would recognize.

FORWARDS

Forwards, or strikers, are positioned farthest forward on a team, nearest the opponent's goal. These players come in all shapes and sizes, from small and agile to large and powerful, but they all have one essential job: to score goals. As the principal goal scorers, forwards are often a team's most celebrated—and expensive—players.

THE FORWARD'S ROLE

In addition to taking advantage of goal-scoring opportunities, forwards are expected to set up goals for other forwards and sometimes for attacking midfielders and playmakers (see pp.46–49). Forwards may also aim to keep possession of the ball until other players can move forward and join the attack. Most teams play with either one or two forwards.

SKILLS REQUIRED

There are many different ways to score a goal and, consequently, many different types of forward. However, certain mental and physical characteristics are common for all. Forwards must have pace (at least over short distances), show great courage, and have an instinctive eye for goal. Excellent shooting ability is a prerequisite, but heading, crossing, and passing skills are also vital in order to engineer goal-scoring opportunities and outmaneuver defenders while advancing up the field.

Forceful shot
A powerful swing of the kicking leg produces a strong shot.

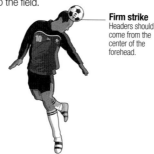

Firm strike
Headers should come from the center of the forehead.

SHOOTING
As the ball will arrive to the forward at a variety of speeds and angles, there are many shooting techniques. However, the most common method is a low, hard shot struck off the instep of the cleat.

HEADING
Used for passing, shooting, or controlling the ball, heading is a versatile and important skill—not just for the forward but for all players. It is a vital skill in both defense and attack.

ROBERT LEWANDOWSKI
One of the best strikers of all time in Germany's Bundesliga, Lewandowski played for Borussia Dortmund and Bayern Munich before joining Barcelona in 2022. He scored 312 Bundesliga goals in 384 appearances.

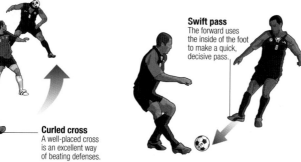

Curled cross
A well-placed cross is an excellent way of beating defenses.

Swift pass
The forward uses the inside of the foot to make a quick, decisive pass.

CROSSING
The cross pass, in which the ball is quickly moved from the edge of the field to the center, is used to deliver the ball toward players in attacking positions. Well-hit crosses are hard to defend against.

PASSING
A well-executed pass consists of three elements: the correct amount of power, appropriate direction, and good timing. A forward will use the inside of the foot to make a swift, short pass.

LIGHTNING FAST

Forwards must be quick. Over short distances, many can run almost as fast as 100 m sprinters:

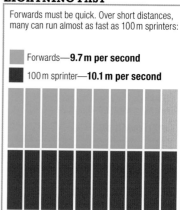

Forwards—**9.7 m per second**

100 m sprinter—**10.1 m per second**

CENTER FORWARD

With the aim of scoring as many goals as possible, center forwards are often tall, and powerful enough to get control of the ball before opponents. Frequently used as "targets" for passes, these players operate as strikers near the goal, waiting to "collect" the ball from teammates in midfield or defense. Height, speed, and strength enable the center forward to head goals from corners and crosses, or to shield the ball from other players while they turn and shoot.

SKILLS REQUIRED

Center forwards must have superior strength and excellent heading ability. They must be accurate shooters, and have the necessary ball control to retain possession of the ball while waiting for other players to provide support. Center forwards often play with their back to the goal, so they must be able to control the ball, often with a defender at their back, while looking to bring teammates into play.

ALAN SHEARER

Famed for celebrating goals with a simple flat-palmed raise of the arm, Shearer scored a hat trick on his full league debut for Southampton in 1988 and never looked back. He was one of the classic English center forwards.

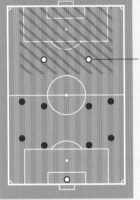

In attack
Center forwards wait near the goal and act as focal points for attacks.

CENTER FORWARD'S DOMAIN
Center forwards range up the field, focusing on the area in front of the goal. From here, they are in the best position to receive balls, turn, and score.

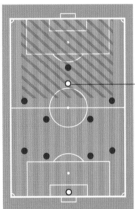

WITHDRAWN STRIKER

Withdrawn strikers have a similar role to the advanced playmaker midfielders (see p.48) in that they play between midfield and the opponent's defense, aiming to set up attacks. However, withdrawn strikers typically have just one player from their team in front of them, while advanced playmakers have two. Many of the greatest players in the game's history have been withdrawn strikers.

Setups
The withdrawn striker retains possession, sets up attacks, or shoots from their position in the "hole."

WITHDRAWN STRIKER'S DOMAIN
The withdrawn striker exploits the space between the midfield and the opponent's defense (the "hole"). They hold up the ball, pass, and shoot.

ROOM TO ROAM

Exceptionally talented players, such as Diego Maradona and Zinedine Zidane, flourished in this position because it allowed them the freedom to roam the field and express their creative instincts. Withdrawn strikers must be aware of the positions of both teammates and opponents and be able to instinctively time runs so that players can pass to them. Withdrawn strikers are excellent passers of the ball and must be able to turn quickly and accelerate.

ROBERTO FIRMINO
Perhaps under appreciated away from Liverpool, Brazilian Firmino became a vital player in The Reds' attacking trio alongside Sadio Mané and Mohamed Salah.

TELEPATHY EXPERIMENT

In the 1970s, Liverpool forwards Kevin Keegan and John Toshack developed such an intrinsic partnership that many people thought they were telepathic. To test the theory, a local TV station invited them into the studio to guess the shape drawn on a card by the other player. They guessed correctly every time. Only later did Toshack confess that they could see the shapes reflected in the cameras.

THE "OFF-THE-SHOULDER" STRIKER

Forwards who specialize in timing runs so that they are only just onside when the ball is played forward to them are known as "off-the-shoulder" strikers. This is because they stay directly parallel with the opposing team's last defender, only moving off the shoulder at the last possible moment.

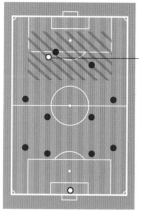

Offside danger
The striker hangs "off the shoulder" of the opponent's deepest-lying defender (shown in blue).

OFF-THE-SHOULDER STRIKER'S DOMAIN
The off-the-shoulder striker positions themself alongside the opposing team's last man (the last defender before the goalkeeper). From this position, they are well placed to break through on goal.

PATIENCE REQUIRED

As the off-the-shoulder striker is often ruled offside (correctly or otherwise), patience is a key requirement. Patience is also required of the fans, as the technique employed by these forwards can be frustrating to watch. However, when it works, the tactic can be highly effective, as it offers the striker a crucial head start over the defenders. AC Milan's Pippo Inzaghi was one of the greatest off-the-shoulder strikers.

THIERRY **HENRY**

Henry played as a forward in his youth but began his professional career as a winger (see p.49). Under the tutelage of Arsène Wenger at Arsenal, he evolved into a mixture of both. His trademark approach was to drift to the left before cutting in and shooting. He frequently played "off the shoulder."

THE "POACHER"

Poachers are penalty-box opportunists who either quickly find space to shoot or who pick up loose balls and toe-poke them into the goal. While poachers may not always look like a conventional forward, they can be very effective strikers, with impressive goal-scoring tallies. The best poachers also possess excellent "off-the-ball" movement, allowing them to shake off defenders and sneak into enough space to shoot. Rarely scoring from outside the penalty area, poachers are renowned for their powerful and accurate close-range finishes.

GERD MÜLLER

Müller was the ultimate opportunist striker, playing for West Germany and Bayern Munich in the 1960s and '70s.

QUICK REACTIONS

While poachers don't have to be particularly strong or skillful, or even have great pace over more than short distances, it helps to possess extremely quick reactions. Above all, the goal-poacher needs to hone the knack of being in the right place at the right time. Such strikers are usually found working in and around the opponent's penalty area hoping to snatch goals.

UNCONVENTIONAL PLAYER

Gerd Müller was once memorably described as "short, squat, awkward-looking, and not notably fast." Nevertheless, his extraordinary acceleration over short distances and unparalleled eye for goal made him one of the greatest strikers of all time. He scored a record 365 Bundesliga goals.

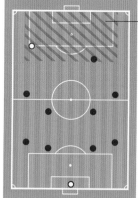

Penalty area
The poacher occupies the penalty area of the opposing team, aiming to score opportunistic goals.

THE POACHER'S DOMAIN
Poachers take up an extreme forward position, focusing their attention on the opponent's penalty area, and looking to exploit any goal-scoring opportunities that present themselves.

UNCLASSIFIABLE STRIKERS

Not all strikers can be neatly pigeonholed. In fact, it can be a positive advantage to a team if they can't. While the defending team can use a tall defender to mark a conventional target, it will struggle to defend against a forward who defies categorization. For this reason, some of the greatest strikers have been mavericks with playing styles all their own.

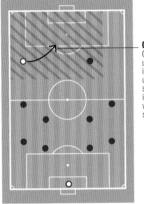

Cutting In
One frequently used ploy is for the unclassifiable striker to "cut in" from the wing before shooting.

UNCLASSIFIABLE STRIKER'S DOMAIN
While by definition it is difficult to place the unclassifiable striker, this player often receives the ball on the wing before "cutting in" toward the center of the field and unleashing a shot.

VERSATILITY REQUIRED

Strikers who can vary their roles during the course of a game are rare but invaluable. Dutch star Robin van Persie was a prime example. Such strikers are quick, and capable of shooting from any angle and distance—attributes that allow them to play with equal effectiveness on the left wing, in the "hole," or as a target. By moving between these positions, the striker can shake off markers and create scoring opportunities.

TOO MANY ROLES

Sometimes a forward can be too versatile for his own good. In Wayne Rooney's early days at Manchester United, manager Sir Alex Ferguson played him as a main striker, a support striker, and on both wings, making it difficult for him to make any one position his own.

ROBIN VAN PERSIE
Netherlands forward Robin van Persie was a creative and "unclassifiable" striker.

STRIKING PARTNERSHIPS

Strikers often work in pairs to form effective partnerships. The best duos consist of players with differing styles, much like the partnerships between central defenders (see p.45). One well-tested formula places a tall, powerful player with a smaller, more agile one. Larger players win headers and set up goals for their partner or try to retain the ball to bring them more into play.

GREAT PAIRINGS

The greatest striking partnerships, however, are based on far more than just complementary playing styles—the players must instinctively know what the other will do in any given situation. This can be achieved by experience, but there is another more elusive ingredient—the pair must "click." Equally, partnerships that look great on paper may fail to come off in reality.

THE TIGER

Born in Brazil in 1892, Arthur Friedenreich is thought to have scored 1,329 goals in his career. Known as "The Tiger," he was the first mixed-race soccer superstar. Playing at a time when soccer in Brazil was the preserve of the white middle classes, Friedenreich spent a lot of time flattening his naturally curly hair with brilliantine.

I LOVE TO SCORE GOALS AFTER PASSING ALL THE DEFENDERS AS WELL AS THE KEEPER. THIS IS NOT MY SPECIALTY ... BUT MY HABIT!

RONALDO
BRAZIL STRIKER, 2003

STAR STRIKERS

STRIKING PARTNERSHIPS

ROMÁRIO AND BEBETO
The front two in Brazil's 1994 World Cup–winning team are the exception that proves the rule that duos with differing styles are best. Both were small, quick, and mobile, making opponents feel like they were seeing double.

LLOYD AND MORGAN
The deadly duo made a powerful partnership for the United States mixing cool finishing with a high work-rate. The pair played in the 2011, 2015, and 2019 Women's World Cup finals.

MORIENTES AND RAÚL
Between 1997 and 2005, Morientes formed a powerful partnership with his close friend Raúl at Real Madrid. In a typical finish, Morientes would win the ball in the air, and Raúl would then slam it into the net.

BERGKAMP AND HENRY
With his intelligent play and silky-smooth passing ability, Dennis Bergkamp was the perfect foil for goal scorer Thierry Henry, his great striking partner at Arsenal from 1999–2006.

GOALKEEPERS

The goalkeeper is the last line of defense between an opponent's attacking players and the goal. As such, the position carries great responsibility—the outcome of a match can depend more on the goalkeeper than any other player. Each team must have a goalkeeper on the field at all times. If the goalkeeper is injured or sent off, a substitute must be used. If no substitutes are available, another outfield player must assume the role.

THE GOALKEEPER'S ROLE

Goalkeeping is the most specialized role in soccer. While inside their own penalty areas, the goalkeepers are the only players who are allowed to touch the ball with any part of the body—including the hands. They must defend their team's goal, prevent the opposition from scoring, and organize the defense. The role requires courage, quick reactions, and the ability to concentrate for the entirety of a match.

ESSENTIAL SKILLS

The essential skills of a goalkeeper include saving, clearing, marshaling the defense, and distributing the ball. In addition to being a "safe pair of hands," goalkeepers must show strength of character. If an outfield player makes a mistake, for example, a teammate may be able to salvage the situation; if a goalkeeper errs, the consequences are usually a confidence-shattering goal. Therefore, the keeper must be strong enough to deal with any flack.

"GOLO!"

Gordon Banks's miraculous clearance of a downward header from Pelé in the 1970 World Cup is often cited as the greatest save in history. The England goalkeeper heard the great Brazilian shout "golo!" as soon as he made contact. However, Banks managed to reach the ball and flick it over the crossbar with one finger and a roll of his hand.

Diving save
Quick reactions and a willingness to dive are important skills for the goalkeeper.

SAVING
Keeping the ball out of the net is the goalkeepers' number-one priority. They must stop and block any shots at goal as well as use the hands to get above opponents and pluck high crosses out of the air.

Punched out
A well-placed punch will clear the ball away.

CLEARING
Goalkeepers need to get the ball away from danger areas quickly, whether with their feet or via a punch. They must make sure that their clearance doesn't offer the ball back to the opposition.

Organization skills
The goalkeeper is instrumental in organizing the defense and relaying advice.

MARSHALING
Goalkeepers are in charge of the goal area and must tell their defenders exactly where they want them. This is particularly important during free kicks, when the goalkeeper organizes the wall.

Quick pass
The goalkeeper quickly decides which player is best placed to receive the ball.

DISTRIBUTION
Once the ball is safely in the goalkeeper's hands, they must make good use of it. They look to see which teammate is available and punt or throw the ball to that player as quickly as possible.

STAR GOALKEEPERS

A World Cup penalty shoot-out is one of the most stressful situations for the goalkeeper. See right for the top three highest goal savers in the tournament.

Some goalkeepers are as adept at scoring goals as they are at saving them. See far right for the most prolific goal scorers in the game.

BEST WORLD CUP PENALTY SAVERS

SERGIO GOYCOCHEA has saved **5** penalty shoot-out goals for Argentina.

CLAUDIO TAFFAREL of Brazil has also saved **5**, although **2** went over the crossbar.

HARALD SCHUMACHER of West Germany is in third place with **4** shoot-out saves.

BEST GOAL-SCORING GOALKEEPERS

NAME	FROM/TO	GOALS
Rogério CENI	1990–2015	131
José Luis CHILAVERT	1982–2004	67
Jorge CAMPOS	1988–2004	46
Dimitar IVANKOV	1995–2011	42
René HIGUITA	1985–2010	41
Johnny FERNANDEZ	1997–2017	39

RENÉ **HIGUITA**

Colombian goalkeeper René Higuita is famous for his "scorpion kick" (pictured). During a friendly match at Wembley in 1995, England midfielder Jamie Redknapp tried to lob the ball over his head. However, Higuita allowed the ball to float over his head and then turned himself into a human scorpion and kicked it back into play with his heels.

TOP 5: ECCENTRIC GOALKEEPERS

Like drummers in rock groups, goalkeepers are well known for their eccentric behavior—both on and off the field. Perhaps their unique position on the field and the amount of character they must show is the reason behind this phenomenon. The following five goalkeepers are among the most eccentric:

FABIEN BARTHEZ

The former Marseilles, Manchester United, and France goalkeeper was as energetic and unpredictable as a bouncing rubber ball. His eccentric antics included taunting dribbles and step overs, and attempts to psyche out opposing strikers.

BRUCE GROBBELAAR

Having served in the Rhodesian Bush War, the Liverpool goalkeeper was fearless—if not always inclined to take the game seriously. During a penalty shoot-out against AS Roma at the 1984 European Cup Final, he put Francesco Graziani off his shot by wobbling his legs like spaghetti.

OLIVER KAHN

Former Germany goalkeeper Oliver Kahn was notorious for arguing with anyone and everyone, from rival goalkeepers and players to managers and even his own teammates. Not surprisingly, he earned a number of nicknames, which included "Genghis Kahn" and "Kung-fu Kahn."

JORGE CAMPOS

Known for his flamboyant, multi-colored shirts (which he designed himself), the Mexican goalkeeper spent as much time out of his area as in it. At club level, he would frequently start between the posts and finish the game as a striker—a position in which he excelled. Campos was talented enough to win 130 caps for his country.

JOSE LUIS CHILAVERT

The former goalkeeper for Paraguay was renowned for his incredible skill at taking free kicks—and for his hotheadedness. His fiery temper led to him being sent off for brawling with Colombia's Tino Asprilla and banned for spitting at Brazil's Roberto Carlos. He was also imprisoned for falsifying club documents.

THE JOY OF SEEING YURI GAGARIN FLY IN SPACE IS ONLY SUPERSEDED BY THE JOY OF A GOOD ... # PENALTY SAVE!

PAT JENNINGS'S HANDS

The success of the former Northern Ireland goalkeeper, who played from 1964–1986, was due in part to his large hand span, which enabled him to make spectacular one-handed catches.

LEV YASHIN

USSR GOALKEEPER, 1954–1967

GIANLUIGI BUFFON

Consistent, commanding, and unflappable, Buffon ranks very high among goalkeeping greats. In 2001, Juventus paid Parma more than $80 million (€52 million) for his signature, a fee that remained the world record for a goalkeeper for 16 years.

THE OFFICIALS

In professional matches, the game is controlled by four officials: the referee (see below), two assistant referees, and the fourth official (see pp.58–59). The referee, aided by the other officials, is tasked with enforcing the 17 Laws of the Game (see pp.62–63). The introduction of the Video Assistant Referee (VAR) system to major tournaments and leagues around 2018 also helped the referee. The VAR team watch the game on a screen and alert referees to any incidents they may have missed.

RISE OF THE REFEREE

During the early days, teams relied on a spirit of fair play and good sportsmanship. As disputes began to escalate, umpires were introduced. But it wasn't until 1881 that an objective and authoritative official, known as the referee, first appeared.

PIERLUIGI COLLINA

Collina became the leading referee in global soccer, setting new standards for authoritativeness, evenhandedness, and tact in this often impossibly complex task. For example, in his refereeing career (1988–2005), he was unique among referees for his willingness to apologize to managers for any mistakes made during the match.

LEADING LIGHT

As the referee's standing grew during the 20th century, influential figures began to emerge. English referee Stanley Rous, for example, was one of the leading referees of the 1930s. In addition to instigating the diagonal system of control (see right), he drafted the 1938 rewrite of the rules, which remain substantially unchanged today. He also championed the provision of referee training by FIFA for all of its new members.

THE REFEREE'S HAND SIGNALS

Referees use a variety of hand signals, which are employed to indicate decisions to the players. The referee also blows a whistle to stop play before making the appropriate signal. A short, quick whistle usually indicates a less-serious offense, while more-serious fouls elicit harder blasts. If the attacking team has a foul committed against one of its players, the referee may signal an advantage in the attacking team's favor without blowing the whistle.

IT'S A KNOCKOUT

Concetto Lo Bello (1924–1991) is one of the most famous Italian referees in the history of the game. Known as "the prince," he was noted for his immaculate dress, a carefully manicured moustache, and such vigorous hand signals that, on numerous occasions, he knocked players to the ground when signaling for a free kick.

YELLOW CARD
A yellow card is held up, above the head, to the player being cautioned.

RED CARD
A red card is held up, above the head, to the player being sent off.

DIRECT FREE KICK
The referee blows the whistle and points in the direction of the kick.

INDIRECT FREE KICK
A hand is held up until the taker and a teammate have touched the ball.

ADVANTAGE
The referee extends both arms to indicate that play can continue.

PENALTY KICK
The referee points to the appropriate penalty mark.

GOAL KICK
The referee points to the appropriate part of the goal area.

CORNER KICK
The referee points to the appropriate corner arc.

OFFICIALS' EQUIPMENT

The referee and the assistant referees (see p.58) make use of several different pieces of equipment. These are all designed to help the referee enforce the Laws of the Game effectively.

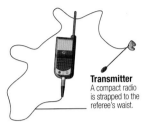

Transmitter
A compact radio is strapped to the referee's waist.

EARPIECE AND RADIO SET
In all top-flight matches, referees and their assistants communicate by using a small radio set. Messages from the Video Assistant Referee (VAR) team can also be sent.

ASSISTANTS' FLAGS
Flags are used by the assistant referees to signal to the referee (see p.58 for assistants' signals).

TIMEPIECE
Referees need at least one timepiece—a wristwatch and stopwatch.

Metal design
A metal whistle is tough and produces a loud, high-pitch sound.

CARDS AND NOTEBOOK
The referee may decide to penalize players by issuing yellow or red cards. Incidents are recorded in a notebook.

WHISTLE
The referee blows the whistle to start play, to stop or delay play due to a foul or injury, and to end each half.

GOAL-LINE TECHNOLOGY
This device alerts the referee within a second of the ball crossing the line (see p.60).

REFEREEING SYSTEMS

Early matches were played without referees. From the 1880s, however, it became clear that a coordinated and more mobile approach to refereeing was needed. Several systems of patrolling the field have since been developed.

LINEAR SYSTEM
The referee patrols one side of the field only, while one or two assistants move along the opposite sideline. The side views afforded are helpful, but the referee is in danger of obstructing wing play.

DIAGONAL SYSTEM
This is the most common system in modern soccer. The referee patrols a diagonal area between two opposing corner flags, while the assistant referees stand on opposite sides. This system means that two people should see any incident on the field.

ZIGZAG-PATH SYSTEM
In lower leagues in which the referee officiates alone, they may choose to move in a steady zigzag path, following a line between the teams' penalty arcs. The referee will, however, have to change positions for corners and penalty kicks.

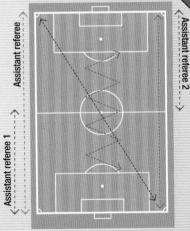

KEY

<- - - ->	Linear system
<- - - ->	Diagonal system
<- - - ->	Zigzag-path system

CHECKLIST

REFEREE'S DUTIES

Referees control the match and have full authority to enforce the rules for the match to which they have been appointed. Their main duties are:

ENFORCE THE RULES
The referee's principal responsibility is to enforce the rules to the appointed match as set out in the Laws of the Game.

CONTROL THE MATCH
The referee must control the match in cooperation with the assistant referees and, for official matches, the fourth official.

CHECK EQUIPMENT
The referee must ensure that the ball and the players' equipment meet the requirements of the Laws of the Game.

KEEP TIME AND MAINTAIN RECORDS
The referee must act as the timekeeper for the match and keep a record of any substitutions and offenses.

STOP PLAY WHEN NECESSARY
The referee must stop, suspend, or abandon the match for any infringements of the Laws of the Game, or because of any other outside interference.

ENSURE PLAYER SAFETY
The referee must stop the match if a player is seriously injured, ensuring that the player is removed from the field of play.

REFEREE'S FITNESS

Officials must have very high levels of fitness. In elite matches, for example, the referee can cover up to 8 miles (13 km) during a game—more than the players themselves. FIFA tests its international referees for the following:

AVERAGE RUNNING SPEED
Candidates run six 44 yd (40 m) sprints, with a maximum recovery time of 90 seconds between each sprint. The average time of the runs is then calculated. Male referees must complete the distance in 6.2 seconds or less; female referees must run it in 6.6 seconds.

HIGH-INTENSITY RUNNING
Male referees must cover 164 yd (150 m) in 30 seconds or less, followed by 35 seconds of recovery time during which they must walk 55 yd (50 m). This distance is repeated to count as one lap. Referees must complete 10 laps. Female referees are allowed 35 seconds to complete the run sections and 40 seconds to complete the walks.

HOW THE GAME IS PLAYED

ASSISTANT REFEREE

The assistant referee is responsible for helping the referee officiate a match. In professional games, two assistants patrol each touchline. They each take responsibility for half of the field, diagonally across from each other (see "Refereeing systems," p.57). The assistants officiate in situations in which the referee is not in a position to make the best decision. While their expertise is often crucial, their role is purely advisory.

THE GENDER AGENDA

The role of "linesman" was added to the Laws of the Game (see pp.62–63) in 1891—at a time when the officials were always male. It wasn't until 1996 that the term was dropped in favor of the gender-neutral "assistant referee."

THE ROLE OF THE ASSISTANTS

The more senior of the two assistants usually oversees the side of the field that contains the technical areas so they can help supervise substitutions in the absence of a fourth official. Typical duties for either assistant include signaling for offside and determining which team should be awarded a throw-in.

FLAG SIGNALS

The flag is the assistant's most important piece of equipment, as flag signals are the standard form of communication with a referee (although a buzzer system is also commonly used). The distinctive red-and-yellow checkered design of the flag has been proven to be the most eye-catching color combination over a long distance. The following signals (see right) are most commonly used during a match.

BEST BEHAVIOR

The referee has the power to relieve an assistant of duties—and make a report to the appropriate authorities—if an assistant acts in an improper way.

OFFSIDE
The flag is held above the head to signal for an offside offense.

OFFSIDE POSITION
A high flag is used for far offside, a horizontal flag for middle offside, and a low flag for near offside.

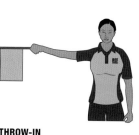

FLAG CARRYING
The assistant referee carries the flag unfurled so that any signals can be clearly seen.

THROW-IN
A flag is held out to one side, pointing in the direction of play of the team awarded the throw.

SUBSTITUTION
A flag is held above the head with both hands to indicate a substitution.

OTHER SIGNALS

In addition to using flag signals and a buzzer system, the assistant referees employ a variety of other forms of communication. Discrete hand signals, for example, let the referee know that a close ball has not gone out of play or that no offense has been committed. In return, the referee can use hand signals to inform an assistant which direction a throw-in should be taken if the assistant is unsure.

21,107 The distance run in yards (19,300 m) by assistants at the World U–17 Championships

20 The percentage of the distance run by assistant referees (see above) at speeds of 8 mph (13 km/h) or faster

CALLING TIME
A clenched fist on the chest means 45 minutes have elapsed in the half.

NO OFFENSE
The assistant referee shows a lowered palm to indicate that no offense has been committed.

FOURTH OFFICIAL

The fourth official assists the referee with administrative duties before and after the game, helps with assessing players' equipment, and may be called on to replace another match official (see below). The fourth official is also responsible for setting and holding up electronic display boards, acts as another pair of eyes for the referee, and keeps an extra set of records.

THE FOURTH OFFICIAL AS SUBSTITUTE

The fourth official may replace the assistant referee or referee if one of the other officials can't continue. If an assistant is injured, for example, the fourth official replaces the assistant automatically. If the referee is unable to continue, the fourth official may replace them directly, or an assistant may replace the referee, with the fourth official taking the vacant assistant's position.

NO IFS OR BUTTS

During the 2006 World Cup final, it was the fourth official, Luis Medina Cantalejo, who spotted Zidane's infamous headbutt—not referee Horacio Elizondo. As a result, Zidane was sent off. The French coach Raymond Domenech argued that Cantalejo had seen the incident on a replay and not as it happened, which would have broken FIFA rules. However, FIFA insisted that Cantalejo had not breached the rules and the decision stood.

THE REFEREE HAS GOT ME THE SACK ... THANK HIM FOR THAT!

GRAHAM TAYLOR
ENGLAND MANAGER, 1993

SUPPORTING ROLE
Among other duties, the fourth official must hold up a display board to indicate any time added on at the end of each half.

KEY DUTIES

ASSISTANT REFEREE

Assistant referees assist with (rather than insist on) refereeing decisions. Their duties include:

SIGNALING FOR OUT OF PLAY
The assistant referee signals to the referee when the ball leaves the field of play.

SIGNALING FOR RESTARTS
The assistant indicates which side is entitled to a goal kick, corner kick, or throw-in.

SIGNALING FOR OFFSIDE
The assistant referee signals when a player is in an offside position.

SIGNALING FOR SUBSTITUTIONS
The assistant referee signals when a substitution has been requested.

SIGNALING FOR MISCONDUCT
The assistant signals when misconduct occurs out of the referee's field of vision.

MONITORING THE GOALKEEPER
The assistant monitors the goalkeeper during penalty kicks, signaling if they move off the line before the kick.

FOURTH OFFICIAL

The fourth official is responsible for the following duties during the course of a professional match:

ASSISTING WITH RECORD KEEPING
The fourth official keeps a duplicate set of records.

CHECKING PLAYERS' EQUIPMENT
The fourth official helps the referee check that the players' equipment meets the requirements set out in the rules.

OVERSEEING SUBSTITUTIONS
The fourth official ensures that substitutions are conducted in an orderly manner.

DISPLAYING INFORMATION
The fourth official uses numbered boards or electronic displays to inform the referee of any substitution and to show the amount of time added on at the end of each half (having been advised by the referee).

MAINTAINING CONTROL
The fourth official maintains control in teams' technical areas, intervening in situations in which coaches, bench personnel, or substitutes become argumentative.

ACTING AS AN INTERMEDIARY
The fourth official acts as the contact point between the match officials and any nonparticipants, such as stadium managers, broadcast crews, and ball retrievers.

SOCCER TECHNOLOGIES

New technology has been transforming soccer for more than a century. The invention of reinforced concrete, for example, swept aside the wooden stadiums of the 19th and early 20th centuries. New materials have also changed the look and feel of every item of gear, virtual soccer worlds have been created, and GPS tracking systems are already in use.

GOAL-LINE TECHNOLOGIES

In 2003, FIFA and two companies began developing systems to assist in goal-line decisions. One system used radio signals sent from a microchip suspended inside the ball to determine its position on the field. Then, in 2010, the International Football Association decided not to pursue these technologies. The debate was reignited at the 2010 World Cup Finals, however, following the controversy around a disallowed goal by England's Frank Lampard against Germany. Video footage showed what the officials had missed—the ball bouncing over the goal line.

THE NEW SOCCER SHIRT

Soccer shirts (see pp.70–71) are becoming lighter, and new materials and weaves are being introduced to allow sweat to escape and air to circulate more efficiently. The latest research makes use of nanotechnology, which allows the manipulation of materials at an atomic level. Shirts have also been created that heal minor abrasions, destroy airborne germs, and are impregnated with the minerals usually lost by the body during a game. A player can even have the composition of the shirt tailored to their individual metabolic patterns.

Microchip
A chip embedded inside the ball sends 100,000 measurements per second to antennae arranged around the field.

Struts
Twelve struts securely hold the microchip and its protective casing in the center of the ball.

GOALCONTROL-4D SYSTEM
After the controversy at the 2010 World Cup, FIFA decided to introduce goal-line technology (GLT), choosing German-produced GoalControl. Its computerized system uses 14 mounted cameras—seven pointed at each goal—to detect the ball's movement around the goal line. This system was successfully used at the 2014 World Cup in Brazil.

PROZONE ET AL

For years, barely any statistics about player and team performance were gathered—the flow of play was just too complex, frenetic, and unpredictable to create systems of record keeping that could match baseball's box scores. New computing technologies, movement sensors, and GPS positioning systems have now been combined to create systems such as Prozone, which can track every player's actions and movements in a game.

GREEN IS THE COLOR

Soccer is not neglecting its environmental obligations. Future stadiums are designed, built, and maintained with energy conservation in mind. They incorporate facilities for recycling water and food waste, and even generate their own energy—through solar panels located on their large roofs, for example. In addition, artificial turf may become an increasingly familiar sight in soccer stadiums where water is scarce.

IPOD COACHING

Before the start of the penalty shoot-out at the end of the 2009 English League Cup Final, Manchester United's goalkeeper Ben Foster watched footage of his opponents taking penalties on a coach's iPod. It seemed to help, as Foster made a brilliant save from Tottenham Hotspur's Jamie O'Hara's spot kick, delivering the cup to United.

GAMES AND SIMULATIONS

Computer software companies have been quick to produce soccer simulation games. Many rapidly achieved cult status, offering fans the tantalizing prospect of taking Bristol Rovers to the Champions League Final, for example, from the comfort of their bedroom. As computing power and connectivity have increased, online multiplayer games have created entire virtual soccer worlds.

57 The percentage of fans who think GLT is the most important recent technological development to be made in soccer

68 The percentage of fans who would welcome the broadcasting of match officials' comments—as is currently the case with football and international rugby

82 The percentage of fans who think that technology, such as goal-line cameras, would considerably improve their enjoyment of the game

CAIROS GLT SYSTEM

This system uses a magnetic field to track the ball, which has a sensor embedded inside it. If the ball crosses the goal line, a radio signal is sent to the referee's watch immediately (see p.57). This system was granted a FIFA license in 2013.

1966 WORLD CUP FINAL—DID THE BALL CROSS THE LINE?

With 12 minutes of extra time played and the score at 2–2, England's Geoff Hurst sent a thundering shot toward the German goal. The ball bounced down from the crossbar and was cleared by a German defender. The referee was unsure whether the ball had crossed the line, but the ruling linesman, Tofik Bakhramov, rushed over and, in the heat of the moment, ruled the shot a goal. Controversy has reigned ever since.

THE RULES

The original Laws of the Game were devised by the FA in 1863 and contained only 13 items. As a testament to the game's simplicity, there are still only 17 laws in place today. The offside rule (see pp.66–67) has proved to be the most complex to create and administer, having been overhauled several times in the rule book's history.

THE INTERNATIONAL FA BOARD

Founded in 1886 by the soccer associations of England, Scotland, Wales, and Ireland, the International Football Association Board (IFAB) is still the game's ultimate rulemaking body. The board now includes four members from outside the UK, as nominated by FIFA, and meets annually to decide potential rule changes. Its decisions are binding for all national soccer associations worldwide.

ROBERTO TROTTA
A former Argentinian defender, Trotta set a new misconduct record by receiving the highest number of red cards in the Argentine Primera. He was sent off 17 times.

LAWS OF THE GAME

1. FIELD OF PLAY

The field (see pp.40–41) must be a rectangle, marked with touchlines, goal lines and areas, a halfway line, a center circle, penalty areas, spots, and arcs, corner arcs, and flag posts. It must be between 100–131 yd (90–120 m) long and between 49–98 yd (45–90 m) wide. For international soccer, the limits are 109–120 yd (100–110 m) and 70–82 yd (64–75 m), respectively.

2. THE BALL

The ball (see pp.76–77) must be made of approved materials. At the start of the game, it must have a diameter of 27–28 in (68–70 cm), weigh between 14–16 oz (410–450 g), and have an internal pressure of between 0.6 and 1.1 atmospheres at sea level. It can be changed only by the referee. If it bursts during a game, play is stopped and restarted with a new drop ball.

3. NUMBER OF PLAYERS

A match consists of two teams of not more than 11 players, each including a goalkeeper. An outfield player may swap with the goalkeeper during a stoppage of play. Teams must have at least seven players to begin or continue a match. In official competitions, a maximum of three player substitutions may be made, with some competitions allowing a fourth substitution in extra time.

4. PLAYERS' EQUIPMENT

Compulsory equipment for players are a shirt, shorts, socks, shin pads, and soccer cleats (see pp.70–73). Goalkeepers must wear a strip that distinguishes them from their own team, their opponents, and the officials. Headgear is permitted if it does not present a threat to other players. Most forms of jewelry are not permitted.

5. THE REFEREE

The referee (see pp.56–57) is the arbiter and interpreter of the rules, whose decision is final. The referee decides whether a game can go ahead and may stop play if a player requires medical treatment. The referee cautions players (yellow card), sends them off (red card), and is responsible for timekeeping, record keeping, and ensuring that all match equipment and strips are correct. The referee can also make decisions as highlighted by the Video Assistant Referee (VAR).

6. ASSISTANT REFEREES

The assistant referees (see pp.58–59)— formerly called linesmen—support the referee, primarily by signaling for corner kicks, throw-ins, and offside infringements. They must also bring the referee's attention to any other fouls or infringements that the referee may not have seen. However, the referee's word is always final.

7. DURATION OF MATCH

There are two equal halves of 45 minutes of play. Additional time may be added—at the discretion of the referee—for injuries, substitutions, and time wasting. Time can also be added to allow a penalty to be taken at the end of normal time. Rules covering extra time are made by national soccer associations and confederations.

8. START/RESTART OF PLAY

A coin is tossed before the start of play; the winners choose ends for the first half and the losers kick off. The other team kicks off in the second half. The kickoff is taken from the center spot. All players must be in their own half, and the opposition must be at least 10 yd (9.15 m) away from the ball. The ball must be touched by a second player before the first player can touch it again.

9. BALL IN AND OUT OF PLAY

The ball is in play when it is inside the field of play and the referee has not stopped the match. The ball is out of play when it has completely crossed the sidelines or the goal lines, whether in the air or on the ground. If the ball rebounds off a goalpost, crossbar, corner flag post, or the referee or one of the assistant referees and remains in the field of play, it is still in play.

ENFORCING THE RULES

The Laws of the Game are enforced by the referee (see pp.56–57), who has the final say in any match disputes. Since 1992, FIFA has stipulated that all referees in international matches must speak English. The referee may be helped by two assistant referees and a fourth official (see pp.58–59). The fourth official is increasingly used in international matches and the leading leagues, primarily to assist the referee with administrative duties.

VARIATIONS IN THE RULES

The Laws of the Game are simple enough to apply to every level of the game. However, there are minor variations between leagues. For example, while the names of substitutes must always be submitted to the referee before kickoff, in lower leagues, the teams can decide between themselves how many substitutions may be made; in FIFA competitions, the maximum is three, unless a fourth is allowed in extra time.

BALL BOY SCORES

Law 5 states that the referee's decision is final—no matter how bizarre. In 2008, when a striker for Brazil's Santacruzense missed an attempted equalizer against Sorocaba, no one could have predicted what happened next. When the referee's back was turned, a cheeky ball boy decided to nudge the ball over the goal line. To everyone's amazement, the goal was allowed.

STAT ATTACK

"DIRTIEST" WORLD CUPS

Some of the most recent men's World Cups have also seen the most sendings off in the history of the tournament. In contrast, the 1950 and 1970 World Cups saw not a single red card.

MOST RED CARDS ISSUED

HOST	YEAR	TOTAL*
GERMANY	2006	28
FRANCE	1998	22
SOUTH AFRICA	2010	17
KOREA/JAPAN	2002	17
ITALY	1990	16

* Total red cards issued per tournament

10. METHOD OF SCORING

A goal is scored when the ball has completely crossed the goal line between the goalposts and under the crossbar, provided that no other infringements have taken place. The team with the most goals wins. If both teams score the same number of goals, or if no goals are scored at all, the match is a draw.

11. OFFSIDE

A player is offside (see pp.66–67), at the moment a ball is passed forward, when they player is: in the opponents' half of the field; closer to the opponents' goal line than the ball; and there are fewer than two defenders (including the goalkeeper) closer to the goal line than the attacking player. When a player is called offside, the opposition is awarded a free kick.

12. FOULS AND MISCONDUCT

A foul (see pp.68–69) has been committed if a player: trips, kicks, pushes, or charges another player recklessly; strikes, attempts to strike, or spits at an opponent; makes a tackle but connects with the player before the ball; deliberately handles the ball (goalkeepers in their area excepted); or obstructs an opponent or prevents an opponent from releasing the ball.

13. FREE KICKS

Free kicks (see pp.64–65, 138–139) restart play after a foul or infringement and are usually taken from the place where the offense was committed. Free kicks can be "direct," in which the taker may score directly, or "indirect," in which the taker and a second player from the same team must touch the ball before a goal can be scored.

14. PENALTY KICK

A penalty kick (see pp.64, 140–141) is awarded for a foul committed by a defending player in the player's own penalty area. The kick is taken from the penalty spot, and all other players—except for the goalkeeper and taker—must be at least 10 yd (9.15 m) from the spot. The taker may touch the ball if it rebounds from the goalkeeper, but not if it rebounds from the post or crossbar.

15. THE THROW-IN

A throw-in (see p.64, pp.138–139) is awarded when the ball has crossed the touchline and an opposition player was the last to touch it. The throw is taken from the point where the ball crossed the line. The taker must have both feet on the ground, use two hands, throw the ball from behind and over the head, and be facing the field of play.

16. GOAL KICK

A goal kick (see pp.142–145) is awarded to the defending team when the ball crosses its goal line, a goal has not been scored, and the last player to touch it was from the opposition. Any player may take the goal kick, placing the ball anywhere in the goal area. The kick must send the ball out of the penalty area or be retaken. The taker may not touch the ball again until it has been touched by a second player.

17. CORNER KICK

A corner kick (see pp.64, 136–137) is awarded to the attacking team when the opposition is last to touch the ball and the ball crosses the goal line without a goal being scored. A corner is also awarded if the ball enters the goal from a throw-in or indirect free kick. The attacking team restarts play by placing the ball in the corner arc closest to where it crossed the goal line.

SEEING RED
Law 5 says that the referee's decision is always final.

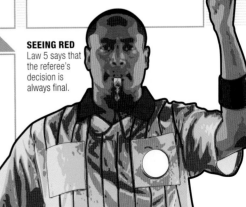

HOW THE GAME IS PLAYED

USING SET PIECES

A set piece is a predetermined, fixed move used to restart play when the referee is forced to halt the game temporarily. There are three occasions when the normally free-flowing game of soccer is stopped: following an infringement, such as a foul or offside; when the ball goes out of play; and following a player injury or other interruption, such as a burst ball.

TYPES OF SET PIECE

There are six different types of set piece: goal kicks, free kicks, throw-ins, penalty kicks, corner kicks, and drop balls. Free kicks can be either "direct," in which the taker can score a goal without another player touching the ball, or "indirect," in which a second player must first touch the ball. In either situation, every member of the opposing team must be at least 10 yd (9.15 m) from the ball at the moment the kick is taken.

GOALS FROM A SET PIECE

England: Premier League—**37** percent

Germany: Bundesliga—**33** percent

Italy: Serie A—**32** percent

Spain: La Liga—**31** percent

HIGH STAKES

Many goals are scored from set pieces (see box, right). As a result, teams spend a lot of time practicing how to attack (and defend) from set pieces. A defending team, for example, will adopt positions and patterns of movement designed to stop an easy goal. If a free kick is awarded near the goal, the defenders will set up a line of players (called a wall) in front of the kicker to try to block the ball.

IN THE SPOTLIGHT

Almost 120 years after William McCrum invented the penalty kick, a memorial was erected in his hometown to celebrate his contribution to soccer. The bust and plinth sits in the small town of Milford in County Armagh, Northern Ireland. McCrum invented the set piece as the ultimate sanction after witnessing violent play.

Goal area
A goal kick is taken from inside the goal area.

GOAL KICK
A goal kick is awarded to a defending team when the ball completely crosses the goal line—either on the ground or in the air—having been kicked by an opposing player without a goal being scored.

The wall
The goalkeeper organizes the defenders into a wall.

Player position
The taker kicks the ball from where the infringement took place.

FREE KICK
Direct free kicks are awarded for serious offenses, such as kicking, tripping, or pushing, while indirect free kicks are awarded for less serious offenses, such as obstruction or offside (see right).

Correct technique
The thrower must face the field of play and have both feet on the ground.

THROW-IN
A throw-in is awarded against the team that last touches the ball before it crosses the touchline. It is made with both feet on or behind the touchline and both hands moving from behind the taker's head.

Great expectations
There can be huge pressure on the taker of a penalty kick, especially during a penalty shoot-out (see pp.140–141).

PENALTY KICK
A penalty kick is awarded for any offense committed inside the penalty area that would otherwise be punished by a direct free kick had it taken place outside the penalty area.

Scoring opportunity
Many goals are scored from corners, often as a result of headers.

Testing time
The keeper must decide whether to defend from the goal line or advance to try to clear the ball.

CORNER KICK
A corner kick is awarded when the whole of the ball crosses the goal line (either on the ground or in the air) having last been touched by a member of the defending team, including the goalkeeper.

SET PIECE ETIQUETTE

If a player is injured, the team in possession is expected to kick the ball into touch. The other side should then return it from the resulting set piece. During an English FA Cup tie in 1999, Sheffield United's goalkeeper kicked the ball out of play so that an injured teammate could receive treatment. But instead of returning the ball, Arsenal midfielder Ray Parlour initiated a move that led to the winning goal. The match was eventually replayed.

DROP BALL

A drop ball is played when a game needs to be restarted following an incident not covered in the rules, such as a serious player injury. The ball is not awarded to either team. Instead, a player from one team stands across from a player from the other team and the referee drops the ball between them.

THE "BANANA SHOT"

LEGENDARY FREE KICK

In 1997, Roberto Carlos (see below) scored from an incredible direct free kick. He hit the ball so far to the right of the French wall that a ball boy between the corner flag and the goalpost ducked. Miraculously, the ball swerved in and landed in the goal. Carlos's "banana shot" has entered soccer folklore.

With a shot that seemed to defy the laws of physics, Carlos swerved the ball around the wall.

- ● Roberto Carlos (Brazil)
- ● Defending team (France)
- — Trajectory of ball

ROBERTO **CARLOS**

Brazilian wingback (see p.44) Roberto Carlos was renowned for his trademark free kicks. His seemingly impossible "banana shot" (see above) is legendary. Carlos played for the Brazil national team in three World Cup tournaments, helping the South American team reach the final in 1998 and win in 2002. He was named as one of the top 125 greatest living players by Pelé in 2004.

OFFENSES

DIRECT FREE KICKS

Direct free kicks are usually awarded for relatively serious offenses (see pp.68–69). The most common are:

KICKING AND TRIPPING
It is an offense for a player to kick or trip—or attempt to kick or trip—an opponent.

JUMPING OR CHARGING
It is an offense for a player to jump or charge at an opponent.

STRIKING AND PUSHING
It is an offense for a player to strike, push, hold, or spit at an opponent.

MAKING CONTACT
It is an offense for a player to touch an opponent before touching the ball when making a tackle.

HANDLING THE BALL
It is an offense for a player to handle the ball deliberately (except for goalkeepers in their area).

INDIRECT FREE KICKS

Indirect free kicks are usually awarded for less serious offenses than direct free kicks. The most common are:

OBSTRUCTION
It is an offense for a player to impede the progress of an opponent deliberately.

DANGEROUS PLAY
It is an offense to make an attempt to kick the ball when an opponent is aiming to head it, especially when the ball is above waist height.

IMPEDING THE GOALKEEPER
It is an offense to prevent the goalkeeper from releasing the ball.

TOUCHING THE BALL TWICE
It is an offense to touch the ball twice at a set piece without an intervening touch from another player.

OFFSIDE
If a player is offside (see pp.66–67), an indirect free kick is given to the opposition.

HOW THE GAME IS PLAYED

THE OFFSIDE RULE

Offside is the most contentious and frequently misunderstood rule in soccer, as decisions often rest on an official's individual interpretation of the law. It is also the most frequently revised rule, as minor changes to the regulations can have dramatic effects on the character of matches.

KEY
- Attacking team
- Defending team
- ○ Goalkeeper
- – – Pass
- — Player movement

WHAT IS THE RULE?

A player is ruled offside at the moment the ball is passed forward by a teammate if the player is in the opponent's half of the field and ahead of the last defender (not including the goalkeeper). Only the head, body, and legs are taken into consideration (not the arms). A player is still onside if that player is level with the last defender from the goal line or if the player receives the ball directly from a throw-in, corner, or goal kick.

THE DEVIL IN THE DETAIL

The situation is complicated, however, by the stipulation that a player in an offside position is deemed to be committing an offense only if they are "active." In 2005, FIFA expanded on the rule by defining an active player as one who is: interfering with play—meaning that they have played a ball passed or touched by a teammate; interfering with an opponent—meaning that they have obstructed the movement or line of vision of an opponent, or distracted them with a gesture or movement; gaining an advantage—meaning that they have used the offside position to benefit from a rebound off a post, crossbar, or an opponent.

OFFSIDE

Here, Player A is offside because there is only one defender—the goalkeeper (1)—between Player A and the goal line when Player B passes the ball. An indirect free kick would be awarded for this offense.

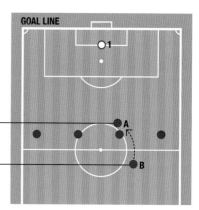

GOAL LINE

Offside
Player A is in an offside position.

Passing forward
Player B passes the ball to Player A, who is offside.

ONSIDE

In the scenario shown here, Player A is not offside. This is because when Player B passed the ball, there was one defender (excluding the goalkeeper) between Player A and the goal line.

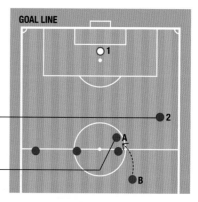

GOAL LINE

Two defenders
Both the goalkeeper (1) and another defender (2) are between Player A and the goal line.

Onside
Player A is in an onside position.

OFFSIDE OR NOT?

The offside rule has various nuances that often make rulings very subjective. There are, for example, many situations in which a player is in an offside position but is not deemed to be violating the offside rule. The following scenarios (right) illustrate some of the peculiarities of the rule.

KEY
- Attacking team
- Defending team
- ○ Goalkeeper
- – – Pass
- — Player movement

SCENARIO ONE

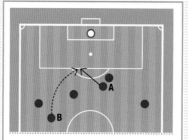

ONSIDE
In this example, Player A is in an onside position when receiving the ball and plays it forward to a teammate. Both are therefore onside.

SCENARIO TWO

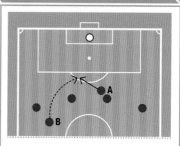

OFFSIDE
In this example, Player A, who is receiving the ball, was in an offside position when the ball was played forward by Player B. Player A is therefore offside.

HISTORY OF THE OFFSIDE RULE

The offside law was introduced to prevent "goal hanging," which usually results in a game degenerating into a series of long kicks from one end of the field to the other. The FA's first set of rules in 1896 stated: "When a player has kicked the ball, anyone of the same side who is nearer to the opponents' goal line is out of play." Three years later, forward passes were permitted, as long as there were three opponents between the receiver and the goal line (or a goalkeeper and the defenders). In 1925, this number was reduced to two. The most significant recent change came in 1990, when attackers were ruled onside if they were level with the second-to-last opponent.

OFFSIDE DECISIONS PER GAME

Of the five major leagues in Europe, the Bundesliga, Serie A, and La Liga had the most offside decisions per game during the 2016–2017 season:

Bundesliga—**4.6** (Germany)

Serie A—**4.6** (Italy)

La Liga—**4.6** (Spain)

Premier League—**3.8** (England/Wales)

FILIPPO **INZAGHI**

Former Italy and AC Milan forward Filippo Inzaghi was a predatory goal scorer with a reputation for playing "off the shoulder" (see p.52). Ex-Manchester United manager Sir Alex Ferguson once joked that he was "born in an offside position." The World Cup–winning player was Italy's top goal scorer during the qualifying rounds of the 2002 World Cup and Euro 2004.

IF A PLAYER ISN'T INTERFERING WITH PLAY OR SEEKING TO GAIN AN ADVANTAGE ...
HE SHOULD BE!

BILL SHANKLY, LIVERPOOL MANAGER, 1960s–'70s
ON "ACTIVE" PLAYERS IN OFFSIDE DECISIONS

SCENARIO THREE

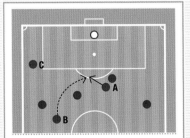

ONSIDE
In this example, Player C on the left wing is in an offside position. However, as C is not interfering with the play between Players A and B, Player C is deemed to be onside.

SCENARIO FOUR

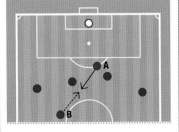

OFFSIDE
In this example, Player A receives the ball in an offside position at the moment it was passed forward by Player B.

SCENARIO FIVE

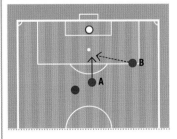

ONSIDE
In this example, despite the fact that Player A receives the ball in an offside position, A is actually onside. This is because A was behind the ball at the moment that it was played.

FOULS AND INFRINGEMENTS

When the FA's Laws of the Game (see pp.62–63) were first drawn up in 1863, one team, Blackheath, decided to withdraw from the association because its favored habit of hacking (forcing the foot into an opponent's ankle) was about to be outlawed. Since then, a host of other offenses have been written into the rule book as fouls, and referees, equipped with red and yellow cards, have been employed to enforce them.

UNRULY RULINGS

In a game between Curitiba and Santos in Brazil in 2003, Curitiba striker Jaba displayed his skill with a flamboyant show of close-ball control. The Santos players thought Jaba was mocking them and, incensed, physically attacked him. But instead of the Santos players being booked for their behavior, Jaba was cautioned for provoking his opponents.

CRIME AND PUNISHMENT

A foul is an act or offense committed by a player who is deemed by the referee to have contravened Law 12 of the Laws of the Game. This includes kicking, tripping, or striking an opponent, connecting with a player before connecting with the ball when tackling, and deliberately handling the ball. Yellow and red cards are used to punish serious fouls (see right), while, for lesser fouls, free kicks are awarded to the opposing side.

> I'M COMMITTING WICKED FOULS ... GOING FOR HIGH BALLS I USE MY ELBOW ...
> ## OR I'M DEAD
>
> **THIERRY HENRY**
> FRANCE STRIKER, 2000

DIRECT AND INDIRECT FREE KICKS

A direct free kick is awarded to the opposing team when a player commits a dangerous or "penal" foul, such as charging at an opponent with excessive force or performing a high tackle. A goal may be scored directly from this type of free kick (see pp.64–65). An indirect free kick is awarded to the opposing team when a player commits a foul other than a dangerous or penal foul, or infringes technical requirements. A goal cannot be scored directly from this type of free kick (a second player must first touch the ball). See below for some typical fouls.

Blocking play
It is a foul for a player to use their body to block another player.

Dangerous play
High tackles are considered to be dangerous play.

OBSTRUCTION
If a player is positioned between the ball and an opponent and makes no attempt to play the ball, this is known as obstruction.

HIGH TACKLE
Whether attempting to play the ball or not, tackles made with "high feet" have become increasingly less acceptable in soccer.

Impeded
It is a foul for a player to hold back an opponent.

Intentional trip
A player who deliberately trips up an opponent is committing a foul.

Dangerous tackle
A sliding tackle can be a serious offense if not executed properly.

HOLDING
It is an offense to pull on a player's shirt to slow them down in an attempt to gain possession of the ball.

TRIPPING
Tripping has long been an offense, but the referee must be sharp-eyed to see if there really has been contact between the players.

SLIDING TACKLE
A sliding tackle, in which the attacking player fails to gain possession of the ball, is considered to be a serious foul.

TOP 5: BAD BOYS

Soccer has always attracted players who are happy to flout the rules—no matter how dangerous their behavior. Here are five of the "best" bad boys.

GERARDO MÚNERA
Colombia's Gerardo Múnera received more red cards (46) than any other player in soccer history.

HARALD SCHUMACHER
Schumacher's moment of infamy came in the 1982 World Cup Semifinal when he smashed into advancing French player Patrick Battiston. The Frenchman was left unconscious by the challenge, but Schumacher wasn't booked.

ANDONI GOIKOETXEA
Dubbed "The butcher from Bilbao," Goiko was a ruthless defender who achieved notoriety for a dangerous tackle on Diego Maradona that resulted in a broken ankle for the Argentinian midfielder.

"CHOPPER" HARRIS
Ron "Chopper" Harris acquired his infamous nickname during 17 bone-crunching seasons at Chelsea between 1963 and 1980.

FRANK BARSON
A player for Barnsley, Aston Villa, and Manchester United between 1911 and 1935, Barson's tackles and barging of goalkeepers produced a strong reaction among rival fans. For his own safety, he was often escorted out by the local police.

HARALD SCHUMACHER
Schumacher injured Patrick Battiston at the 1982 World Cup by deliberately colliding into him.

FOUL, REF!
A tackle should take the ball, not the opponent. Referees judge whether foul play merits a yellow or red card, as well as a free-kick.

THE CARD SYSTEM

In addition to awarding free kicks, the referee can penalize an individual player by issuing either a yellow or red card. A yellow card (or caution) is issued for serious offenses or dissent. A red card is issued for very serious or violent offenses and results in the player being sent off immediately. Players receiving two yellow cards in the same game will also be sent off.

CARD HISTORY

A system of colored cards was first developed by English referee Ken Aston following the 1966 World Cup. He was inspired by stop lights, and the red and yellow cards were tried out at the 1968 Olympic Games and the 1970 World Cup. They became compulsory in 1982.

OFFENSES

A player is shown a yellow card for relatively serious offenses, such as those listed (see right). A player is shown a red card for very serious offenses, including those listed here (see far right). A player who has been dismissed may not remain on or in the vicinity of the field of play or the technical area.

YELLOW CARD OFFENSES

Dissent by word or action

Persistent infringement of the rules

Delaying the restart of play, and deliberate time wasting

Making a poorly timed, dangerous tackle

Entering or leaving the field without the referee's permission

Unsporting behavior

RED CARD OFFENSES

Serious foul play

Violent conduct, or using offensive language

Spitting at an opponent or other person

Denying the opposing team a goal or potential chance at goal by deliberately handling the ball (does not apply to goalkeepers inside their own penalty area)

Receiving two cautions in the same match

SHIRTS, SHORTS, AND SOCKS

For official games, it is compulsory for players to wear a shirt or jersey (with short or long sleeves), shorts, and socks. Shin pads and cleats must also be worn (see pp.72–73). All the players on a team (except for the goalkeeper, who wears a distinguishing shirt) must wear matching uniforms. While shirts may feature stripes, hoops, or other patterned designs, shorts arc usually one color, sometimes with a stripe down the sides. Undergarments may be worn for added comfort and protection, but they must be the same main color as the shirt or shorts.

HOME AND AWAY

The first clash of uniforms in the world came in 1890 when Sunderland played Wolverhampton Wanderers (both teams wore red and white stripes at the time). Sunderland was the home team and, in accordance with the rules of the English league, was required to change uniform. In 1921, however, the rules were reversed, with the away team required to change (although both teams had to change in FA Cup games played at a neutral ground).

REFEREE'S DECISION

A player who is not wearing the correct uniform will be asked to leave the field by the referee and may return only when the referee has confirmed that the uniform is correct. No uniform was specified in the first set of rules in 1863, however, when players could wear whatever they liked.

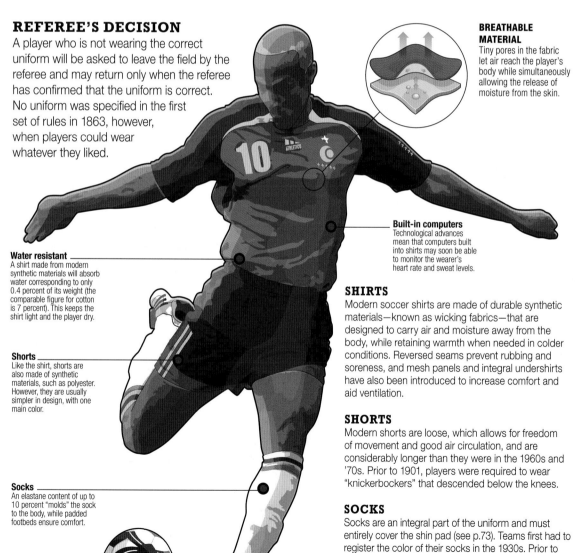

BREATHABLE MATERIAL
Tiny pores in the fabric let air reach the player's body while simultaneously allowing the release of moisture from the skin.

Built-in computers
Technological advances mean that computers built into shirts may soon be able to monitor the wearer's heart rate and sweat levels.

Water resistant
A shirt made from modern synthetic materials will absorb water corresponding to only 0.4 percent of its weight (the comparable figure for cotton is 7 percent). This keeps the shirt light and the player dry.

Shorts
Like the shirt, shorts are also made of synthetic materials, such as polyester. However, they are usually simpler in design, with one main color.

Socks
An elastane content of up to 10 percent "molds" the sock to the body, while padded footbeds ensure comfort.

SHIRTS

Modern soccer shirts are made of durable synthetic materials—known as wicking fabrics—that are designed to carry air and moisture away from the body, while retaining warmth when needed in colder conditions. Reversed seams prevent rubbing and soreness, and mesh panels and integral undershirts have also been introduced to increase comfort and aid ventilation.

SHORTS

Modern shorts are loose, which allows for freedom of movement and good air circulation, and are considerably longer than they were in the 1960s and '70s. Prior to 1901, players were required to wear "knickerbockers" that descended below the knees.

SOCKS

Socks are an integral part of the uniform and must entirely cover the shin pad (see p.73). Teams first had to register the color of their socks in the 1930s. Prior to this, players could choose their own, which would often result in a lack of color coordination across the team.

GOALKEEPER'S SHIRT

As the only player who is allowed to handle the ball, it is important that the goalkeeper is easily identifiable. For this reason, in 1909 goalkeepers could wear white, scarlet, or blue shirts. In 1912, the green shirt was introduced as an option and quickly became the most popular choice. Then, in the 1970s, regulations were relaxed, allowing manufacturers to experiment with designs.

SHIRT NUMBERS

Shirt numbers were first used in 1928 to help referees and the crowd identify players. Historically, they corresponded to fixed playing positions, with the center forward (see p.51), for example, always allocated the number nine. As formations have evolved, however, this practice has become rare. Today "squad" numbers are used, with individual players being designated a number for the whole season.

SQUAD NUMBERS

The relaxation of the rules relating shirt numbers to playing positions has led some players to choose unique squad numbers for themselves. When Inter Milan signed the Brazilian striker Ronaldo, giving him Chilean forward Ivan Zamorano's number-nine shirt, Zamorano was allocated the number 18 shirt. However, because he liked to think of himself as a "number nine," he inserted a plus sign between the two digits (1+8=9).

RAHEEM STERLING
The exciting forward is shown wearing Manchester City's 2019–2020 uniform made by Puma. It is said to reflect the team's industrial and cultural heritage.

HISTORICAL NUMBERING SYSTEM
This "classic" numbering system was based on the positions in the 2-3-5 formation (see p.86) that was dominant when shirt numbers were first introduced.

A HISTORY OF KIT

In 1891, the English league called for all clubs to register their shirt colors, and, by the early 20th century, most of the biggest soccer clubs from Europe and Latin America had decided on their current uniform design. However, while shirt colors and designs may have remained largely unchanged since the early days of soccer, the materials used, the cut, and the details of those early shirts would be almost unrecognizable to the modern player.

SOCK TAGS AND SMILEY FACES

In 1961, Leeds United manager Don Revie changed the color of his team's uniform from royal blue to all white, in emulation of Real Madrid, whose success he hoped to copy. In 1973, he tried another tack and introduced numbered sock tags to the Yorkshire team. In another innovation, he changed the badge so that the letters "LU" formed a smiley face.

1890s
Early shirts were heavy, long-sleeved, woolen jerseys. Some had no collar while others had a laced crew neck. Long shorts were standard.

1930s
Typically made from cotton, shirts became lighter with a more generous cut. Most had a player number, and collars were popular.

1960s
With the introduction of the first synthetic materials, shirts became even lighter. V-necks and short sleeves were common.

1970s
Manufacturer's logos started to take up more space on shirts. Club emblems were redesigned as logos and shorts became very short.

1980s–1990s
Sponsorship logos became widespread. Shadow stripes and pinstripes appeared, as did players' names on the backs of shirts.

2000s
Shorts are very light, and skintight lycra shirts with piping and trim have been introduced. Sales of replica uniforms have exploded.

CLEATS AND PROTECTIVE GEAR

Players need comfortable, lightweight, and durable footwear that grips the playing surface. In addition, players need some protective gear. Shin pads, which are made from plastic, are worn to protect the shins and must be covered entirely by socks. Goalkeepers can wear protective headgear and gloves that provide grip and hand protection when catching the ball.

FIT FOR A KING

Despite issuing a series of laws that banned the playing of soccer in England—it was blamed for inciting riots—King Henry VIII (1491–1547) owned a pair of soccer cleats. In an inventory of the king's wardrobe made after his death, there is an entry for a pair of cleats made from sturdy Spanish leather.

SOCCER CLEATS

The soccer cleat should be flexible enough to maximize performance but sturdy enough to reduce the risk of injury. On grass, players wear studded cleats (see right for types of studs); on artificial turf, players wear sneakers with rubber pimples on the sole.

TECHNOLOGICAL DEVELOPMENTS

While innovations in modern soccer cleat design may appear to be limited to a profusion of often garish colors and logos, there have in fact been a number of significant technological developments. These have had wide-ranging implications for performance and play.

SCREW-IN STUDS
Detachable studs are used for wet conditions. Different lengths of stud can be fitted.

FIXED STUDS
Cleats with fixed or "molded" studs are used for standard turf conditions.

BLADED STUDS
Boots with fixed "blades" provide a stable base on firm natural turf that is too hard for studs.

MODERN SOCCER CLEATS
Modern cleats are extremely light and flexible and are made from an array of synthetic fabrics and plastics. Kangaroo leather, which is markedly stronger, lighter, and more supple than other leathers, is widely used in cleat manufacture.

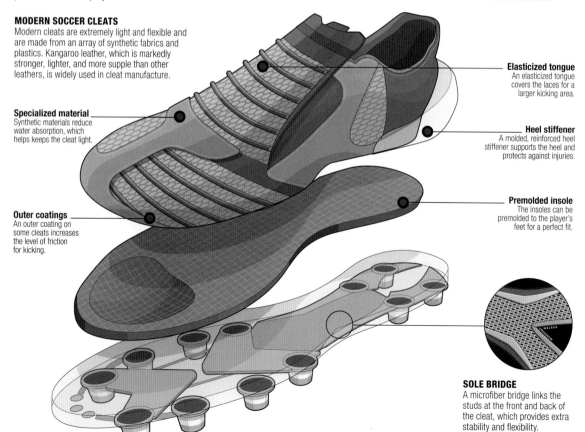

Elasticized tongue
An elasticized tongue covers the laces for a larger kicking area.

Heel stiffener
A molded, reinforced heel stiffener supports the heel and protects against injuries.

Specialized material
Synthetic materials reduce water absorption, which helps keeps the cleat light.

Premolded insole
The insoles can be premolded to the player's feet for a perfect fit.

Outer coatings
An outer coating on some cleats increases the level of friction for kicking.

SOLE BRIDGE
A microfiber bridge links the studs at the front and back of the cleat, which provides extra stability and flexibility.

A HISTORY OF THE CLEAT

While the FA made no comment about balls or shirts in its first set of rules, it had strict rules about the use of cleats (see quote below). By the 1880s, specialized cleats were being made to supply both the professional and burgeoning amateur markets. With only minor developments, these early cleats were the industry standard until the appearance of the low-cut design in the 1950s.

ALL WHITE ON THE NIGHT

In the early 1970s, Alan Ball (who had been the youngest player on England's 1966 World Cup–winning side) wanted to be the first player to wear white soccer cleats. He daubed his black Adidas cleats with paint, but the moment was short-lived as rain washed them clean.

Thick leather
The earliest cleats were made from thick, stiff leather that offered little "give."

Fewer eyelets
In the 1930s, soccer cleats were being laced using fewer eyelets.

Conical stud
This popular cleat from the late 1970s featured fixed conical-shaped studs.

EARLY CLEAT—1880s
The first specially designed cleats were produced in small batches in the 1880s. Individual styles varied, but all cleats had nailed-in studs, full ankle protection, and extra toe coverings.

CLASSIC CLEAT—1930s
Although the basic cleat design inherited from the 19th century had changed very little, by the 1930s the tops and tongue were often left loose. Lighter leather and synthetic materials were used.

CLEATS FROM 1954 ONWARD
Cleats cut below the ankle were first manufactured in 1954, creating the distinct profile of all modern soccer cleats. Screw-in studs (see p.72) were also pioneered at this time.

PROTECTIVE GEAR

Shin pads, which are designed to prevent fractures to the tibia resulting from rough tackles, were made compulsory by FIFA in 1990. Goalkeepers can, and always do, wear protective gloves (see below, right). Players are permitted to wear protective headgear as long as it doesn't jeopardize the safety of other players.

NO ONE WEARING PROJECTING NAILS ... IS ALLOWED TO PLAY!

LAW 13
FA RULES, 1863

SHIN PADS

Pads are made from plastic polymers and fiberglass and protect the shins from other players' tackles. They strap to the shin, under the sock. The first shin pads were cut-down cricket pads and are thought to have been invented in 1874 in England by Sam Widdowson, who played soccer for Nottingham Forest and cricket for Nottinghamshire.

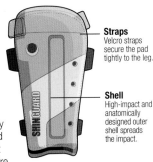

Straps
Velcro straps secure the pad tightly to the leg.

Shell
High-impact and anatomically designed outer shell spreads the impact.

HEADGEAR

Protective headgear is designed to cushion the head from collisions with other players, the ground, or the goalposts. Protective headgear is now worn by many goalkeepers.

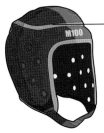

Flexible cap
Soccer headgear is flexible but tough enough to prevent injuries.

GOALKEEPER'S GLOVES

All players may wear gloves, although up until the 1970s, few chose to do so. Gloves are now universally worn by goalkeepers to increase grip on the ball and protect the hands. They are made from strong synthetic materials and are segmented to aid flexibility. Protectors prevent the fingers from bending backward.

PALM PROTECTION
The palm area of the glove is made from material designed to enhance grip and protection.

SOCCER SHIRTS

The humble soccer shirt has come a long way since the heavy woolen jerseys and thick cotton smocks of the 19th century. For almost a century, a narrow range of colors, designs, and motifs was used. Over the last few decades, however, manufacturers have been pursuing ever more complex—and colorful—designs in an effort to innovate and sell more shirts. The results have not always been edifying.

VOCABULARY OF THE SOCCER SHIRT

Although in recent years manufacturers have experimented with the range of colors and the complexity of designs used in their soccer shirts, for much of the last century there were surprisingly few visual devices in use. Many of these designs were drawn from the language of European heraldry. Here are some of the most popular shirt designs.

CHECKERS
Checkered shirts are a useful strategy for confusing the opposition. The Croatian team's colors appear on Croatia's national coat of arms.

TEAMS: Croatia and Boavista

STRIPES
While stripes may look great, they do nothing for the waistline. Two colors are the norm, but some teams, such as Rio's Flamengo, have three.

TEAMS: Celtic, Flamengo, Queens Park Rangers, and Sporting Lisbon

SASH
Rarely found in Europe, Latin American teams have a fondness for the cross-body sash shirt. The simple, bold design certainly adds panache.

TEAMS: Peru, Vasco de Gama, Rayo Vallecano, and River Plate

VERTICAL STRIPES
When soccer shirts were first made, the cheapest available material had vertically striped patterns (often the remnants from material for mattresses).

TEAMS: Argentina, Athletic Bilbao, Internazionale, Juventus, Milan, Newcastle, Sunderland

HALVES
A favorite among English public schools, other clubs around the world that use the motif often have a strong English connection.

TEAMS: Basel, Blackburn Rovers, Cagliari, Genoa, Grasshopper, and Newell's Old Boys

CONTRASTING ARMS
The uniform was made popular by Herbert Chapman's Arsenal in the 1920s and '30s, although Aston Villa and West Ham were already sporting the look.

TEAMS: Arsenal, Aston Villa, Rapid Vienna, and Stade de Reims

CENTRAL STRIPE
Amsterdam club Ajax considers itself unique in many ways, and few other clubs have followed its distinctive centrally striped shirt.

TEAMS: Ajax, Paris Saint-Germain, and Southampton

WEIRD-LOOKING SHIRTS

Not only can the imagination run wild, but—as with these extraordinary shirts—it can also turn nasty. Feast your eyes on the world's strangest shirts.

MEXICO
Jorge Campos, Mexico's goalkeeper for much of the 1990s, was renowned for his frequent bizarre and psychedelic adventures in shirt design.

MANCHESTER UNITED
Gray was the color of Manchester United's change shirt in 1995–1996. Unfortunately, on the five occasions they played in it, they lost four matches and tied the fifth.

COLORADO CARIBOUS
In 1978, the Caribous lasted just one season in the North American Soccer League. With a unique leather-fringed shirt, it was just like the Wild West on the field.

CAMEROON 2004
Cameroon unveiled the first one-piece soccer uniform at the African Nations Cup in 2004. It was banned by FIFA, who then deducted six points after Cameroon continued to wear it.

INTERNAZIONALE
In 2007, Internazionale wore a change shirt in white with a red cross—the symbol of Milan. But opponents in the Muslim world took exception to the design, feeling it was redolent of the crusades.

ATHLETIC BILBAO
Bilbao has reinvented itself as the home of the critically acclaimed Guggenheim art museum. A similar reinvention of the club's shirt has been less well received.

ODD COUPLES

Some of the most unlikely teams in world soccer have been united by their shirts. The distance between Juventus, the superstars of Italian soccer, and Notts County, forever mired at the bottom of the English league, is huge—but the teams are still connected. Here are five of soccer's oddest couples.

(2013–14)

(2013–14)

JUVENTUS AND NOTTS COUNTY
In 1903, one of the English members of Juventus arranged for a new shirt to be sent from Nottingham. It must have come from Notts County's tailors.

(2013–14)

(2013–14)

BLACKBURN ROVERS AND GRASSHOPPERS
English biology student Tom Griffiths gave the Zurich team its zoological title and the same shirt as his home team—Blackburn Rovers.

(2011–12)

(2013–14)

BARCELONA AND BASEL FC
The itinerant Swiss-born founding member of Barcelona didn't just take soccer to Barcelona; he also took his home club's shirt.

(2016–17)

(2013–14)

BOCA JUNIORS AND SWEDEN
The founders of Boca are said to have waited by the harbor in Buenos Aires and taken the colors of the first ship that entered port—it was Swedish.

(2011–12)

(2013–14)

ATHLETIC BILBAO AND SUNDERLAND
Red and white stripes arrived in the Basque country in the 1890s when English workers at the port showed the locals how to play their game.

THE BALL

Modern soccer balls consist of an outer covering of synthetic leather panels bonded by heat to form a spherical surface. Real leather, which was used until the 1980s, tended to absorb water, making the ball very heavy (see box, far right). Inside the outer covering is the air bladder, which is usually made from latex or butyl. Between the bladder and the outer cover is an inner lining, which gives the ball its bounce.

FIFA REQUIREMENTS

According to the Laws of the Game (see pp.62–63), the ball must be spherical, made from leather or other suitable materials, and have a circumference of 27–28 in (68.5–71 cm). At the start of the match, the ball should weigh 14½–16 oz (410–450 g) and be inflated to a pressure of 8½ lb/sq in (600–1,100 g/sq cm). These requirements were set in 1872 and have remained largely unchanged ever since.

WHAT'S IN A NAME?

Brazilian soccer commentator Washington Rodriguez has said: "In Brazil, you can call the ball anything except the ball." In fact, there are more than 30 synonyms for the ball in Brazilian Portuguese. Five are women's names and others include: baby, balloon, bladder, chestnut, capricious one, sphere, infidel, demon, doll, and pellet plum.

LABORATORY TESTING

A ball's level of bounce, its ability to swerve through the air, its air retention, and its overall longevity can all be altered by its design. Recent developments in the use of synthetic materials and production techniques, for example, have produced balls that maximize the transfer of energy from the kicker to the ball and are flight accurate. FIFA-approved balls are all laboratory tested for balance, bounce, shape, trajectory, velocity, and water absorption.

SOCCER BALL CONSTRUCTION

There are three main components of a ball: the outer cover, the inner lining, and the bladder. The quality of the materials used for each of these elements can affect how it behaves.

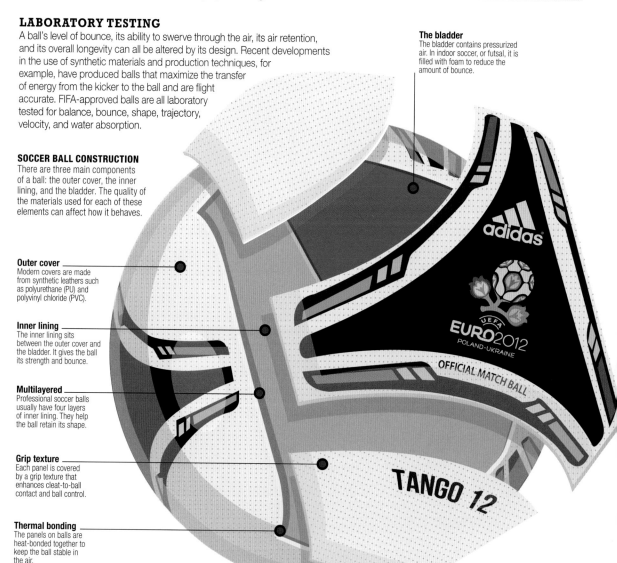

The bladder
The bladder contains pressurized air. In indoor soccer, or futsal, it is filled with foam to reduce the amount of bounce.

Outer cover
Modern covers are made from synthetic leathers such as polyurethane (PU) and polyvinyl chloride (PVC).

Inner lining
The inner lining sits between the outer cover and the bladder. It gives the ball its strength and bounce.

Multilayered
Professional soccer balls usually have four layers of inner lining. They help the ball retain its shape.

Grip texture
Each panel is covered by a grip texture that enhances cleat-to-ball contact and ball control.

Thermal bonding
The panels on balls are heat-bonded together to keep the ball stable in the air.

adidas

UEFA EURO 2012
POLAND-UKRAINE

OFFICIAL MATCH BALL

TANGO 12

BALL DIMENSIONS

Soccer balls for official match use come in a range of standard sizes, depending on the type of soccer being played and the respective age of the players. These variations include professional soccer, indoor soccer or futsal, children's leagues, and beach soccer (see pp.22–27).

27–28 in (68.5–71 cm)

SIZE 5 BALL
This is the international standard ball for professional competitions, from the U12 to adult age ranges.

25–26 in (63.5–66 cm)

SIZE 4 BALL
This is the standard size for futsal (see pp.22–23). It weighs 14–15½ oz (400–440 g).

23–24 in (58.5–61 cm)

SIZE 3 BALL
The smallest official ball, this is used for U8 matches. It weighs between 11–12 oz (310–340 g).

27–28 in (68.5–71 cm)

BEACH SOCCER BALL
The ball used in official beach soccer matches is a size 5 (see above) but is lighter at 14–15½ oz (400–440 g).

A HISTORY OF THE BALL

Medieval soccer was played using a ball stuffed with an inflated pig's bladder. Unsurprisingly, these balls lacked bounce, or bounced irregularly, and were prone to collapsing. In 1836, Charles Goodyear patented vulcanized (cured) rubber and, in 1855, designed and made the first balls with vulcanized-rubber bladders. This provided the ball with a consistent bounce—a key development.

SOCCER INJURIES
A coroner's report into the death of England striker Jeff Astle—a prolific header of the ball who died of a brain disease in 2002—suggested that he suffered from long-term damage caused by heading old-style leather balls that would grow heavy when wet.

Glued seams
Rubber panels (shaped like a modern basketball), were glued together at the seams.

Interlocking panels
Seven or eight interlocking leather panels helped the ball retain its shape.

Multi-sectioned panels
Balls from this period had heavy leather covers comprising six panels of three sections each.

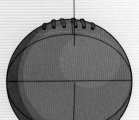
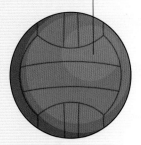

1850s BALL
Goodyear's invention meant that the dimensions of the ball could be set, rather than depending on the size and shape of the pig's bladder.

1880s BALL
The first mass-produced ball arrived after the founding of the English Football League in 1888. Its cover was made from cow leather.

1920s BALL
By the 1920s, the soccer ball's bladder was made from stronger rubber than its predecessors so could be inflated to a higher pressure.

Waterproofing
Synthetic paints and other nonporous materials were used to stop water absorption.

Hexagonal panels
The buckyball consists of 20 hexagonal and 12 pentagonal panels fitted together.

Thermal bonding
Replacing stitching with thermal bonding creates a more aerodynamic surface.

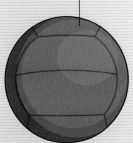

1940s–1950s BALL
The introduction of a carcass, made from strong cloth and placed between the bladder and outer cover, increased strength.

1970s "BUCKYBALL"
The buckyball (named after inventor Richard Buckminster Fuller) marked a new era in ball design. Its black panels helped players detect swerve.

21ST CENTURY BALL
Manufacturers have reduced the number of panels and have replaced stitching with thermal bonding for a smoother surface.

THE GOALKEEPER LIKES THE BALL BEST. EVERYONE ELSE KICKS IT. ONLY THE ...

KEEPER HUGS IT!

POMPIA
BRAZILIAN GOALKEEPER

HOW THE GAME IS PLAYED

THE GOAL

Soccer would be nothing without goals, so great importance is placed on the design of these structures. They must be safe and reliable and must not obscure the spectators' view. They also need to be durable. Nets, for example, used to be made of string and had to be taken down between matches to prevent them from rotting. Today they are made from weatherproof synthetic fibers.

GOAL REQUIREMENTS

The Laws of the Game (see pp.62–63) state that a goal must be placed on the center of each goal line and consist of two upright posts joined at the top by a crossbar. It should be placed equidistant from the corner flag posts and may be made of wood, metal, or other approved material. The posts and crossbar must be white, and the goal should be securely anchored.

BARBECUE OF REVENGE

When Brazil lost the final match of the 1950 World Cup at home in front of a record-breaking crowd and having been 1–0 up against Uruguay, angry fans looked for a scapegoat. They chose their goalkeeper, Barbosa. Still shunned by the 1994 World Cup squad at their training camp, Barbosa is said, in Brazilian popular legend, to have burned the goalposts at the Maracana stadium and enjoyed a "barbecue of revenge" on the embers.

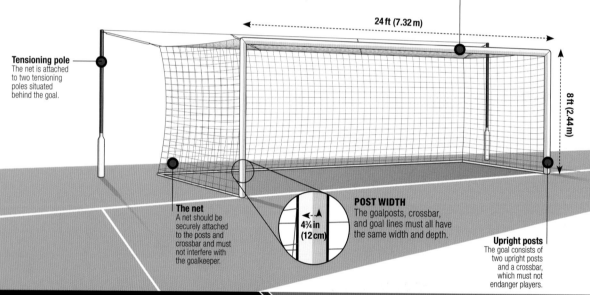

Crossbar
The crossbar must be the same width and color as the upright posts.

24 ft (7.32 m)

8 ft (2.44 m)

Tensioning pole
The net is attached to two tensioning poles situated behind the goal.

The net
A net should be securely attached to the posts and crossbar and must not interfere with the goalkeeper.

4¾ in (12 cm)

POST WIDTH
The goalposts, crossbar, and goal lines must all have the same width and depth.

Upright posts
The goal consists of two upright posts and a crossbar, which must not endanger players.

A HISTORY OF THE GOAL

Despite the obvious importance of the goal to soccer, the FA's first set of rules in 1863 was surprisingly vague about its size and construction. The posts were the first elements to be introduced, although their dimensions and shape could vary. There was also no mention of the crossbar, which meant that a goal was permitted at any height as long as the ball passed between the posts.

RAISING THE BAR

In 1888, London team Swifts were disqualified from the FA Cup when opponents Crewe Alexandra complained about one of the crossbars. Crewe claimed the bar was 2 in (5 cm) lower at one end—below the required height.

1860s GOAL
Early goals consisted of two vertical posts with no crossbar, which led to contentious goals from high balls.

1870s GOAL
A form of crossbar was introduced in the 1870s, when tape was hung between the tops of the posts.

1880s GOAL
In 1882, all soccer teams were required to replace the flimsy tape with a sturdier crossbar.

1890s GOAL
The net was introduced to avoid the need to retrieve the ball after a goal was scored.

DIFFERENT GOAL SIZES

The required dimensions of the goal vary depending on the type of soccer being played. In five-a-side, for example, the ball must not go above head height, so the goal is low. Equally, in beach soccer, the goal is slightly smaller than it is for professional matches because the sand makes it difficult for the goalkeeper to cover large distances quickly.

SIZE MATTERS

Clubs occasionally still make mistakes when setting up their goalposts. In 1998, for example, one of the crossbars at Real Mallorca's old ground—the Luis Sitjer Stadium—was found to be significantly lower than the other.

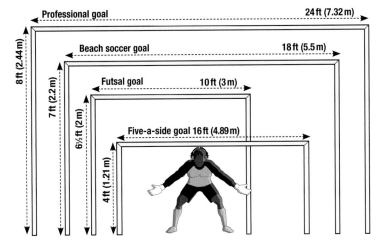

Professional goal — 24 ft (7.32 m) — 8 ft (2.44 m)
Beach soccer goal — 18 ft (5.5 m) — 7 ft (2.2 m)
Futsal goal — 10 ft (3 m) — 6½ ft (2 m)
Five-a-side goal 16 ft (4.89 m) — 4 ft (1.21 m)

750 The number of nets made each year by inmates of Durham prison, England; many are sold to top clubs

13 The distance in feet (4 m) that the nets at Real Zaragoza's La Romareda stadium extend back from the goal line

75 The delay in minutes during Real Madrid's European Cup Semifinal against Borussia Dortmund in 1998, when the crowd damaged the posts

4 Diameter in inches (10 cm) of a professional goalpost with round posts and crossbar

CROSSBAR AND POST PROFILE

Early posts and crossbars, which were usually made from wood (often Douglas fir), were typically either round or square in profile. This was largely because these were the easiest shapes for manufacturers to produce. In 1922, John Claude Perkins of the Standard Goals Company in Nottingham, England, patented a goal frame with a much stronger elliptical profile. He also reinforced his crossbars with metal rods drilled through the core, which helped prevent them from sagging in the middle. Elliptical posts are now standard in top-flight games.

ELLIPTICAL
Most modern goals have this profile, which offers strength and reasonably predictable rebounds.

CIRCULAR
The major drawback with this shape was that the ball might bounce off in any direction.

SQUARE
Some Scottish clubs retained square posts long after they had been abandoned elsewhere.

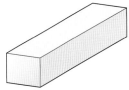

RECTANGULAR
The sharp edges of these posts and crossbars posed an injury threat now considered unacceptable.

HOW THE NET IS HUNG

Several net-hanging systems have been developed over the years. There are two main considerations for the design of these systems: the tension of the net should be such that it is clear when a goal has been scored; and the ball should not rebound off, or become lodged in, the back stanchion.

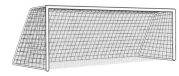

BALL-AND-SOCKET SYSTEM
In the 1970s, net extensions were plugged into "female" sockets that screwed into the posts and crossbar.

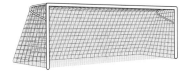

EXTRUSION SYSTEM
In the 1980s, triangular brackets projecting back from the corners of the goal were used to tighten the net.

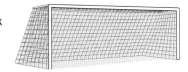

NET-TENSIONING SYSTEM
In the 1990s, goal nets were clipped onto fixed aluminum mounts that functioned in a similar way to curtain rails.

IN (AND OUT) OF THE NET

The "net pocket" was invented by a civil engineer from Liverpool named John Brodie. It was patented in 1889 for goals used in soccer, lacrosse, and other games. Early nets were occasionally strung so tautly that the ball would rebound. In 1909, for example, West Bromwich Albion missed out on promotion after a referee disallowed a goal, thinking that the ball had hit the crossbar— it had in fact rebounded off the net.

SING WHEN YOU'RE WINNING

Soccer is nothing without the crowd—is there any silence grimmer than that of a game played behind closed doors? Soccer crowds have been offering commentary, shouting criticism, and singing for more than a century, drawing on their distinct popular cultures, from the Edwardian music hall and Brazilian carnival, to Viennese oompah bands and Nigerian highlife. Soccer crowds have fused a love of music and rhyme to produce some memorable chants, many of which have inspired the players themselves (see pp.208–209).

FLARES
Although they are banned from all stadiums, fans cannot resist the theatrical swirl of the smoke bomb and the pyrotechnic magic of fireworks and big naval flares.

SOLO ARTISTES
Some people can sing well, and some people are completely tone-deaf, and together they provide the essential catalyst for singing—striking up the first bar alone, unperturbed by the thought that no one might join in.

CHANT ENTREPRENEURS
The poets of the terrace compose their odes in the shower and test them out in the stands. Wit and bravery are required, but the buzz these chant entrepreneurs experience when the chorus picks up their words keeps the songs coming.

DRUMMERS
In Mediterranean countries and across Latin America, singing is often well orchestrated. Most groups will have at least one drummer to keep time and a network of chant leaders, equipped with megaphones, who are strategically positioned throughout the bleachers.

BRASS BANDS
African soccer crowds, especially those in Nigeria, have specialized in the use of horns and brass instruments. Brass bands and instruments are also popular in central and northern Europe, while in Brazil they play sambas.

THE CHORUS
When the mood takes them and the song is right, the crowd provides the volume during the chorus, although some crowds and stands are notoriously hard to "get going." At some clubs, calls between groups of fans across the field form a key component of the singing. Call and response also shapes the interaction between home and away fans.

SCARVES AND FLAGS
In addition to singing, Spanish fans like to take off their scarves and wave them around their heads at moments of excellence on the field. Huge flags are also passed around the crowd like blankets before the game in stadiums around the world.

SUPPORTING ACTORS
Long-standing groups of season ticket holders and fans who practice in the pubs and bars before the game form key parts of the singing crowd. They lend real weight to songs on their second and third lines and keep a tune going when the rest of the crowd is flagging.

SECOND IN COMMAND
Chant entrepreneurs (see left) often have acolytes and friends who lend their support to new chants.

TOP 5: SOCCER ANTHEMS

YOU'LL NEVER WALK ALONE (LIVERPOOL, ENGLAND)
The gold standard of collective solidarity in song, this was originally a tune from the Rodgers and Hammerstein musical *Carousel*. Gerry and the Pacemakers took it to number one in the UK charts in 1963, and it was quickly adopted by their fellow Liverpudlians in the Kop at Anfield.

LA ROMA NON SI DISCUTE, SI AMA (ROMA, ITALY)
The anthem of the club, which translates as "Roma is not to be questioned, it is to be loved," was penned by local singer Antonello Venditti.

HORTO MAGIKO (PANATHINAIKOS, GREECE)
Titled "Magic Weed," the song is a hypnotic dirge of praise that was first sung by the fans of Panathinaikos and notionally refers to the club's emblem, the shamrock.

CANT DEL BARÇA (BARCELONA, SPAIN)
Translated as "Song of Barcelona," this is the official hymn of FC Barcelona, commissioned in 1974 to celebrate the club's 75th anniversary. It was given its official debut that year before a game between Barça and East Germany.

I'M FOREVER BLOWING BUBBLES (WEST HAM, ENGLAND)
Originally a song in a Broadway musical and then a huge hit in the British music hall, this song was introduced to West Ham United in the 1920s by former player and manager Charlie Paynter. It is the perfect anthem for a club whose aspirations invariably exceed performance. The song is often accompanied by mass bubble blowing.

TEAMWORK

TEAMWORK: KEY CONCEPTS

There are many commonly used strategies in soccer, but certain principles can be applied to them all. Players need to have a grasp of these fundamentals if they are to succeed on the field. For a lucky few, it is a process that comes instinctively; for everyone else, a little theory, coupled with plenty of hard work on the training ground, is invaluable.

THE TEAM IS EVERYTHING

There is no "I" in "team." Individual brilliance is useless unless it is harnessed for the good of the team. Whenever players are on the pitch, they should bear five things in mind: find some space so that teammates can pass to them; offer teammates support whenever they are on the ball; guard possession of the ball; move to a new position after they have made a pass; and keep teammates informed of their intentions.

SUPPORT

Players must always look to support their colleagues. This may involve joining them in attack, running back to help out in defense, or filling in for a teammate who has abandoned their usual playing position after joining an attack. Strikers should always follow up shots looking for rebounds off the goalkeeper.

COMMUNICATION

Communication on the field is vital. A player in possession of the ball isn't always aware of teammates' intentions. Therefore, it is essential they make known where they are, where they are heading, and where they want the ball to be played. A player can make a teammate aware by using one of a number of calls.

EMPTY SPACES AND SILENCES ARE AS IMPORTANT AS THOSE THAT ARE FILLED

FORMER INTER MILAN MANAGER **HELENIO HERRERA**

PLAYER CALLS

In theory, players are allowed to shout out anything as long as they aren't deliberately attempting to deceive the opposition. In practice, referees will award an indirect free kick against a player calling out ambiguous phrases like "leave it!" or "mine!"

GLOBAL STYLES

The way soccer should be played is a much-discussed topic, and the opinion given varies from country to country. The descriptions below are generalizations, but they certainly have some validity.

Central American
Mexico (1986)
Crashed out of the
World Cup on penalties
without losing a game.

ROY KEANE
The midfielder was an ultimate team player during his distinguished career with Nottingham Forest, Manchester United, Celtic, and the Republic of Ireland.

CENTRAL AMERICAN

Players (type): Clever, but sometimes excessive, dribblers

Characteristics: Ball tends to be moved around the field in a series of short passes; all players have good one-on-one skills; tempo of matches is often slow

Success: Mexico is the primary representative of this style

USE OF SPACE

When children play soccer, they all tend to follow the ball. Then they realize they will be more useful to their team if they get away from the pack and find some space. The history of soccer can be seen as a process of gradual enlightenment when it comes to space; today, it is given the importance it deserves.

POSSESSION

In soccer, possession is nine-tenths of the law. Barring own goals, no one can score against you if they don't have the ball. Chasing the play also tires and frustrates opponents. Possession soccer has developed into a fully fledged tactic and one that is related to the "pass-and-move" philosophy (see right). It is particularly popular in Latin countries, not least because the patient approach makes excellent sense in a hot climate.

PASS AND MOVE

The pass-and-move philosophy is based on the idea that if a player is static it is easy for opponents to pick them up. Brazil and Spain in the men's game, and the United States in women's soccer, have built reputations for this style, frustrating opponents by retaining possession of the ball in free-flowing patterns.

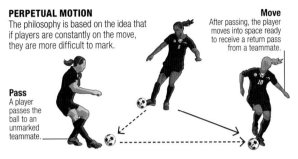

PERPETUAL MOTION
The philosophy is based on the idea that if players are constantly on the move, they are more difficult to mark.

Move
After passing, the player moves into space ready to receive a return pass from a teammate.

Pass
A player passes the ball to an unmarked teammate.

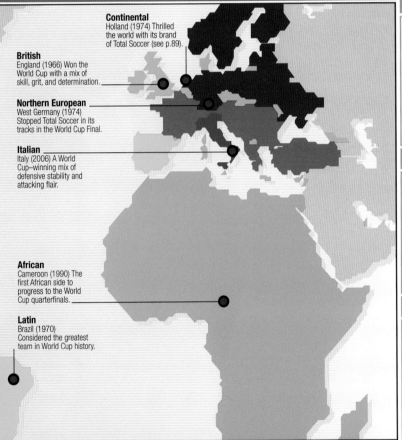

Continental
Holland (1974) Thrilled the world with its brand of Total Soccer (see p.89).

British
England (1966) Won the World Cup with a mix of skill, grit, and determination.

Northern European
West Germany (1974) Stopped Total Soccer in its tracks in the World Cup Final.

Italian
Italy (2006) A World Cup–winning mix of defensive stability and attacking flair.

African
Cameroon (1990) The first African side to progress to the World Cup quarterfinals.

Latin
Brazil (1970) Considered the greatest team in World Cup history.

NORTHERN EUROPEAN

Players (type): Aggressive, fast-paced, hardworking, and highly organized

Characteristics: Direct game with forceful, although sometimes predictable, attacks; defenses are typically hard to break down

Success: Germany remains the ultimate standard-bearer for the Northern European style of play

BRITISH

Players (type): Traditionally physical, athletic, fast tempo, and direct

Characteristics: Attacks are set up quickly with few touches on the ball; the game plan is based on substance over style

Success: Despite success at club level, the national teams flatter to deceive on the world stage

CONTINENTAL

Players (type): A combination of the Latin and Northern European games

Characteristics: All players are comfortable on the ball; emphasis is on creativity combined with composure and team coordination

Success: Spain, Netherlands, and France are the style's leading representatives

LATIN

Players (type): Confident with the ball, good dribblers, and creative

Characteristics: The Latin game style has a possession-oriented character suited to the hot, draining climates in which matches are typically played

Success: Brazil, Argentina, Spain, and Portugal are among the world's best teams

AFRICAN

Players (type): Athletic, physical

Characteristics: Touch-and-move soccer similar to the Latin style; emphasis is on stylish attacking soccer and displays of individual skill

Success: African teams continue to threaten to reach the latter stages of the World Cup

ITALIAN

Players (type): Skillful, inventive, cautious

Characteristics: Reluctance to commit too many players forward in attack due to great emphasis on defense

Success: Italian clubs often feature in the latter stages of all major European competitions; the national side is a regular contender at major championships

TEAMWORK

FORMATIONS

The formation of a team is determined by the positions allocated to players and their relationship to each other. Managers and coaches select formations with two main aims: to neutralize the opposition, and to exploit its weaknesses. Formations are listed in numbers, with the defenders listed first and the strikers listed last (goalkeepers are never listed). The following are some of the most influential formations in soccer's formative years.

HERBERT CHAPMAN

English manager Herbert Chapman (below) redefined the role of manager and pioneered the use of organized tactics. His best achievement was to perfect the W-M (see right), which dominated soccer for a generation and brought him English league titles at Huddersfield and Arsenal.

1-2-7

In soccer's earliest days, forward passes were not permitted. Players could pass the ball sideways or backward, although this was seen as contrary to the spirit of the game. Instead, players moved up the field using a kind of charge-dribble, with several teammates in attendance.

2-3-5 (THE PYRAMID)

In 1866, the rules were changed to allow forward passing (provided there were at least three opponents between the player receiving the ball and the goal). This put more pressure on defenses, and, by the 1880s, the standard formation had evolved into the more defensive 2-3-5.

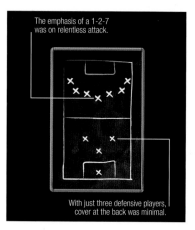

The emphasis of a 1-2-7 was on relentless attack.

With just three defensive players, cover at the back was minimal.

Five forwards gave teams ample scope in attack.

Center halves were responsible for breaking down play and instigating attacks.

THE DEATH OF THE 1-2-7

In 1872, Queen's Park, representing Scotland, lined up against a much bigger and stronger England team at Hampden Park. Realizing they would have little chance if they played dribble-and-charge soccer, Queen's Park decided to adopt a 2-2-6 formation and attempted to pass the ball around their opponents. It was deemed a success, as they held out for a famous 0–0 draw.

DEVELOPMENT OF FORMATIONS

The way teams have lined up on a field has changed radically throughout the game's history.

1867
Offside rule first introduced

1872
Royal Engineers win the FA Cup with a 1-2-7 formation

1889
Preston North End wins the English league and FA Cup playing a 2-3-5

1925
Changes in the offside rule give birth to the W-M

1934
Vittorio Pozzo's Italy wins the World Cup with a 2-3-2-3 formation, known as *il metodo* ("the method")

1860   1870   1880   1900   1920   1930   1940

3-2-2-3 (W-M)

The offside rule (see pp.66–67) was amended in 1925 to encourage more attacking soccer. A player receiving the ball was now onside provided there were two opponents ahead. To deal with the increased attacking threat, Herbert Chapman (see left) developed the 3-2-2-3 (or W-M) formation.

3-2-3-2 (M-U)

In November 1953, Hungary (the reigning Olympic soccer champions) lined up against England at Wembley in a revolutionary M-U formation. They gave their hosts, who were playing a rigid W-M, a soccer lesson and went on to win the match 6–3—it was England's first-ever defeat at Wembley.

4-2-4

Developed to reinforce the defense without sacrificing attacking play, the 4-2-4 exploded onto the international scene with Brazil's victory at the 1958 World Cup. On paper, it looks as though it would leave a team light in midfield; in practice, it operates as a 3-3-4 when in possession and as a 4-3-3 in defense.

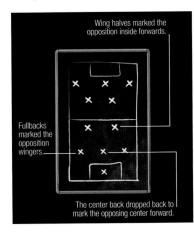

Wing halves marked the opposition inside forwards.

Fullbacks marked the opposition wingers

The center back dropped back to mark the opposing center forward.

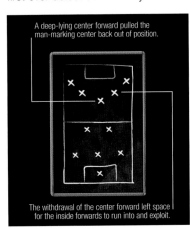

A deep-lying center forward pulled the man-marking center back out of position.

The withdrawal of the center forward left space for the inside forwards to run into and exploit.

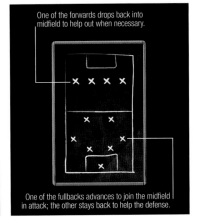

One of the forwards drops back into midfield to help out when necessary.

One of the fullbacks advances to join the midfield in attack; the other stays back to help the defense.

OTHER FORMATIONS

Several theories on how to play the game abounded throughout Europe in the 1920s and '30s—the following are among the most famous of those systems.

DANUBIAN SCHOOL

A modification of the pyramid (2-3-5) formation, utilized by the Austrians, Czechs, and Hungarians in the 1920s, this formation relied on short passing and individual skills. It reached its peak in the early 1930s with the Austrian national side, who finished fourth at the 1934 World Cup.

IL METODO ("THE METHOD")

Devised by Vittorio Pozzo, coach of the Italian national side in the 1930s, il metodo was a derivation of the Danubian School. Pozzo, seeking to gain midfield dominance, pulled back two of the forwards to just in front of midfield to create a 2-3-2-3 formation. It was a huge success: Italy won back-to-back World Cups using this formation in 1934 and 1938, and Pozzo remains the only manager to have won two successive World Cups.

THE DIAGONAL

During the 1940s, Brazil manager Flávio Costa developed a curiously lopsided system known as the diagonal. It was similar to the W-M, except that the two left-sided midfielders were stationed further forward than their equivalents on the right. Costa enjoyed considerable success with the system but abandoned it halfway through the 1950 World Cup campaign in favor of a conventional W-M. Many blamed his decision for Brazil's sensational loss to Uruguay in the final match that cost them the trophy. The defeat is considered the darkest day in Brazilian sporting history.

IT WAS LIKE PLAYING PEOPLE FROM OUTER SPACE

ENGLAND'S **SYD OWEN** AFTER A 7–1 DEFEAT AGAINST HUNGARY IN 1954

1953
Hungary exposes the weaknesses in the W-M by playing an innovative M-U formation

1958
Brazil wins the World Cup playing 4-2-4

1966
England's "wingless wonders" win the World Cup with a midfield diamond

1970
Ajax wins the first of three consecutive European Cups playing "Total Soccer"

1990
AC Milan deploys the definitive modern 4-4-2

2010s
The dominant contemporary formations are fluid variants of 4-5-1 and 4-2-3-1, even 4-6-0

1950   1960   1970   1980   1990   2000   PRESENT

TEAMWORK

MODERN FORMATIONS

During the first 100 years of soccer's existence, only a handful of formations were regularly used. There also tended to be just one used in a given era. Since the 1960s, the tactical side of the game has been blown wide open. Flexibility has become the watchword, with the team increasingly tailored to the opposition and to the way a match is panning out.

ARRIGO SACCHI

Although he never played professional soccer, Arrigo Sacchi managed the great AC Milan side of the early 1990s. His success came through perfecting the 4-4-2. The formation can leave big gaps between the ranks, but Sacchi solved the problem by making his players move up and down the field as a packed unit.

4-4-2

The basic modern formation, the 4-4-2, places a burden on midfielders: one of the central pair must go up and support attacks, while the other drops back. Wide players help out in defense and attack, creating a temporary 4-2-4. The two strikers work in tandem and need to have a good understanding of each other.

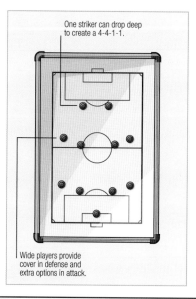

One striker can drop deep to create a 4-4-1-1.

Wide players provide cover in defense and extra options in attack.

3-5-2/5-3-2

The difference between 3-5-2 and 5-3-2 is one of emphasis, with the former being more attack-oriented than the latter since it has more midfielders. In either variant, the key individuals are the wide players, usually described as wingbacks, who are expected to help out with both attack and defense.

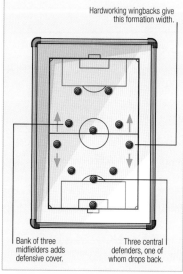

Hardworking wingbacks give this formation width.

Bank of three midfielders adds defensive cover.

Three central defenders, one of whom drops back.

OTHER MODERN FORMATIONS

While the majority of formations have been adopted as standard throughout the soccer world, others—such as *catenaccio* and "Total Soccer"—have become synonymous with a particular team or nation.

CATENACCIO (1-4-3-2)

Catenaccio, which means "door bolt" in Italian, relied on a *libero*, or sweeper (see p.43) stationed in front of the goalkeeper to counter the risk of an opposing forward breaking through the main line of defense. It was fundamentally a defensive system, but by forcing opponents to commit extra players forward, it left them vulnerable to rapid counterattacks.

THE BIRTH OF *CATENACCIO*

Catenaccio first became popular in Italy in the late 1940s. Gipo Viani, the former Salernitana manager, claimed to have invented the formation after seeing fishermen using two nets, with a reserve net placed behind the main net to pick up any fish that had managed to evade it.

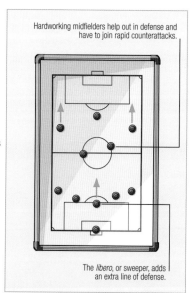

Hardworking midfielders help out in defense and have to join rapid counterattacks.

The *libero*, or sweeper, adds an extra line of defense.

4-3-3

Essentially a more defensive version of the 4-2-4, the 4-3-3 was first pioneered by Brazil at the 1962 World Cup. The three midfielders could be staggered in various ways and tended to move across the field as a unit. Lots of teams now start with this system, or adopt it late in a match if they need a goal.

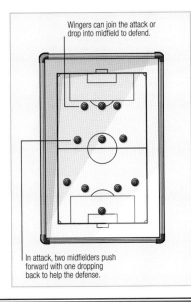

Wingers can join the attack or drop into midfield to defend.

In attack, two midfielders push forward with one dropping back to help the defense.

4-5-1

This is essentially a defensive formation, with a packed midfield and a lone striker left to fend for themself, or hold the ball up, until support arrives, usually from the wide players. English team Chelsea used this system to great effect during its back-to-back Premier League title successes in 2005 and 2006.

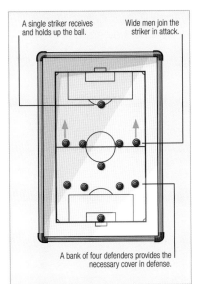

A single striker receives and holds up the ball.

Wide men join the striker in attack.

A bank of four defenders provides the necessary cover in defense.

4-2-3-1

This was arguably the dominant formation on either side of the millennium. It revolves around the midfield, with two of the central players in holding roles and the other one concentrating on attack. France beat Brazil 3–0 in the 1998 World Cup Final using this formation. It is popular in continental Europe.

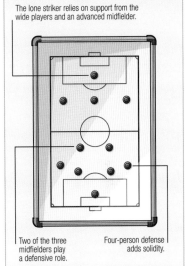

The lone striker relies on support from the wide players and an advanced midfielder.

Two of the three midfielders play a defensive role.

Four-person defense adds solidity.

TOTAL SOCCER

Rinus Michels, manager of the great Ajax and Netherlands teams of the early 1970s, gave his players unprecedented freedom to express themselves on the field and adapt to the circumstances of a game. In Total Soccer, outfield players had no fixed positions, although the team did have a structure (a variant of 4-3-3); each player had to be prepared to occupy any position as the need arose. Although they thrilled, and influenced, a generation of fans, the Dutch ultimately failed in its attempt to win the World Cup, losing to West Germany in the 1974 Final and to Argentina in the 1978 Final.

THE TRUTH IS ... SOCCER MAKES ITSELF ON THE FIELD

FORMER NETHERLANDS MANAGER **RINUS MICHELS**

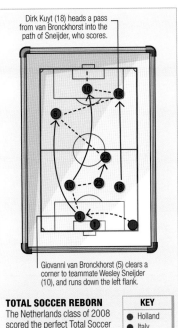

Dirk Kuyt (18) heads a pass from van Bronckhorst into the path of Sneijder, who scores.

Giovanni van Bronckhorst (5) clears a corner to teammate Wesley Sneijder (10), and runs down the left flank.

TOTAL SOCCER REBORN
The Netherlands class of 2008 scored the perfect Total Soccer goal vs. Italy at Euro 2008, turning defense into instant attack in the blink of an eye.

KEY	
●	Holland
●	Italy
- -	Pass
—	Player movement

VARIATIONS

THE DIAMOND

Alf Ramsey's "wingless wonders," England, won the 1966 World Cup with this formation, one that gives a side great solidity in midfield, with the fullbacks providing the width in attack. AC Milan won the Champions League in 2007 playing with the same system.

THE CHRISTMAS TREE

Named after its pointed shape, the 4-3-2-1 formation is a more attacking adaptation of 4-3-3, with two players playing behind a lone striker ("in the hole"). Terry Venables's England side used the Christmas Tree formation to great effect at Euro 1996.

THE FUTURE: 4-6-0

At a 2003 coaching conference in Rio de Janeiro, former Brazil manager Carlos Alberto Parreira declared the 4-6-0 to be the formation of the future. His prediction seems to be coming true: Spain won Euro 2012 playing with no dedicated striker, and top club teams such as Barcelona and Manchester City have had success with attacking midfielders bursting forward.

DEFENSIVE STRATEGIES

Defenders, like all other players, need to master the basic skills of the game, like passing and ball control, but in some departments—notably tackling—they have to be considerably better than average. Individual technical ability, though, is only part of the story. Defenders also need to address how they are going to work together as a unit.

DEFENDING AS A UNIT

A good defense provides the foundation for every great team, and if a defense wants to become impenetrable, it needs to become a coherent unit. That means working together to regain possession of the ball, holding a tight defensive line, claiming responsibility for marking attacking players, and disrupting the opposing side's organization as much as possible.

HOLDING THE LINE

Defenders tend to form a line across the field exactly parallel to the goal line, particularly when the opposition has possession of the ball. This line serves two very important functions. It increases the chances of catching opposing forwards offside, unless one of them makes a well-timed run and is found by a teammate. It also dictates how far up the field the team as a whole plays. Midfielders should base themselves a certain distance ahead of the defensive line, and the same is true of forwards in relation to the midfielders.

THE OFFSIDE TRAP

Holding a good defensive line is a deterrent in itself, but the offside trap takes matters a stage further. It involves all the defenders stepping forward just before an opponent passes the ball to a forward-running striker, thus playing the opponent offside at the moment the ball is struck (see pp.66–67). It is a high-risk strategy but can be particularly effective if performed properly. The Arsenal back four of the late 1980s and early '90s were masters of the offside trap, raising their arms simultaneously to alert the referee's assistant as they stepped forward in unison. The maneuver was reenacted in the 1997 film *The Full Monty*.

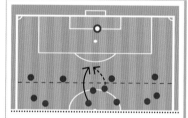
HIGH DEFENSIVE LINE Danger of opponents breaking offside trap with a well-timed through ball. ● Attacking team ● Defensive team -- Player movement — Pass

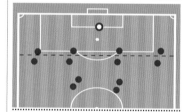
LOW DEFENSIVE LINE Danger of allowing opposition players to get too close to goal. ● Attacking team ● Defensive team

MARKING

Marking, or "picking up," is about preventing the ball from being passed easily from one opposing team member to another. Picking up an opponent, whether from set pieces or in open play, is one of the defender's most important tasks. Clearly, if several defenders decide to mark one opponent at the same time, they will leave other opponents dangerously unmarked. Therefore, a system has to be worked out. There are two options when it comes to a team's marking strategy: they can use either zonal marking or man-to-man marking.

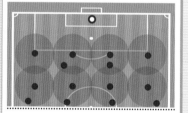
ZONAL MARKING Players occupy an area of the field and do not directly mark an opponent. ● Attacking team ● Defensive team

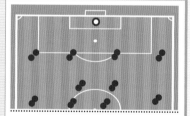
MAN-TO-MAN Each player marks a single opponent. ● Attacking team ● Defensive team

ZONAL MARKING

Zonal marking was developed in the 1950s to deal with the problem of playing against a team using withdrawn strikers. In zonal marking, defenders are responsible for specific areas of the field rather than particular opponents.

MAN-TO-MAN MARKING

Man-to-man marking is simple: a defender is allocated an opponent and has to stick to that opponent no matter where they run. The system's advantage is its clarity. The disadvantage is that it allows attacking players to pull defenders out of position.

[SOCCER] IS A SIMPLE GAME BASED ON THE GIVING AND TAKING OF PASSES … IT IS TERRIBLY SIMPLE

FORMER LIVERPOOL MANAGER **BILL SHANKLY**

TOP 5: PARTNERSHIPS

Successful teams are invariably built on the foundations of a great defensive partnership. Here are five of the finest:

BARESI AND COSTACURTA (AC MILAN)
The pair played together for so long at the heart of AC Milan's defense that they instinctively knew where the other would be. When Baresi retired, Paolo Maldini stepped effortlessly into his shoes.

HANSEN AND LAWRENSON (LIVERPOOL)
The cornerstone of the great Liverpool team of the early 1980s. Lawrenson was the quicker, Hansen the more stylish, but both had the priceless ability to bring the ball out of defense.

ADAMS AND KEOWN (ARSENAL)
The Arsenal center backs were formidable to begin with but got even better with age. Born in the same year, they won a league and FA Cup double aged 31 and another in 2002 aged 35.

LEBOEUF AND DESAILLY (CHELSEA)
A World Cup–winning center-back partnership with France in 1998, Leboeuf and Desailly were also a formidable force at Chelsea.

SCHWARZENBECK AND BECKENBAUER (BAYERN MUNICH)
Beckenbauer's elegance and attacking libero style was perfectly complemented by Schwarzenbeck's no-nonsense traditional approach to the game.

GREAT DEFENSIVE PARTNERSHIPS

Most formations pair two central defenders together at the back, and their partnership is one of the most important on the field. It helps if they are not too similar in playing style (so they can offer more than one skill), and there are various theories about the ideal combination.

THE PERFECT MIX
One tried-and-true formula is a ball winner plus a ball player, with the former doing most of the tackling and the latter picking up the ball and passing (such as Italy's Fabio Cannavaro and Alessandro Nesta). The most important ingredient is mutual understanding.

NESTA AND CANNAVARO
Cannavaro's positional sense and superb reading of the game broke up opposition attacks. Nesta, supremely quick and elegant on the ball, picked up the pieces and instigated new attacks.

517 Number of minutes Italy goalkeeper Walter Zenga and his defense went without conceding a goal at the 1990 World Cup—a tournament record

14 Most goals conceded in one tournament by a team that has gone on to win the World Cup—West Germany in 1954

NESTA AND CANNAVARO

- Matches won—**54%**
- Matches tied—**30%**
- Matches lost—**16%**

THE BEREZUTSKI TWINS

Understanding is arguably the most important component of a defensive partnership, and no two people understand each other better than identical twins. Aleksei and Vasili Berezutski of CSKA Moscow and Russia are living proof that such a formula can work at the highest level of the sport. Born 20 minutes apart, on June 20, 1982, Aleksei is the younger brother and is also half an inch (1 cm) shorter. The pair played together at the heart of the CSKA defense and Russia's national side, and went on to work together as coaches.

TEAMWORK

DEFENDING FROM THE FRONT

It's not just defenders who need to defend. Forwards today are expected to help out even when their side does not have the ball, putting pressure on the opposing defenders and doing the same to the goalkeepers when receiving a back pass. The purpose of this is to force a defensive error. If forwards achieve this, they stand a good chance of being in a goal-scoring position.

CONDENSING PLAY

When the attacking team has possession of the ball, the defending team can make life difficult for them by quickly filling the gaps between players. Condensing the play in this way makes the field appear smaller, denies the attacking team room in which to operate efficiently, and increases the chances of forcing them to make a mistake. It is a major weapon to use when trying to regain possession of the ball.

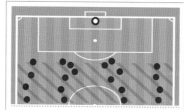

CONDENSING PLAY
Team B condenses the play, putting pressure on attacking Team A.

● Attacking team A
● Defensive team B
⬡ Action area

SHIELDING

Shielding the ball involves a player positioning their body between an opponent and the ball without actually obstructing the opponent. It is a useful skill and one that can be used all over the field, from a lone striker holding the ball up to a defender shielding the ball from an attacker to ensure that it goes out of play for a goal kick or a throw-in.

PROTECTION
When defenders place their bodies between the ball and an opponent, it is known as "shielding."

Shielded ball
Facing away from the attacker, the defender protects the ball.

Ball skills
Close control is essential when shielding.

TOP 5: HARDMEN

Defensive hardmen are there to terrify opponents. A type of anti-strategy, it can be very effective. The notion of having a hardman in the team is not a new one, but the following players can be viewed as being among the toughest players the game of soccer has ever seen.

CLAUDIO GENTILE
Gentile—which means "gentle" in Italian—was an inappropriate last name for one of the toughest defenders of all time. "Soccer is not for ballerinas," the Juventus hardman said, after famously kicking a young Diego Maradona into submission at the 1982 World Cup. Remarkably, despite his hardman reputation, he never received a red card.

TOMMY SMITH
According to Bill Shankly, the man they called the "Anfield Iron" wasn't born; he was "quarried." Smith, who enjoyed a 16-year career with Liverpool, once handed opposing striker Jimmy Greaves a piece of paper before a match. It was the lunch menu from the Liverpool Infirmary.

STUART PEARCE
Known as "Psycho," the giant-thighed England fullback used to listen to the Sex Pistols to get himself into the right mood for matches. Pearce (right) once tried to run off a broken leg, and when Basile Boli headbutted him at Euro 1992, it was the Frenchman who came off worse.

SHEPHERDING

Just as a shepherd uses a dog to move and control sheep without touching them, a defender "shepherds" an attacker by attempting to maneuver the opponent away from danger zones, without ever actually trying to take the ball from them. The two main purposes of shepherding are to channel attacking players away from the goal and to force them to play the ball with their weaker foot.

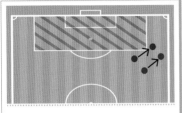

SHEPHERDING I
The defender shepherds a left-footed striker onto their weaker right foot.

- ● Attacking team
- ● Defensive team
- — Player movement
- ▨ Danger zone

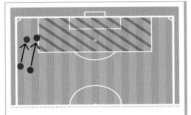

SHEPHERDING II
The defender prevents the winger from getting in a cross.

- ● Attacking team
- ● Defensive team
- — Player movement
- ▨ Danger zone

BOBBY MOORE
The classic calm defender, relying on positional sense rather than speed or muscle, Moore was rarely ruffled.

IF I WANTED TO BE AN INDIVIDUAL, I WOULD HAVE TAKEN UP TENNIS

FORMER HOLLAND CAPTAIN **RUUD GULLIT**

DOUBLING UP

If an opponent becomes isolated, the defenders can improve their chances of dispossessing the opponent by "doubling up"—putting two defenders on one attacker. Defenders need to be careful: if two of them are attending to one attacker, other attackers are likely to be left unguarded.

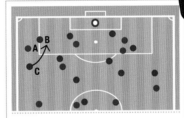

DOUBLING UP
Player C runs back to assist player B against opponent player A.

- ● Attacking team
- ● Defensive team
- — Player movement

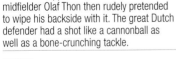

RONALD KOEMAN
After the Netherlands beat hosts West Germany in the semifinal of Euro 1988, Koeman swapped his shirt with German midfielder Olaf Thon then rudely pretended to wipe his backside with it. The great Dutch defender had a shot like a cannonball as well as a bone-crunching tackle.

DUNGA
Brazilians are not known for their hard tackling, but the captain of the 1994 World Cup–winning team played like a naval destroyer and also looked particularly scary. Capped 91 times, he added much-needed strength to Brazil's traditionally attacking style of play.

WORLD CUP—GOALS CONCEDED PER MATCH

Brazil are the only nation to play at every World Cup final, but they have still conceded only 108 goals in the 114 games they have played, including those at the 2022 tournament. Germany have let in the most World Cup goals—130 in total—in 112 games, including the 2022 World Cup.

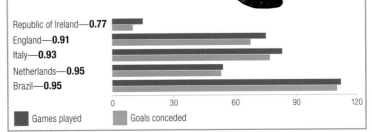

Republic of Ireland—**0.77**
England—**0.91**
Italy—**0.93**
Netherlands—**0.95**
Brazil—**0.95**

0   30   60   90   120

- ■ Games played
- ■ Goals conceded

A QUICK FIX ON THE PITCH

If you think "what you see is what you get," think again. Since 2000, more than 30 countries have seen criminal investigations into allegations of match fixing at soccer games. From China to South Africa, Italy to Portugal, and Brazil to England, there is evidence (and plenty of rumors) to suggest that games are being thrown. However, governing bodies, soccer associations, and the police are all handing out severe penalties to convicted offenders.

WHAT YOU SEE IS WHAT YOU GET?

If it takes two to tango, it often takes a lot more people to fix a soccer match. The fixers—the people with the money and power—tend to be club bosses, big-time gamblers, organized criminals, or all three. If they can get past the sentries of the media and the soccer authorities, there are a variety of ways that match fixers—intent on breaking the law—can ensure that officials, coaches, and players see things their way.

THE DIRECTORS
If they are not directly involved in a betting scam, directors fix matches for a variety of reasons. They can bribe other teams to lose to avoid relegation, for example, or ask other teams to "go easy" on them in order to save their own players' energies for bigger matches to come.

THE GAMBLERS
Big-money gamblers and bookmakers actually prefer certainty to chance. The global soccer betting markets are growing fast, especially in East and Southeast Asia.

THE ORGANIZED CRIMINALS
Both gamblers and bookmakers are tied to networks of organized crime, so match fixing is on the rise. Fixes include attempts to guarantee wins and defeats, but, as the betting market becomes more complex, fixes also turn on arranging corners, throws, and the number and timing of goals.

CASH, GIFTS, AND INCENTIVES
Money, particularly good old-fashioned cash, is the most usual means of influence. Incentives might include cars, expensive watches, vacations, and very soft loans.

BLACKMAIL
Simply produce some incriminating evidence about a key official and blackmail him.

VIOLENCE
There may be direct threats to the person or indirect threats to their families. Officials and players who have crossed the fixers have faced kidnappings, attacks, and assignations.

DIRECT INTERVENTION
Simply stop the match. In some betting markets, games abandoned at halftime stand as the final result. One way of ensuring your winnings, if the score is right at halftime, is to simply turn off the lights.

THESE PEOPLE MIGHT TRY TO FIX A MATCH ... **BY USING THESE METHODS ...**

30,000

The value of the loan in dollars (£20,000) made by Anderlecht's president to the referee in charge of their UEFA Cup tie with Nottingham Forest in 1984

2
The number of games UEFA is certain were fixed between 2004 and 2009: a 2004 UEFA Cup match and a 2007 Intertoto Cup match

10
The length of prison sentence given to Chinese referee Gong Jianping by a Beijing court in 2001 for accepting bribes

2005
The year a huge match-fixing scandal rocked Brazil—11 matches were declared null and void

THE MEDIA
The media can't fix a match, but they can make sure that nobody talks about it too much once it has been played. In many countries, much of the press is in thrall to the most powerful clubs, officials, and individuals.

THE REGULATORS
From the smallest associations to FIFA and the regional confederations, soccer bureaucracies have only begun to scratch the surface of the match-fixing problems. In countries where many of the most senior officials are involved in these practices, any form of regulation and investigation is obstructed and watered down.

TOP 5: MATCH FIXES

OLYMPIQUE MARSEILLES
Bernard Tapie, the flamboyant businessman, politician, and president of Olympique de Marseille, saw his team win a French league and European Cup double in 1993. It turned out that he had paid a small team called Valenciennes to go easy against Marseilles in a league game before his side's big matches. Marseilles was stripped of its French title, and Tapie served six months in jail.

MOGGIOPOLY
"Moggiopoly" wasn't just one fix; it was a system of fixes that affected almost the whole of Italian soccer. It centered around Luciano Moggi, the general manager at Juventus, and included players, agents, referees, and officials. Moggi's networks of pressure, influence, and power shaped Italian soccer in Juventus's favor for a decade. When the case was exposed in 2006, Juventus was relegated to serie B and stripped of its 2006 title.

AC ALLIANSSI
In 2005, tiny Finnish first division team AC Allianssi lost its first game under new ownership 8–0. Unlike most games in the Finnish first division, more than $600,000 (€500,000) staked on this one. New owner Ye Zheyun did not take any chances: the goalkeeper was sent to Belgium for nonexistent training; six new players, all of whom were injured and unfit, had been brought in to play; and, just for good measure, players wore short studs on their cleats—highly inappropriate for the rain-drenched field.

WEST GERMANY VS. AUSTRIA
West Germany and Austria played each other in the final game of their group at the 1982 World Cup. A 0–0 draw was all that was needed to see both teams safely through to the next round—at the expense of Algeria. The least-competitive game in World Cup history was disgracefully played out, and Algeria went home.

MANCHESTER UNITED VS. LIVERPOOL
In spring 1915, relegation-threatened Manchester United beat Liverpool 2–0. Players on both sides visibly abused a Liverpool player (who wasn't in on the fix) after he almost scored when the match was standing at 2–0. The players, fearing the economic consequences of the coming suspension of professional soccer due to World War I, had organized a tiny betting coup among themselves. The ruse, however, was obvious.

THE OFFICIALS
Want things to go your way? Go straight to the top and the men and women in black.

THE ASSISTANT REFEREES
The assistants aren't much use by themselves, but they can make a very helpful addition to the team if the referee is already on board. The assistant referees can give those offside decisions real authenticity.

THE REFEREE
Score looking lopsided? How about a penalty. Wrong side on form? Simply disallow that goal. The referee is the most important person to "get" if you want to fix a game. They are in total control of the match, and, with so much resting on a few key decisions, a referee who knows what they are doing can fix almost any game.

THE TEAM
They are paid to play, but the players can also be paid to play badly if the price is right.

THE COACH
With the coach in your pocket, you can be sure that the weakest team gets picked or that injured players get their chance to fail.

GOALKEEPER
The goalkeeper can be a great asset if you want to lose the game, but is less useful if you're trying to win.

DEFENDERS
With so many close decisions and penalty chances, center backs make great targets for the fixers.

MIDFIELDERS
Best bought in groups, a lackluster midfield shirking a tackle and misplacing passes can easily produce a draw—and any wrongdoing is hard to spot.

STRIKERS
Strikers are useful only if you need someone to keep on missing shots set up by an incorruptible midfield.

TO TRY TO INFLUENCE THESE GROUPS

TEAMWORK

SET PIECES

Set pieces are free kicks, corners, and throw-ins. About 20 percent of goals are scored directly or indirectly from set piece situations, so they are extremely important for both the attacking and defending side. Modern teams spend hours on the training ground practicing, creating, and honing set piece routines, from both an attacking and defensive point of view.

CORNERS: THE ATTACKING TEAM

A corner provides an attacking team with a fantastic opportunity to create a goal-scoring chance. Numerous moves have been devised over the years—some more innovative than others—all of which fall into one of three categories: a short corner, a near-post corner, or a far-post corner.

SHORT CORNERS

Unlike a standard corner, no attempt is made to cross the ball directly into the penalty area; instead the corner taker makes a short pass to a teammate, moves into an onside position, receives the ball back, and only then delivers the cross. The aim is to confuse the defenders' plans.

NEAR-POST CORNERS

A near-post corner is played to the goalpost nearest the taker. It is good because it eliminates the goalkeeper, since the ball does not reach them. A usually tall attacking player is stationed on the near post to flick the ball on with their head, hoping an incoming teammate will pick it up and score.

SHORT CORNERS
Player B comes for the ball then returns it to player A who crosses it.

- Attacking team
- Defensive team
- -- Pass/cross
- — Player movement

NEAR-POST CORNER
Player A crosses to player B, who flicks the ball on for teammates.

- Attacking team
- Defensive team
- -- Pass/cross
- — Player movement

FAR-POST CORNERS

A far-post corner is played to the goalpost farthest away from the taker. The aim is to bypass the goalkeeper. The ball is struck with pace, and the plan is for a teammate is to escape their marker, meet the ball, and score.

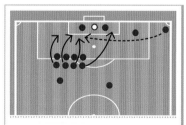

FAR-POST CORNER
Attackers try to avoid their markers to meet the deeper corner

- Attacking team
- Defensive team
- -- Pass/cross
- — Player movement

WHAT SHOULD THE GOALKEEPER DO?

A goalkeeper has two main choices: to come and meet the ball (either by catching or punching it) or to stay on the goal line and hope to make a save. It requires excellent judgment to decide what to do in the heat of the moment.

THE DEFENSIVE WALL

The number of players in a wall depends on the area of the field from which a free kick is taken. It will range from between one and five players.

CORNERS: THE DEFENDING TEAM

Although a defending team has no idea what kind of corner an attacking side will deliver, it should always follow certain principles—such as adopting a marking strategy (be it zonal or man-to-man marking) and putting a defender on the inside of each of the goalposts.

MARKING

Tactics vary depending on whether a team uses zonal or man-to-man marking, but the basic principle is to stick to your opponent and stay goal-side. If a defender lets the attacker get in front of them, the latter will have a chance to direct a header on goal.

GUARDING THE POSTS

The defending team should place one player on each post. As the ball comes in, these defenders position themselves on the goal line, just inside the post they are guarding. If they do this, they will be ready to clear any goal attempts heading for the inside of their posts.

FREE KICKS: THE DEFENDING TEAM

Because free kicks provide an opponent with an ideal opportunity to shoot on goal, it is vital that defenses are organized to deal with the impending threat. Every defender needs to be on guard. Marking (be it zonal or man-to-man) needs to be tight, and then a wall needs to be created that directly blocks the route to goal.

DEFENSIVE WALLS

If a free kick is given in a scoring position, the defending team will set up a wall. The goalkeeper is in charge of positioning the wall, which may have as many as five members or as few as one, depending on how close to goal the free kick is. The goalkeeper needs to ensure that one side of the goal is covered, leaving them free to concentrate on the other side.

ANTICIPATING FREE KICKS

Defenders need to be alert to quickly taken free kicks or ones delivered to an unmarked opponent. If the free kick is indirect, a player should be nominated to close the ball down as soon as it has been touched by an opponent.

THROW-INS

The defending team needs to mark every opponent, including the thrower. The thrower's teammates should move around, looking to escape the attentions of their markers. Long throws (see p.139) can provide a dangerous attacking option.

> # IT'S AMAZING ... JUST HOW MANY GOALS COME FROM SET PIECES
>
> **GORDON STRACHAN**
> FORMER SCOTLAND MANAGER

FREE KICKS: THE ATTACKING TEAM

Some free kicks awarded in advanced positions invite crosses, in which case—because the ball is crossed into the box—the tactics for both sides are similar to those in the corners section (see left). Others provide opportunities for a direct shot on goal.

REHEARSED FREE KICKS

Rehearsed free kicks can take various forms, from simple taps to the side to complex passing routines, but all have the same intention: to catch an opponent unawares. A classic example of a perfectly executed free kick was given by Argentina in its second-round clash against England at the 1998 World Cup (see right). In a move honed on the training ground, Gabriel Batistuta made a dummy run, Javier Zanetti peeled into space from behind the defensive wall, was found by Juan Sebastian Veron, shot, and scored.

FREE KICK TRICKS
Javier Zanetti positioned himself behind England's defensive wall.

- ● Argentina
- ● England
- - - Pass/shot
- — Player run

SET PIECE SUCCESS
A cleverly worked free kick resulted in an Argentinian goal for Javier Zanetti in his country's clash against England at the 1998 World Cup in France.

ATTACKING STRATEGIES

There are three main choices when it comes to attacking play. How many strikers do you employ? Do you try to get into a scoring position via the sides of the field ("the flanks") or through the middle? And do you seek to get there through intricate or direct passing? The answers depend on the strength of your team, the weaknesses of the opposition, and the way the game is unfolding.

THROUGH THE MIDDLE: THE LONG-BALL GAME

The long-ball game involves getting the ball from the defenders to the forwards as quickly as possible. This entails passing the ball two-thirds of the length of the field or more in the air, and for this reason, the approach is also known as "route-one soccer."

IDEAL REQUIREMENTS

The long-ball game works best with a tall forward (the "target player"), who is likely to win the long aerial balls, or with wingers stationed near the touchlines ready to receive long passes. Teams resort to the long-ball game to get the ball rapidly out of defense to minimize the risk of losing possession in a dangerous area and to get the ball up to the forwards before the defending team has had a chance to organize its defense.

Bergkamp

Ayala

De Boer

ROUTE-ONE PERFECTION
There is nothing attractive or particularly skillful about the long-ball game, and it is usually not pretty to watch, but there are exceptions, such as Dennis Bergkamp's exquisite 89th-minute, match-winning goal for the Netherlands against Argentina in the 1998 World Cup quarterfinals.

KEY
- Netherlands
- Argentina
- -- Pass
- — Player movement

ONE STRIKER OR TWO?

In the modern game, teams are unlikely to use more than two forwards through fear of leaving themselves too vulnerable in other parts of the field. The question then becomes whether you play with one, two, or conceivably with no strikers at all. This is a matter of formation (see pp.90–93) and will have an important impact on a team's attacking strategy. Typically, a team plays with two strikers, one of whom features in a more advanced position (called a center forward—see pp.50–53). The second striker plays in a slightly deeper role—often called "playing in the hole"—and will act as a link between the midfielders and the center forward.

INTRICATE PASSING/BUILDUP PLAY

Well-marshaled defenders can render the long-ball game ineffective by packing the defense with extra players to leave attacking forwards hopelessly outnumbered. When teams face such a defense, they have to rely on intricate passing to break through. It helps if they have players who are skillful enough to pass the ball accurately and quickly in confined spaces.

PLAYER MOVEMENT

Static players are easy for defenders to mark. Successful intricate passing depends on attackers moving around and the player in possession of the ball anticipating teammates' movements. The passer should also move into space as soon as they have played the ball to provide teammates with another passing option.

ELEMENT OF SURPRISE

Tricks, such as backheels, are invaluable in and around the penalty area. They are almost impossible for defenders to anticipate and so can buy the attackers time and space. Ideally, all attackers will be alert to their teammates' tricks, but even if they aren't, they may still find themselves in a position to capitalize on them.

IT WAS A VERY **SIMPLE TEAM TALK**. ALL I USED TO SAY WAS "WHENEVER POSSIBLE, GIVE THE BALL TO **GEORGE BEST**"

MANCHESTER UNITED'S **MATT BUSBY** ON ATTACKING TACTICS

CHARLES REEP: THE LONG-BALL GAME

The guru of the long-ball game was Charles Reep. The former Royal Air Force wing commander first became convinced of the merits of route-one soccer in the 1930s and, after World War II, began to analyze matches to discover what strategies actually led to goals. After studying 578 games between 1953 and 1967, he figured he had discovered several "laws" (see numbers below).

BIG-NAME FOLLOWERS

Reep's theories were extremely influential on a generation of managers, particularly in the UK. Graham Taylor was one notable disciple. Another was Norway boss Egil Olsen, who was still turning to Reep for advice when Reep was over 90 years old.

FALLING OUT OF FASHION

Reep's ideas on the game have fallen out of fashion in recent years. The Latin/Continental-style passing game has tended to win out in the end, with the emphasis in the modern era placed on skillful, technical players.

60 Percentage of goals resulting from regaining possession in the final third of the field

12.3 Optimum distance in yards (11.2 m) for a successful shot on goal

80 Percentage of goals that resulted from a sequence of three passes or less

1 Number of goals scored from every 10 shots taken on goal

TOP 5: LONG-BALL TEAMS

Teams playing the long-ball game are unlikely to win friends among purists, but the tactic has helped less-gifted sides punch above their weight.

WATFORD (1980s)
At the start of the 1977–1978 season, rock star owner Elton John appointed Graham Taylor as manager of his club, Watford. Using a relatively cultured version of the long-ball game, Taylor took the "Hornets" from the Fourth Division to second place in the top flight in just six years.

WIMBLEDON (1988)
The unfashionable southwest London side pulled off one of the biggest shocks in FA Cup history when they beat Liverpool 1–0 in the 1988 final. Known as the "Crazy Gang," their rough-and-tumble, route-one style kept them in the top division for an unlikely 16 years.

REPUBLIC OF IRELAND (1990)
Manager Jack Charlton took the Republic of Ireland to the knockout stages of two World Cup tournaments in the early 1990s, employing long-ball tactics to make the best of limited resources. The team's finest hour was a 1–0 victory over Italy at the 1994 World Cup.

NORWAY (1998)
Egil Olsen, who managed Norway between 1990 and 1998, was an unrepentant disciple of Charles Reep (see left). His devotion to the long-ball game was vindicated when his team beat mighty Brazil 2–1 in the 1998 World Cup. Appropriately, Olsen later managed Wimbledon.

NETHERLANDS (1998)
During the World Cup in 1998, Frank de Boer launched a cross-field pass from his own half that cleared almost the entire Argentina side. Landing on the edge of the six-yard box, a supreme piece of skill from Dennis Bergkamp saw him turn the last defender and drill home to book a place in the semifinals.

SLIDE-RULE PASSES

A slide-rule pass is a pass that has been weighted so precisely that it arrives at the feet of a forward-running attacker at the exact moment they arrive in the desired position. It is a vital tool for breaking even the most stubborn of defenses and can be used for beating offside traps and for finding players making overlapping runs. If a slide-rule pass is to work, however, the player receiving the ball will need to time their run to perfection.

KEVIN DE BRUYNE
The Manchester City attacking midfielder is one of the neatest passers in modern football.

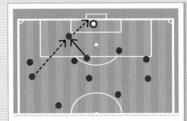

SLIDE-RULE PASS
The forward takes the ball in stride and shoots on goal.

● Attacking team
● Defensive team
-- Pass
— Player movement

TEAMWORK

NEYMAR
An expert finisher, Brazilian forward Neymar is also known for his exceptional playmaking skills and his ability to create lots of chances for his teammates.

THE ONE-TWO

The one-two is an excellent way to get past a defender who is standing between the attacker (who has the ball) and the goal. It needs two attackers: one of them stationary and one running with the ball. The running attacker passes to a stationary teammate, continues to run forward past the defender, then receives the ball back from the stationary teammate. Also known as the "wall pass," the one-two is particularly effective around the edge of the penalty area.

INNOVATIVE IDEAS

Former Liverpool manager Bill Shankly introduced several unusual training methods to get the best out of his players. To increase their passing accuracy, he had an artificial goal painted on a convenient brick wall and split into eight segments, which he would then order his players to hit on demand.

THE ONE-TWO
Player A passes to player B, continues the run, and receives a return pass

- ● Attacking team
- ● Defensive team
- - - Pass/shot
- — Player movement

PRESSING

The pressing game involves never giving an opponent a moment's rest when their team has the ball, thereby pressuring them into making an error. In the modern game, all players are expected to press, including the forwards, who are expected to harry an opponent's goalkeeper and central defenders.

PROBING

If a team is comfortable in possession, there is no need to rush into an all-out attack. Instead, the attacking team can "probe" their opponents' defense, passing the ball between themselves until a clear shooting opportunity presents itself. The longer the move, the more tired and frustrated the defending team will become.

THE PERFECT GOAL

Argentina's second goal in its 6–0 thrashing of Serbia at the 2006 World Cup was a master class on patient buildup play. It had almost everything—one-touch passing, a neat one-two, superb movement, and support. The move began with Javier Mascherano tackling an opponent deep in his own half. It ended, 24 passes later, with Esteban Cambiasso slamming the ball high into the Serbian net.

The move begins when Javier Mascherano collects a misplaced Serbian pass and feeds the ball to teammate Maxi Rodriguez.

KEY
- ● Argentina
- ● Serbia
- → Player movement
- -→ Ball movement
- ⇢ Player with ball

Left back Juan Pablo Sorín collects the ball in an advanced position on the left wing.

Hernán Crespo backheels the ball into the path of the onrushing Cambiasso

USING THE FLANKS

The alternative to playing the ball through the middle is to use wide players who have pace, dribbling skills, the ability to run past defenders to the goal line, and accurate crosses.

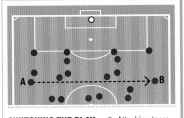

USING WINGERS
Player A beats the defender and delivers a dangerous cross.

- ● Attacking team
- ● Defensive team
- – – Pass/shot
- — Player movement

SWITCHING THE ATTACK

If one side of the field looks a better attacking proposition, the team in possession can "switch the play," i.e., change the focus to a less well-defended area of the field.

SWITCHING THE PLAY
Player A plays a cross-field pass to player B on the opposite flank.

- ● Attacking team
- ● Defensive team
- – – Pass

STRETCHING PLAY

Just as teams condense play when their opponents have the ball (see p.92), they seek to stretch the play in attack by increasing the distance between their players to create more time and space.

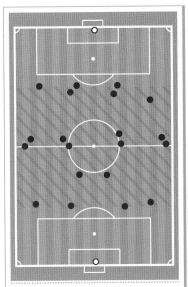

STRETCHING PLAY
The attacking team increases the distance between its players.

- ● Attacking team
- ● Defensive team
- \\\ Action area

BENEFITS OF FIVE-A-SIDE SOCCER

Arsène Wenger and Bill Shankly were just two of the managers who used five-a-side soccer in training sessions to develop ball skills and close control.

COUNTERATTACKING

An instant switch from defense to attack, the counterattack can place an opponent's defense under huge pressure. To work, one or two counterattacking players must stay upfield during an opposition attack.

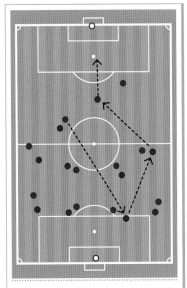

COUNTERATTACKS
An intercepted pass in defense can lead to an instant attack.

- ● Attacking team
- ● Defensive team
- – – Pass

ESTEBAN CAMBIASSO
The Argentine midfielder celebrates scoring one of the greatest goals in World Cup history.

MASCHERANO, RODRIGUEZ, SORIN, RIQUELME, SORIN, MASCHERANO, RODRIGUEZ, AYALA, CAMBIASSO, MASCHERANO, RODRIGUEZ, SORIN, RODRIGUEZ, CAMBIASSO, RIQUELME, MASCHERANO, SORIN, SAVIOLA, RIQUELME, SAVIOLA, CAMBIASSO, CRESPO, CAMBIASSO...**GOAL!**

AN ARGENTINIAN COMMENTATOR DESCRIBES THE 24-PASS GOAL AT THE 2006 WORLD CUP

TEAMWORK

MANAGERS AND COACHES

The language of soccer is packed with military terminology. A season is often described as a "campaign," and an individual game as a "battle." In this spirit, a soccer team can be compared to an army. If the players are the troops, operating under a captain, the coach is the drill sergeant and the manager is the general.

THE MANAGER

RESPONSIBILITIES

The 21st-century soccer manager has to juggle a bewildering number of tasks. The following are just a handful of them.

TEAM AND PLAYERS
Team selection
Motivating the players
Deciding on formations
Making substitutions
Giving team talks

BEHIND THE SCENES
Signing new players
Maintaining player discipline
Overseeing player development
Monitoring player fitness
Running training sessions

RUNNING THE CLUB
Appointing ancillary staff
Delegating responsibilities
Attending board meetings
Setting club coaching policy
Scouting for new players

IN THE SPOTLIGHT
Dealing with the media
Appearing on club's social media channels
Preparing program notes
Helping club sponsors
Attending club functions

THE MODERN MANAGER

The role of the modern soccer manager was defined by three key figures in the late 1920s and early 1930s: the Englishman Herbert Chapman at Arsenal; Vittorio Pozzo, coach of the Italian national team; and Hugo Meisel, coach of Austrian Wien and Austria. Prior to their arrival, boardroom directors had picked squads and handled transfers and contracts, while players had determined tactics.

A NEW DIRECTION

With the arrival of professionalism in the early 20th century, all three of these managers carved out a new zone of control within their respective soccer clubs. Chapman added showmanship to the mix, inviting film stars to Highbury and calling for floodlit games; Pozzo and Meisel created new levels of tactical sophistication in their squads. All three also possessed another key ingredient: an aura of almost magical, charismatic authority.

A MANAGER HAS A RESPONSIBILITY TO **CREATE A TEAM** AND **USE HIS IDEAS** TO ACHIEVE THAT

FORMER JUVENTUS MANAGER **GIOVANNI TRAPATTONI**

SILVIA NEID
Germany's Silvia Neid won seven league titles and three Euros as a player before picking up the World Cup, Olympic, and Euro trophies as a coach.

THE GREAT MANAGERS

A number of managers have achieved unparalleled success in the game, but here are perhaps the 10 best managers ever to have taken charge of a team.

HERBERT CHAPMAN

The man who invented and personified the idea of the modern, autocratic, media-savvy manager, he won titles with Huddersfield and Arsenal.

SIR ALEX FERGUSON

Ferguson took his grit and cunning to Aberdeen and led them to the top of Scottish soccer. He then headed south and transformed Manchester United into England's dominant club.

BÉLA GUTTMANN

The Hungarian is the only coach to have won the European Cup and the Copa Libertadores (see pp.362–363)—with Benfica and Peñarol respectively—and was a key figure in bringing tactical innovations to Latin America.

HELENIO HERRERA

The man they called "The Magician" conjured up titles and trophies at Barcelona and Inter Milan with his mix of lock-tight defense and surreal motivational techniques.

RINUS MICHELS

"Iron" Rinus brought discipline and coherence to Dutch soccer, turned Ajax into a global force with his Total Soccer (see p.89), and coached the Dutch national side to Euro 1988 success.

BOB PAISLEY

Twenty years in the famous Liverpool "boot room" before he became the club's manager, Bob Paisley may have appeared avuncular, but he ruled Anfield with a rod of iron and won six league titles and three European Cups.

BILL SHANKLY

Shankly's Liverpool teams delighted, his words inspired, and his memory is treasured. No other coach has been hoisted into and across the Kop in scenes of jubilation.

VITTORIO POZZO

Pozzo brought modern soccer management to Italy. He enjoyed success with Torino, but two World Cup wins and an Olympic gold for Italy are hard to beat.

JOSÉ MOURINHO

The former manager of Porto, Inter Milan, Chelsea, Real Madrid, and Manchester United, Mourinho has won numerous honors with all four clubs. He is renowned for his tactical knowledge and his charismatic, if controversial, style.

GIOVANNI TRAPATTONI

In the excruciating hothouse of Italian soccer, one man stays cool: Trapattoni (right) won it all with Juventus in the 1980s and again with Bayern Munich in the 1990s.

THE MANAGERIAL MERRY-GO-ROUND

The job of a top-flight soccer manager is one of the least secure in the world. Even the most talented boss can face being fired after a string of bad results or if there is the slightest hint of losing the confidence of the players, known as "losing the dressing room."

MANAGERIAL MADNESS

There is no hotter seat in world sports than that of the soccer manager. The graphic on the right shows how many managers lost their job in the top five divisions of European soccer—Italy, Spain, England, Germany, and France—in just one season, 2015–2016. They reveal just how tenuous a manager's position can be and that this phenomenon is not isolated to one particular country.

MANAGER CHANGES IN 2015–2016

- Serie A (Italy)—22
- La Liga (Spain)—14
- Premier League (England)—13
- La Ligue (France)—13
- Bundesliga (Germany)—11

13 11 22 13 14

SHORTEST MANAGERIAL REIGN

On May 17, 2007, Torquay United announced that Leroy Rosenior would be joining the club for a second stint as head coach (he had led "The Gulls" to promotion to League One in 2004). Moments later, news emerged that the club had changed ownership, and that the new owners had appointed their own manager. Officially, Rosenior's second stint as Torquay manager lasted 10 minutes—it is thought to be the shortest managerial reign in soccer history.

1 Number of managers to have won back-to-back World Cups—Italy's Vittorio Pozzo

7 Number of Spanish and Italian managers to have won the European Cup—more than all other nations

63 Total number of managerial changes in all four divisions of top-flight English soccer during the 2012–2013 season—out of a total of 92 clubs

MANAGEMENT STYLES

Managers and coaches come in every shape, size, and emotional disposition. At one end of the spectrum, you find the icemen—coaches who barely flinch when their side has scored a goal—and at the other end of the scale are the fire-breathers and ecstatic shamans who patrol their technical zones as if they were in an endless war dance.

The Intimidator
(e.g. Alex Ferguson, right) Revitalizes a sluggish team performance with an inspirational, but terrifying, head-to-head, halftime tongue-lashing.

The Disciplinarian
(e.g. Fabio Capello) Runs the team with a rod of iron. There is no room in the team for the pampered star—the rules are the same for every player.

The Motivator
(e.g. Bill Shankly) Gives players the belief that they are on top of their game and that they are capable of beating any team in the world.

The Philosopher
(e.g. Arsène Wenger) Maintains an unflinching belief in how the game should be played. The emphasis is always on style over substance.

The Resolute
(e.g. Pep Guardiola, below) A bold, principled manager, strong in convictions, especially when it comes to the harmony and culture within the squad. Does not tolerate unruly players and their pushy agents.

THE HAIRDRYER TREATMENT

The former Manchester United striker Mark Hughes came up with the phrase "hairdryer treatment" to describe the tongue-lashings dished out by Alex Ferguson in his halftime team talks.

The Ranter
(e.g. Nereo Rocco) Communicates an all-consuming passion for the game to every one of the players, who invariably live in fear.

The Charismatic
(e.g. Brian Clough) Demands exacting standards from the players; constantly keeps players, club officials, and the media on their toes.

The Mind-Games Expert
(e.g. José Mourinho) Takes the pressure off the team by making themselves, and the opposing side, the center of the media spotlight.

The Wheeler-Dealer
(e.g. Harry Redknapp) Forges a team in their own image, and at limited cost, by making a series of shrewd acquisitions in the transfer market.

The Innovator
(e.g. Vittorio Pozzo) Seeks to surprise the opposition by utilizing specific, and unusual, tactics that have been honed on the training ground.

The Parent Figure
(e.g. Bobby Robson) Provides a comforting arm around the shoulder in the bad times and words of wisdom when things are going well.

The Tactician
(e.g. Rafa Benítez) More likely to scribble notes in a notepad when their side scores a goal than to celebrate with the players.

The Iceman
(e.g. Sven-Goran Eriksson) Remains unflappable under any circumstances, whether the team is 5–0 up in a crunch clash or about to crash out of a major tournament.

°F 122
104
86
68
50
32
14

MOTIVATIONAL TECHNIQUES

Managers have used numerous techniques to try to encourage and cajole the players under their charge, from screaming and shouting at their players while marching up and down the sideline, to a more placid approach. Whichever technique is used, the intention is the same: to get the players to perform to the best of their ability on the field.

MOTIVATION THE ARSENAL WAY

In September 2008, the *Guardian* newspaper in England obtained a copy of a motivational handout prepared by Arsenal manager Arsène Wenger for his players to take away and digest before big matches. The text of the handout is printed below.

BIZARRE MOTIVATIONAL TECHNIQUES

Many managers have been known to use a number of unusual techniques to get the best out of their players; others have simply crossed the boundaries of normality. Former Nottingham Forest manager Brian Clough used to order his players to run through stinging nettles. Most bizarre of all, however, was Giovanni Trapattoni. The former Juventus manager was famously eccentric on the sideline, gesticulating frantically, and even showering his players with holy water.

OUR TEAM BECOMES STRONGER BY:
DISPLAYING A POSITIVE ATTITUDE ON AND OFF THE FIELD
EVERYONE MAKING THE RIGHT DECISIONS FOR THE TEAM
HAVE AN UNSHAKABLE BELIEF THAT WE CAN ACHIEVE OUR TARGET
BELIEVE IN THE STRENGTH OF THE TEAM
ALWAYS WANT MORE—ALWAYS GIVE MORE
FOCUS ON OUR COMMUNICATION
BE DEMANDING WITH YOURSELF
BE FRESH AND PREPARED TO WIN
FOCUS ON BEING MENTALLY STRONGER AND ALWAYS KEEP GOING UNTIL THE END
WHEN WE PLAY AWAY FROM HOME, BELIEVE IN OUR IDENTITY AND PLAY THE SOCCER WE LOVE TO PLAY AT HOME
STICK TOGETHER
STAY GROUNDED AND HUMBLE AS A PLAYER AND A PERSON
SHOW THE DESIRE TO WIN IN ALL THAT YOU DO
ENJOY AND CONTRIBUTE TO ALL THAT IS SPECIAL ABOUT BEING IN A TEAM

IF I HAD AN ARGUMENT WITH A PLAYER WE WOULD ... TALK ABOUT IT ... AND THEN DECIDE **I WAS RIGHT!**

FORMER NOTTINGHAM FOREST MANAGER **BRIAN CLOUGH**

TOP 5: MANAGER SPEAK

Modern managers are exposed to extreme pressures and often say things they should not.

JOSÉ MOURINHO
While manager of Chelsea, Mourinho offered this recipe for success: "If you have no eggs, you have no omelet. And it depends upon the quality of the eggs. Some are more expensive than others and some give you better omelets. So when the class-one eggs are in [UK supermarket] Waitrose and you cannot go there, you have a problem."

JAVIER CLEMENTE
When one journalist tried to validate his opinion by saying he'd "seen a lot of soccer," the much-traveled Spanish manager cut him down with the following observation: "The cows at Lezama [Athletic Bilbao's training ground in the country] watch soccer every day, and they haven't got a ... clue."

JOEL SALDANHA
The former journalist became Brazil's manager prior to the 1970 World Cup. When Brazil's military president, General Medici, said he didn't like Saldanha's selections, Saldanha replied: "I don't choose the president's ministry ... he can't choose my front line." He was promptly fired.

KEVIN KEEGAN
Newcastle boss Keegan (below) fired off a tirade at Manchester United's Alex Ferguson's mind games in the climax to the 1995–1996 Premier League season: "But I'll tell ya—you can tell him now if you're watching it—we're still fighting for this title, and ... and I tell you honestly, I'd love it if we beat them, just love it!" United took the title by four points.

SILVIA NEID
Asked about the chances of a woman coach in the Bundesliga, she replied, "When I was asked about the chances of that happening 10 years ago, I thought the time might be ripe in 10 years' time. But nothing has really changed. It would be a lie to say the battle is over."

32,700,000
Yearly salary (in dollars) of then Manchester United manager José Mourinho in 2016–2017

3 Number of men who won World Cup as both a player and manager—Mario Zagallo (Brazil), Franz Beckenbauer (Germany), and Didier Deschamps (France)

TEAMWORK

THE ANATOMY OF A CLUB

Since Sheffield FC was established in northern England in 1857, the club has been at the center of soccer cultures all over the world. But clubs come in many shapes and sizes, and methods of ownership have changed, too. In England, clubs moved from being private organizations to private limited companies. Socio clubs emerged in southern Europe and Latin America. In communist societies, state organizations and trade unions ran teams.

TYPES OF CLUB OWNERSHIP

A soccer club is no longer solely represented by 11 players taking to a field up to twice a week wearing a familiar jersey; the modern club extends far beyond the confines of the sidelines. It is a business, a potential vehicle for political advancement, and in some cases even a billionaire's toy. Clubs have evolved in various ways in different parts of the world.

FOREIGN INVESTMENT

Following a trend kicked off largely by Russia's Roman Abramovich, who took control of Chelsea in 2003, many Premier League clubs are now under the command of foreign owners. Manchester City was purchased by the Abu Dhabi United Group in 2008, and many US-based companies or individuals have control of other Premier League teams.

THE SOCIO MODEL

In Latin America and southern Europe, the original sports/social clubs out of which so many teams grew left a legacy in which all members have an annual vote for the elected officers of the club's board. The club itself can neither be bought nor sold.

FC UNITED OF MANCHESTER

When American tycoon Malcolm Glazer acquired a controlling interest in Manchester United in May 2005, supporters who opposed the takeover decided to form their own club. FC United entered the 10th tier of English soccer in the fall of 2005.

I LOVE THIS SPORT, I LOVE THIS LEAGUE. WHY DON'T I GET MY OWN TEAM?

FORMER CHELSEA OWNER **ROMAN ABRAMOVICH**

OTHER TYPES OF CLUB

In countries like Germany, soccer clubs are owned and controlled by the original amateur sports associations out of which they grew. In the US, Australia, and Mexico, clubs are operated on a franchise basis. A recent innovation has been the e-club (such as Ebbsfleet United in England) where anyone can buy a stake in the club.

WORLD'S RICHEST CLUBS 2022

- Man City—**$766m**
- Real Madrid—**$761m**
- Bayern Munich—**$726m**
- Barcelona—**$692m**
- Man Utd—**$663m**
- Paris Saint-Germain—**$661m**
- Liverpool—**$654m**
- Chelsea—**$586m**
- Juventus—**$515m**
- Tottenham—**$483m**

682
621 715
623
551
484 454
720 615 650

TOP 5: TYCOONS AND TYRANTS

Money and power just can't keep away from the game, and soccer associations and soccer clubs have been owned, run, embarrassed, and even ruined by business tycoons and political tyrants. Here are five of the biggest and baddest tycoons and tyrants in the history of the game, some of whom have made Genghis Khan seem like a benign dictator.

JOÃO HAVELANGE (Brazil, FIFA)
The Sun King of global soccer, Havelange started in the Brazilian bus business and ran the Brazilian FA in its golden era before destroying Sir Stanley Rous in FIFA's 1974 presidential election. A master of power politics, Havelange revolutionized, expanded, and commercialized both FIFA and the World Cup—but he would brook no opposition. He is known to have blanked Rupert Murdoch and compared himself to the Pope.

IRVIN KHOZA (South Africa, Orlando Pirates)
The "Iron Duke" made his money and his reputation in the townships of South Africa under apartheid, running a whole variety of "business interests." He became a commanding, controversial, and headline-grabbing figure in the whole of the African soccer scene, running his club, Orlando Pirates (Free State province in South Africa), with the same single-mindedness he devoted to his businesses.

WHO'S IN CHARGE?

The power structures and lines of command in soccer clubs are an endless source of intrigue. The relationships between presidents, coaches, technical directors, and directors of soccer serve to create as much friction as they do cooperation and have generated as many newspaper headlines in recent years as the action on the field.

PRESIDENT, PRIME MINISTER, AND PUNDIT

Former Italian prime minister Silvio Berlusconi bought AC Milan in 1986. Never one to keep away from the television cameras, he was often seen bemoaning his manager Carlo Ancelotti's tactics. The manager's insistence on playing 4-3-2-1 was a constant source of anguish for Berlusconi, who believed that soccer is a game requiring two strikers.

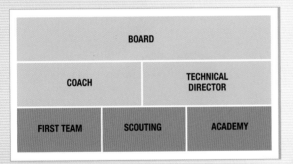

TRADITIONAL SETUP
The classic setup that hinges on an all-powerful manager who takes charge of all aspects of the club's first team transfer policy, scouting, and youth development.

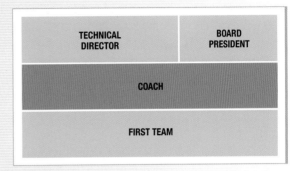

ALL-POWERFUL TECHNICAL DIRECTOR
Increasingly common in Europe, the technical director has total control of the club's transfer policy. The coach can ask for certain players but has to make do with what is given by the technical director.

CLASSIC CONTINENTAL
In this setup, the club is run by the board, the technical director (who is responsible for dealings on the transfer market), and the coach (who is responsible for first-team affairs).

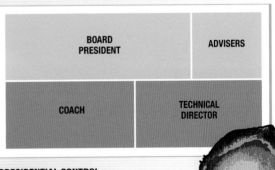

PRESIDENTIAL CONTROL
The board president, assisted by a number of advisers, calls all the shots, from team selection to transfer policy. The coach answers to only one person: the board president.

LAVRENTIY BERIA
(USSR, Dynamo Moscow)
The man who ran the KGB under Stalin and a key figure in the purges and the Gulag (the government agency that administered the penal labor camps in the USSR), Beria brought his own style of terror-based management to the KGB's very own soccer team—Dynamo Moscow.

ROMAN ABRAMOVICH
(England, Chelsea)
After making millions in oil and aluminum, the Russian turned his attention to soccer. He bought Chelsea in June 2003, spent big money, and, although managers have come and gone, trophies soon followed. Chelsea won the Champions League for the second time in 2021. He sold the club in 2022.

JESÚS GIL Y GIL
(Spain, Atlético Madrid)
A building magnate who was imprisoned after a hotel he made collapsed on its residents and who was wanted in courts across Spain on corruption charges, Gil (right) didn't care. He kept Atlético Madrid in the headlines for two decades.

INDIVIDUAL
SKILLS

INDIVIDUAL SKILLS

ANATOMY OF A PLAYER

Like dancers and singers, soccer players' bodies are their instruments, their means of performance and expression. Although men and women professionals are generally getting stronger and fitter, the game still offers space for a variety of physiques and specialties. Above all, the game still demands the secret soccer biology of "guts" and "heart."

EDGAR DAVIDS

The hard-tackling Dutch international is best remembered for protective goggles, worn following an operation on his right eye for glaucoma in 1999. He required permission from FIFA to wear the glasses and to use eyewash that contained a banned substance.

KEY REQUIREMENTS

Although the size and shape of players does vary, there are certain anatomical requirements that all top-level players have in common. Because soccer players use their legs and feet more than anything else, strong lower-body muscles—the calf, thigh muscles (quadriceps), and hamstrings—are the most important. Upper-body strength is also key, in order to facilitate both powerful running and resisting tackles from opposing players.

CHANGING SHAPE

Soccer players are changing shape. One study looked at the height, weight, and body mass index (BMI) of male players in the top English division between 1974 and 2004. Over those 40 years, players on average got taller and leaner—and the top six teams in the league each season consistently had more of these kinds of players.

AVERAGE HEIGHTS

Average heights of male professionals in Europe by position.

Forwards—**5 FT 10 IN**

Midfielders—**5 FT 9 IN**

Defenders—**6 FT**

Goalkeepers—**6 FT 2 IN**

BODY STRENGTH

A soccer player's leg muscles do much of the work (and are most prone to injury), but a strong neck, spine, chest, abdominals, and deltoids are all important.

Eyes
Players need to read the game and judge speeds and distances.

Deltoids
Built by bench presses and weight lifting, these muscles power the arms and are useful for cushioning high balls.

Chest muscles
Players need this large area of muscle, just one of three glutei muscles, to run and pass the ball.

Abdominals
Core inner-body strength is a prerequisite of the balance and posture required for top-level soccer.

Quadriceps
The four muscles at the front of the thigh are the player's engine room, essential for running and kicking.

Groin
Takes much of the muscle stress caused by shooting, so pre-match stretching is vital.

Ankles
Must be strong to cope with the stress of constant changes of direction.

750,000,000

The total cost in dollars (£663 million) to insure Lionel Messi's legs when he was at Barcelona

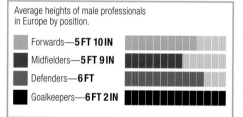

66 Percentage of daily caloric intake burned in a match

23.3 Average Body Mass Index of Premiership players 2003–2004

6 ft 1 in Average man-height (185.8 cm) of the tallest team at Euro 2016—Sweden

177 Average man-weight in lb (80.3 kg) of the heaviest team at Euro 2016—Germany

SHAPES AND SIZES

Soccer does not favor one body type or one kind of player, but, because it demands such a complex range and mixture of skills, it can accommodate all shapes and sizes of both sexes. People of different physical makeups have become stars, from the tall and thin to the short and stocky.

THE LONG ...

6 ft 10 in (2.08 m) Kristof van Hout (Belgium)

6 ft 9 in (2.05 m) Yang Changpeng (China)

6 ft 8 in (2.04 m) Tor Hogne Aarøy (Norway)

... AND THE SHORT

5 ft 3 in (1.60 m) Brian Flynn (Wales)

5 ft 2 in (1.58 m) Élton Jose Xavier Gomes (Brazil)

5 ft 1 in (1.55 m) Jafal Rashed (Qatar)

6 ft 7 in (2.01 m)

5 ft 4 in (1.62 m)

6 ft 4 in (1.93 m)

5 ft 8 in (1.73 m)

PETER CROUCH
Tall, gangly, but surprisingly mobile and was a regular for England

MARTA
Her low center of gravity gives her amazing balance

WILLIAM FOULKE
At his peak in the 1920s, Foulke weighed 280 lb (127 kg)

PELÉ
The perfect player, a balance of height, speed, and power

Neck muscles
The key to powerful heading, players need to work specifically on these muscles to strengthen them.

Spine
Liable to take a lot of stress in a match, as a player braces and stretches for every turn.

Hamstrings
Give flexibility to the knee and hip and allow the leg to stretch. These are easily torn, so players need them to be long, supple, and tough.

Calves
Raise the heel when running, walking, and jumping. The calf muscles are very prone to cramp.

Achilles heel
Has to take all the strain of soccer's bursts of speed, stop and start motion, and sharp turns.

PERFECTION?

Despite 150 years of top-flight soccer, the perfect player has yet to grace the field. Hypothetically, however, it would be rewarding to create the perfect stereotyped male player by fusing together the best physical attributes of some of the game's greats.

PART	WHO AND WHY?
BRAIN	Johan Cruyff—dubbed "Pythagoras in Boots"; no player ever saw the angles and spaces of a game more quickly.
HANDS	Pat Jennings—huge, long-fingered, and reliable, the Northern Ireland keeper even scored a goal in 1967.
UPPER BODY	Cristiano Ronaldo—the powerful chest of the Portuguese star gives him the strength to out-jump and out-muscle defenders.
THIGHS	Ronald Koeman—very muscular upper legs, so the Dutch player delivered shots and free kicks with great force.
RIGHT FOOT	David Beckham—a foot that could caress and coax the ball as well as slam it is the perfect tool.
LEFT FOOT	Lionel Messi—his lethal left foot made him the record scorer for both Barcelona and Argentina.

GARRINCHA

The brilliant Brazilian midfielder who won two World Cups in 1958 and 1962 was born with several disabilities. His spine was abnormally shaped, his right leg curved inward, and his left leg was bent and 2 in (6 cm) shorter than the right leg. Yet, from an early age, he demonstrated complete mastery of the ball and developed a fierce shot.

MIND OF A PLAYER

Soccer players are often portrayed as stupid, perhaps by people who are jealous of the wealth and adulation they receive. In fact, top players do not lack intelligence. Soccer demands a wide range of cognitive and creative skills, including imagination, spatial awareness, and speed of thought. All great players need to demonstrate high levels of creativity and application.

MENTAL TRAINING

Many of the most important mental attributes of a top-class player are instinctive, such as spatial awareness and quick reactions. Various training methods are used to enhance these qualities. One of the most effective is a board on which are mounted several lights that switch on and off at random. The player's task is to touch them as soon as they come on. Performances are timed and compared to assess improvement.

PSYCHOLOGY

Natural abilities are only half the story. Big clubs routinely employ the services of sports psychologists to get their players in the optimum mental condition. Techniques regularly employed include visualization, relaxation, and positive thinking exercises. Players capable of calm and rational thought on the field are prized assets for any team.

CLEVER KEEPER

The Algerian-born French author and philosopher Albert Camus (1913–1960) was a highly promising goalkeeper until his career was ruined by tuberculosis at the age of 17.

ALBERT CAMUS

The French novelist played for Racing Universitaire Algerois, which won four trophies during the 1930s.

SOCRATES

A player with a name like Socrates ought to have had a powerful brain. The former Brazil captain held two doctorates, in medicine and philosophy. Socrates was also blessed with a great ability to read the game and make astute passes.

YOU'RE BOOKED

Soccer attracts the literary mind. Alongside Albert Camus, these are some leading lights of literary soccer:

VLADIMIR NABOKOV (RUSSIA/US)

Before becoming a novelist, Nabokov learned goalkeeping skills at the Tenishev School in St. Petersburg, Russia. He mused about the "blessing of the ball hugged to one's chest."

ORHAN PAMUK (TURKEY)

"Soccer is faster than words," Pamuk said in 2008, meaning that literature struggles to keep up with the visual medium of sports.

NAGUIB MAHFOUZ (EGYPT)

As a child, Mahfouz played street soccer in Cairo's Abbassia section on land also used to stage Islamic festivals.

EDUARDO GALEANO (URUGUAY)

Galeano has said that he reserves for the page what he could not, as an "irredeemable klutz," manage on the field.

BARRY HINES (ENGLAND)

Hines brought a soccer player's awareness to his writing. He played for Barnsley, England, in the 1950s.

GEORGE BEST
He was the best player of his generation but psychologically flawed.

MAD, BAD, OR JUST PLAIN CRAZY?

For all the efforts of managers and psychologists to mold the personality of their players, once they walk onto the field, their emotions can sometimes take over. Soccer has had its fair share of unpredictable characters over the years, from George Best to Zinedine Zidane.

OFF THE RAILS

Some of the best players in the history of the game have gone spectacularly off the rails. George Best abandoned Manchester United for the bottle, Paul Gascoigne descended into a spiral of self-harm, and Diego Maradona shot a reporter with an air gun. Certainly madness and genius are closely related, although the pressure to perform and obsessive media attention players are subjected to are contributing factors.

I SPENT MOST OF MY MONEY ON BOOZE, BIRDS, AND FAST CARS; THE REST I JUST ... SQUANDERED

FORMER MANCHESTER UNITED STAR, **GEORGE BEST**

LIMBIC LOSS

Certain players have found it hard to control their aggression during games. The career of French legend Zinedine Zidane ended in disgrace after the midfielder headbutted Italian defender Marco Materazzi during the 2006 World Cup Final. The scientific explanation for these lapses lies with the limbic system—the area of the brain that controls emotions. Yoga and relaxation techniques can help keep this under control.

THE RED MIST

In 1995, Manchester United's Eric Cantona was sent off in an away game against Crystal Palace. As he was walking off the field, he suddenly launched himself into the crowd, flooring Palace fan Matthew Simmons with a spectacular kung fu kick. Mr. Simmons's claim that he had merely shouted, "An early bath for you, Cantona!" seems unlikely.

FASTEST SENDINGS OFF

3 SECONDS—Chippenham Town striker David Pratt was sent off for a wild tackle in an English minor league game in 2008.

10 SECONDS—Bologna's Giuseppe Lorenzo hit an opponent in a 1990 Italian league game.

13 SECONDS—Sheffield Wednesday keeper Kevin Pressman was sent off in 2000.

TOP 5: LUCKY CHARMS

Superstition plays a significant role in the mental makeup of many players. Here are five of the most famous characters through the years.

CARLITO ROCHA

The President of Rio Club Botafogo in the 1940s and '50s owned a dog named Biriba. One day the dog ran onto the field during a match, and Botafogo scored in the ensuing disruption. From then on, Biriba was permanently on the bench and regularly used to disrupt games.

IVORY COAST

Before the 1984 Africa Cup of Nations, the Ivory Coast squad was joined at its hotel by more than 150 healers and witch doctors. Each player was invited to "say his wishes privately into the ear of a living pigeon."

JOHN TERRY

The Chelsea captain and England defender has more pregame superstitions than any other player in the English game. These range from listening to the same CD in his car to tying tape around his socks three times.

SERGIO GOYCOCHEA

The former Argentina goalkeeper believes, "If you have any natural human urges, you have to go (urinate) on the field." He relieved himself ahead of the 1990 World Cup Semifinal against Italy and went on to make two spectacular saves.

DON REVIE

The former Leeds United manager wore the same blue suit for every match, touched a bus stop before each home game, and sincerely believed that the club's stadium, Elland Road, had been cursed.

MARTIAL LAW
Manchester United's Eric Cantona took the law into his own hands at Selhurst Park (see left).

INDIVIDUAL SKILLS

WARMING UP

Every game of soccer should start with a warm-up. Soccer's twists and turns and its demand for fast accelerating movements will quickly pull or damage cold muscles and stiff joints and tendons. Similarly, the body's metabolism works best if it is gradually coaxed into life, by systematically raising the heart rate and body temperature of the player.

RUNNING LATE

In 2006, Spartak Moscow was stuck in traffic on the way to a match against Internazionale. With time running short, the team had to warm up by jogging through the streets to the nearest metro station and received their team talk in a packed commuter car.

THE ROUTINE

There are four stages to the typical warm-up routine used by professional teams—jogging and gentle stretches, static stretches, dynamic stretches, and footwork and agility. The session is always followed by a cooldown.

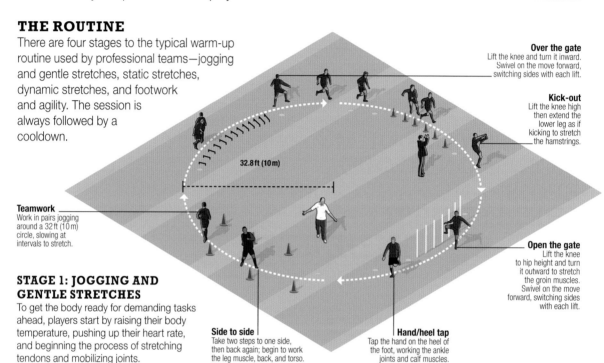

Over the gate
Lift the knee and turn it inward. Swivel on the move forward, switching sides with each lift.

Kick-out
Lift the knee high then extend the lower leg as if kicking to stretch the hamstrings.

32.8 ft (10 m)

Teamwork
Work in pairs jogging around a 32 ft (10 m) circle, slowing at intervals to stretch.

Open the gate
Lift the knee to hip height and turn it outward to stretch the groin muscles. Swivel on the move forward, switching sides with each lift.

Side to side
Take two steps to one side, then back again; begin to work the leg muscle, back, and torso.

Hand/heel tap
Tap the hand on the heel of the foot, working the ankle joints and calf muscles.

STAGE 1: JOGGING AND GENTLE STRETCHES

To get the body ready for demanding tasks ahead, players start by raising their body temperature, pushing up their heart rate, and beginning the process of stretching tendons and mobilizing joints.

STAGE 2: STATIC STRETCHES

The body is warm, but the big muscle groups are not yet ready for a full workout. The key muscles in the leg need extra work. The quadriceps in the front of the thigh and the hamstrings in the back of the leg need stretching before running, while groins, calves, and ankles are prone to damage if used when cold.

SPIRITUAL SOCCER

Yoga, the ancient Indian art of stretching, breathing, and meditation, has been used by several famous players to help them recover from injury and to prolong their careers. Practitioners have included Manchester United winger Ryan Giggs and England goalkeeper David James.

Both legs
Repeat the stretch to work both legs.

QUAD STRETCH
Hold the heel against the buttock for at least 30 seconds. Use a wall to aid balance.

Keep straight
The back should be straight.

CALF STRETCH
Stand with the back foot flat on the floor and transfer weight to the front foot. Hold for about 10 seconds.

Tight muscles
Feel the muscles of the front leg tighten.

HAMSTRING STRETCH
Extend one leg in front with the foot flexed. Bend the other knee and lean forward slightly.

Knee bend
Knee should not be bent beyond the ankle.

GROIN STRETCH
Good for inner thigh and groin muscles—should be held for 10–20 seconds.

STAGE 3: DYNAMIC STRETCHES

Players pick up the pace and combine aerobic work (which raises the activity rate of the heart and lungs) with full muscle stretches. Players work in pairs, moving through a series of routines that push their heart rates upward. Each player uses his partner for balance during the moves. The intention is also to raise the body's temperature by approximately 2°F (1°C).

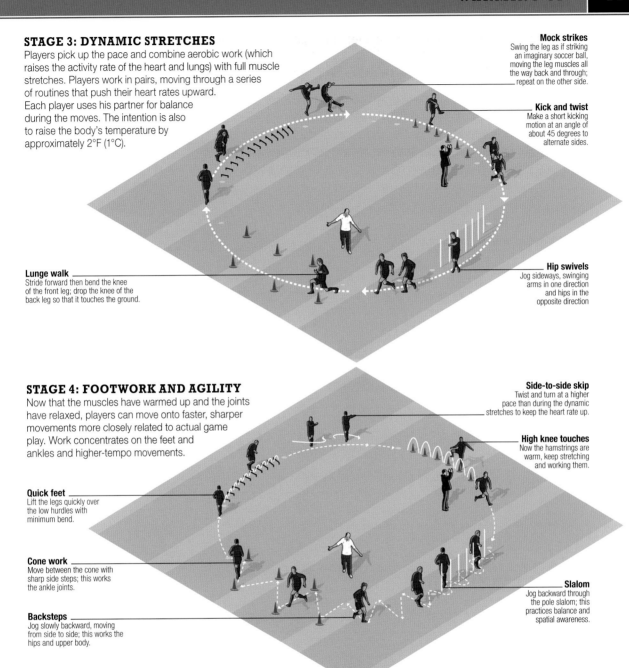

Mock strikes
Swing the leg as if striking an imaginary soccer ball, moving the leg muscles all the way back and through; repeat on the other side.

Kick and twist
Make a short kicking motion at an angle of about 45 degrees to alternate sides.

Hip swivels
Jog sideways, swinging arms in one direction and hips in the opposite direction

Lunge walk
Stride forward then bend the knee of the front leg; drop the knee of the back leg so that it touches the ground.

STAGE 4: FOOTWORK AND AGILITY

Now that the muscles have warmed up and the joints have relaxed, players can move onto faster, sharper movements more closely related to actual game play. Work concentrates on the feet and ankles and higher-tempo movements.

Side-to-side skip
Twist and turn at a higher pace than during the dynamic stretches to keep the heart rate up.

High knee touches
Now the hamstrings are warm, keep stretching and working them.

Quick feet
Lift the legs quickly over the low hurdles with minimum bend.

Cone work
Move between the cone with sharp side steps; this works the ankle joints.

Slalom
Jog backward through the pole slalom; this practices balance and spatial awareness.

Backsteps
Jog slowly backward, moving from side to side; this works the hips and upper body.

THE COOLDOWN

At the end of training, players need to lower their heart rate and body temperature steadily and allow the body to disperse the buildup of lactic acid that forms in well-worked muscles. Soreness and stiffness will last for longer otherwise. Players repeat many of the gentle stretches but at a steadily lower pace. They then repeat long static and dynamic stretching of all the key muscle groups.

COOLDOWN ROUTINE		
STAGE ONE GENTLE MOVEMENTS	STAGE TWO STATIC STRETCHES	STAGE THREE DYNAMIC STRETCHES
OVER THE GATE	QUADS	MOCK STRIKES
OPEN THE GATE	HAMSTRINGS	KICK AND TWIST
HAND TAP	CALVES	HIP SWIVELS
KICK-OUT	GROIN	LUNGE WALK
SIDE STEP		

TRAINING

Top teams spend a great deal of time practicing with the ball. Some of this is devoted to rehearsing set pieces (see pp.64–65), but a major part of the average training session is given over to honing basic ball skills so that they become instinctive.

BALL WORK

A good training session encompasses a variety of skills, exercises all the key muscle groups, and encourages teamwork. The drills below represent only some of the infinite choices available to coaches.

POST WARM-UP

Ball work drills should be practiced after the players have warmed up and stretched their muscles. Depending on the desired intensity, there should be one ball for every two or three players, and these should remain in play throughout the session.

KEY
- ● Player
- — Player motion
- ○ Ball
- --- Ball motion
- ▲ Cone

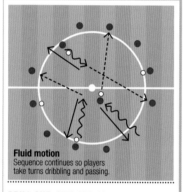

Fluid motion
Sequence continues so players take turns dribbling and passing.

DRILL ONE: GIVE AND GO
Each player lines up on the edge of a circle. Those with a ball dribble into the center, pass to a teammate without the ball, and run back.

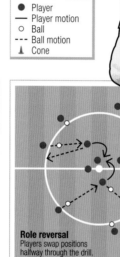

Role reversal
Players swap positions halfway through the drill.

DRILL TWO: IN THE MIDDLE
Half of the players stand on the outside of the circle; the other half toward its center. The two sets exchange passes using several balls.

Swap
Both sets of players swap positions during the dribble.

DRILL THREE: AROUND THE CONE
Players inside the circle dribble around a cone on the edge and pass to players who have run to the first player's original starting point.

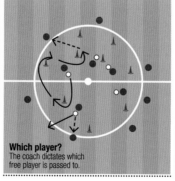

Which player?
The coach dictates which free player is passed to.

DRILL FOUR: MORE CONE WORK
Players in the center dribble around cones. When instructed, they pass to a free player on the outside of the circle and swap positions.

KAKÁ

The Brazil legend was renowned for his close control and ball skills, a talent honed on the training field through his career from junior level. Training with the ball is now standard with men and women, and far removed from the basic running and jumping exercises of former eras.

WITHOUT THE BALL

There are two aspects to training without the ball. The first consists of running and building stamina; players recovering from injuries also do strength work in the gym. The second concerns how players look after themselves away from the training ground: diet, rest, and self-discipline are all important (see box below).

BUILDING STAMINA

If a player runs out of energy toward the end of a match, the team is likely to suffer. Soccer players need considerable stamina, and their training should help them develop it. A typical stamina-building session might consist of three 985 yd (900 m) runs followed by three of 660 yd (600 m) and three of 330 yd (300 m) with a two- to three-minute break between each run.

SPRINT TRAINING

During matches, players sprint in quick bursts and spend the rest of the time jogging or walking. Sprint training is designed to reflect this. Players run flat out for 5 to 10 seconds then walk back to the start and repeat the procedure. One of the advantages of this kind of training is that it gets the body to work anaerobically. This means that it is temporarily producing energy without oxygen, which is what happens when a player suddenly has to run flat-out at the end of 90 exhausting minutes. Anaerobic exercise is hard on the body, so it should be practiced only occasionally, perhaps once every two weeks.

COACHING
Top coaches and managers, such as Carlo Ancelotti, help motivate players during training sessions.

PLYOMETRICS

Players need to run quickly over short distances. Plyometric training is designed to develop the explosive muscle power needed for sudden bursts of acceleration, such as forward chasing a ball. A good example of this kind of exercise is players jumping over a series of hurdles set narrowly apart.

WE TRAIN ALL WEEK WITH A BALL THAT IS ABOUT ...
TWICE THE SIZE!

JUVENTUS DEFENDER **NICOLA LEGROTTAGLIE**
COMPARES THE SIZE OF THE TEAM'S TRAINING BALL TO THE MATCH BALL

WHAT TO EAT, DRINK, AND AVOID

If the wrong kind of fuel is put into a car, it will underperform. The same is true of players with regard to their diets. Players should carefully choose what to eat and drink to perform at their best on match days.

EAT

Players should consume plenty of carbohydrates (such as potatoes and pasta), because these provide the body with energy; easily digestible proteins, such as fish and chicken; and vegetables rich in iron, such as broccoli.

• **AFTER TRAINING**—The body stores energy in the form of a substance called glycogen. Players need to replenish their glycogen levels within two to five hours of exercising. The best way to do this is to eat plenty of carbohydrates.

• **THREE DAYS BEFORE A MATCH**—Players should start "carbohydrate-loading." This means eating meals that are 75 percent complex carbohydrates.

• **MATCH DAY**—An easily digestible meal high in carbohydrates and low in protein and fat should be eaten three to four hours before kickoff. This will optimize the energy available to the player during the game.

DRINK

Soccer players should drink lots of water, particularly before and after training sessions. Players can lose seven pints (four liters) or more of water during a match and will need to rehydrate themselves as quickly as possible. In addition to water, isotonic drinks containing vital nutrients and sugars are particularly easy for the body to absorb. There are several commercial varieties, but a simple version consists of fruit juice and water in equal measures.

AVOID

Players should avoid all caffeine (tea and coffee), alcohol, and junk foods (such as potato chips and deep-fried foodstuffs). Consumption of dairy products and fatty and high-sugar foods should also be limited.

CONTROLLING THE BALL

Possession is the key to controlling a game, and a team can only be said to be in possession when one of its players has the ball under control. Achieving this is one of the fundamental skills of soccer. No matter how perfectly a pass is delivered, it will be wasted if the receiver fails to control the ball effectively.

FLEXIBILITY AND FIRST TOUCH

Controlling the ball is easiest when it is passed gently to the feet, but players must be prepared for it to reach them at any height, from any angle, and at any speed. The quality of a player's first touch is crucial. The best players are able to put the ball exactly where they want it with the same touch they use to bring it under control, giving them time and space to consider their next move.

SYLVAIN WILTORD

The former French international was known for excellent coordination and suppleness involved in certain ball-control maneuvers. Wiltord was one of the few able wingers who could effectively catch the ball at shoulder height with the toe of their boot.

> ## HE DOMINATES THE BALL AND HE PLAYS AS IF HE HAS SILK GLOVES ...
> ## IN EACH BOOT
>
> REAL MADRID LEGEND **ALFREDO DI STEFANO**, ON ZINEDINE ZIDANE, 2006

USING THE FEET

As with most skills, players will find it easiest to control the ball with the feet by getting into position to receive the ball early. The simplest way to practice the art is to kick a ball against a wall at varying heights, strengths, and angles and try to control the rebound. As their skills improve, players should ask friends to rebound the ball for them so they have to make quick adjustments to cope with the unknown deliveries. Basic foot-trapping techniques involve the sole and inside of the foot. With experience, players can move on to the top, outside, and side volley trap.

FOOT TENNIS

One of the best ways to learn ball control is to use a tennis ball. Many of the greatest players in history grew up too poor to afford a proper soccer ball but honed their techniques in this way. If players can master a small bouncy object such as a tennis ball, a regular soccer ball will seem as big as a pumpkin.

Soft landing
Pull the foot back slightly to cushion impact.

INSIDE OF FOOT
This is the easiest way to control the ball. Ideally, the ball will land about a stride ahead of the receiver rather than directly at the feet.

Not too relaxed
Relaxing the leg too much at the moment of impact could result in a jarred knee.

OUTSIDE OF FOOT
If the close proximity of opponents precludes using the inside of the favored foot, the player should use the outside of the other foot.

USING THE BODY

If the ball arrives at a player too high to control it with the feet, there are three main options: to use the thigh, chest, or head. An excellent way to practice these skills is via a game of "head tennis." Played over a volleyball net, players must keep the ball from touching the ground and return it over the net by using their head, chest, thighs, and feet. The more frequently a player plays this enjoyable game, the better their skills will become.

SHANKLY'S SWEAT BOX

Liverpool's legendary manager Bill Shankly used an innovative but exhausting device to improve his players' ball control and stamina. Known as the "sweat box," it consisted of an area bounded by four numbered boards, which players shot against, in between controlling the rebounds, corresponding to the number shouted out by the trainer.

Relax
Relax the neck muscles to cushion the ball.

Lean back
Lean back to take away the ball's momentum.

Leap
Jump up to anticipate the ball.

Angle of receipt
The thigh should be about 45 degrees to the ground when the ball arrives.

CONTROL WITH THIGH
If a player can "catch" the ball with the upper part of the thigh, they can bring it under control very effectively.

CONTROL WITH CHEST
Using the chest to control the ball is easier than it sounds. The receiver must take care to avoid the ball hitting too low and winding them.

CONTROL WITH HEAD
This technique is difficult because the skull is hard, making a degree of bounce inevitable, but sometimes a player will have no alternative.

Foot down
As the ball lands, bring the foot down on it gently but firmly.

Cushion impact
Bend the knee and cushion the ball on the foot.

Pay attention
Pay more attention than usual to the flight of the ball.

And relax
Relax the foot as the ball lands on it.

SOLE OF FOOT
A ball dropping near the feet of the receiver is best controlled by pinning it to the ground with the underside of the foot.

SIDE VOLLEY TRAP
This is used when the ball arrives too high to trap but too low to chest down. The technique requires flexibility to execute well.

TOP-OF-FOOT CUSHION
An alternative to the trap for controlling a dropping ball, this is difficult to perform correctly, as the player is using the narrowest part of the foot.

PASSING

Passing is the lifeblood of any team and a vital skill for all players to learn, including goalkeepers. There are several good reasons why a player might choose to pass—to clear the ball from a danger area, to help the team keep possession, or to try to set up a scoring opportunity. There is only one good time for that player to make the pass, however—whenever there is a teammate in a better position.

TYPES OF PASS

Players pass in order to develop attacks or to work the ball away from opponents. These passes can be along the ground or in the air, over short distances or long range. Short passes are the easiest to execute; long-range airborne passes, the most difficult. Each type of pass has its advantages and disadvantages.

PASSING OPTIONS
Short passes are sometimes made in tight situations near the opponent's goal or laterally between defenders prior to a searching forward pass. Inswinging, outswinging, and driven passes are made over long distances, usually from the player's own half of the field.

KEY	
– – –	Inswinging pass
– – –	Outswinging pass
– – –	Driven pass
– – –	Short pass
– – –	Channel pass
●	Player

SHORT PASS

The short pass is the most accurate kind for two reasons: the ball is struck with the side of the foot and any slight miscue is likely to be masked by the small distance the ball has to travel.

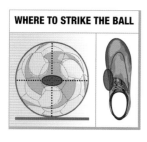

WHERE TO STRIKE THE BALL

Standing leg
Place the leg alongside the ball with the toes pointing in direction of travel.

1 Approach the ball at a 30-degree angle, giving room to swing the passing leg.

Side foot
Strike the ball with the side of the foot for maximum control.

2 Strike the ball with the side of the foot and keeps the ball down. The ankle stays firm.

Eyes ahead
Watch the ball closely as it heads to its target.

3 The length of follow-through reflects the weight the player wants to give the pass.

MAKING A LONG PASS

Long passes or crosses can be very effective, largely because it is normal for defenders to guard their opponents less thoroughly the further away they are from the action. Accuracy is crucial as any error will be magnified.

WHERE TO STRIKE THE BALL

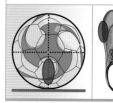

Support
Standing leg should be grounded solidly before the strike.

1 Fix eyes on the ball and approach it at an angle of about 30 degrees.

Instep
Strike the ball with the instep at its central point to keep it low.

2 To keep the pass low, make sure the knee of the striking leg is over the ball at impact.

Sweep
Push the foot in the direction of the ball after impact.

3 The follow-through is more pronounced than for a short pass.

USING THE CHANNELS

Sometimes a player in possession will have no obvious teammate to pass to. In such cases, they should either run with the ball or pass it into a "safe" channel (usually directly ahead of—see left), which gives a teammate a realistic chance of winning the race with the defender to collect it.

THE SCIENCE OF SPIN

You don't have to be an expert in physics to bend a ball—just a good quality player—but the science behind the ball's movements in the air is fascinating. Once struck, the ball naturally seeks the path of least resistance, so it will tend to swerve in the direction of the spin—to the right if the ball is spinning clockwise and the left if it is spinning counterclockwise.

SIDEWAYS SPIN

If a ball is spinning through the air sideways, one side of it will be moving in the direction of its flight while the other is moving counter to it. The forward-spinning side develops a greater force than the backward-spinning one. This is called the Magnus force.

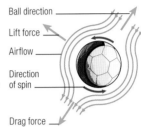

Ball direction
Lift force
Airflow
Direction of spin
Drag force

TOP- AND BACKSPIN

If a ball is rotating forward or backward, the same principle applies, but it has different effects. A ball given topspin will move downward faster than it otherwise would, while the reverse is true of a ball given backspin.

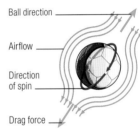

Ball direction
Airflow
Direction of spin
Drag force

ADDING CURVE TO A LONG PASS OR CROSS

Putting curve onto the ball can be useful during attacking moves because the path of a curving ball is much harder to anticipate, and therefore defend, than one that flies straight.

OUTSWINGING PASS OR CROSS
To get the ball to swing left to right, a right-footed player strikes the left side of the ball with the outside of the foot.

INSWINGING PASS OR CROSS
To get the ball to swing right to left, a right-footed player strikes the ball on its right side with the instep.

Strength
Keep the striking foot strong through impact.

Ball edge
Strike the right-hand side of the ball.

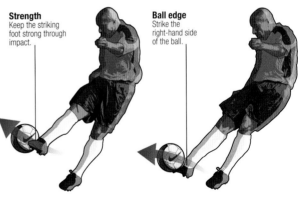

LUKA MODRIĆ

The Real Madrid and Croatia playmaker's measured and varied passing allows him to dominate games despite his diminutive stature. Modrić's vision, accuracy, and intelligence have made him one of the most coveted players in world soccer.

WHERE TO STRIKE THE BALL

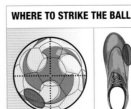

WHERE TO STRIKE THE BALL

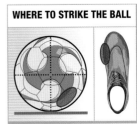

RUNNING WITH THE BALL

Running with the ball under control is known as dribbling. In its basic form, the skill involves a player kicking the ball ahead, running to catch up with it, kicking it forward again, and so on. In practice, however, players rarely have clear spaces ahead of them for long as opposing defenders arrive to try to check their runs. They therefore need to keep the ball close to their feet and develop a repertoire of skills to avoid would-be tacklers.

BEATING OPPONENTS

Dribblers employ a variety of techniques to get past opponents without checking their runs. One of the most important is the shoulder drop, in which the player lowers the level of one shoulder to fool the defender into thinking he is heading in that direction. Another is having the ability to anticipate tackles and the dexterity to jump over them.

HE ... FLOATED OVER THE GROUND LIKE A COCKER SPANIEL CHASING A PIECE OF PAPER ... IN THE WIND

FORMER MANCHESTER UNITED MANAGER **SIR ALEX FERGUSON**
DESCRIBING THE FIRST TIME HE SAW RYAN GIGGS PLAY

BETH **MEAD**

The skillful and fast English forward, Beth Mead, is known for great control of the ball and her quick thinking on the field. She helped her team win the Women's Euro 2022 and was named the Player of the Tournament by UEFA. She was also runner-up for the Ballon d'Or in 2022.

HOW TO DRIBBLE

The best dribblers give the impression that the ball is tied to their cleats. These players also have the ability to alternate between both feet equally well (using the inside and outside of the feet). A dribble is executed as follows.

Look down and up
Keep eyes alternately on the ball and the space ahead.

Softly softly
Don't kick the ball too hard with either foot.

Close range
Keep the ball close by.

Right foot
Push the ball forward with the right foot.

1 Using the left foot, gently kick the ball between 12–19 in (30–50 cm) ahead and to the right.

2 Keep eyes on the ball while running forward, occasionally looking up to assess the situation ahead.

3 When reaching the ball, continue the dribble, using the right foot. Repeat this sequence, using left foot then right.

STOP-TURNS WHILE RUNNING

A player dribbling with the ball will often want to change direction, either to develop a different angle of attack, to run into space, or to evade the challenge of an incoming defender. There are several means of changing direction with the ball. Among the most popular are the inside and outside hooks and the Puskás turn, also known as the drag back.

THE NUTMEG

The nutmeg is a maneuver in which an attacking player passes the ball through an opponent's legs, weighting it to continue the dribble on the other side. Defenders dislike being nutmegged, but if they keep their legs too close together to prevent it, they invite the attacker to kick the ball past them and get around them to the side.

INSIDE HOOK

This hook technique is the easiest of the two hooks. It is used to move inside (to the left for a right-footer) when an opponent is on the player's outside.

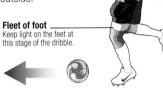

Fleet of foot
Keep light on the feet at this stage of the dribble.

Bend it
Twist the foot around the outside of the ball.

Spin secret
Ensure the standing foot is planted solidly for the spin.

1 Start the inside hook by dribbling forward with the ball under close control, attentive to the presence of defenders.

2 Place one foot slightly ahead of the ball and uses the instep to push the ball back in the direction of the turn.

3 Spin to the left, push off the back foot, and use the front foot to continue the dribble away from the opponent.

OUTSIDE HOOK

This hooking skill is more demanding than the inside hook because it requires the player to use the outside of the right foot to move 180 degrees to the right (for a right-footer).

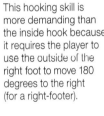

Balance
Use the arms to keep steady.

Turn
Use the outside of the foot.

Drive
Use the arms to power the run.

Kick it
Kick the ball to the front.

1 As with the inside hook turn, start the maneuver by dribbling forward, feeding the ball between each foot alternately.

2 Using the outside of the foot, hook the ball back in the direction you wish to go.

3 Turn 180 degrees to the right then push off with the back foot and accelerate away, using the front foot to dribble.

PUSKÁS TURN

Named after the great Hungarian striker Ferenc Puskás, this trick involves a quarter turn that allows the player in possession to move rapidly at right angles to the direction in which they were originally facing.

Fake kick
Make as if to kick the ball forward.

Stop it
Abbreviate the kick and rest the studs on the ball.

Drag
Pull the ball back with the studs then move into space.

1 Starting with the ball in line with the center of the body, swing one foot as if to kick the ball forward.

2 However, instead of kicking it forward, move the foot slightly over the ball and bring the studs into contact with the top of it.

3 Putting weight on the other foot, drag the ball back and then knock it sideways with the outside of the cleat.

STEP OVERS

The step over, also known as the scissors maneuver, is one of the most visually striking moves in the game. It is used to fool an opponent into thinking the player in possession is about to pass sideways, whereas in fact the run is continued, throwing the defender off balance. Step overs used to be considered an exotic skill, but they have become almost commonplace.

TYPES OF STEP OVER

The classic step over involves the player in possession making to move the ball one way with the outside of one foot but actually passing the foot over and around the ball (from inside to outside) without touching it before picking it up with the other foot and moving in the opposite direction. There are also two more developed styles of step over; the double step over (below) and the Rivelino (opposite).

CRISTIANO **RONALDO**

The Portuguese winger Cristiano Ronaldo is the undisputed master of the step over. Criticized for excessive showmanship early in his career, he is now recognized as one of the world's greatest players. By the end of the 2021–2022 season, he had scored more than 800 career goals.

THE PEDALADA …IS A TRICK I LIKE TO DO …
WITH SPEED

ROBINHO, BRAZIL ATTACKING MIDFIELDER, 2008

DOUBLE STEP OVER

In the double step over, the player performs the trick twice in quick succession, once with each foot. This is more difficult to master, technically.

THE PEDALADA

In South America, the continent that gave birth to the step over, it is known as the "pedalada" and was a common skill used by Brazilian legend Pelé.

The eyes
Look straight ahead.

Dribble
Dribble forward at a slow pace.

1 Dribble the ball forward and prepare to set the standing leg.

Drop it
Drop the left shoulder.

Swivel
Lift and rotate the right foot through 360 degrees.

2 Move the right foot around and over the ball in a clockwise direction.

3 This brings the player back to the starting point but further forward than before.

Look
Keep the eyes on the ball.

Rotate
Lift the left foot in a circle over the ball.

Rolling on
Ball keeps moving forward.

4 Perform a second step over, this time with the left foot and in a counterclockwise direction.

THE RIVELINO

In this variation of the step over, named after the Brazilian winger, the legs move around the ball in the opposite direction—that is, from outside to inside. The Rivelino requires very precise balance.

Eyes peeled
Keep eyes fully focused on the ball to avoid contact with either foot.

Shoulder
Raise the right shoulder and move to the left.

Hip
Move the left hip forward.

Right leg
Place weight on the right side before springing off.

Slow
Dribble slowly at first.

Foot down
Put the left foot down.

1 Dribble the ball slowly and precisely toward the defender, planting the front foot and bringing the trailing leg toward the ball.

2 Instead of making contact with the ball, bring the trailing leg up and over the ball, placing it on the other side.

3 Swivel 180 degrees, placing weight on the right foot, then play the ball with the left.

---

11 The average number of Cristiano Ronaldo step overs performed per game during the 2007–2008 season

25 The typical amount of space created, in inches (63 cm), by an effective step over move

6 Number of step overs Brazil winger Denílson made before evading France midfielder Emmanuel Petit during the 1998 World Cup

7 Number of step overs made by Santos striker Robinho before he won the penalty that clinched the match for his side in the 2002 Brazilian league final

STEP IT UP

In 2007, Roma's Alessandro Mancini performed a total of six step overs in rapid succession en route to scoring a goal in a Champions League match against Olympique Lyonnais.

Push off
Spring off from the left side to travel quickly to the right.

5 The player is again back to the starting position but further forward than before.

6 Knock the ball forward with the right foot and continue the dribble.

EDEN HAZARD

The Belgium and Real Madrid forward has an array of tricks to get beyond defenders and either score or assist a teammate. Hazard's low center of gravity helps him bamboozle players with a few skillful step overs.

SPINS AND TURNS

Some of the most spectacular moves in soccer involve players spinning or turning in unexpected ways. The skills below are much more technically demanding than the regular turns covered in the dribbling section (see pp.122–123) and often only the world's best-known and most skillful players use them successfully in a match situation.

FINDING SPACE

Complex turns require large amounts of practice, but they aren't executed simply to show off (at least not during a match). Making a successful turn is a great way to lose a marker or throw off an opponent, both of which buy the player precious time to run into space or make a considered pass to a teammate. Two of the best maneuvers for achieving this are the Zidane spin and the Cruyff turn.

Balance
Use outstretched arms for balance during the spin and to repel the advances of opponents

JOHAN CRUYFF
The Dutch maestro perfected a move known as the "Cruyff turn" (see right).

THE ZIDANE SPIN

The Zidane spin or turn is a form of pirouette in which the player spins through 360 degrees while keeping the ball under close control. It is almost as difficult to describe as it is to do, but the trick can be broken down into four stages. Zinedine Zidane performed this technique on many occasions at the highest level. When executed well, it buys the player in possession much-needed time in crowded midfield situations.

ZINEDINE **ZIDANE**

The former French international came to worldwide prominence at Juventus in Italy and then Real Madrid in Spain. His personal accolades include being a World Cup winner in 1998 and a three-time FIFA World Player of the Year.

Fleet of foot
Players need to be agile when performing this maneuver.

Position play
Stop the ball with the favored foot to start the spin.

1 Dribble forward with the ball as normal then stop and puts the stronger foot on top of it.

THE CRUYFF TURN

Many famous soccer tricks are named after the players who introduced or perfected them. This silky maneuver, a complex drag back that always leaves defenders behind, is named after the great Ajax and Netherlands forward Johan Cruyff, who first performed it in 1974. When executing the maneuver, the player feigns execution of a long pass or cross but instead spins 180 degrees and continues the dribble.

COERVER COACHING METHOD

During the 1970s, the Feyenoord manager Wiel Coerver pioneered a training technique that involved analyzing films of great players in action and breaking their moves down into stages that could be taught to young players. His approach earned him the nickname "the Albert Einstein of soccer." In 1998, Boudewijn Zenden became the first player schooled by the Coerver method to appear in a World Cup final.

Fake it
Pass the foot over the ball rather than striking it.

Drag back
Push the ball gently behind you with the right foot.

Solid base
Plant the standing foot solidly as this forms a strong base for the move.

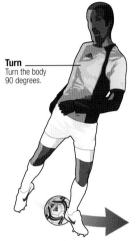

Turn
Turn the body 90 degrees.

Weight shift
Plant the weight on the right side and use this as a springboard.

1 Plant one foot by the ball and make as if to shoot or hit a long pass with the other leg.

2 Bring the leg toward the ball but, instead of kicking the ball, pass the foot over it.

3 Using the inside of the same foot, drag the ball back behind and turn your body.

4 Complete the turn through 180 degrees and run off with the ball.

THE HALF-PREKI

Predrag Radosavljevic began his career with Red Star Belgrade and ended it in Major League Soccer in America, where he shortened his name to Preki. In this maneuver, named after him, a dribbling player puts space between themselves and an approaching defender by rolling the ball across the front of the body with the sole of the dominant foot. When they lift their foot to begin the move, there is a chance that the defender will think they are going to pass. Another version of the trick starts with a half-Preki and ends with a step over (see pp.124–125).

[CRUYFF] IS THE BEST PLAYER I HAVE SEEN IN MY ...
LIFETIME

MICHEL PLATINI, FORMER FRANCE MIDFIELDER

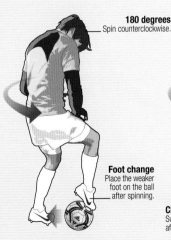

180 degrees
Spin counterclockwise.

Foot change
Place the weaker foot on the ball after spinning.

Turn
Complete the spin.

Change feet
Swap feet again after spinning.

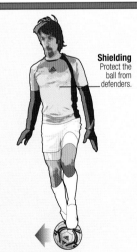

Shielding
Protect the ball from defenders.

Continue
Keep dribbling in the same direction as you started the spin.

2 Roll the ball backward, spin 180 degrees around it, then hold it with the weaker foot.

3 Roll the ball back gently with the weaker foot and turns 180 degrees in the same direction.

4 After completing the full spin, get the ball again with the stronger foot.

5 Finally, continue the run, leaving the opposition defenders perplexed.

FAKES

Deception is a vital ingredient in top-class soccer. Many of the most effective moves rely on players fooling their opponents into thinking they are going to do one thing and actually doing another. When this works, it cons members of the other team into moving out of position and buys crucial time for the team in possession.

TYPES OF FAKE

"Selling" someone a dummy—acting as if to kick the ball but in fact leaving it to run on, usually to a teammate—is one of the most common forms of fakes in soccer. But there are also several others, including shuffles, fake kicks, and "flip-flaps." All have the effect of confusing and throwing off the opponent.

PELÉ'S DUMMY

Most dummies involve leaving the ball to run on to another player. Pelé's legendary dummy against Uruguay during the 1970 World Cup was different—he left the ball to run on so he could gather it up himself, and he narrowly missed scoring.

MY GAME IS BASED ON IMPROVISATION ... IT IS INSTINCT THAT GIVES THE ORDERS

RONALDINHO,
BRAZILIAN INTERNATIONAL PLAYER

RONALDINHO

Few players have had as many tricks at their disposal as the Brazilian striker Ronaldinho. Born in Puerto Alegre in 1980, he was a master of deception, using his eyes and a bewildering range of tricks, flicks, and dummies to confuse defenders. "Little Ronaldo," as his name means in Portuguese, was one of the few players who used freestyle techniques in top-flight matches.

JADON SANCHO

After leaving Manchester City as a 17-year-old to get more playing time at Borussia Dortmund, the exciting winger soon developed his world-class skills. Sancho loves to drive at defenders, using step-overs to race into the box. He joined Manchester United in 2021.

Balance
Use the arm for balance.

Left leg
Plant the left leg on the ground as a brace to start the maneuver.

1 Jogging slowly with the ball under close control, bring the right leg toward the ball as if feigning to pass it or change direction.

THE FAKE KICK

A player mimes a shot or pass, causing the defenders to flinch, but actually passes the foot over or just to the side of the ball. This affords time and space to turn or deliver a pass.

Prestrike
Wind up the foot for a strong kick.

Look down
Keep the eyes on the ball.

Slow down
Practice slowing down the foot before the ball.

The drag
Drag the ball away from the opponent.

1 Give every indication of taking a long-range shot at goal or making a long pass. Draw back the leg in preparation for a strike.

2 Swing the foot down hard, but as it approaches the ball, slow it down rapidly and pass the foot over the ball.

3 While the opponent turns away in anticipation of a shot, place the foot lightly on top of the ball and drag it back quickly.

THE ELASTICO OR FLIP-FLAP

The Brazil striker Ronaldinho is particularly associated with the "elastico" or "flip-flap," which was invented by his fellow countryman Rivelino in the 1970s. The elastico involves the player moving the foot very quickly from right to left while dribbling, keeping the ball in such close proximity that it appears connected to the foot by elastic.

WHY BRAZIL?

Brazilian players are famous for their eye-catching tricks on the field. Why they are so famous is down to their unique soccer philosophy. As well as being tactically astute, Brazilian players like to produce the unexpected, doing simple things with flair and playing for the sheer fun and joy of the game.

Look right
Make the defender think you're heading to the right.

Rolling
Ball should be rolling forward.

Fake move
Align the body as if moving to the right.

Push it
Initially push the ball to the right.

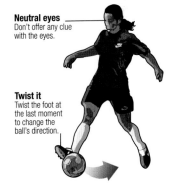

Neutral eyes
Don't offer any clue with the eyes.

Twist it
Twist the foot at the last moment to change the ball's direction.

1 Prepare for the elastico by looking in the direction you want the approaching defender to think you are about to play the ball.

2 Push the ball with the outside of the right foot as though about to dribble to the right.

3 At the last moment, gather the ball in with the instep of the same foot and pull it back in the other direction, confusing the defender.

Turn in
Twist the torso in conjunction with the right leg.

Weight shift
Move the weight to the left side.

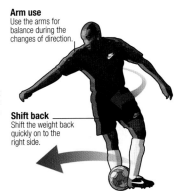

Arm use
Use the arms for balance during the changes of direction.

Shift back
Shift the weight back quickly on to the right side.

Move off
Push the left foot through the ball and move off.

2 Bring the right foot very close to the ball so the defender is convinced you are changing direction.

3 In one rapid, fluid movement, shift balance back to the right side, leaving the defender confused as to the chosen path.

4 Move away quickly with the ball in the direction you were traveling in step 1. You will gain precious space as a result.

SHOOTING

ELLEN WHITE

Former England striker Ellen White scored six goals at the 2019 Women's World Cup. Cool and calm when through on goal, she is able to beat the goalkeeper with power or a delicate finish.

Soccer would be nothing without goals. Besides heading the ball or benefiting from an own goal or a lucky deflection, the only way to score is to shoot. This can be done from almost any position on the field (goals are occasionally scored from the shooter's own half), but the closer players are to the opponents's goal when they take a shot, the higher the chances of success.

PLACEMENT OR POWER?

Sometimes the only way to beat the keeper is to strike the ball as hard as possible. At other times, it may be possible to pass the ball into the net. A player should strike the ball as hard as possible without sacrificing accuracy.

THE BASIC SHOT

Certain principles apply whether a shot is long- or short-range, placed or blasted. The shooter should aim the ball on either side of the goalkeeper and keep the ball down so it doesn't fly over the crossbar.

WHERE TO STRIKE THE BALL

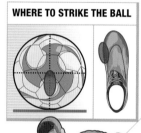

Sweep
Sweep the striking leg through on a plane consistent with the ball's direction.

1 Place the standing foot firmly next to the ball and pointing toward the goal.

Open up
Open the leg and strike the ball on the instep.

2 Make contact with the center of the ball or a spot slightly below it.

POWER SHOTS

Although attempts on goal aren't all about power (see above), spectacular strikes are real crowd-pleasers. Here are six of the best.

David Hirst (England) 1996—**114 mph (183.5 km/h)**

David Beckham (England) 1997—**97.9 mph (157.6 km/h)**

David Trezeguet (France) 1998—**96 mph (154.5 km/h)**

Alan Shearer (England) 1997—**85.8 mph (138.1 km/h)**

Roberto Carlos (Brazil) 1997—**85.2 mph (137.1 km/h)**

Tugay (Turkey) 2001—**84.2 mph (135.5 km/h)**

0 mph   25 mph   50 mph   75 mph   100 mph   125 mph

THE CURVING SHOT

The curving shot is difficult to execute well because it requires a highly precise strike, both in respect of the part of the foot used and the impact position on the ball. For the inswinging strike (see right), connect with the instep on the base of the ball; for the far more difficult outswinger, use the same spot on the outside of the foot (see also p.121).

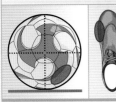

WHERE TO STRIKE THE BALL

Ball watching
Focus on the part of the ball you want to strike.

Follow-through
Keep the striking leg firm and straight through impact.

Solid base
Use the standing foot as a solid base from which to swing the striking leg.

Shoe in
Get the toes under the ball for more lofted shots.

Lean back
Lean back slightly at impact.

1 Approach the ball and ensure that the standing leg is about 18 in (45 cm) to the side.

2 Sweep the leg on an in-to-out arc and connect with the bottom-right portion of the ball.

3 Follow the path of the ball with the foot to stand a better chance of curving it.

TOP 5: GOAL CELEBRATIONS

Back in the early 20th century, players scoring goals used to be congratulated with a handshake from teammates, but in recent years, the goal celebration has become an art in itself.

BRANDI CHASTAIN
The US defender celebrated scoring the winning penalty in the 1999 Women's World Cup Final by removing her top. She revealed the most photographed sports bra in history.

PAUL GASCOIGNE
Gazza's sensational goal against Scotland at Euro 1996 was followed by a reconstruction (using water) of a pretournament incident in which England players had been photographed having tequila poured down their throats while sitting in a dentist's chair during late-night revelry.

JULIUS AGHAHOWA
At the 2002 Africa Cup of Nations, the Nigerian striker celebrated scoring a winning goal against Algeria with a series of six flips and an immaculately executed double somersault.

ROGER MILLA
Cameroon's elder statesman stole the show at the 1990 World Cup with goal celebrations that involved a run to the corner flag and some snake-hipped gyrations to follow.

BEBETO
During the 1994 World Cup, the Brazilian striker's wife gave birth to a son. When he scored in the quarterfinal against the Netherlands, Bebeto mimed rocking the baby and his teammates joined in (below).

THE CHIP, LOB, AND SCOOP

When a goalkeeper is off the line, there is a chance of beating them by lofting the ball over their head and weighting the shot so that the ball drops under the crossbar. The three methods by which this can be achieved—the chip, scoop, and lob—are all about touch, timing, and judgment.

Spinning
With backspin the ball gains height quickly.

Strike
Strike the ball with finesse on the top of the foot.

THE CHIP AND SCOOP
The chip and the scoop are used when the ball is on the ground as the shot is taken. The chip requires back lift and the scoop doesn't.

THE LOB
The lob is used when the ball arrives at a player full toss or after bouncing. The ball needs to be struck with enough height to clear the goalkeeper.

WOODCOCK WOULD HAVE SCORED, BUT HIS SHOT WAS TOO ... PERFECT

RON ATKINSON, COMMENTATING ON AN ENGLAND MATCH IN THE 1980s

INDIVIDUAL SKILLS

VOLLEYING

There are few sights in soccer as satisfying as seeing a cleanly hit volley fly into the net. This technique, which is defined as striking a ball that is in full flight, is also used to make rapid crosses, clearances, and passes. A high level of foot-eye coordination is essential for volleying. When it is executed well, the results can be spectacular.

MARCO VAN BASTEN

Marco Van Basten's strike for the Netherlands against the USSR in 1988 was probably the greatest-ever volleyed goal. He received a high cross-field pass on the edge of the six-yard box and, from an almost impossible angle, sent a looping volley into the opposite corner of the net.

VOLLEYING STYLES

There are two main styles of volley. The first is the full volley—the most visually arresting— where the ball is struck "on the fly." The second is the half volley, where the ball is struck very shortly after it has bounced. There is also a third technique, the bicycle (or overhead) kick, but this is normally performed only by experienced, very athletic players.

EVERYONE IS STILL TALKING ABOUT THAT GOAL ... IN THE 1988 FINAL

DUTCH MIDFIELDER **RAFAEL VAN DER VAART** ON VAN BASTEN'S WONDER STRIKE, 2008

THE FULL VOLLEY

The full version of the volley is used when the ball arrives at the kicker without touching the ground. It is therefore likely to be traveling quickly, giving the kicker less time to get into the right position to make his strike. The key ingredients for a well-executed volley are timing, composure, and concentration. Repeatedly striking a ball suspended at chest height from a crossbar via a piece of rope is an excellent way to practice this skill.

CHAMPIONS LEAGUE FINAL, 2002

In the 44th minute, Real Madrid's Zinedine Zidane was just outside the penalty area, perfectly positioned to receive a high looping cross from Roberto Carlos. Pirouetting exquisitely, his fully outstretched leg hit the ball chest high and sent it blasting into the net. It was a worthy winning goal.

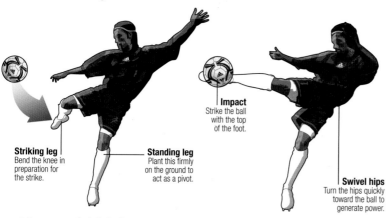

Striking leg
Bend the knee in preparation for the strike.

Standing leg
Plant this firmly on the ground to act as a pivot.

Impact
Strike the ball with the top of the foot.

Swivel hips
Turn the hips quickly toward the ball to generate power.

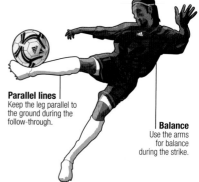

Parallel lines
Keep the leg parallel to the ground during the follow-through.

Balance
Use the arms for balance during the strike.

1 Keep eyes on the ball. Position yourself in its line of flight to have the best chance of making good contact.

2 Starting with the knee, bring the leg toward the ball and turn the hips. Strike the ball above center to keep it down.

3 Follow through with the kicking leg parallel to the ground and rotate the hips through the impact area.

BICYCLE KICK

Also known as the overhead kick, the bicycle kick is one of soccer's most spectacular techniques. It was invented in the Peruvian port of Callao during a game between locals and some European sailors in the early 1900s. Residents of the city are known as Chalacos and "Chalaca," the Latin American term for the trick, literally means "from Callao."

DIDIER DROGBA
The Ivorian striker's muscular frame makes him adept at finding space to perform overhead kicks.

MAKING AN OVERHEAD KICK

The bicycle kick is often used when an apparently misplaced cross arrives behind an attacker. Alternatively, a player can "tee" up for an overhead kick with their back to the goal by flicking the ball up to strike.

Head and body
Throw the head back to aid lift and the body will follow.

Launch
Use the striking leg as a springboard.

Sweep
Sweep the leg toward the ball with controlled pace.

Fall
Use the hand to soften the impact of the landing.

1 Launch into the air by raising the non-kicking leg and pushing off the ground with the other foot.

2 Once airborne, swing the kicking leg beyond the other leg and toward the ball.

3 Make contact with the ball with the back parallel to the ground. Players practice this in training before attempting it in a match.

THE HALF VOLLEY

The half volley is performed when the ball bounces just before the kicker strikes it. It is, therefore, sometimes on the rise at the moment of impact. Sometimes, a player is able to hit the ball at the exact moment it touches the ground. When this happens, the shot gains more momentum as the ball has lost less energy through not bouncing.

RAW POWER

One of the most memorable half volleys was Steven Gerrard's goal for Liverpool against Olympiacos in the 2005 Champions League. He struck the ball sweetly from the edge of the area. Liverpool went on to win the tournament.

Poise
Prepare the body for the dropping ball; timing is everything.

Composure
Keep everything smooth through impact.

Center strike
Connect with the middle of the ball to control the strike.

1 Watch the ball closely as it drops. Position the body and pull back the striking leg before connecting with the ball.

2 Strike the ball with the top of the foot, either on the rise or as it drops toward the ground heading for a second bounce.

HEADING

Heading the ball is counterintuitive for any young players learning the game, because they think it will hurt. However, it is an essential skill to master because, in an average match, the ball is in the air for 30 percent of the time.

TYPES OF HEADER

There are many different types of headers—basic, flick, tactical, defensive, and diving. Players need to practice all of them so they know which one to use in a match situation.

BASIC HEADER

The basic header is used for passing and attempts on goal. It is made with the forehead as this provides the most power and accuracy. It also doesn't hurt, unlike heading the ball with the top (crown) of the head. To get power on a header, players bends their knees and arch their backs as they jump for the ball, turning themselves into the shape of a bow. Their heads are the "arrow," initially tilted back then brought forward rapidly using the neck muscles.

WAYNE ROONEY

Former England and Manchester United striker Wayne Rooney was one of world soccer's most skillful and powerful players. Heading skill comes from powerful neck muscles, and knowing how to time a leap to meet the ball.

Focus
Keep eyes on the ball.

Pull up
Use arms to pull yourself into the air if you're jumping for the ball.

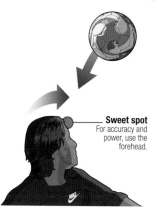

Sweet spot
For accuracy and power, use the forehead.

Good timing
Head needs to swing downward at moment of impact.

1 Get into position early and watch the ball onto the head, keeping eyes open throughout.

2 Without taking eyes off the ball, tense the neck muscles to provide maximum power.

3 To head the ball downward, rise above the ball when jumping.

FLICK PASSES

The flick header is used to head the ball sideways or backward. It is particularly useful in three situations: when a defender facing upfield wants to head the ball back to the goalkeeper; when a midfielder wants to flick the ball back to a defender; or when a forward wants to get the ball into the penalty area from a near-post cross or corner without revealing intentions.

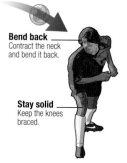

Bend back
Contract the neck and bend it back.

Stay solid
Keep the knees braced.

Turn the head
Twist the neck muscles to get power and direction.

Flick on
The ball skims off the forehead.

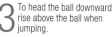

1 Arch the body forward when making contact with the ball.

2 Use the forehead if the neck is supple; otherwise, use the side of the head.

3 The ball bounces off the head and continues on its new path.

HEADING AWARENESS

In recent years, concerns have been raised about the long-term health effects of repeated heading of the ball by professionals, with possible links to brain damage and dementia in later life. Medical research and awareness campaigns continue, with the possibility of future restrictions on heading, for instance by children.

TACTICAL HEADERS

The flick header is a staple part of the tactics of most professional teams. It is used on crosses, free kicks, and corners to change the direction of the ball and confuse the opposition defenders.

NEAR-POST HEADER
A player needs to time the run to be in front of the marker when it arrives, then flick the ball behind into the area for a teammate.

FAR-POST HEADER
A player may need to step backward to lose the marker. Then direct the header back across goal toward the far post.

KEY
- ● Attacker
- ● Defender
- ○ Goalkeeper
- - - - Ball motion
- —— Player movement

DEFENSIVE HEADER

The most important thing when making a defensive header is to get good height and distance on the ball. It is usually safer to direct it away from the center of the field.

Timing
Time the jump so you connect with the ball before the attacker does.

Air time
Head the ball as high and as far forward as possible.

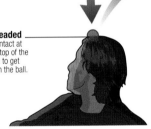

High-headed
Make contact at the very top of the forehead to get height on the ball.

Direction
Pass the ball to a teammate if possible.

Landing
Take care when landing.

1 The defender needs to get in position early because they will probably be competing with an attacker to get to the ball.

2 Contact should be made with the bottom half of the ball on the very top part of the forehead. Keep the neck braced.

3 If the defender approaches the ball from a sideways position, there is less chance of clashing with the attacker.

DIVING HEADER

Players use their whole body as a battering ram to strike the ball. This skill is not for the fainthearted—players stand a risk of getting a kick in the face from a defender—and for that reason it is usually used only to attempt to score. It is an option when the ball arrives in front of a player at a height between the neck and the knee.

LONGEST GOAL

The longest-range goal scored with the head was by Peter Aldis of Aston Villa. In September 1952, he headed the ball into the Sunderland net from an astonishing distance of 35 yd (32 m).

Watch the ball
Pay close attention to the flight of the ball.

Watch out
Make sure that the ball doesn't strike the face.

Soft landing
Break your fall with the hands.

1 Keeping both eyes on the ball, launch into the air with the foot closest to the goal.

2 When making contact with the ball, the player is parallel to the ground. Head the ball with the top of the forehead.

3 After heading the ball toward goal, stretch out the arms to cushion the impact of falling to the ground.

THROW-INS AND CORNERS

Statistically, corners and throw-ins are the most commonly awarded set pieces (see pp.96–97). A team is likely to be awarded several of each during the course of a game. These can often lead to scoring opportunities—about a third of all goals are scored from set pieces—so coaches make sure that players practice them extensively on the training ground.

RULES ON SCORING

Goals cannot be scored directly from a throw-in. The rules concerning corners are ambiguous, however. FIFA regulations state that "A corner kick falls under the same guidelines as a direct free kick," implying that such goals are legitimate.

RORY DELAP
Known as the "Delapidator" the former Republic of Ireland player terrorized defenses with his long throws. Delap threw the ball, on average, 86 ft (38 m).

THROW-INS

Throw-ins are used to restart play from the sideline. They can be taken either short or long. The thrower needs to be alert to the movements of teammates and have a good aim. Throwing onto the field can be risky—if the opponents win possession, they may quickly counterattack—so the majority of throws are aimed upfield along the sideline, out of harm's way. The exception is the long throw aimed directly into the penalty area. This can be more potent than a corner, since the thrown ball can be delivered more accurately.

IT'S LIKE A ...
HUMAN SLING!

FORMER EVERTON MANAGER **DAVID MOYES** ON RORY DELAP'S THROW-IN STYLE

TAKING A THROW-IN

Throw-ins awarded in a team's own half are usually taken as a means of getting the ball back in play. But those taken near the opposition's penalty area can be as effective as a free kick. There are three basic rules for taking throw-ins: the player is permitted a run-up; the ball must be thrown from behind the head with both hands; and both feet must be on the ground at the moment of release.

Follow-through
Arms should follow the path of the ball.

Launch
Launch angle is usually about 30 degrees.

Grip it
Keep the hands evenly spaced on the ball.

Momentum
A short run-up provides momentum.

Stay grounded
Both feet must stay on the ground.

1 Hold the ball fully behind the head with both hands. You are permitted to make a short run-up.

2 Bring the arms over the head and whip the body forward as you release the ball. This generates the power for the throw.

CORNER KICKS

As with free kicks in general (see pp.138–139), there are several options open to a player taking a corner. Aside from the classic inswinging and outswinging corners, there are five key variations.

FIVE CORNER STYLES

A corner represents a good opportunity to score a goal, so teams always work on these set piece routines. The following corner techniques are all practiced during training sessions: penalty spot, near post, far post, long, and short.

SINIŠA **MIHAJLOVIĆ**

The former Serbian international was described by manager Roberto Mancini, as "extraordinary at dead-ball situations." His accurate left foot made Mihajlović the perfect corner taker.

KEY

○ Goalkeeper
● Attackers
--- Ball motion

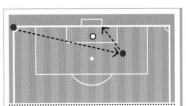

LONG CORNER

Used when the corner taker notices a teammate hovering unmarked outside the six-yard box. A quick pass can set up a strike on goal.

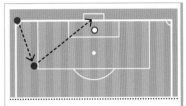

SHORT CORNER

A short-range pass to a teammate creates a different crossing or shooting angle. Defenders have no time to readjust themselves.

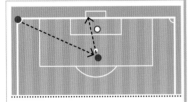

PENALTY-SPOT CORNER

A corner aimed at the penalty spot may lure the keeper from the goal. The ball must travel fast to reach a teammate before the keeper intercepts it.

NEAR-POST CORNER

The corner is aimed at the near goalpost so that it can be flicked on by a teammate to alter the ball's path and confuse the defenders.

FAR-POST CORNER

Usually delivered as an outswinger, the ball will be curving toward the teammate attacking it, helping to get power into the header.

TAKING A CORNER

The rules of taking a corner are simple: players are permitted to place the ball anywhere within the segment (the quarter circle between the goal line and the touchline); they are not permitted to remove the corner flag. For more detailed technique on taking a corner, see "Passing" (pp.120–121) and "Free kicks" (pp.138–139).

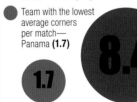

BALL POSITIONING
❶ Right-footed player takes a corner from the left-hand side
❷ Left-footed player takes a corner from the left-hand side

CORNERS PER MATCH

The total number of corners awarded at the 2018 World Cup was **604**.

● Team with the highest average corners per match—Brazil **(8.4)**

● Team with the lowest average corners per match— Panama **(1.7)**

8.4

1.7

Eyes down
Keep the head still and eyes focused on the ball.

Standing foot
Plant the nonstriking foot firmly next to the ball.

Strike
Connect with the ball before the ground.

1 Place the ball anywhere in the segment, step back, pick a target (a teammate in the penalty area), and take a short run-up.

2 Connect with the bottom of the ball on the right- or left-hand side, depending on the intended curve, if any, and follow through.

THE OLIMPICO

A goal scored directly from a corner with a curving shot is known as an "Olimpico" in South America. The shot is named in honor of Cesáreo Onzari of Uruguay, who scored against Argentina in this manner in 1924 when his team were reigning Olympic champions.

FREE KICKS

All free kicks are awarded against the team that has committed an infringement. There are various options open to the player who takes the free kick. The ball can be struck directly at the goal with force, chipped, curved, or passed to a teammate—anything, in fact, that catches the opposing team unawares.

Direct free kick   Indirect free kick

TYPES OF FREE KICK

There are two types of free kicks—direct and indirect. Many direct free kicks that are taken from the edge of the opposition penalty area give good goal-scoring opportunities, while most indirect free kicks (except those taken from inside the penalty area) are little more than a means of restarting play.

INDIRECT FREE KICK

An indirect free kick is awarded against a team for committing a foul, other than a penalty foul (for example, dangerous play) or for infringing certain technical requirements of the laws (for example, offside). An indirect free kick requires the ball to be touched by more than one player on the same team before it can enter the goal.

HOW TO TELL THE DIFFERENCE
If in doubt about whether a free kick is direct or indirect, watch the referee. A direct kick is indicated with an outstretched arm (horizontal) and an indirect with a vertical arm position.

THE QUICK FREE KICK

Usually, a player standing over a free kick must wait for the referee's whistle before starting play. But the player is permitted to ask the referee if they can take a "quick" kick without the whistle signal, to try to gain an advantage.

YOU REALLY ARE ...
CAPTAIN FANTASTIC

COMMENTATOR **MARTIN TYLER** ON DAVID BECKHAM'S FREE KICK AGAINST GREECE, 2001

AVERAGE SPEEDS

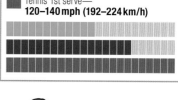

Soccer free kick—
60–70 mph (96–112 km/h)

Baseball pitch—
90–100 mph (144–160 km/h)

Tennis 1st serve—
120–140 mph (192–224 km/h)

DIRECT FREE KICK

A direct free kick is awarded against a team for committing a penalty foul, such as kicking a player instead of the ball, pushing, tripping, and similar infringements. If the referee deems the foul to be too malicious or dangerous, they will issue a yellow or red card. Direct free kicks can be struck directly into the goal without the need for another teammate to touch the ball. The most punitive direct free kicks a team can face is a kick from the penalty spot (see pp.140–141).

THE CURVING FREE KICK

If the free kick is awarded close to the goal, the defending team will build a defensive wall (see p.97). If the player taking the free kick gives the ball enough curve, it will bend around the wall. It will also make it difficult for the goalkeeper to judge its flight. The principles of getting the ball to curve are the same whether the kick is taken from a dead-ball situation or on the move (see p.131).

WHERE TO STRIKE THE BALL

Run-up
Approach the ball from an angle of about 45 degrees.

Long strides
Make sure the last stride before impact is a long one.

Nonstriking foot
Plant the standing leg firmly on the ground.

It's a wrap
Wrap the instep around the bottom right section of the ball to generate spin.

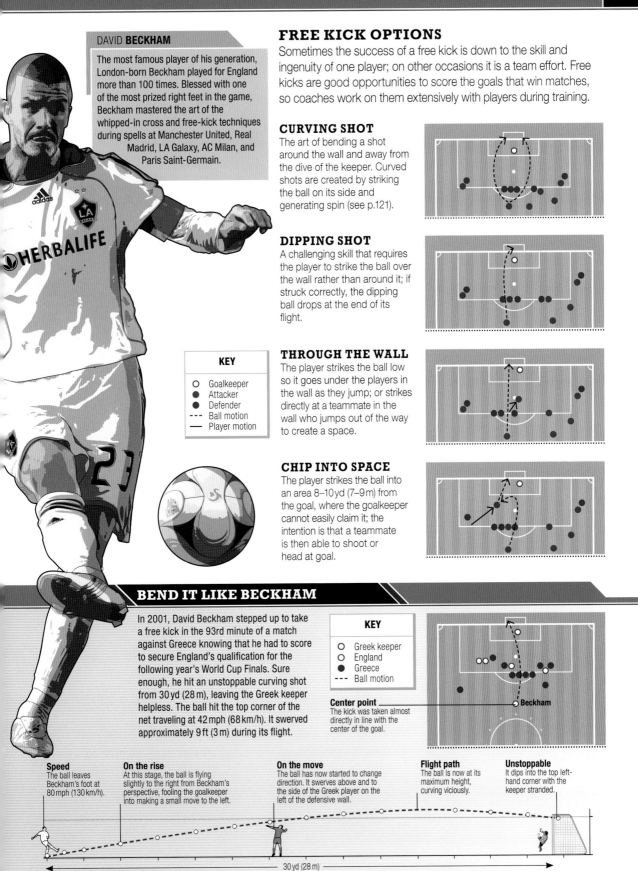

DAVID BECKHAM

The most famous player of his generation, London-born Beckham played for England more than 100 times. Blessed with one of the most prized right feet in the game, Beckham mastered the art of the whipped-in cross and free-kick techniques during spells at Manchester United, Real Madrid, LA Galaxy, AC Milan, and Paris Saint-Germain.

FREE KICK OPTIONS

Sometimes the success of a free kick is down to the skill and ingenuity of one player; on other occasions it is a team effort. Free kicks are good opportunities to score the goals that win matches, so coaches work on them extensively with players during training.

CURVING SHOT

The art of bending a shot around the wall and away from the dive of the keeper. Curved shots are created by striking the ball on its side and generating spin (see p.121).

DIPPING SHOT

A challenging skill that requires the player to strike the ball over the wall rather than around it; if struck correctly, the dipping ball drops at the end of its flight.

THROUGH THE WALL

The player strikes the ball low so it goes under the players in the wall as they jump; or strikes directly at a teammate in the wall who jumps out of the way to create a space.

CHIP INTO SPACE

The player strikes the ball into an area 8–10 yd (7–9 m) from the goal, where the goalkeeper cannot easily claim it; the intention is that a teammate is then able to shoot or head at goal.

KEY

- ○ Goalkeeper
- ● Attacker
- ● Defender
- - - Ball motion
- — Player motion

BEND IT LIKE BECKHAM

In 2001, David Beckham stepped up to take a free kick in the 93rd minute of a match against Greece knowing that he had to score to secure England's qualification for the following year's World Cup Finals. Sure enough, he hit an unstoppable curving shot from 30 yd (28 m), leaving the Greek keeper helpless. The ball hit the top corner of the net traveling at 42 mph (68 km/h). It swerved approximately 9 ft (3 m) during its flight.

KEY

- ○ Greek keeper
- ○ England
- ● Greece
- - - Ball motion

Center point
The kick was taken almost directly in line with the center of the goal.

Beckham

Speed
The ball leaves Beckham's foot at 80 mph (130 km/h).

On the rise
At this stage, the ball is flying slightly to the right from Beckham's perspective, fooling the goalkeeper into making a small move to the left.

On the move
The ball has now started to change direction. It swerves above and to the side of the Greek player on the left of the defensive wall.

Flight path
The ball is now at its maximum height, curving viciously.

Unstoppable
It dips into the top left-hand corner with the keeper stranded.

30 yd (28 m)

PENALTIES

Penalties provide the most nerve-racking moments in soccer. They are awarded for fouls committed in the penalty area, such as tripping and pushing. They are taken from the penalty spot, which is located directly between the goalposts, 12 yd (11 m) from the goal line. Scoring from penalties requires composure and skillful ball placement, and saving penalties requires agility and anticipation. Goalkeepers are rarely expected to save penalties.

PIRES'S POOR PENALTY

In October 2005, Arsenal was awarded a penalty in a match against Manchester City. Instead of shooting, Robert Pires opted for the unorthodox but perfectly legal option of knocking the ball for Thierry Henry to strike. However, Pires's touch was so feeble that the ball failed to move and a defender cleared it.

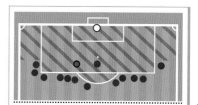

PENALTY DO'S AND DON'TS	
DO	**DON'T**
KEEP YOUR WEIGHT OVER THE BALL	TAKE TOO LONG A RUN-UP
MAKE A PLAN AND STICK TO IT	LET THE KEEPER PSYCHE YOU OUT
FOOL THE KEEPER WITH YOUR EYES	HIT THE BALL AT CHEST HEIGHT …
STRIKE THE BALL FIRMLY	… OR TOO CLOSE TO THE KEEPER

PENALTY SHOOT-OUTS

Draws are acceptable in some matches (almost all league games), but not in matches where a winner has to be found in order for a tournament to progress or reach a conclusion (cup ties, cup finals, and playoffs). Penalty shoot-outs are a way of forcing a result when the scores are level at the end of such a game, usually after a period of overtime.

FINDING A WINNER

Shoot-outs were introduced by UEFA in 1970 and FIFA in 1976. Each team takes five penalties against the other, with the kicks alternating. The team that's ahead at the end wins the match. If the scores are still level, the match goes into "sudden death." The first team to fall behind when an equal number of penalties has been taken by each side loses. Penalty shoot-outs are often considered an unsatisfactory way of deciding matches, but no better alternative has yet been found.

PENALTY RULES
The penalty is not just a battle of wits between the taker and the keeper; there are various rules and restrictions to be adhered to for other players, too.

EXCLUSION ZONE
All players bar the taker and the goalkeeper must stay outside the penalty area

- ● Defender
- ● Attacker
- ○ Goalkeeper
- ● Referee

On the move
The keeper will usually calculate that the best chance of saving the kick is to dive early to one side.

Second chances
Attackers need to be ready to pounce on any rebounds.

On alert
Defenders must be ready to run in to make a clearance if there's a rebound.

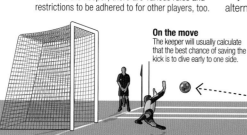

6 yd (5.5 m)   12 yd (11 m)   18 yd (16.5 m)

STAT ATTACK

WORLD CUP HITS AND MISSES

The team shooting first has won 19 of the 30 shoot-outs (63 percent)

Twenty one players have scored in two separate shoot-outs, but none in three

Sergio Goycochea of Argentina has saved five penalties—a record

THE LONGEST

THE LONGEST SHOOT-OUTS

TEAMS	YEAR	SCORE
Argentinos Juniors vs. Racing Club	1988	20–19
KK Palace vs. Civics	2005	17–16
Gençlerbirliği SK vs. Galatasaray SK	1996	17–16
Obernai vs. Wittelsheim	1996	16–15

… AND THE BEST

THE BEST SHOOT-OUT RECORDS

COUNTRY	PEN. TAKEN / SCORED	%
Belgium	5 / 5	100
Paraguay	5 / 5	100
South Korea	5 / 5	100
Germany	18 / 17	94.4
Sweden	6 / 5	83.3
Costa Rica	10 / 8	80

ALESSANDRO **DEL PIERO**

The Juventus and Italy striker had a good penalty-taking record. Del Piero often used delicate chips to outwit the keeper. He was brought on near the end of the 2006 World Cup Final against France in order to take a penalty—which he scored.

WHERE TO SHOOT

Success or failure with the penalty kick is partly determined by the strength of the shot, but if a penalty is poorly placed, the goalkeeper may reach it, and its power will be largely irrelevant. So where should a player aim to guarantee the greatest chance of success?

SCIENTIFIC STUDY

Research carried out at Liverpool University concluded that the perfect penalty was one hit into the top corner of the net. This has a 100 percent success rate, but there is a high chance of missing such a kick, hence, the conventional advice given by coaches to aim for the bottom of the goal.

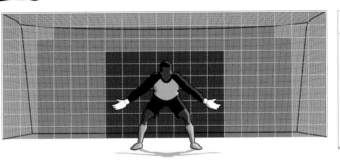

KEY

Goalkeeper will save unless overcommitted

Goalkeeper may save if shot is struck weakly

Goalkeeper is highly unlikely to save

I STUCK IT IN THE CORNER AND IF THE KEEPER WENT THE RIGHT WAY, IT WAS HARD ENOUGH ...
TO BEAT HIM

MATT LE TISSIER, OF SOUTHAMPTON AND ENGLAND, ON HIS SUCCESS RATE OF 48 FROM 49 PENALTIES

TYPES OF PENALTY

Penalty takers have three basic options when taking a spot kick: to attempt to pass the ball into the net, to try a chip, or to strike the ball very firmly. A penalty struck firmly into the bottom or top corner will register a goal, but there is very little margin for error—players must be very confident that they will not kick the ball wide.

WOBBLY KNEES

In the 1984 European Cup Final penalty shoot-out, Liverpool goalkeeper Bruce Grobbelaar famously wobbled his legs in mock terror, causing two AS Roma players to miss. Liverpool won the trophy.

PENALTY PASS

When players place a penalty, they effectively pass the ball into the net. This provides accuracy and is a good option if the keeper has dived early.

PENALTY CHIP

The most audacious kind of penalty, but extremely risky. The taker relies on the goalkeeper diving before the strike is made.

POWER SHOT

Takers sacrifice accuracy for speed with this option, and stand a good chance of success if they don't blast the ball wide or high.

PENALTY SHOOT-OUTS

Thirty-six penalty shoot-out kicks were taken in the 2014 World Cup.

Right foot—**25** (68% scored)

Left foot—**11** (82% scored)

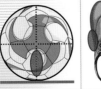

WHERE TO STRIKE THE BALL

WHERE TO STRIKE THE BALL

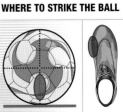
WHERE TO STRIKE THE BALL

GOALKEEPING

Goalkeeping is so different from other soccer roles that it almost seems to belong to another sport. All players need agility, bravery, a strong physical presence, and good distribution and decision-making abilities, but keepers have to have these characteristics in abundance. The special demands of the position require them to master a set of skills peculiarly their own.

GOAL-FREE MINUTES

- Matos Filho Mazarópi, Vasco de Gama, 1978–1979: **1,816**
- Thabet El-Batal, Al-Ahly (Cairo), 1975–1976: **1,486**
- Dany Verlinden, Club Brugge, 1990: **1,390**

1,390

1,816

1,486

BASIC TECHNIQUES

The three fundamentals for any aspiring goalkeeper to master are: stance (being "athletically primed"); body positioning (being aware of angles of attack and position in relation to the goal); and shot stopping.

STANCE

Keepers need to be continually alert to the possibility of a shot, leaning slightly forward so that their weight is on their toes rather than their heels. This places them in the optimum position to dive quickly or run toward an attacker if the situation demands it.

BODY POSITIONING

Keepers always need to know where they and the ball are relative to the goal. As they can't afford to turn around to check, they need to construct a mental image. One effective way to do this is to imagine a capital "T" with the shaft running through the penalty spot and the cross stroke stretching between the posts.

Fingers and thumbs
When the ball is caught, the thumbs should be almost touching.

SHOT STOPPING

The key task for any goalkeeper is knowing how to catch or stop the ball. There are two differing techniques for this depending on whether the ball is traveling along the ground or in the air—the "W" and the "M" (see left). All saving techniques are based from these two starting points. Whenever possible, a goalkeeper should attempt to use both hands when gathering the ball or making a save. Two hands together are stronger and cover more area than one.

THE "W"

The basic hand position when dealing with a shot close to the body and above the waist forms the letter "W," with the thumbs touching and the fingers pointing upward—a good position to catch the ball.

Bend the knees
Bend the knees to "close the gate" and prevent the ball from going through the legs.

THE "M"

When dealing with a ball below waist height and close to the body, a goalkeeper should form a downward pointing "M" with the hands, with the four fingers in the middle squeezed together.

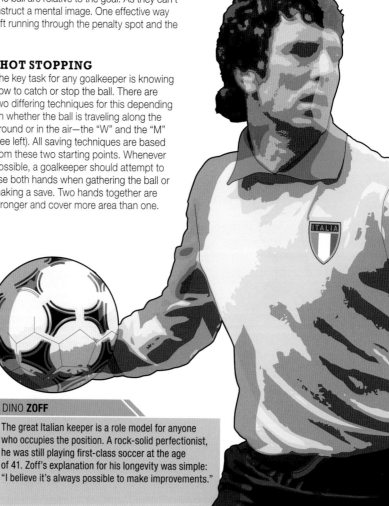

DINO ZOFF

The great Italian keeper is a role model for anyone who occupies the position. A rock-solid perfectionist, he was still playing first-class soccer at the age of 41. Zoff's explanation for his longevity was simple: "I believe it's always possible to make improvements."

MAKE YOURSELF BIG—NARROW THE ANGLE

The closer a goalkeeper is to an attacker running toward them with the ball, the less of the goal the attacker will be able to see. This method is known as "narrowing the angle." When an attacker is running toward the goal with the ball or charging onto a through pass, the keeper needs to decide instantly whether to stay back or run forward. They do not want to be caught in no-man's-land, where they have run away from the goal but are not close enough to the ball to prevent or block a shot.

THE COLOR [DISTRACTS]... THE STRIKER

CZECH GOALKEEPER **PETR ČECH** ON WHY HE WEARS AN ORANGE SHIRT

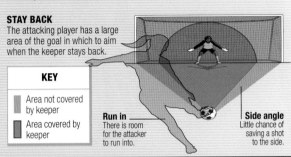

STAY BACK
The attacking player has a large area of the goal in which to aim when the keeper stays back.

KEY

▨	Area not covered by keeper
▦	Area covered by keeper

Run in
There is room for the attacker to run into.

Side angle
Little chance of saving a shot to the side.

MOVE FORWARD
By maintaining height and having arms outstretched, the keeper presents a large obstacle.

No option
The attacker's only real option here is to dribble around the keeper.

Got it covered
The keeper has narrowed the angle well.

GROUNDING

When a keeper catches a ball but has no chance of staying on their feet, they need to ground the ball as soon as possible to bring it under control and avoid spilling it into the path of incoming attackers.

A WORD IN YOUR EAR

In the Belgian league in January 2004, Racing Genk's Jan Moons became the first goalkeeper to receive instructions from the bench via an earpiece. His side beat FC Bruges 1–0.

Hands on
Prepare the hands for the catch.

Stay straight
Keep the torso fairly rigid during the dive.

Weighed down
Focus all upper body weight down onto the ball.

1 Dive with the hands in the "W" position, watching the ball closely as it approaches.

2 Go to ground, landing on one knee with the other leg outstretched, and catch the ball slightly above its center.

3 Bring the ball firmly down to the ground, holding it tightly, still with the hands in the "W" position.

DIVING SAVE

The diving save is the most spectacular in a goalkeeper's repertoire. The keys to success are quick reactions, good footwork, and getting into position early.

Eye on the ball
Watch the ball closely to make sure you judge the distance.

Lift off
Launch the body toward the ball.

Stretch out
Get the fingertips to the ball.

1 Bend the leg closest to the ball and watch its flight. Spring to the side with one arm outstretched and the wrist held firm.

2 Push the ball away from the goal to prevent attackers from capitalizing on a rebound then brace for landing.

CATCH OR PUNCH?

Goalkeepers have to decide whether to deal with high balls played into the penalty area by catching them, punching them, or staying on the goal line. They should do the latter only if they believe they have a poor chance of getting to the ball first.

LEV YASHIN

The only keeper to be voted European Player of the Year, Yashin played for Dynamo Moscow. He represented the USSR at three World Cups and was noted for his domination of the goal area, and his amazing arm-reach, hence his nickname "the Black Spider."

Hold on
Keep a grip on the ball as you land on the ground.

Challenging
Opposition players jump in front of the keeper.

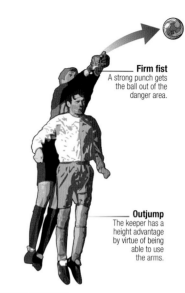

Firm fist
A strong punch gets the ball out of the danger area.

Outjump
The keeper has a height advantage by virtue of being able to use the arms.

CATCHING THE BALL
The best option is to catch the ball, as doing so ends the attack. Whether you can will depend on your ability to reach the ball unimpeded.

PUNCHING THE BALL
The second-best option is to punch the ball. This can be done with two arms, but more often, you will be able to get only one to the ball.

DEALING WITH CROSSES

The task of catching a cross or corner is ostensibly a simple one—follow the flight of the ball clearly and time the jump. Complications arise, however, with the number of players in the penalty area. Keepers must shout loudly to indicate their intentions to the defenders. They must also be strong enough to compete with the opposition's attackers.

DEFENDING A CROSS
The secret of defending a cross is all about organization. Defenders need to pick up the players they're supposed to be marking, and the keeper needs to be authoritative.

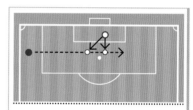

COMING OUT
The keeper comes out to catch crosses in different parts of the penalty area.

○ Goalkeeper
● Attacker
-- Ball motion
— Player motion

THE PENALTY IS THE ONE THING KEEPERS DON'T FEAR ... IF IT IS SCORED, NO ONE BLAMES HIM. IF HE SAVES IT ...

HE'S A HERO

DAVE SEXTON, FORMER QUEENS PARK RANGERS MANAGER, 1975

GOALKEEPER'S ROLES

Being a good goalkeeper isn't all about eye-catching saves and a strong physical presence. Keepers have a duty to start attacks by distributing the ball well and being the unofficial captain of the team's defense.

DISTRIBUTION

A goalkeeper who catches or picks up the ball has exactly six seconds to put it down again and restart play; otherwise they are at risk of being penalized. The aim should be to launch a speedy counterattack, so they needs to look up quickly to see where a teammate might be free. There are four methods by which a goalkeeper can start a new attack. Each has its own merits.

DISTRIBUTION DISTANCES

The goalkeeper needs to tailor distribution method to the player they are trying to reach. Often the target will be on the other side of the halfway line, which will usually necessitate a long punt or a half volley.

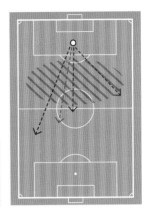

KEY

---	Punt	---	Roll out
---	Half volley	O	Goalkeeper
---	Long throw	⧄	Danger area

Good contact
Connect cleanly with the middle part of the foot.

Timing
Good timing is paramount with this technique.

Serve
Technique is similar to a bowler's action in cricket.

Bowling
Technique is similar to 10-pin bowling

THE PUNT
The keeper drops the ball from the hands and volleys it. Long distances are possible with this technique.

THE HALF VOLLEY
Similar to the punt, but the keeper lets the ball hit the ground a fraction of a second before making contact.

THE OVERARM THROW
Gripping the ball tightly, the throwing arm comes around in an arc over the shoulder to launch the ball upfield.

THE ROLL OUT
Rolling the ball out is a good option over short to medium distances and is extremely accurate.

TOP 5: GOALKEEPING MOMENTS

EL DIVINO'S CIGARS
Spain's Ricardo Zamora first came to public attention at the 1920 Olympics for his excellent goalkeeping and his attempts to smuggle Cuban cigars into the country on the way home, which led to the first of a number of prison sentences.

BERT TRAUTMANN'S NECK
Germany's Trautmann came to England as a prisoner of war and signed for Manchester City in 1949. He secured cult status at Maine Road when it was discovered that he had played most of the 1956 FA Cup Final with a broken neck.

A GUST OF WIND
One of the most famous goalkeeping goals was scored by Tottenham Hotspur's Pat Jennings in the 1967 Charity Shield. His clearance was caught by a gust of wind and sailed past Manchester United's Alex Stepney.

CARELESS HANDS
In a 1967 match away at Liverpool, Leeds United keeper Gary Sprake was about to throw the ball to a teammate, changed his mind, and inadvertently hurled the ball into his own net.

THE SCORPION KICK
Former Colombian keeper René Higuita earned notoriety in September 1995 during a friendly match against England at Wembley. He performed a clearance with the "Scorpion kick," bouncing forward onto his hands, arching his back, and kicking the ball away with his heels (see p.55).

MARSHALING THE DEFENSE

Goalkeepers are the only players able to see the whole game in front of them. They are best placed to organize their defenses for the general benefit of the team.

UNDER ORDERS

Quiet keepers are not doing the job well. They should be extremely vocal in warning teammates when an opponent is unmarked and in announcing intention to clear or catch a ball.

Good keepers also bark orders at the defense when setting up defensive walls, as they alone know where they should stand to give them the best chance of saving a shot.

PETER SCHMEICHEL
The Denmark and Manchester United keeper was a huge physical presence on the field, at 6 ft 4 in (1.93 m) and wore size XXXL shirts.

TACKLING

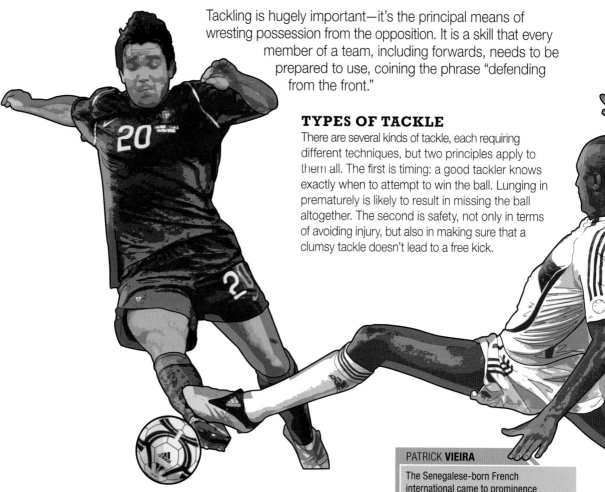

Tackling is hugely important—it's the principal means of wresting possession from the opposition. It is a skill that every member of a team, including forwards, needs to be prepared to use, coining the phrase "defending from the front."

TYPES OF TACKLE

There are several kinds of tackle, each requiring different techniques, but two principles apply to them all. The first is timing: a good tackler knows exactly when to attempt to win the ball. Lunging in prematurely is likely to result in missing the ball altogether. The second is safety, not only in terms of avoiding injury, but also in making sure that a clumsy tackle doesn't lead to a free kick.

PATRICK VIEIRA

The Senegalese-born French international came to prominence during his time at Arsenal, then later Juventus, Inter Milan, and Manchester City, where his height, stamina, physical strength, and excellent tackling ability made him a formidable player.

BLOCK TACKLE

The block tackle is made when a defending player meets an attacker head on. Both players use the inside of their tackling foot, forcibly making contact with the ball. Both players stay on their feet. The block tackle is used more often than any other kind of tackle.

Pivot
Use back leg as a pivot to move sideways during jockeying.

1 Before the tackler makes a challenge, they "jockey" their opponent. This involves standing in front of the other player and denying room.

Weight shift
Move weight forward into the tackle.

2 When the opponent draws a leg back to kick the ball, the defending player brings their tackling foot toward the ball.

Firm ankle
Keep the ankle firm throughout the tackle.

3 Once the tackle is engaged, the defending player still has to work hard to control the ball and win possession.

IF PLAYERS DON'T WANT **TO GET KICKED,** THEY SHOULD BECOME ACCOUNTANTS

ROBERTO MANCINI
FORMER ITALIAN PLAYER AND MANAGER

THE "HOOK" TACKLE

This is a variation of the slide tackle in which the tackler "hooks" a foot around the ball. The tackler begins behind the player in possession at an angle of about 45 degrees. They challenge the attacker, hooking a foot around the ball and stealing possession, then pass to a teammate.

RECOVERY TACKLE

Similar in many ways to the slide tackle, the recovery tackle is not intended to gain possession or set up a pass to a teammate. It's usually made when an attacker has the ball near the touchline and needs to be stopped from advancing. The tackler's best option is to kick the ball into touch.

SLIDE TACKLE

Both dramatic and emphatic, this technique should be used only when there are no alternatives. This is because the defender always ends up on the ground and invariably out of the game.

Stay up
Stay on your feet until the last possible moment.

Heading for a fall
The player in possession will fall over the legs of the tackler.

Knee slide
Slide on the knee of the nonstriking leg.

1. Approaching from the side, make the tackle with the leg furthest forward. Bend the other leg to allow you to slide in.

2. Knock the ball away, ideally to a teammate. Get back on your feet as soon as possible after making the tackle.

POKE TACKLE

The tackler stays on their feet and pokes or prods the ball away from the opponent into the path of a teammate. It is best used when the ball has bounced up between knee and waist height.

Right moment
Wait for the ball to drop before making the move.

Element of surprise
Player in possession is often unaware challenge is about to be made.

Find the gap
Aim for the gap between the player's legs.

1. Gets as close as possible to the opponent before making the tackle and wait for the ball to come into view.

2. Choosing the moment carefully, flick the foot out and through the opponent's legs to poke the ball away.

Stumble
The attacking player stumbles over the challenge.

Support
Use the arm to support the body on the ground.

Get in front
Get the body in front of the player in possession.

Clear it
Slide in and kick the ball into touch.

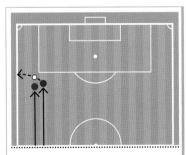

OUT OF PLAY
The recovery tackle is used to dispossess an opponent and put the ball out of play.

● Defender
● Attacker
-- Ball motion
— Player motion

FREESTYLE SKILLS

Most of the skills associated with freestyle soccer (see pp.28–29) are not directly relevant to match play, as they require more space and time on the ball than are ever likely to be available in competitive situations. Nevertheless, they are well worth mastering because they develop ball control and encourage creativity and improvisation. They are also a lot of fun to perform.

THE MOVES

There are many different moves that an aspiring freestyler can learn, and, as with other freestyle sports (such as skateboarding), new tricks are constantly being invented. Tricks usually fall into three main categories: juggling (keeping the ball airborne), flick-ups, and catches.

SHOWING OFF

Sometimes a player uses a freestyle skill during a match. In April 1967, Scotland's Jim Baxter taunted the then–World Champions England by juggling the ball near the corner flag during his country's 3–2 victory at Wembley.

MILENE DOMINGUES

Known as Ronaldinha, the ex-wife of Brazilian star Ronaldo was one of the best female players in Europe. With 55,198 touches, she holds the women's record for ball juggling.

Pay attention
It is vital to watch the ball closely at all times.

Balancing act
Readjust the neck to make head as flat as possible.

Control
Small and subtle foot movements are best.

Poised
Remain agile and light on the feet.

JUGGLING (KEEPIE UPPIE)
In its simplest form, this fundamental freestyle skill involves keeping the ball from touching the ground for as long as possible, usually with the feet and head.

HEAD STALL
This trick involves balancing the ball on the forehead. The performer keeps eyes on the ball and makes small neck and body adjustments to keep it in place.

PEOPLE ARE ALWAYS KICKING, OLD OR YOUNG. EVEN AN UNBORN BABY IS KICKING

SEPP BLATTER, FORMER FIFA SECRETARY GENERAL, 1990

AROUND THE WORLD

With this trick, a player kicks the ball up in the air during a juggling session and circles the kicking foot around it before it begins to drop. This must be done smoothly enough to get the foot back in position to continue the juggling at the end of the maneuver. The kicking foot can go around the ball either on the outside (away from the center of the body) or on the inside.

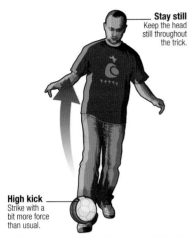

Stay still
Keep the head still throughout the trick.

Balance
Stretch out arms to maintain balance.

No contact
Keep the foot away from the ball.

High kick
Strike with a bit more force than usual.

1 The player starts by juggling as normal, keeping the ball under close control, then begins the trick by kicking the ball higher than usual.

2 As the ball rises, the player circles the foot over the ball then controls it and continues juggling as it drops.

26 The world record (in hours) for the longest juggling session, held by Dan Magness

2 The number of European Freestyle Championships won by Ireland's "Nam the Man"

26¼ The distance in miles (42 km) covered by Dr. Jan Skorkovsky while juggling the ball at the Prague marathon. He ran the race in 7 hours and 18 minutes

THE RAINBOW

In this trick, players flick the ball behind them and then backheel the ball over their heads before bringing it under control at the front of their bodies. The flight of the ball forms an arc over the players' heads, hence the trick's name.

Trap it
Trap the ball between the heel and toes.

1 Place the weaker foot in front of the ball, touching the heel. Roll the ball a short distance up the back of the ankle with the other foot.

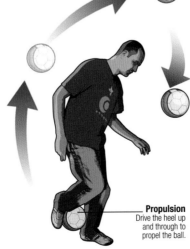

Propulsion
Drive the heel up and through to propel the ball.

2 When the ball is just above the heel, hop forward, leading with the stronger foot, and flick it up over the head with the weaker one.

Anticipate
Follow the flight of the ball carefully.

3 Concentration and skill are required to anticipate the path of the ball over the head and onto the feet. Then start juggling.

TOP 5: MOVIES

ESCAPE TO VICTORY (1981)
A group of Allied prisoners of war, played by most of Ipswich Town FC, Michael Caine, Sylvester Stallone, Ossie Ardiles, Pelé, and Bobby Moore, plan a bid to abscond at halftime in a game against their German guards.

ZIDANE: A 21ST CENTURY PORTRAIT (2006)
Seventeen cameras are trained on Zidane in a 2005 La Liga game against Villarreal. Footage of the player is cut with stadium shots and a haunting soundtrack to present a unique and kaleidoscopic picture of the man, the game, and the media.

GINGA: THE SOUL OF BRAZILIAN SOCCER (2006)
Shot like a sportswear commercial, Ginga is a brilliant collection of short soccer stories from Brazil—from the beach, the Amazon, and the favelas (shanty towns). It showcases Brazilian soccer and society in all its guises.

THE MIRACLE OF BERNE (2003)
Sentimental story of soccer-obsessed Matthias whose family, split by World War II and the imprisonment of his father in the Soviet Union, are redeemed by West Germany's victory in the 1954 World Cup.

6:3 (1999)
Soccer-crazed garbage collector Tutti puts on the shirt of Hungarian legend Hidegkuti and is transported back in time to Budapest on the day of the great game against England in 1953—and he's the only man who knows the score.

SOCCER AND CAPOEIRA

Young urban South Americans have developed a soccer version of Capoeira, the Afro-Brazilian dance-based martial art.

INJURIES

Soccer does not have the frequency of contact injuries sustained in rugby and football. However, players' twists and turns put huge stresses on their joints, and collisions and tackles at high speed can be serious. At the top level, injuries are inevitable but can still affect a side's season or even shape a player's entire career.

INJURY RESEARCH

Medical staff at 91 professional clubs examined the number and type of injuries sustained by their players over two seasons, 1997–1999. They found more than 3,000 injuries per season, approximately 1.5 per player per year, leading to roughly 24 days a season lost per player.

INJURY FACTS

The most common months for injuries are during preseason training and the season's early months, when muscles are comparatively untrained. The most common moments in games to get injured are the two 15-minute periods at the end of both halves. Eighty percent of injuries are severe enough to rule players out of at least one match—the average number of matches missed is as high as four.

DJIBRIL CISSÉ

Cissé had played only 19 games for Liverpool when, in October 2004, a tackle from Blackburn Rovers' Jay McEveley broke two bones in his leg. Then, playing for France against China on June 7, 2006, he suffered another broken leg.

IT IS TOUGH TO HEAR DJIBRIL SCREAM ... ## LIKE THAT

THIERRY HENRY, ON CISSÉ'S INJURY IN 2006

STRETCHERED OFF

Stretchers and stretcher-bearers have long been a feature of soccer's touchlines, and they are now recognized and required at matches under FIFA regulations. The motorized stretcher or "soccer ambulance" first made its appearance at the 1994 World Cup in the US—the home of the golf cart on which it was modeled. It provides an increased level of comfort for the player prior to receiving further medical attention off the field.

CASUALTY
An injured player leaves the field of play.

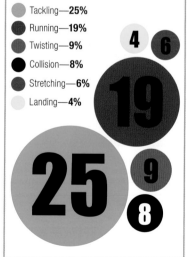

TOP CAUSES OF INJURY

- Tackling—**25%**
- Running—**19%**
- Twisting—**9%**
- Collision—**8%**
- Stretching—**6%**
- Landing—**4%**

COMMON SOCCER INJURIES

AREA OF BODY	INJURY/DESCRIPTION
HEAD	CUTS—general abrasions suffered in the course of play CONCUSSION—result of an impact to the head
BACK	MUSCLE STRAIN—caused by excessive spinal stretching SLIPPED DISK—the pain of a vertebrae pushing on a nerve
ARMS	FRACTURE—usually as a result of an awkward fall DISLOCATION—whereby a bone is dislodged from its socket
LEGS (UPPER)	GROIN STRAIN—overstretching of the groin muscles DEAD LEG—loss of feeling of movement from hard blow HAMSTRING STRAIN OR TEAR—usually incurred while running at high speed
KNEES	CRUCIATE LIGAMENT DAMAGE—overbending or rotation of the knee TORN CARTILAGE—damage to the knee's shock absorbers
LEGS (LOWER)	CALF STRAIN—overstretching of the lower leg SHIN SPLINTS—tiny fractures due to repeated hard impact to the shin
ANKLES AND FEET	TWISTED OR BROKEN ANKLE—caused by rapid turning or a bad tackle ACHILLES STRAIN—strained tendon in the heel METATARSAL FRACTURE—fractured foot bones

REHABILITATION

When top players get injured, they have a team of medical experts to guide them through the painful process of rehabilitation. In the case of a broken leg, after approximately four weeks in a cast, the player will begin a grueling session of gym work, focused on rebuilding the muscle tissue. Usually, the injured body part ends up stronger than it was before the injury.

MEND IT LIKE BECKHAM

In April 2002, David Beckham broke the second metatarsal in his right foot—a long tubular bone in the instep. With just six weeks before the beginning of the World Cup, all England fans (and some of the soccer world) became focused on the complex rehabilitation of bone fractures. While some players have been out for many months, Beckham, albeit treading tentatively, was able to play again quickly.

HYPERBARIC CHAMBER

Studies have proved the recovery period from certain injuries is reduced by 70 percent when players are treated with Hyperbaric Oxygen Therapy—essentially time spent in an oxygen tent.

BIZARRE INJURIES

MATCH INJURIES

SHUT IT:
In 1975, Manchester United goalkeeper Alex Stepney was yelling at his defense so hard that he dislocated his jaw and had to be replaced.

BARKING MAD:
The career of Chic Brodie, Brentford goalkeeper, ended in October 1970. He had collided with a sheepdog that had run onto the field and shattered his kneecap while the dog got the ball.

TRAINING INJURIES

LOOSE MOOSE:
The Norwegian defender Svein Grondalen had to withdraw from an international game in the 1970s after colliding with a moose during his daily run.

PAY ATTENTION:
In 2003, Everton's Richard Wright twisted his ankle falling over a sign that warned players not to warm up in the goalmouth.

INJURIES AT HOME

HOME HELP:
Danish goalkeeper Michael Stensgaard retired in 1999 after suffering an injury to his shoulder while he attempted to fold down an ironing board.

CLOSE SHAVE:
Spanish goalkeeper Santiago Cañizares missed out on the 2002 World Cup when he dropped a bottle of cologne and a shard of glass severed the tendon in his right foot.

WATCH OUT:
In 1998, American goalkeeper Kasey Keller knocked out his front teeth while removing the golf clubs from his car.

AND THE AWARD GOES TO ...

WORLD'S GREATEST PLAY-ACTOR

In Brazil's opening round game against Turkey at the 2002 World Cup, Hakan Ünsal kicked the ball at the legs of Brazilian Rivaldo. Rivaldo, standing at the corner flag, grasped his face and fell to the ground, Ünsal was then sent off. FIFA later fined Rivaldo $7,350 (£5,000) for play-acting.

FAKING IT
Brazil's Rivaldo was a brilliantly gifted player, but prone to acts of simulation.

PLANET
SOCCER

FIFA CONFEDERATIONS

The Fédération Internationale de Football Association (FIFA) is the global governing body of soccer. Based in Zurich, Switzerland, it was founded in 1907 by Belgium, Denmark, France, the Netherlands, Spain, Sweden, and Switzerland. The British home nations had turned down an invitation to lead the creation of a global organization five years earlier but did eventually join the founding seven, only to resign and rejoin twice in the 1920s.

A GLOBAL GIANT

FIFA is the affiliating body for all the major global soccer competitions, first among which is the World Cup, and has acquired more than 200 member countries. These soccer nations are organized into six geographical confederations that each run their own tournaments. FIFA was a small and relatively poorly resourced organization until the 1970s, but under the presidency of Brazilian João Havelange, the World Cup was transformed into a premier global sporting event. Despite its unique position as the custodian of the world's most popular game, FIFA regularly ranks at the bottom of global surveys on the transparency and accountability of global NGOs.

THE CONFEDERATIONS

The unique geography of planet soccer has seen Israel and Kazakhstan join Europe, Australia leave Oceania for Asia, and South America reduced to its 10 largest members with the three minnows of Surinam, Guyana, and French Guyana packed off to the Caribbean.

NORTH AND CENTRAL AMERICA

CONCACAF
Founded: 1961
Headquarters:
Miami, US

SOUTH AMERICA

CONMEBOL
Founded: 1916
Headquarters:
Luque, Paraguay

NON-FIFA SOCCER

FIFA may appear to cover the world, but a substantial amount of soccer is played beyond its control. Such teams include those of stateless ethnic groups, such as the Sami of Scandinavia and the European Roma; micronations including Vatican City, Monaco, and the Marshall Islands; minorities within bigger states; and regions seeking autonomy, such as Padania in Italy.

STAT ATTACK

FIFA

FÉDÉRATION INTERNATIONALE DE FOOTBALL ASSOCIATION COMPETITIONS INCLUDE:
FIFA World Cup, FIFA Women's World Cup, FIFA Under-17 World Cup, FIFA Under-20 World Cup, FIFA Club World Cup, FIFA Confederations Cup
AWARDS: The Best FIFA Football Awards

CONCACAF

CONFEDERATION OF NORTH, CENTRAL AMERICAN, AND CARIBBEAN ASSOCIATION FOOTBALL
NUMBER OF MEMBERS: 41
COMPETITIONS INCLUDE: CONCACAF Gold Cup, CONCACAF Women's Championship, CONCACAF Champions League

CONMEBOL

CONFEDERACIÓN SUDAMERICANA DE FÚTBOL
NUMBER OF MEMBERS: 10
COMPETITIONS INCLUDE: Copa América, Copa Libertadores, Copa Sudamericana

UEFA

UNION DES ASSOCIATIONS EUROPÉENNES DE FOOTBALL
NUMBER OF MEMBERS: 55
COMPETITIONS INCLUDE: European Championship, UEFA Champions League, UEFA Europa League, UEFA Super Cup, UEFA Women's Champions League

HE WAS JUST A MASTER OF POWER

GUIDO TOGNONI,
FORMER MEMBER OF FIFA EXECUTIVE COMMITTEE
ON JOÃO HAVELANGE, PRESIDENT OF FIFA 1974–1998

SEATS ON THE FIFA EXECUTIVE

- UEFA—**9**
- CAF—**7**
- AFC—**7**
- CONMEBOL—**5**
- CONCACAF—**5**
- OFC—**3**
- President—**1**

EXTRATERRESTRIAL SOCCER?

Although the exact number fluctuates from time to time due to political factors, the number of nations in the world is listed by the UN as 193. So where exactly does FIFA get the extra 18 countries? The answer lies in the practice of awarding member status to nonsovereign countries, such as the four constituent parts of the UK—England, Scotland, Wales, and Northern Ireland.

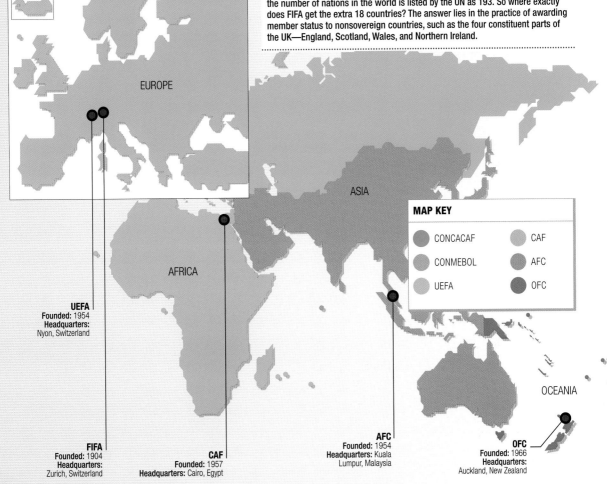

EUROPE

ASIA

AFRICA

OCEANIA

MAP KEY

- CONCACAF
- CONMEBOL
- UEFA
- CAF
- AFC
- OFC

UEFA
Founded: 1954
Headquarters:
Nyon, Switzerland

FIFA
Founded: 1904
Headquarters:
Zurich, Switzerland

CAF
Founded: 1957
Headquarters: Cairo, Egypt

AFC
Founded: 1954
Headquarters: Kuala
Lumpur, Malaysia

OFC
Founded: 1966
Headquarters:
Auckland, New Zealand

CAF

CONFÉDÉRATION AFRICAINE DE FOOTBALL
NUMBER OF MEMBERS: 56
COMPETITIONS INCLUDE: Africa Cup of Nations, CAF Champions League, CAF Confederation Cup, CAF Super Cup

AFC

ASIAN FOOTBALL CONFEDERATION
NUMBER OF MEMBERS: 47
COMPETITIONS INCLUDE: AFC Asian Cup, AFC Champions League, AFC Women's Asian Cup

OFC

OCEANIA FOOTBALL CONFEDERATION
NUMBER OF MEMBERS: 14
COMPETITIONS INCLUDE: OFC Nations Cup, OFC Champions League, OFC Women's Nations Cup

EUROPE: UEFA

EUROPE

ENGLAND

HOME

AWAY

POPULATION: 55.6 MILLION
CAPITAL: LONDON
LICENSED PLAYERS:
MALE: 1.8 MILLION
FEMALE: 50,000
PROFESSIONALS: 6,000
REGISTERED CLUBS: 42,500

English soccer is heavily colored by the fact that it was the birthplace of the professional sport. The strength of the domestic game meant that the nation was slow to pick up on international soccer— England didn't bother to enter the World Cup until 1950. Despite an influx of foreign coaches and players, English soccer is rooted in the Victorian values of hard work.

BOBBY CHARLTON
With a thunderous shot and distinctive "comb-over" haircut, Charlton was a key member of England's 1966 World Cup–winning team.

THE GOOD AND THE BAD

As the "originators" of soccer and the joint-oldest international team—founded in 1872, the same year as Scotland's team—England plays under a huge weight of expectation. Although one of an elite group of only eight nations to have won the World Cup, England is prone to under-achievement at the highest level. Aside from winning the trophy in 1966, their World Cup high points have been emotional semifinal penalty defeats to Germany, in both Italia 1990 (in which Paul Gascoigne memorably wept) and Euro 1996, plus a World Cup semifinal appearance in 2018. England's typical performance—a quarterfinal exit—has been about right.

1966 AND ALL THAT

England's finest hour came in 1966 when, as hosts of the eighth World Cup, Sir Alf Ramsey's side triumphed 4–2 over West Germany to lift the Jules Rimet trophy. Geoff Hurst became the first and only player to score a hat trick in the final, when he scored in the dying seconds of the game.

HARRY KANE

England's striker has an impressive goals per game ratio, and is also noted for accurate passing. Captain of his national team, Kane can create and finish, and is effective at long-range shooting as well as goal-poaching.

SOME PEOPLE ARE ON THE PITCH. THEY THINK IT'S ALL OVER ...

... IT IS NOW!

KENNETH WOLSTENHOLME
ENGLISH COMMENTATOR ON ENGLAND'S
FINAL GOAL, WORLD CUP FINAL 1966

WINNING MANAGERS

Name	Games lost/drawn	Games won
Fabio Capello	33%	67%
Sir Alf Ramsey	39%	61%
Glenn Hoddle	39%	61%
Gareth Southgate	39%	61%
Ron Greenwood	40%	60%
Sven-Göran Eriksson	40%	60%

STAT ATTACK

GOVERNING BODY:
The Football Association
FOUNDED: 1863
NATIONAL STADIUM:
Wembley, London, 90,000
FIRST MATCH: 0–0 vs. Scotland, 1882
BIGGEST WIN: 13–0 vs. Ireland, 1882
BIGGEST DEFEAT: 1–7 vs. Hungary, 1954

THE LEGENDS

MOST CAPPED PLAYERS

Name	From/To	Caps
Peter SHILTON	1970–1990	125
Wayne ROONEY	2003–2018	120
David BECKHAM	1996–2009	115
Steven GERRARD	2000–2014	114
Bobby MOORE	1962–1973	108
Ashley COLE	2001–2014	107

TOP GOAL SCORERS

Name	From/To	Goals
Harry KANE	2015–present	53
Wayne ROONEY	2003–2018	53
Bobby CHARLTON	1958–1970	49
Gary LINEKER	1984–1992	48
Jimmy GREAVES	1959–1967	44
Michael OWEN	1997–2008	40

THE PREMIER LEAGUE

Lured by media mogul Rupert Murdoch's millions, the clubs in the old English top division (Division 1) split from its governing body, the Football League, in 1992 to form the Premier League. It has grown into the most lucrative league in the world, attracting a global television audience and the best players and managers on the planet. It's easy to forget that the English Football League has been running since 1888.

WHEN IT ALL GOES WRONG

Following considerable success in the late 1990s, Leeds United borrowed heavily against assumed future revenue from the UEFA Champions League. When they failed to qualify in 2001, everything started to unravel. The best players were sold, and the club went into administration and languished in the lower divisions before returning to the top in 2020.

FA CUP MAGIC

The growing importance of qualification for the Champions League has reduced the importance of the FA Cup, but young boys still dream of lifting the trophy at Wembley in May. The world's oldest soccer competition has thrown up legends galore, from the giant-killing exploits of nonleague teams to Manchester City keeper Bert Trautmann playing on in the 1956 final with a broken neck.

DAVID BECKHAM

Dubbed "Goldenballs," Beckham was a dead-ball expert with a pop-star wife who became a national icon. He overcame the shame of a red card that led to England's exit from the 1998 World Cup to later captain his country.

BORN: MAY 2, 1975, LONDON, ENGLAND
HEIGHT: 6 FT (1.83 M)
CLUBS: MANCHESTER UNITED, REAL MADRID, LA GALAXY, AC MILAN, PARIS SAINT-GERMAIN
INTERNATIONAL CAPS: 115

STAT ATTACK

PREMIER LEAGUE / DIV 1

LEAGUE STRUCTURE: 20 Teams
TOP SCORER: Jimmy Greaves, **357** goals
MOST SUCCESSFUL TEAM:
Manchester United, **20** titles
BIGGEST WIN: 12–0, West Brom vs. Darwen, 1891; Nottingham Forest vs. Leicester Fosse, 1908
HIGHEST ATTENDANCE: 83,260, Manchester United vs. Arsenal, 1948 (played at Maine Road)
DIVISIONS BELOW PREMIER LEAGUE:
Football League Championship (**24** teams), Leagues One and Two (**24** teams each)

FA CUP

Inaugurated in 1872, the FA Cup is the most prestigious knockout competition. All clubs from the English League system are eligible, as well as six clubs from the Welsh League.
TOP SCORER: Henry Cursham (Nottingham County), **49** goals
MOST WINS: Arsenal, **13** wins
BIGGEST WIN: 26–0, Preston North End vs. Hyde, 1887

LEAGUE CUP

A knockout competition. 92 clubs can enter—the 20 clubs of the FA Premier League, and the 72 clubs of the Football League.
TOP SCORERS: Ian Rush and Geoff Hurst, **49** goals each
MOST WINS: Liverpool, **8** wins
BIGGEST WINS: 10–0, Liverpool vs. Fulham, 1986; West Ham vs. Bury, 1983

13 Paying spectators at Stockport County vs. Leicester City in 1921

139 Total number of England matches managed by Walter Winterbottom—a national record

21 Number of different last names—such as United, City, Rovers, or Villa—of clubs playing in the English Premier and Football Leagues

WORLD CUP

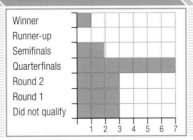

EURO CHAMPIONSHIPS

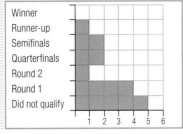

WEMBLEY STADIUM

The old Wembley Stadium, built in 1923 for the British Empire Exhibition, had been the home of English soccer for more than 80 years. However, despite regular refurbishment, it was tired, dilapidated, and inadequate. In a rare act of boldness, the FA decided to knock it down (including the two iconic towers) and start again. Although plagued by cost and time overruns, the new Wembley opened in 2007 and is one of the largest and most generously appointed soccer stadiums in the world.

WEMBLEY NATIONAL STADIUM

WEMBLEY STADIUM, LONDON, ENGLAND

OWNER:
THE FOOTBALL ASSOCIATION (FA)

ARCHITECTS:
FOSTER AND PARTNERS
HOK SPORT VENUE EVENT

OPENED: 2007

CONSTRUCTION COST:
$1.6 BILLION (£798 MILLION)

CAPACITY: 90,000

HUGE INVESTMENT

The new Wembley Stadium is a fitting architectural expression of modern English soccer. Its size and cost are testament to the vast sums of money and waves of euphoria that surrounded the Premiership and national team. Its funding was complex and international, relying at one point on a German bank for key funds. Ultimately, the stadium's finances rested on selling a significant number of expensive, long-term commercial and hospitality contracts and using the stadium for other sporting events and rock concerts.

Field dimensions
At 115 x 75 yd (105 x 69 m), the field is slightly narrower than the old Wembley

Roof
The roof covers an area of more than 484,00 sq ft (45,000 sq m), of which 172,000 sq ft (16,000 sq m) is retractable

Foundations
The foundations comprise 4,000 driven piles, up to 115 ft (35 m) deep

FIELD PROBLEMS

Although spectators love the new Wembley for its sight lines and atmosphere, there have been problems with the quality of the field—perhaps as a result of its multipurpose use.

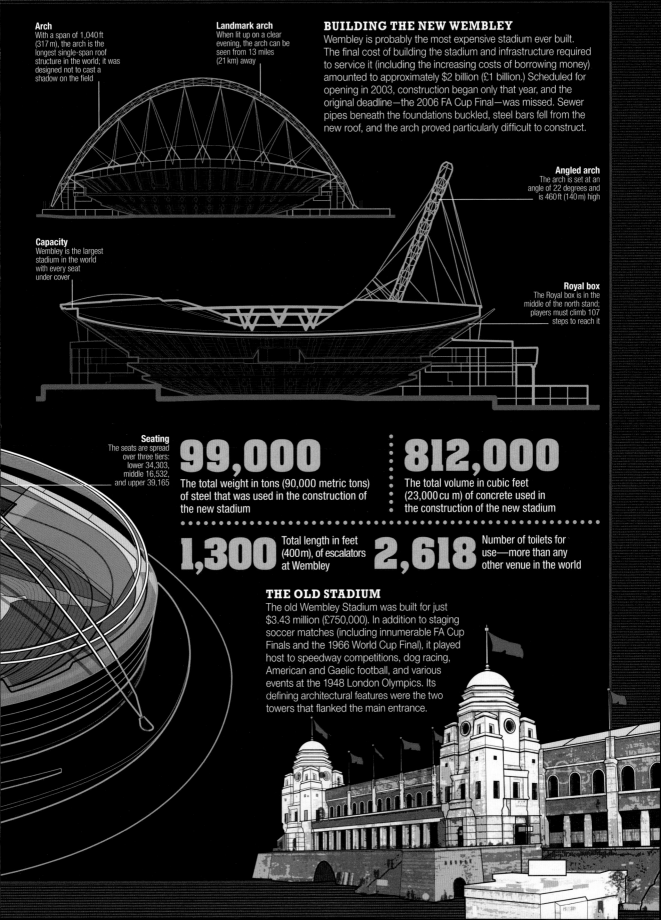

Arch
With a span of 1,040 ft (317 m), the arch is the longest single-span roof structure in the world; it was designed not to cast a shadow on the field

Landmark arch
When lit up on a clear evening, the arch can be seen from 13 miles (21 km) away

BUILDING THE NEW WEMBLEY

Wembley is probably the most expensive stadium ever built. The final cost of building the stadium and infrastructure required to service it (including the increasing costs of borrowing money) amounted to approximately $2 billion (£1 billion.) Scheduled for opening in 2003, construction began only that year, and the original deadline—the 2006 FA Cup Final—was missed. Sewer pipes beneath the foundations buckled, steel bars fell from the new roof, and the arch proved particularly difficult to construct.

Angled arch
The arch is set at an angle of 22 degrees and is 460 ft (140 m) high

Capacity
Wembley is the largest stadium in the world with every seat under cover

Royal box
The Royal box is in the middle of the north stand; players must climb 107 steps to reach it

Seating
The seats are spread over three tiers: lower 34,303, middle 16,532, and upper 39,165

99,000
The total weight in tons (90,000 metric tons) of steel that was used in the construction of the new stadium

812,000
The total volume in cubic feet (23,000 cu m) of concrete used in the construction of the new stadium

1,300
Total length in feet (400 m), of escalators at Wembley

2,618
Number of toilets for use—more than any other venue in the world

THE OLD STADIUM

The old Wembley Stadium was built for just $3.43 million (£750,000). In addition to staging soccer matches (including innumerable FA Cup Finals and the 1966 World Cup Final), it played host to speedway competitions, dog racing, American and Gaelic football, and various events at the 1948 London Olympics. Its defining architectural features were the two towers that flanked the main entrance.

EUROPE

ENGLAND: THE NORTHERN CLUBS

Soccer was born in the universities and public (private) schools of southern England, but it was in the industrial north that it first became a mass spectator sport. The game remains close to a religion in the urban centers of Merseyside (the Liverpool area), Manchester, Yorkshire, and the Northeast.

NICKNAME: REDS
FOUNDED: LIVERPOOL, 1892
STADIUM: ANFIELD, 54,074   HOME
DOMESTIC HONORS: LEAGUE 19; FA CUP 8
INTERNATIONAL HONORS: CHAMPIONS LEAGUE 1977, 1978, 1981, 1984, 2006, 2019; UEFA CUP 1973, 1976, 2001

LIVERPOOL FC

One of the most successful clubs in the history of English soccer, the Reds enjoyed an unprecedented period of dominance during the 1970s and '80s, winning seven league titles and four European Cups between 1976 and 1984, mostly under Bob Paisley. Since the 1990s, league success passed to the rival city of Manchester, with Liverpool almost a sleeping giant. But by the standards of most clubs, they have been wide awake, winning FA Cups, League Cups, UEFA Cups, and the Champions League.

IAN RUSH
Despite supporting Merseyside rivals Everton as a child, Rush went on to become Liverpool's highest scorer, netting 346 times in 469 games.

PEOPLE BELIEVE [SOCCER] IS A MATTER OF LIFE AND DEATH ... I CAN ASSURE YOU, **IT IS MUCH, MUCH MORE IMPORTANT THAN THAT**

BILL SHANKLY, LIVERPOOL MANAGER, 1959–1974

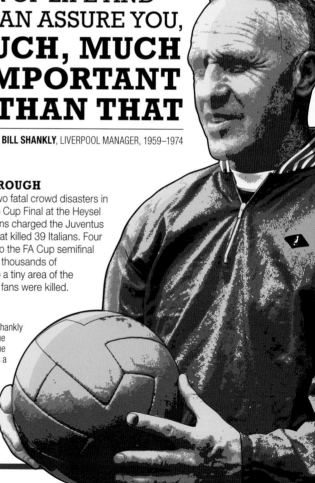

HEYSEL AND HILLSBOROUGH

Liverpool fans were involved in two fatal crowd disasters in the 1980s. At the 1985 European Cup Final at the Heysel Stadium in Brussels, Liverpool fans charged the Juventus fans, leading to a wall collapse that killed 39 Italians. Four years later, a policing error prior to the FA Cup semifinal against Nottingham Forest led to thousands of Liverpool fans being diverted into a tiny area of the Hillsborough Stadium. Ninety-six fans were killed.

THE KOP AT ANFIELD

The Kop, or to give it its full name the "Spion Kop," is the most famous field in world soccer. Named after a steeply sloping Boer War battlefield, it is a single-tier structure that once held 28,000 delirious fans. All-seater regulations have reduced capacity to 12,390 seats, but it remains an intimidating place, capable—in the words of Bill Shankly—of "sucking the ball into the net."

BILL SHANKLY
A short, wiry Scotsman, Shankly led Liverpool to two League titles, two FA Cups, and the UEFA Cup. His legacy was a simple but effective "pass and move" philosophy.

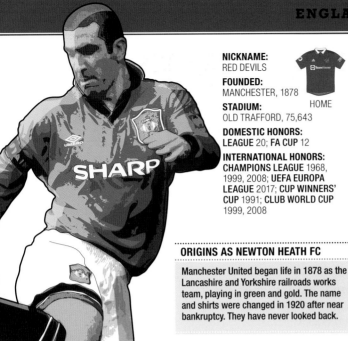

NICKNAME:
RED DEVILS
FOUNDED:
MANCHESTER, 1878
STADIUM:
OLD TRAFFORD, 75,643
HOME
DOMESTIC HONORS:
LEAGUE 20; FA CUP 12
INTERNATIONAL HONORS:
CHAMPIONS LEAGUE 1968,
1999, 2008; **UEFA EUROPA
LEAGUE** 2017; **CUP WINNERS'
CUP** 1991; **CLUB WORLD CUP**
1999, 2008

MANCHESTER: UNITED AND CITY

United was by far the most successful club of the 1990s and early 2000s, with league titles in double figures, as well as Champions League glory. Their manager Sir Alex Ferguson has won more trophies than any other British manager. Rivals Manchester City have benefited from wealthy owners, lavish spending on players, and the skills of coaches such as Roberto Mancini and Pep Guardiola.

ORIGINS AS NEWTON HEATH FC

Manchester United began life in 1878 as the Lancashire and Yorkshire railroads works team, playing in green and gold. The name and shirts were changed in 1920 after near bankruptcy. They have never looked back.

THE BUSBY BABES

The man who took Manchester United to greatness once played for Liverpool. Sir Matt Busby became manager in 1945 and began bringing youth players into the first team, the greatest of whom was the wing half Duncan Edwards. The "Babes" won the league in 1956 and 1957 and were set to take on Europe when, on February 6, 1958, their plane crashed in Munich. Seven players died, followed a week later by Edwards.

ERIC CANTONA

Ferguson's surprise 1992 signing of Cantona, a maverick French striker with a reputation for trouble, turned out to be an inspired move. More than a decade of domestic dominance was to follow, and Cantona was voted "Greatest United Player of the 20th Century" in 2001.

BORN: **MAY 24, 1966, MARSEILLE, FRANCE**
HEIGHT: **6 FT 2 IN (1.88 M)**
MAIN CLUBS: **AUXERRE, MARSEILLE, NIMES, LEEDS UNITED, MANCHESTER UNITED**
INTERNATIONAL CAPS: **43**

PREMIER LEAGUE TITLE WINS

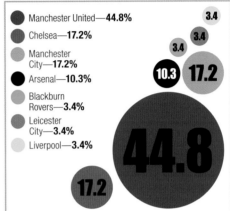

- Manchester United—**44.8%**
- Chelsea—**17.2%**
- Manchester City—**17.2%**
- Arsenal—**10.3%**
- Blackburn Rovers—**3.4%**
- Leicester City—**3.4%**
- Liverpool—**3.4%**

THE TREBLE

In 1968, Sir Matt Busby's second great United team, featuring the talents of George Best, Denis Law, and Bobby Charlton, became the first English side to lift the European Cup. Its achievements were surpassed, however, when the team of 1999 became the first English club to win the treble of the Champions League, the Premier League, and the FA Cup in a single season. The victory over Bayern Munich in the Champions League Final was particularly memorable. United was a goal down after 90 minutes but scored twice in stoppage time to win the game.

FAMOUS OLD NAMES

EVERTON (1878)

Once the dominant Merseyside team, in modern times Everton has had to stomach Liverpool's success. Its last FA Cup win was in 1995.

HONORS: LEAGUE 9, FA CUP 5; CUP WINNERS' CUP 1985

LEEDS UNITED (1919)

At the start of the 21st century, Leeds came within a whisker of becoming a top European club. It reached the semifinal of the Champions League in 2001.

HONORS: LEAGUE 3, FA CUP 1; UEFA CUP 1968, 1971

MANCHESTER CITY (1887)

City had lived in the shadow of United until, in 2008, the club was bought by the Abu Dhabi Royal Family. With wealth came success and titles. Armed with a big squad of expensive players, City won their first Premier League title in 2012, dramatically beating rivals Manchester United to the crown on the very last day. They also became League champions in 2014, 2018, and 2019 and continue to attract world-class talent in the transfer windows. In 2019, manager Pep Guardiola captured the treble of Premier League, FA Cup, and EFL Cup.

HONORS: LEAGUE 8, FA CUP 6; UEFA CUP WINNERS' CUP 1970

NEWCASTLE UNITED (1881)

"The Toon," as the club is known to its fanatical fans, regularly attracts home crowds of more than 52,000. With wealthy Saudi Arabian–backed owners, the club has huge potential.

HONORS: LEAGUE 4, FA CUP 6; UEFA CUP 1969

PRESTON NORTH END (1881)

Preston secured immortality by winning the first two league titles. Success has been thin on the ground since the 1890s, but the Lancashire club finished as league runner-up in 1953 and 1958.

HONORS: LEAGUE 2, FA CUP 2

EUROPE

ENGLAND: THE SOUTHERN CLUBS

Although London is almost 10 times the size of the next biggest city in the UK, it was not until 1931 that the English league title went to the capital. Liverpool alone has won roughly the same number of titles as all of the London teams combined. However, Chelsea or Arsenal won eight of the 20 league titles between 1998 and 2017.

NICKNAME:
THE BLUES
FOUNDED:
LONDON, 1905
STADIUM:
STAMFORD BRIDGE, 41,663
HOME
DOMESTIC HONORS:
LEAGUE 6, CUP 7
INTERNATIONAL HONORS:
CHAMPIONS LEAGUE 2012; 2021
CUP WINNERS' CUP 1971, 1998;
EUROPEAN SUPER CUP 1998;
EUROPA LEAGUE 2013, 2019

CHELSEA
Prior to 2005, Chelsea had won just one league title—in 1955. The club's past is checkered: the 1971 Cup Winners' Cup victory had been the high point, and near bankruptcy and hooliganism in the early 1980s were the low points. Bankrolled by the super-wealthy Roman Abramovich since 2003, the club went on to win the Champions League in 2012 and 2021.

KINGS OF THE KING'S ROAD
During the 1960s, London's King's Road became one of the most fashionable streets in the world and the center of the "swinging" music scene. Stamford Bridge, Chelsea's stadium, is located in the area and became a magnet for celebrities, including Steve McQueen, Michael Caine, and Raquel Welch. The Chelsea team of the era played glamorous, stylish soccer, epitomized by talismanic striker Peter Osgood.

THE ITALIAN CONNECTION
Chelsea had already met with recent success by the time Abramovich arrived, having won the FA Cup in 1997 and the Cup Winners' Cup in 1998. Much of this success was the result of the purchase of a series of top-class Italians, notably Gianluca Vialli (who became player-manager in 1998), Roberto di Matteo, and the great Gianfranco Zola.

HE CAME FROM IT-ALY TO PLAY FOR CHE-ELSEA

CHELSEA FANS SING THEIR APPRECIATION OF **GIANLUCA VIALLI**

THE ABRAMOVICH ERA
In June 2003, Chelsea fans woke up to find that their club had become the richest in the world. Wily chairman Ken Bates, who purchased the debt-ridden club for $2 million in the early 1980s, had sold it to Roman Abramovich, a Russian billionaire, for $280 million. Abramovich then spent hundreds of millions of dollars to build one of the strongest teams in world soccer, before selling the club in 2022.

GIANFRANCO **ZOLA**
Applauded in his pomp as a soccer wizard, Zola learned his trade from Diego Maradona while the pair played for Italian champions Napoli. Moving to Chelsea in 1996, he thrilled fans with a wealth of breathtaking ball tricks.

BORN: **JULY 5, 1966, OLIENA, ITALY**
HEIGHT: **5 FT 5½ IN (1.66 M)**
MAIN CLUBS: **TORRES, NAPOLI, PARMA, CHELSEA, CAGLIARI**
INTERNATIONAL CAPS: **35**

NICKNAME:
THE GUNNERS
FOUNDED:
LONDON, 1886
STADIUM:
THE EMIRATES, 60,432
HOME
DOMESTIC HONORS:
LEAGUE 13, CUP 14
INTERNATIONAL HONORS:
CUP WINNERS' CUP 1994; UEFA
CUP 1970

ARSENAL

Founded in 1886 as Dial Square FC, a factory team from the Royal Arsenal in Woolwich, Arsenal took its current name in 1914. Its first golden era was under manager Herbert Chapman, who won three league titles and persuaded the authorities to rename the local underground station, Gillespie Road, to Arsenal. Following the arrival of French manager Arsène Wenger, Arsenal shed its defensive, conservative past and emerged as one of the most attractive passing teams in the world.

TONY ADAMS

Adams was made Arsenal captain at the age of just 21 and spent his entire playing career at the club. A tall, gangly defender, he was a courageous, masterful reader of the game. He became an Arsenal legend during his 19-year, 504-game playing career.

BORN: OCTOBER 10, 1966, LONDON, ENGLAND
HEIGHT: 6 FT 3 IN (1.91 M)
MAIN CLUBS: ARSENAL
INTERNATIONAL CAPS: 66

THE NORTH LONDON DERBY

Few local derbies match the intensity of an Arsenal vs. Tottenham Hotspur tie. The roots of the rivalry can be traced to 1913, when Arsenal moved to north London from its former south-London home in Woolwich, and 1919, when it joined the top tier. Arsenal, who had finished fifth in Division 2, won a place at the expense of Tottenham, who had come 20th in Division 1.

ONE NIL TO THE ARSENAL

Under manager George Graham (1986–1995), Arsenal was known for eking out 1–0 wins with efficient, defensively minded displays. Arsène Wenger (1996–2018) changed things completely, introducing flowing, attacking soccer.

MIDLANDS CLUBS

Clubs from the Midlands, an area of central England known for its industrial heritage, have enjoyed notable success in the past. Aston Villa (see right) won five titles between 1894 and 1900, and Wolverhampton Wanderers won three during the 1950s. Leicester City provided one of soccer's greatest stories in 2016. Tipped for relegation at the start of the season, it went on a captivating run and ended up winning the Premier League.

BEST OF THE REST

TOTTENHAM HOTSPUR (1882)
Spur's greatest achievement was winning the Double in 1961. Since then, success has been limited to cup competitions, but the club has a reputation for attractive soccer.
HONORS: LEAGUE 2, CUP 8; CUP WINNERS' CUP 1963; UEFA CUP 1972, 1984

WEST HAM UNITED (1895)
"The Hammers" have won three FA Cups and the Cup Winners' Cup. The club is renowned for producing great players who move on to better things at bigger clubs.
HONORS: CUP 3; CUP WINNERS' CUP 1965

ASTON VILLA (1874)
In the first 12 years of English professional soccer, Villa won 5 league titles and 3 FA Cups. In 1982, the club became the fourth English club to win the European Cup.
HONORS: LEAGUE 7, CUP 7; EUROPEAN CUP 1982

LEICESTER CITY (1884)
A side that became renowned for swinging between the top two tiers of English soccer, Leicester sent shock waves around the world when it won the Premier League in 2016.
HONORS: LEAGUE 1, CUP 1

IPSWICH TOWN (1878)
Nicknamed "The Tractor Boys," this small East Anglian club punches above its weight. It has supplied England with two great managers—Alf Ramsey and Bobby Robson.
HONORS: LEAGUE 1, CUP 1; UEFA CUP 1981

NOTTINGHAM FOREST (1865)
Nottingham Forest has won as many European Cups as Juventus and Benfica, thanks to the genius of Brian Clough, who led the unfashionable side to greatness in the late 1970s and early '80s.
HONORS: LEAGUE 1, CUP 2; EUROPEAN CUP 1979, 1980

BRIAN CLOUGH
One of the greatest-ever English managers, Clough was a true maverick who managed Leeds, Derby, and Nottingham Forest. His nickname of "Old Big 'Ed" was justified; "They say Rome wasn't built in a day, but I wasn't on that job," he once quipped.

EUROPE

HOME   AWAY

POPULATION: 5.4 MILLION
CAPITAL: EDINBURGH
FA: SCOTTISH FOOTBALL ASSOCIATION
LICENSED PLAYERS:
MALE: 374,000
FEMALE: 4,500
PROFESSIONALS: 4,000
REGISTERED CLUBS: 6,500

SCOTLAND

Scotland's contribution to the emergence of professional soccer is on par with its old rivals, England. The game was played in private schools in Glasgow and Edinburgh in the 1850s, and Queen's Park became the first soccer club to be founded, in 1867. By 1875, a network of teams had emerged in Scotland, the first international game had been played against England, and the Scottish FA had been founded.

WORLD CUP WOES

Scotland qualified for five consecutive World Cups from 1974 to 1990 but suffered a series of near misses in the contest. It went out on goal difference in 1974, 1978, and 1982, and its most recent outing at France 1998 was no luckier, losing to Brazil thanks to an own goal, and exiting in the first round.

SCOTTISH SOCCER FIRSTS

Scotland boasts a number of soccer firsts. The first international match to be played was held at the West of Scotland Cricket Ground, Glasgow, in 1872 against England. The first penalty in an official match was taken by Airdrieonians in 1891, and the first stadium disaster occurred at Ibrox in 1902.

THE TARTAN ARMY

Scotland beat England at Wembley to win the 1977 British Home Championships, the round-robin tournament between the UK national sides, triggering a huge Scottish field invasion. Since then, Scotland's band of traveling fans has become known as the "Tartan Army," and while English traveling fans became more violent in the 1980s and '90s, the Scottish fans won several UEFA awards for good behavior.

THE SPL

The structure of domestic soccer revolves around the domination of rival Glasgow teams, Celtic and Rangers. The two-division system of the 1970s was deemed too uncompetitive and shrank in 1976 to a 10-team premier league, a cup, and a league cup. In 1998, the teams of the top tier split from the Scottish FA in a similar move to the English clubs (see p.161), forming the Scottish Premier League (SPL), which then became the Scottish Premiership.

KENNY **DALGLISH**

The first player to score 100 goals in both the English and Scottish leagues, during a playing career that spanned four decades, Dalglish was equally successful as a manager.

BORN: **MARCH 4, 1951, GLASGOW, SCOTLAND**
HEIGHT: **5 FT 8 IN (1.73 M)**
MAIN CLUBS: **CELTIC, LIVERPOOL**
INTERNATIONAL CAPS: **102**

STAT ATTACK

NATIONAL TEAM

NATIONAL STADIUM:
Hampden Park, 51,866
WORLD CUP FINALS:
8 appearances
EUROPEAN CHAMPIONSHIPS:
3 appearances
BIGGEST WIN: 11–0 vs. Northern Ireland, 1901
BIGGEST DEFEAT: 0–7 vs. Uruguay, 1954
MOST CAPS: Kenny Dalglish, **102**
MOST GOALS: Kenny Dalglish and Denis Law, **30**

25 The number of fatalities at the Ibrox Stadium disaster in 1902

The number of copies of "Ally's Tartan Army" sold—a record released for Scotland's 1978 World Cup campaign **360,000**

Attendance at the 1937 Scottish Cup Final between Celtic and Aberdeen at Hampden Park—a European record for a club match **146,433**

RANGERS

Rangers is the team of Glasgow's Protestant community and particularly of the Unionists. By World War I, it had become a major club quietly committed to not signing Catholic players—a ban that held until Mo Johnston joined the club in 1989. The club stands against sectarianism, but tensions can run high, especially when playing Celtic (see below).

NICKNAME: GERS
FOUNDED: GLASGOW, 1873
STADIUM: IBROX, 50,817

HOME

DOMESTIC HONORS: LEAGUE 55, CUP 34
INTERNATIONAL HONORS: EUROPEAN CUP WINNERS' CUP 1972

ALLY McCOIST
McCoist played for Rangers for 15 seasons and was the key goal scorer in the side that won nine titles in a row (1989–1997).

LIQUIDATION

In 2012, Rangers were found guilty of financial irregularities and entered a process of administration, leading to liquidation. Renamed The Rangers Football Club, they were demoted to the lowest tier of Scottish soccer for the start of the 2012–2013 season but were back in the top division by 2016.

NICKNAME: THE BHOYS
FOUNDED: GLASGOW, 1888
STADIUM: CELTIC PARK, 60,411

HOME

DOMESTIC HONORS: LEAGUE 52, CUP 40
INTERNATIONAL HONORS: EUROPEAN CUP 1967; UEFA CUP RUNNER-UP 2003

CELTIC

Founded in 1888 in a Glasgow church hall, Celtic provided soccer and a social club for Irish immigrant boys in the poorest parts of Glasgow. Despite its links with the nationalist cause in Ireland—Irish tricolors are regularly flown by the crowd—the club has never banned Protestants. Jock Stein, manager of the great sides of the 1960s, came from a Protestant background.

THE LISBON LIONS

Many Celtic fans claim to have witnessed the club's famous 1967 European Cup Final win in Lisbon. Celtic's 2–1 victory over Inter Milan started a tradition of European pilgrimage. When the team played Porto in the UEFA Cup Final in 2003, more than 80,000 fans—less than half with tickets—made the trip.

HENRIK **LARSSON**

Larsson was a key figure at Celtic for seven seasons. The prolific striker was hugely popular with the crowd as he helped Celtic to four league titles, breaking the Rangers' long stranglehold on the championship.

BORN: SEPTEMBER 20, 1971, HELSINGBORG, SWEDEN
HEIGHT: 5 FT 10 IN (1.78 M)
MAIN CLUBS: HELSINGBORG, FEYENOORD, CELTIC, BARCELONA, MANCHESTER UNITED
INTERNATIONAL CAPS: 106

THE OLD FIRM DERBY

Celtic and Rangers are known collectively as "The Old Firm"—as the two largest Scottish clubs, it became clear from an early stage that they would benefit financially from cooperating to ensure huge ticket sales. The Old Firm derby occurs four times a season in the SPL and is historically an intense affair.

BEST OF THE REST

ABERDEEN (1903)
Alex Ferguson's Aberdeen in the 1980s has been the only real challenge to the Glasgow hegemony, but it couldn't dislodge the Old Firm.
HONORS: LEAGUE 4, CUP 7; EUROPEAN CUP WINNERS' CUP 1983

HEART OF MIDLOTHIAN (1874)
The club's name was taken from the Edinburgh dance hall where the club began, and after winning the Scottish Cup in 2006, they had something to dance about.
HONORS: LEAGUE 4, CUP 8

HIBERNIAN (1875)
"Hibs" was the first team to be founded by the Irish immigrant community in Scotland. Fans had been waiting half a century for a title win, until the team won the Scottish Cup in 2016.
HONORS: LEAGUE 4, CUP 3

EUROPE

HOME

AWAY

POPULATION: 3 MILLION
CAPITAL: CARDIFF
FA: FOOTBALL ASSOCIATION OF WALES
LICENSED PLAYERS:
MALE: 157,500
FEMALE: 16,000
PROFESSIONALS: 550
REGISTERED CLUBS: 1,900

WALES

Soccer took off in north Wales in the late 19th century then spread to the cities and coal-mining valleys of south Wales. Following World War I, the leading Welsh sides—Cardiff City, Swansea Town, Newport, and Wrexham—joined the English league system and played in the English FA Cup. Although Wales has consistently produced players of the highest caliber, including John Charles, Ryan Giggs, and Gareth Bale, it has inevitably been with English clubs that they have made their mark.

CROSS-BORDER COMPETITION

The anomalous system of clubs playing in both English and Welsh competitions ended in the 1990s, when the League of Wales (renamed the Welsh Premier League in 2002) and FAW Premier Cup were set up. The Welsh clubs playing in England were excluded.

CARDIFF CITY VS. EUROPE

As winners of the Welsh Cup, Cardiff City won a place in the 1968 Cup Winners' Cup and—amazingly for a team fighting relegation—reached the semifinals. It met Shamrock Rovers, Dutch side NAC Breda, and traveled deep into the USSR to play Torpedo Moscow in Tashkent but was beaten 3–2 by Hamburg in the semifinal.

STAT ATTACK

NATIONAL TEAM

NICKNAME: The Dragons
NATIONAL STADIUM: Principality Stadium, 74,500
WORLD CUP FINALS: 1 appearance, quarterfinals **1958**
EUROPEAN CHAMPIONSHIPS: 2 appearances, semifinals **2016**
BIGGEST WIN: 11–0 vs. Northern Ireland, 1888
BIGGEST DEFEAT: 0–9 vs. Scotland, 1878
MOST CAPS: Chris Gunter, **101**
MOST GOALS: Gareth Bale, **33**

MAIN DOMESTIC CLUBS

CARDIFF CITY
FOUNDED: Cardiff, 1899
STADIUM: Cardiff City Stadium
CAPACITY: 33,280   HOME
INTERNATIONAL HONORS: None
LEAGUE: 0 **CUP:** 1

SWANSEA CITY
FOUNDED: Swansea, 1912
STADIUM: Liberty Stadium
CAPACITY: 21,088   HOME
INTERNATIONAL HONORS: None
LEAGUE: 0 **CUP:** 0

WREXHAM
FOUNDED: Wrexham, 1872
STADIUM: Racecourse Ground
CAPACITY: 10,771   HOME
INTERNATIONAL HONORS: None
LEAGUE: 0 **CUP:** 0

1927 FA CUP

Cardiff City's 1–0 victory over Arsenal in the 1927 FA Cup is the only time a Welsh club has won the trophy. The first FA Cup Final to be broadcast live by the BBC, it featured one of the worst goalkeeping mistakes ever as Arsenal's Dan Lewis let the ball squirm out of his hands and over the line for an own goal.

EURO 2016

After reaching the quarterfinals of the 1958 World Cup, it was not until 2016 that Wales qualified for another major tournament—the European Championship. There it topped its group, winning against England, Slovakia, and Russia. Wales then beat Northern Ireland and Belgium to reach the semifinals, where its dream of a first European Cup Final was shattered by Portugal, who won 2–0.

GARETH BALE

The Wales legend displays exceptional close control while running with the ball. His skills certainly impressed Real Madrid, who in 2013 paid Tottenham Hotspur £85 million—a then world record—to acquire his services.

BORN: **JULY 16, 1989, CARDIFF, WALES**
HEIGHT: **6 FT (1.85 M)**
MAIN CLUBS: **REAL MADRID, TOTTENHAM HOTSPUR**
INTERNATIONAL CAPS: **111**

NORTHERN IRELAND

Politics and religion have shaped the geography and culture of soccer in Northern Ireland. The game's strongest roots were in industrial Belfast, and, following partition from the Republic in 1921, the game was dominated by Unionist teams, such as Linfield, while nationalist teams, such as Belfast Celtic, withdrew.

GEORGE **BEST**

Best was Northern Ireland's greatest player and one of the best, anywhere, ever. He had everything—pace, courage, two equally good feet, superb balance, and an ability, in the words of a Manchester United teammate, to leave opposing defenders with "twisted blood."

BORN: **MAY 22, 1946, BELFAST, NORTHERN IRELAND**
HEIGHT: **5 FT 8 IN (1.73 M)**
MAIN CLUBS: **MANCHESTER UNITED, LOS ANGELES AZTECS, FULHAM, FORT LAUDERDALE STRIKERS, SAN JOSE EARTHQUAKES**
INTERNATIONAL CAPS: **37**

HOME   AWAY

POPULATION: 1.8 MILLION
CAPITAL: BELFAST
FA: IRISH FOOTBALL ASSOCIATION
REGISTERED PLAYERS:
MALE: 83,000
FEMALE: 9,000
PROFESSIONALS: 220
REGISTERED CLUBS: 820

THE PREMIERSHIP

The top level of competition in Northern Ireland consists of the 12-team Premiership, the Irish Cup, and the Irish League Cup. Attendances are low due to the high level of local support for Scottish rivals Rangers and Celtic, as well as for English Premier League teams. The constant flow of talented young players from Northern Ireland to England and Scotland has also affected the quality of the domestic teams in Northern Ireland.

BELFAST CELTIC

The first nationalist club in Northern Ireland, Belfast Celtic were modeled on their Glasgow namesake. They played in Northern Ireland's Irish League, which led to trouble with Unionist fans. In 1912, a game against Linfield was abandoned after gunfire in the stands. A field invasion following another Linfield tie in 1948 saw many of the team's players badly hurt, and the club withdrew from the Irish League.

THE MAZE

Attempts to build a national stadium in Belfast for soccer, rugby, and Gaelic sports have foundered. Plans to use land formerly occupied by the Maze prison, which held paramilitaries from both sides during the Troubles (the period of violence and protest from the 1960s to late '90s), were blocked by Unionist parties.

STAT ATTACK
NATIONAL TEAM

NICKNAME: "Norn Iron"
NATIONAL STADIUM: Windsor Park, 18,167
WORLD CUP FINALS: 3 appearances, quarterfinals **1958**
EUROPEAN CHAMPIONSHIPS: 1 appearance, second round **2016**
BIGGEST WIN: 7–0 vs. Wales, 1930
BIGGEST DEFEAT: 0–13 vs. England, 1882
MOST CAPS: Pat Jennings, **119**
MOST GOALS: David Healy, **36**

MAIN DOMESTIC CLUBS

LINFIELD
FOUNDED: Belfast, 1886
STADIUM: Windsor Park
CAPACITY: 18,167
INTERNATIONAL HONORS: None
LEAGUE: 56 **CUP:** 44
HOME

GLENTORAN
FOUNDED: Belfast, 1882
STADIUM: The Oval
CAPACITY: 15,000
INTERNATIONAL HONORS: None
LEAGUE: 23 **CUP:** 23
HOME

CLIFTONVILLE
FOUNDED: Belfast, 1879
STADIUM: Solitude
CAPACITY: 3,200
INTERNATIONAL HONORS: None
LEAGUE: 5 **CUP:** 8
HOME

REPUBLIC OF IRELAND

HOME   AWAY

POPULATION: 4.7 MILLION
CAPITAL: DUBLIN
FA: FOOTBALL ASSOCIATION OF IRELAND
LICENSED PLAYERS:
MALE: 390,000
FEMALE: 31,000
PROFESSIONALS: 500
REGISTERED CLUBS: 5,500

Soccer has always occupied an unusual space in Ireland. The game grew in Dublin under British rule in the 19th century, and a number of teams competed in the all-Ireland cups and leagues. However, the creation of the Gaelic Athletics Association—which aligned nationalism with the revival of Gaelic sports—had the effect of casting soccer as a foreign sport. Further marginalized following Partition in 1921, another 70 years passed before the national team met with any success.

STAT ATTACK

NATIONAL TEAM

NICKNAME: Boys in Green
NATIONAL STADIUM: Aviva, 51,700
WORLD CUP FINALS: 3 appearances, quarterfinals **1990**
EUROPEAN CHAMPIONSHIPS: 3 appearances, second round **2016**
BIGGEST WIN: 8–0 vs. Malta, 1983
BIGGEST DEFEAT: 7–0 vs. Brazil, 1982
MOST CAPS: Robbie Keane, **146**
MOST GOALS: Robbie Keane, **68**

MAIN DOMESTIC CLUBS

SHAMROCK ROVERS
FOUNDED: Dublin, 1901
STADIUM: Tallaght Stadium
CAPACITY: 6,000
HOME
INTERNATIONAL HONORS: None
LEAGUE: 20 **CUP:** 25

SHELBOURNE
FOUNDED: Dublin, 1895
STADIUM: Tolka Park
CAPACITY: 9,681
HOME
INTERNATIONAL HONORS: None
LEAGUE: 13 **CUP:** 7

BOHEMIANS
FOUNDED: Dublin, 1890
STADIUM: Dalymount Park
CAPACITY: 7,995
HOME
INTERNATIONAL HONORS: None
LEAGUE: 11 **CUP:** 7

THE LEAGUE OF IRELAND
The top-flight FAI League of Ireland contains 10 teams which, since 2003, play over spring and summer. There are also two cup contests, the FAI Cup and League Cup. Attendances are low, especially compared to the sell-out crowds of the national team's games.

SHAMROCK ROVERS
Ireland's biggest club, and the first to play in Europe, Shamrock Rovers have an interesting past. The club spent much of 1967 in the US, playing in the NASL as Boston Rovers. In 1987, the club's stadium was controversially sold to housing developers. In 2005, Rovers were relegated and on the brink of bankruptcy but reentered the top flight under fan ownership.

ROY KEANE
The leading Irish player of the modern era, Keane was an uncompromising midfielder with a volcanic temper and high standards. He became the linchpin of the hugely successful Manchester United teams of the 1990s.

BORN: AUGUST 10, 1971, CORK, IRELAND
HEIGHT: **5 FT 10 IN (1.78 M)**
MAIN CLUBS: **NOTTINGHAM FOREST, MANCHESTER UNITED, CELTIC**
INTERNATIONAL CAPS: **66**

WORLD CUP 1990
The Irish national team finally qualified for a major tournament under manager Jack Charlton, going to the 1988 European Championships and two World Cups—1990 and 1994. Ireland reached the quarterfinals of Italia 1990 on the back of vast traveling support and was the only national team to be granted an audience with the Pope during the contest.

CROKE PARK
Named after a nationalist, anti-soccer Archbishop, Croke Park is the largest stadium in Dublin. Formerly off-limits to soccer, following peace in Northern Ireland, it was made available to the Ireland soccer team in 2007 while a new national stadium was being built.

BELGIUM

HOME

AWAY

POPULATION: 11.4 MILLION
CAPITAL: BRUSSELS
FA: UNION ROYALE BELGE DES SOCIÉTÉS DE FOOTBALL ASSOCIATION
LICENSED PLAYERS:
MALE: 745,000
FEMALE: 71,300
PROFESSIONALS: 1,500
REGISTERED CLUBS: 2,000

Soccer was played in the English schools of Brussels, and among British textile workers in Antwerp and Liège, as early as the 1870s. As clubs began to emerge in the 1880s, a national association was founded in the 1890s, followed by a Brussels league. The 1970s were marked by professionalization and a short golden age, when Belgian teams won European titles and the national team was a World Cup contender.

WORLD CUP GLORY

The Belgian national team had languished in obscurity until Guy Thys became manager in the late 1970s. It reached the final of the 1980 European Championship but was beaten by a very late West German goal. The core of this squad, reinforced by midfield playmaker Enzo Scifo, went on to achieve fourth place at the 1986 World Cup. A new generation of stars reached the quarterfinals in 2014 and third place in 2018.

STAT ATTACK
NATIONAL TEAM

NICKNAME: The Red Devils
NATIONAL STADIUM: King Baudouin, 50,093
WORLD CUP FINALS: 14 appearances, third place **2018**
EUROPEAN CHAMPIONSHIPS: **6** appearances, runner-up **1980**, third place **1972**, quarter-finals 2020
BIGGEST WIN: 10–1 vs. San Marino, 2001
BIGGEST DEFEAT: 2–11 vs. England, 1909
MOST CAPS: Jan Vertonghen, **142**
MOST GOALS: Romelu Lukaku, **68**

EDEN **HAZARD**

An attacking midfielder, Hazard is renowned for his creativity, technical ability, and superb passing skills. He was instrumental in Belgium reaching the quarterfinals of the UEFA Euro 2016, and has won awards in both the French (2010–2011, 2011–2012) and English (2014–2015, 2016–2017) premier leagues.
BORN: JANUARY 7, 1991, LA LOUVIÈRE, BELGIUM
HEIGHT: 5 FT 8 IN (1.73 M)
MAIN CLUBS: LILLE, CHELSEA, REAL MADRID
INTERNATIONAL CAPS: 123

DOMESTIC CHALLENGES

The Belgian domestic game has struggled with financial problems and a lack of competition for more than two decades. The big three clubs—Anderlecht, Brugge, and Standard Liège—receive the majority of honors and wealth. Despite local government subsidies and TV revenues, many clubs have been in debt, for which the penalty is relegation, have merged with other clubs, or gone bankrupt and disappeared completely.

1930 WORLD CUP

Belgium's first World Cup appearance was under duress from FIFA, which was intent on increasing the number of teams from Europe. The Belgians lost to the US in their first game.

MAIN DOMESTIC CLUBS

RSC ANDERLECHT
FOUNDED: Brussels, 1908
STADIUM: Vanden Stock
CAPACITY: 28,063   HOME
INTERNATIONAL HONORS: Cup Winners' Cup **1976** and **1978**; UEFA Cup **1983**
LEAGUE: 34 **CUP:** 9

CLUB BRUGGE
FOUNDED: Brugge, 1891
STADIUM: Jan Breydel
CAPACITY: 29,042   HOME
INTERNATIONAL HONORS: European Cup runner-up **1978**; UEFA Cup runner-up **1976**
LEAGUE: 18 **CUP:** 11

STANDARD LIÈGE
FOUNDED: Liège, 1898
STADIUM: Sclessin
CAPACITY: 28,272   HOME
INTERNATIONAL HONORS: Cup Winners' Cup runner-up **1982**
LEAGUE: 10 **CUP:** 8

MONEY MADNESS

Soccer rarely obeys the laws of economics. When buying players, for example, businesspeople are willing to make far riskier investments than they ever would in their normal dealing lives. For much of soccer's history, owners have had control, to the extent of imposing maximum wages and ruling the transfer system. Today, however, players and their agents command vast salaries over which owners have little control.

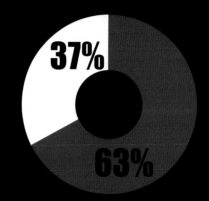

BOOM TIME

The economics of soccer changed dramatically in the 1990s with the arrival of new forms of pay-per-view TV and sky-high broadcasting rights in the big European leagues. The smaller and lower leagues, however, haven't seen much of this new money—most of which goes to a handful of top-tier clubs.

SLICE OF THE PIE
Almost two-thirds of a club's spending is eaten up by players' salaries. The rest goes to operating costs, grounds maintenance, and transfer fees.

TELEVISION REVENUE PER LEAGUE (€ MILLION)

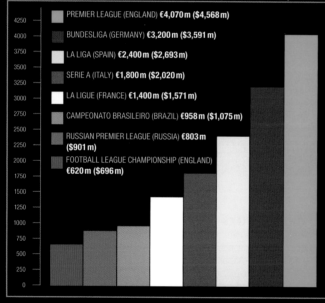

PREMIER LEAGUE (ENGLAND) €4,070 m ($4,568 m)

BUNDESLIGA (GERMANY) €3,200 m ($3,591 m)

LA LIGA (SPAIN) €2,400 m ($2,693 m)

SERIE A (ITALY) €1,800 m ($2,020 m)

LA LIGUE (FRANCE) €1,400 m ($1,571 m)

CAMPEONATO BRASILEIRO (BRAZIL) €958 m ($1,075 m)

RUSSIAN PREMIER LEAGUE (RUSSIA) €803 m ($901 m)

FOOTBALL LEAGUE CHAMPIONSHIP (ENGLAND) €620 m ($696 m)

WHERE THE MONEY COMES FROM

A club receives most of its income from four main sources—game-day revenue, broadcasting rights, sponsorship deals, and commercial activities (see left). Where necessary, clubs may add to their coffers with money borrowed from the banks.

IN DEBT

An awful lot of clubs have an awful lot of debt. Many clubs, for example, have been "propped up" by soft loans from generous owners. Equally, banks with political connections to particular clubs (especially in Spain) have extended huge overdrafts, which have been stretched beyond normal breaking points.

BIG NUMBERS

In 2019, the Premier League awarded Manchester City, the Premier League champions, $187.9 million (£150.9 million) in broadcast revenue. Liverpool actually received slightly more ($190.3 million/£152.4 million) as they played three more live TV games.

$1,184,27

WHERE THE MONEY GOES

Clubs used to spend less than 40 percent of their income on players' salaries, but players are now able to claim a much larger slice of the pie (see left). A club must also pay staff such as coaches and caterers as well as spend money on maintaining the stadium and training grounds.

TRANSFERS

For the club buying, transfers are a huge drain on resources. Premier League clubs spent a record $1.5 billion (£1.2 billion) during the 2016 summer transfer window.

INVESTMENTS

Since 1992, UK Premiership clubs have invested a combined total of more than $3.5 billion (£2.4 billion) in new facilities.

PROFITS

In September 2011, Manchester United announced a record annual operating profit of $166.4 million (£110.9 million).

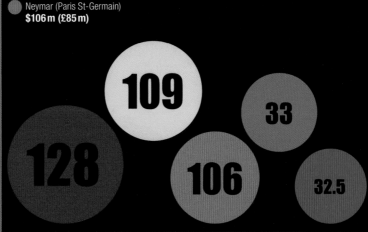

Lionel Messi (Barcelona)
$128 m (£103 m)

Cristiano Ronaldo (Juventus)
$109 m (£88 m)

Neymar (Paris St-Germain)
$106 m (£85 m)

Paul Pogba (Manchester United)
$33 m (£26.7 m)

Andrés Iniesta (Vissel Kobe)
$32.5 m (£26.3 m)

TOP FIVE BIGGEST TRANSFER FEES ($ MILLION)

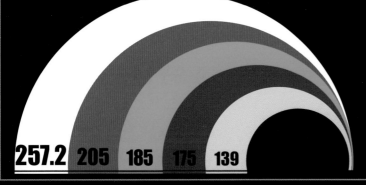

Neymar: Barcelona to Paris Saint-Germain in 2017—**$257.2 m (£199 m)**

Kylian Mbappé: Monaco to Paris Saint-Germain in 2017—**$205 m (£166 m)**

Eden Hazard: Chelsea to Real Madrid in 2019—**$185 m (£150 m)**

Philippe Coutinho: Liverpool to Barcelona in 2018—**$175 m (£142 m)**

João Félix: Benfica to Atletico Madrid in 2019—**$139 m (£113 m)**

257.2 205 185 175 139

2

The number of days Cristiano Ronaldo had owned his $300,000 (£200,000) Ferrari 599 GTB before he crashed it

350,000

The average cost in dollars (£240,000) of each of the handful of games Thomas Brolin played for Leeds United after his expensive transfer and collapse in form

111 million

The amount of money in dollars (£82 million) made by Cristiano Ronaldo on and off field in 2016

,316

THE MONEY COMING INTO THE GAME IS INCREDIBLE. BUT ... IT COMES IN AND GOES OUT STRAIGHT AWAY

ALAN SUGAR, FORMER CHAIRMAN OF TOTTENHAM HOTSPUR

FRANCE

HOME

AWAY

POPULATION: 66.8 MILLION
CAPITAL: PARIS
LICENSED PLAYERS:
MALE: 1.7 MILLION
FEMALE: 49,000
PROFESSIONALS: 2,000
REGISTERED CLUBS: 19,000

After its arrival in France in the late 19th century, soccer jostled for popularity with rugby and was restricted by the small size of the nation's cities. Nevertheless, a nationwide, professional game was introduced by the 1930s. French soccer has always been marked by stylish passing and a passion for international soccer, which have led to World Cup and European Championship wins.

ANTOINE **GRIEZMANN**

A creative forward who was prolific in Madrid before a big move to Barcelona, Antoine Griezmann is highly effective in France's front three. He scored in the victorious 2018 World Cup final.
BORN: **MARCH 21, 1991, MACON, FRANCE**
HEIGHT: **5 FT 9 IN (1.76 M)**
MAIN CLUBS: **REAL SOCIEDAD, ATLETICO MADRID, BARCELONA**
INTERNATIONAL CAPS: **117**

A SYMPHONY IN BLUE

The French team's fortunes revived in the early 1980s. Having lost an epic World Cup semifinal to West Germany in 1982, France hosted and won the 1984 European Championship with a midfield of exquisite skill—Jean Tigana, Alain Giresse, and Luis Fernández. They scored 15 goals in five games, including a 5–0 victory over Belgium. At the 1986 World Cup, it beat Brazil in the game of the tournament, only to lose again to West Germany in the semifinal.

VIVE LA DIFFERENCE

Under Aimé Jacquet, France's multiethnic team—hailing from as far afield as Senegal, Ghana, and New Caledonia—won its first World Cup as host in 1998. It beat Croatia in the semifinal after defender Thuram scored his two sole international goals, then triumphed over Brazil in the final, triggering the biggest street party in Paris since the Liberation in 1944. France went on to win their second world crown at Russia 2018, but also suffered heartbreak in the 2006 and 2022 finals.

A SYMPHONY OF WONDERFUL PASSES ... OF PERFECT THROUGH BALLS

JEAN PIERRE LECLAIRE
ON FRANCE VS. BRAZIL, SEVILLA, 1986

STAT ATTACK

GOVERNING BODY:
Fédération Française de Football
FOUNDED: 1919
NATIONAL STADIUM:
Stade de France, Paris, 81,838
FIRST MATCH: 3–3 vs. Belgium, **1904**
BIGGEST WIN: 11–0 vs Greece, **1919**
BIGGEST DEFEAT: 1–17 vs. Denmark, **1908**

THE LEGENDS

MOST CAPPED PLAYERS

Name	From/To	Caps
Hugo LLORIS	2008–present	145
Lilian THURAM	1994–2008	142
Thierry HENRY	1997–2010	123
Olivier GIROUD	2011–present	120
Antoine GRIEZMANN	2014–present	117
Marcel DESAILLY	1993–2004	116

DEFENSIVE PLAY

Despite France's reputation for developing exciting attackers, Ligue 1 produces the lowest number of goals per game of the five major European leagues.

- Spain—**2.9**
- Italy—**2.9**
- Germany—**2.8**
- England—**2.8**
- France—**2.6**

LIGUE 1

Established in 1932 as France's first national professional league, La Ligue has been played continuously except during World War II (1939–1945). As of 2023–2024 it has 18 teams, and a standard three up, three down promotion and relegation format. The first title was won by Olympique Lillois, who later became Lille. The league has a reputation for tightly monitored finances, but the acquisition of Paris Saint-Germain by the high-spending sovereign wealth fund of Qatar in 2011 may have changed the ethos forever.

COUPE DE FRANCE

First played in 1918, the Coupe de France is the second-most-important competition in French soccer. It was originally named the Coupe Charles Simon after a player who was killed during World War I, and, since 1927, the final has been attended by the French president. The cup was played in a restricted format during World War II but has been canceled only once, due to a stadium disaster in 1992 in which a temporary stand collapsed during a semifinal, killing 18 and injuring thousands, at Bastia's ground in Corsica.

MARCEL DESAILLY
A formidable defender who won almost every honor for both club and country, Desailly also received the dubious distinction of being sent off in a World Cup Final.

STAT ATTACK

LIGUE 1

LEAGUE STRUCTURE: 18 teams
TOP SCORER: Delio Onnis, **299** goals
MOST WINS: Saint Étienne, PSG, **10** titles
BIGGEST WIN: 12–1, Sochaux vs. Valenciennes, 1935–1936
HIGHEST ATTENDANCE:
77,840, Lille vs. Lyon, 2007–2008
DIVISIONS BELOW LIGUE 1:
Ligue 2 (**20** teams), National (**20** teams)

COUPE DE FRANCE

First played in 1918, the Coupe de France is open to every professional and nonprofessional team in France.
MOST FINAL DEFEATS: Marseille, **9** defeats
MOST WINS: Paris Saint-Germain, **14** wins
BIGGEST WIN: 5–0, Saint Étienne vs. Nantes, 1970

COUPE DE LA LIGUE

Introduced in 1994, the Coupe de la Ligue is contested by France's 45 professional clubs, and the winner qualifies for the Europa League.
TOP SCORER: Pauleta, Edinson Cavani **15**
MOST WINS: Paris Saint-Germain, **9** wins
BIGGEST WIN: 4–0, Bordeaux v Vannes, 2009; Paris Saint-Germain v Bastia, 2015

8,008
The population of Guingamp, a Breton administrative region whose team—En Avant Guingamp—topped Ligue 1 in 2002

44
The number of goals scored by Croatian striker Josip Skoblar for Marseilles in the 1970–1971 season, a total that is still unbeaten

1922
The year a French Women's XI played the first informal women's international against England in Paris—the score was 1–1

TOP GOAL SCORERS

Name	From/To	Goals
Olivier GIROUD	2011–present	53
Thierry HENRY	1997–2010	51
Antoine GRIEZMANN	2014–present	42
Michel PLATINI	1976–1987	41
Karim BENZEMA	2007–present	37
Kylian MBAPPÉ	2017–present	36

WORLD CUP

Winner
Runner-up
Semifinals
Quarterfinals
Round 2
Round 1
Did not qualify
1 2 3 4 5 6 7

EURO CHAMPIONSHIPS

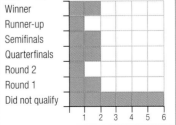

Winner
Runner-up
Semifinals
Quarterfinals
Round 2
Round 1
Did not qualify
1 2 3 4 5 6

FRENCH CLUBS

French law used to forbid the sale of soccer clubs, so each one was primarily owned by the amateur clubs and associations from which professional soccer grew. For 100 years, this ensured that no single club could pull too far ahead of the others and allowed the very smallest of clubs, such as Auxerre, to triumph occasionally. In recent times, however, foreign money has poured into the French game, notably at Paris Saint-Germain (PSG).

SOCCER AS GEOGRAPHY

The soccer clubs of France reflect the country's pattern of dispersed urbanization. Reims and Saint Étienne are small provincial towns, but they have been able to support teams at the top of French soccer. Similarly, the island of Corsica is a soccer hotbed with two leading teams—Bastia and Ajaccio.

NICKNAME:
LES GONES
("THE KIDS")
FOUNDED:
LYON, 1950
HOME
STADIUM:
PARC OLYMPIQUE LYONNAIS,
59,186
DOMESTIC HONORS:
LEAGUE 7, CUP 5
INTERNATIONAL HONORS:
INTERTOTO CUP 1997

OLYMPIQUE LYONNAIS

With just three French Cup wins to their name, Olympique Lyonnais was a small provincial club until 1987, when businessman Jean Michel Aulas took over the club. Seven consecutive league titles since 2002 followed, as did sell-out crowds, which have given Lyon the financial muscle to be a powerful force in French soccer in the 21st century.

DERBY DU RHÔNE

Saint Étienne, located just 25 miles (40 km) from Lyon, dominated the French league in the 1970s, just as Olympique Lyonnais did at the start of the 21st century. The "Derby du Rhône" between the two clubs became a highlight of the French season.

NICKNAME: L'OM
FOUNDED:
MARSEILLE, 1899
STADIUM: STADE
VELODROME,
HOME
67,394
DOMESTIC HONORS:
LEAGUE 9, CUP 10
INTERNATIONAL HONORS:
CHAMPIONS LEAGUE 1993;
INTERTOTO CUP 2005, 2006

OLYMPIQUE DE MARSEILLE

Always a big club, Olympique de Marseille (OM) rose to the top of French soccer under the presidency of the eccentric businessman and politician, Bernard Tapie. Four league titles culminated in the 1993 European Cup, only for the 1993 league title to be stripped and the team demoted after a series of match-fixing allegations were proved true and financial irregularities were exposed.

ULTRA CULTURE

L'OM has the most voluble fans in France, and their ethnic mix reflects the population of the port city. Different groups inhabit different parts of the Stade Velodrome: the Yankee Nord Marseille, Fanatics, and Dodgers in the north curve, the Commando Ultras 1984 in the south bleachers, the South Winners in the center, and Amis de l'OM in the wings.

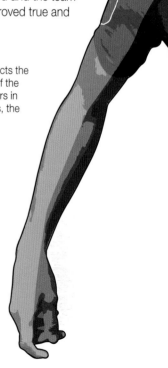

ABEDI **PELE**

Legendary Ghanaian international Pele was a pioneering African soccer player in Europe during the 1980s and '90s. The attacking midfielder enjoyed most success with Marseille, which won the Champions League in 1993.

BORN: **NOVEMBER 5, 1964, DOME, GHANA**
HEIGHT: **5 FT 8½ IN (1.74 M)**
MAIN CLUBS: **MARSEILLE, LILLE, LYON, TORINO, 1860 MUNICH**
INTERNATIONAL CAPS: **67**

NICKNAME: PSG
FOUNDED:
PARIS, 1970
STADIUM:
PARC DES
PRINCES, 48,712

HOME

DOMESTIC HONORS:
LEAGUE 10, CUP 14
INTERNATIONAL HONORS:
CUP WINNERS' CUP 1996;
INTERTOTO CUP 2001

PARIS SAINT-GERMAIN

Paris found itself without a major team for the first time in the 1960s, with the demise of Racing Club. A group of some 20,000 Parisians put up the money to buy a small club in 1970, transforming it into Paris Saint-Germain (PSG). Backed by Qatari money since 2011, PSG has become the dominant force in French football.

BACK FROM THE BRINK

Canal Plus, the giant French TV company, pumped money into PSG after buying the club in 1991. Although it won three French league cups, five French cups, and—under coach Luis Fernández—the European Cup Winners' Cup, the Ligue 1 title eluded it, despite being offered in 1993. PSG had finished second to Marseille, which was stripped of the title for match fixing, but PSG refused to accept it. In 2011, PSG was bought by a Qatari investment company.

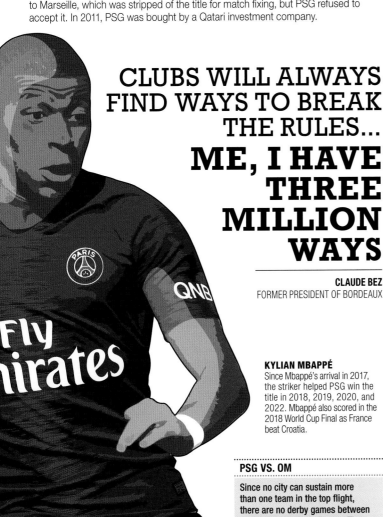

CLUBS WILL ALWAYS FIND WAYS TO BREAK THE RULES... ME, I HAVE THREE MILLION WAYS

CLAUDE BEZ
FORMER PRESIDENT OF BORDEAUX

KYLIAN MBAPPÉ

Since Mbappé's arrival in 2017, the striker helped PSG win the title in 2018, 2019, 2020, and 2022. Mbappé also scored in the 2018 World Cup Final as France beat Croatia.

PSG VS. OM

Since no city can sustain more than one team in the top flight, there are no derby games between neighboring clubs in France. The game between two of the richest clubs and loudest fans—PSG and Marseille—serves as the national derby, pitting Paris and the center against the outlying peripheries, such as Marseille.

BEST OF THE REST

SAINT-ÉTIENNE (1919)
With seven league titles between 1967 and 1976, Saint-Étienne was the first French team to gain national television coverage. The home crowd is nicknamed "Le Cauldron Vert."
HONORS: LEAGUE 10, CUP 6

LILLE OSC (1944)
Successful in the 1940s and '50s, Lille Olympique Sporting Club rose again to win the Ligue 1 title in 2011 and 2021. Their nickname is "les Dogues" (the Bulldogs).
HONOURS: LEAGUE 4, CUP 6

NANTES (1943)
Nantes is famed for its youth system, which has helped the peripheral Breton side to a series of titles in the 1960s, as well as recent success in the 1990s.
HONORS: LEAGUE 8, CUP 4

AUXERRE (1905)
Auxerre won a league title and four French cups under Guy Roux, who was club manager for more than 40 years.
HONORS: LEAGUE 1, CUP 4
INTERTOTO CUP 1997, 2006

SOCHAUX-MONTBÉLIARD (1928)
Founded as the factory team of the huge Peugeot factory in Montbéliard, the club had a commercial ethos that led it to become the first professional side in France in 1935.
HONORS: LEAGUE 2, CUP 2

LENS (1906)
The team of France's northern coalfields, Lens' large and stalwart crowds bravely wear the team colors of blood and gold.
HONORS: LEAGUE 1;
INTERTOTO CUP 2005, 2007

MONACO (1924)
The team of the Riviera tax haven, Monaco is backed by the royal Grimaldi family and the Monaco government. Plenty of titles have resulted, most recently in 2017.
HONORS: LEAGUE 8, CUP 5

ARSÈNE WENGER
The thinking man's manager of choice and Arsenal's most successful manager in terms of silverware, Wenger cut his teeth with considerable success in Ligue 1 with Monaco.

EUROPE

NETHERLANDS

HOME   AWAY

POPULATION: 17 MILLION
CAPITAL: AMSTERDAM
LICENSED PLAYERS:
MALE: 1.1 MILLION
FEMALE: 84,000
PROFESSIONALS: 1,000
REGISTERED CLUBS: 4,000

Professional soccer came late to the Netherlands. Yet a mere 20 years after its arrival, the national team was unlucky to lose the 1974 World Cup Final to West Germany—still a painful memory for Dutch fans. A sparkling win in the 1988 European Championship gave some consolation. The Dutch do not play in the typically high-tempo, tough-tackling northern European style but are famed for attractive, inventive play. They are widely regarded as the best team never to have won the World Cup.

DUTCH MASTERS

The Dutch national team has produced some of the most sublime moments in international soccer: from the pioneering "total soccer"—featuring Cruyff and Neeskens—of the 1970s to the successive World Cup Final defeats in 1974 and 1978, and from Marco van Basten's volley on the way to the 1988 European Championship win to Dennis Bergkamp's amazing goal against Argentina in the 1998 World Cup. When the team is good, it is superb.

THE DARK SIDE

The Dutch national team is also, on occasion, capable of falling to pieces. This was never more true than at Euro 2000, which it cohosted with Belgium. In the quarterfinals, it decimated a good Yugoslav team 6–1, and Patrick Kluivert scored a hat trick. But in the semifinals, the team seemed to freeze, despite winning two penalties and even though its opponent, Italy, had been reduced to 10 men. Italy eventually ground out a 0–0 draw and, in the shoot-out that followed, scored the first three penalties. The dispirited Dutch scored just one penalty out of four.

DENNIS BERGKAMP
An ice-cool, withdrawn striker with a phobia of flying, Bergkamp formed deadly partnerships with Thierry Henry at Arsenal and with Patrick Kluivert in the Dutch national team.

ORANGE POWER

Wearing the national shirt is almost compulsory for Netherlands fans, and whenever the Dutch team plays, the crowd is a sea of orange. The national color is derived from the coat of arms of Prince William of Nassau-Orange (1533–1584), the nobleman who instigated the revolt against the ruling Spanish Empire that ultimately led to Dutch independence in 1648.

SOCCER IS SIMPLE, BUT THE HARDEST THING IS ...
TO PLAY SOCCER IN A SIMPLE WAY

JOHAN CRUYFF
LEGENDARY DUTCH PLAYER AND MANAGER

STAT ATTACK

GOVERNING BODY:
Koninklijke Nederlandse Voetbal Bond (KNVB)
FOUNDED: 1889
NATIONAL STADIUM: None
FIRST MATCH: 4–1 vs. Belgium, 1905
BIGGEST WIN: 11–0 vs. San Marino, 2011
BIGGEST DEFEAT: 2–12 vs. England, 1907

THE LEGENDS

MOST CAPPED PLAYERS

Name	From/To	Caps
Wesley SNEIJDER	2003–2018	134
Edwin VAN DER SAR	1995–2008	130
Frank DE BOER	1990–2004	112
Rafael van der VAART	2001–2013	109
Giovanni VAN BRONCKHORST	1996–2010	106

TOP GOAL SCORERS

Name	From/To	Goals
Robin VAN PERSIE	2005–2017	50
Memphis DEPAY	2013–present	4
Klaas-Jan HUNTELAAR	2006–2015	42
Patrick KLUIVERT	1994–2004	40
Dennis BERGKAMP	1990–2000	37
Arjen ROBBEN	2003–2017	37

DUTCH COMPETITIONS

The 18 best teams in the Netherlands compete in the Eredivisie ("honorary division"), which began in 1956 and has been dominated by Ajax, PSV Eindhoven, and Feyenoord. Since 1965, they have won the majority of titles, although AZ and FC Twente have interrupted their dominance in recent years. The main knockout competition is the KNVB Beker, organized by the Royal Netherlands Football Association (KNVB). Also known as the Dutch Cup, it was founded in 1898 and was deliberately modeled on the FA Cup in England. Ajax has won it more times than any other club.

RUUD GULLIT

Few players caught the eye like the dreadlocked Ruud Gullit. Big, athletic, and superbly balanced, he could play in any position and still dominate a match.

STAT ATTACK

EREDIVISIE

LEAGUE STRUCTURE: 18 teams
TOP SCORER: Willy van der Kuijlen, **311** goals
MOST WINS: 36, Ajax
BIGGEST WIN: 12–1, Ajax vs. Vitesse Arnhem, 1972
HIGHEST ATTENDANCE: 65,150, Feyenoord vs. Ajax, 1970
DIVISIONS BELOW EREDIVISIE: Eerste Divisie (**18** teams)

KNVB BEKER

Eighty-eight teams participate; every Eredivisie and Eerste Divisie club, the top four from the six third-level leagues, and the remainder from the fourth tier.
MOST WINS: 20, Ajax
BIGGEST WIN: 9–2, Willem II vs. Groene Ster, 1943–1944

0.5 Average number of goals scored per game by Robin van Persie, the Dutch national team's top scorer, in 102 appearances

7 Goals scored by Afonso Alves in Heerenveen's 9–0 thrashing of Heracles Almelo in 2007

73 Percentage of Dutch fans who admit to having hugged or kissed a stranger during a match

111 Eredivisie goals conceded by SHS Den Haag in the 1958–1959 season

4 Penalties awarded to PSV Eindhoven in a 2005 Eredivisie match vs. RBC Roosendaal; they missed two of them

JOHAN CRUYFF

Cruyff was the most complete player in the Dutch and Ajax teams famous for "total soccer." Nominally a striker, he bamboozled markers by dropping into midfield. His vision and passing skill led to the accolade "Pythagoras in boots."

BORN: **APRIL 25, 1947, AMSTERDAM, NETHERLANDS**
HEIGHT: **5 FT 11 IN (1.8 M)**
MAIN CLUBS: **AJAX, BARCELONA, FEYENOORD**
INTERNATIONAL CAPS: **48**

GULL KICK

During the derby match between Sparta Rotterdam and Feyenoord on November 15, 1970, Feyenoord goalkeeper Eddy Treytel made a long clearance that has gone down in club history. His kick knocked a passing seagull out of the sky, and the unfortunate bird was stuffed and put on display in the club's trophy room. At least that's what Feyenoord fans believe—Sparta fans are not so sure. They were supported by a biologist who stated that the exhibit looks nothing like a gull in its late fall plumage.

WORLD CUP

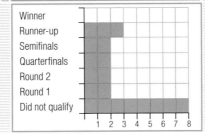

EURO CHAMPIONSHIPS

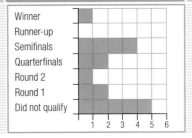

DUTCH CLUBS: THE BIG THREE

In the early days of soccer in the Netherlands, small clubs like Den Haag and Deventer won titles. However, since the professional era, Dutch soccer has been dominated by three big clubs—Ajax, PSV Eindhoven, and Feyenoord. In the 1960s and 1970s, the game underwent a major period of consolidation and club mergers. Many teams remain reliant on support and subsidy from local and city governments.

NICKNAME:
GODENZONEN ("SONS OF THE GODS")

HOME

FOUNDED:
AMSTERDAM, 1900

STADIUM:
JOHAN CRUYFF ARENA, 53,748

DOMESTIC HONORS:
LEAGUE 36, CUP 20

INTERNATIONAL HONORS:
CHAMPIONS LEAGUE 1971, 1972, 1973, 1995; **UEFA CUP** 1992; **CUP WINNERS' CUP** 1987; **UEFA SUPER CUP** 1973, 1995; **CLUB WORLD CUP** 1972, 1995

AFC AJAX

Ajax is at the center of Dutch soccer. The club has won the European Cup four times, including three consecutive wins between 1971 and 1973, and is one of only five teams to have been awarded the trophy permanently. In the 1960s, Ajax pioneered "total soccer," a revolutionary strategy in which teammates exchanged playing positions rapidly and fluidly.

THE JEWISH CLUB

Amsterdam's complex relationship with its Jewish community is reflected by the Ajax fans, very few of whom are Jewish. Fans have taken to waving the Israeli flag, spray-painting stars of David around the city, and claiming Ajax as a Jewish club.

FRANK RIJKAARD

As a player, Rijkaard was a ferocious midfielder. As a top-flight manager, he became the polar opposite—cool, calm, and collected—but no less successful, as proven by his 2006 Champions League triumph with Barcelona.

BORN: **SEPTEMBER 30, 1962, AMSTERDAM, NETHERLANDS**
HEIGHT: **6 FT 3 IN (1.9 M)**
MAIN CLUBS: **AJAX, MILAN**
INTERNATIONAL CAPS: **73**

NICKNAME:
BOEREN ("FARMERS")

HOME

FOUNDED:
EINDHOVEN, 1913

STADIUM:
PHILIPS STADION, 35,000

DOMESTIC HONORS:
LEAGUE 23, CUP 10

INTERNATIONAL HONORS:
EUROPEAN CUP 1988; UEFA CUP 1978

PSV EINDHOVEN

In 1913, electronics giant Philips held a sports day to celebrate the centenary of the Netherlands. It proved so popular that it decided to start a soccer team, which was named Philips Sport Vereniging ("Philips Sports Union") Eindhoven. Considerable sponsorship and solid home support have seen PSV win two European trophies and more than 20 Dutch titles. The Philips Stadion has often showcased the company's latest products.

VICTORY DRAW

PSV's finest hour was the 1988 European Cup Final against Benfica, which it won on penalties after Hans van Breukelen made a crucial save. Amazingly, PSV had failed to win either of the two-leg quarter- and semifinal ties, going through on away goals after drawing both games. The Intercontinental Cup Final went the same way later in the year, but PSV lost on penalties after a 2–2 draw with Nacional of Uruguay.

RUUD VAN NISTELROOY

A former central defender, van Nistelrooy became a striker at FC den Bosch. He was the Eredivisie's top scorer for two seasons running at PSV then signed for Manchester United for $36 million in 2001.

NICKNAME:
DE CLUB VAN
HET VOLK ("THE
PEOPLE'S CLUB")

HOME

FOUNDED:
ROTTERDAM, 1908

STADIUM:
DE KUIP, 51,177

DOMESTIC HONORS:
LEAGUE 15, CUP 13

INTERNATIONAL HONORS:
EUROPEAN CUP 1970;
UEFA CUP 1974, 2002;
CLUB WORLD CUP 1970

FEYENOORD

Feyenoord was founded in 1908 in the heart of Rotterdam's docks by a group of youths who played outside the Wilhelmina church. The team still plays in the area in the newly refurbished De Kuip stadium. Support is drawn from across the region, and although it is the country's second club, Feyenoord was the first Dutch club to win a European title, beating Celtic to take the European Cup in 1970.

FEYENOORD FANATICS

The fans of Feyenoord are among the most fervent in European soccer. When the team won the Dutch championship in 1999, more than a quarter of a million people gathered in Rotterdam to celebrate. Ever since more than 3,000 fans traveled by boat to Lisbon to see the team play Benfica in the 1963 European Cup, support at European away matches has been huge. The fans also like their music, and the song "Hand in Hand" has been their unofficial hymn since the 1960s.

DIE KLASSIKER

Whatever the league standings, the games between Ajax and Feyenoord—Die Klassiker—are the biggest of the Dutch season. Ajax holds the lead in this derby and, as the country's most successful club, attract the ire of not just Feyenoord but much of the rest of the soccer nation. During the 1997–1998 season, all fans were banned from the stadium after extensive disorder the previous year.

GIOVANNI VAN BRONCKHORST

A gifted, ever-present playmaker who has won league and cup honors in four countries, van Bronckhorst also appeared in two World Cup and three European Championship finals.

DIE KLASSIKER RECORD

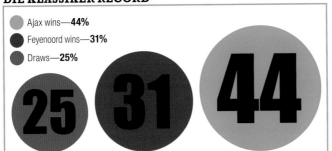

- Ajax wins—**44%**
- Feyenoord wins—**31%**
- Draws—**25%**

25   31   44

THE YEAR OF MAGIC

In 1983–1984, Johan Cruyff left Ajax and crossed over to Feyenoord for a single scintillating season. At 37 he played brilliantly and carried Feyenoord to its most unlikely Dutch league and cup double, dubbed "The Year of Magic."

BEST OF THE REST

VITESSE ARNHEM (1892)
The new team of the 1980s, backed with municipal money and recipient of a futuristic stadium, it challenged the big three but was struck by debt and recrimination.
HONORS: LEAGUE 0, CUP 1

SPARTA ROTTERDAM (1888)
An old team from the working-class heart of Rotterdam, Sparta's golden years were before World War I. In recent years, staying in the top flight has been its major ambition.
HONORS: LEAGUE 6, CUP 3

SC HEERENVEEN (1920)
Virtually a village team, Heerenveen's youth system has lifted it to the top six of the Dutch league, and even into European competition. Ruud van Nistelrooy began his career here.
HONORS: LEAGUE 0, CUP 1

FC TWENTE (1965)
Formed in Enschede, FC Twente challenged Feyenoord for the league title in 1973 then lost the 1974 UEFA Cup Final to Spurs, having already beaten Juventus in the semifinal.
HONORS: LEAGUE 1, CUP 3

FC UTRECHT (1970)
Formed from the fusion of three clubs, FC Utrecht has won two Dutch cups since 2003 and has demonstrated its ambition to challenge for the league title.
HONORS: LEAGUE 1, CUP 3

AZ ALKMAAR (1967)
The team that finally broke the dominance of the big three, Alkmaar won the Dutch league in 1981 but has been unable to repeat the performance since.
HONORS: LEAGUE 2, CUP 4

WILLEM II TILBURG (1896)
Named after the 19th-century Dutch King, the team wears the Dutch national colors. Without a title win since 1955, it played in the 1999 Champions League group stage.
HONORS: LEAGUE 3, CUP 2

HOME

AWAY

POPULATION: 5.6 MILLION
CAPITAL: COPENHAGEN
FA: DANSK BOLDSPIL-UNION
LICENSED PLAYERS:
MALE: 420,000
FEMALE: 91,000
PROFESSIONALS: 1,000
REGISTERED CLUBS: 1,500

DENMARK

Denmark was the first country in continental Europe to embrace soccer and boasts of the oldest national association—one of the seven founding members of FIFA in 1904—outside the UK. Denmark won silver at the 1908 and 1912 Olympics, but further success was limited until the lifting in the early 1980s of a selection ban on players signed to overseas teams.

THE DANISH SUPERLIGA

The Danish national league started in 1913, although it wasn't until the 1950s that a team from outside the capital won it. The league was restricted and reduced to the 12-team Danish Superliga in 1991, which then expanded to 14 teams in 2016, eventually coming down to 12 again in 2020.

DERBY DAY

Danish soccer has been dominated by the two big Copenhagen teams, which have won more than half the titles since the inception of the Superliga in 1991. Brøndby, from the south of the city, styles itself as the authentic, working-class, community club, whereas uptown FC København is perceived as the brash, nouveau-riche, commercial club.

MICHAEL LAUDRUP
One of the game's most dazzling and creative playmakers, Laudrup's teammates commented "Just run, he will always find a way of passing you the ball."

STAT ATTACK

NATIONAL TEAM

NICKNAME: Danish Dynamite, Olsen-Banden ("The Olsen Gang")
NATIONAL STADIUM: Parken, 38,065
WORLD CUP FINALS: 6 appearances, quarterfinals **1998**
EUROPEAN CHAMPIONSHIPS: 8 appearances, winners **1992**, semifinals **1964, 1984, 2020**
BIGGEST WIN: 17–1 vs. France, 1908
BIGGEST DEFEAT: 0–8 vs. Germany, 1937
MOST CAPS: Peter Schmeichel, **129**
MOST GOALS: Poul Nielson, Jon Dahl Tomasson **52**

ROOLIGANS

Best translated as "fool-igan" or "fun-igan," Denmark's fans redefined the image of the soccer fan. Colorful, drunken, and friendly, they pioneered the mass-happiness, singing, and odd headgear that have come to flavor the modern soccer tournament.

EURO 1992

Denmark failed to qualify for the 1992 European Championship, and the team was on vacation when it was called up to replace Yugoslavia, which had withdrawn due to the civil war. It scraped through the first round but made it all the way to the final where, to everyone's amazement, it beat Germany.

PETER SCHMEICHEL

One of the most formidable keepers the game has ever seen, Peter not only dominated his goal area and berated fellow-defenders when roused, but also scored nine goals. His son Kasper emulated Peter's success, also becoming Denmark's goalkeeper.

BORN: NOVEMBER 18, 1963, GLADSAXE, DENMARK
HEIGHT: 6 FT 4 IN (1.93 M)
MAIN CLUBS: BRØNDBY, MANCHESTER UNITED, ASTON VILLA, MANCHESTER CITY
INTERNATIONAL CAPS: 129

MAIN DOMESTIC CLUBS

FC KØBENHAVN
FOUNDED: Copenhagen, 1992
STADIUM: Parken
CAPACITY: 38,065
INTERNATIONAL HONORS: None
LEAGUE: 14 CUP: 8

HOME

BRØNDBY
FOUNDED: Copenhagen, 1964
STADIUM: Brøndby Stadium
CAPACITY: 28,000
INTERNATIONAL HONORS: None
LEAGUE: 11 CUP: 7

HOME

AGF AARHUS
FOUNDED: Aarhus, 1880
STADIUM: Ceres Park
CAPACITY: 20,032
INTERNATIONAL HONORS: None
LEAGUE: 5 CUP: 9

HOME

HOME   AWAY

POPULATION: 9.9 MILLION
CAPITAL: STOCKHOLM
FA: SVENSKA FOTBOLLFÖRBUNDET
REGISTERED PLAYERS:
MALE: 791,500
FEMALE: 215,500
PROFESSIONALS: 2,000
REGISTERED CLUBS: 3,000

SWEDEN

The first Swedish soccer clubs and leagues were established in the 1890s among the middle and upper classes. Working-class soccer arrived in the early 20th century, and conflict between the two groups was resolved only by the introduction of an amateur code in the 1930s. The national team has challenged for international silverware, although in modern times, the best of Sweden's players have played overseas.

STAT ATTACK

NATIONAL TEAM

NICKNAME: Blågult ("Blue and Yellow")
NATIONAL STADIUM: Friends Arena, 54,329
WORLD CUP FINALS: 12 appearances, runner-up **1958**, semifinals **1950**, **1994**
EUROPEAN CHAMPIONSHIPS: 7 appearances, semifinals **1992**, quarterfinals **2004**
BIGGEST WIN: 12–0 vs. Latvia, 1927 and vs. South Korea, 1948
BIGGEST DEFEAT: 1–12 vs. England Amateurs, 1908
MOST CAPS: Anders Svensson, **148**
MOST GOALS: Zlatan Ibrahimović, **62**

MAIN DOMESTIC CLUBS

IFK GÖTEBORG
FOUNDED: Gothenburg, 1904
STADIUM: Ullevi
CAPACITY: 18,416

HOME
INTERNATIONAL HONORS: European Cup semifinals **1986**, **1993**; UEFA Cup winners **1982**, **1987**
LEAGUE: 18 **CUP:** 8

MALMÖ FF
FOUNDED: Malmö, 1910
STADIUM: Swedbank Stadion
CAPACITY: 24,000

HOME
INTERNATIONAL HONORS: European Cup runner-up **1979**
LEAGUE: 22 **CUP:** 15

AIK
FOUNDED: Stockholm, 1891
STADIUM: Friends Arena
CAPACITY: 54,329

HOME
INTERNATIONAL HONORS: None
LEAGUE: 12 **CUP:** 8

ALLSVENSKAN

The national league was founded in 1900 and was renamed Allsvenskan ("All-Swedish") in 1924. Unusually for a European nation, playoffs between the top teams have been used to determine the winner, most recently from 1982 to 1990. The Swedish league was one of the only leagues in Europe to continue during either of the world wars, and the Swedish Cup was actually started during World War II.

HARD TO PLEASE

In 2001, Hammarby IF, a small team from the south of Stockholm, finally managed to win the championship, leading to delirium among the club's long-suffering fans. Nevertheless, the board of the club had already decided to fire the coach, Sören Cratz, on the grounds that he didn't play attacking soccer.

THE ENGLISH CONNECTION

Both the 1948 Olympic gold-medal-winning team and the 1958 World Cup–losing finalists were coached by Englishman George Raynor. An ex-professional player, Raynor later managed the Swedish team that beat his home nation 3–2 at Wembley in a 1959 friendly match.

ZLATAN **IBRAHIMOVIĆ**

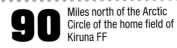

Ibrahimović was born of Yugoslav-Bosnian immigrants in the toughest part of Malmö. A sharp-minded striker, he brought an arrogance and invention—honed at Inter Milan—that had been missing from the Swedish team.

BORN: OCTOBER 3, 1981, MALMÖ, SWEDEN
HEIGHT: 6 FT (1.83 M)
MAIN CLUBS: MALMÖ, AJAX, JUVENTUS, INTER, BARCELONA, MILAN, PARIS SAINT-GERMAIN, MANCHESTER UNITED
INTERNATIONAL CAPS: 121

GRE-NO-LI

Sweden's most famous trio of players—Gunnar Gren, Gunnar Nordahl, and Nils Liedholm—became known as Gre-No-Li. They formed the backbone of Sweden's Olympic gold-medal-winning team in 1948 but were later banned from the national team after signing for clubs in Italy.

0 Games won by Billingsfors IK in 1946–1947, its sole season in the Swedish top division

7 Number of goals scored in a single game by IFK Norrköping's Gunnar Nordahl, in 1944

11 Seconds it took for Hjalmar Lorichs to score for Sweden vs. Finland in 1912

90 Miles north of the Arctic Circle of the home field of Kiruna FF

EUROPE

HOME

AWAY

POPULATION: 5.2 MILLION
CAPITAL: OSLO
FA: NORGES FOTBALLFORBUND
REGISTERED PLAYERS:
MALE: 409,000
FEMALE: 135,000
PROFESSIONALS: 1,000
REGISTERED CLUBS: 1,800

NORWAY

Norway caught the soccer bug in the late 19th century and took up the sport at once; the national association was founded in 1902, three years before Norway's independence from Sweden. The country's fierce Arctic conditions and national love of skiing initially hindered the growth of the game, but since the Norwegian government began to invest in elite soccer in the early 1990s, the men's and women's national teams have flourished.

WOMEN'S WORLD CUP

Norway is at the forefront of women's soccer and was one of the first countries in Europe to incorporate the women's game. Norway was runner-up at the first Women's World Cup in 1991, winner in 1995, and Olympic champion in 2000.

THE TIPPELIGAEN

The Norwegian playing season is centered around the summer months and lasts from mid-March to early November. The top tier was renamed the Tippeligaen ("Premier League") in 1991 and then Eliteserien in 2017. It has been dominated by Rosenborg, which won the title 13 consecutive times between 1992 and 2004. The Norwegian Cup is a knockout contest open to teams from almost every level of soccer in Norway.

CITY OF KINGS, CLUB OF THE PEOPLE

The Norwegian club that has prospered most from the arrival of professionalism and European money has been Rosenborg. The club was founded in 1917 as a people's team in the city of Trondheim, the seat of the ancient Norwegian kings. After establishing domestic dominance in the 1990s, it went on to win money and games in Europe, and even reached the quarterfinals of the Champion's League in 1996.

BEATING ENGLAND

Norway's first triumph over England came with a 2–1 victory in a 1981 World Cup qualifier. It is remembered in Norway for an extraordinary outburst from radio commentator Bjørge Lillelien: "Lord Nelson, Sir Winston Churchill, Henry Cooper, Lady Diana, we have beaten them all! Maggie Thatcher, can you hear me? Your boys took a hell of a beating!"

JOHN CAREW

Of Gambian descent, "Big John Carew" was the first black player to appear for Norway. A hardworking and determined striker, he won league titles in two countries: Spain (with Valencia) and France (with Lyon).

BORN: **SEPTEMBER 5, 1979, LØRENSKOG, NORWAY**
HEIGHT: **6 FT 4 IN (1.93 M)**
MAIN CLUBS: **ROSENBORG, VALENCIA, BESIKTAS, LYON, ASTON VILLA, WEST HAM**
INTERNATIONAL CAPS: **91**

STAT ATTACK

NATIONAL TEAM

NICKNAME: Vikingene ("The Vikings")
NATIONAL STADIUM:
Ullevaal Stadion, 28,972
WORLD CUP FINALS:
3 appearances
EUROPEAN CHAMPIONSHIPS:
1 appearance
BIGGEST WIN: 12–0 vs. Finland, 1946
BIGGEST DEFEAT: 0–12 vs. Denmark, 1917
MOST CAPS: John Arne Riise, **110**
MOST GOALS: Jørgen Juve, **33**

MAIN DOMESTIC CLUBS

ROSENBORG BK
FOUNDED: Trondheim, 1917
STADIUM: Lerkendal
CAPACITY: 21,405
HOME
INTERNATIONAL HONORS:
Champions League quarterfinals **1997**
LEAGUE: 26 CUP: 12

SK BRANN BERGEN
FOUNDED: Bergen, 1908
STADIUM: Brann Stadion
CAPACITY: 17,686
HOME
INTERNATIONAL HONORS:
Cup Winners' Cup quarterfinals **1996**
LEAGUE: 3 CUP: 6

VÅLERENGA IF
FOUNDED: Oslo, 1913
STADIUM: Intility Arena
CAPACITY: 28,972
HOME
INTERNATIONAL HONORS: None
LEAGUE: 5 CUP: 4

HOME

AWAY

FINLAND

POPULATION: 5.4 MILLION
CAPITAL: HELSINKI
FA: SUOMEN PALLOLIITTO
REGISTERED PLAYERS:
MALE: 304,000
FEMALE: 58,500
PROFESSIONALS: 400
REGISTERED CLUBS: 1,000

Soccer may have arrived early in Finland—the first club, Reipas Lahti, was set up in 1897, and a Helsinki league soon followed—but soccer has had to compete with the weather, ice hockey, and ski jumping ever since. Success for the national team has consisted of a semifinal appearance at the 1912 Olympics. Semi-professionalism arrived in the 1990s, and a few players, including Jari Litmanen, Sami Hyypiä, and Mikael Forssell, moved to the leading leagues of Europe.

THE VEIKKAUSLIIGA

Finland's winter is long and harsh, so the playing season runs from late April to early October, and teams in the 12-team Veikkausliiga are often forced to play two games a week to fit them all in. The Finnish Cup has been running since 1955, and cup-final day forms a fitting climax to the season in November. During the winter, a more informal league is played indoors.

EUROPEAN HEIGHTS

In 1998, HJK Helsinki qualified for the group stages of the Champions League, becoming the first Finnish side to do so. It beat Benfica but failed to progress from the group stage. Prior to this, the only Finnish success in Europe was a 1987 UEFA Cup-tie win over Inter Milan in the San Siro by Turun Palloseura.

JARI LITMANEN

Unusually for a Finn, Litmanen turned down the chance to play ice hockey in favor of being a soccer striker. After blooming in the Finnish league, he moved to Ajax in 1993, where he won a Champions League medal in 1995.

BORN: FEBRUARY 20, 1971, HOLLOLA, FINLAND
HEIGHT: 6 FT (1.82 M)
MAIN CLUBS: REIPAS, HJK HELSINKI, MYPA, AJAX, BARCELONA, LIVERPOOL, FC LAHTI, HANSA ROSTOCK
INTERNATIONAL CAPS: 137

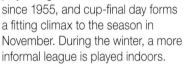

EAGLE OWLS

The Finnish national team acquired the nickname "Huuhkajat," Finnish for "eagle owl," from a bird named Bubi who lived near the Helsinki Olympic Stadium. His first showing at a match was a 2007 fixture between Finland and Belgium. Finland won 2–0, and Bubi was named Helsinki's Resident of the Year.

STAT ATTACK

NATIONAL TEAM

NICKNAME: Huuhkajat ("Eagle Owls")
NATIONAL STADIUM:
Helsingin Olympiastadion, 42,062
WORLD CUP FINALS: No appearances
EUROPEAN CHAMPIONSHIPS:
1 appearance
BIGGEST WIN: 10–2 vs. Estonia, 1922
BIGGEST DEFEAT: 0–13 vs. Germany, 1940
MOST CAPS: Jari Litmanen, **137**
MOST GOALS: Teemu Pukki, **37**

MAIN DOMESTIC CLUBS

HJK HELSINKI
FOUNDED: Helsinki, 1907
STADIUM: Telia 5G-areena
CAPACITY: 10,770
INTERNATIONAL HONORS: None
LEAGUE: 32 **CUP:** 14

HOME

FC HAKA
FOUNDED: Valkeakoski, 1934
STADIUM: Tehtaan Kenttä
CAPACITY: 3,516
INTERNATIONAL HONORS:
Cup Winners' Cup quarterfinals **1984**
LEAGUE: 9 **CUP:** 12

HOME

FOUR NAMES, TWO HOMES, ONE TEAM

Klubi-04 was formerly named Pallo-Kerho-35, PK35, and FC Jokerit, was based in Viipuri until World War II, and is now HJK's reserve team.

19 Number of goals conceded by Reipas Lahti over two legs vs. Levski Spartak in the 1976–1977 Cup Winners' Cup

0 Number of players in the Euro 2020 Finland squad who played for a Finnish side

29 Number of different clubs that have won the Finnish league title

2,900 Average attendance at Veikkausliiga (premier division) matches

EUROPE

GERMANY

HOME

AWAY

POPULATION: 82.9 MILLION
CAPITAL: BERLIN
LICENSED PLAYERS:
MALE: 5.4 MILLION
FEMALE: 871,000
PROFESSIONALS: 1,000
REGISTERED CLUBS: 26,000

Soccer was first played in Germany in elite Anglophile circles but soon spread to white-collar workers in the 1890s. Endorsed by the kaiser before World War I, the game boomed following the war as it finally spread to the working classes. After World War II, soccer, like everything else, was split between East and West Germany before reunification in 1990.

WORLD BEATERS

Germany's international record is exceptional, winning both the World Cup and European Championship several times and finishing as runner-up a total of seven times. Even when playing poorly, the team grinds out results and is notoriously effective at penalties. The stability and order that have characterized the team were shaped by manager Sepp Herberger, who won the 1954 World Cup and coached the side for nearly 30 years.

THOMAS MÜLLER
Attacking midfielder or forward, Müller burst onto the world scene in 2010. At the 2010 World Cup, aged 20, he won the Golden Boot. He scored five goals when Germany won the Cup four years later.

FRANZ **BECKENBAUER**

Known as Der Kaiser ("The Emperor"), Beckenbauer was a midfielder but transformed himself into the definitive modern sweeper, dictating play from the back. He won all the major honors as a player then managed West Germany to World Cup success in 1990.

BORN: **SEPTEMBER 11, 1945,**
MUNICH, GERMANY
HEIGHT: **5 FT 11 IN (1.81 M)**
CLUBS: **BAYERN MUNICH, NEW YORK COSMOS, HAMBURG**
INTERNATIONAL CAPS: **103**

SAARLAND

A tiny corner of western Germany, the Saar was an independent soccer nation between 1948 and 1956. Placed under French control after World War II, Saarland entered the 1952 Olympics and 1954 World Cup qualifiers, losing twice to West Germany. In 1957, Saarland was unified with West Germany, and the national team disbanded. The Saar was coached by Helmut Schön, who went on to coach the West German national team.

6 Most own goals in Bundesliga, by Manfred Kaltz of Hamburger SV

53 Most Bundesliga goals scored by penalties— by Manfred Kaltz

9 Seconds to score the Bundesliga's fastest goal: Karim Bellarabi (Bayer Leverkusen) vs. Borussia Dortmund, 2014–2015; Kevin Volland (Hoffenheim) vs. Bayern München, 2015–2016

STAT ATTACK

GOVERNING BODY:
Deutscher Fußball-Bund
FOUNDED: 1900
NATIONAL STADIUM: None
FIRST MATCH: 3–5 vs. Switzerland, 1908
BIGGEST WIN: 16–0 vs. Russia, 1912
BIGGEST DEFEAT: 0–9 vs. England, 1909

THE LEGENDS

MOST CAPPED PLAYERS

Name	From/To	Caps
Lothar MATTHÄUS	1980–2000	150
Miroslav KLOSE	2001–2014	137
Lukas PODOLSKI	2004–2017	130
Bastian SCHWEINSTEIGER	2004–2016	121
Thomas MULLER	2010–present	118
Manuel NEUER	2009–present	114

TOP GOAL SCORERS

Name	From/To	Goals
Miroslav KLOSE	2001–2014	71
Gerd MÜLLER	1966–1974	68
Lukas PODOLSKI	2004–2017	49
Rudi VÖLLER	1982–1994	47
Jürgen KLINSMANN	1987–1998	47
Karl-Heinz RUMMENIGGE	1976–1986	45

STAT ATTACK

BUNDESLIGA

LEAGUE STRUCTURE:
18 clubs

TOP SCORER: Gerd Müller, **365** goals

MOST SUCCESSFUL TEAM:
Bayern Munich, **30** league titles

BIGGEST WIN: 12–0, Borussia Monchengladbach vs. Borussia Dortmund, 1978

HIGHEST ATTENDANCE: 88,075, Hertha Berlin vs. 1FC Köln, 1969

DIVISIONS BELOW BUNDESLIGA:
Bundesliga 2 (**18** teams), Regionalliga Nord and Sud (**18** teams each)

DFB POKAL

The cup unites the major professional clubs with semiprofessional and amateur teams.

HIGHEST SCORING FINAL: 5–2, Bayern Munich vs. VFB Stuttgart, 1986 and Borussia Dortmund vs. Bayern Munich, 2012

MOST SUCCESSFUL TEAM:
FC Bayern Munich **20** wins

BIGGEST WIN: 5–0, FC Schalke 04 vs. FC Duisburg, 2011

THE NEXT GAME
IS ALWAYS THE TOUGHEST ONE ...

JOSEF "SEPP" HERBERGER
MANAGER, WEST GERMANY, 1936–1964

BUNDESLIGA

The Bundesliga was created as a professional national league in West Germany in 1963 and is operated by the Deutscher Fußball-Bund. In 1990, after the reunification of Germany, two leading teams from the former East Germany were admitted to the top division as the old East German leagues were disbanded.

DFB POKAL

First played in 1935, the DFB Pokal is a knockout tournament cup contest that includes the top professional clubs and the best of the lower league clubs. It was designed to embarrass the big clubs, with single legs decided by shoot-outs. More recently, the top professional clubs have been granted a bye to the later rounds.

EAST GERMAN NOSTALGIA

East Germany and its own particular soccer culture are long gone but remain legendary. Until the late 1970s, soccer retained a semblance of autonomy from the state. In 1978, Erich Mielke, head of the Stasi and president of Dynamo Berlin, decided it was time for his team to win. Their turn went on for 10 unbroken years. Support for soccer collapsed, and most fans secretly watched the Bundesliga on TV.

AVERAGE ATTENDANCES—EUROPE

Germany: Bundesliga—**43,300**
England: Premier League—**36,451**
Spain: La Liga—**28,191**
Italy: Serie A—**22,644**
France: La Ligue—**20,976**
Netherlands: Eredivisie—**19,412**

LOTHAR MATTHÄUS

The most capped German player of all time, Matthäus was a gifted and versatile outfield player who appeared in five World Cups. Renowned for his hard tackling, imperious passing, and fierce shot, he played for the national side to the age of 39.

RULE 1: SHOW UP

Karlsruhe, the favorite for the first German national championship held in 1904, was thrown out at the semifinal stage. It was duped by a fake telegram purporting that the game, against Bohemians of Prague, had been canceled, so the team failed to show up.

WORLD CUP

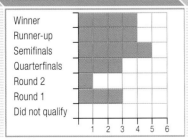

	1	2	3	4	5	6
Winner						
Runner-up						
Semifinals						
Quarterfinals						
Round 2						
Round 1						
Did not qualify						

EURO CHAMPIONSHIPS

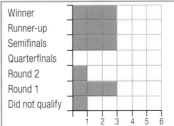

	1	2	3	4	5	6
Winner						
Runner-up						
Semifinals						
Quarterfinals						
Round 2						
Round 1						
Did not qualify						

EUROPE

GERMAN CLUBS

Soccer first boomed in Germany in the ports and northern cities of Hamburg, Bremen, and Berlin. While both regions still boast major clubs, the real powerhouse clubs are in the Ruhr valley, home to Schalke 04 and Borussia Dortmund, and in Munich, home to Bayern as well as TSV München. Many of the leading postwar West German clubs—such as Nürnberg, 1FC Köln, Eintracht Frankfurt, and Kaiserslautern—struggled after Germany's reunification.

MIROSLAV KLOSE

A deadly marksman who scored in every other game for Germany, former Bayern Munich striker Klose is the World Cup's all-time leading goal scorer.

NICKNAME: DER FCB, DIE BAYERN ("THE BAVARIANS")
FOUNDED: MUNICH, 1900
HOME
STADIUM: ALLIANZ ARENA, 75,000
DOMESTIC HONORS: LEAGUE 32, CUP 20
INTERNATIONAL HONORS: CHAMPIONS LEAGUE 1974, 1975, 1976, 2001, 2013, 2020; CUP WINNERS' CUP 1967; UEFA CUP 1996; UEFA SUPER CUP 2013, 2020

BAYERN MUNICH

Known in Germany as FC Hollywood, Bayern is the team everyone loves to hate but still boasts legions of German fans and more than 1,000 supporters' clubs outside the country. Founded in 1900 in Schwabing, a working-class district of Munich, the club acquired significant Jewish membership. Despite missing the first year of the Bundesliga in 1963, the club has won more league titles than any other team.

THEY'RE BEHIND YOU

Bayern was caught making a secret TV deal without the other teams in the Bundesliga but threatened to switch to Serie A—the Italian top tier—if punished.

KINGS OF EUROPE

Bayern Munich won the European Cup three times in a row from 1974 to 1976, with an extraordinary squad that boasted Sepp Maier in goal, Frank Beckenbauer everywhere, and Gerd Müller up front. Bayern went on to lose another three finals in the 1980s and 1990s before winning the trophy for the fourth time in 2001, with a fifth success coming in 2013.

NICKNAME: DIE SCHWARZGELBEN ("THE BLACK AND YELLOWS")
FOUNDED: DORTMUND, 1909
HOME
STADIUM: WESTFALENSTADION, 81,359
DOMESTIC HONORS: LEAGUE 8, CUP 5
INTERNATIONAL HONORS: CHAMPIONS LEAGUE 1997; CUP WINNERS' CUP 1966

BORUSSIA DORTMUND

Founded in 1909 from the fusion of three clubs—Trinity, Rhenania, and Britannia—Borussia Dortmund spent the next 50 years in the shadow of neighboring Schalke 04. That changed in the 1980s and 1990s, when a new commercial strategy made them the Ruhr's biggest club and the second biggest club in the country.

A GRANDSTAND VIEW

The Westfalenstadion attracts the biggest regular crowds in Europe. Uniquely for such a large arena, the stadium retains a safe standing section for Bundesliga games only, the Südtribüne. For internationals the section is fitted with temporary seats, reducing the overall capacity to 67,000. During building work ahead of the 2008 European Championships, a 1,000 lb (450 kg) unexploded wartime bomb was discovered buried beneath the halfway line, leading to an evacuation of the surrounding area while the bomb was defused.

MATTHIAS SAMMER

Sammer was one of the few East German players to make the transition to the Bundesliga. An adaptable sweeper and midfielder, he was the linchpin of Borussia Dortmund's 1997 European Cup–winning team.

BORN: **SEPTEMBER 5, 1967, DRESDEN, GERMANY**
HEIGHT: **5 FT 11 IN (1.8 M)**
MAIN CLUBS: **DYNAMO DRESDEN, VFB STUTTGART, BORUSSIA DORTMUND**
INTERNATIONAL CAPS: **23 (EAST GERMANY), 51 (GERMANY)**

NICKNAME:
ROTHOSEN
("RED SHORTS")

FOUNDED:
HAMBURG, 1887

HOME

STADIUM:
VOLKSPARKSTADION, 57,000

DOMESTIC HONORS:
LEAGUE 6, CUP 3

INTERNATIONAL HONORS:
EUROPEAN CUP 1983; CUP
WINNERS' CUP 1977;
INTERTOTO CUP 2005, 2007

HAMBURGER SV

Uniquely among German clubs, Hamburger's biggest shareholders are the fans, whose representatives sit on the board of directors. However, fan power has yet to return the team to the heady days of the late 1970s and early 1980s, when the club won three league championships, the 1977 Cup Winners' Cup, and the 1983 European Cup.

HAMBURGER TO THE CORE

Hamburger SV is personified by the graft of striker Uwe Seeler, who played 476 league games and scored 404 goals in a club career that spanned three decades. He turned down a lucrative move to Inter Milan in 1961 and went on to play for another 10 years then became club president after retiring.

SOMETIMES YOU LOSE ...
SOMETIMES THE OTHERS WIN

OTTO REHHAGEL
FORMER BAYERN MUNICH, KAISERSLAUTERN, AND GREECE MANAGER

THE RUHR DERBY

First played in 1925, games between the two Ruhr clubs, Schalke 04 and Borussia Dortmund, are known as the Revierderby or "District Derby" and attract the biggest crowds of any German league tie. In 2007, on the penultimate weekend of the Bundesliga, Dortmund won the derby and killed off Schalke's best chance to win a league title for almost 50 years.

MANUEL NEUER
Goalkeeper Manuel Neuer joined Bayern Munich from Schalke in 2011. He went on to win more than 20 major honors with the club.

CHAMPIONS LEAGUE WINS

- Bayern Munich – **75%**
- Hamburg – **12.5%**
- Borussia Dortmund – **12.5%**
- The rest—**0%**

12.5
12.5
75

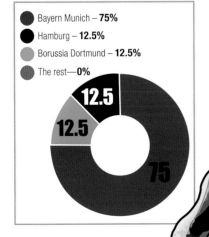

BEST OF THE REST

SCHALKE 04 (1904)
With a huge stadium in the tiny Ruhr town of Gelsenkirchen, Schalke is the worker's club and won four championships in the 1930s.
HONORS: LEAGUE 7, CUP 5; UEFA CUP 1997; INTERTOTO CUP 2003, 2004

BAYER LEVERKUSEN (1904)
Founded—and still funded—by the Bayer chemical company, Leverkusen has a reputation for choking in the big games.
HONORS: LEAGUE 0, CUP 1; UEFA CUP 1988

HERTHA BERLIN (1892)
Champions in the final years of the Weimar Republic, Hertha spent the Cold War at the Gesundbrune stadium, next to the Berlin Wall.
HONORS: LEAGUE 2, CUP 0; INTERTOTO CUP 1971, 1973, 1976, 1978, 2006

BORUSSIA MÖNCHENGLADBACH (1900)
A tiny team from the Ruhr, the club rose to prominence in the 1970s and contested five European finals, winning two of them.
HONORS: LEAGUE 5, CUP 3; UEFA CUP 1975, 1979

WERDER BREMEN (1899)
One of Germany's oldest clubs, Bremen was one of the leading clubs in the 1980s and '90s, winning the Cup Winners' Cup in 1992.
HONORS: LEAGUE 4, CUP 6; CUP WINNERS' CUP 1992; INTERTOTO CUP 1998

FC NÜRNBERG (1900)
The first great German soccer club, Nürnberg ruled the 1920s and won titles in every decade up to the 1960s but then won nothing until the DFB-Pokal (see p.187) in 2007.
HONORS: LEAGUE 9, CUP 4

VFB STUTTGART (1893)
Five-time champions Stuttgart is backed by the huge combined powers of local politicians and the German car industry.
HONORS: LEAGUE 5, CUP 3; INTERTOTO CUP 2000, 2002, 2008

HOME

AWAY

POPULATION: 8.7 MILLION
CAPITAL: VIENNA
FA: ÖSTERREICHISCHER FUßBALL-BUND
LICENSED PLAYERS:
MALE: 912,600
FEMALE: 55,500
PROFESSIONALS: 900
REGISTERED CLUBS: 2,200

AUSTRIA

The roots of Austrian soccer lie in a match between the Vienna Cricket Club and a team of Scottish gardeners from the Rothschilds' estate in 1894. Soccer in Austria never looked back, and the two teams became Wiener Amateur and First Vienna. The national team attracted gates of 60,000 by the 1920s and reached a peak with the "Wunderteam" that achieved a record run of 14 unbeaten games during the early 1930s. Vienna's unique soccer culture withered with the Nazi Anschluss (1938).

DOMESTIC STRIFE

The road to establishing a truly domestic game in Austria was marked by turbulence. Teams from Vienna played separately from those in the provinces until 1938, when the Austrian game was absorbed into German soccer. Rapid Vienna went on to win the German title in 1941, while Austria Wien won the German Cup in 1943. A truly national Austrian league—now known as the Bundesliga—has run only since 1949. The Austrian Cup is a minor affair and even disappeared from the fixture list for most of the 1950s.

THE TANK

Josef Uridil was the first star of Austrian soccer. A huge, marauding forward affectionately nicknamed "The Tank," he played for Rapid Vienna in the early 1920s. His popularity was marked by a fox-trot, "Uridil Will Play Today," and his face was used to sell soap, underwear, and chocolates.

STAT ATTACK

NATIONAL TEAM

NICKNAME: Das Team, Wunderteam (1930s)
NATIONAL STADIUM: Ernst Happel Stadion, Vienna, 51,428
WORLD CUP FINALS: 7 appearances, 3rd place, **1954**
EUROPEAN CHAMPIONSHIPS: 3 appearances, **2008, 2016, 2020**
BIGGEST WIN: 9–0 vs. Malta, 1977
BIGGEST DEFEAT: 1–11 vs. England, 1908
MOST CAPS: Marko Arnautovic, **104**
MOST GOALS: Anton Polster, **44**

MAIN DOMESTIC CLUBS

SK RAPID WIEN
FOUNDED: Vienna, 1899
STADIUM: Allianz Stadion
CAPACITY: 28,345
INTERNATIONAL HONORS: Intertoto Cup 1992, 1993
LEAGUE: 32 **CUP:** 14

HOME

FK AUSTRIA WIEN
FOUNDED: Vienna, 1911
STADIUM: Horr Stadion
CAPACITY: 17,565
INTERNATIONAL HONORS: Cup Winners' Cup runner-up **1978**
LEAGUE: 24 **CUP:** 27

HOME

SK STURM GRAZ
FOUNDED: Graz 1909
STADIUM: UPC-Arena
CAPACITY: 15,400
INTERNATIONAL HONORS: Intertoto Cup **2008**
LEAGUE: 3 **CUP:** 4

HOME

MAN OF PAPER

Nicknamed "die Papierene," the man of paper, Matthias Sindelar was the greatest of a great generation of soccer players. Personifying the graceful, intelligent Viennese style, he was described as playing soccer like a grand master played chess. He refused to play for the newly "unified" German team after Austria's annexation by the Nazis.

HAKOAH CHAMPIONS

The first professional Austrian championship was held in 1925 and won by Hakoah ("strength" in Hebrew) Wien, the city's leading Jewish sports club. The team toured the US, playing in front of a crowd of 45,000 at the Polo Fields in New York. Most of the squad enjoyed the tour—and the pay—so much that they stayed in US soccer, and the team never won the league again. After 1938, the club was closed by Nazi Germany and expunged from their records.

DER WUNDERTEAM

The so-called "wonder team," coached by the brilliant Hugo Meisel, was the all-conquering Austrian side that played a mesmerizing passing game that captivated Europe. Between 1931 and 1934, it played 33 games, lost just three, and scored 101 goals. However, its decline was marked by losing to host Italy at the 1934 World Cup.

9 Number of goals Austria conceded in a European Championship qualifier against Spain in 1999

1941 Year in which Rapid Vienna won the German league title

12 Number of clubs in the Austrian Bundesliga

2005 The year Red Bull bought SV Austria Salzburg and rebranded it as Red Bull Salzburg. Major honors soon followed

6 Goals scored by the losing team in the 1924 Austrian Cup Final—the winners scored 8

SWITZERLAND

HOME

AWAY

POPULATION: 8.1 MILLION
CAPITAL: BERN
FA: SFV-ASF (SWISS FOOTBALL ASSOCIATION)
LICENSED PLAYERS:
MALE: 507,900
FEMALE: 63,800
PROFESSIONALS: 550
REGISTERED CLUBS: 1,500

Soccer came early to Switzerland, with Geneva Cricket Club playing the game in the 1860s. A league championship was first held in 1895, and Swiss players played for French and Italian teams for the next 20 years. Despite being the home of UEFA and FIFA, hosting the 1954 World Cup, and cohosting Euro 2008, Switzerland has won little internationally, but reached the last eight of Euro 2020.

STAT ATTACK

NATIONAL TEAM

NICKNAME: La Nati
NATIONAL STADIUM:
Stade de Suisse, Bern, 32,000
WORLD CUP FINALS: 11 appearances, quarterfinals **1934**, **1938**, **1954**
EUROPEAN CHAMPIONSHIPS:
5 appearances, quarter-finals 2020
BIGGEST WIN: 9–0 vs. Lithuania, 1924
BIGGEST DEFEAT: 0–9 vs. Hungary, 1911; vs. England, 1909
MOST CAPS: Heinz Hermann, **118**
MOST GOALS: Alexander Frei, **42**

FIXTURE FREEZE

The national league, known as the Super League, has been running since 1933. From 2023–2024, it will consist of 12 teams playing each other four times during a year-round 36-game season. During the winter, from the end of November to late February, fans must be content with watching an indoor league.

LATE STARTERS

FC Basel was founded in 1893 (its first captain, Joan Gamper, also founded Barcelona in 1899). It had to wait until 1953 for its first league title. In recent years, along with Young Boys, it has been the most successful Swiss soccer team and progressed to the last 16 of the Champions League in 2018.

MAIN DOMESTIC CLUBS

GRASSHOPPER CLUB
FOUNDED: Zurich, 1886
STADIUM: Letzigrund Stadion
CAPACITY: 26,104
INTERNATIONAL HONORS: None
LEAGUE: 27 **CUP:** 19
HOME

FC BASEL
FOUNDED: Basel, 1893
STADIUM: St. Jakob-Park
CAPACITY: 38,512
INTERNATIONAL HONORS: UEFA Europa League semifinals **2013**
LEAGUE: 20 **CUP:** 13
HOME

SERVETTE FC
FOUNDED: Geneva, 1890
STADIUM: Stade de Geneve
CAPACITY: 30,084
INTERNATIONAL HONORS: None
LEAGUE: 17 **CUP:** 7

HOME

HAKAN YAKIN

Attacking midfielder Hakan Yakin, along with his brother Murat, was a key player in the revival of Swiss soccer. Of Turkish descent, he became the public face of Switzerland's real ethnic mix.

BORN: FEBRUARY 22, 1977, BASEL, SWITZERLAND
HEIGHT: 5 FT 11 IN (1.8 M)
MAIN CLUBS: **AL-GHARAFA, GRASSHOPPERS, YOUNG BOYS BERN, LUCERNE, BASEL**
INTERNATIONAL CAPS: **87**

GOING, GOING, GONE

Three top clubs in Switzerland suffered deep financial problems as the 21st century began. FC Lugano and Lausanne Sports both dropped out of the top league before working their way back. Servette FC, with its 117-year history and 1999 championship win, also fell from grace due to financial woes.

SO MUCH FOR THE CLEAN SHEET

At the 2006 World Cup, Switzerland tied 0–0 with France and then beat South Korea and Togo 2–0 to progress to the second round. It then tied 0–0 with Ukraine and was beaten in a penalty shoot-out, making it the first team to be knocked out of the World Cup finals without conceding a single goal.

EUROPE

SPAIN

HOME

AWAY

POPULATION: 48.5 MILLION
CAPITAL: MADRID
LICENSED PLAYERS:
MALE: 629,000
FEMALE: 18,000
PROFESSIONALS: 1,300
REGISTERED CLUBS: 18,000

There is one word to describe the Spanish attitude to soccer—"passionate." At both domestic and national levels, the game is heavily influenced by regional identities and past political conflicts within the country. Games between Catalan and Castilian clubs are charged with historical significance, and the nation's ethnic and geographic diversity has produced a fascinating mix of playing styles.

CAUTION TO THE WIND

Prior to 2008, Spain had a reputation as the great underachievers of international soccer. Given the excellence of La Liga and the country's wealth of talent, its poor record was puzzling. Possible explanations included the fact that cautious play was simply not in the Spanish makeup. However, it then set the record straight in style, winning the 2008 and 2012 European Championships and the 2010 World Cup—an unprecedented hat trick.

IKER CASILLAS

Arguably Spain's greatest-ever goalkeeper, Casillas made his debut for the national team at the age of 19. He became the captain of the team in 2008 and led his side to its historic World Cup win in 2010 and UEFA Euro wins in both 2008 and 2012.

BORN: **MAY 20, 1981, MOSTÓLES, SPAIN**
HEIGHT: **6 FT 1 IN (1.81 M)**
MAIN CLUBS: **REAL MADRID, PORTO**
INTERNATIONAL CAPS: **167**

LUIS SUÁREZ

Often described as Spain's greatest-ever player, Barcelona midfielder Luis Suárez became the only Spanish-born player to be voted European Soccer Player of the Year, winning the award in 1960.

REGIONAL TEAMS

Spain is made up of several autonomous regions, three of which field teams of their own. The Catalonian, Basque, and Galician XIs play only friendly games, and their star players also turn out for Spain, but they still have fervent followings in their home provinces. The Catalonian team regularly attracts crowds of 60,000-plus and, in recent years, has played teams as illustrious as Argentina and Brazil. FIFA and UEFA have so far resisted requests to grant them full international status.

69 Percentage of Spanish fans who perform superstitious rituals to help their teams win

14 La Liga titles won by Real Madrid from 1961 to 1980

99,354 Capacity of Barcelona's Nou Camp stadium, the largest soccer stadium in Europe

STAT ATTACK

GOVERNING BODY:
Real Federación Española de Fútbol
FOUNDED: 1913
NATIONAL STADIUM: None
FIRST MATCH: 1–0 vs. Denmark, 1920
BIGGEST WIN: 13–0 vs. Bulgaria, 1933
BIGGEST DEFEAT: 1–7 vs. Italy, 1928, vs. England, 1931

THE LEGENDS

MOST CAPPED PLAYERS

Name	From/To	Caps
Sergio RAMOS	2005–present	180
Iker CASILLAS	2000–2016	167
Xavi HERNÁNDEZ	2000–2014	133
Andrés INIESTA	2006–2018	131
Andoni ZUBIZARRETA	1985–1998	126
David SILVA	2006–2018	125

TOP GOAL SCORERS

Name	From/To	Goals
David VILLA	2005–2017	59
RAÚL	1996–2006	44
Fernando TORRES	2003–2014	38
David SILVA	2006–2018	35
Fernando HIERRO	1989–2002	29
Fernando MORIENTES	1998–2007	27

STAT ATTACK

LA LIGA PRIMERA

LEAGUE STRUCTURE: 20 clubs
TOP SCORER: Lionel Messi, **474**
MOST SUCCESSFUL TEAM: Real Madrid,
35 League titles
BIGGEST WIN: 12–1 Athletic Bilbao vs.
Barcelona, **1931**
HIGHEST ATTENDANCE: 125,000
(maximum past capacity of Real Madrid's
Bernabeu Stadium)
DIVISIONS BELOW LA LIGA PRIMERA:
Segunda A—**22**, Segunda B—**80** (four
groups of 20), Tercera—**360** (18 groups of 20)

COPA DEL REY

First played in 1902 as the Copa del
Ayuntamiento de Madrid, the Copa del Rey
is a limited-entry knockout contest.
HIGHEST SCORING FINAL:
6–2 Sevilla vs. Rácing Ferrol, 1939
MOST SUCCESSFUL TEAM: Barcelona,
31 wins
BIGGEST FINAL WIN: 6–1 Real Madrid vs.
Castilla CF, **1980**

LA LIGA

La Liga is the name for the professional soccer leagues in Spain. There
are two divisions—the Primera and the Segunda. The idea of a national
professional league was proposed in 1927, and the first games were played
in 1928 with just 10 teams. Three of the founding teams—Real Madrid,
Barcelona, and Athletic Bilbao—have never been relegated from the Primera.

LA LIGA TITLE WINS

- Real Madrid—**38%**
- Others—**33%**
- Barcelona—**29%**

WHEN I STRUCK IT, IT JUST HAD ... TO GO IN

ANDRÉS INIESTA
ON HIS 2010 WORLD CUP–WINNING GOAL FOR SPAIN

COPA DEL REY

Known as the Copa de España during the Second Republic (1930s)
and the Copa del Generalísimo during the Franco dictatorship (1939–1975),
the Copa del Rey is Spain's main domestic knockout competition. All the
Primera Division and Segunda A clubs take part plus around 23 from
Segunda B. They are joined by the champions of the Tercera Division, or
the runner-up if the champions are the reserve team of a bigger club.

EL PICHICHI

Every year since 1953, the Spanish newspaper *La Marca*
has awarded the Trofeo Pichichi ("Pichichi Trophy") to
the top scorer in La Liga. It is named after the diminutive
Athletic Bilbao striker Rafael Moreno Aranzadi, who
was known as "Pichichi" and scored 170 goals in 200
matches before dying of typhus in 1922, aged just 29.

DAVID VILLA
Outstanding striker David
Villa is Spain's all-time
leading goal scorer, with 59
goals in 98 appearances.

WORLD CUP

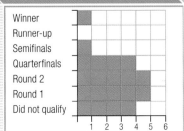

EURO CHAMPIONSHIPS

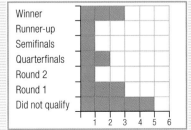

EUROPE

SPAIN'S BIG TWO

Considering the wealth and success of Real Madrid and Barcelona, La Liga is remarkably competitive—five other clubs have won the title since 1980. The Copa del Rey is even less predictable, and the Big Two do not dominate. The game in Spain has a strong regional character, with the Basque, Catalan, and Galician clubs liking nothing better than victory over the giants from the capital.

NICKNAME:
LOS BLANCOS
("THE WHITES")

HOME

FOUNDED:
MADRID, 1902

STADIUM:
SANTIAGO BERNABÉU, 81,044

DOMESTIC HONORS:
LEAGUE 35; CUP 19

INTERNATIONAL HONORS:
CHAMPIONS LEAGUE 1956–1960, 1966, 1998, 2000, 2002, 2014, 2016, 2017, 2018, 2022; UEFA CUP 1985, 1986; CLUB WORLD CUP 1960, 1998, 2002, 2014, 2016, 2017, 2018

REAL MADRID

Real Madrid consistently sits near the top of the global revenue table, and the team has won more La Liga titles and European Cups than any other team. Founded in 1902 as Madrid FC, the club was granted the use of the title Real ("royal") by King Alfonso XIII in 1920. Under Santiago Bernabéu (the club president 1945–1978), after whom its stadium is named, Real Madrid became the dominant force in Spain and Europe. The fans of Los Blancos expect their team not only to win but to win with style.

FIVE OUT OF FIVE

Santiago Bernabéu was one of the three men responsible for the creation of the European Cup, so the club's victory in the inaugural tournament in 1956 was singularly appropriate. With the first truly international team of players in soccer history, Real won the competition for the next four years, earning the right to keep the original trophy.

IT WANTS THE TEAM TO WIN FIRST ... THEN TO PLAY!

ALFREDO DI STEFANO
DESCRIBING THE MADRID CROWD

THE YE-YÉ GENERATION

When former captain Miguel Muñoz became manager in 1959, he ended the policy of buying foreign players. Seven years later, Real won the 1966 European Cup with an all-Spanish side, captained by Francisco Gento. With Beatlemania in full swing, the victors were christened the Ye-Yé team after the "Yeah yeah yeah" chorus of the band's hit "She Loves You."

ALFREDO DI STEFANO
Legendary Argentinian striker Alfredo di Stefano joined Real Madrid in 1953, winning eight La Liga titles and five European Cups and scoring 216 goals in his 11 years at the club.

THE GALÁCTICOS

Florentino Pérez, president of Real in 2000, followed up his election pledge of buying Luís Figo from archrivals Barcelona by building a team of Galácticos ("superstars"). Pérez resigned in 2006 but returned in 2009 to build a new generation of Galácticos including Kakà and Cristiano Ronaldo.

RAÚL

When Raúl González Blanco made his Real Madrid debut in 1994, he became the club's youngest ever player. A prolific striker, he went on to captain Real, making 550 appearances for Los Blancos and is one of the Champions League's all-time top scorers.

BORN: **JUNE 27, 1977, MADRID, SPAIN**
HEIGHT: **5 FT 11 IN (1.8 M)**
MAIN CLUBS: **REAL MADRID, SCHALKE 04**
INTERNATIONAL CAPS: **102**

NICKNAME:
BARÇA

FOUNDED:
BARCELONA, 1899

STADIUM:
NOU CAMP, 99,354

HOME

DOMESTIC HONORS:
LEAGUE 26; **CUP** 31

INTERNATIONAL HONORS:
CHAMPIONS LEAGUE 1992, 2006, 2009, 2011, 2015; **CWC** 1979, 1982, 1989, 1997; **FAIRS CUP** 1958, 1960, 1966; **CLUB WORLD CUP** 2009, 2011, 2015

FC BARCELONA

Founded in 1899 by a group of Swiss, English, and Spanish enthusiasts led by Swiss émigré Joan Gamper (also called Hans Gamper), Barcelona is a symbol of Catalonia, the semiautonomous Spanish province of which it is the capital. Barcelona (Barça) is co-owned by more than 150,000 fanatical members (known as the "socios"), and it plays at the biggest stadium in Europe, the 99,354-capacity Nou Camp. It is Spain's second most successful side, having won fewer La Liga titles but more Spanish Cups than its great rival Real Madrid.

A POETIC PERFORMANCE

Rafael Alberti, a member of the "Generation of '27" group of Spanish poets, was so impressed by Ferenc Platko's courage during the 1928 Copa del Rey Final that he wrote "Oda a Platko" as a tribute. The goalkeeper's outstanding performance secured Barcelona's victory, earning him legendary status.

"MÉS QUE UN CLUB"

The motto "more than a club" describes Barça's symbolism of the Catalan identity, which successive Spanish regimes tried to stamp out. Barça was a center of resistance to the Madrid government. In 1925, the Royal March was jeered at Barça's Les Corts stadium—as a result, the ground closed for three months, and the club's president, Joan Gamper, was forced to resign. With Francisco Franco in power, the Catalan flag and language were banned, but Barça's stadium remained one of the few places where Catalan was spoken openly.

THE DREAM TEAM

The team assembled under manager Johan Cruyff featured legends Gheorghe Hagi, Michael Laudrup, Hristo Stoichkov, and the Brazilian goal-machine Romário. Named after the US basketball team of the 1992 Olympics, it won four successive La Liga titles (1991–1994) and Barça's first European Cup (1992).

XAVI HERNÁNDEZ

A World Cup winner and double European champion with Spain, midfielder Xavi was one of the most gifted playmakers of his generation, with superb spacial awareness and an eye for a killer pass. He made 767 appearances in all competitions for Barcelona—a number beaten only by Lionel Messi (778).

BORN: JANUARY 25, 1980, TERRASSA, SPAIN
HEIGHT: 5 FT 7 IN (1.7 M)
MAIN CLUBS: **BARCELONA, AL SADD**
INTERNATIONAL CAPS: **133**

ROMÁRIO

In his first season at Barça, Romário won the La Liga title and the Pichichi, with 30 goals in 33 games. If friendly games are included, the tiny Brazilian's goal tally is well over 1,000.

EL CLÁSICO

Real Madrid and Barcelona embody the opposites of the character of Spain: capital versus provinces, conservative versus liberal, establishment versus the fringe. As a result, any clash between Real and Barça, known as *El Clásico*, is charged with meaning. It is one of the most-watched sporting events on earth.

EL CLÁSICO—WINS

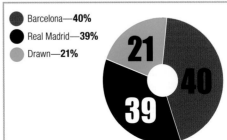

- Barcelona—**40%**
- Real Madrid—**39%**
- Drawn—**21%**

21
40
39

BRAGA STADIUM

New football stadiums can look functional rather than architecturally innovative, but there are standouts. For Euro 2004 (see p.334), Portugal built 10 new stadiums, and Braga's municipal arena was in a league of its own from an engineering angle. Carved out of a disused quarry, it is open at the goal ends, while its two stands form an elegant canyon. At one end, the stadium hugs the mountainous rock, while at the other end it is open. The roofs of the stands join over the pitch and are supported by a thin net of steel cables.

ESTÁDIO MUNICIPAL DE BRAGA

PARQUE NORTE,
DUME, 4710
BRAGA, PORTUGAL

OWNER:	MUNICIPALITY OF BRAGA
ARCHITECT:	EDUARDO SOUTO DE MOURA
OPENED:	DECEMBER 30, 2003
CONSTRUCTION COST:	$94 MILLION (€83.1 MILLION)
CAPACITY:	30,286

ONE STADIUM, THREE NAMES

In 2007, SC Braga agreed to a sponsorship deal with French insurance company AXA and began referring to the stadium as Estádio AXA. However, the Braga local government has not officially sanctioned the new name. Colloquially, it is known as simply "the quarry."

ROCK BLASTING

A huge amount of rock had to be blasted and removed to build the stadium. A construction cost of $94 million made it the third most expensive of the 10 new stadiums built for Euro 2004. Only the Estádio da Luz in Lisbon (capacity: 65,647) and Estádio do Dragão in Porto (capacity: 50,035) cost more.

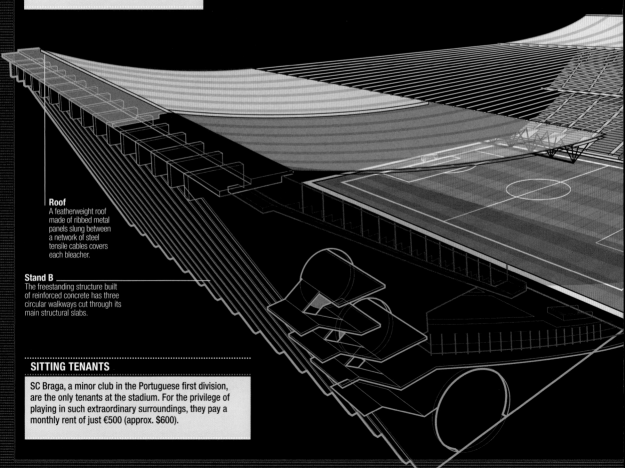

Roof
A featherweight roof made of ribbed metal panels slung between a network of steel tensile cables covers each bleacher.

Stand B
The freestanding structure built of reinforced concrete has three circular walkways cut through its main structural slabs.

SITTING TENANTS

SC Braga, a minor club in the Portuguese first division, are the only tenants at the stadium. For the privilege of playing in such extraordinary surroundings, they pay a monthly rent of just €500 (approx. $600).

THE SETTING

The stadium was carved out of a quarry called Monte do Castro, which overlooks the city of Braga. It is located to the north of the city and is intended to be the centerpiece of a broader development called Parque Urbano de Braga. The process of removing huge amounts of rock contributed to the total cost of the build. The results, however, were worth the expense—the stadium is often cited as one of the most beautiful in the world.

Exposed rock wall
The area behind one of the goals is exposed granite, which is studded by a series of steel pins to prevent landslides.

Bleachers
The bleachers are parallel with the sidelines, rather than behind the goals as is typical at more conventional grounds.

Wired for sound
The leading edges of each roof are supported by steel gantries that carry lighting and sound.

Entrances
The entrances to the stands are located in the bottom tier of the building.

The Plaza
Once inside the stadium, spectators move between stands via an under-field plaza 54,000 sq ft (5,000 sq m) in area.

Drainage
Water drains off the roof at two points and runs into freestanding concrete troughs mounted on the granite cliff face. Water runs down the hillside in a snaking open channel.

ACCORDING TO ME, SOCCER IS WATCHED
... LIKE THIS!

EDUARDO SOUTO DE MOURA, BRAGA'S ARCHITECT
MOVING HIS HAND FROM LEFT TO RIGHT AND BACK AGAIN

EURO 2004

Denmark beat Bulgaria 2–0 at Braga Stadium in the group stage of Euro 2004, although Denmark's coach, Morten Olsen, complained that his players couldn't see the goal properly. "Because of that mountain wall," he said, "players found it tough to distinguish the goalposts."

Stand A
The stand rests against the blasted rock wall. The entrances to the stand are positioned along the top tier of the building.

Cables
Dozens of steel strings are connected over the field, a design which, according to the architects, was inspired by ancient Inca bridges.

16 The number of vertical concrete slabs that form the spine of Stand A

500 The monthly rent, in euros ($600), paid by SC Braga to play at the stadium

730 The number of days it took to build the Braga stadium

0 The number of full houses SC Braga has attracted since taking occupation of the ground

EUROPE

SPAIN: THE CHASING PACK

While Real Madrid and Barcelona are easily the biggest teams in Spain, a whole pack of other clubs are snapping at their heels, making La Liga more unpredictable than many other big leagues. In recent years, Atlético Madrid, Deportivo la Coruña, and Valencia have topped the league, and consistent pressure, fueled by regional pride, has come from the leading teams of Andalucia (Betis and Sevilla) and the Basque country (Real Sociedad and Athletic Bilbao).

NICKNAME: LOS COLCHONEROS ("THE MATTRESS MAKERS")

HOME

FOUNDED: MADRID, 1903

STADIUM: WANDA METROPOLITANO, 68,000

DOMESTIC HONORS: LEAGUE 11; CUP 10

INTERNATIONAL HONORS: CUP WINNERS' CUP 1962; EUROPA LEAGUE 2010, 2012, 2018; INTERTOTO CUP 2007; UEFA SUPER CUP 2010, 2012, 2018; CLUB WORLD CUP 1974

ATLÉTICO MADRID

Founded by Basque students in 1903 as a branch of Athletic Bilbao, Atlético Madrid took off in 1939 after a merger with the Spanish Air Force team Aviaçion Nacional. Although Atlético has won 10 La Liga titles, it lives in the shadow of Real Madrid. Nevertheless, the club's followers emphasize that they, rather than their famous neighbors, are Madrid's authentic soccer fans.

JESÚS GIL

Property tycoon, ex-mayor of Marbella, and owner of Atlético Madrid, Gil was one of the most colorful and controversial characters in Spanish soccer. During his 16 years as club president, Gil hired and fired 23 managers, served time in jail for fraud, and outraged the soccer authorities with foul-mouthed verbal attacks. His greatest triumph came in 1996, when Atlético won the league and cup double. Gil upstaged his players at the celebratory parade by riding through the streets of Madrid on horseback. He died in 2004 aged 71.

FERNANDO TORRES

Deadly in front of goal, Torres originally wanted to be a goalkeeper. Thankfully he was persuaded otherwise, joining Atlético Madrid at the age of 11, where he was always a favorite. He then moved to Liverpool (and Chelsea) and scored the winning goal for Spain to lift the Euro 2008 title, before returning in 2015 for a second stint at Atlético Madrid before retiring.

VICTORY IN THE SHADOWS

For more than a decade, Atlético played in the shadow of Real Madrid, whose dominance included five European Cups. Even when Atlético won the 1962 Cup Winners' Cup, hardly anyone noticed: it drew with Fiorentina in the final, and by the time the replay took place four months later, a new season had already started.

FIRING A COACH IS LIKE HAVING A BEER TO ME ... I CAN SACK 20 IN A YEAR, EVEN A HUNDRED IF I HAVE TO

JESÚS GIL
PRESIDENT OF ATLÉTICO MADRID, 1987–2003

NICKNAME:
LOS LEONES
("THE LIONS")
FOUNDED:
BILBAO, 1898
STADIUM: SAN MAMES, 53,289
DOMESTIC HONORS:
LEAGUE 8; CUP 23
INTERNATIONAL HONORS:
NONE

HOME

ATHLETIC BILBAO

The most important Basque team in Spain, Athletic Bilbao won two of the first three La Liga titles and went on to win six more. Famed for bringing youth players through the ranks, the club also has a policy of signing only players with a Basque connection. Success at the club was largely achieved under manager Javier Clemente, whose tough tackling teams of the 1980s became feared. However, success has recently been hard to find, despite Clemente returning to the club for two further spells in charge.

THROWN TO THE LIONS

Athletic Bilbao's stadium is named after St. Mames, an early Christian who was thrown to the lions in the Colosseum in Rome, but the lions refused to eat him—thus, the team's nickname "the lions" and the stadium's nickname "the cathedral."

ANDONI GOIKOETXEA

Goikoetxea (pronounced "goykochea") was one of the fiercest tacklers of all time. Although he had a distinguished international career, he is notorious for breaking Diego Maradona's ankle in 1983.

BORN: **MAY 23, 1956, ALONSOTEGI, SPAIN**
HEIGHT: **6 FT 1 IN (1.85 M)**
MAIN CLUBS: **ATHLETIC BILBAO, ATLÉTICO MADRID**
INTERNATIONAL CAPS: **39**

NICKNAME:
LOS CHES
("THE LADS")
FOUNDED:
VALENCIA, 1919
STADIUM: MESTALLA, 55,000
DOMESTIC HONORS:
LEAGUE 6; CUP 8
INTERNATIONAL HONORS:
CWC 1980; INTERTOTO CUP
1998; UEFA CUP
1962, 1963,
2004

HOME

VALENCIA

Fourth in the all-time La Liga table, Valencia have won a host of European trophies. The 1980s and 1990s were relatively lean times at the Mestalla Stadium, but the club made up for them in the early years of the 21st century, appearing in consecutive Champions League finals under the Argentinean manager Héctor Cúper (2000 and 2001) and winning the UEFA Cup and two La Liga titles under his successor Rafa Benítez.

ECCENTRIC SUPPORT

Valencia is also home to Manuel Cáceres Artesero, better known as Manolo el del Bombo. This infamous, rotund, drum-beating fan sports a distinctive beret, attends every game played by the Spanish national team, and is also a passionate Valencia supporter. He has a bar near the Mestalla Stadium.

MARIO KEMPES

Although best remembered for his winning goal in the 1978 World Cup Final, Kempes played some of his best soccer at Valencia, 1977–1981. While there he scored an amazing 95 goals in 143 games and was the top scorer in the league two years running.

BEST OF THE REST

ESPANYOL (1900)
Barcelona's second team, Espanyol was one of the 10 original teams to be included in the first La Liga in 1928 but has never won the league title.
HONORS: CUP 4

SEVILLA (1905)
Although founded by British miners in 1905, Sevilla is wholly Spanish. It won the Copa del Rey in 2007, the first domestic trophy in 60 years, and six Europa League crowns.
HONORS: LEAGUE 1, CUP 5

DEPORTIVO LA CORUÑA (1906)
A force in the early 2000s, Deportivo won La Liga in 2000 and finished runner-up in both successive seasons.
HONORS: LEAGUE 1, CUP 2; INTERTOTO CUP 2008

REAL SOCIEDAD (1909)
Based in the northern city of San Sebastián, Real Sociedad won consecutive league titles in 1981 and '82. It dropped a Basque-only policy in 1989, unlike rival Athletic Bilbao.
HONORS: LEAGUE 2, CUP 3

VILLARREAL (1923)
With a population of just 48,000, Villarreal is a surprise success story. Promoted to La Liga in 1998, the club came third in 2005 and beat Barcelona to second place in 2008.
HONORS: EUROPA LEAGUE 1

REAL BETIS (1907)
The first Andalusian team to play in La Liga, Seville's "other" team won the league title in 1935 and the Copa del Rey in 1997 and 2005. It has also played in the UEFA Cup.
HONORS: LEAGUE 1, CUP 3

REAL ZARAGOZA (1932)
Cup specialists Zaragoza finished runner-up in La Liga in 1975 but has since been relegated twice, most recently in 2008.
HONORS: CUP 6, CUP WINNERS' CUP 1 UEFA CUP 1

PORTUGAL

HOME

AWAY

POPULATION: 10.8 MILLION
CAPITAL: LISBON
LICENSED PLAYERS:
MALE: 489,000
FEMALE: 59,000
PROFESSIONALS: 1,500
REGISTERED CLUBS: 2,500

Portugal's intimate connections with Britain led to soccer being played there as early as the 1860s. The game really took off in the early 20th century, but it was not until the 1960s that Portugal developed into an international power. After a long fallow period, the 21st century has seen the nation win the European Championships, its clubs win in Europe, and a host of gifted players emerge.

FOOTBALL, FADO, FATIMA

During its long dictatorship (1932–1974), "Football, Fatima, and Fado" was commonly heard in Portugal. Football (soccer), which was permitted after a defeat to Spain in 1933, the Catholic cult of Fatima, and the melancholy Fado style of music combined to distract the people from politics.

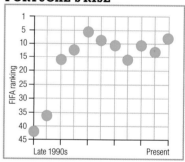

CRISTIANO RONALDO
Portugal's dribbling magician, Cristiano Ronaldo has become one of the world's leading players, winning the Ballon d'Or on multiple occasions.

THE GOLDEN GENERATIONS

Portugal won the FIFA World Youth Cup twice in the space of three years (1989 and 1991). The victorious team—including Luís Figo, Nuno Gomes, Rui Costa, Sérgio Conceição, Fernando Couto, Vítor Baía, and Jorge Costa—was dubbed the "golden generation" by the Portuguese press. While each of the players went on to have successful club careers, the success Portugal expected (semifinalists at the 2006 World Cup and winners of Euro 2016) came only after the emergence of a second golden generation, including Deco, Cristiano Ronaldo, and Ricardo Carvalho.

THE PORTUGUESE PREVAIL

Portugal won an unexpected victory over host France in the Euro 2016 Championship. Starting the match as underdogs, Portugal's chances of victory seemed even more remote when captain Cristiano Ronaldo was stretchered off in the first half. However, Portugal managed to thwart France's attempts to break the deadlock, and forward Eder Lopes, who came in as a substitute, eventually settled the game in the 109th minute, sealing Portugal's first-ever triumph in a major tournament.

PORTUGAL'S RISE

FIFA ranking chart, y-axis: 1, 5, 10, 15, 20, 25, 30, 35, 40, 45; x-axis: Late 1990s to Present

THERE'S NOT ENOUGH BUM
FOR TWO CHAIRS

BÉLA GUTTMAN, BENFICA COACH
ON WHY THE CLUB COULD NOT WIN THE EUROPEAN CUP
AND PORTUGUESE TITLE IN THE SAME SEASON

STAT ATTACK

GOVERNING BODY:
Federação Portuguesa de Futebol
FOUNDED: 1914
NATIONAL STADIUM: None
FIRST MATCH: 1–3 vs. Spain, 1923
BIGGEST WIN: 8–0 vs. Lichtenstein, 1994, and vs. Kuwait, 2003
BIGGEST DEFEAT: 0–10 vs. England, 1947

THE LEGENDS

MOST CAPPED PLAYERS

Name	From/To	Caps
Cristiano RONALDO	2003–present	196
João MOUTINHO	2005–present	146
PEPE	2007–present	129
Luís FIGO	1991–2006	127
NANI	2006–2017	112
Fernando COUTO	1990–2004	110

TOP GOAL SCORERS

Name	From/To	Goals
Cristiano RONALDO	2003–present	118
PAULETA	1997–2006	47
EUSÉBIO	1961–1973	41
Luís FIGO	1991–2006	32
Nuno GOMES	1996–2011	29
Hélder POSTIGA	2003–2014	27

LIGA

Founded in 1935 as a national professional league, the top division replaced regional tournaments and a knockout competition that formerly decided the national title. It was renamed the Primeira Liga in 1999. Only five clubs have ever won the title, and the big three—Benfica, Sporting Lisbon, and Porto—account for 85 of the 88 title wins since the league's foundation.

CUP COMPETITIONS

Portugal has two major cup competitions. The Taça de Portugal ("Cup of Portugal") is a knockout contest with amateur teams contesting the first three rounds before the top-flight teams join in. The final is held close to the National Day, June 10. The Taça da Liga ("League Cup") is a more limited knockout contest that was played for the first time in 2007. Entry is confined to clubs in Portugal's top two divisions.

RUI COSTA
Attacking midfielder Rui Costa was an outstanding player in Portugal's first golden generation.

OPERATION GOLDEN WHISTLE

At the end of the 2004 season, the Portuguese police arrested and interviewed more than 60 players, referees, and club presidents—including the president of the Primeira Liga—over allegations of match fixing. No cases were brought to trial.

STAT ATTACK

LIGA

LEAGUE STRUCTURE: 18 teams
TOP SCORER: Fernando Peyroteo, **330** goals
MOST WINS: Benfica, **36** titles
BIGGEST WIN: 14–0, Sporting Lisbon vs. Leça, 1941–1942
HIGHEST ATTENDANCE: 135,000 Benfica vs. Porto, 1987
DIVISIONS BELOW PRIMEIRA LIGA: Liga Pro (**20** teams)

TACA DE PORTUGAL

The eight-round cup is open to all four national divisions as well as nonleague champions.

MOST WINS: Benfica, **26** wins
MOST FINAL DEFEATS: Porto, **14** losses
BIGGEST WIN: 8–0, Benfica vs. GD Estoril-Praia, 1944

LUÍS FIGO

An incredibly skillful winger, Figo was one of the true greats, but he was also no stranger to controversy. His record-breaking $76 million transfer in 2000 from Barcelona to archrival Real Madrid was a source of great ire among the Catalan fans.

BORN: **NOVEMBER 4, 1972, ALMADA, PORTUGAL**
HEIGHT: **5 FT 11 IN (1.8 M)**
MAIN CLUBS: **BARCELONA, REAL MADRID, INTER MILAN**
INTERNATIONAL CAPS: **127**

5 The number of titles Porto won in a row, between 1995–1999

715 The number of games Eusébio played for Benfica

1875 The year the first club in Portugal—Lisbon FC—was founded

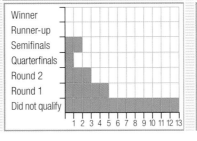

WORLD CUP

	1	2	3	4	5	6	7	8	9	10	11	12	13
Winner													
Runner-up													
Semifinals	■	■											
Quarterfinals			■										
Round 2				■									
Round 1					■								
Did not qualify						■	■	■	■	■	■	■	■

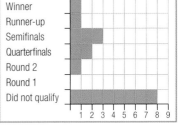

EURO CHAMPIONSHIPS

	1	2	3	4	5	6	7	8	9
Winner									
Runner-up	■								
Semifinals		■	■						
Quarterfinals				■					
Round 2									
Round 1									
Did not qualify					■	■	■	■	■

EUROPE

PORTUGUESE CLUBS

Portuguese soccer has been dominated by just three clubs since it turned professional in the 1930s—Benfica and Sporting, both from the capital city Lisbon, and Porto, from the great northern city of the same name. The rivalry between Porto and Benfica dramatizes the national divisions between north and south, contrasting the second city with the hedonistic capital.

NICKNAME:
O GLORIOS
("THE GLORIOUS")

HOME

FOUNDED:
LISBON, 1904

STADIUM:
ESTÁDIO DA LUZ, 64,642

DOMESTIC HONORS:
LEAGUE 37, CUP 26

INTERNATIONAL HONORS:
EUROPEAN CUP 1961, 1962

BENFICA

The best-resourced and best-supported club in Portugal, Benfica was founded by nationalists who stipulated a ban on foreign players. The club rose to prominence after overturning the ban in the 1960s, signing the Mozambique striker Eusébio, who helped it win two European Cups. Mismanagement in the 1990s led to a barren period that finally ended with the Primeira Liga title in 2005.

THE GOLDEN ERA

Benfica's golden era began when club president De Brito lured Hungarian coach Béla Guttman away from Porto in 1959. Guttman brought a level of professional organization and tactical sophistication that were new to the club. His squad came of age in 1961 when they won the league and beat Barcelona to win the European Cup, having scored three goals a game in the first four rounds. Eusébio signed the following year, and a league and European Cup double followed.

EUSÉBIO

One of the finest center forwards the game has ever seen, Eusébio's strike rate was phenomenal. In 15 years at Benfica, he scored 317 goals in 301 appearances.

BORN: JANUARY 25, 1942, LOURENÇO MARQUES, MOZAMBIQUE
HEIGHT: 5 FT 9½ IN (1.77 M)
MAIN CLUBS: SPORTING LOURENÇO MARQUES, BENFICA
INTERNATIONAL CAPS: 64

NICKNAME:
LEOES ("LIONS")

FOUNDED:
LISBON, 1906

HOME

STADIUM:
ESTÁDIO JOSÉ ALVALADE, 50,095

DOMESTIC HONORS:
LEAGUE 19, CUP 17

INTERNATIONAL HONORS:
CUP WINNERS' CUP 1964

SPORTING LISBON

Sporting was founded in 1906 by disenchanted members of Benfica with the assistance of the Viscount of Alvalade, who gave land for the team's first ground and after whom the club's current stadium, which was built in 1954 and redeveloped in 2004, is named. The 1930s and 1960s—which brought a European Cup Winners' Cup win and three Liga titles—were Sporting's glory days, but despite a focus on nurturing new talent, the club remains the poorer of Portugal's big three clubs.

BY PRESIDENTIAL DECREE

Under coach Bobby Robson, Sporting reached the top of the league at Christmas 1993 and stood an excellent chance of winning the title. New club president José de Sousa Cintra, drawing on his business experience as a mineral water millionaire, decided to fire the coach. Sporting lost the league, and Robson went to Porto. He had the last laugh when Porto beat his old club in the Portuguese Cup final in the same season.

PORTUGUESE LEAGUE WINS

- Benfica – **43%**
- Porto – **33%**
- Sporting Lisbon – **22%**
- The rest – **2%**

43   33   22   2

NICKNAME:
DRAGÕES ("DRAGONS")

HOME

FOUNDED:
PORTO, 1893

STADIUM:
ESTÁDIO DO DRAGÃO, 50,434

DOMESTIC HONORS:
LEAGUE 30, CUP 18

INTERNATIONAL HONORS:
CHAMPIONS LEAGUE 1987, 2004; **UEFA CUP** 2003; **EUROPA LEAGUE** 2011; **CLUB WORLD CUP** 1987, 2004

THE CHAMPIONS LEAGUE TROPHY, GOD, AND AFTER GOD ... ME

JOSÉ MOURINHO
ON HIS PRIORITIES AT PORTO

PORTO

Although Porto has always been a big club, it was only in the 1990s that the team rose to the top of Portuguese soccer. An unprecedented record since 1995—five consecutive titles (1995–1999) and five of six between 2003 and 2008—was capped by the club's first UEFA Cup win in 2003 and its second European Cup in 2004 under then-coach Mourinho.

POWER BEHIND PORTO

For most of the modern era, the power behind Porto has been chairman Jorge Nuno Pinto da Costa, a brilliant organizer and man of quiet maneuvers. Nicknamed Papa—"the Pope"—for his authoritarian infallibility, he was banned from holding office for two years after the 2007 Golden Whistle police investigation into soccer corruption.

PORTO VS. BENFICA

The derby between the big clubs of Portugal's major northern and southern cities, Porto and Lisbon, has eclipsed all other games in the fixture list. The Porto vs. Benfica game pits urban identities against each other that are economically and culturally at odds. Lisbon is the city of glamour and hedonism, while Porto is the city that gets up and goes to work. The characters of Benfica and Porto are close to these attributes.

JOSÉ MOURINHO
"The Special One" is one of the greatest managers in the modern game. Charismatic and controversial, Mourinho has proved to be as entertaining as his stylish teams.

BEST OF THE REST

BOAVISTA (1903)
Always Porto's second club, Boavista's stadium is packed into the inner-city neighborhood of Bessa. Founded by an Anglo-Portuguese textile firm, the club finally hit the big time in 2001, winning Primeira Liga.
HONORS: LEAGUE 1, CUP 5

OS BELENENSES (1919)
Tucked away in the upper-class Lisbon suburb of Restiro, Belenenses was the only club to break the Liga monopoly of Portugal's three big clubs in the 20th century, with a single title win in 1946.
HONORS: LEAGUE 1, CUP 3

MARITIMO (1910)
Founded by dockworkers in Funchal, Maritimo is the biggest team on the Portuguese Madeira islands. With strong foreign support, the team has fan clubs in Brazil, Angola, and Venezuela.
HONORS: LEAGUE 0, CUP 0

BRAGA (1921)
A club on the up, Braga acquired an amazing new stadium carved out of a mountainside for Euro 2004. The club won its first-ever European trophy in 2008, the Intertoto Cup.
HONORS: LEAGUE 0, CUP 3; INTERTOTO CUP 2008

VITORIA SETUBAL (1910)
After a decade of successes in the 1960s, Setubal sank low until the Cup win of 2004. Fans are known as the "Eighth Army" after their 1943 cup-final revelry as the British Eighth Army fought in the Mediterranean.
HONORS: LEAGUE 0, CUP 3

ACADEMICA DE COIMBRA (1876)
Founded by college students in Coimbra in 1876, Academica plays in an all-black uniform that mirrors the formal wear of the university scholars. The club won the Portuguese Cup in 1939 and 2012.
HONORS: LEAGUE 0, CUP 2

HOME   AWAY

POPULATION: 62 MILLION
CAPITAL: ROME
LICENSED PLAYERS:
MALE: 1.5 MILLION
FEMALE: 16,000
PROFESSIONALS: 3,500
REGISTERED CLUBS: 16,000

ITALY

Soccer plays a huge role in Italian life. Three national newspapers—*La Gazzetta dello Sport*, *Tuttosport*, and *Corriere dello Sport*—are devoted to the game, soccer shows rule the airwaves, and the game is a constant source of conversation. Fortunately, the nation's teams can justify the devotion. The Azzurri have won four World Cups—only Brazil has won more—and Italian clubs have won over 30 major European trophies.

ANCIENT ORIGINS

Although the modern game was invented in Britain, Italians claim that the violent medieval form, known as "calcio" in Italy, came from the Roman ball-sport Harpastum (see pp.14–15).

SAFETY FIRST

The first rule of Italian soccer is "do not concede a goal." Italian teams are typically cautious and defensive, aiming to hit opponents on the break. If they manage to get ahead, their default tactic is to put men behind the ball and "close up shop." At the same time, Italian players are known for their technical excellence. Skill and guile are highly valued, as exemplified by attacking players including Alessandro Del Piero and Roberto Baggio.

SLOW OUT OF THE BLOCKS

Despite its impressive reputation, Italy is a notoriously slow starter. It drew all its group matches on the way to World Cup victory in 1982, and reached the final in 1994 despite losing its opening game to Ireland. Meanwhile, every Italian knows the name Pak Doo-Ik, the North Korean dentist whose goal sent Italy out of the 1966 World Cup. That said, adversity can bring the best out of the side—Italy won the 1982 and 2006 World Cups and triumphed in the COVID-delayed 2020 European Championship.

SILVIO PIOLA
Famous for his overhead kicks, which he helped pioneer, Piola became the highest scorer in Serie A history and was the star of Italy's 1938 World Cup–winning team.

DINO **ZOFF**

Zoff once said, "If I hadn't been a goalkeeper, I would have used the hands God gave me to be a farm worker or mechanic." Instead, he developed into an unflappable goalkeeper with six Serie A titles and captained Italy to victory at the 1982 World Cup aged 40.

BORN: **FEBRUARY 28, 1942, MARIANO DEL FRIULI, ITALY**
HEIGHT: **6 FT (1.83 M)**
MAIN CLUBS: **UDINESE, MANTOVA, NAPOLI, JUVENTUS**
INTERNATIONAL CAPS: **112**

SOCCER IS NOT FOR BALLERINAS

CLAUDIO GENTILE, HARDMAN ITALIAN DEFENDER
AFTER SUBDUING MARADONA IN THE 1982 WORLD CUP

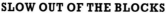

STAT ATTACK

NICKNAME: Azzurri ("Blues")
GOVERNING BODY:
Federazione Italiana Giuoco Calcio
FOUNDED: 1898
NATIONAL STADIUM: None
FIRST MATCH: 6–2 vs. France, 1910
BIGGEST WIN: 9–0 vs. USA, 1948
BIGGEST DEFEAT: 1–7 vs. Hungary, 1924

THE LEGENDS

MOST CAPPED PLAYERS

Name	From/To	Caps
Gianluigi BUFFON	1997–2018	176
Fabio CANNAVARO	1997–2010	136
Paolo MALDINI	1988–2002	126
Leonardo BONUCCI	2010–present	119
Daniele De ROSSI	2004–2017	117
Andrea PIRLO	2002–2015	116

TOP GOAL SCORERS

Name	From/To	Goals
Luigi RIVA	1965–1974	35
Giuseppe MEAZZA	1930–1939	33
Silvio PIOLA	1935–1952	30
Roberto BAGGIO	1988–2004	27
Alessandro DEL PIERO	1995–2008	27
Adolfo BALONCIERI	1920–1930	25

SERIE A

A national Italian soccer league was created from preexisting regional tournaments and national knockout competitions in 1929. The top division is known as Serie A and the second division as Serie B. The schedule for both leagues pits teams against their opponents once in the first half of the season—the "andata"—and then again in exactly the same order in the second half—"the ritorno"—but switching from home to away and vice versa. Internazionale is the only team to have played continuously in Serie A since its foundation.

PROMOTING THE ITALIAN CUP

The Coppa Italia is usually a low-key affair, with teams regularly fielding their reserve sides and with attendances sometimes half that of Serie A fixtures. In an attempt to raise the profile of the competition, the Italian FA has made a Europa League place available to the winner, and champions are allowed to sport a roundel on their shirt in the Italian tricolor. The two-leg final has been cut to one game, and a seeding system has been put in place.

FRANCO BARESI
"Il Capitano" spent his entire career at AC Milan, orchestrating play as sweeper. Baresi's timing and reading of the game were superlative.

STAT ATTACK

SERIE A

LEAGUE STRUCTURE: **20** teams
TOP SCORER: Silvio Piola, **274** goals
MOST WINS: Juventus, **36** titles
BIGGEST WIN: **10–0**, Torino vs. Alessandria, 1947–1948
HIGHEST ATTENDANCE: **89,365** Napoli vs. Perugia, 1979–1980
DIVISIONS BELOW SERIE A: Serie B (**22** teams), Lega Pro (3 divisions, **60** teams in total), Serie D

1949 Year in which Italy lost 10 first-team players in the Torino air disaster

44 Age at which Lazio goalkeeper Marco Ballotta made his last Serie A appearance, in 2008

6 Goals scored by Italy against France in its first international match, in 1910

2022 The year that Italy, the European champions, failed to reach the World Cup

COPPA ITALIA

Entry to the knockout Coppa Italia was restricted to the 42 Serie A and Serie B clubs from the 2007–2008 season onward.
MOST GOALS IN A SEASON: Gianluca Vialli, **13** goals, Sampdoria 1988–1989
MOST SUCCESSFUL TEAM: Juventus, **14** wins
BIGGEST WIN: **6–1** Sampdoria vs. Ancona, 2nd-leg tie, 1994

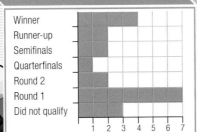

WORLD CUP — Winner, Runner-up, Semifinals, Quarterfinals, Round 2, Round 1, Did not qualify (1–7)

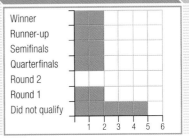

EURO CHAMPIONSHIPS — Winner, Runner-up, Semifinals, Quarterfinals, Round 2, Round 1, Did not qualify (1–6)

ITALY: JUVENTUS AND INTER

Italian domestic soccer is dominated by teams from the industrial North, with clubs from outside the region having won only eight Serie A titles (*scudetti*) by the end of the 2021–2022 season. Yet *calcio*, as the sport is called in Italy, is an obsession throughout the country. Despite having less money to spend now than in the 1990s, Italian clubs continue to attract a fair proportion of the world's top players.

NICKNAME:
LA VECCHIA SIGNORA ("THE OLD LADY")

HOME

FOUNDED:
TURIN, 1897

STADIUM:
JUVENTUS STADIUM, 41,507

DOMESTIC HONORS:
LEAGUE 36, CUP 14

INTERNATIONAL HONORS:
CHAMPIONS LEAGUE 1985, 1996; CUP WINNERS' CUP 1984; INTERTOTO CUP 1999; UEFA CUP 1977, 1990, 1993

JUVENTUS

Despite a name that means "youth" in Latin, Juventus (or Juve) is widely known as the *La Vecchia Signora* ("The Old Lady"). Some say that the nickname came about because the team's uniform recalls the black clothes and pale faces of the more elderly female members of Italian society. What's not in doubt is that Juventus is the most successful club in Italian soccer, with 36 *scudetti* and 14 Coppa Italias.

EUROPEAN MILESTONE

In 1985, a goal by Michel Platini gave Juventus a 1–0 victory over Liverpool in the final of the European Cup. It meant that the Italian club became the first team to win all three major European club competitions: the UEFA Cup, European Cup, and European Cup Winners' Cup.

THE TRAPATTONI ERA

Giovanni Trapattoni has had two spells as manager of Juventus. During the first, most successful one, between 1976 and 1986, the team won every major tournament for which it was eligible. Trapattoni built a primarily defensive outfit sprinkled with the creative talent of players like the Irishman Liam Brady and the French genius Michel Platini, who was European Player of the Year three times in succession (1983–1985).

THE GIRLFRIEND OF ITALY

While Juve is Italy's best-supported club, average home attendances are lower than those of most other top European teams. The reason is that the majority of the club's fans live elsewhere in Italy, particularly in the South, where local teams have traditionally been weaker and affection for Juventus has been acquired by workers who have migrated north to Turin. As a result of its widely distributed fan base, Juventus is sometimes called *La Fidanzata d'Italia* ("The Girlfriend of Italy").

THE DERBY OF ITALY

Prior to Juve's demotion to Serie B in 2006, the Turin club and Inter were the only teams never to have been relegated from the Italian top flight. Because of this and the fact that the clubs are ranked first and second in the all-time Serie A table, in 1967 a journalist coined the name "*Derby d'Italia*" for the intense meetings between the two giants.

ROBERTO **BAGGIO**

One of the few men to have played for each of the Italian Big Three (Juventus, AC Milan, and Inter), ponytailed Buddhist Roberto Baggio was for a time the best player in the world. Small and light, he had great technical ability.

BORN: FEBRUARY 18, 1967, CALDOGNO, ITALY
HEIGHT: 5 FT 9 IN (1.74 M)
MAIN CLUBS: **FIORENTINA, JUVENTUS, AC MILAN, BOLOGNA, INTER**
INTERNATIONAL CAPS: **56**

NICKNAME:
NERAZZURRI
("BLACK-BLUES")

FOUNDED:
MILAN, 1908

HOME

STADIUM:
SAN SIRO (GIUSEPPE MEAZZA),
80,018

DOMESTIC HONORS:
LEAGUE 19, CUP 8

INTERNATIONAL HONORS:
CHAMPIONS LEAGUE 1964, 1965,
2010; UEFA CUP 1991, 1994, 1998

INTERNAZIONALE

Inter (or, erroneously, Inter Milan) was formed in 1908 by members of the Milan Cricket and Soccer Club (the forerunner of AC Milan, see p.210) unhappy about its bias toward Italian players. The club has played in the top flight since its formation and tied with AC Milan on 19 titles each by the end of 2021–2022, although both lag behind Juventus.

LA GRANDE INTER

Helenio Herrera managed Inter from 1960 to 1968 and was given as much credit for his team's performances as the players. He dictated every aspect of his players' lives, from their diet to the air that they breathed (he made them inhale pure oxygen the night before games). Herrera's Inter players were defensive, ultra-fit, and ruthless. They were also more successful than at any other period in the club's history, winning three Serie A titles and two European Cups in four years. Under José Mourinho, they won the European Cup again in 2010.

CHRISTIAN VIERI

A powerful, old-fashioned striker, Vieri was one of the few players to have represented each of the principal Milan and Turin teams. He joined Inter in 1999 for a then-world-record fee of $46.5 million and scored 103 goals in 144 league matches for the *Nerazzurri*.

THE TWO MILANS

So close is their rivalry that, by 2008, Inter and AC Milan had scored and conceded exactly the same number of goals (270) against each other in the three main competitions. In Serie A, Inter won the title in 2021, followed by AC Milan in 2022.

HERRERA WAS THE FIRST MODERN MANAGER ... A SUPERSTAR

JOHN FOOT
AUTHOR OF *CALCIO: A HISTORY OF ITALIAN FOOTBALL*

MILANESE GROUND-SHARE

Inter and AC Milan share the 80,018-seat San Siro stadium, or the Stadio Giuseppe Meazza as it is officially called. Traditionally, AC Milan is the team of the working class, with a large contingent of southern Italian fans, while Inter supporters are more likely to be middle class and local. Two of the most eagerly contested games in the Italian soccer calendar occur when the Milan teams play the *Derby della Madonnina*, named after the statue of the Virgin Mary on top of the city's cathedral.

AVERAGE ATTENDANCES 2018–2019

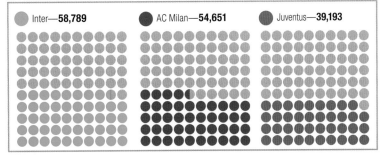

Inter—**58,789**   AC Milan—**54,651**   Juventus—**39,193**

AC MILAN VS. LIVERPOOL

"Make us dream," a banner at Anfield had pleaded during the knockout stages of the 2005 Champions League, as Liverpool fought its way to its first final of Europe's biggest club tournament in 20 years. The Reds certainly obliged in Istanbul. In the first half, AC Milan—the favorites, appearing in its second final in three years and 10th overall—was utterly dominant and raced into a three-goal lead. But then Liverpool came back to equalize in six dazzling second-half minutes. Both teams probed for a winning goal in overtime, but ultimately it took a penalty shoot-out to decide a winner.

AC MILAN 3 (PEN 2)	LIVERPOOL 3 (PEN 3)
FORMATION: 5-3-2	FORMATION: 5-3-2
MANAGER: CARLO ANCELOTTI	MANAGER: RAFAEL BENITEZ
ATATÜRK STADIUM, ISTANBUL, TURKEY MAY 25, 2005	
ATTENDANCE: 70,024	
REFEREE: MEJUTO GONZÁLEZ (SPAIN)	

1 Dudek
2 Finnan   5 Carragher   16 Alonso   14 Hyypiä   6 Traoré
4 Luis García   17 Gerrard   18 Riise
10 Baroš   20 Kewell
11 Crespo   10 Kaká   16 Shevchenko
14 Seedorf   7 Gattuso
2 Maldini   5 Nesta   12 Pirlo   9 Stam   19 Cafu
1 Dida

SUBS: 21 Serginho   21 Rui Costa   21 Tomasson   11 Hamann   19 Smicer   19 Cissé

1 M Liverpool starts nervously and is immediately punished. Djimi Traoré gives away a needless free kick on Liverpool's left-hand side, and defender Paolo Maldini volleys home Andrea Pirlo's angled cross: 1–0.

38 M Andriy Shevchenko and Hernán Crespo combine in the area to give AC Milan what already appears to be an unassailable lead, 2–0. AC Milan, as a British commentator states, is now playing soccer out of this world.

43 M Kaká plays an exquisite defense-splitting pass to Crespo, who flicks it over Jerzy Dudek and into the net: 3–0. For Liverpool, the cause seems hopeless.

45 M During the interval, the Liverpool fans sing the club anthem—"You'll Never Walk Alone"—in a way they had never done before. When the teams re-emerge, the AC Milan players are nonplussed, their opponents inspired.

54 M Liverpool's efforts are rewarded when Steven Gerrard jumps to head home a cross from John Arne Riise: 3–1. The captain windmills his arms as a signal to the Liverpool fans to turn up the volume. Hope is back in their hearts.

56 M While Kaká ties up his boot laces, perhaps unaware that Liverpool has not yet given up, the ball is played to Vladimír Šmicer on the edge of the Italian's penalty area. The Czech midfielder, playing his last match for the Reds, fires home from 20 yards: 3–2.

60 M Gerrard bursts into the box with unstoppable momentum, and Gennaro Gattuso clips his ankles. The referee awards a penalty. Dida saves Xabi Alonso's first effort, but the Liverpool player scores on the rebound and is buried under a pile of delirious teammates: 3–3.

FT* When Gerrard hoists the Cup, the predominant feeling among Liverpool fans is blissful relief. Their club is back at the top table, European champions for the fifth time.

120+ M Before the shoot-out, Jamie Carragher encourages Dudek to repeat Bruce Grobbelaar's antics at the 1984 Final, when the keeper had put off the Roma penalty takers by wobbling his legs. Serginho blasts the first penalty over the bar. Shevchenko steps up to take Milan's fifth penalty knowing that a miss will mean defeat; his nerves are shot, and the Pole denies him. The "Miracle of Istanbul" is complete.

*Full-time

ITALY: AC MILAN AND ROMA

The Juventus–Inter fixture may be known as The Derby of Italy, but from an international perspective, the nation's most important club is the last member of Italy's Big Three, AC Milan. Between them, the trio have won more than 60 percent of the *scudetti* contested to date. However, Italian soccer is much more than a three-horse race—several other teams, including the two principal clubs from Rome, have also risen to the top.

AC MILAN

The Rossoneri ("red-blacks") lag behind Juventus in *scudetto* wins, but in the sphere of international club competitions they are the undisputed aristocrats of Italian soccer. Only Real Madrid surpass AC Milan's haul of seven Champions League titles. The club has also won the Club World Cup a record four times.

HOME

NICKNAME:
ROSSONERI
("RED-BLACKS")

FOUNDED:
MILAN, 1899

STADIUM:
SAN SIRO (GIUSEPPE MEAZZA), 80,018

DOMESTIC HONORS:
LEAGUE 19; CUP 5

INTERNATIONAL HONORS:
CHAMPIONS LEAGUE 1963, 1969, 1989, 1990, 1994, 2003, 2007; CLUB WORLD CUP 1969, 1989, 1990, 2007; CUP WINNERS' CUP 1968, 1973

SILVIO BERLUSCONI

After billionaire media tycoon Silvio Berlusconi purchased AC Milan in 1986, he went on to become the Prime Minister of Italy four times, and the club secured seven Serie A titles and five Champions League titles. When he needed a name for his new political party in 1993, Berlusconi adapted the words of a Milan chant and came up with "Forza Italia." The club is now owned by a Chinese-led consortium.

GOING DUTCH

The best of several great Milan sides was assembled by manager Arrigo Sacchi (1987–1991) and built on by his successor Fabio Capello (1991–1996). At the heart of the team was a trio of top Dutch players: all-arounder Ruud Gullit, holding midfielder Frank Rijkaard, and striker Marco van Basten. While they were at the club, Milan won two European Cups and three *scudetti*.

PAOLO **MALDINI**

An elegant and reliable defender, Paolo Maldini made his debut for Milan as a 16-year-old and played regularly for the club until the age of 40. He appeared more than 1,000 times for Milan and Italy combined and competed in eight Champions League finals.

BORN: **JUNE 26, 1968, MILAN, ITALY**
HEIGHT: **6 FT 1 IN (1.86 M)**
MAIN CLUBS: **AC MILAN**
INTERNATIONAL CAPS: **126**

EUROPEAN TITLE WINS

- AC Milan—**14**
- Juventus—**9**
- Inter—**6**

6

9

14

NICKNAME:
GIALLOROSSI
("YELLOW-REDS")

HOME

FOUNDED:
ROME, 1927

STADIUM:
STADIO OLIMPICO, 70,634

DOMESTIC HONORS:
LEAGUE 3; **CUP** 9

INTERNATIONAL HONORS:
UEFA CUP 1961

ROMA

The Giallorossi ("yellow-reds") have occasionally been good enough to break the stranglehold that Juventus and the two Milan teams have had on the title. The last time Roma did it (in 2002), the cost of mounting the challenge almost bankrupted the club. Roma, who share the Stadio Olimpico with Lazio, hold Francesco Totti as their 21st-century hero.

I LUPI ("THE WOLVES")

As the Eternal City's dominant team, Roma's colors are packed with symbolism. The maroon shirts represent Rome's imperial past, while the orange/yellow trim stands for God (the city is the home of the papacy). The club badge features an image of a she-wolf suckling a pair of infants. According to legend, Rome's twin founders Romulus and Remus were raised by a female wolf who rescued them from the Tiber River.

VOCAL SUPPORT

Roma has two club anthems, both written by local singer Antonello Venditti. The first, *La Roma non si discute, si ama* ("Roma is not to be discussed, it is to be loved") is sung before every home game, while *Grazie Roma* ("Thank you Rome") is played only when the club wins. Venditti also penned a satirical song about former AC Milan owner Silvio Berlusconi.

THEY CALLED ME A FOOL WHEN I SAID THIS TEAM COULD CHALLENGE FOR THE TITLE. NOW THEY CAN THINK AGAIN!

FRANCESCO TOTTI
PRESS INTERVIEW, 2001

FRANCESCO TOTTI
Famous for his passing skills, the former Roma captain has scored more goals for the club than any other player. He loved to wind up opposing supporters, particularly Lazio fans.

BEST OF THE REST

LAZIO (1900)
Named after the province in which Rome is situated, Roman club Lazio draws its support from the north of the city. A cash injection after a 1992 buyout led to Lazio winning the Cup Winners' Cup in 1999 and the *scudetto* in 2000.

HONORS: LEAGUE 2 CUP 7; CWC 1999

FIORENTINA (1926)
Only four clubs have spent more seasons in Serie A than Fiorentina. However, in 2002 Florence's premier club went bankrupt. The club was reestablished in the lowest division and has since climbed back up to the top flight.

HONORS: LEAGUE 2 CUP 6; CWC 1961

SAMPDORIA (1946)
Genoa's "other" club was formed from the merger of Sampierdarenese and Andrea Doria. Most of its first few decades were spent in Serie B, but success came with a Cup Winners' Cup win in 1990 and the *scudetto* in 1991.

HONORS: LEAGUE 1 CUP 4; CWC 1990

TORINO (1906)
Torino was founded in 1906 by a group of defectors from Juventus. Between 1943 and 1949, *Il Grande Torino* was the greatest team in Italy, but most of the squad were tragically killed in a 1949 air disaster.

HONORS: LEAGUE 7 CUP 5

NAPOLI (1926)
Napoli is the only mainland team south of Rome to have won the *scudetto*. True success came after Diego Maradona joined the club for a world record fee in 1984.

HONORS: LEAGUE 2 CUP 6;
UEFA CUP 1989

GENOA (1893)
Genoa Cricket and Soccer Club was founded in 1893, making it one of the oldest outfits in Italy. The club won the first three national championships (1898–1900) but has spent most of the post-World War II period in Serie B.

HONORS: LEAGUE 9 CUP 1

HELLAS VERONA (1903)
Given the prefix Hellas ("Greece") by a classics professor at the university where the club was founded, Verona's biggest claim to fame is winning the 1985 *scudetto* (the last team from outside Rome, Turin, and Milan to do so).

HONORS: LEAGUE 1

EUROPE

GREECE

HOME

AWAY

POPULATION: 10.7 MILLION
CAPITAL: ATHENS
FA: HELLENIC FOOTBALL FEDERATION
LICENSED PLAYERS:
MALE: 705,000
FEMALE: 55,500
PROFESSIONALS: 1,800
REGISTERED CLUBS: 5,500

Soccer was first played in Greece in the late 19th century by British sailors and diplomats and also featured at the 1896 Athens Olympics. Initially the preserve of the wealthy, who founded Panathinaikos, the game soon spread to the working class, and Olympiacos was born. Greek refugees from Turkey started new clubs in the 1920s, including AEK Athens.

SLOW BEGINNINGS

The Greek Cup was established in 1932, but because intercity communication was poor, it was only in 1960 that the Greeks were able to establish a truly national soccer league. Named the Alpha Ethniki ("First National Division"), it remained an amateur league until 1979 and was replaced by Super League Greece in 2006.

STAT ATTACK

NATIONAL TEAM

NICKNAME:
The Pirate Ship
NATIONAL STADIUM:
Olympic Stadium, Athens, 69,618
WORLD CUP FINALS:
3 appearances
EUROPEAN CHAMPIONSHIPS:
4 appearances, winner **2004**
BIGGEST WIN: 8–0 vs. Syria, 1949
BIGGEST DEFEAT: 1–11 vs. Hungary, 1938
MOST CAPS: Giorgios Karagounis, **139**
MOST GOALS: Nikos Anastopoulos, **29**

MAIN DOMESTIC CLUBS

OLYMPIACOS
FOUNDED: Athens, 1925
STADIUM: Karaiskakis
CAPACITY: 32,115
HOME
INTERNATIONAL HONORS: None
LEAGUE: 47 **CUP:** 28

PANATHINAIKOS
FOUNDED: Athens, 1908
STADIUM: Apostolos Nikolaidis
CAPACITY: 16,003
HOME
INTERNATIONAL HONORS: None
LEAGUE: 20 **CUP:** 19

AEK ATHENS
FOUNDED: Athens, 1924
STADIUM: Olympic
CAPACITY: 69,618
HOME
INTERNATIONAL HONORS: None
LEAGUE: 12 **CUP:** 15

ON A WING AND A PRAYER

In 1971, Panathinaikos made it all the way to the European Cup Final—the most successful run in a European club competition by a Greek team. They arrived in London for the final with an array of holy Greek Orthodox relics. Sadly, they were beaten 2–0 by Ajax at Wembley.

HOW DO THEY DO IT?

The economics of Greek soccer are unfathomable. In 2002, the government reported that the top division had debts of more than $180 million and an income of less than $7 million. Little has changed. Until recently, Olympiacos was bankrolled by its former owner, Greek tycoon Socrates Kokkalis.

EURO 2004

After failing to win a point in any previous international competition, Greece won the 2004 European Championship in Portugal under the German coach Otto Rehhagel. Schooled in the no-nonsense Bundesliga, he created a team characterized by tight marking, an exemplary work rate, and drilled set pieces. It proved a potent combination; they beat the hosts in the opening game and the final.

THEODOROS **ZAGORAKIS**

A defensive midfielder who understood how to control a game, Theo's finest hour came when he captained his country to glory in Euro 2004. On top of the shock win, he won the UEFA Player of the Tournament.

BORN: OCTOBER 27, 1971, KAVALA, GREECE
HEIGHT: 5 FT 10 IN (1.78 M)
MAIN CLUBS: **KAVALA, PAOK SALONIKA, LEICESTER CITY, AEK ATHENS, BOLOGNA**
INTERNATIONAL CAPS: **120**

TURKEY

HOME   AWAY

POPULATION: 85.3 MILLION

CAPITAL: ANKARA

FA: TÜRKIYE FUTBOL FEDERASYONU

LICENSED PLAYERS:
MALE: 2,400,000
FEMALE: 345,000

PROFESSIONALS: 4,500

REGISTERED CLUBS: 4,300

Soccer was viewed with suspicion by the last sultan of the Ottoman Empire and judged to be foreign, dangerous, and illegal. However, after the Turkish revolution of the early 1920s, soccer bloomed. Turkey's first president, Kemal Atatürk, is claimed by all three of Istanbul's big teams—Galatasaray, Fenerbahçe, and Besiktas—as a supporter.

CAPITAL DOMINATION

Soccer spread rapidly around the country after the Turkish soccer federation was founded in 1923. Only two non-Istanbul clubs, Trabzonspor and Bursaspor, have ever won the league title. Victory in the Cup, which started in 1963, has been more widely spread.

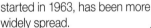

HAKAN **SÜKÜR**

Scorer of the fastest-ever World Cup goal, during Turkey's third-place playoff in 2002, Sükür has a raft of league titles and cup winners' medals to his name. It's no coincidence that Turkish soccer came of age during Sükür's glittering playing career.

BORN: SEPTEMBER 1, 1971, SAKARYA, TURKEY
HEIGHT: 6 FT 3 IN (1.91 M)
MAIN CLUBS: GALATASARAY, INTER MILAN, PARMA FC, BLACKBURN ROVERS
INTERNATIONAL CAPS: **112**

TURKISH PASSION

Always noisy and exuberant, Turkish crowds are passionate about their team—visiting fans have been met by flags reading "Welcome to Hell." The national team, too, can get exuberant—a tunnel-mouth brawl followed Turkey's 2006 World Cup playoff defeat to Switzerland.

LOCAL RIVALRY

Fenerbahçe versus Galatasaray is the most fiercely contested of the nation's derbies and always begins with the "buruya," a ritual in which every player of each team is called by name to salute their fans, and be saluted in return. Despite the intensity of the occasion, it only rarely boils over, as in 1996 when Graeme Souness, Galatasaray's victorious Scottish manager, planted his club's flag in the center of Fenerbahçe's field.

WORLD CUP 2002

Turkey first went to the World Cup in 1954 but was knocked out after the first round. It failed to qualify for another tournament until Euro 1996, then reached the quarterfinals in 2000 and semifinals in 2008. The national team's greatest achievement was third place at the 2002 World Cup in Japan, after a close-fought semifinal against Brazil. A national holiday was declared on the team's return.

EUROPE

BULGARIA

HOME   AWAY

Under Ottoman rule, soccer in Bulgaria was subject to official curbs, but the game flourished once the country had achieved independence after the Balkan Wars of 1912 and 1913. Sofia's leading clubs soon emerged: Slavia, founded by intellectuals in 1913; and Levski, started by a group of teenagers in 1914. Following the 1944 communist takeover, the Bulgarian army created CSKA Sofia, which came to dominate the domestic game.

POPULATION: 7.1 MILLION
CAPITAL: SOFIA
FA: BULGARIAN FOOTBALL UNION
LICENSED PLAYERS:
MALE: 289,500
FEMALE: 38,000
PROFESSIONALS: 1,000
REGISTERED CLUBS: 500

SMALL YET MIGHTY

The surprise package of the post-communist era, Litex Lovech is a tiny provincial club that won Bulgaria's top division in 1998 and 1999.

IT'S ALL IN THE NAME

The first truly national league was established in 1949 and has been through various formats but currently consists of 16 teams. The Bulgarian Cup was established as the Czars Cup in 1924 and was renamed the Soviet Army Cup following World War II. It took its current name in 1981.

STAT ATTACK

NATIONAL TEAM

NICKNAME: The Lions
NATIONAL STADIUM:
Vasil Levski, 43,320
WORLD CUP FINALS: 7 appearances, 4th place **1994**
EUROPEAN CHAMPIONSHIPS:
2 appearances
BIGGEST WIN: 10–0 vs. Ghana, 1968
BIGGEST DEFEAT: 0–13 vs. Spain, 1933
MOST CAPS: Stiliyan Petrov, **106**
MOST GOALS: Dimitar Berbatov, **48**

HRISTO **STOICHKOV**

An explosive left-sided attacker, Stoichkov was as famous for his fiery temperament as for his soccer skills. He received an eight-game ban for stamping on a referee's foot and a lifetime suspension in 1985 (later rescinded).

BORN: FEBRUARY 8, 1966, PLOVDIV, BULGARIA
HEIGHT: 5 FT 10 IN (1.78 M)
MAIN CLUBS: **HEBROS HARMANLI, CSKA SOFIA, FC BARCELONA, PARMA, KASHIWA REYSOL, CHICAGO FIRE**
INTERNATIONAL CAPS: **83**

MAIN DOMESTIC CLUBS

CSKA SOFIA
FOUNDED: Sofia, 1948
STADIUM: Bulgarian Army Stadium
WINBET
HOME
CAPACITY: 22,995
INTERNATIONAL HONORS: European Cup semifinals **1967**, **1982**; Cup Winners' Cup semifinals **1989**
LEAGUE: 31 **CUP:** 21

LEVSKI SOFIA
FOUNDED: Sofia, 1914
STADIUM:
Georgi Asparuhov
HOME
CAPACITY: 25,000
INTERNATIONAL HONORS: Cup Winners' Cup quarterfinals **1970**, **1977**, **1987**; UEFA Cup quarterfinals **1976**, **2006**
LEAGUE: 26 **CUP:** 26

THE UNFINISHED CUP FINAL

The 1985 Bulgarian Cup Final between Levski and CSKA Sofia descended into a 22-man fist fight on national television. The game was abandoned, both teams were dissolved on the order of the Politburo, and then renamed—although a year later they reverted to their original names.

WORLD CUP 1994

Bulgaria began the 1994 World Cup with a defeat to Nigeria but, contrary to prior form, went on to beat Greece, Argentina, and Mexico to win a quarterfinal slot. Led by Stoichkov, Bulgaria came from behind to beat Germany 2–1, and ignited a national celebration. That was the peak, as it lost to Italy in the semifinal.

HOME   AWAY

POPULATION: 21.5 MILLION
CAPITAL: BUCHAREST
FA: FEDERATIA ROMÂNA DE FOTBAL
LICENSED PLAYERS:
MALE: 929,500
FEMALE: 105,000
PROFESSIONALS: 1,100
REGISTERED CLUBS: 2,800

ROMANIA

An 1888 newspaper report of "two youths running with a ball" in the city of Arad was the first recorded instance of soccer in Romania. A club was founded in Arad in 1899 after students and professionals brought the game from Vienna and Budapest, while employees of British and German oil companies played soccer in Bucharest and Ploesti. King Carol I was a driving force behind the founding of the soccer association in 1909.

CAPITAL DOMINATION

A national league began in 1909 and, aside from a break during World War II, has been played ever since. In 2007, FC Cluj broke a 17-year domination of the domestic championships by the Bucharest trio—Dinamo, Steaua, and Rapid. The Romanian Cup, played since 1953, has been dominated by the same trio.

GHEORGHE **HAGI**

Dubbed the "Maradona of the Carpathians," Hagi was a supremely gifted player and one of only a few to have played for both Barcelona and Real Madrid. His best years arguably came at Galatasaray.

BORN: **FEBRUARY 5, 1965, SACELE, ROMANIA**
HEIGHT: **5 FT 8½ IN (1.74 M)**
MAIN CLUBS: **CONSTANTA, SPORTUL STUDENTESC, STEAUA BUCHAREST, REAL MADRID, BRESCIA CALCIO, BARCELONA, GALATASARAY**
INTERNATIONAL CAPS: **125**

EUROPEAN CUP TRIUMPH

Steaua Bucharest made it to the 1986 European Cup Final in Seville, Spain, and faced Barcelona, who was effectively playing at home. Steaua held out for a draw and won the game on penalties, becoming the first eastern-European team to lift the European Cup. A crowd of 30,000 met them on their return to Bucharest airport, while 40 communist party members who had followed the team to Spain took the opportunity to defect.

TAKING ON THE WORLD

Romania impressed at Italia '90, and were the most entertaining team at US 1994. A 3–2 victory over Argentina was its finest hour, graced by a delicate lob from Hagi, and an amazing full-team counterattack. It lost to Sweden on penalties in the quarterfinal.

4 Different names under which Universitatea Cluj have played in their four Romanian Cup final appearances

733 Armchairs at Steaua Stadium, home of Steaua Bucharest

17 Consecutive games won by Dinamo Bucharest, between June and November 1988

STAT ATTACK

NATIONAL TEAM

NICKNAME: Tricolorii ("The Tricolors")
NATIONAL STADIUM: The National Arena, 55,600
WORLD CUP FINALS: 7 appearances, quarterfinals **1994**
EUROPEAN CHAMPIONSHIPS:
5 appearances, quarterfinals **2000**
BIGGEST WIN: 9–0 vs. Finland, 1973
BIGGEST DEFEAT: 0–9 vs. Hungary, 1948
MOST CAPS: Dorinel Munteanu, **134**
MOST GOALS: Gheorghe Hagi, Adrian Mutu, **35**

GIVE US SOCCER

Under Nicolae Ceausescu's communist regime, soccer was one of the few areas in which attacks on authority were possible. In 1985, when a live transmission of the game between Rapid and Steaua Bucharest was canceled, tens of thousands of disgruntled fans descended upon the stadium, broke through police lines, and entered the stands. At the end of the afternoon, there was a pitched battle with the police.

MAIN DOMESTIC CLUBS

FC FCSB (PREVIOUSLY STEAUA BUCHAREST)

HOME

FOUNDED: Bucharest, 1947
STADIUM: The National Arena
CAPACITY: 55,600
INTERNATIONAL HONORS: European Cup **1986**, runner-up **1989**
LEAGUE: 26 **CUP:** 24

DINAMO BUCHAREST

HOME

FOUNDED: Bucharest, 1948
STADIUM: Dinamo Stadium
CAPACITY: 15,032
INTERNATIONAL HONORS:
European Cup semifinals **1984**; Cup Winners' Cup semifinals **1990**
LEAGUE: 18 **CUP:** 13

EUROPE

CROATIA

HOME AWAY

POPULATION: 4.3 MILLION
CAPITAL: ZAGREB
FA: HRVATSKI NOGOMETNI SAVEZ
LICENSED PLAYERS:
MALE: 340,000
FEMALE: 22,500
PROFESSIONALS: 300
REGISTERED CLUBS: 1,500

Soccer came to Zagreb, now capital of Croatia, from other cities in the Austro-Hungarian Empire. The first club, HASK, was founded in 1903, and a Zagreb league was set up before World War I. After the war, Croatian clubs played in Yugoslavia's interconnected football leagues, until they set up their own league and cup competitions after Croatia's independence in 1991.

DOMESTIC TRANSITION

The Croat top-flight league, known as the Prva HNL, has been through many formats and numbers of teams. For much of its existence, teams played each other until March and then split into two mini-leagues—one to determine relegation, the other to decide the championship. In 2013, the league shifted to a standard season with the 10 teams playing each other four times. NK Zagreb and HNK Rijeka are the only two teams to have broken the duopoly of the big two—Dinamo Zagreb and Hajduk Split.

ZVONIMIR BOBAN

In his native country, Zvonimir Boban is loved as much for his patriotism as for his superlative midfield performances for the national team. He scored 12 goals in 51 appearances for his country.

BORN: OCTOBER 8, 1968, IMOTSKI, CROATIA
HEIGHT: 6 FT (1.83 M)
MAIN CLUBS: DINAMO ZAGREB, AC MILAN, AS BARI, CELTA VIGO
INTERNATIONAL CAPS: 8 (YUGOSLAVIA), 51 (CROATIA)

STAT ATTACK

NATIONAL TEAM

NICKNAME: Vatreni ("The Blazers")
NATIONAL STADIUM: Maksimir, Zagreb, 35,123
WORLD CUP FINALS: 6 appearances, 3rd place **1998**
EUROPEAN CHAMPIONSHIPS: 6 appearances, runners-up **2018**
BIGGEST WIN: 10–0 vs. San Marino, 2016
BIGGEST DEFEAT: 1–5 vs. Germany, 1941 and 1942, vs. England 2009
MOST CAPS: Luka Modrić, **157**
MOST GOALS: Davor Suker, **45**

MAIN DOMESTIC CLUBS

DINAMO ZAGREB
FOUNDED: Zagreb, 1945
STADIUM: Maksimir
CAPACITY: 35,123   HOME
INTERNATIONAL HONORS: Fairs Cup (now UEFA Cup) **1967**, runner-up **1963**
LEAGUE: 23 **CUP:** 16

HAJDUK SPLIT
FOUNDED: Split, 1911
STADIUM: Poljud
CAPACITY: 35,000   HOME
INTERNATIONAL HONORS: Cup Winners' Cup semifinals **1973**, UEFA Cup semifinals **1984**
LEAGUE: 6 **CUP:** 7

WHAT'S IN A NAME?

After Croatia gained independence, President Franjo Tudjman took control of Dinamo Zagreb. The team had been an icon of Croat identity during the Yugoslav era, but, against the wishes of the fans, Tudjman renamed the club Croatia Zagreb. After his exit from politics, however, the club reverted to Dinamo.

BOBAN'S KICK

In 1990, Serbian police clashed with Croat fans in Dinamo Zagreb's stadium. Zvonimir Boban, Zagreb's star defender, infamously launched a karate kick at a policeman. The game was abandoned, and the civil war began soon after. Relations have remained tense; the 1997 Champions League qualifier between Dinamo Zagreb and Partisan Belgrade was played behind closed doors.

WORLD CUP SUCCESS

In their first World Cup—France '98—Croatia's coach Miroslav Blaževic wore a French policeman's "Kepi" cap for luck. The brilliance of Davor Suker and Robert Prosinečki helped sweep Germany aside 3–0 in the quarter-final. Losing to France in the semi-finals, Croatia beat Holland to finish third. They did even better at the 2018 World Cup finals, finishing second behind France.

CZECH REPUBLIC

HOME   AWAY

POPULATION: 10.6 MILLION
CAPITAL: PRAGUE
FA: ČESKOMORAVSKÝ FOTBALOVÝ SVAZ
LICENSED PLAYERS:
MALE: 976,400
FEMALE: 64,000
PROFESSIONALS: 1,500
REGISTERED CLUBS: 4,000

In the late 19th century, soccer came to Prague, and the two dominant teams—Slavia and Sparta—were founded in 1892 and 1893. Adopting a central-European short-passing style, the Czechs—then playing as Czechoslovakia—were good enough to reach two World Cup finals, losing in 1934 and 1962, and to win the European Championship in 1976.

EARLY STARTERS

The popularity of soccer in Prague led to a citywide league in 1896 and a charity cup in 1906. After World War I, both league and cup became Czechoslovak competitions and went professional in 1922. The Czech League was first played in 1993, after separation from Slovakia, and consists of 16 teams.

SPARTA VS. SLAVIA

Slavia Praha was formed by students and intellectuals, whereas cross-town rival Sparta attracted working-class fans, as reflected by its nickname, "Iron Sparta."

DON'T SCORE FIRST

Czechoslovakia twice took the lead in World Cup finals and twice finished runner-up. In 1934, against host Italy, the Czechs held a one-goal lead for 70 minutes and even hit the woodwork, before losing 2–1. Against Brazil in 1962, an early Czech goal opened the floodgates for three Brazilian goals, and the team lost 3–1.

EURO 1976

Czechoslovakia won the 1976 European Championship the hard way, beating an exceptional Dutch team in overtime in the semifinal, and then triumphing over world champion West Germany in a penalty shoot-out.

STAT ATTACK

NATIONAL TEAM

NICKNAME: Locomotiva ("Locomotive")
NATIONAL STADIUM: None
WORLD CUP FINALS: 2 appearances, runner-up **1934**, **1962**
EUROPEAN CHAMPIONSHIPS:
10 appearances, winner **1976**, runner-up **1996**
BIGGEST WIN: 8–0 Czechoslovakia vs. Thailand, 1968; **8–1** Czech Republic vs. Andorra, 2005
BIGGEST DEFEAT: 3–8 Czechoslovakia vs. Hungary, 1937
MOST CAPS: Petr Čech, **124**
MOST GOALS: Jan Koller, **55**

PAVEL NEDVED

Starting out at Sparta Praha, Nedved caught the eye of the world with his midfield displays for the Czech Republic at Euro 1996. Incredibly fit and with a remarkable shot, he also won European Soccer Player of the Year in 2003.

BORN: **AUGUST 30, 1972, CHEB, CZECHOSLOVAKIA**
HEIGHT: **5 FT 9 IN (1.77 M)**
MAIN CLUBS: **DUKLA PRAHA, SPARTA PRAHA, LAZIO, JUVENTUS**
INTERNATIONAL CAPS: **91**

MAIN DOMESTIC CLUBS

SPARTA PRAHA
FOUNDED: Prague, 1893
STADIUM: Generali Arena
CAPACITY: 19,416   HOME
INTERNATIONAL HONORS: None
LEAGUE: 33 **CUP:** 15

SK SLAVIA PRAHA
FOUNDED: Prague, 1892
STADIUM: Sinobo
CAPACITY: 21,000   HOME
INTERNATIONAL HONORS: None
LEAGUE: 20 **CUP:** 9

EUROPE

SERBIA

In 1896, Hugo Bale, son of a Belgrade tailor, returned home from Vienna with a soccer ball. The game took off in Belgrade among students, artisans, the middle class, and then Serb nationalists. While part of Yugoslavia (1919–1941 and 1945–1991), Belgrade clubs played in Yugoslav leagues; when Yugoslavia dissolved in 1991, the Serbs set up their own Superliga.

HOME

AWAY

POPULATION: 7.1 MILLION
CAPITAL: BELGRADE
FA: FUDBALSKI SAVEZ SRBIJE
LICENSED PLAYERS:
MALE: 400,800
FEMALE: 40,800
PROFESSIONALS: 1,500
REGISTERED CLUBS: 2,000

STAT ATTACK

NATIONAL TEAM

NICKNAME: Beli Orlovi ("The Eagles")
NATIONAL STADIUM: Rajko Mitić Stadium, Belgrade, 55,538
WORLD CUP FINALS: 13 appearances, (including as Yugoslavia), semifinals **1930** and **1962**
EUROPEAN CHAMPIONSHIPS: 5 appearances, runner-up, **1960** and **1968**
BIGGEST WIN: 10–0 vs. Venezuela, 1972
BIGGEST DEFEAT: 0–7 Yugoslavia vs. Czechoslovakia 1920 and 1925; Yugoslavia vs. Uruguay 1924
MOST CAPS: Branislav Ivanović, **105**
MOST GOALS: Aleksandar Mitrovic, **51**

MAIN DOMESTIC CLUBS

RED STAR BELGRADE
FOUNDED: Belgrade, 1945
STADIUM: Rajko Mitić Stadium
CAPACITY: 55,538
INTERNATIONAL HONORS: European Cup **1991**
LEAGUE: 33 CUP: 26

HOME

PARTIZAN BELGRADE
FOUNDED: Belgrade, 1945
STADIUM: Partizana
CAPACITY: 32,710
INTERNATIONAL HONORS: European Cup runner-up **1966**
LEAGUE: 27 CUP: 16

HOME

RED STAR VS. PARTIZAN

Red Star Belgrade was founded in 1945 by the communist party with support from the university, police, and political elite. Partizan Belgrade was created in the same year by the federal, Yugoslav-minded national army. Rivalry between the two teams is intense, and games are known as "the eternal derby."

THE SUPERLIGA

Until 2007, the Serbian Superliga was decided by an end-of-season playoff. This was replaced by a standard league with 12 clubs, cut from 22. In 2009, the league was expanded to 16 teams.

EUROPEAN CUP 1991

In the final year of Yugoslavia's existence, Red Star Belgrade made it to the final of the European Cup. Despite the Serbian affiliation of the fans, the team was resolutely multiethnic, including Robert Prosinecki (a Croat), Refik Sabanadzovic (a Bosnian Muslim), and Darko Pancev (a Macedonian). The title was really won in a monumental 4–3 semifinal against Bayern Munich; they won a disappointing final against Marseilles on penalties.

SAVO MILOSEVIC

After bagging 74 goals in 98 games for Partizan, Milosevic moved to Aston Villa in 1995, where he gained the unfortunate moniker "Miss-a-lot-evic" due to his erratic behavior in front of goal. He played for four national sides as the borders of the Balkans shifted.

BORN: SEPTEMBER 2, 1973, BIJELJINA, BOSNIA AND HERZEGOVINA
HEIGHT: 6 FT 1 IN (1.87 M)
MAIN CLUBS: PARTIZAN BELGRADE, ASTON VILLA, REAL ZARAGOZA, PARMA, CA OSASUNA
INTERNATIONAL CAPS: **102**

YUGOSLAV SOCCER

Both FIFA and the Football Association of Serbia consider Serbia to be the official descendant of both the Yugoslav and Serbian and Montenegrin national teams, despite the fact that the Yugoslav team was always multiethnic in composition. Yugoslav soccer enjoyed a golden era between the 1950s and 1970s, winning the gold medal at the 1952 Helsinki Olympics, and contesting four World Cup quarterfinals.

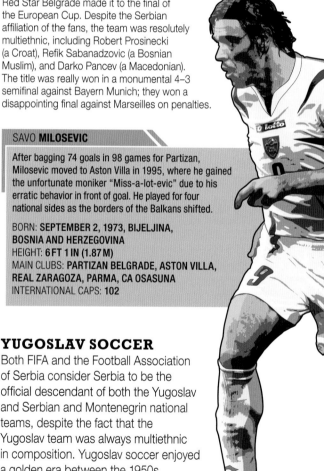

HUNGARY

HOME

AWAY

POPULATION: 9.8 MILLION
CAPITAL: BUDAPEST
FA: MAGYAR LABDARÚGÓ SZÖVETSÉG
LICENSED PLAYERS:
MALE: 477,500
FEMALE: 50,000
PROFESSIONALS: 450
REGISTERED CLUBS: 2,800

Soccer took off in Budapest in the 1890s, and clubs soon sprang up—MTK in 1898, Ferencváros in 1899, and Újpest in 1905. The game flourished: club sides competed all over central Europe, the national team made it to the final of the 1938 World Cup, and the remarkable golden generation of the 1950s marked the high point of Hungarian soccer.

THE NATIONAL CHAMPIONSHIP

Organizational problems and poor financing of Hungarian soccer in modern times has allowed teams outside the capital, Budapest, to prosper. In recent seasons, the league has been won by tiny provincial teams, such as Debreceni and Videoton.

STAT ATTACK

NATIONAL TEAM

NICKNAME: The Magical Magyars (1950s)
NATIONAL STADIUM:
Puskás Aréna, Budapest, 67,889
WORLD CUP FINALS: 9 appearances, runner-up **1938** and **1954**
EUROPEAN CHAMPIONSHIPS:
4 appearances, 3rd place **1964**
BIGGEST WIN: 13–1 vs. France, 1927
BIGGEST DEFEAT: 0–7 vs. England 1908, and vs. Germany 1941
MOST CAPS: Balázs Dzsudzsák, **109**
MOST GOALS: Ferenc Puskás, **84**

MAIN DOMESTIC CLUBS

FERENCVÁROSI TC
FOUNDED: Budapest, 1899
STADIUM: Groupama Arena
CAPACITY: 22,000
HOME
INTERNATIONAL HONORS:
Fairs Cup (now Europa League) **1965**
LEAGUE: 33 **CUP:** 23

MTK BUDAPEST
FOUNDED: Budapest, 1888
STADIUM: Hidegkuti Nándor
CAPACITY: 5,322
HOME
INTERNATIONAL HONORS:
Cup Winners' Cup runner-up **1964**
LEAGUE: 23 **CUP:** 12

WORLD-RECORD RUN

Hungary held the record for the longest unbeaten run of any international side, with 33 games between 1950 and 1954. The record held for 55 years but was finally beaten by Spain in 2009 after 35 winning games.

MTK VS. FERENCVÁROS

From its origins, MTK was the team of Budapest's liberals, intellectuals, and Jews. Most of Hungary's Jews perished during World War II, and, under the communists, MTK became Red Banner. Ferencváros, named after a city suburb, is the team of the working classes. Favored by the Nazis during World War II, it was punished by the post-war communists, consequently making it the team of the opposition.

GOLDEN GENERATION

Coached by Gustáv Sebes, and boasting the talents of Puskàs, Czibor, and Kocsis, the Hungarian team of the 1950s combined the best of the traditional passing game with Sebes's tactical innovations. They swept all rivals aside in 1952 and 1953 but lost to West Germany in the World Cup Final of 1954.

FERENC PUSKÁS

A genuine soccer legend, Puskás was one of the greatest strikers of all time. Playing in the Hungarian and Spanish leagues between 1943 and 1966, he scored 514 goals in 529 appearances, a record bettered only by his international career, where he netted in all but one of his 85 outings.

BORN: APRIL 2, 1927, BUDAPEST, HUNGARY
HEIGHT: 5 FT 10 IN (1.78 M)
MAIN CLUBS: KISPEST, AC HONVÉD, REAL MADRID
INTERNATIONAL CAPS: 85

33 Unbeaten games by national team, 1950–1954

114 Goals scored by Ferenc Deák of Szentlornic in 64 games between 1945 and 1947

105 Years Ferencváros spent in Hungarian first division before being relegated for financial irregularities in 2006

10 Goals scored vs. El Salvador in 1982 World Cup

ENGLAND VS. HUNGARY

England's assumption that it was the best team in the world had been knocked by a shock defeat to the US and an early exit from the 1950 World Cup, but it had never been beaten at home. Meanwhile, the golden generation of Hungarian players had demonstrated to anyone who was watching that Hungary was forging a new and extraordinary form of soccer. Olympic Champions in 1952, Hungary was unbeaten throughout 1953. But England hadn't been paying attention and expected to win with ease. After 90 minutes of exhilarating Hungarian play, world soccer had new stars.

ENGLAND 3	HUNGARY 6
FORMATION: 2-3-5	FORMATION: 4-2-4
MANAGER: WALTER WINTERBOTTOM	MANAGER: GUSTÁV SEBES
WEMBLEY STADIUM, LONDON, ENGLAND NOVEMBER 25, 1953	
ATTENDANCE: 100,000	
REFEREE: LEO HORN (HOLLAND)	

1 Grosics
2 Lóránt 4 Buzánszky 5 Zakariás 3 Lantos
6 Bozsik 9 Hidegkuti
7 Budai 8 Kocsis 10 Puskás 11 Czibor
11 Matthews 10 Taylor 9 Mortensen 8 Sewell 7 Robb
6 Wright 5 Johnston 4 Dickinson
3 Ramsey 2 Eckersley
1 Merrick

SUBS: 12 Geller (76)

0 M

England captain Billy Wright was taken aback by the appearance of the Hungarian team. "I looked down and noticed that the Hungarians had on these strange, lightweight boots. I turned to big Stan Mortensen and said: 'We should be all right here, Stan, they haven't got the proper gear.'"

I CAME AWAY WONDERING ... WHAT WE HAD BEEN DOING ALL THESE YEARS!

TOM FINNEY ENGLAND STRIKER, 1946–1958

2 M

The Hungarians start the match on the attack. They put together a slalom of one-touch passes from the halfway line to Hidegkuti, who is totally unmarked. He rifles the soaked ball into the net: 1–0.

TACTICS

England lost the tactical battle completely. The host played the standard W-M formation (see p.87); Hungary was playing a flexible 4-2-4 formation. Further confusion resulted from Hidegkuti wearing the No. 9 shirt—always the center forward in England, but Hidegkuti played deep in midfield, and his marker, center half Harry Johnston, was constantly drawn out of position.

England ties on 13 minutes when Jackie Sewell intercepts a Mortensen pass and strikes a left-footed shot into the far corner: 1–1.

13 M

The situation gets worse for England when Billy Wright totally mistimes a tackle on Puskás, who has dragged the ball back and away from him with his studs. Nonchalantly, Puskás knocks the ball over England goalkeeper Merrick: 3–1. Hungarian commentator György Szepesi demands that a plaque be installed at Wembley to commemorate the drag-back goal.

24 M

20 M

Seven minutes later, and Hungary is back in front. Hidegkuti pounces on a loose ball after a series of ricochets: 2–1.

27 M Puskás diverts a Bozsik free kick into the net, making it 4–1. Hungary has stamped its authority on the match with less than half an hour played.

38 M Stan Mortensen scores just on halftime, making it 4–2 and giving England the illusion of hope, but the gap between the teams is obvious.

50 M

57 M

Alf Ramsey scores a penalty to make it 6–3. On the final whistle, the crowd applauds the new masters of world soccer.

Hungary has complete control and finishes the job. Bozsik makes it 5–2 five minutes into the second half with a long-range shot, seconds after Puskás has hit the post. Hidegkuti completes his hat trick on 53 minutes with a half volley from eight yards after a lofted pass from the edge of the area: 6–2.

EUROPE

POLAND

HOME

AWAY

POPULATION: 38.5 MILLION

CAPITAL: WARSAW

FA: POLSKI ZWIĄZEK PIŁKI NOŻNEJ

LICENSED PLAYERS:
MALE: 1.8 MILLION
FEMALE: 182,500

PROFESSIONALS: 1,200

REGISTERED CLUBS: 5,700

Soccer arrived late in Poland, with Krakow becoming the first hotbed. Cracovia and Wisla Krakow were formed by students in 1906, but there was no national team until after World War I. Success was rare under communism, the exceptions being when they knocked England out of the 1974 World Cup qualifiers and a 1982 World Cup semifinal place.

THE EKSTRAKLASA

The Polish top flight is the Ekstraklasa ("Top League") and is a standard 18-team league that was founded in 1927. Dominated by Wisla Krakow from the late 1990s onward, it has suffered a spate of match-fixing scandals in recent years, leading to teams being demoted. In 1993, the title was awarded to third-place Lech Poznan after the top two, Legia Warsaw and ŁKS Łódź, were penalized for match fixing.

FIRST-TIME THRILLS

Poland first qualified for the World Cup in 1938, where they played Brazil in France, cheered on by thousands of fans. Down 0–3, the Poles brought the game back to 4–4 by halftime, only to lose 5–6 in the end.

WARSAW RIVALS

Legia Warsaw may be the biggest team in Poland's capital city, but it was not the first team to win a league title. Polonia Warsaw, its smaller neighbor and the oldest team in the city, emerged from the wreckage of postwar Warsaw and won the league in 1946. Originally the team of the railroad workers and then the city's liberal intelligentsia, Polonia was steadily sidelined by the communist authorities.

ROBERT **LEWANDOWSKI**

From his international debut for Poland in 2008, Lewandowski went on to become captain and the national side's leading goal scorer. He netted 312 goals in 384 games in Germany's Bundesliga, before joining Barcelona in 2022.

BORN: AUGUST 21, 1988, WARSAW, POLAND
HEIGHT: 6 FT 1 IN (1.85 M)
MAIN CLUBS: ZNICZ PRUSZKÓW, LECH POZNAN, BORUSSIA DORTMUND, BAYERN MUNICH, BARCELONA
INTERNATIONAL CAPS: 137

THE LAST GAME

The so-called "Last Game" was played on August 27, 1939, four days before World War II broke out. Poland beat one of the best teams of the time—1938 World Cup runner-up, Hungary—4–2 in Warsaw. It is still remembered as the last match before the war and the biggest win yet for Polish soccer.

STAT ATTACK

NATIONAL TEAM

NICKNAME: Biale Orly ("The White Eagles")

NATIONAL STADIUM:
National Stadium, Warsaw, 58,145

WORLD CUP FINALS: 9 appearances, 3rd place **1974** and **1982**

EUROPEAN CHAMPIONSHIPS:
4 appearances, quarterfinal **2016**

BIGGEST WIN: 10–0 vs. San Marino, 2009

BIGGEST DEFEAT: 0–8 vs. Denmark, 1948

MOST CAPS: Robert Lewandowski, **137**

MOST GOALS: Robert Lewandowski, **77**

MAIN DOMESTIC CLUBS

LEGIA WARSAW
FOUNDED: Warsaw, 1916
STADIUM:
Polish Army Stadium   HOME
CAPACITY: 31,800
INTERNATIONAL HONORS:
Cup Winners' Cup semifinal **1991**;
European Cup semifinal **1970**
LEAGUE: 15 CUP: 19

WISLA KRAKOW
FOUNDED: Krakow, 1906
STADIUM: Stadion Miejski
im. Henryka Reymana   HOME
CAPACITY: 33,130
INTERNATIONAL HONORS:
European Cup quarterfinal **1979**;
Intertoto Cup **1969**, **1970**, **1973**
LEAGUE: 14 CUP: 4

UKRAINE

HOME   AWAY

POPULATION: 44.2 MILLION
CAPITAL: KYIV
FA: FOOTBALL FEDERATION OF UKRAINE
LICENSED PLAYERS:
MALE: 2 MILLION
FEMALE: 232,000
PROFESSIONALS: 2,500
REGISTERED CLUBS: 68

Soccer was first played in Ukraine under czarist rule, prior to World War I. The game grew under Soviet rule, and Dynamo Kyiv was the first non-Russian team to win the Soviet championships in 1961. Since independence in 1991, Ukraine has struggled internationally but qualified for the World Cup finals in 2006. It missed out on qualifying for the 2022 World Cup, falling in the play-off to Wales.

THE PREMIER LEAGUE

Founded in 1991, the Ukrainian Premier League consists of 16 teams playing each other twice through the season. However, the season is split by a three-month winter break.

LOBANOVSKY'S DYNAMO KYIV

Dynamo Kyiv under coach Valeri Lobanovsky in the 1970s and '80s was notionally Soviet but became the pride of Ukraine. With support from the Ukrainian communists, Lobanovsky developed an immaculately planned method of training and playing that was reliant on endless rehearsal. His Dynamo team won six Soviet championships and the European Cup Winners' Cup twice.

ANDRIY **SHEVCHENKO**

A raft of honors for club and country set Shevchenko out as one of the finest strikers of his generation. A transfer tug-of-war between Chelsea and AC Milan saw him move to London for $39 million in 2006, only to return to Milan, before moving back to Dynamo Kyiv in 2009. In 2016 he became Ukraine's national coach.

BORN: **SEPTEMBER 29, 1976, DVIRKIVSCHYNA, SOVIET UNION**
HEIGHT: **6 FT (1.83 M)**
MAIN CLUBS: **DYNAMO KYIV, AC MILAN, CHELSEA**
INTERNATIONAL CAPS: **111**

SHAKHTAR DONETSK

Shakhtar Donetsk is the club that broke Dynamo Kyiv's hold on Ukrainian soccer. Based in the huge Donbass coal and steel region, the club was bought by the area's dominant oligarch and nation's richest man, Rinat Akhmetov. With immense financial backing, the club has won 13 Ukrainian titles since the turn of the century.

11 Ukraine's highest ever FIFA ranking, achieved in February 2007

9 Number of different stadiums in which Ukraine have played their home matches since 1992

18 The percentage of mistakes in moves a team can make and still be unbeatable, according to Valeri Lobanovsky

STAT ATTACK

NATIONAL TEAM

NICKNAME: Zhovto-Blkytni ("Yellow and Blues")
NATIONAL STADIUM: Olympic Stadium, Kyiv, 70,050
WORLD CUP FINALS: 1 appearance, quarterfinals **2006**
EUROPEAN CHAMPIONSHIPS: 3 appearances, quarterfinal 2020
BIGGEST WIN: 9–0 vs. San Marino, 2013
BIGGEST DEFEAT: 0–4 vs. Croatia 1995; vs. Spain 2006; vs. Czech Republic 2011
MOST CAPS: Anatoliy Tymoshchuk, **144**
MOST GOALS: Andriy Shevchenko, **48**

MAIN DOMESTIC CLUBS

DYNAMO KYIV
FOUNDED: Kyiv, 1927
STADIUM: Olympic Stadium
CAPACITY: 70,050
INTERNATIONAL HONORS: Cup Winners' Cup **1975**, **1986**
LEAGUE: 29   **CUP:** 22

HOME

SHAKHTAR DONETSK
FOUNDED: Donetsk, 1936
STADIUM: Donbass Arena
CAPACITY: 52,187
INTERNATIONAL HONORS: UEFA Cup **2009**
LEAGUE: 14   **CUP:** 17

HOME

GAME OF DEATH

Kyiv was taken by the invading Nazis in 1942 and subjected to a brutal occupation. The Luftwaffe and other German military teams played a series of games against the remnants of Dynamo Kyiv's team, decimated by deaths in the war.

EUROPE

RUSSIA

Soccer was first played in Czarist Russia by British sailors in Odessa and expatriates in St. Petersburg. The game spread in the cities, and city leagues were formed in Moscow and St. Petersburg. Following the 1917 Russian Revolution, soccer was controlled by the communist state. After the breakup of the USSR, the game in Russia boomed as newly-rich oligarchs invested in their country's league.

HOME   AWAY

POPULATION: 146 MILLION
CAPITAL: MOSCOW
FA: RUSSIAN FOOTBALL UNION
LICENSED PLAYERS:
MALE: 5,100,000
FEMALE: 697,500
PROFESSIONALS: 3,500
REGISTERED CLUBS: 14,000

THE RUSSIAN LEAGUE

The 16-team Russian League was founded in 1991 and was dominated by Spartak Moscow for the first decade. In recent years, Spartak has been eclipsed by CSKA Moscow, Lokomotiv Moscow, and Zenit St. Petersburg—funded by the nation's large energy company, Gazprom.

THE BOOM PAYS OFF

The Russian soccer boom finally paid off in 2008. Zenit St. Petersburg beat Glasgow Rangers 2–0 to win the UEFA Cup in some style. Meanwhile, the Russian national team, coached by Dutchman Guus Hiddink, reached the semifinals of the European Championships, Russia's best placing since the fall of communism.

THE COMEBACK OF ALL TIME

It's the final 20 minutes of a 1952 Olympics Round of 16 match. The Soviet Union is down 0–5 to Tito's Yugoslavia—at that time the bête noire of Stalin. The losing team is facing a long and unpleasant session in the gulag. Miraculously, it manages to find five goals and forces a replay but loses the second game. Despite these superhuman exertions, the CSKA Moscow team, from which most of the Soviet Olympic team was drawn, was disbanded as a punishment.

LEV **YASHIN**

Known as "The Black Spider" due to his all-black uniform and agility in keeping the ball out of the net, Yashin won five Soviet Championships with Dynamo Moscow, the 1960 European Championship, and Olympic Gold in 1956.

BORN: OCTOBER 22, 1929, MOSCOW, USSR
HEIGHT: 6 FT 2 IN (1.88 M)
MAIN CLUBS: DYNAMO MOSCOW
INTERNATIONAL CAPS: 74

CAUSE FOR COMPLAINT

The national soccer team was one of the few aspects of Soviet life on which citizens were brave enough to protest. When the USSR capitulated in the quarterfinals of the 1970 World Cup, *Izvetia*—a national paper—received more than 300,000 complaint letters.

ISRAEL

HOME

AWAY

POPULATION: 8.1 MILLION
CAPITAL: JERUSALEM
FA: ISRAEL FOOTBALL ASSOCIATION
LICENSED PLAYERS:
MALE: 251,500
FEMALE: 32,500
PROFESSIONALS: 1,500
REGISTERED CLUBS: 280

Soccer was played in Palestine by Jewish immigrants and Turkish soldiers prior to 1917, but the game took off under the British mandate from 1922. Palestine was FIFA-affiliated in 1929 on the condition that Jews and Arabs would be incorporated. Following the creation of Israel in 1948, the nation entered FIFA, and regular league soccer commenced. The Israeli league and national team include Jewish and Israeli-Arab players.

ONE AND ONLY

Beating New Zealand and Australia to qualify through the Oceania group, Israel made it to its one and only World Cup Final in 1970 in Mexico. Ties with Sweden and Italy and defeat to Uruguay were not enough to prevent a first-round exit, having scored just one goal.

HAPOEL, MACCABI, BEITAR

Most Israeli clubs bear the prefix Hapoel, Maccabi, or Beitar. All three were Zionist organizations committed to the creation of an Israeli state, and, among their many social functions, they created sports teams. Hapoel clubs were rooted in the trade union movement; the Maccabi clubs represented a more liberal, European Jewish tradition; while Beitar clubs represented Sephardic Jews from Asia and Africa, tending to be more militantly conservative. Official ties between clubs and these organizations have ended, but some of their ethos and attitude remains.

ISRAELI PREMIER LEAGUE

Founded in 1999, the Israeli Premier League consists of 14 teams, which play each other three times in a season. There are also two cup competitions—the Israel State Cup and the preseason Toto Cup. Although Maccabi Tel Aviv is one of the oldest teams in Israel and boasts the most title wins (21), the most successful teams in the late 1990s and 2000s have been Maccabi Haifa and Beitar Jerusalem. The latter especially was boosted by the lavish funding of its Russian-Israeli billionaire owner Arcadi Gaydamak, before he sold the club in 2009.

THE LOST CONTINENT

Israel has switched soccer continents three times in its short history. It was initially a member of the Asian Football Confederation, but after a series of national federations and teams, such as Iran and Indonesia, refused to play Israel on political grounds, FIFA moved Israel into the Oceania Football Confederation, where they played World Cup qualifiers from the early 1970s until the late 1980s. The situation was resolved when Israel joined UEFA in 1992 and came under European jurisdiction.

NATIONAL TEAM

NATIONAL STADIUM: Ramat Gan, Tel Aviv, 41,583
WORLD CUP FINALS: 1 appearance, **1970**
EUROPEAN CHAMPIONSHIPS: None
BIGGEST WIN: 9–0 vs. Chinese Taipei, 1988
BIGGEST DEFEAT: 1–7 vs. Egypt 1934; vs. Germany 2002
MOST CAPS: Yossi Benayoun, **102**
MOST GOALS: Mordechai Spiegler, Eran Zahavi, **33**

MAIN DOMESTIC CLUBS

BEITAR JERUSALEM
FOUNDED: Jerusalem, 1936
STADIUM: Teddy Stadium
CAPACITY: 31,733
HOME
INTERNATIONAL HONORS: None
LEAGUE: 6 **CUP:** 7

MACCABI HAIFA
FOUNDED: Haifa, 1913
STADIUM: Sammy Ofer Stadium
CAPACITY: 30,870
HOME
INTERNATIONAL HONORS: Cup Winners' Cup quarterfinals **1999**
LEAGUE: 14 **CUP:** 6

HAPOEL TEL AVIV
FOUNDED: Tel Aviv, 1927
STADIUM: Bloomfield Stadium
CAPACITY: 29,150
HOME
INTERNATIONAL HONORS: Asia Champions Cup winners **1967**
LEAGUE: 13 **CUP:** 16

EUROPEAN ENTRY

Israel's most popular and successful Arab club, Bnei Sakhnin has fielded Jewish players and counts Israeli Jews among its fans. The team was promoted to the Israeli Premier League for the first time in 2003 and went on to win the State Cup in 2004. It subsequently qualified for the UEFA Cup, becoming the first Arab side to play in a European competition.

28 Record number of goals scored in league season by Shlomi Arbeitman in 2009–2010

48 Consecutive league games in which Maccabi Haifa was unbeaten, 1993–1994

3 Different continents Israel has been deemed part of for organizational purposes (Asia, Oceania, Europe)

1932 Year British police won the Palestine league title

5 Number of titles won consecutively by Hapoel Petah Tikva, 1958–1963

0 Number of points won by Maccabi Nes Tziona in the 1949–1950 season

EUROPE

UEFA MINNOWS

The contours of medieval Europe left a legacy of small nations, while the breakup of the USSR and Yugoslavia has added to the diversity. Not all of the lesser nations are pushovers—they are playing smarter and making the going harder for the big countries. Some of these minnows have teeth.

LIECHTENSTEIN

The Alpine microstate of Liechtenstein is a lasting remnant of the Holy Roman Empire. Its best result yet was a 2–2 home draw with Portugal in a 2006 World Cup qualifier.

LITTLE GIANTS

In Europe, the minnows are mainly confined to the principalities dotted around both the north and south of the continent, ranging from Luxembourg to Andorra. The other participants are made up of small or sparsely populated islands, such as the Faroe Islands or Iceland. The big countries regard a visit to the smaller ones as a certain win. Traditionally, very large scorelines are the norm, placing the minnows at the bottom of all the World Cup and European Championship qualifying groups. However, the smaller countries live in hope that one day they will become giant killers and pull off a sensational win.

EIDUR GUDJOHNSEN
Iceland's leading player, Gudjohnsen helped take the islanders to the European Championship in 2016.

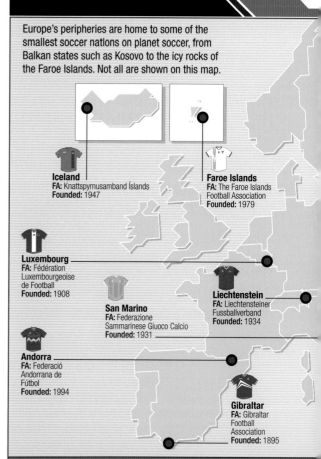

Europe's peripheries are home to some of the smallest soccer nations on planet soccer, from Balkan states such as Kosovo to the icy rocks of the Faroe Islands. Not all are shown on this map.

Iceland
FA: Knattspyrnusamband Íslands
Founded: 1947

Faroe Islands
FA: The Faroe Islands Football Association
Founded: 1979

Luxembourg
FA: Fédération Luxembourgeoise de Football
Founded: 1908

San Marino
FA: Federazione Sammarinese Giuoco Calcio
Founded: 1931

Liechtenstein
FA: Liechtensteiner Fussballverband
Founded: 1934

Andorra
FA: Federació Andorrana de Fútbol
Founded: 1994

Gibraltar
FA: Gibraltar Football Association
Founded: 1895

STAT ATTACK

NATIONAL TEAMS

ICELAND
POPULATION: 335,800
CAPITAL: Reykjavik
NATIONAL STADIUM: Laugardalsvöllur, 15,000
BIGGEST WIN: 9–0 vs. Faroe Islands, 1985
BIGGEST DEFEAT: 2–14 vs. Denmark, 1967
MOST CAPS: Birkir Bjarnason, **113**
MOST GOALS: Eidur Gudjohnsen and Kolbeinn Sigborsson, **26**

FAROE ISLANDS
POPULATION: 50,400
CAPITAL: Tórshavn
NATIONAL STADIUM: Tórsvøllor, 6,000
BIGGEST WIN: 3–0 vs. San Marino, 1995, and Liechtenstein, 2018; 4–1 vs Gibraltar, 2014
BIGGEST DEFEAT: 1–8 vs. Yugoslavia, 1996
MOST CAPS: Fróði Benjaminsen, **95**
MOST GOALS: Rógvi Jacobsen, **10**

LUXEMBOURG
POPULATION: 582,200
CAPITAL: Luxembourg City
NATIONAL STADIUM: Stade Josy Barthel, 9,000
BIGGEST WIN: 6–0 vs. Afghanistan, 1948
BIGGEST DEFEAT: 0–9 vs. England, 1960 and 1982
MOST CAPS: Mario Mutsch, **102**
MOST GOALS: Léon Mart, **16**

NATIONAL TEAMS

GIBRALTAR
POPULATION: 29,000
CAPITAL: Gibraltar
NATIONAL STADIUM: Victoria Stadium, 2,000
BIGGEST WIN: 1–0 vs. Malta, 2014
BIGGEST DEFEAT: 0–9 vs. Belgium, 2017,
MOST CAPS: Liam Walker, **41**
MOST GOALS: Lee Casciaro, Jake Gosling, **2**

MALTA
POPULATION: 415,000
CAPITAL: Valletta
NATIONAL STADIUM: Ta' Qali National Stadium, 17,797
BIGGEST WIN: 7–1 vs. Liechtenstein, 2008
BIGGEST DEFEAT: 1–12 vs. Spain, 1983
MOST CAPS: Michael Mifsud, **139**
MOST GOALS: Michael Mifsud, **41**

NATIONAL TEAMS

MOLDOVA
POPULATION: 3.5 million
CAPITAL: Chisinau
NATIONAL STADIUM: Zimbru Stadium, 10,400
BIGGEST WIN: 5–0 vs. Pakistan, 1992
BIGGEST DEFEAT: 0–6 vs. Sweden, 2001
MOST CAPS: Alexandru Epureanu, **100**
MOST GOALS: Serghei Clescenco, **11**

SLOVAKIA
POPULATION: 5.4 million
CAPITAL: Bratislava
NATIONAL STADIUM: Štadión Antona Malatinského, 19,200
BIGGEST WIN: 7–0 vs. Liechtenstein, 2004, and San Marino 2007, 2009
BIGGEST DEFEAT: 0–6 vs. Argentina, 2005, and Sweden, 2017
MOST CAPS: Marek Hamsik, **136**
MOST GOALS: Marek Hamsik, **26**

SLOVENIA
POPULATION: 1.9 million
CAPITAL: Ljubljana
NATIONAL STADIUM: Stadion Ljudski vrt, Maribor, 12,702
BIGGEST WIN: 7–0 vs. Oman, 1999
BIGGEST DEFEAT: 0–5 vs. France, 2002
MOST CAPS: Boštjan Cesar, **101**
MOST GOALS: Zlatko Zahovic, **35**

CYPRUS
POPULATION: 1.2 million
CAPITAL: Nicosia
NATIONAL STADIUM: GSP Stadium, 22,859
BIGGEST WIN: 5–0 vs. Andorra, 2000, 2014; vs San Marino, 2019
BIGGEST DEFEAT: 0–12 vs. West Germany, 1969
MOST CAPS: Yiannakis Okkas, **106**
MOST GOALS: Michalis Konstantinou, **32**

Moldova — FA: Football Association of Moldova — Founded: 1990
Slovakia — FA: Slovak Football Association — Founded: 1993
Slovenia — FA: Slovenian à la Federazione Sammarinese Giuoco Calcio — Founded: 1992
Malta — FA: Malta Football Association — Founded: 1900
Cyprus — FA: Cyprus Football Association — Founded: 1934

LIECHTENSTEIN
POPULATION: 38,022
CAPITAL: Vaduz
NATIONAL STADIUM: Rheinpark Stadion, 5,873
BIGGEST WIN: 4–0 vs. Luxembourg, 2004
BIGGEST DEFEAT: 1–11 vs. FYR Macedonia, 1996
MOST CAPS: Peter Jehle, **132**
MOST GOALS: Mario Frick, **16**

ANDORRA
POPULATION: 85,600
CAPITAL: Andorra La Vella
NATIONAL STADIUM: National Stadium, 3,306
BIGGEST WIN: 0–3 vs San Marino, 2021
BIGGEST DEFEAT: 1–8 vs. Czech Rep., 2005
MOST CAPS: Ildefons Lima, **134**
MOST GOALS: Ildefons Lima, **11**

SAN MARINO
POPULATION: 33,200
CAPITAL: San Marino City
NATIONAL STADIUM: San Marino Stadium, 6,664
BIGGEST WIN: 1–0 vs. Liechtenstein, 2004
BIGGEST DEFEAT: 0–13 vs. Germany, 2006
MOST CAPS: Matteo Vitaioli, **81**
MOST GOALS: Andy Selva, **8**

SOUTH AMERICA: CONMEBOL

SOUTH AMERICA

ARGENTINA

HOME   AWAY

POPULATION: 45.5 MILLION
CAPITAL: BUENOS AIRES
LICENSED PLAYERS:
MALE: 2.35 MILLION
FEMALE: 30,900
PROFESSIONALS: 3,500
REGISTERED CLUBS: 3,500

LIONEL MESSI
Tiny but strong and skillful, the forward is considered to be one of the game's all-time greats. Messi always dreamed of winning the World Cup, and he did so by leading his team from the front in the nail-biting final of the 2022 Men's World Cup.

Soccer has been around in Argentina for a long time—as early as 1867, a group of Englishmen formed the Buenos Aires Football Club. The game really took off when it spread beyond the expatriate community, and by 1907, there were more than 300 clubs in the country. It would be fair to describe Argentinians as soccer crazy—90 percent of the population supports a club, and when the national team plays, the country comes to a halt.

LA NUESTRA ("OUR WAY")

The style of play that has evolved in Argentina is a mixture of South American flair, Anglo-Saxon pragmatism, and *criolla viveza* ("cunning"). Argentinians play to win, and for every super-skillful Lionel Messi, there is a no-nonsense hardman such as Roberto Ayala. The nation has also developed playing positions peculiarly its own, such as the *trequartista* (three-quarter forward). The result of all these combined styles and approaches is extremely effective— Argentina is always a formidable opponent.

GOD MAKES ME PLAY WELL ...
I ALWAYS MAKE THE SIGN OF A CROSS WHEN I WALK ON THE FIELD

DIEGO MARADONA

CROSS-BORDER SKIRMISHES
In 1901, Argentina beat Uruguay 3–2 in the first official international match contested outside the UK. The two have since met in excess of 180 times, more than any other pair of nations. In the early 20th century, they sometimes played two matches in a day, one in Buenos Aires and one across the Plate River in Montevideo. The countries are separated only by the width of the river, and Uruguayans sound more like residents of Buenos Aires than the rest of Argentina's citizens.

IGLESIA MARADONIANA
Diego Maradona is often described as being like a god to Argentinians, but some take this quite literally. In 1998, the Iglesia Maradoniana ("Maradonian Church") was founded in Rosario, a city northwest of Buenos Aires. The claimed 100,000 church members celebrate Christmas on Maradona's birthday (October 30), worship in the Hand of God chapel, and date their calendars from their idol's year of birth (1960). Maradona died in 2020 and the football world paid respects to an all-time great.

STAT ATTACK

GOVERNING BODY: Asociación del Fútbol Argentino (Argentine Football Association)
FOUNDED: 1893
NATIONAL STADIUM:
El Monumental, Buenos Aires, 61,688
FIRST MATCH: 3–2 vs. Uruguay, 1901
BIGGEST WIN: 12–0 vs. Ecuador, 1942
BIGGEST DEFEAT: 6–1 vs. Bolivia, 2009

THE LEGENDS

MOST CAPPED PLAYERS

Name	From/To	Caps
Lionel MESSI	2005–present	172
Javier MASCHERANO	2003–2018	147
Javier ZANETTI	1994–2011	145
Angel Di Maria	2008–present	129
Roberto AYALA	1994–2007	115
Diego SIMEONE	1988–2002	104

TOP GOAL SCORERS

Name	From/To	Goals
Lionel MESSI	2005–present	98
Gabriel BATISTUTA	1991–2002	54
Sergio AGÜERO	2006–present	41
Hernán CRESPO	1995–2007	35
Diego MARADONA	1977–1994	34
Gonzalo HIGUAÍN	2009–2018	31

DIEGO **MARADONA**

Arguably the greatest player in history, Diego Maradona's bewitching ball control, strength, speed, and low center of gravity marked him out as unique. His eventful career includes a World Cup win, drug addiction, a heart attack, and becoming manager of Argentina.

BORN: **OCTOBER 30, 1960, LANÚS, ARGENTINA**
HEIGHT: **5 FT 5 IN (1.65 M)**
MAIN CLUBS: **ARGENTINOS JUNIORS, BOCA JUNIORS, BARCELONA, NAPOLI, SEVILLA**
INTERNATIONAL CAPS: **91**

DOMESTIC SETUP

The structure of Argentinian domestic soccer—particularly the intricacies of relegation and promotion, and qualification for the major South American club tournaments—is very complicated. The formula has been changed several times over the years. Currently, the main features are the absence of a domestic Cup—league soccer is everything in Argentina—and a division that comprises of 28 teams, all of whom play each other. River Plate head the field in league titles.

RACING CLUB AND THE BLACK CATS

Black cats are considered extremely unlucky in Argentina. In 1967, fans of the Buenos Aires club Independiente buried seven of them at the stadium of champions Racing Club while their rivals were away beating Scottish club Celtic in the Intercontinental Cup. Racing didn't win another title for 35 years, and only when the seventh cat was exhumed in 2001 did the club's fortunes begin to change.

STAT ATTACK

PRIMERA A

LEAGUE STRUCTURE: 28 teams
TOP SCORER: Arsenio Erico, **295**
MOST SUCCESSFUL TEAM: River Plate, **37** League Titles
BIGGEST WIN: 13–1, Banfield vs. Puerto Commercial, 1974
DIVISIONS BELOW PREMIER LEAGUE: Primera B Nacional (**32** teams); third tier made up Torneo Federal A (**35** teams) and Primera B Metropolitana (**19** teams)

BARRA BRAVAS

Some clubs have hard-core groups of fans known as the *barra bravas* ("tough gangs"). These organizations have an unhealthy influence on Argentinian soccer—in addition to allegedly being hired by would-be club directors to intimidate rival candidates, they reportedly extort protection money from players and commit acts of violence.

GABRIEL BATISTUTA
A quiet family man away from the field, yet lethal on it, the adored Batistuta scored 56 goals for Argentina in his international career of 11 years.

17 Red cards shown to defender Roberto Trotta during his Primera División career

2 Minutes played by Argentina's Marcelo Trobbiani during the 1986 World Cup tournament

44 Number of penalties it took to decide a 1988 match between Argentinos Juniors and Racing Club

7 Years between caps for striker Ariel Ortega, who was called up for a friendly in 2010

WORLD CUP

	1	2	3	4
Winner				
Runner-up				
Semifinals				
Quarterfinals				
Round 2				
Round 1				
Did not qualify				

COPA AMÉRICA

	1	2	3	4	5	6	7	8	9	10	11	12	13	14	15
Winner															
Runners-up															
Semi-finals															
Quarter-finals															
Round 2															
Round 1															
Did not qualify															

ARGENTINIAN CLUBS

Club soccer in Argentina has always been centered on Buenos Aires. In fact, there were no provincial teams in the national championships until the 1930s, and they still occupy less than half of the slots in the top division. *Los Cincos Grandes* ("The Big Five") won every title for nearly 40 years, with Boca Juniors and River Plate way ahead of Racing, San Lorenzo, and Independiente in terms of money and popularity. Smaller clubs such as Argentinos Juniors and Estudiantes have also had periods of success.

EL SUPERCLÁSICO

The Boca-River derby—*El Superclásico*—is a maniacal affair that is often marked by disturbances both inside and outside the stadia. Following Boca's 2–1 defeat of River at the latter's stadium in 2002, the away fans refused to leave, and heavy-handed policing precipitated a stadium-wide riot. This was then replicated among the fans of both clubs in provincial cities.

NICKNAME: LOS XENEIZES ("THE GENOESE")
FOUNDED: BUENOS AIRES, 1905
STADIUM: LA BOMBONERA, 49,000
DOMESTIC HONORS: LEAGUE 35 CUP 3
INTERNATIONAL HONORS: COPA LIBERTADORES 1977, 1978, 2000, 2001, 2003, 2007; COPA SUDAMERICANA 2004, 2005; CLUB WORLD CUP 1977, 2000, 2003

HOME

BOCA JUNIORS

Though founded by Italian immigrants, Boca took its colors from the Swedish flag—the first flag seen on a ship by early members of this port-side team. Since then, Boca has always seen itself as the team of the people—a fact not lost on former Argentinian leader General Juan Perón, who was a fan. Though the club boasts a fanatical local support, Boca is able to draw on a fan base that is countrywide. Its run of international success is unequaled in Argentine soccer.

LOS BOSTEROS

Boca's La Bombonera stadium is built on the site of a former horse manure factory. For this reason, supporters of the club are known as Bosteros ("manure handlers"). The name was originally meant as an insult, but Boca fans have embraced it with pride. The team itself is nicknamed Los Xeneizes ("the Genoese"), a reference to the Italian founders of the club.

MARTÍN PALERMO

Despite regular periods out due to injury, Palermo was regarded as a Boca Juniors legend thanks to his deadly finishing. He also makes an appearance in the record books for missing three penalties for Argentina in a single Copa América game against Colombia in 1999.

BORN: **NOVEMBER 7, 1973, LA PLATA, ARGENTINA**
HEIGHT: **6 FT 1 IN (1.87 M)**
MAIN CLUBS: **ESTUDIANTES, BOCA JUNIORS, VILLARREAL, REAL BETIS, ALAVÉS**
INTERNATIONAL CAPS: **15**

THE BOMBONERA DOESN'T TREMBLE ... ## IT BEATS!

SAYING DERIVED FROM THE FACT THAT THE BOCA JUNIORS STADIUM VIBRATES WHEN ITS FANS JUMP UP AND DOWN

BEST OF THE REST

RACING (1903)
In and out of bankruptcy for many years, Racing is one of the old greats of Argentinian soccer and the team of Eva Perón in the 1940s and '50s.
HONORS: LEAGUE 18; COPA LIBERTADORES 1967

SAN LORENZO (1908)
Formed from a street team in the Almagro barrio of Buenos Aires in 1908, San Lorenzo grew into one of the biggest clubs in the city before it relocated in the 1990s.
HONORS: LEAGUE 15; COPA LIBERTADORES 2014

INDEPENDIENTE (1905)
Founded by employees of a British store, it had great success in the Copa Libertadores.
HONORS: LEAGUE 16; COPA LIBERTADORES 1964–1965, 1972–1975, 1984; CLUB WORLD CUP 1973, 1984

ESTUDIANTES (1905)
The tiny club from La Plata surprised—and then enraged—the world with its brutal version of anti-soccer.
HONORS: LEAGUE 6; COPA LIBERTADORES 1968–1970, 2009; CLUB WORLD CUP 1968

NICKNAME: LOS MILLIONARIOS ("THE MILLIONAIRES")

FOUNDED: BUENOS AIRES, 1901

STADIUM: EL MONUMENTAL, 61,688

DOMESTIC HONORS: LEAGUE 37

INTERNATIONAL HONORS: COPA LIBERTADORES 1986, 1996, 2015, 2018; CLUB WORLD CUP 1986

HOME

RIVER PLATE

Originally based in the Boca area of Buenos Aires, River Plate always had ambition, shifting first to Palermo and then to Nuñez. Boca stayed in the docks, and River Plate became the classy team from the better part of town. In 1931, the club earned its enduring nickname *Los Millonarios* after it went on the first great spending spree in Argentine professional soccer. River Plate's style of play was defined in the 1940s and '50s by the great *La Maquina*—an elegant passing side that dominated Argentine soccer for a decade.

FLUCTUATING FORTUNES

Although River Plate is the most successful club in Argentinian soccer history, in recent years it has been in the shadow of archrival Boca Juniors. River Plate reached a nadir in 2011, when it was relegated to the second tier of Argentine soccer for the first time.

LAS GALLINAS

River Plate's title drought from 1957 to 1975 led rival fans to nickname the club *Las Gallinas* ("chickens") for a tendency to lose its head. The team came second in the league 11 times and famously squandered a 2–0 lead in the 1966 Copa Libertadores Final to lose 4–2 to Peñarol.

CLAUDIO CANIGGIA
One of the fastest players in the world, *El Pájaro* ("The Bird") once completed 109 yards in 10 seconds. Famously, the striker was not selected for national duty for several years after refusing to cut his flowing locks.

EL SUPERCLÁSICO

- Boca Juniors—**40%**
- River Plate—**33%**
- Drawn—**27%**

27 33 40

VÉLEZ SARSFIELD (1910)
Based in the west of Buenos Aires, Vélez got a new stadium from the Junta in 1978—built on a garbage-filled lagoon.

HONORS: LEAGUE 10; COPA LIBERTADORES 1994; CLUB WORLD CUP 1994

ARGENTINOS JUNIORS (1904)
A small but tough inner-city team, with a following to match. A 15-year-old Diego Maradona got his break into the club's first team.

HONORS: LEAGUE 3; COPA LIBERTADORES 1985

NEWELL'S OLD BOYS (1903)
Formed by students of the English High School in Rosario and named after a British teacher, Isaac Newell. Lost two Copa Libertadores finals during the early 1990s.

HONORS: LEAGUE 6

ROSARIO CENTRAL (1889)
Founded by English railroad workers as the Central Argentine Railroad Athletic Club. Said to have got the nickname *Callanas* ("Scoundrels") after refusing to play a charity match.

HONORS: LEAGUE 4

BRAZIL

HOME

AWAY

POPULATION: 214 MILLION
CAPITAL: BRASILIA
LICENSED PLAYERS:
MALE: 11.7 MILLION
FEMALE: 190,000
PROFESSIONALS: 16,200
REGISTERED CLUBS: 29,000

British sailors were seen playing soccer on the Rio docks during the 1870s, but it was rich European Brazilians who brought the game home in the 1890s—Charles Miller from Southampton to São Paulo and Oscar Cox from Switzerland to Rio. By the 1920s, the game was especially popular with the then-marginalized African-Brazilians. Attempts to exclude them from the professional game failed and thereafter Brazilian soccer has never looked back.

SÓCRATES
The midfielder captained Brazil at two World Cups and played for an English nonleague team. Appropriately, he had a doctorate in medicine.

WORLD CUP LEGENDS
Brazil's reputation and global popularity rest on its World Cup performances. The team dazzled at the 1938 World Cup and were favorites at home in 1950, only to lose to Uruguay. Redemption and the famous yellow shirts finally arrived with Pelé in Sweden in 1958 and Garrincha in 1962, and in 1970, the team won for the third time. Further World Cup wins came in 1994 and 2002.

STATE CHAMPIONSHIPS
In the early months of the year, before the national league starts, there are state championships around the country. Before the league was founded in 1971, these were the principal tournaments, and they remain popular.

PELÉ
Edson Arantes do Nascimento (better known as Pelé) made his debut for Santos at 15 and won the first of three World Cup winners' medals at 17. He scored over 1,000 goals, and became a global icon. The soccer legend died in 2022.

BORN: **OCTOBER 23, 1940, TRÊS CORAÇÕES, BRAZIL**
HEIGHT: **5FT 8IN (1.73M)**
MAIN CLUBS: **SANTOS, NEW YORK COSMOS**
INTERNATIONAL CAPS: **92**

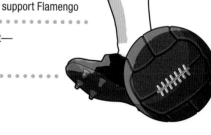

94 The number of teams in the Brazilian national championship in 1979

19.1 The percentage of Brazilian fans who support Flamengo

7,000 Members of Athletes for Christ—including six players from the 1994 World Cup squad

5 The number of Brazilian high-court judges taken on all-expenses paid trip to the 1994 World Cup Final by the Brazilian FA

STAT ATTACK

GOVERNING BODY:
Confederação Brasileira de Futebol
FOUNDED: 1914
NATIONAL STADIUM: None
FIRST MATCH: 0–3 vs. Argentina **1914**
BIGGEST WIN: 14–0 vs. Nicaragua **1975**
BIGGEST DEFEAT: 0–6 vs. Uruguay **1920**;
1–7 vs. Germany, **2014**

THE LEGENDS

MOST CAPPED PLAYER

Name	From/To	Caps
CAFU	1990–2006	142
Dani ALVES	2006–present	127
Roberto CARLOS	1992–2006	125
NEYMAR	2010–present	124
Thiago SILVA	2008–present	113
LUCIO	2000–2011	105

TOP GOAL SCORERS

Name	From/To	Goals
PELÉ	1957–1971	77
RONALDO	1994–2006	77
NEYMAR	2010–present	68
ROMÁRIO	1987–2005	55
ZICO	1971–1989	52
BEBETO	1985–1998	39

JUST THE TICKET

Brazil is so huge and its transportation infrastructure so inadequate that no national league could be played before 1970. In 1969, the government started a soccer game lottery to raise money as well as teach some geography—the tickets included games from all over the country. The lottery's popularity pressured the soccer authorities into creating a national league, resulting in the Campeonato Brasileiro kicking off in 1971.

COPA DO BRASIL

Brazil's premier knockout competition was introduced in 1989 to give the nation's smaller clubs an opportunity to compete with the big boys. The tournament is contested by 92 teams, most of them qualifying via various state championships. All stages of the cup are over two legs and the away goals rule applies. Any team that wins an away match by two goals or more in the first two rounds automatically goes through to the next round.

THE GAMA AFFAIR

Brazil's big clubs will do almost anything to avoid relegation. In 1996, Fluminense avoided relegation by having the league conveniently expanded by four teams. Three years later, Botafogo was relegated until it persuaded the CBF to reallocate some points on a technicality. This meant that a small team—Gama—was relegated instead, but the club then went to court and was reinstated. The situation was resolved only by creating a complex new one-time tournament made up of 116 clubs.

STAT ATTACK

CAMPEONATO BRASILEIRO

LEAGUE STRUCTURE: 20 teams
TOP SCORER: Roberto Dinamite, **190** goals
MOST SUCCESSFUL TEAM:
Palmeiras, **11** titles
BIGGEST WIN: 10–1 Corinthians vs. Tiradentes PI, 1983
HIGHEST ATTENDANCE: 155,523, Flamengo vs. Santos, 1983
DIVISIONS BELOW PREMIER LEAGUE:
Serie B (**20** teams), Serie C (**20** teams split into two leagues of 10), Serie D (**68** teams)

COPA DO BRASIL

The Copa was first contested in 1989. The final is a two-legged affair.
MOST SUCCESSFUL TEAMS:
Cruzeiro, **6** wins
BIGGEST WIN: 5–3, Grêmio vs. Corinthians, 2001

IN BRAZIL EVERY KID STARTS PLAYING STREET SOCCER VERY EARLY ... IT'S IN OUR BLOOD

RONALDO

WORLD CUP WINS

	Tournaments played	Tournaments won
Brazil	22	5
Italy	18	4
Germany	20	4
Argentina	18	3
Uruguay	14	2
France	16	2
England	16	1
Spain	16	1

WHERE'S THE MONEY?

Despite a record-breaking national team deal with a shirt sponsor (Nike paid around $160 million in 1996), Brazil's soccer association remained in debt for a decade and grassroots funding saw no benefit. A 2002 investigation by the Senate recommended that 17 leading CBF figures should be prosecuted.

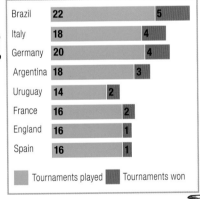

RONALDO
Blessed with lightning feet and a supernatural eye for goal, Ronaldo has scored in more World Cup finals than any other player.

WORLD CUP

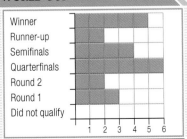

Winner
Runner-up
Semifinals
Quarterfinals
Round 2
Round 1
Did not qualify

1 2 3 4 5 6

COPA AMÉRICA

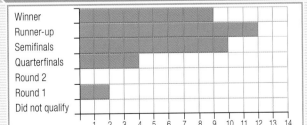

Winner
Runner-up
Semifinals
Quarterfinals
Round 2
Round 1
Did not qualify

1 2 3 4 5 6 7 8 9 10 11 12 13 14

BRAZILIAN CLUBS

Until the 1970s, Brazilian soccer was dominated by clubs from Rio and São Paulo. With the arrival of the national championship and the growth of new cities, other teams from across Brazil have since challenged them.

NICKNAME:
MENGÃO
("BIG MENGO")

FOUNDED:
RIO, 1895   HOME

STADIUM: MARACANÃ STADIUM, 78,838

DOMESTIC HONORS:
NATIONAL 7; COPA DO BRASIL 4; STATE LEAGUE 37

INTERNATIONAL HONORS:
COPA LIBERTADORES 1981; 2019, 2022 COPA MERCOSUR 1999; INTERCONTINENTAL CUP 1981

FLAMENGO

Flamengo is the biggest, best supported, and most chaotic club in Brazil. Founded in 1895 as an elite rowing club, defectors from Fluminense joined in 1911 and began playing soccer at the club. Despite these origins, Flamengo is unashamedly "the people's team," a symbolic tribune of the poor.

NICKNAME:
FLUZÃO
("BIG FLU")

FOUNDED:
RIO, 1902   HOME

STADIUM: MARACANÃ, 78,838

DOMESTIC HONORS:
NATIONAL 4; COPA DO BRASIL 1; STATE LEAGUE 32

FLUMINENSE

The most unashamedly aristocratic club in the country, Fluminense was founded by Oscar Cox, a Swiss-Brazilian from one of the city's richest families. In the early days, the ground's elegant wooden bleachers were filled with Rio's high society, who cheered in English "hip-hip-hooray."

NICKNAME:
GIGANTE DA COLINA
("HILL'S GIANT")

FOUNDED:
RIO, 1898

STADIUM: ESTÁDIO   HOME VASCO DA GAMA, 21,880

DOMESTIC HONORS:
NATIONAL 4; CUP 1; STATE LEAGUE 24

INTERNATIONAL HONORS:
COPA LIBERTADORES 1998; COPA MERCOSUR 2000

VASCO DA GAMA

Founded as a rowing club for Portuguese immigrants in 1898, the club has always had a less aristocratic and more commercial cast than the other Rio clubs. The second generation of members preferred to play soccer and to win. In the 1920s, Vasco was the first Rio club to field a black player; it was a key force in the emergence of the professional game in Brazil and ending racial discrimination in Rio soccer.

ZICO

Zico was among the greatest Brazilians to emerge in the generation after Pelé. He excelled at home with Flamengo and in Italy and Japan, boasting an extraordinary shot and miraculous free kicks.

BORN: **MARCH 3, 1953, RIO DE JANEIRO, BRAZIL**
HEIGHT: **6 FT (1.83 M)**
MAIN CLUBS: **FLAMENGO, UDINESE**
INTERNATIONAL CAPS: **88**

BEST OF THE REST

BOTAFOGO (1904)
Students from the Alfredo Gomez College founded Botafogo in the glamorous neighborhood of the same name, just north of Copacabana beach.

HONORS: NATIONAL 2; STATE LEAGUE 21; COPA CONMEBOL 1993

INTERNACIONAL (1909)
Formed in opposition to Grêmio, the team's name reflects its open recruitment policy. The Libertadores triumphs marked a new high for the club.

HONORS: NATIONAL 3; COPA DO BRASIL 1; STATE LEAGUE 45; COPA LIBERTADORES 2006, 2010; CLUB WORLD CUP 2006

PALMEIRAS (1914)
Palestra Italia started from São Paulo's Italian community. The name changed when Brazil joined the Allies during World War II.

HONORS: NATIONAL 11; COPA DO BRASIL 4; STATE LEAGUE 25; COPA LIBERTADORES 1999, 2020, 2021; COPA MERCOSUR 1998

GRÊMIO (1903)
Founded by German immigrants and established merchants, Grêmio achieved great success in the 1980s when managed by Luiz Felipe Scolari.

HONORS: NATIONAL 2; COPA DO BRASIL 5; STATE LEAGUE 41; COPA LIBERTADORES 1983, 1995, 2017

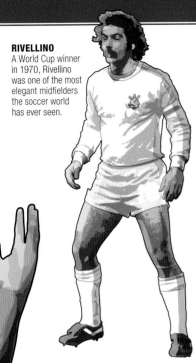

RIVELLINO
A World Cup winner in 1970, Rivellino was one of the most elegant midfielders the soccer world has ever seen.

NICKNAME:
TIMÃO ("GRAND TEAM")
FOUNDED:
SÃO PAOLO, 1910
HOME
STADIUM: ARENA CORINTHIANS, 49,205
DOMESTIC HONORS:
NATIONAL 7; COPA DO BRASIL 3; STATE LEAGUE 30
INTERNATIONAL HONORS:
COPA LIBERTADORES 2012; WORLD CLUB CUP 2000, 2012

CORINTHIANS

Founded by railroad workers in the Bom Retiro district of São Paulo, the club was named after an amateur English side that played in the city. Corinthians has retained its blue collar character and claims almost as many fans across Brazil as Flamengo.

NICKNAME:
O MAIS QUERIDO ("THE MOST LOVED")
FOUNDED:
SÃO PAULO, 1930
HOME
STADIUM:
MORUMBI, 67,053
DOMESTIC HONORS:
NATIONAL 6; STATE LEAGUE 22
INTERNATIONAL HONORS:
COPA LIBERTADORES 1992, 1993, 20F05; COPA CONMEBOL 1994; CLUB WORLD CUP 2005

SÃO PAULO

The last-formed of the big clubs from São Paulo, the team emerged from the wreckage of earlier amateur outfits in the west of the city. After living in Corinthians' shadow, it is now the strongest team in the city.

NICKNAME:
PEIXE ("THE FISH")
FOUNDED:
SANTOS, 1912
HOME
STADIUM:
VILA BELMIRO, 16,068
DOMESTIC HONORS:
NATIONAL 8; COPA DO BRASIL 1; STATE LEAGUE 22
INTERNATIONAL HONORS:
COPA LIBERTADORES 1962, 1963, 2011; COPA CONMEBOL 1998; CLUB WORLD CUP 2011

SANTOS

A short drive south of São Paulo, Santos is the city's port. The club played second fiddle to those in Rio until the arrival of Pelé, who played most of his career here and for a short period in the early 1960s made it the best team in the world.

CARLOS ALBERTO
Defender Carlos Alberto captained the legendary World Cup–winning Brazil team of 1970.

RECORD CROWD

In December 1963, Fluminense played Flamengo in the second leg of the final of the Carioca state championship. In addition to 177,656 paying spectators, another 16,947 entered without tickets, to make a grand total of 194,603 fans. The score was 0–0.

BRAZILIAN SUPPORT

The rest—**45%**
Rio Clubs—**30%**
São Paulo Clubs—**25%**

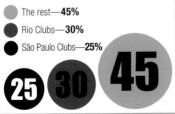

ATLÉTICO MINEIRO (1908)
Won the first national championship in 1971. A period of success from 2000 culminated in the 2013 Copa Libertadores.

HONORS: NATIONAL 1 COPA DO BRASIL 1; STATE LEAGUE 47; COPA CONMEBOL 1992, 1997; COPA LIBERTADORES 2013

CRUZEIRO (1921)
Founded by Italian immigrants as Palestra Mineiro, it originally played in the colors of the Italian flag. During World War II, it changed its name to Cruzeiro.

HONORS: NATIONAL 4; COPA DO BRASIL 6; STATE LEAGUE 40; COPA LIBERTADORES 1976, 1997

BAHIA (1931)
Bahia is the biggest club in northern Brazil. In recent years, it has suffered calamitous bankruptcies and numerous relegations but still manages to draw the biggest crowds in all of Brazilian soccer.

HONORS: NATIONAL 2; STATE LEAGUE 49

RECIFE (1905)
Known locally as "Sport," the club won the chaotically mismanaged 1987 national championship. Recife climbed out of the lower divisions and won the Copa Do Brasil in 2008.

HONORS: NATIONAL 1; COPA DO BRASIL 1; STATE LEAGUE 42

GLOBAL MIGRATION

Soccer was introduced to the world by waves of English and Scottish migrants in the 19th century. The earliest non-British clubs, such as Genoa and Milan in Italy or Barcelona in Spain, had a truly cosmopolitan makeup. By the 1930s, Latin American players began to travel across the globe, with African players following suit in the 1940s and '50s. Today the migration patterns of players are truly global and involve virtually every league—from the poorly resourced to the super-rich.

KEY
● Major importer of players
○ Major exporter of players

EUROPE (UEFA)

○ **England**
Since the arrival of the Premier League, England has become the biggest importer of foreign players.

● **France**
A great youth-training system has seen France become a major exporter.

● **Netherlands**
A "conveyor belt" of talent has created players that have outgrown their home country.

○ **Spain**
Spain's transfer market once had a ban on foreign players; it now embraces internationalism.

● **Sweden and Denmark**
Swedish and Danish players' diligence and adaptability has seen them flourish as soccer migrants.

○ **Portugal**
Portuguese clubs first drew on the talent of the country's African colonies in the 1950s and '60s.

○ **Italy**
For decades, Italian clubs attracted elite global players, but today they are often out-bid by English and Spanish clubs.

○ **Turkey**
Istanbul's biggest clubs, such as Fenerbahçe and Galatasaray, have the money to entice players from all over the world.

○ **Russia**
The arrival of the new super-rich in the early 2000s, with their oil and gas money, started a wave of migration.

● **Serbia and Croatia**
Serbia and Croatia are among the biggest exporters of players in Europe.

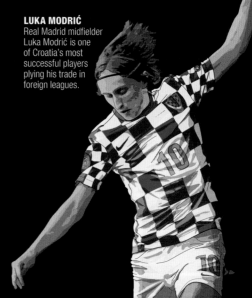

LUKA MODRIĆ
Real Madrid midfielder Luka Modrić is one of Croatia's most successful players plying his trade in foreign leagues.

PERCENTAGE OF FOREIGN PLAYERS IN EUROPE'S BIGGEST LEAGUES

● Premier League—England: **69%**
● Serie A—Italy: **55%**
○ Bundesliga—Germany: **49%**
● Ligue 1—France: **47%**
○ La Liga—Spain: **44%**

47

44

49 55 69

FROM MINNOWS TO MAJORS

NORTHAMPTON TOWN
Until 1961, the small English club had been promoted out of the bottom league only twice. In that year, however, it set out on a roller-coaster ride of success and failure. Promoted in successive years from 1962 to '64, the club reached its zenith in 1965–1966, when it played its only season of top-flight soccer. The club was then relegated every year until 1968, when "normal service" was resumed in division four.

COTON SPORT
For years Coton Sport was just the amateur works team of Cameroon's largest cotton company. However, in 1986, it joined the Cameroonian league and, in 1993, was promoted to the top level. The team has been in the top two leagues ever since. Coton Sport played its first African Champions League Final in 2008, narrowly losing to Cairo's venerable Al Ahly.

TSG 1899 HOFFENHEIM
In the late 1990s, TSG 1899 Hoffenheim—an amateur club from the suburbs of small-town Sinsheim in southern Germany—was languishing in the fifth level of German soccer. Dietmar Hopp, founder and owner of the software giant SAP, had played for the club in his youth, and it was his financial backing that took them all the way to the Bundesliga in 2008. The club was at the top of the league by Christmas of the first season, no mean feat given that it was all achieved away from home (Hopp was still building a new 30,000-seat stadium).

SÃO CAETANO
São Caetano is an anonymous suburb of São Paulo, Brazil, and the team was founded only in 1989. In 2000, however, the madness of the Brazilian league saw teams from the second and third divisions play the top teams of the first division for the national title—São Caetano made it to the final. Although the club lost, it continued its top-flight run the following year, making it to the finals of the Copa Libertadores.

SOUTH AMERICA (CONMEBOL)

Argentina
Argentinians of Italian descent were first enticed to Europe in the 1930s by the promise of huge wages.

Brazil
Few players left the country during the golden era of the 1950s and '60s, but Brazilians have been heading overseas ever since.

Uruguay
With a population of only 3 million, Uruguay exports more players per capita than anywhere else in the world.

Colombia, Ecuador, and Peru
As players from Argentina and Brazil have left for Europe, Colombians, Ecuadorians, and Peruvians have stepped into the breach.

ASIA (AFC)

China
China's growing wealth has made the country's top division an attractive prospect for international superstars.

Japan
The J-League attracts talent from Korea, Australia, and Brazil.

Qatar
Qatar's clubs have big budgets but very little home-grown talent.

NORTH AND CENTRAL AMERICA, AND THE CARIBBEAN (CONCACAF)

Mexico
The rising wealth and ambition of Mexican clubs has seen an influx of foreign players to its leagues.

USA
With a growing interest in the sport and deep pockets, the US is able to attract world-class players.

AFRICA (CAF)

Egypt and Tunisia
Egypt, Tunisia, and the surrounding region, have a long history of exporting players throughout Europe.

Nigeria and Cameroon
West African countries, most notably Nigeria and Cameroon, have been supplying talent to Europe since the 1930s.

1,500 The number of Brazilian players transferred abroad in 2011—more than any other nationality

23 The most common age for a player to be transferred to a foreign club

0 The number of foreign players at Guadalajara and Athletic Bilbao—both have Mexican- and Basque-only policies respectively

9 The number of English Premier League teams who bought exclusively foreign players in 2013

SOUTH AMERICA

PARAGUAY

HOME   AWAY

POPULATION: 6.8 MILLION
CAPITAL: ASUNCIÓN
FA: ASOCIACIÓN PARAGUAYA DE FÚTBOL

Soccer arrived in the Paraguayan capital Asunción in the late 1890s with the Dutch teacher William Paats. In 1902, Paats helped found the nation's first club, Olimpia, and in 1903 a second club, Guaraní, was founded to provide some opposition.

COPA AMÉRICA HOST

In 1953, Paraguay had the honor of hosting its first Copa América. However, the state of Paraguay's soccer infrastructure was so poor that despite retaining administrative control of the tournament, the Paraguayan governing body relocated it to Lima, Peru.

CAPITAL TEAM

Olimpia won three Copa Libertadores under the presidency of Osvaldo Dibb, a successful businessman and central figure in Paraguayan politics. Olimpia's many trophies include six consecutive league championships.

HOME   AWAY

POPULATION: 3.3 MILLION
CAPITAL: MONTEVIDEO
FA: ASOCIACIÓN URUGUAYA DE FÚTBOL

URUGUAY

Soccer came to Montevideo in the 1880s before a Scottish teacher founded the first team in 1893. By the early 20th century, a league had been formed, followed by professionalism in the 1930s. Uruguay has won two World Cups and two Olympic gold medals.

EL MUNDIALITO

In 1980, the ruling military dictatorship decided to promote themselves and celebrate the 50-year anniversary of the first World Cup by staging a mini "world cup" of past champions. England would not go, so the Dutch went instead. Not surprisingly, Uruguay won.

CHAMPIONSHIP COW

For most of the 20th century, all the soccer teams in the Uruguayan top division were from Montevideo. In 1998, a provincial team was finally promoted, and since then places have been allocated to teams from outside of the capital. In 2004, Rocha was the first provincial side to win the league and celebrated by parading a cow around its field.

LUIS SUÁREZ
A versatile and highly coveted striker, Suárez made his national team debut in 2007. He won the Copa América with Uruguay in 2011.

UNIVERSITY VS. THE RAILROADS

Domestic soccer has been dominated by a century-long struggle between two teams. Nacional plays in the national colors and is founded by rich students. Peñarol, founded as a railroad club, is seen as the team of the poor.

CHILE

Soccer arrived in Chile in the late 19th century via British sailors. The first club, Santiago Wanderers, was founded in Valparaíso in 1892. A Santiago league was in place by 1895, although the provincial teams did not join until the 1950s.

HOME   AWAY

POPULATION: 18.9 MILLION
CAPITAL: SANTIAGO
FA: FEDERACIÓN DE FÚTBOL DE CHILE

MIXED HISTORY

In November 1973, two months after General Pinochet's military coup, Chile qualified for the 1974 World Cup by scoring a goal with no opposition on the field. The Soviet Union, its opponent, had refused to play the match because the national stadium was also being used as a prison camp.

BANKRUPTCY BENEFITS

In 2002, Colo-Colo, the nation's biggest soccer club, went bankrupt with debts of at least $30 million. The players were forced to arrange friendlies and benefit concerts to raise funds. They were rewarded by larger turnouts than the club had been getting before the collapse.

MARCELO SALAS
One of Chile's most famous soccer sons, Salas was known as *El Matador* ("The Killer") thanks to his lethal left foot and slew of spectacular goals.

STAT ATTACK

NATIONAL TEAM

NICKNAME: La Roja ("The Red One")
NATIONAL STADIUM: El Nacional, 48,665
WORLD CUP FINALS: 9 appearances
COPA AMÉRICA: Winners **2015**, **2016**

MAIN DOMESTIC CLUBS

COLO-COLO
FOUNDED: Santiago, 1925
STADIUM: El Monumental, 47,347

UNIVERSIDAD DE CHILE
FOUNDED: Santiago, 1911
STADIUM: El Nacional, 48,665

COBRELOA
FOUNDED: Calama, 1977
STADIUM: Zorros del Desierto, 12,000

BOLIVIA

HOME   AWAY

POPULATION: 10.9 MILLION
CAPITAL: LA PAZ
FA: FEDERACIÓN BOLIVIANA DE FÚTBOL

Bolivian soccer began in 1896 with the formation of Royal Oruro Club, using teams of railroad workers. Traditionally, Bolivar and The Strongest from high in the Andes dominate. More recently, the teams from the lowlands, such as Jorge Wilstermann, have challenged them.

THE ALTITUDE GAME

In 2007, FIFA banned international matches being played above 9,022 ft (2,750 m), which meant that Bolivia could not play home games in La Paz. A campaign by President Evo Morales saw the ban rescinded a year later.

WORLD CUP GOAL

Bolivia's appearance at the 1994 World Cup tournament was its best yet. Although it didn't win a match, it did score in its 3–1 defeat by Spain. In 1930, Bolivia lost 4–0 to both Yugoslavia and Brazil and in 1950 lost 8–0 to Uruguay.

STAT ATTACK

NATIONAL TEAM

NICKNAME: La Verde ("The Green One")
NATIONAL STADIUM: Estadio Hernando Siles, 41,143
WORLD CUP FINALS: 3 appearances
COPA AMÉRICA: Winners **1963**

MAIN DOMESTIC CLUBS

BOLIVAR
FOUNDED: La Paz, 1925
STADIUM: Estadio Hernando Siles, 41,143

JORGE WILSTERMANN
FOUNDED: Cochabamba, 1949
STADIUM: Félix Capriles, 32,000

THE STRONGEST
FOUNDED: La Paz, 1908
STADIUM: Estadio Hernando Siles, 41,143

SOUTH AMERICA

PERU

HOME AWAY

POPULATION: 33.2 MILLION
CAPITAL: LIMA
FA: FEDERACIÓN PERUANA DE FÚTBOL

By 1900, the wealthy elite of Lima had adopted soccer from British expatriates. The urban poor were also quick to join in, creating Alianza Lima in 1901 in La Victoria, the working-class area of the capital. Peru peaked with the 1970s side led by Teófilo Cubillas. The side attended two World Cups and won the Copa América, although needing the toss of a coin to beat Brazil in the semifinal.

1936 OLYMPICS
Peru's exuberant, multiracial team beat Austria 4–2 in the quarterfinals of the 1936 Berlin Olympics. The Nazi authorities were desperate for a Germanic team to progress so insisted on a replay due to Peruvian fan celebrations on the field. Peru went home in disgust.

THE ESTADIO NACIONAL DISASTER
Angry scenes among Peru fans at the end of a 1964 Olympic qualifying defeat to Argentina led police to fire tear gas into the crowd at Lima's Estadio Nacional ground. More than 350 people died in the resulting stampede, the highest fatality of any stadium disaster.

NATIONAL STADIUM: Estadio Nacional, 50,000
WORLD CUP FINALS: 5 appearances, second round **1970** and **1978**
COPA AMÉRICA: Winners **1939, 1975**

MAIN DOMESTIC CLUBS

UNIVERSITARIO DE DEPORTES
FOUNDED: Lima, 1924
STADIUM: Monumental "U," 80,093

ALIANZA LIMA
FOUNDED: Lima, 1901
STADIUM: Alejandro Villanueva, 35,000

SPORTING CRISTAL
FOUNDED: Lima, 1955
STADIUM: Estadio Alberto Gallardo, 18,000

TEÓFILO CUBILLAS
Nicknamed "The Babe," midfielder Cubillas scored in every Peru game at the 1970 World Cup and won South American Player of the Year in 1972.
BORN: MARCH 8, 1949, LIMA, PERU
HEIGHT: 5 FT 8 IN (1.73 M)
MAIN CLUBS: ALIANZA LIMA, PORTO
INTERNATIONAL CAPS: 81

NATIONAL STADIUM: Olímpico Atahualpa, 35,724
WORLD CUP FINALS: 4 appearances
COPA AMÉRICA: 27 appearances, semifinals **1959, 1993, 2021**

MAIN DOMESTIC CLUBS

EL NACIONAL
FOUNDED: Quito, 1964
STADIUM: Olímpico Atahualpa, 35,724

BARCELONA
FOUNDED: Guayaquil, 1925
STADIUM: Monumentall, 57,267

LDU QUITO
FOUNDED: Quito, 1918
STADIUM: Casa Blanca, 41,575

ECUADOR

HOME AWAY

POPULATION: 13.5 MILLION
CAPITAL: QUITO
FA: FEDERACIÓN ECUATORIANA DE FÚTBOL

Soccer came to Ecuador in 1898 with European students in the port of Guayaquil. A citywide league was in existence by 1908, and the game spread to the capital city, Quito, by the 1930s. Ecuador's international results have improved since 2002.

WORLD CUP 2002
Ecuador has been a minor player for much of its history, but the 21st century has brought a change in fortunes. The national team qualified for the World Cup for the first time in 2002 and reached the second round in 2006.

FOUNDING ORIGINS
Barcelona, Ecuador's leading club, was founded by Catalan immigrants. El Nacional is the team of the Ecuadorian armed forces, while LDU Quito have ties to the city's university.

VENEZUELA

HOME

AWAY

POPULATION: 28.5 MILLION
CAPITAL: CARACAS
FA: FEDERACIÓN VENEZOLANA DE FÚTBOL

Soccer in Venezuela suffers from competition with baseball, the national sport. The game has improved in the 2000s, though only relatively, with modest World Cup qualifying wins for the national side and first-round victories in the Copa Libertadores.

SLOW STARTERS

Venezuela has been called the *Cenicienta* ("Cinderella") team of South American soccer, winning just two games in its first 30 years. In 2007, Venezuela hosted the Copa América for the first time and reached the quarterfinals. In 2011, it got to the semifinals but lost to Paraguay on penalties.

STAT ATTACK

NATIONAL TEAM

NATIONAL STADIUM: None
WORLD CUP FINALS: No appearances
COPA AMÉRICA: 19 appearances; semifinals **2011**; quarterfinals **2007**

MAIN DOMESTIC CLUBS

CARACAS FC
FOUNDED: Caracas, 1967
STADIUM: Estadio Olímpico, 23,940

DEPORTIVO TÁCHIRA
FOUNDED: San Cristóbal, 1974
STADIUM: Polideportivo de Pueblo Nuevo, 42,500

COLOMBIA

Soccer was slow to gain popularity in Colombia, first catching on in the ports in the early 20th century before spreading to the big cities in the 1930s and 1940s. Ever since the national league was set up in 1948, the domestic game has been plagued by corruption.

HOME

AWAY

POPULATION: 47.2 MILLION
CAPITAL: BOGOTÁ
FA: FEDERACIÓN DE COLOMBIANA DE FÚTBOL

INTERNATIONAL SUCCESS

Colombia has been to six World Cups and reached the quarterfinals in 2014. The 2001 Copa América win was wildly celebrated, but the country's finest hour was a 5–0 World Cup qualifying win over Argentina in 1993.

DOMESTIC CORRUPTION

Soccer in Colombia has had a history of being tinged by corruption. Opposing teams were controlled by rival drug cartels in the 1970s, and betting scams and intimidation of officials escalated to the extent that Colombia gave up the right to host the 1986 World Cup.

RADAMEL **FALCAO**

Considered one of the world's most prolific strikers, Falcao averaged almost a goal per game during his second season at Atlético Madrid (2012–2013).

BORN: FEBRUARY 10, 1986, SANTA MARTA, COLOMBIA
HEIGHT: 5 FT 10 IN (1.78 M) **MAIN CLUBS:** RIVER PLATE, ATLÉTICO MADRID, MONACO, MANCHESTER UNITED, CHELSEA, GALATASARAY, RAYO VALLECANO
INTERNATIONAL CAPS: 102

STAT ATTACK

NATIONAL TEAM

NATIONAL STADIUM: Metropolitano, 49,692
WORLD CUP FINALS: 5 appearances, quarterfinals 2014
COPA AMÉRICA: 21 appearances, winners **2001**; runner-up **1975**; semifinals **2021**

MAIN DOMESTIC CLUBS

MILLONARIOS
FOUNDED: Bogotá, 1946
STADIUM: El Campín, 36,343

AMÉRICA DE CALI
FOUNDED: Cali, 1927
STADIUM: Pascual Guerrero, 35,402

ATLÉTICO NACIONAL
FOUNDED: Medellín, 1947
STADIUM: Atanasio Girardot, 40,043

NORTH AND CENTRAL AMERICA AND THE CARIBBEAN: CONCACAF

CONCACAF

US

Soccer arrived in the US in the 1870s, by which time football had been invented and baseball was the national sport. Strongest among immigrant communities from European countries, "soccer" acquired an ethnic, working-class identity. It also became popular in colleges, but until the 1990s and the MLS, the professional game did not take off.

HOME

AWAY

POPULATION: 329.4 MILLION
CAPITAL: WASHINGTON, D.C.
FA: UNITED STATES SOCCER FEDERATION
LICENSED PLAYERS:
MALE: 17.4 MILLION
FEMALE: 7.1 MILLION
PROFESSIONALS: 1,500
REGISTERED CLUBS: 5,000

WORLD CUP AMBITIONS

The US entered the first World Cup in 1930, beating Belgium and Paraguay 3–0 to reach the semifinals. Its 6–1 loss to Argentina, which FIFA lists as third place, remains the team's highest-ever World Cup finish.

STAT ATTACK

NATIONAL TEAM

NATIONAL STADIUM: None
WORLD CUP FINALS: 11 appearances, semifinals **1930**, quarterfinals **2002**
CONCACAF CHAMPIONSHIPS/GOLD CUP: Winners **1991, 2002, 2005, 2007, 2013, 2017, 2021**
BIGGEST WIN: 8–0 vs. Barbados, 2008
BIGGEST DEFEAT: 0–11 vs. Norway, 1948
MOST CAPS: Cobi Jones, **164**
MOST GOALS: Landon Donovan, **57**

MAIN DOMESTIC CLUBS

DC UNITED
FOUNDED: Washington, D.C. 1995
STADIUM: Audi Field
CAPACITY: 20,000
HOME
INTERNATIONAL HONORS: CONCACAF Club Championship winners **1998**
LEAGUE: 4 CUP: 3

LA GALAXY
FOUNDED: Los Angeles, 1994
STADIUM: Dignity Health Sports Park
CAPACITY: 27,000
HOME
INTERNATIONAL HONORS: CONCACAF Club Championship winners **2000**
LEAGUE: 5 CUP: 2

CHICAGO FIRE
FOUNDED: Chicago, 1997
STADIUM: Soldier Field
CAPACITY: 61,500
HOME
INTERNATIONAL HONORS: CONCACAF Champions League 3rd place **1999, 2004**
LEAGUE: 1 **CUP:** 4

MAJOR LEAGUE SOCCER

Set up in 1996 as a condition of hosting the 1994 World Cup, Major League Soccer (MLS) started small, with just 10 sides. It steadily expanded to include 29 teams, the top 14 of which compete in postseason playoffs to determine who wins the championship.

THE SOCCER LEAGUE

The North American Soccer League (NASL) was founded in 1967 to revive the professional game in the US. Early attendance and viewing figures were low, and a number of foreign teams had to be imported and renamed to keep the show on the road. However, after the New York Cosmos signed an aging Pelé in 1975, the NASL instantly acquired glamour and fans. Pelé stayed for five years, but by 1985, NASL was reduced to an indoor tournament, and it ultimately folded.

COBI JONES

Starting out at England's Coventry City, Jones was one of the American stars who returned to the US to join the inaugural MLS season in 1996. He became an MLS legend, playing for LA Galaxy for 11 seasons. When he retired in 2007, the club also retired his "13" shirt.

BORN: JUNE 16, 1970, DETROIT, MICHIGAN
HEIGHT: 5 FT 7 IN (1.7 M)
MAIN CLUBS: COVENTRY CITY, VASCO DA GAMA, LA GALAXY
INTERNATIONAL CAPS: 164

THE BECKS EFFECT

When England star David Beckham, nicknamed "Becks," joined LA Galaxy in 2007, it hugely lifted the profile of MLS. Without his arrival, other superstars such as Thierry Henry and David Villa might not have switched to the US in later years. In 2014, Beckham began creating his own MLS team, and Inter Miami finally kicked off in March 2020.

1894
The year owners of US baseball franchises tried to run a professional winter soccer league in their ballparks—it lasted a single season

8
The number of goals scored by the New York Cosmos in their 1977 championship playoff victory over Fort Lauderdale—the 77,000-strong crowd at Giants Stadium was also a new record for soccer in the US

CANADA

HOME   AWAY

POPULATION: 37.3 MILLION
CAPITAL: OTTAWA
FA: CANADA SOCCER ASSOCIATION
LICENSED PLAYERS:
MALE: 1.8 MILLION
FEMALE: 86,000
PROFESSIONALS: 150
REGISTERED CLUBS: 7,000

With just two Men's World Cup appearances and no national professional league, Canada remains small in soccer terms. The arrival of European migrants after World War II enlivened the soccer scene for a time, but ultimately soccer has to compete against established sports such as baseball, basketball, Canadian football, and ice hockey.

CANADIAN PREMIER LEAGUE

The country has suffered from a lack of professional soccer, with teams such as Toronto FC and Vancouver Whitecaps competing in the MLS in the US. The Canadian Soccer League folded in the early '90s, and it took until 2019 for the new Canadian Premier League (CPL) to finally kick off. Forge FC, from Hamilton, Ontario, won three of the four titles.

WHO IS THE CHAMPION?

Traditionally, Canada's biggest clubs play in the MLS and second-tier USL-1 leagues in the US. As a consequence, there was no Canadian national champion to compete in the CONCACAF Championship until 2008, when a round-robin playoff between the Montreal Impact, Toronto FC, and the Vancouver Whitecaps—the country's three pro teams at the time—was started. Montreal emerged victorious, becoming Canada's first representative in 33 years.

INTERNATIONAL PLAYERS

The Canadian national team would possibly do better if more of the best players eligible to join them did so; but the best often seem to have relatives elsewhere. The excellent Jonathan de Guzmán, playing with Feyenoord, chose Holland, while his brother Julian remained a mainstay of the Canadian midfield. Owen Hargreaves, of Manchester United, chose England.

WORLD CUP 1986

Canada secured its spot at the 1986 World Cup by beating Honduras 2–1 in St. John's, Newfoundland, in 1985. In the final, however, Canada lost its first match 1–0 to France and, after further defeats by 2–0 to both Hungary and the USSR, it went home without gaining a single point or scoring a single goal.

PAUL **PESCHISOLIDO**

A well-traveled player, Peschisolido played for several clubs on both sides of the Atlantic. He scored 10 goals in his 53 appearances for Canada.

BORN: **MAY 25, 1971, SCARBOROUGH, ONTARIO, CANADA**
HEIGHT: **5 FT 7 IN (1.7 M)**
MAIN CLUBS: **TORONTO BLIZZARD, BIRMINGHAM CITY, STOKE CITY, FULHAM, SHEFFIELD UNITED, DERBY COUNTY**
INTERNATIONAL CAPS: 53

THE FLIP OF A COIN

Canada won the 2000 CONCACAF Gold Cup, beating Colombia 2–0 in the final. However, the victory ultimately rested on the toss of a coin. Having finished level with South Korea in the group stage, a coin had to be flipped to determine who went through to the knockout stages.

STAT ATTACK

NATIONAL TEAM

NICKNAME: The Canucks, Les Rouges
NATIONAL STADIUM: BMO Field
CAPACITY: 30,000
WORLD CUP FINALS: 2 appearances, **1986, 2022**
CONCACAF CHAMPIONSHIPS/GOLD CUP: 15 appearances, winners **1985, 2000**
BIGGEST WIN: 8–0 vs. US Virgin Islands, 2018
BIGGEST DEFEAT: 0–8 vs. Mexico, 1993
MOST CAPS: Atiba Hutchinson, **100**
MOST GOALS: Cyle Larin, **25**

MAIN DOMESTIC CLUBS

TORONTO FC
FOUNDED: Toronto, 2005
STADIUM: BMO Field
CAPACITY: 30,000
INTERNATIONAL HONORS: None
LEAGUE: 7 **CUP:** 4

MONTREAL IMPACT
FOUNDED: Montreal, 2010
STADIUM: Saputo
CAPACITY: 20,801
INTERNATIONAL HONORS: None
LEAGUE: 3 **CUP:** 0

VANCOUVER WHITECAPS
FOUNDED: Vancouver, 1974
STADIUM: BC Place
CAPACITY: 54,313
INTERNATIONAL HONORS: None
LEAGUE: 2 **CUP:** 3

MEXICO

Soccer was brought to Mexico City in the late 19th century by British expatriates and French and Spanish immigrants. The first club, Pachuca Athletic, was founded in 1900 by British engineers and was soon joined by other teams from Mexico City. After the Mexican Revolution of 1920–1930, key Mexican teams emerged—América, Atlanta, and Necaxa. UNAM followed in the 1950s, Cruz Azul in the 1970s, and Toros Neza in 1991.

HOME   AWAY

POPULATION: 130.2 MILLION
CAPITAL: MEXICO CITY
FA: FEDERACIÓN MEXICANA DE FÚTBOL ASOCIACIÓN
LICENSED PLAYERS:
MALE: 325,000
FEMALE: 13,000
PROFESSIONALS: 4,500
REGISTERED CLUBS: 311

STAT ATTACK

NATIONAL TEAM

NICKNAME: El Tri ("Three-colored Flag")
NATIONAL STADIUM: Estadio Azteca, 87,000
WORLD CUP FINALS: 16 appearances, quarterfinals 1970 and 1986
CONCACAF CHAMPIONSHIPS: Winners **1965**, **1971**, **1977**, **1993**, **1996**, **1998**, **2003**, **2009**, **2011**, **2015**, **2019**
COPA AMÉRICA: Runner-up **2001**
BIGGEST WIN: 13–0 vs. Bahamas, 1987
BIGGEST DEFEAT: 0–8 vs. England, 1961
MOST CAPS: Andres Guardado, 178
MOST GOALS: Javier Hernández, 52

OLYMPIC PLAYERS

Mexico was absent from the 1990 World Cup following a ban from international competition after fielding over-age players in the qualifiers for the 1988 Olympics under-20 competition.

A NATIONAL LEAGUE

The difficulties of getting teams around Mexico because of its sheer size and the lack of transportation meant there were only regional leagues and cup competitions until a national league was created in 1944. In the 1970s, the league format shifted to its current structure, in which many small groups of teams compete for places in a playoff system to determine the championship. In 1996, the league was split into two separate championships—an *Apertura* ("Opening") and a *Clausura* ("Closing"). The Mexican Cup was discontinued in 1998 but reinstated in 2012.

NORTH, SOUTH, OR CENTRAL AMERICA

Mexico's geographical position means teams compete in a variety of continental competitions, such as the North-American, the Pan-American, and the Central-American games. Since CONCACAF was formed, Mexico has played in its Gold Cup and club competitions but regularly attends South American tournaments.

HOSTS BUT NOT CHAMPIONS

Mexico has a fine World Cup pedigree, especially at home. The national team has made it to the quarterfinals of the tournament twice—in 1970, losing to Italy, and in 1986, losing to Germany. On both occasions, it was the host nation.

JAVIER **HERNÁNDEZ**

Nicknamed "Chicharito" (Little Pea)—his father, also a Mexican international, was dubbed "Chicharo" (Pea) on account of his green eyes—Hernández made his debut for Mexico in 2009. He finished the 2011 Gold Cup, which Mexico won, as the tournament's top scorer (seven goals) and went on to become Mexico's all-time leading goal scorer.

BORN: **JUNE 1, 1988, GUADALAJARA, MEXICO**
HEIGHT: **5 FT 9 IN (1.75 M)**
MAIN CLUBS: **GUADALAJARA, MANCHESTER UNITED, REAL MADRID, BAYER LEVERKUSEN, WEST HAM UNITED**
INTERNATIONAL CAPS: **109**

NICKNAME
AZULCREMAS ("BLUE AND CREAMS")

HOME

FOUNDED: MEXICO CITY, 1916

STADIUM: ESTADIO AZTECA, 87,000

DOMESTIC HONORS: LEAGUE: 13 CUP: 6

INTERNATIONAL HONORS: CONCACAF CHAMPIONS LEAGUE 1977, 1987, 1990, 1992, 2006, 2014, 2015, 2016

CF AMÉRICA

For half a century, CF América was the team of the ruling order and its twin pillars, the main political party, the PRI, and Televisa—the main TV station. The giant TV conglomerate Televisa has shaped the landscape of Mexico City's soccer, and for many years, the club received privileged network coverage.

JORGE CAMPOS
Well known for his self-designed garish goalkeeping shirts, Campos sometimes played as striker.

EL CLÁSICO

El Clásico is the derby game between CF América and Guadalajara—the two biggest and best supported teams in Mexico. The competition is all the greater as it is the team from the capital playing the one from the provinces.

EL CLÁSICO
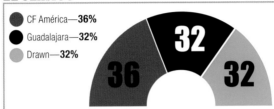

- CF América—**36%**
- Guadalajara—**32%**
- Drawn—**32%**

36 / 32 / 32

NICKNAME: LOS CHIVAS ("THE GOATS")

HOME

FOUNDED: GUADALAJARA, 1906

STADIUM: ESTADIO AKRON, 49,850

DOMESTIC HONORS: LEAGUE: 12 CUP: 4

INTERNATIONAL HONORS: CONCACAF CHAMPIONS LEAGUE 1962, 2018

GUADALAJARA

More commonly known as *Los Chivas* or "the goats," Guadalajara has never been out of the Mexican top flight, and it has done so fielding only Mexican-born players—a recruitment policy the club began in 1943. Ironically, Guadalajara began life as Club Union founded by a Belgian and a Frenchman. From 2002, the fortunes of the club were transformed by billionaire owner-president Jorge Vergara.

1985 The year of the Azteca disaster—10 were killed and 29 injured in a crash at the Mexican Cup final between UNAM and América

24 The number of different clubs who have won the Mexican national championships

4 The number of Pan-American Games titles won by the Mexican national team

107,412 Official attendance at the 1970 World Cup Final in the famous Estadio Azteca, Mexico City

BEST OF THE REST

CRUZ AZUL (1927)
Founded in 1927, this team of working-class Mexico City was the first Mexican team to reach the final of the Copa Libertadores.
HONORS: LEAGUE 9, CUP 4; CONCACAF CHAMPIONS LEAGUE 1969–1971, 1996–1997, 2014

ATLANTE (1916)
Founded in 1916, the club began as Sinaola, switched to Lusitania and U-53 before settling on Atlante. It draws its support from its roots in the inner-city zones of Mexico City.
HONORS: LEAGUE 3, CUP 3; CONCACAF CHAMPIONS LEAGUE 1983, 2009

TOLUCA (1917)
Founded in 1917, Toluca was successful in the 1960s and 1970s. In 2003, this provincial team won the CONCACAF Champions League in the first all-Mexican final against Morelia.
HONORS: LEAGUE 10, CUP 2; CONCACAF CHAMPIONS LEAGUE 1968, 2003

UNAM (1954)
The club was founded as the team of the University of Mexico. No longer run by the university, nor fielding students, it retains its commitment to supporting young players.
HONORS: LEAGUE 7, CUP 1; CONCACAF CHAMPIONS LEAGUE 1980, 1982, 1989

PACHUCA (1901)
The oldest Mexican club reached the top flight in 1998, won the national championship in 1999, and won the Copa Sudamericana in 2006.
HONORS: LEAGUE 6; CONCACAF CHAMPIONS LEAGUE 2002, 2007, 2008, 2010, 2017; COPA SUDAMERICANA 2006

NECAXA (1923)
For nearly 80 years, Necaxa was based in Mexico City. It was bought by Televisa and, in 2002, was moved north to a town without a top-flight team—Aguascalientes.
HONORS: LEAGUE 3, CUP 8; CONCACAF CHAMPIONS LEAGUE 1975, 1999

DOMESTIC CLUBS

LA GALAXY
The second US team to win an international competition, LA Galaxy has also won five MLS titles. The team was hit hard by the death of general manager Doug Hamilton at the start of the 2006 season. The Galaxy's greatest coup was the signing of David Beckham in 2007; in 2011 he helped create the goal that clinched the Galaxy's first MLS title in six years.

HONORS: LEAGUE 5, **CUP** 2; **CONCACAF CHAMPIONS LEAGUE** WINNERS 2000

DC UNITED
One of the 10 founding members of the MLS in 1996, DC United has four domestic titles to its name, most recently in 2004. In 1998, DC became the first US team to win both the CONCACAF Champions League and the Copa Interamerica in the same year, famously beating CONMEBOL team Vasco de Gama of Rio 2–1 in the latter.

HONORS: LEAGUE 4 **CUP** 3; **CONCACAF CHAMPIONS LEAGUE** WINNERS 1998

MUNICIPAL
Founded by workers of Guatemala City Council, Municipal is the most successful team in Guatemalan soccer. It has never been out of the top division ever since the club was founded in 1942 and has won the title a record 31 times. Occasional competitors in CONCACAF contests, Municipal won the Champions League title in 1974.

HONORS: LEAGUE 31, **CUP** 8; **CONCACAF CHAMPIONS LEAGUE** WINNERS 1974

COMUNICACIONES
Nicknamed Los Cremas ("The Creams"), Comunicaciones is Guatemala City's second team behind Municipal. That said, it has twice been runner-up in the CONCACAF Champions League and has won 31 domestic league titles. Comunicaciones has always been owned by the Garcia-Granados, a powerful industrial and political family.

HONORS: LEAGUE 31, **CUP** 8; **CONCACAF CHAMPIONS LEAGUE** WINNERS 1978

CONCACAF: TOP CLUBS

Mexican clubs, traditionally the strongest in the sides in CONCACAF, viewed the rest of the federation with disdain for many years, even refusing to play in the Champions League. Since reversing this decision, teams from Mexico have regularly won the contest. The next-best clubs are those from the US, Costa Rica, Honduras, El Salvador, Surinam, and Trinidad.

UNITED STATES
Given the dominance of the US over international soccer in the region, the fact that US clubs have yet to stamp their authority on CONCACAF competitions is all the more surprising. Only Seattle Sounders, LA Galaxy, and DC United have proved good enough to push the Mexican teams aside and challenge for the CONCACAF Champions League, each winning the trophy once.

THE LOST WORLD
Surinam is the forgotten powerhouse of CONCACAF club soccer. Robin Hood, the leading team, has played and lost five CONCACAF Champions Cup Finals, although the last was in 1982. SV Transvaal, Surinam's second team, has reached five finals of the CONCACAF Champion's Cup and managed to win two of them.

CHRISTIAN PULISIC
Captaining the US national team at the age of just 20, creative forward Pulisic has the skills and intelligence to trouble the best defenders.

DOMESTIC CLUBS

CLUB FAS
Club FAS—or to give its full title, Club Deportivo Futbolistas Asociados Santanecos—is the most successful and best-supported Salvadorian club. The team's high point was winning the CONCACAF Champions League in 1979. Nicknamed Tigrillos ("Tigers"), the club has a long history of importing Argentinian and Brazilian players.

HONORS: LEAGUE 19, **CUP** 0; **CONCACAF CHAMPIONS LEAGUE** WINNERS 1979

OLIMPIA
The leading club in Honduras, Olimpia is based in the capital city, Tegucigalpa. The Leones ("Lions") are the only Honduran club to win two CONCACAF Champions League titles. Olimpia is also notable as the first Honduran club to export a player to a European team, selling striker David Suazo to Italian Serie A side Cagliari in 1999.

HONORS: LEAGUE 34, **CUP** 3; **CONCACAF CHAMPIONS LEAGUE** WINNERS 1972, 1988

MARATHÓN
The second-most-successful team in Honduras, Marathón acquired its name after the founders ordered a soccer ball from a Chicago mail-order company—a ball arrived stamped with the name "marathon," which the team took for themselves. In 1981, Marathón became the first Honduran team to beat a Mexican team in an official match, defeating Cruz Azul 3–1 in the Champions Cup.

HONORS: LEAGUE 9, **CUP** 2

THE CLUBS

CONCACAF is composed of three distinct regions. Mexican teams—not included on this map—are in a different world, being much richer and better supported than any others in the region. US teams are approaching the success of the Mexicans, but lagging behind both are the Caribbean and Central American clubs.

DC United
Country: United States
Founded: Washington, D.C., 1995
Stadium: Audi Field
Capacity: 20,000

Marathón
Country: Honduras
Founded: San Pedro Sula, 1925
Stadium: Estadio Yankel Rosenthal
Capacity: 15,000

Olimpia
Country: Honduras
Founded: Tegucigalpa, 1912
Stadium: Estadio Tiburcio Carias Andino
Capacity: 35,000

Saprissa
Country: Costa Rica
Founded: San Jose, 1935
Stadium: Ricardo Saprissa
Capacity: 23,112

LA Galaxy
Country: United States
Founded: Los Angeles, 1994
Stadium: Dignity Health Sports Park
Capacity: 27,000

Club FAS
Country: El Salvador
Founded: Santa Anna, 1947
Stadium: Estadio Oscar Quiteño
Capacity: 15,000

Cartaginés
Country: Costa Rica
Founded: Cartago, 1906
Stadium: Estadio José Rafael Fello Meza Ivankovich
Capacity: 10,500

Comunicaciones
Country: Guatemala
Founded: Guatemala City, 1949
Stadium: Estadio Doroteo Guamuch Flores
Capacity: 26,000

Municipal
Country: Guatemala
Founded: Guatemala City, 1936
Stadium: Estadio Manuel Felipe Carrera
Capacity: 7,500

Alajuelense
Country: Costa Rica
Founded: Alajuela, 1919
Stadium: Alejandro Morera Soto
Capacity: 17,895

CENTRAL AMERICA

Central America has a wealth of soccer talent, but the sport has suffered from competition from baseball, desperate economic conditions, and even civil war in several countries, factors that have combined to make the task of creating great clubs even harder. Currently, the Costa Rican duo of Saprissa and Alajuelense are the regions' strongest clubs.

[AT FIFA] I HAVE NEVER SEEN ...
ONE IOTA OF CORRUPTION

JACK WARNER, FORMER PRESIDENT OF CONCACAF
REPORTED IN THE TRINIDAD EXPRESS, DECEMBER 12, 2004

DOMESTIC CLUBS

ALAJUELENSE
Starting out as El Once de Abril ("The Eleventh of April"), Alajuelense was formed by a group of friends in the city of Alajuela, Costa Rica. In addition to many domestic titles, the club has won two CONCACAF Champions League titles. The club mascot is a lion, but in previous years, it was a mango, in homage to the town of Alajuela, which is nicknamed "The City of Mangoes."

HONORS: LEAGUE 30, CUP 10; CONCACAF CHAMPIONS LEAGUE WINNERS 1986, 2004

SAPRISSA
Based in San José, Costa Rica, Saprissa is nicknamed "The Purple Monster," and its stadium is known as La Cueva del Monstruo ("The Monster's Cave"). It has won numerous domestic titles and three CONCACAF Champions League titles. Saprissa finished third at the 2005 World Club Cup.

HONORS: LEAGUE 37, CUP 8; CONCACAF CHAMPIONS LEAGUE WINNERS 1993, 1995, 2005

CARTAGINÉS
The oldest club in Costa Rica, Cartaginés is the most recent challenger to the Saprissa-Alajuelense duopoly, winning the CONCACAF Champions League in 1994. Its last domestic title was in 1940, and its failure to win another has been ascribed to the curse of a priest at the Basilica de Los Ángles, where players celebrated the 1940 title on horseback.

HONORS: LEAGUE 3, CUP 5; CONCACAF CHAMPIONS LEAGUE WINNERS 1994

AFRICA: CAF

AFRICA

ALGERIA

HOME

AWAY

POPULATION: 43.2 MILLION
CAPITAL: ALGIERS
FA: FÉDÉRATION ALGÉRIENNE DE FOOTBALL

Soccer was popular in Algeria before World War I, with clubs strictly aligned to French colonists or Algerians. In the 1950s, the Algerian FA became a section of the French FA. Since independence in 1962, Algerian soccer has enjoyed major success.

AMBASSADORS FOR INDEPENDENCE

In 1958, at the height of the Algerian War of Independence, a group of French-Algerian players left France to form a team representing FNL—the leading force behind the Algerian struggle for independence. This team included Rachid Mekloufi, also a member of the French World Cup squad.

OUTSTANDING SUCCESS

JS Kabylie is the most successful and best-supported team in modern Algerian soccer. From the Berber region of Algeria, it is an icon of ethnic pride and identity. Its recent form in African club cups has been exceptional.

STAT ATTACK

NATIONAL TEAM

NICKNAME: Les Fennecs ("Desert Foxes")
NATIONAL STADIUM: Stade Mustapha Tchaker, 37,000
WORLD CUP FINALS: 4 appearances
AFRICA CUP OF NATIONS: Winners **1990**, **2019**

MAIN DOMESTIC CLUBS

JS KABYLIE
FOUNDED: Tizi Ouzou, 1946
STADIUM: 1er Novembre 1954, 20,000

USM ALGER
FOUNDED: Algiers, 1937
STADIUM: Stade Omar Hamadi, 17,000

MC ALGER
FOUNDED: Algiers, 1921
STADIUM: Stade Omar Hamadi, 17,000

EGYPT

HOME

AWAY

POPULATION: 104 MILLION
CAPITAL: CAIRO
FA: EGYPTIAN FOOTBALL ASSOCIATION

British soldiers based in Egypt in the late 19th century brought soccer to Cairo. Al Ahly, the oldest club in Africa, was founded in 1907. A second team, Farouk (later Zamalek)—named after the king of Egypt—was formed soon after. Egypt was the first African team to be represented at the Olympics and the World Cup.

STAT ATTACK

NATIONAL TEAM

NICKNAME: The Pharaohs
NATIONAL STADIUM: Cairo Stadium, 75,000
WORLD CUP FINALS: 3 appearances
AFRICA CUP OF NATIONS: Winners **1957, 1959, 1986, 1998, 2006, 2008, 2010**

MAIN DOMESTIC CLUBS

AL AHLY
FOUNDED: Cairo, 1907
STADIUM: Cairo Stadium, 75,000

ZAMALEK
FOUNDED: Cairo, 1911
STADIUM: Cairo Stadium, 75,000

FAMOUS YELLOW CARD

Political pressure from the highest levels of the Egyptian government at the 1986 Africa Cup of Nations saw a yellow card against Egyptian star Taher Abouzaid rescinded. Abouzaid had initially been booked for his wild celebrations after scoring a goal in the semifinals and he was due to miss the final against Cameroon. Egypt won the final on penalties.

DOMESTIC RIVALRY

Al Ahly means "the nation." Initially the club founded by wealthy Egyptians attracted elite liberal republicans who were opposed to the conservative royalists grouped around Zamalek. Now both clubs draw support from every level of Egyptian society, and between them they have made Egypt the most successful country in African club soccer. The rivalry between the two clubs has dominated Egyptian soccer since they were founded.

MOHAMED SALAH
Although the retired Hossam Hassan is Egypt's all-time top scorer, Liverpool FC striker Mohamed Salah won fame at Liverpool and became Egypt's most celebrated player. His goals led The Pharaohs to qualification for the 2018 World Cup finals after 28 years.

MOROCCO

HOME   AWAY

POPULATION: 36.5 MILLION
CAPITAL: RABAT
FA: FÉDÉRATION ROYALE MAROCAINE DE FOOTBALL

The French played soccer in Morocco but excluded the locals. The first Arab club, Wydad Casablanca, was founded in 1937 and was joined in 1949 by a workers' club, Raja Casablanca. The army team, FAR Rabat, has since joined them at the top of Moroccan soccer.

STAT ATTACK

NATIONAL TEAM

NICKNAME: Lions of the Atlas
NATIONAL STADIUM:
Stade de Marrakech, 45,240
WORLD CUP FINALS: 5 appearances
AFRICA CUP OF NATIONS:
Winners **1976**

MAIN DOMESTIC CLUBS

FAR RABAT
FOUNDED: Rabat, 1958
STADIUM: Moulay Abdallah, 52,000

WYDAD CASABLANCA
FOUNDED: Casablanca, 1937
STADIUM: Stade Mohammed V, 45,981

RAJA CASABLANCA
FOUNDED: Casablanca, 1949
STADIUM: Stade Mohammed V, 45,981

WORLD CUP FIRSTS

Morocco was the first African team to win a group at the World Cup. In 1986, it finished ahead of Portugal, Poland, and England. It was also the first African team to make it to the second round of the tournament. However, it lost to a late West German goal. In 2022, they made history by becoming the first African and Arab nation to reach the semi-finals.

ROYAL SUPPORT

King Mohammed IV was such a big fan of Wydad Casablanca that he persuaded the French colonial authorities to install a phone line between his palace and the club's dressing room.

NEW TERRITORIES

The club Jeunesse Sportive El Massira, founded in 1977, plays in the Moroccan league, but it is based in Laayoune, the capital of the Western Sahara. When Morocco first occupied this territory in 1975, the government sponsored the building of a 30,000-seat sports stadium in an effort to integrate the territory with the rest of the country.

TUNISIA

HOME   AWAY

POPULATION: 10.28 MILLION
CAPITAL: TUNIS
FA: FÉDÉRATION TUNISIENNE DE FOOTBALL

The French and Italian colonists played soccer in Tunisia after World War I. Other migrant groups, including the Maltese, Jews, and Greeks, also formed teams. Arab clubs were established alongside these, including Esperance and its great rival Club Africain.

STAT ATTACK

NATIONAL TEAM

NICKNAME: The Eagles of Carthage
NATIONAL STADIUM: Stade Olympique de Radès, 60,000
WORLD CUP FINALS: 5 appearances
AFRICA CUP OF NATIONS: Winners **2004**

MAIN DOMESTIC CLUBS

ESPÉRANCE SPORTIVE
FOUNDED: Tunis, 1919
STADIUM: Stade Olympique de Radès, 60,000

CLUB AFRICAIN
FOUNDED: Tunis, 1920
STADIUM: Stade Olympique de Radès, 60,000

ÉTOILE SPORTIVE DU SAHEL
FOUNDED: Sousse, 1925
STADIUM: Stade Olympique, 28,000

CS SFAXIEN
FOUNDED: Sfax, 1928
STADIUM: Stade Taieb-Mhiri, 11,000

AFRICAN TEAM FIRST

Tunisia was the first African team to win a game at a World Cup. In Argentina in 1978, it beat Mexico 3–1 after going down 1–0 to a questionable penalty. Tunisia's coach Chetali remarked, "The world has laughed at Africa, but now the mockery is over." In recent years, Tunisian soccer has become among the strongest in Africa, with four more World Cup appearances. In 2004, it hosted and won the Africa Cup of Nations.

PRESIDENT'S TEAM

Espérance Sportive has been the leading team in Tunisian soccer since before the nation achieved independence in 1956. It was the first Arab team to win the national championship in 1941 and has traditionally been the team of the Tunisian President.

AFRICA

NIGERIA

HOME

AWAY

POPULATION: 210 MILLION
CAPITAL: ABUJA
FA: NIGERIA FOOTBALL ASSOCIATION
LICENSED PLAYERS:
MALE: 35,000
FEMALE: 660
PROFESSIONALS: 1,400
REGISTERED CLUBS: 365

Nigerian soccer was first played at a school in Calabar when Englishman James Luke took up the post of headmaster in 1902, bringing a soccer ball with him. The game's popularity soon spread across the country. In 1960, independence was celebrated in the new national stadium in Lagos, but civil war (1967–1970) meant that a league was not established until 1972.

PREMIER LEAGUE

Nigeria runs a 20-team premier league and national cup competition. The majority of top clubs come from the cities of the south, although Kano Pillars' league victory in 2008 was the first for a northern team in more than a decade.

SCHOOLBOY VICTORY

The first recorded game in Nigeria was played in June 1904 between the barefoot Nigerian schoolboys of Reverend Luke's Hope Waddell Training Institute in Calabar and the crew of the visiting Royal Navy ship HMS Thistle. The schoolboys won the match 3–2.

SUPERSTITION

In 1993, on the advice of a traditional healer, the Nigerian national team refused to shake hands with the Prime Minister and Sports Minister of Ivory Coast before playing a game in Abidjan.

JAY-JAY OKOCHA

Former Nigerian team captain, midfielder Okocha started his career with a local team. He moved to Europe and played for third-division German side Borussia Neunkirchen. Eight years later, Paris Saint-Germain paid $24 million for his services.

BORN: **AUGUST 14, 1973, ENUGU, NIGERIA**
HEIGHT: **5 FT 8 IN (1.73 M)**
MAIN CLUBS: **BORUSSIA NEUNKIRCHEN, EINTRACHT FRANKFURT, FENERBAHÇE, PARIS SAINT-GERMAIN, BOLTON WANDERERS, QATAR SC, HULL CITY**
INTERNATIONAL CAPS: **75**

STAT ATTACK

NATIONAL TEAM

NICKNAME: Super Eagles
NATIONAL STADIUM: Abuja Stadium, 60,491
WORLD CUP FINALS: 6 appearances, Round of 16 **1994, 1998, 2014**
AFRICA CUP OF NATIONS: Winners **1980, 1994, 2013**
BIGGEST WIN: **10–1** vs. Dahomey, 1959
BIGGEST DEFEAT: **0–7** vs. Ghana, 1955
MOST CAPS: Ahmed Musa, **107**
MOST GOALS: Rashidi Yekini, **37**

MAIN DOMESTIC CLUBS

SHOOTING STARS
FOUNDED: Ibadan, 1963
STADIUM:
Lekan Salami, 18,000

HOME
INTERNATIONAL HONORS: African Cup Winners' Cup **1976**; CAF Cup **1992**
LEAGUE: 5 **CUP:** 4

ENUGU RANGERS
FOUNDED: Enugu, 1970
STADIUM:
Nnamdi Azikiwe, 30,000
HOME
INTERNATIONAL HONORS:
African Cup Winners' Cup **1977**
LEAGUE: 7 **CUP:** 6

ENYIMBA
FOUNDED: Aba, 1976
STADIUM:
Enyimba International, 16,000

HOME
INTERNATIONAL HONORS:
African Champions League **2003, 2004**
LEAGUE: 8 **CUP:** 4

INTERNATIONAL CLUB COMPETITIONS

Turbulence in Nigeria made it a late starter in international soccer. It hosted and won its first Africa Cup of Nations in 1980, beating Algeria in the final 3–0. The mid-1990s were the Super Eagles' best years. The team won the Africa Cup of Nations and reached the quarterfinals of the World Cup in 1994 and then won Olympic Gold in 1996. It won the Africa Cup of Nations again in 2013.

CAMEROON

HOME

AWAY

POPULATION: 24.3 MILLION
CAPITAL: YAOUNDÉ
FA: FÉDÉRATION CAMEROUNAISE DE FOOTBALL
LICENSED PLAYERS:
MALE: 750,500
FEMALE: 36,000
PROFESSIONALS: 540
REGISTERED CLUBS: 220

Soccer was first played in Cameroon by French colonial administrators, but teams formed along ethnic lines by the 1930s, with Beti, Bamileke, and English speakers supporting different sides. In the 1970s, Cameroon clubs began to win major African trophies, and in 1982, the national team first went to the World Cup. Cameroon has been among the elite of African soccer ever since.

DOMESTIC COMPETITION

Cameroon plays a standard league and cup competition and had a short-lived "super cup" for the winners of the two. Coton Sport, once a tiny workers' social club from the north, has won six titles in a row from 2003–2008.

WORLD CUP 1990

Cameroon earned its nickname—The Indomitable Lions—with three drawn games at the 1982 World Cup. However, at Italia 1990, it sparkled and made it all the way to the quarterfinals—the first African team to do so.

MVF REMEMBERED

Marc-Vivien Foé (MVF) died while playing for Cameroon at the 2003 Confederations Cup. In his honor, the whole team's warm-up gear carried his name in the final of the competition.

SAMUEL ETO'O
Striker Eto'o is the Africa Cup of Nations' all-time top scorer and was the first man to be voted African Player of the Year three times in a row.

ROGER **MILLA**

Milla toiled in the lower reaches of French soccer for more than a decade. But at the age of 38, he came to the world's attention as Cameroon's key goal scorer at Italia 1990.

BORN: MAY 29, 1952, YAOUNDÉ, CAMEROON
HEIGHT: 6 FT 1 IN (1.85 M)
MAIN CLUBS: **AS MONACO, BASTIA, SAINT-ÉTIENNE, MONTPELLIER, JS SAINT-PIERROISE, TONNERRE YAOUNDÉ, PELITA JAYA**
INTERNATIONAL CAPS: **77**

STAT ATTACK

NATIONAL TEAM

NICKNAME: The Indomitable Lions
NATIONAL STADIUM: Stade Ahmadou Ahidjo, 40,122
WORLD CUP FINALS: 8 appearances, quarterfinals 1990
AFRICA CUP OF NATIONS: Winners **1984, 1988, 2000, 2002, 2017**
BIGGEST WIN: 9–0 vs. Chad, 1965
BIGGEST DEFEAT: 1–6 vs. Norway, 1990; vs. Russia, 1994
MOST CAPS: Rigobert Song, **137**
MOST GOALS: Samuel Eto'o, **56**

MAIN DOMESTIC CLUBS

CANON YAOUNDÉ
FOUNDED: Yaoundé, 1930
STADIUM: Stade Ahmadou, 40,122
HOME
INTERNATIONAL HONORS: African Champions League **1971**, **1978**, **1980**; African Cup Winners' Cup **1979**
LEAGUE: 10 **CUP:** 12

UNION DOUALA
FOUNDED: Douala, 1958
STADIUM: Stade de la Reunification, 30,000
HOME
INTERNATIONAL HONORS: African Champions League **1979**
LEAGUE: 5 **CUP:** 6

COTON SPORT
FOUNDED: Garoua, 1986
STADIUM: Omnisports Roumdé-Adjia, 22,000
HOME
INTERNATIONAL HONORS: None
LEAGUE: 17 **CUP:** 6

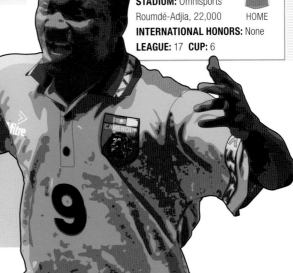

AFRICA

IVORY COAST

HOME

AWAY

POPULATION: 25.7 MILLION
CAPITAL: YAMOUSSOUKRO
FA: FÉDÉRATION IVOIRIENNE DE FOOTBALL
LICENSED PLAYERS:
MALE: 801,500
PROFESSIONALS: 100
REGISTERED CLUBS: 220

Soccer was introduced to the Ivory Coast in the 1920s by French colonial officials and migrants. Locals soon joined in, and the first African teams were formed in the 1930s. The national team's greatest success to date was winning the Africa Cup of Nations in 1992 after a marathon penalty shoot-out (11–10) against Ghana. In recent years, the national team has prospered, but the best of the talent plays in Europe. Domestic soccer suffered during the country's civil war.

WORLD-RECORD RUN

Between 1989 and 1994, ASEC Mimosas went a world-record 108 games without defeat. Their run finally ended in a 2–1 loss to SO Armée. They also have a record of nurturing top players, including Kolo and Yaya Touré.

STAT ATTACK

NATIONAL TEAM

NICKNAME: The Elephants
NATIONAL STADIUM: Stade Félix Houphouët Boigny, 45,000
WORLD CUP FINALS: 3 appearances
AFRICA CUP OF NATIONS: Winners **1992, 2015**
BIGGEST WIN: **11–0** vs. Central African Republic, 1961
BIGGEST DEFEAT: 0–5 vs. Netherlands, 2017
MOST CAPS: Didier Zokora, **123**
MOST GOALS: Didier Drogba, **65**

MAIN DOMESTIC CLUBS

ASEC MIMOSAS
FOUNDED: Abidjan, 1948
STADIUM: Stade Félix Houphouët Boigny, 45,000
HOME
INTERNATIONAL HONORS: African Champions League **1998**
LEAGUE: 27 **CUP:** 20

AFRICA SPORTS
FOUNDED: Abidjan, 1947
STADIUM: Stade Robert Champroux, 20,000
HOME
INTERNATIONAL HONORS: Cup Winners Cup 1992, **1999**
LEAGUE: 18 **CUP:** 17

STADE D'ABIDJAN
FOUNDED: Abidjan, 1936
STADIUM: Stade Robert Champroux, 3,000
HOME
INTERNATIONAL HONORS: African Champions League **1966**
LEAGUE: 5 **CUP:** 5

DOMESTIC SUCCESS

ASEC Mimosas, or ASEC Abidjan, have been the strongest domestic team and won the 1998 African Champions Cup—the country's first continental trophy since Stade d'Abidjan's 1966 African Champions League win. They also run the most successful soccer academy in Africa. Since the end of the civil war in 2006, the domestic game has progressed. AS Tanda have grown to become a strong team recently, winning the title in 2015, 2016, and 2017.

WORLD CUP 2006

In its first World Cup finals appearance, the Ivory Coast had the misfortune to be placed in the most deadly "group of death" yet, containing Argentina, Holland, and Serbia and Montenegro. It lost its two opening games, but the Ivorians were not outclassed. In their final game, an extraordinary second half rally saw them come back down 2–1 to beat Serbia 3–2.

DIDIER **DROGBA**

Drogba was only 5 years old when he left Abidjan to live in France. He played in the lower divisions, initially as a defender then as a forward. He made his breakthrough at Guingamp before stardom at Chelsea.

BORN: MARCH 11, 1978, ABIDJAN, IVORY COAST
HEIGHT: **6 FT 2 IN (1.89 M)** MAIN CLUBS: **LE MANS, GUINGAMP, MARSEILLE, CHELSEA, GALATASARAY**
INTERNATIONAL CAPS: **105**

GHANA

HOME

AWAY

POPULATION: 26.9 MILLION
CAPITAL: ACCRA
FA: GHANA FOOTBALL ASSOCIATION
LICENSED PLAYERS:
MALE: 27,500
FEMALE: 1,700
REGISTERED CLUBS: 280

The first recorded game of soccer in Ghana (the Gold Coast) was played in 1903. Boys at the Government Boys School were so entranced they created their own side, Cape Coast Excelsior. In 1911, Hearts of Oak, the oldest club in sub-Saharan Africa, was founded. The independence celebrations in Ghana in 1957 included a tour by English legend Stanley Matthews. But it took until 2006 to get to the World Cup.

STAT ATTACK

NATIONAL TEAM

NICKNAME: Black Stars
NATIONAL STADIUM: Various
WORLD CUP FINALS: 4 appearances
AFRICA CUP OF NATIONS: Winners **1963**, **1965**, **1978**, **1982**
BIGGEST WIN: **13–2** vs. Kenya, 1965
BIGGEST DEFEAT: **0–10** vs. Bulgaria, 1968
MOST CAPS: Andre Ayew, **110**
MOST GOALS: Asamoah Gyan, **51**

THE BIG CLUBS

Both league and cup are "owned" by the big two clubs in Ghana, Hearts of Oak and Asante Kotoko—no other club has enjoyed the success that these two teams have. The Cup was abandoned in 2001.

REAL REPUBLICANS

The Real Republicans were created in 1962 at the behest of independent Ghana's first president, Kwame Nkrumah. They had access to the best players and won the title in 1963, but he wanted them to dominate a continent and win the newly created African Champions Cup—they never did. The team was dissolved after Nkrumah's overthrow.

ACCRA STADIUM DISASTER

On May 9, 2001, Ghana suffered a terrible soccer stadium disaster. In the old Accra sports stadium, when a game between Hearts of Oak and Asante Kotoko reached the 91st minute, the police fired tear gas toward the restless Kotoko fans. Many fans were killed or injured in the resulting stampede.

BLACK STARS

The Ghanaian national team is known as the Black Stars. It was given the name by President Nkrumah, who named the team after the Black Star Line, the shipping line set up in 1919 by Marcus Garvey to take African Americans to Africa.

MAIN DOMESTIC CLUBS

HEARTS OF OAK
FOUNDED: Accra, 1911
STADIUM:
Accra Sports Stadium, 40,000   HOME
INTERNATIONAL HONORS: African Champions League **2000**, CAF Confederations Cup **2004**
LEAGUE: 21 **CUP:** 12

ASANTE KOTOKO
FOUNDED: Kumasi, 1935
STADIUM: Baba Yara, 40,528
INTERNATIONAL HONORS: HOME
African Champions League **1970**, **1983**
LEAGUE: 24 **CUP:** 9

ASAMOAH **GYAN**

Gyan played a pivotal role in three of Ghana's World Cup campaigns. In addition to being Ghana's all-time leading goal scorer, he also holds the honor of being the all-time leading African goal scorer in the World Cup, with a total of six goals.
BORN: NOVEMBER 22, 1985, ACCRA, GHANA
HEIGHT: **6 FT 1 IN (1.86 M)**
MAIN CLUBS: LIBERTY PROFESSIONALS, UDINESE, RENNES, SUNDERLAND, AL AIN, SHANGHAI SIPG, KAYSERISPOR
INTERNATIONAL CAPS: 106

29
Sequence of games in which Ghana scored a goal, from 1963 to 1967

3
The number of times Ghana won the Africa Cup of Nations, after which it was permitted to keep the Abdelaziz Abdallah Salem Trophy permanently

1963
The year Ghana beat Italy 5–2 on a European friendly tour

24
The average age of Ghana's squad at the 2006 World Cup—the youngest of any team

DR CONGO

HOME   AWAY

POPULATION: 92.2 MILLION
CAPITAL: KINSHASA
FA: FÉDÉRATION CONGOLAISE DE FOOTBALL-ASSOCIATION
LICENSED PLAYERS:
MALE: 2.5 MILLION
REGISTERED CLUBS: 770

Soccer was introduced to the Democratic Republic of Congo (DRC) by Belgian administrators and missionaries after World War I. It spread fastest among the Congolese in the southern mining cities, and mining company–backed teams played in the 1940s. The national team now suffers from a lack of financial support.

DOMESTIC LEAGUE

The leading teams in the DRC play a national league that has had several format changes over the years. In 2019–2020, the top division was contested by 19 teams after FC Renaissance were expelled. Some of DRC's best players play in other countries.

SHABANI NONDA

Nonda is DRC's top-scoring striker—his tally could have been higher, but he exiled himself from international soccer from 2005 to 2007. On his return, he scored a hat trick against Djibouti.

BORN: MARCH 6, 1977, BUJUMBURA, BURUNDI
HEIGHT: 5 FT 11½ IN (1.82 M)
MAIN CLUBS: FC ZURICH, STADE RENNAIS, AS MONACO, AS ROMA, BLACKBURN ROVERS, GALATASARAY
INTERNATIONAL CAPS: 49

STAT ATTACK

NATIONAL TEAM

NICKNAME: The Leopards
NATIONAL STADIUM:
Stade des Martyrs, 80,000
WORLD CUP FINALS: 1 appearance
AFRICA CUP OF NATIONS: Winners **1968**, **1974**
BIGGEST WIN: 10–1 vs. Zambia, 1969
BIGGEST DEFEAT: 0–9 vs. Yugoslavia, 1974
MOST CAPS: Issama Mpeko, **76**
MOST GOALS: Shabani Nonda, **32**

PRESIDENT MOBUTU

When President Mobutu took power in 1965 of what was then Zaire, he invested heavily in the team. It won two African Champions Cups and the Africa Cup of Nations in 1968 and 1974. Mobutu abandoned soccer after its dismissal from the 1974 World Cup.

WORLD CUP 1974

The Leopards, as Mobutu called them, arrived at West Germany 1974 as the first sub-Saharan nation at the tournament. They lost all three games, 2–0 to Scotland, 3–0 to Brazil, and 9–0 to Yugoslavia. When the team returned home, no one met them at the airport.

AFRICA CUP OF NATIONS

Money was so short for the DRC before the 2004 Africa Cup of Nations, which was held in Egypt, that members of the Congolese squad were living in hostels in Cairo while training for the games. They were moved to better accommodations, thanks to the Egyptian FA. However, in their game against Egypt, the Congolese players were off the field celebrating an equalizer when the Egyptians restarted the game and scored a winning goal.

MAIN DOMESTIC CLUBS

DARING CLUB MOTEMA PEMBE
FOUNDED: Kinshasa, 1936
STADIUM:
Stade Tata Raphaël, 50,000
INTERNATIONAL HONORS:
Cup Winners' Cup **1994**
LEAGUE: 12   **CUP:** 14

HOME

AS VITA CLUB
FOUNDED:
Kinshasa, 1935
STADIUM:
Stade des Martyrs, 80,000
INTERNATIONAL HONORS:
African Champions League **1973**
LEAGUE: 15   **CUP:** 8

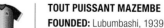

HOME

TOUT PUISSANT MAZEMBE
FOUNDED: Lubumbashi, 1939
STADIUM: Stade TP Mazembe, 18,500
INTERNATIONAL HONORS: African Champions League **1967**, **1968**, **2009**, **2010**, **2015**
LEAGUE: 19   **CUP:** 5

HOME

SOUTH AFRICA

 HOME AWAY

POPULATION: 54.3 MILLION
CAPITAL: PRETORIA
FA: SOUTH AFRICAN FOOTBALL ASSOCIATION
LICENSED PLAYERS:
MALE: 1.5 MILLION
FEMALE: 5,000
PROFESSIONALS: 1,000
REGISTERED CLUBS: 450

Soccer began in South Africa in the 1860s among Europeans, and by 1882 a governing body had been set up in Natal along with three clubs. The game spread among Africans working in the mining areas alongside soccer-playing white miners. Later, the apartheid regime banned sports between races. South Africa was expelled from CAF and FIFA and was not readmitted until 1992.

SOCCER IN THE TOWNSHIPS

In 1961, a group of independent owners, clubs, and administrators broke from the apartheid soccer authorities. They created their own soccer league in the black townships—the SASL (South African Soccer League), which was led by clubs like Cape Town Ramblers and Moroka Swallows. Their games were a gigantic success and a source of great pride to the teams and people of the townships. However, the South African state steadily closed down teams and dissolved the township league in 1966.

SOUTH AFRICAN LEAGUE

The Premier League has grown out of the National Professional Soccer League (NPSL)—a black league that merged with its white counterpart in 1978 to create one of the very earliest mixed-race institutions in South Africa. The clubs also play a cup competition and, until recently, a tournament for the top eight teams, too.

2010 FIFA WORLD CUP HOST

Following an all-African bidding process, South Africa won the honor of being the first country on the continent to host the FIFA World Cup finals. Despite a memorable 2–1 win against France in the final group game, the plucky Bafana Bafana missed out on making it to the knockout stages on goal difference alone.

BENNI McCARTHY

McCarthy made his name with Ajax Cape Town and then moved to Europe. He famously scored two goals in Porto's win against Manchester United on the way to winning the 2004 Champions League.

BORN: **NOVEMBER 12, 1977, CAPE TOWN, SOUTH AFRICA**
HEIGHT: **6 FT (1.83 M)**
MAIN CLUBS: **SEVEN STARS/AJAX CAPE TOWN, AJAX, CELTA VIGO, FC PORTO, BLACKBURN ROVERS, WEST HAM**
INTERNATIONAL CAPS: **80**

STAT ATTACK

NATIONAL TEAM

NICKNAME: Bafana Bafana
NATIONAL STADIUM: FNB Stadium, 94,736
WORLD CUP FINALS: 3 appearances
AFRICA CUP OF NATIONS: Winners **1996**
BIGGEST WIN: 8–0 vs. Australia, 1955
BIGGEST DEFEAT: 0–5 vs. Brazil, 2014
MOST CAPS: Aaron Mokoena, **107**
MOST GOALS: Benni McCarthy, **32**

MAIN DOMESTIC CLUBS

KAIZER CHIEFS
FOUNDED: Krugersdorp, 1970
STADIUM: FNB Stadium, 94,736
 HOME
INTERNATIONAL HONORS: African Cup Winners' Cup **2001**
LEAGUE: 13 **CUP:** 13

ORLANDO PIRATES
FOUNDED: Johannesburg, 1937
STADIUM: Orlando, 40,000
HOME
INTERNATIONAL HONORS: African Champions League **1995**
LEAGUE: 9 **CUP:** 8

MAMELODI SUNDOWNS
FOUNDED: Pretoria, 1970
STADIUM: Loftus Versfeld, 51,762
 HOME
INTERNATIONAL HONORS: African Champions League **2016**
LEAGUE: 14 **CUP:** 5

AFRICA

AFRICA: TOP CLUBS

The development of pan-African club competitions in the 1960s enabled a generation of big clubs previously known only at home to shine internationally. Since the 1990s, North African clubs—initially the Egyptian sides but later the Moroccan, Tunisian, and Algerian teams, too—have become more successful and wealthy, although the recent success of Enyimba of Nigeria and Coton Sport of Cameroon show that West African soccer is also thriving.

HAFIA CONAKRY

Once Guinea's biggest and Africa's strongest club, Hafia Conakry was acquired by President Sékou Touré in 1970. With an injection of funds and control of players, the team won three African Champions Cups. After losing the 1976 final to Mouloudi Algiers, Touré sent players to prison for "political re-education."

NORTH AFRICA

North African soccer is so strong that Egypt's third-best team, Ismaily, was actually the first to win a continental trophy. The side has fierce hometown support and has been bankrolled by the powerful Osman family, with links to Egyptian politics and construction. Morocco's leading teams are not far behind: led by Raja Casablanca, the team of the working class; and FAR Rabat, founded by the late King Hassan II and team of the Moroccan armed forces.

1974 Year in which a Congolese team last won the Champions Cup

9 Algerian club JS Kabylie's rank in CAF's African club of the century poll

0 East African clubs that have won a continental African trophy

MOHAMED ABOUTRIKA
A midfielder for both Al Ahly and Egypt, Aboutrika was a world-class player who chose to play his whole career in Egypt.

WEST AFRICA

The recent rise of Coton Sport from Cameroon is a measure of West Africa's soccer strength. Founded as recently as 1986 as a textile factory's workers team, Coton Sport won the first of its many domestic titles in 1997 and has now made it all the way to the final of the African Champions League.

STAT ATTACK

DOMESTIC TEAMS

JS KABYLIE
The top club in Algeria, JS Kabylie's form in African competitions places the club among the continent's elite. Kabylie comes from the city of Tizi Ouzou in Berber country—an ethnic group distinct from the nation's Arab majority.

HONORS: LEAGUE 14, CUP 4; AFRICAN CHAMPIONS LEAGUE WINNERS 1981, 1990; AFRICAN CUP WINNERS' CUP WINNERS 1995; CAF CONFEDERATIONS CUP WINNERS 2000, 2001, 2002

ÉTOILE SPORTIVE DU SAHEL
Étoile was founded in 1925 as a multisport club for Muslims in the French colonial city of Sousse, in Tunisia. It has won at least one title every decade since independence from France in 1956.

HONORS: LEAGUE 10, CUP 10; AFRICAN CHAMPIONS LEAGUE WINNERS 2007 AFRICAN CUP WINNERS' CUP WINNERS 1997, 2003; CAF CONFEDERATIONS CUP WINNERS 2006, 2015

ESPÉRANCE SPORTIVE
The premier team of Tunis, Espérance Sportive remains the favored team of the Tunisian nation as a whole. However, the number and quality of domestic challengers is threatening the team's number-one status.

HONORS: LEAGUE 32, CUP 15; AFRICAN CHAMPIONS LEAGUE WINNERS 1994, 2011, 2018, 2019; AFRICAN CUP WINNERS' CUP WINNERS 1998; CAF CONFEDERATIONS CUP WINNERS 1997

THE TEAMS

Africa's top teams are clustered in the north and west of the continent. The South Africans, such as Orlando Pirates and the Kaizer Chiefs, have fallen from grace, although Angolan clubs, buoyed by oil money, are progressing.

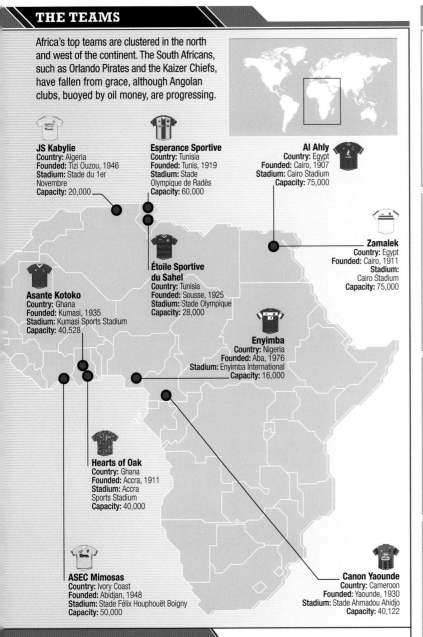

JS Kabylie
Country: Algeria
Founded: Tizi Ouzou, 1946
Stadium: Stade du 1er Novembre
Capacity: 20,000

Esperance Sportive
Country: Tunisia
Founded: Tunis, 1919
Stadium: Stade Olympique de Radès
Capacity: 60,000

Al Ahly
Country: Egypt
Founded: Cairo, 1907
Stadium: Cairo Stadium
Capacity: 75,000

Zamalek
Country: Egypt
Founded: Cairo, 1911
Stadium: Cairo Stadium
Capacity: 75,000

Étoile Sportive du Sahel
Country: Tunisia
Founded: Sousse, 1925
Stadium: Stade Olympique
Capacity: 28,000

Asante Kotoko
Country: Ghana
Founded: Kumasi, 1935
Stadium: Kumasi Sports Stadium
Capacity: 40,528

Enyimba
Country: Nigeria
Founded: Aba, 1976
Stadium: Enyimba International
Capacity: 16,000

Hearts of Oak
Country: Ghana
Founded: Accra, 1911
Stadium: Accra Sports Stadium
Capacity: 40,000

ASEC Mimosas
Country: Ivory Coast
Founded: Abidjan, 1948
Stadium: Stade Félix Houphouët Boigny
Capacity: 50,000

Canon Yaounde
Country: Cameroon
Founded: Yaounde, 1930
Stadium: Stade Ahmadou Ahidjo
Capacity: 40,122

DOMESTIC TEAMS

ENYIMBA
Founded in 1976, Enyimba means "People's Elephant" in Igbo and is the nickname for the city of Aba, in which the team is based. The team became the property of the Nigerian government in 1991, and it has recently risen to the top of both Nigerian and African soccer. Enyimba memorably won back-to-back Champions League titles in 2003 and 2004.

HONORS: LEAGUE 8, **CUP** 4; **AFRICAN CHAMPIONS LEAGUE** 2003, 2004

CANON YAOUNDE
In its heyday, Canon Yaounde was the leading team in Cameroon and among the leading sides in Africa, winning four continental titles between 1971 and 1980. Recent success, however, has been limited to a single domestic league win in 2002.

HONORS: LEAGUE 10, **CUP** 12; **AFRICAN CHAMPIONS LEAGUE WINNERS** 1971, 1978, 1980, **AFRICAN CUP WINNERS CUP WINNERS** 1979

HEARTS OF OAK
The oldest club in sub-Saharan Africa, Ghanaian side Hearts of Oak finally sealed its status among the continent's elite with a Champions Cup victory in 2000. It hit the record books by winning the Ghanaian domestic league six consecutive times between 1997 and 2002.

HONORS: LEAGUE 21, **CUP** 12; **AFRICAN CHAMPIONS LEAGUE WINNERS** 2000, **CAF CONFEDERATIONS CUP WINNERS** 2004

ASANTE KOTOKO
Asante is the main rival to Hearts of Oaks' Ghanaian crown. Founded in the 1930s as Asante United, it acquired the name Kotoko, meaning "porcupine," in 1935. By this time, the club's patrons and key supporters were the mainly elite Ashanti of northern Ghana, and the club has remained an icon of ethnic identity for supporters in the region.

HONORS: LEAGUE 24, **CUP** 9; **AFRICAN CHAMPIONS LEAGUE WINNERS** 1970, 1983

AL AHLY
Voted by CAF as the top African club of the 20th century, Cairo-based Al Ahly has continued to be the biggest and most successful African club.

HONORS: LEAGUE 42, **CUP** 37; **AFRICAN CHAMPIONS LEAGUE WINNERS** 1982, 1987, 2001, 2005, 2006, 2008, 2012, 2013, 2020, 2021 **AFRICAN CUP WINNERS' CUP WINNERS** 1984, 1985, 1986, 1993; **CAF SUPER CUP WINNERS** 2002, 2006, 2007, 2009, 2013, 2014, 2021

ZAMALEK
In any other country, Cairo-based Zamalek would be the top dog, and its nine African titles makes it a potent force in the continental game. But Egyptian soccer also contains the mighty Al Ahly, in whose shadow Zamalek is forced to toil.

HONORS: LEAGUE 14, **CUP** 28; **AFRICAN CHAMPIONS LEAGUE WINNERS** 1984, 1986, 1993, 1996, 2002; **CAF SUPER CUP WINNERS** 1994, 1997, 2003, 2020

ASEC MIMOSAS
Ivory Coast side ASEC Mimosas has a long history and a brilliant domestic record. However, it is best known for its exceptional youth academy, which successfully and profitably sends players to Europe, and is a model to which much of Africa aspires. The export of talent accounts for the fact that it has just a single Champions Cup to its name.

HONORS: LEAGUE 26, **CUP** 20; **AFRICAN CHAMPIONS LEAGUE WINNERS** 1998

ASIA AND OCEANIA: AFC AND OFC

HOME AWAY

POPULATION: 85 MILLION

CAPITAL: TEHRAN

FA: ISLAMIC REPUBLIC OF IRAN FOOTBALL FEDERATION

IRAN

Played in Iran since the early 20th century, soccer boomed in the 1960s as oil money flowed in. Iran then won three Asian Cups and competed at the 1978 World Cup just a year before its Islamic revolution. The game survived restrictions and still flourishes.

STAT ATTACK

NATIONAL TEAM

NATIONAL STADIUM: Azadi, 78,116

WORLD CUP FINALS: 6 appearances

ASIAN CUP: 14 appearances, winners **1968**, **1972**, **1976**

MAIN DOMESTIC CLUBS

ESTEGHLAL
FOUNDED: Tehran, 1945
STADIUM: Azadi Stadium

PERSEPOLIS
FOUNDED: Tehran, 1963
STADIUM: Azadi Stadium

PAS TEHRAN (NOT IN EXISTENCE NOW)
FOUNDED: Tehran, 1963
STADIUM: Shahid Dastgerdi Stadium

WORLD CUP 1998

Iran won its first game at the World Cup in 1998, where the team was placed in the same group as the US. After almost 20 years of political and rhetorical conflict between the two countries, the Iranians disarmed the world by handing bouquets of white flowers to the US team, who reciprocated with a gift of pennants. Iran won the match 2–1, but lost its remaining two matches and was knocked out of the competition.

THE TEHRAN DERBY

The two biggest clubs in Iranian soccer are Persepolis, previously known as Pirouzi, who has won the top-tier Iran Pro League on 13 occasions, and Esteghlal, previously Taj or Crown, who has won the title eight times. Under the Shah, Persepolis became the team of the poor, while Taj was the team of the establishment. Games between the two Tehran teams attract huge crowds, with more than 90,000 fans flocking to the teams' shared ground, the Azadi Stadium.

SOCCER AS PROTEST

Soccer has been a lightning rod for politics in Iran and especially the contentious issue of the place of women in Iranian society. Women have been banned from entering stadiums to watch men play, though women's soccer is popular. FIFA has been assured the ban on women spectators will be lifted, after fans and activists staged frequent protests outside the national stadium while the men's side was playing international matches.

IRAQ

HOME AWAY

POPULATION: 39.5 MILLION

CAPITAL: BAGHDAD

FA: IRAQI FOOTBALL ASSOCIATION

Soccer came to Iraq with foreign armies and oil workers, above all the British. The game is immensely popular, and the Iraqi team is one of the few institutions to survive the US-led invasion that began in 2003. The team retains the support of most of an otherwise divided nation.

STAT ATTACK

NATIONAL TEAM

NATIONAL STADIUM: Basra Sports City, 65,227

WORLD CUP FINALS: 1 appearance

ASIAN CUP: 9 appearances, winners **2007**

MAIN DOMESTIC CLUBS

AL-ZAWRA'A
FOUNDED: Baghdad, 1969
STADIUM: Al-Shaab Stadium

AL-QUWA AL-JAWIYA
FOUNDED: Baghdad, 1931
STADIUM: Al-Quwa Al-Jawiya Stadium

ERBIL FC
FOUNDED: Erbil, 1968
STADIUM: Franso Hariri Stadium

THINGS CAN ONLY GET BETTER

Despite the destabilization caused by the invasion of Iraq, the national team qualified for the 2004 Athens Olympics. Coach Berndt Stange resigned after receiving death threats, but the team reached the semifinals, which led to celebrations at home. It went one better in 2006, finishing runner-up in the Asian Games, then went on to win the 2007 AFC Asian Cup.

POLITICS BEFORE SOCCER

Al-Shorta—previously Police Club—made it to the final of the 1971 Asian Champions Cup, where it faced Israel's Maccabi Tel Aviv. In protest over Israel's national status and oppression of the Palestinians, the Iraqi team boycotted the game, so Tel Aviv was awarded the title.

HOME

AWAY

POPULATION: 34.1 MILLION
CAPITAL: RIYADH
FA: SAUDI ARABIAN FOOTBALL FEDERATION

SAUDI ARABIA

Soccer has been embraced with enthusiasm in Saudi Arabia despite conservative religious opposition, especially to the participation of women. The game arrived in the interwar period, and a national FA was founded in 1959.

STAT ATTACK

NATIONAL TEAM

NATIONAL STADIUM: King Fahd, 67,000
WORLD CUP FINALS: 6 appearances
ASIAN CUP: 10 appearances, winners **1984**, **1988**, **1996**; runner-up **1992**, **2000**, **2007**

MAIN DOMESTIC CLUBS

AL-HILAL
FOUNDED: Riyadh, 1957
STADIUM: King Saud University Stadium

AL-ITTIHAD
FOUNDED: Jeddah, 1927
STADIUM: King Abdullah Sports City Stadium

AL-NASSR
FOUNDED: Riyadh, 1955
STADIUM: King Fahd Stadium

WORLD CUP HIGHS AND LOWS

After winning the Asian Cup in the 1980s, Saudi Arabia rose to prominence with four consecutive World Cup appearances, starting in 1994. On the first occasion, it beat Belgium and Morocco to qualify for the second round but went home early in 2002 after losing 8–0 to Germany. Their 2–1 win over Argentina in the 2022 group stage was a huge shock.

CUPS AND KINGS

The presence of the Saudi royal house is felt everywhere in Saudi football. The winners of the Prince Faisal Cup, which started in 2008, and the Crown Prince's Cup join six other teams to contest the big-money prize of the Saudi Champions Cup, officially known as the "Custodian of The Two Holy Mosques Champions Cup."

MOHAMED **AL-DEAYEA**

Goalkeeper for the Saudi Arabia national team for more than 18 years, Al-Deayea holds the world record for the most number of international caps by a goalkeeper.

BORN: **AUGUST 2, 1972, TABUK, SAUDI ARABIA**
HEIGHT: **6 FT 3 IN (1.91 M)**
MAIN CLUBS: **AL-TA'EE, AL-HILAL**
INTERNATIONAL CAPS: **178**

UAE

HOME

AWAY

POPULATION: 9.7 MILLION
CAPITAL: ABU DHABI
FA: UNITED ARAB EMIRATES FOOTBALL ASSOCIATION

The United Arab Emirates (UAE) is making its presence felt in world soccer. The 2009 and 2010 FIFA World Club Cups were hosted in Abu Dhabi, and national airline Emirates was the first World Cup sponsor. Neighboring Qatar hosted the 2022 FIFA World Cup.

STAT ATTACK

NATIONAL TEAM

NATIONAL STADIUM:
Mohammed Bin Zayed Stadium, 42,056
WORLD CUP FINALS: 1 appearance
ASIAN CUP: 10 appearances, runner-up **1996**

MAIN DOMESTIC CLUBS

AL-AIN FC
FOUNDED: Al-Ain, 1968
STADIUM: Hazza Bin Zayed Stadium

SHARJAH SC
FOUNDED: Sharjah, 1966
STADIUM: Sharjah Stadium

AL-AHLI
FOUNDED: Dubai, 1970
STADIUM: King Abdullah Sports City

PUNCHING ABOVE ITS WEIGHT

The UAE is one of the smallest nations to have played in a World Cup finals, qualifying for Italia 1990 but losing all three games. The side also progressed to the final of the 1996 Asian Cup only to lose on penalties. It won the Gulf Cup for the first time in 2007 and again in 2013.

AL-AIN FC

Leading side Al-Ain is the only UAE team to have won the Asian Champions League. It has won the top-flight UAE League 14 times as well as 7 UAE President's Cups, partly thanks to direct sponsorship from the Royal Al-Nahyan family since 1968. The club changed its uniform from red and green to the purple of Belgian side Anderlecht, with whom it shared a training camp in 1977.

KING FAHD STADIUM

KING FAHD INTERNATIONAL STADIUM

AL AMIR BANDAR, BIN ABDUL AZIZ ST., RIYADH, SAUDI ARABIA

HOME TEAMS:
SAUDI ARABIA NATIONAL TEAM, AL-SHABAB

ARCHITECT:
IAN FRASER, JOHN ROBERTS AND PARTNERS

OPENED: 1987

CONSTRUCTION COST:
$80 MILLION (£55 MILLION)

CAPACITY: 67,000

Riyadh's extraordinary King Fahd International Stadium is the largest stadium in the Middle East. Completed in 1987, its iconic roof is both functional and symbolic. In addition to shielding spectators from the harsh Arabian sun, the roof is redolent of the royal crown of the stadium's patrons and evokes the folds of a Bedouin desert tent—the heart and hearth of traditional Saudi society.

HOME STADIUM

The stadium serves as the home ground of two Saudi clubs (Al-Hilal play some games here) and the national team. Built to the highest FIFA standards, it has hosted a number of international tournaments, including the FIFA World Youth Cup in 1989 and the FIFA Confederations Cup in 1992 and 1997.

MULTIPURPOSE VENUE

No expense was spared by the Saudi royal family in building a national stadium. In addition to being a top-class soccer venue, the stadium's athletic track and other facilities allow it to host a variety of international sporting events. Designed as an unbroken ellipse, all seats offer an unimpeded view of the field.

Women were not allowed to watch stadium events involving men until Saudi law was relaxed in 2017–2018, to permit mixed family enclosures. Before this, foreign women visitors to the national stadium could have watched from a reserved area near the press stand.

Concourse
A continuous concourse runs around the top of the stands; the VIP areas and press stand are located above it.

Running track
The athletics running track was designed to Olympic standards.

Roof
The roof covers an area of 506,000 sq ft (47,000 sq m), making it the largest of any soccer stadium in the world.

Columns
Twenty-four supporting columns are arranged around a circle, which has a diameter of 810 ft (247 m). A flag pole sits on top of each column, above the roof line.

TENTLIKE ROOF

Set in an ocean of parking lots, the King Fahd International Stadium is located on the northeastern edge of Riyadh, the capital city of Saudi Arabia. Widely regarded as one of the most spectacular and beautiful stadia in the world, it is noted for its vast, tentlike roof structure.

SHOOTING MATCH

Although the King Fahd Stadium has an official capacity of 67,000, the biggest games regularly attract larger crowds. When Manchester United played a friendly against Al-Hilal in 2008, for example, the stadium was full beyond capacity five hours before kickoff. Adding to the noise of so many fans was the sound of celebratory gunfire.

Ramps
Eight concrete ramps lead fans from the outside ticket booths to the stadium.

Seating
Every one of the 70,000 seats is shaded from the sun by the stadium's vast roof.

Sight lines
The stadium's design allows for every spectator to enjoy an uninterrupted view.

Boxes
The press stand and sumptuous VIP boxes are across from the halfway line.

Facilities
There are three levels of support services beneath the stands, which include communications equipment, changing rooms, and catering facilities.

Masts
Each of the 24 Teflon-coated masts stand at a height of 190 ft (58 m).

Medical facilities
Medical suites are located under the stands, providing specialist sports medicines and surgical facilities.

3 The number of years it took to build the stadium

24 The carat of gold used to make the faucets and fittings in the stadium's VIP bathrooms

5,400,000 The total area, in sq ft (500,000 sq m), covered by the King Fahd stadium

506,000 The area in sq ft (47,000 sq m) of the membrane roof—making it the largest stadium roof in the world

THE BEAUTY OF KING FAHD STADIUM WILL NOT BE COMPLETED UNLESS THE CROWDS ATTEND ... THE SUPPORTERS ARE THE FIRST PLAYER

PRINCE FAHD BIN SALMAN, FORMER PRESIDENT OF AL-HILAL

HOME AWAY

POPULATION: 1.3 BILLION
CAPITAL: DELHI
FA: ALL INDIA FOOTBALL FEDERATION
LICENSED PLAYERS:
MALE: 19 MILLION
FEMALE: 1.5 MILLION
PROFESSIONALS: 400
REGISTERED CLUBS: 6,500

INDIA

The first recorded soccer game in India was between British colonialists in 1854, and a Kolkata league existed by the 1870s. A nationwide federation came in 1936, but the game fared poorly after independence in 1947. The first professional league, the National Football League (1996) became the I-League in 2007. The Indian Super League started in 2013.

THE INDIAN SUPER LEAGUE

Indian soccer consists of a range of leagues and tournaments. The Indian Super League is the top flight, but all the leading clubs also play in local state divisions. The Durand Cup, founded in 1888, is the oldest national tournament; the Federation Cup ran from 1999 until 2017.

THE NEHRU CUP

Set up by the All India Football Federation (AIFF) in 1982, the Nehru Cup was an annual international soccer tournament. The event was not held between 1997 and 2007. It took India 25 years to win the trophy in 2007, beating Syria 1–0.

BAICHUNG **BHUTIA**

The leading Indian player of his generation, Bhutia was born in the Himalayas. He played three seasons of English soccer with the Lancashire club, Bury, and is the only player to score a hat trick in the Kolkata Derby.

BORN: DECEMBER 15, 1976, TINKITAM, SIKKIM, INDIA
HEIGHT: 5 FT 8 IN (1.73 M)
MAIN CLUBS: EAST BENGAL CLUB, JCT MILLS, MOHUN BAGAN
INTERNATIONAL CAPS: 107

THE GOLDEN AGE

The 1950s and early 1960s were the golden age of Indian international soccer. India won the Asian Games in 1951 and 1962 and came fourth at the 1956 Olympics. It even qualified for the 1950 World Cup but did not compete due to FIFA's insistence that the team could not play barefoot.

KOLKATA ALLEGIANCES

The big teams in Kolkata draw support from three groups: Mohun Bagan from Hindu Bengalis, Mohammedan Sporting from the Muslims, and East Bengal from refugee communities from Bangladesh.

106 India's FIFA world ranking in 2022

300 Crowd that watched the national team beat Afghanistan 1–0 in Hyderabad, December 2007

7,000,000 The annual fee, in US dollars, for television rights, paid by Zee TV to the I-League—the deal was canceled after three seasons

MOHUN BAGAN 2, BRITISH EMPIRE 1

The most politically charged game in Indian soccer was in 1911, when Mohun Bagan won the Durand Cup. It beat the East Yorkshire Regiment—a symbol of the British Raj—with two late goals. The game drew a crowd of more than 60,000.

STAT ATTACK

NATIONAL TEAM

NICKNAME: Blue Tigers
NATIONAL STADIUM: None
WORLD CUP FINALS: 0 appearances
BIGGEST WIN: 7–1 vs. Australia, 1956
BIGGEST DEFEAT: 1–11 vs. USSR, 1955
MOST CAPS: Sunil Chhetri, **131**
MOST GOALS: Sunil Chhetri, **84**

MAIN DOMESTIC CLUBS

MOHUN BAGAN
FOUNDED: Kolkata, 1889
STADIUM: Salt Lake Stadium
CAPACITY: 85,000   HOME
INTERNATIONAL HONORS: AFC Champions League group stages, 1987, 1989
LEAGUE: 5 **FEDERATION CUP:** 14

EAST BENGAL
FOUNDED: Kolkata, 1920
STADIUM: Salt Lake Stadium
CAPACITY: 85,000   HOME
INTERNATIONAL HONORS: None
LEAGUE: 5 **FEDERATION CUP:** 8

MOHAMMEDAN SPORTING
FOUNDED: Kolkata, 1891
STADIUM: Mohammedan Sporting Ground   HOME
CAPACITY: 15,000
INTERNATIONAL HONORS: None
LEAGUE: 0 **FEDERATION CUP:** 2

HOME

AWAY

POPULATION: 1.4 BILLION
CAPITAL: BEIJING
FA: CHINESE FOOTBALL ASSOCIATION
LICENSED PLAYERS:
MALE: 24.2 MILLION
FEMALE: 1.9 MILLION
PROFESSIONALS: 2,000
REGISTERED CLUBS: 1,500

CHINA

The history of soccer in China has been as turbulent as that of the nation itself. Played in the port enclaves of late-Imperial China, the game had sufficient support to send a Chinese team to the 1913 Far East Asian games. Not until the establishment of the communist state in 1949 was soccer organized nationwide. A cash-rich professional league was set up following the economic boom of the 1990s and 2000s.

CHINESE SUPER LEAGUE

China's first professional league, the Jia A, ran from 1994 to 2003, replacing a collection of national and regional tournaments. This was relaunched and rebranded in 2004 as the Chinese Super League. This consists of 18 teams in a standard league. There is also a knockout competition, the Chinese FA Cup.

IN OR OUT?

The Chinese FA first joined FIFA in 1931 but left in 1959 in protest at FIFA's recognition of Taiwan. In the 1970s, China began to reengage with the world, rejoining the AFC in 1974 and FIFA in 1979. The process was crowned with Chinese tours by Pelé's New York Cosmos and England's West Bromwich Albion.

SUN JIHAI

One of the first Chinese to play for a top European team, Sun moved to Manchester City in 2002. The 2003 tie between City and Everton, who fielded Chinese defender Li Tie, attracted a TV audience in China of 150 million.

BORN: SEPTEMBER 30, 1977, DALIAN, CHINA
HEIGHT: 6 FT (1.83 M); MAIN CLUBS: DALIAN WANDA, CRYSTAL PALACE, DALIAN SHIDE, MANCHESTER CITY, SHEFFIELD UNITED, CHENGDU BLADES, SHAANXI CHANBA; INTERNATIONAL CAPS: 80

ONE NATION, THREE CHINAS

After the transfer of sovereignty of Hong Kong from the UK in 1997, and Macau from Portugal in 1999, these two special administrative regions have continued to field their own national teams. They play as Hong Kong, China, and Macau, China, respectively.

ASIAN CUP 2004

In 2004, China hosted the Asian Cup, its first major soccer tournament. A showcase for China's growing economic success, the Cup was seen as a barometer for the 2008 Olympic Games. China made it to the final but lost an acrimonious game to Japan.

THE MAY 19TH INCIDENT

In May 1985 in Beijing, China was up 1–0 against Hong Kong in a key World Cup qualifier. The team then froze, lost 2–1, and triggered the first-ever Chinese soccer riot as exasperated fans smashed windows and burned buses downtown.

STAT ATTACK

NATIONAL TEAM

NICKNAME: Team Dragon
NATIONAL STADIUM: None
WORLD CUP FINALS: 1 appearance
BIGGEST WIN: 19–0 vs. Guam, 2000
BIGGEST DEFEAT: 0–8 vs. Brazil, 2012
MOST CAPS: Li Weifeng, **112**
MOST GOALS: Hao Haidong, **41**

MAIN DOMESTIC CLUBS

GUANGZHOU EVERGRANDE
FOUNDED: Guangzhou, 1954
STADIUM: Tianhe Stadium
CAPACITY: 58,500

HOME
INTERNATIONAL HONORS: AFC Champions League **2013**, **2015**
LEAGUE: 7 **CUP:** 2

SHANDONG LUNENG
FOUNDED: Jinan, 1956
STADIUM: Jinan Olympic Sports Center
CAPACITY: 56,808
HOME
INTERNATIONAL HONORS: None
LEAGUE: 4 **CUP:** 7

SHANGHAI SHENHUA
FOUNDED: Kangqiao, Shanghai, 1951
STADIUM: Hongkou Football Stadium
CAPACITY: 33,060
HOME
INTERNATIONAL HONORS: None
LEAGUE: 3 **CUP:** 5

HOME

AWAY

POPULATION: 126.7 MILLION
CAPITAL: TOKYO
FA NAME: JAPAN FOOTBALL ASSOCIATION
LICENSED PLAYERS:
MALE: 4.5 MILLION
FEMALE: 304,500
PROFESSIONALS: 976
REGISTERED CLUBS: 1,000

JAPAN

Soccer came to Japan in the 19th century and was initially the preserve of elite university students. A national league was founded in 1965 with teams from major corporations, such as Mitsubishi and Nissan, but there were no full-time professional players. The league was rebranded, professionalized, and relaunched in 1992 as the J-League, with hometown affiliations replacing corporate branding for the teams. Professional soccer culture has now taken root in Japan.

THE J-LEAGUE

The J-League initially used a combination of overtime, the golden goal, and penalty shoot-outs to decide every match. Penalty shoot-outs were dropped in 1999, as was overtime in 2003. Until 2005, the season was divided into two, with the leading teams from each playing each other home and away to decide the champion.

THE NAME GAME

Many of Japan's top sides changed their names to enter the J-League. Verdy Kawasaki became Tokyo Verdy 1969, Mitsubishi Heavy Industrial became Urawa Red Diamonds, and Nissan Motors became Yokohama F. Marinos.

STAT ATTACK

NATIONAL TEAM

NICKNAME: Samurai Blue
NATIONAL STADIUM: None
WORLD CUP FINALS: 7 appearances
ASIAN CUP: 9 appearances, winners **1992, 2000, 2004, 2011**
BIGGEST WIN: 15–0 vs. Philippines, 1967
BIGGEST DEFEAT: 2–15 vs. Philippines, 1917
MOST CAPS: Yasuhito Endo, **152**
MOST GOALS: Kunishige Kamamoto, **80**

MAIN DOMESTIC CLUBS

TOKYO VERDY 1969
FOUNDED: Tokyo, 1969
STADIUM: Ajinomoto
CAPACITY: 49,970
INTERNATIONAL HONORS: 1
LEAGUE: 7 CUP: 6

HOME

YOKOHAMA F. MARINOS
FOUNDED: Yokohama, 1972
STADIUM: Nissan Stadium
CAPACITY: 72,400
INTERNATIONAL HONORS: 2
LEAGUE: 7 CUP: 7

HOME

URAWA RED DIAMONDS
FOUNDED: Saitama, 1950
STADIUM: Saitama 2002
CAPACITY: 63,700
INTERNATIONAL HONORS: 2
LEAGUE: 5 CUP: 8

HOME

ADORING FANS

In the early years of the J-League, it was not unusual to see fans clap for the opposing team and encourage underperforming players, in an atmosphere closer to a pop concert than a soccer match. More conventional forms of fan behavior have had to be learned in Japan, with the fans of Urawa Red Diamonds taking the lead. They were the first to introduce booing and hummed Elvis's "I can't help falling in love with you" as their team's performances deteriorated in the early 1990s.

BOYS FROM BRAZIL

In the early 20th century, more than a million Japanese peasants migrated to the coffee fields of Brazil. As a consequence, there have been close links between the two countries. The Japanese national team has been coached by the Brazilian Zico, and Brazilian players—such as Dunga—have signed for Japanese teams.

HIDETOSHI **NAKATA**

The most gifted of the more recent Japanese players, Nakata's skills were matched by a determination to break with the traditions of Japanese soccer. He left Japan in 1995 for a series of Italian clubs.

BORN: JANUARY 22, 1977, KOFU, JAPAN
HEIGHT: 5 FT 9 IN (1.75 M)
MAIN CLUBS: BELLMARE HIRATSUKA, PERUGIA, PARMA, FIORENTINA, BOLTON WANDERERS
INTERNATIONAL CAPS: 77

SOUTH KOREA

HOME

AWAY

POPULATION: 51.2 MILLION
CAPITAL: SEOUL
FA: KOREA FOOTBALL ASSOCIATION
LICENSED PLAYERS:
MALE: 1 MILLION
FEMALE: 72,500
PROFESSIONALS: 550
REGISTERED CLUBS: 864

South Korean soccer has always faced stiff competition from baseball, due to US influence following the 1949–1953 Korean War. The country joined FIFA in 1948, but it was not until the creation of the K-League in 1983 that the game blossomed. The South Korean national side qualified for 10 consecutive Men's World Cups between 1986 and 2022, reaching the semifinals in 2002.

THE K-LEAGUE

There are two domestic tournaments in South Korea: the 12-club K-League and the Korean FA Cup, which is open to nonprofessional teams. In the early years of the K-League, there were no home and away games—instead, a circus of teams traveled throughout the country.

SON **HEUNG-MIN**

A gifted forward who can play across the front positions, Son Heung-Min proved excellent in the Premier League with 70 goals and 39 assists for Tottenham in fewer than 200 appearances. He also averages a goal in every three games for South Korea.

BORN: **JULY 8, 1992, CHUNCHEON, SOUTH KOREA**
HEIGHT: **6 FT (1.83 M)**
MAIN CLUBS: **HAMBURG, BAYER LEVERKUSEN, TOTTENHAM**
INTERNATIONAL CAPS:**104**

THE LORD'S TEAM

Seongnam Ilhwa Chunma, one of the most successful clubs in South Korea, were once owned by the Unification Church. Other Christian teams have had success—the first K-League was won by Hallelujah, a Seoul team sponsored by evangelical protestants.

CLEANING UP THE NATION'S ACT

The organizers of the 2002 World Cup left nothing to chance. They exhorted the South Korean people to smile more, organized anti-spitting campaigns, took traditional food stalls off the street, and attempted to close down the "pojangmachas"—the tented drinking clubs normally found in the alleyways of the nation's cities.

STAT ATTACK

NATIONAL TEAM

NICKNAME: Taegeuk Jeonsa ("Taegeuk Warriors")
WORLD CUP FINALS: 11 appearances, semifinals **2002**
ASIAN CUP: 14 appearances, winners **1956**, **1960**
BIGGEST WIN: 16–0 vs. Nepal, 2003
BIGGEST DEFEAT: 0–12 vs. Sweden, 1948
MOST CAPS: Hong Myung Bo, Cha Bum-kun, **136**
MOST GOALS: Cha Bum-kun, **58**

MAIN DOMESTIC CLUBS

SEONGNAM ILHWA CHUNMA
FOUNDED: Seongnam, 1989
STADIUM: Tancheon
CAPACITY: 16,146   HOME
INTERNATIONAL HONORS: Asian Champions League winners **1996**, **2010**
LEAGUE: 7 **CUP:** 3

SUWON SAMSUNG BLUEWINGS
FOUNDED: Suwon, 1995
STADIUM: World Cup Stadium   HOME
CAPACITY: 43,959
INTERNATIONAL HONORS: Asian Champions League winners **2001**, **2002**
LEAGUE: 4 **CUP:** 5

BUSAN I'PARK
FOUNDED: Busan, 1983
STADIUM: Busan Gudeok Stadium
CAPACITY: 12,349   HOME
INTERNATIONAL HONORS: Asian Champions League winners **1985**
LEAGUE: 4 **CUP:** 1

WORLD CUP 2002

South Korea's performance at the 2002 World Cup was their best ever. The Korean FA cleared the domestic schedule to allow coach Guus Hiddink and the squad to focus on the tournament. The team displayed an awesome work rate, matched only by the zeal of their feverish fans. They beat Portugal, Spain, and Italy to reach the semifinals, only to lose to Germany. No team has ever played so hard in the usually flat playoff for third place.

HOME   AWAY

POPULATION: 32 MILLION
CAPITAL: KUALA LUMPUR
FA: FOOTBALL ASSOCIATION OF MALAYSIA

MALAYSIA

Soccer arrived in Malaysia with the British, and a league was running in Kuala Lumpur by 1905. A national association was set up in 1933, initially based in Singapore. In spite of considerable public and political enthusiasm—the nation's president was head of the FA from 1957–1975—Malaysia has yet to make an impact on world soccer. It did qualify for the Olympics in 1972 and 1980.

STAT ATTACK

NATIONAL TEAM

NICKNAME: Harimau Malaya ("Malayan Tigers")
NATIONAL STADIUM: Stadium Nasional Bukit Jalil, 87,411
WORLD CUP FINALS: None

MAIN DOMESTIC CLUBS

SELANGOR
FOUNDED: Selangor, 1936
STADIUM: Shah Alam Stadium, 80,000

PERAK
FOUNDED: Ipoh, 1921
STADIUM: Perak, 32,000

KEDAH
FOUNDED: Alor Setar, 1924
STADIUM: Darul Aman, 32,387

MERDEKA—HONORING INDEPENDENCE

The Merdeka tournament was first held in 1957 to honor Malaysian Independence day. It is the oldest international tournament in Asia and was an annual invitation event for 30 years. Malaysia has won nine times, although it has also been won by Hamburg SV, Austria's Admira Wacker, and a Buenos Aires XI. The tournament has been held only nine times since 1988.

M-LEAGUE MATCH FIXING

In 1996, the Malaysian authorities arrested more than 100 domestic players all linked to systematic match fixing. The police found that more than 90 percent of games in the inaugural season of the M-League were fixed.

SWITCHING OFF THE LIGHTS

In 1999, British police arrested three Malaysians as they attempted to break into Charlton Athletic's Valley stadium in south London. The trio were part of a conspiracy linked to gangs in Malaysia attempting to fix the result of a Charlton game by turning off the floodlights.

VIETNAM

STAT ATTACK

NATIONAL TEAM

NATIONAL STADIUM: My Đình National Stadium, 40,192
WORLD CUP FINALS: None

HOME   AWAY

POPULATION: 96.4 MILLION
CAPITAL: HANOI
FA: VIETNAM FOOTBALL FEDERATION

The French administration brought soccer to Saigon in the late 19th century and a league for European expatriates was played there before World War I. Later wars limited progress, and since Vietnam's unification and development, local interest in soccer has plummeted because of corruption.

MAIN DOMESTIC CLUBS

SONG LAM NGHE AN
FOUNDED: Nghe An, 1979
STADIUM: Vinh Stadium, 18,000

THE CONG FC
FOUNDED: Hanoi, 1954
STADIUM: Hàng Đẫy Stadium, 40,192

BECAMEX BINH DUONG
FOUNDED: Thu Dau Mot, 1976
STADIUM: Go Dau, 18,250

LEAGUE HISTORY

The Vietnamese were running a league by the 1920s and in 1932 created a league with European colonialists. Soccer, like much else, was a casualty of World War II and the wars that followed. Vietnam returned to international competition in 1989 and created a professional V-league in 2000, but it has been plagued by setbacks.

INTERNATIONAL VICTORY

In 2008, Vietnam won its first international tournament in a victory against Thailand and became South East Asian Champions. The win was widely celebrated around the country.

MATCH-FIXING CULTURE

In 1997, players from Ho Chi Minh City Customs were convicted of match fixing. Their arrest was triggered when a goalkeeper allowed a defender to score an own goal. Song Lam Nghe An lost the 2004 Samsung Cup to the Cong club; players were fined for playing badly.

NORTH KOREA

HOME

AWAY

POPULATION: 25.1 MILLION
CAPITAL: PYONGYANG
FA: DPR KOREA FOOTBALL ASSOCIATION

North Korea first made its mark on the international stage at the 1966 World Cup, where it led Portugal 3–0 but missed out on a quarterfinal place after losing 5–3. Clubs have begun to compete in Asian contests, despite the current regime's isolationist policies.

GIANT KILLERS

North Korea's 1–0 victory over Italy during the 1966 World Cup was one of the biggest upsets in the history of sports, never mind soccer. "The fall of the Roman Empire had nothing on this" the *Northern Echo* aptly proclaimed in a newspaper article. For many years, the North Korean heroes of the match went unrecognized, but in 2001 a British film crew interviewed seven of the surviving players in Pyongyang.

ENFORCED EXILE

Crowd trouble after a 2005 World Cup qualifier against Iran in Pyongyang meant that the team was forced to play its next home game in an empty stadium in Bangkok, Thailand.

NO SONG, NO FLAG, NO WAY

North and South Korea were due to play each other in the qualifiers for the 2010 World Cup. North Korea insisted that the South could not show its flag or play its national anthem. Despite endless negotiations, the North Koreans would not give in so FIFA moved the game to Shanghai, China.

STAT ATTACK

NATIONAL TEAM

NICKNAME: Chollima (a mythical horse)
NATIONAL STADIUM: Kim Il Sung, 50,000
WORLD CUP FINALS: 2 appearances
AFC ASIAN CUP: 5 appearances, semifinals 1980

MAIN DOMESTIC CLUBS

PYONGYANG CITY SPORTS GROUP
FOUNDED: Pyongyang, 1956
STADIUM: Kim Il Sung, 50,000

4:25 (APRIL 25)
FOUNDED: Nampo, 1949
STADIUM: Yanggakdo, 30,000

KIGWANCHA SPORTS CLUB
FOUNDED: Pyongyang, 1956
STADIUM: Yanggakdo, 30,000

THAILAND

HOME

AWAY

POPULATION: 69.6 MILLION
CAPITAL: BANGKOK
FA: FOOTBALL ASSOCIATION OF THAILAND

The earliest recorded match in Thailand, known as Siam then, took place in 1915 between locals and Europeans. A soccer association was founded in 1916. Although Thailand has never made it to the World Cup, it has qualified for the Asian Cup six times.

BETTER TO LOSE THAN TO WIN

When Thailand and Indonesia played their final group game of the 1998 Tiger Cup, both had already qualified for the semifinals. Winning the game and the group would leave the victor facing Vietnam and the loser facing Singapore, a weaker team. The game ended 2–2 as both sides stopped defending. Indonesian defender Mursyid Effendi deliberately scored an own goal, and both teams were fined for "violating the spirit of the game."

BAD START

Thailand's first official outing in international competition was at the 1956 Olympics. Sadly, the team lasted only one game, losing 9–0 to Great Britain.

LOOKING OUTSIDE

Although interest in the Thai Premier League is growing steadily, foreign soccer is incredibly popular. Despite gambling being illegal in Thailand, estimates suggest that 5 percent of the country's GDP was gambled on the 2006 World Cup tournament. Thailand's ex-prime minister Thaksin Shinawatra also bought English club Manchester City then sold it a year later.

STAT ATTACK

NATIONAL TEAM

NICKNAME: The War Elephants
NATIONAL STADIUM: Rajamangala, 49,722
WORLD CUP FINALS: None
AFC ASIAN CUP: 7 appearances, semifinals 1972

MAIN DOMESTIC CLUBS

CHONBURI
FOUNDED: Chonburi, 1997
STADIUM: Chonburi Stadium, 8,680

AIRFORCE CENTRAL (NOW UTHAI THANI FC)
FOUNDED: Rangsit, 1937
STADIUM: Thupatemee, 25,000

BURIRAM UNITED FC
FOUNDED: Buriram, 1970
STADIUM: Chang Arena, 32,600

ASIA AND OCEANIA

ASIA: TOP CLUBS

The sheer size and poor transportation networks of Asia have, until recently, made regular competition between the region's teams—and comparison between them—difficult. The Asian Champions League is an imperfect guide to the elite— the big clubs from Iran, Saudi Arabia, the Gulf, and Far East Asia are all represented, but some of the biggest teams are not, such as Mohun Bagan of Kolkata, India.

MIDDLE EAST

The clubs of the Middle East used to be also-rans, but in recent years the region's oil money and soccer obsession has produced clubs good enough to join the continent's elite. Al-Ittihad was founded in Jeddah in 1928, making it the oldest surviving club in Saudi Arabia, and is the main rival to Al-Hilal at the top of Saudi soccer. Al-Arabi is the leading club in Qatar and the first from the country to reach an Asian continental final.

NAKAMURA SHUNSUKE
Starting out at Japanese powerhouse Yokohama Merinos, Nakamura followed the best Asian players by moving to Europe. He joined Reggina (Italy) in 2002, Celtic (Scotland) in 2005, and Espanyol (Spain) in 2009.

THE CLUBS

Asia's top clubs are clustered around the fringes of the continent—the Iranian and Gulf clubs to the west, and the Japanese and South Korean teams to the east. South Asia boasts a number of big clubs, but they have yet to register success beyond their borders.

Esteghlal
Country: Iran
Founded: Tehran, 1945
Stadium: Azadi
Capacity: 78,116

Persepolis
Country: Iran
Founded: Tehran, 1963
Stadium: Azadi
Capacity: 78,116

Al-Hilal
Country: Saudi Arabia
Founded: Riyadh, 1957
Stadium: King Saud University Stadium
Capacity: 25,000

Al-Ain
Country: UAE
Founded: Dubai, 1968
Stadium: Hazza bin Zayed Stadium
Capacity: 22,717

STAT ATTACK

DOMESTIC TEAMS

ESTEGHLAL
Founded by a group of military cycling enthusiasts, Esteghlal was originally named Taj—"crown" in Persian. After the 1979 Islamic Revolution, the name was changed to Esteghlal, which means "independence." The club forms one-half of the Tehran Derby and has been the most successful Iranian club in Asian club competitions.

HONORS: LEAGUE 9, CUP 7; ASIAN CHAMPIONS LEAGUE WINNERS 1970, 1991

PERSEPOLIS
Founded in 1963 as Persepolis by Ali Abdo, an American-Iranian boxer, the team steadily improved throughout the 1970s and won its first national title in 1972. After the Islamic Revolution, the club was renamed Pirouzi ("victory"), but the fans still call it Persepolis, and, in 2012, the old name was officially restored.

HONORS: LEAGUE 10, CUP 5; ASIAN CUP WINNERS' CUP WINNERS 1991

AL-HILAL
Founded as Olympic Club, the then-King Saud insisted on changing its name to Al-Hilal. They are the Bayern Munich of the Middle East— easily the most successful, if not the most loved, team. It has won four Asian Champions Leagues and many Arab and Middle Eastern trophies.

HONORS: LEAGUE 18, CUP 9; ASIAN CHAMPIONS LEAGUE WINNERS 1992, 2000, 2019, 2021; **ASIAN CUP WINNERS' CUP** 1997, 2002

FAR EAST

Alongside the Japanese and South Korean giants is China's Guangzhou Evergrande, who made an appearance in 2013's Club World Cup—the first Chinese club to do so. Life at the once-great Liaoning has not been so good—this club fell on such hard financial times that it had to be bailed out by stand-up comedian Zhao Benshan, who lent them a training ground.

THE RISING GENERATION

A new generation of clubs is rising in Asian soccer to challenge the old guard—Gamba Osaka from Japan came from obscurity to win the Asian Champions League in 2008 and its beaten finalist—Adelaide United—suggest that Australian teams will soon be challenging the Asian soccer elite.

DOMESTIC TEAMS

POHANG STEELERS

Established in 1973 and originally called the Pohang Steelworks, the club turned professional in 1984, adopting its current name in 1997. It finished in the top four of the K-League from 1985 to 1998. The club has three Asian Champions League titles and were third in the FIFA Club World Cup in 2009.

HONORS: LEAGUE 5, CUP 4; ASIAN CHAMPIONS LEAGUE WINNERS 1997, 1998, 2009

URAWA RED DIAMONDS

Beginning life in 1950 as Mitsubishi Motors' factory team, Urawa took its current name as a founding member of the J-League in 1993. Despite patchy success, it has the biggest, most consistent, and raucous support in Japan, which was rewarded when Urawa won the J-League in 2006 and the Asian Champions League the following year.

HONORS: LEAGUE 5, CUP 8; ASIAN CHAMPIONS LEAGUE WINNERS 2007, 2017

JÚBILO IWATA

Júbilo—"exultation" in Portuguese—has won the Japanese J-League title three times, as well as finishing runner-up on three occasions. The club holds the distinction of being Japan's most successful team in international club soccer, making three successive appearances in the Asian Champions Cup final, winning the title once.

HONORS: LEAGUE 4, CUP 2; ASIAN CHAMPIONS LEAGUE WINNERS 1999

SUWON SAMSUNG BLUEWINGS

With the money of the giant Samsung Chaebol behind them, the Bluewings established themselves as one of Asia's biggest clubs with back-to-back Champions Cup victories in 2001 and 2002. They can also boast some of the largest and most organized crowds and supporters' clubs in the continent—particularly the official club, Grand Bleu.

HONORS: LEAGUE 5, CUP 4; ASIAN CHAMPIONS LEAGUE WINNERS 2001, 2002

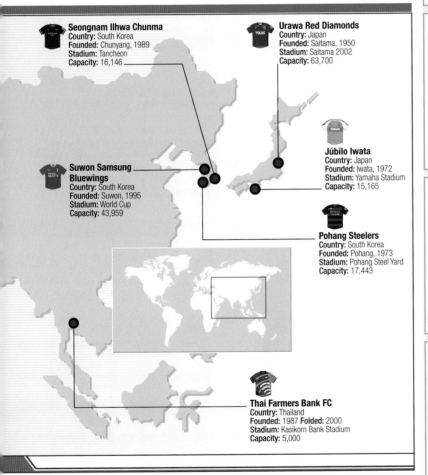

Seongnam Ilhwa Chunma
Country: South Korea
Founded: Chunyang, 1989
Stadium: Tancheon
Capacity: 16,146

Urawa Red Diamonds
Country: Japan
Founded: Saitama, 1950
Stadium: Saitama 2002
Capacity: 63,700

Júbilo Iwata
Country: Japan
Founded: Iwata, 1972
Stadium: Yamaha Stadium
Capacity: 15,165

Suwon Samsung Bluewings
Country: South Korea
Founded: Suwon, 1995
Stadium: World Cup
Capacity: 43,959

Pohang Steelers
Country: South Korea
Founded: Pohang, 1973
Stadium: Pohang Steel Yard
Capacity: 17,443

Thai Farmers Bank FC
Country: Thailand
Founded: 1987 Folded: 2000
Stadium: Kasikorn Bank Stadium
Capacity: 5,000

AL-AIN

Despite coming from one of the smaller cities of the United Arab Emirates, Al-Ain ("The Spring") is the UAE's leading soccer club and its only Asian champion. The team's uniform has changed several times since its foundation, first from green to red, then to purple, inspired by a training match with Belgian side Anderlecht), and now gray.

HONORS: LEAGUE 14, CUP 7; ASIAN CHAMPIONS LEAGUE WINNERS 2003

THAI FARMERS BANK FC

With two consecutive Asian Champions Cups in 1994 and 1995, Thai Farmers Bank FC was the only Thai side to win the tournament. Unfortunately, the major Asian financial crisis of 1997 led to the club sponsor's stock price collapsing. The club was taken over by foreign investors, finance was withdrawn, and in 2000 the club finally folded.

HONORS: LEAGUE 5, CUP 4; ASIAN CHAMPIONS LEAGUE WINNERS 1994, 1995

SEONGNAM ILHWA CHUNMA

The South Korean club began life as Ilhwa Chunma in Seoul but was relocated to the provincial city of Cheonon in 1995 by the soccer authorities. Four disastrous seasons followed, and the club returned to Seongnam, a satellite town of Seoul. Four K-League titles soon followed, and the club returned to the highest levels of Asian competition.

HONORS: LEAGUE 7, CUP 3; ASIAN CHAMPIONS LEAGUE WINNERS 1995, 2010

ASIA AND OCEANIA

AUSTRALIA

HOME

AWAY

POPULATION: 25.3 MILLION
CAPITAL: CANBERRA
FA: FOOTBALL FEDERATION AUSTRALIA
LICENSED PLAYERS:
MALE: 780,000
FEMALE: 190,000
PROFESSIONALS: 200
REGISTERED CLUBS: 2,300

Association soccer arrived in Australia in the 1870s and faced competition from Australian rules football, rugby union, and cricket. The game was boosted by Greek, Serb, and Croat immigrants after World War II, but it was not until the 21st century that a wave of Australians playing in the top overseas leagues raised the bar, culminating in qualification for the 2006 Men's World Cup.

WORLD CUP 2006

The Socceroos' trip to Germany in 2006 was their most successful World Cup. They progressed from the group stage only to be knocked out by Italy. A 95th-minute penalty left Australia with the unenviable record of being the first team to be knocked out of a World Cup with the very last kick of the match.

A MATTER OF CHOICE

Playing for Australia has been passed up by a number of players eligible to play for other nations, including Christian Vieri (Italy); Tony Dorigo and Craig Johnston (England); Joey Didulica, Anthony Šerić, and Josip Šimunić (Croatia); and Saša Ilić and Ivan Ergić (Serbia).

DISASTER IN MELBOURNE

Prior to joining the Asian Football Confederation in 2006, qualification for the World Cup was a tortuous process for Australia, requiring it to win the Oceania group and then enter a playoff with either an Asian or South American team. In 1997, Australia faced Iran in a playoff for a berth at the 1998 World Cup in France and managed a 1–1 draw in Tehran. At home, it was up 2–0 when a man notorious for disrupting Australian public events ran onto the field and broke a crossbar. After a long-enforced break, Iran grabbed two late goals to win the World Cup place.

MARK VIDUKA
Captain of the Socceroos at the 2006 World Cup, Viduka was the leading player of his generation and played in the top divisions of Croatia, Scotland, and England.

STAT ATTACK

NATIONAL TEAM

NICKNAME: Socceroos
NATIONAL STADIUM: None
WORLD CUP FINALS: 6 appearances
BIGGEST WIN: 31–0 vs. American Samoa, 2001
BIGGEST DEFEAT: 0–8 vs. South Africa, 1955
MOST CAPS: Mark Schwarzer, **109**
MOST GOALS: Tim Cahill, 50

A-LEAGUE

ADELAIDE UNITED
CITY: Adelaide, SA
FOUNDED: 2003
STADIUM: Coopers Stadium
CAPACITY: 17,000
HONORS: Asian Champions League Runner-up **2008**; A-league **2006**

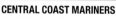
HOME

CENTRAL COAST MARINERS
CITY: Gosford, NSW
FOUNDED: 2004
STADIUM: Central Coast Stadium
CAPACITY: 20,059
HONORS: A-League **2008**, **2012**

HOME

MELBOURNE VICTORY
CITY: Melbourne, VIC
FOUNDED: 2004
STADIUM: AAMI Park
CAPACITY: 30,050
HONORS: A-League **2007**, **2009**, **2015**

HOME

BRISBANE ROAR
CITY: Brisbane, QLD
FOUNDED: 2004
STADIUM: Suncorp Stadium
CAPACITY: 52,500
HONORS: A-League **2011**, **2012**, **2014**

HOME

MELBOURNE CITY
CITY: Melbourne, VIC
FOUNDED: 2009
STADIUM: AAMI Park
CAPACITY: 30,050
HONORS: A-League **2021**

HOME

NEWCASTLE JETS
CITY: Newcastle, NSW
FOUNDED: 2000
STADIUM: McDonald Jones Stadium
CAPACITY: 33,000
HONORS: A-League **2008**

HOME

A-LEAGUE

The A-League is the most recent and successful attempt to set Australian professional soccer on a sustainable commercial footing. It was first played in 2005 with eight teams, expanded to 10 in 2009, and currently has 12. Crowds have been consistent, and the league is competitive.

The league imposes a strict salary cap on clubs but, to ensure a sprinkling of minor stars, allows each a marquee player who can be paid above the salary cap. The top three teams in the league qualify for the Asian Champions League.

HARRY KEWELL

The only Australian-born player to win the UEFA Champions League—with Liverpool in 2005—attacking midfielder Kewell later became a favorite at the Turkish club Galatasaray, before signing for Melbourne Victory.

BORN: **SEPTEMBER 22, 1978, SYDNEY, AUSTRALIA**
HEIGHT: **5 FT 11 IN (1.8 M)**
MAIN CLUBS: **LEEDS UNITED, LIVERPOOL, GALATASARAY, MELBOURNE VICTORY**
INTERNATIONAL CAPS: **56**

THE OLD SCHOOL

Prior to the A-League, Australian soccer was more loosely organized, and leagues and clubs regularly rose and fell, although the top-tier National Soccer League (NSL) ran from 1977 to 2004. Shunned by conservative Australians, the game was rejuvenated by postwar European migrants. Marconi Stallions and Adelaide City—known as Juventus until the mid-1960s—were Italian clubs, South Melbourne was Greek, and Sydney City began as the Jewish club Sydney Hakoah.

PERTH GLORY

CITY: Perth, WA
FOUNDED: 1995
STADIUM: Perth Oval   HOME
CAPACITY: 20,500
HONORS: Premiers **2000**, **2003**, **2004**, **2019**

SYDNEY FC

CITY: Sydney, NSW
FOUNDED: 2004
STADIUM: Allianz Stadium   HOME
CAPACITY: 20,500
HONORS: A-league **2006**, **2010**, **2017**, **2019**

WELLINGTON PHOENIX

CITY: Wellington, NZ
FOUNDED: 2007
STADIUM: Sky Stadium   HOME
CAPACITY: 34,500
HONORS: None

WESTERN SYDNEY WANDERERS

CITY: Sydney, NSW
FOUNDED: 2012
STADIUM: CommBank Stadium   HOME
CAPACITY: 24,000
HONORS: A-League **2013**; AFC Champions League **2014**

STAT ATTACK

THE OLD SCHOOL

SYDNEY CITY
FOUNDED: Sydney, 1939
STADIUM: Hensley Athletic Field
CAPACITY: 1,000
INTERNATIONAL HONORS: OFC Cup Winners' Cup **1987**
LEAGUE: 4 CUP: 2

SOUTH MELBOURNE
FOUNDED: Melbourne, 1959
STADIUM: Lakeside Stadium
CAPACITY: 12,000
INTERNATIONAL HONORS: OFC Champions League **1999**
LEAGUE: 4 CUP: 2

ADELAIDE CITY
FOUNDED: Adelaide, 1946
STADIUM: Adelaide City Park
CAPACITY: 5,000
INTERNATIONAL HONORS: OFC Champions League **1987**
LEAGUE: 3 CUP: 3

MARCONI STALLIONS
FOUNDED: Sydney, 1958
STADIUM: Marconi Stadium
CAPACITY: 10,000
INTERNATIONAL HONORS: None
LEAGUE: 4 CUP: 1

OCEANIA

Covering the widely dispersed islands of the Pacific, Oceania is so vast that promoting soccer was always going to be problematic. The confederation was founded in 1966 by Australia (who left in 2006), New Zealand, and Fiji and has steadily incorporated most of the Polynesian and Micronesian island chains. It became a full FIFA member in 1996, but World Cup qualification requires a playoff with a South American or Asian team.

NEW ZEALAND

In the last quarter of the 19th century, New Zealand was exposed to the formalized rules of soccer, Gaelic football, Australian rules football, rugby league, and rugby union. A national FA was established out of the ensuing melee in 1891, and a Glaswegian whiskey merchant created a national competition called the Brown Shield, which was later superceded by the Chatham Cup. The trophy was provided in 1922 by HMS *Chatham*, a passing British naval ship.

THE ALL WHITES

It soon became clear that rugby union, above all else, would be the national sport in New Zealand, so soccer was confined to the small industrial and mining towns of the islands. However, the New Zealand Football Championship has been contested since 2004, becoming the National League in 2021. Despite soccer's minority status in the country, New Zealand did qualify for the 1982 and 2010 World Cups, but the "All Whites" failed to progress to the knockout stages in either tournament. In the country's top league, Auckland City has become the dominant force, winning 12 titles. Another team, Wellington Phoenix, now plays in Australia's A-League.

CHRIS WOOD

The powerful New Zealand striker has a wealth of experience playing in England with clubs such as Burnley, Leeds, West Brom, and Newcastle. Wood appeared at the 2010 World Cup for the All Whites, aged just 18, and is his country's record goal scorer.

UNBEATEN RECORD

Oceania's biggest moment on the global soccer stage came at the 2010 World Cup finals in South Africa. During the tournament, New Zealand managed to hold defending World Champions Italy to a 1–1 draw and emerged from the tournament as the only unbeaten side.

I CALL ON ALL NATIONS [TO] WORK TOGETHER FOR THE DEVELOPMENT OF SOCCER IN THE SOUTH PACIFIC

SIR WILLIAM WALKLEY
FOUNDING PRESIDENT OF OCEANIA FOOTBALL CONFEDERATION (OFC), 1968

STAT ATTACK

NATIONAL TEAMS

NEW ZEALAND	SOLOMON ISLANDS	FIJI
GOVERNING BODY: New Zealand Football	**GOVERNING BODY:** Solomon Islands Football Federation	**GOVERNING BODY:** Fiji Football Association
FOUNDED: 1891	**FOUNDED:** 1979	**FOUNDED:** 1938
NATIONAL STADIUM: Sky Stadium, 34,500	**NATIONAL STADIUM:** Lawson Tama Stadium, 15,000	**NATIONAL STADIUM:** ANZ National Stadium, 4,300
BIGGEST WIN: 13–0 vs. Fiji, 1981	**BIGGEST WIN:** 17–0 vs. Wallis and Futuna Islands, 1991	**BIGGEST WIN:** 24–0 vs. Kiribati, 1979
BIGGEST DEFEAT: 1–10 vs. Australia, 1936	**BIGGEST DEFEAT:** 0–18 vs. Tahiti, 1963	**BIGGEST DEFEAT:** 0–13 vs. New Zealand, 1981

SOLOMON ISLANDS

The Solomon Islands are the rising force in Oceanic soccer. In a tightly contested mini-league to determine an Oceanic playoff for World Cup 2006 qualification, they managed an amazing 2–2 tie with Australia that pushed out New Zealand. However, in the final playoff with Australia, they lost 0–7 and 1–2.

FIJI

Soccer arrived in Fiji at the turn of the 20th century and was initially played by European expatriates. However, rugby union became more popular in the 1930s, after which the Indian community of Fiji took up the sport, creating its own Indian soccer association. The game and the association were ethnically broadened in the 1960s.

NEW CALEDONIA

New Caledonia's most famous son, Christian Karembeu, won the 1998 World Cup with France. He refused to sing the French national anthem because two of his uncles had been exhibited in a "human zoo" at the 1931 Paris Expo.

VANUATU

What do Vanuatu and Latvia have in common? By 2008, both had produced a team that had won 14 championships in a row—Tafea FC and Skonto Riga.

TONGA

Tonga can boast the services of former Red Star Belgrade and Real Madrid player Milan Jankovic, who took over as the national association's technical director and coach in 2002. His main task was to end the days of losing 22–0.

ASSOCIATE MEMBERS

The OFC includes a number of smaller nations that are classed as Associate Members because they are not full members of FIFA, including Kiribati, Micronesia, Niue, Northern Mariana Islands, Palau, and Tuvalu. They can enter the OFC Nations Cup but are not eligible to qualify for the World Cup.

AMERICAN SAMOA

American Samoa can claim an international victory—against the Wallis and Futuna Islands in 1983—but FIFA has deemed it unofficial. Consequently, the best, if unwanted, soccer record it possesses is that in 2001 it suffered the heaviest defeat in competitive international play, losing 0–31 to Australia.

SAMOA

A more technical approach to coaching combined with FIFA investment in infrastructure has ended the days of disastrous results for Samoa. With some professional facilities and the arrival of foreign coaches, Samoa is improving.

PAPUA NEW GUINEA

With a population bigger than New Zealand, there is no shortage of players. But as a developing nation, investment is limited, so results remain poor.

TAHITI

Encompassing the whole of French Polynesia, Tahiti achieved an amazing third-place finish at the 2002 OFC Nations Cup after beating Vanuatu 1–0 in the playoff. The country is still the highest-ranked island nation, according to FIFA.

0.5 World Cup Qualifying places allocated to OFC

3,000 Number of licensed soccer officials in the Oceania confederation

2000 Year Tahiti hosted its first Oceania Nations Cup

197 Tonga's place in FIFA World Ranking (2022)

NATIONAL TEAMS

AMERICAN SAMOA
GOVERNING BODY:
Football Federation American Samoa
FOUNDED: 1984
NATIONAL STADIUM:
Veterans Memorial Stadium, 10,000
BIGGEST WIN:
3–0 vs. Wallis and Futuna Islands, 1983
BIGGEST DEFEAT:
0–31 vs. Australia, 2001

SAMOA
GOVERNING BODY:
Football Federation Samoa
FOUNDED: 1968
NATIONAL STADIUM: National Soccer Stadium, 3,500
BIGGEST WIN:
8–0 vs. American Samoa, 2001
BIGGEST DEFEAT:
0–13 vs. Tahiti, 1981

PAPUA NEW GUINEA
GOVERNING BODY:
Papua New Guinea Football Association
FOUNDED: 1962
NATIONAL STADIUM:
Hubert Murray Stadium, 25,000
BIGGEST WIN:
20–0 vs. American Samoa, 1987
BIGGEST DEFEAT:
2–11 vs. Australia, 1980

TAHITI
GOVERNING BODY:
Fédération Tahitienne de Football
FOUNDED: 1989
NATIONAL STADIUM:
Stade Hamuta, 10,000
BIGGEST WIN:
30–0 vs. Cook Islands, 1971
BIGGEST DEFEAT: 0–10 vs New Zealand, 2004, and vs. Spain, 2013

NEW CALEDONIA
GOVERNING BODY:
Fédération Calédonienne de Football
FOUNDED: 1928
NATIONAL STADIUM: Stade Numa-Daly Magenta, 16,000
BIGGEST WIN:
18–0 vs. Guam, 1991 and Micronesia, 2003
BIGGEST DEFEAT:
0–11 vs. Australia, 2002

VANUATU
GOVERNING BODY:
Vanuatu Football Federation
FOUNDED: 1934
NATIONAL STADIUM:
Port Vila Municipal Stadium, 10,000
BIGGEST WIN:
18–0 vs. Kiribati, 2003
BIGGEST DEFEAT:
0–9 vs. New Zealand, 1951

TONGA
GOVERNING BODY:
Tonga Football Association
FOUNDED: 1965
NATIONAL STADIUM:
Loto-Tonga Soka Center, 1,000
BIGGEST WIN:
7–0 vs. Micronesia, 2003
BIGGEST DEFEAT:
0–22 vs. Australia, 2001

THE
COMPETITIONS

THE WORLD CUP

URUGUAY 1930

When FIFA met in 1929 to decide where to hold the inaugural World Cup, only Uruguay was ready to foot the bill, paid for by its huge beef exports. The government decided to celebrate the centenary of the country's constitution and hold the World Cup at the same time in the great stadium that was specially built for the tournament—the Estadio Centenario.

JULES RIMET
With 33 years' service, Rimet is FIFA's longest-serving president. The trophy for the winners of the competition he initiated was originally called Victory. In 1946, it was renamed in his honor.

A HAPHAZARD AFFAIR

The Uruguayan FA wrote to everyone, but not everyone came. The Germans turned down the offer, as did the Scandinavians and the English, Irish, Scottish, and Welsh teams. Jules Rimet insisted that his home team, France, should attend, but the coach stayed home. The Romanians came only because Prince Carol paid for a boat and his mistress persuaded the oil companies that employed most of the team to let them have a month off.

GOALS GALORE

Argentina and Uruguay predictably swept the opposition aside. Yugoslavia were the only Europeans who put up any resistance, and the US made its first and only World Cup semifinal. The game between Romania and Peru recorded what became the lowest-ever attendance at a World Cup game—just 300. Remarkably, both semifinals finished 6–1, and six goals were scored in the final.

	SEMIFINALS		FINAL	
ARGENTINA	6			
US	1		URUGUAY	4
URUGUAY	6		ARGENTINA	2
YUGOSLAVIA	1			

A GAME OF TWO HALVES

Ahead of the final, the participants argued about which ball to use. They decided to play the first half with Argentina's favored ball and use Uruguay's in the second. The teams picked wisely—both won the half that featured "their" ball.

THE FINAL

No one knows exactly how many Argentinians crossed the Plate River from Buenos Aires to Montevideo, but 15,000 is a reasonable guess. Six members of the Argentinian Chamber of Deputies requisitioned a government barge and tugboat to get them there. A fifth of the adult male population of Uruguay watched from the bleachers. The home side trailed 2–1 at halftime, but then came back with three goals in the second half to win the first World Cup.

JOSÉ LEANDRO ANDRADE
As a mainstay of the dominant Uruguay team of the 1920s, the skillful midfielder was one of the first black players to gain international recognition. He topped his international career during his country's victory in the 1930 final.

Lineup diagram

- GK Ballestrero
- DF Nasazzi
- DF Mascheroni
- MF Andrade
- MF Fernández
- MF Gestido
- FW Dorado
- FW Scarone
- FW Castro
- FW Cea
- FW Iriarte
- FW Evaristo, M
- FW Ferreira
- FW Stábile
- FW Varallo
- FW Peucelle
- MF Suárez
- MF Monti
- MF Evaristo, J
- DF Paternoster
- DF Della Torre
- GK Botasso

SUBS: No tactical substitutions at this World Cup

URUGUAY 4	ARGENTINA 2
30 JULY, ESTADIO CENTENARIO: 93,000	
MANAGER: ALBERTO SUPPICI	MANAGERS: FRANCISCO OLAZAR & JUAN JOSE TRAMUTOLA
FORMATION: 2-3-5	FORMATION: 2-3-5

ITALY 1934

By 1934, Uruguay, the first country to host the World Cup and the defending champions, had so little money that it couldn't afford to send a team to defend its title. However, Italy, which was under the control of Benito Mussolini, decided being hosts would be good for national pride. The resulting tournament consequently set the standard for turning sports events into political propaganda.

THE WUNDERTEAM FINALLY LOSE

The Italian government generously paid three-quarters of foreign fans' travel expenses, and transportation within Italy was free. Once again the British decided not to come. The Secretary of the FA, Sir Fredrick Wall, wrote of his invitation, "I have no desire to be a guest of the Italian Football Federation."

The team everyone really wanted to watch were the Austrians, who arrived in Italy on the back of a long, unbroken series of victories. Known as the *Wunderteam*, they met the host in the semifinals, going down to a single goal bundled over the line on a rain-soaked San Siro field in Milan.

NO GROUP STAGE

The 1934 World Cup seemed especially cruel as there was no group stage, so each team faced elimination after just one game. In the opening match of the tournament, Italy thrashed the US 7–1. Egypt, the first African team to play at a World Cup final, gave Hungary a good game. France took the Austrian *Wunderteam* into overtime—the first World Cup game to do so.

TWO TROPHIES

After winning the final, the Italian team was presented with two trophies. One was FIFA's Coupe de Jules Rimet, and the other was La Coppa del Duce, which Mussolini had specially commissioned. Each player received a gold medal in recognition of the conquest of soccer and a signed photograph of Il Duce.

GIUSEPPE MEAZZA
The Italian George Best, Meazza was a supremely talented striker whose antics both on and off the field made him the first superstar of the Italian game.

MAY 27 • JUNE 10, 1934

SEMIFINALS		FINAL	
ITALY	1	**ITALY**	**2°**
AUSTRIA	0	**CZECHOSLOVAKIA**	**1**
		3RD/4TH PLACE	
CZECHOSLOVAKIA	3	GERMANY	3
GERMANY	1	AUSTRIA	2

No group stage at the 1934 World Cup   ° After extra time

THE FINAL

The only World Cup Final to have two goalkeepers as captains—Combi for the Italians and Plánička for the Czechs—was goalless for 71 minutes. After being taken off and revived with ammonia, the Czech striker Puč returned to the field to score the opening goal just two minutes later. The Italians survived five minutes of panic and recovered their poise when Orsi curled the ball from the edge of the area into the Czech goal. Schiavio's winner came five minutes into overtime.

CZECHOSLOVAKIA ①	ITALY ②
10 JUNE, STADIO NAZIONALE: 45,000	
MANAGER: KAREL PETRU	MANAGER: VITTORIO POZZO
FORMATION: 2-3-5	FORMATION: 2-3-5

ITALY
- GK Combi
- DF Monzeglio — DF Allemandi
- MF Ferraris — MF Monti — MF Bertolini
- FW Guaita — FW Meazza — FW Schiavio — FW Ferrari — FW Orsi

CZECHOSLOVAKIA
- FW Puč — FW Nejedlý — FW Sobotka — FW Svoboda — FW Junek
- MF Krčil — MF Čambal — MF Kost'álek
- DF Čtyřoký — DF Ženišek
- GK Plánička

SUBS: No tactical substitutions at this World Cup

FRANCE 1938

The third World Cup was played in the shadow of World War II. Germany had swallowed Austria, and the Japanese and Chinese were fighting each other. Brazil was the only South American team who could afford to come, and the British sent a delegation to watch the games. Italy, the defending champion, was met by large anti-fascist protests, but it was unbothered, because the team secured four wins in a row.

ALL ABOUT BRAZIL

The Brazilians gripped the soccer world's imagination. They played an open attacking game against Poland, but their quarterfinal against the Czechs was a spiteful draw and the replay a strange, lethargic match. With striker Leônidas injured, however, they lost to Italy in the semifinals, although they won the third place playoff in some style.

ALFREDO FONI
Foni formed a formidable defensive partnership with Juventus teammate Pietro Rava. Their match-winning performances brought Italy World Cup success.

ATTACKING FLAIR

Brazil brought attacking flair to the World Cup, exemplified by its striker Leônidas—one of only two black players on the squad. Its opening game against Poland in Strasbourg went to overtime with the score at 4–4. Brazil eventually won the game 6–5 on a rain-soaked field. Leônidas scored a hat trick.

VICTORY ... OR NOTHING!

BENITO MUSSOLINI
TELEGRAM TO THE NATIONAL TEAM

SOCCER NEW BOYS

Two teams, the Dutch East Indies and Cuba, made their World Cup debut. The former was thrashed by Hungary, losing 6–0, but then nine of the team were winning their first cap and the captain played in glasses. Cuba surprised Romania in a 3–3 tie and then won the replay. The Swedes proved tougher, thrashing Cuba 8–0 in the next round. Switzerland's victory over Germany was popular, coming back from 2–0 down to win 4–2.

1ST ROUND		QUARTERFINALS		SEMIFINALS		FINAL	
FRANCE	3						
BELGIUM	1	FRANCE	1				
ITALY	2•	ITALY	3				
NORWAY	1			ITALY	2		
BRAZIL	6•			BRAZIL	1		
POLAND	5	BRAZIL	2*			ITALY	4
CZECHOSLOVAKIA	3•	CZECHOSLOVAKIA	1			HUNGARY	2
NETHERLANDS	0						
GERMANY	2*						
SWITZERLAND	4	SWITZERLAND	0				
HUNGARY	6	HUNGARY	2				
DUTCH EAST INDIES	0			HUNGARY	5	**3RD/4TH PLACE**	
SWEDEN (WALKOVER)				SWEDEN	1		
AUSTRIA (WITHDREW)		SWEDEN	8			BRAZIL	4
CUBA	2*	CUBA	0			SWEDEN	2
ROMANIA	1						

* After replays • After overtime

MEAZZA AND SÁROSI
Captaining their respective countries in the 1938 final, the Italian superstar and the versatile Hungarian led their teams in a memorable final. Meazza and teammate Giovanni Ferrari dominated the game, while Sárosi's 70th-minute goal ensured the Italians had to work for their win.

THE VENUES

Ten stadiums in nine different cities were selected for the tournament, but only nine were used. The first-round match between Sweden and Austria in Lyon's Stade Gerland was canceled after Austria withdrew.

Lille
Stade Victor Boucquey
Capacity: 15,000

Reims
Vélodrome Municipal
Capacity: 10,000

Strasbourg
Stade de la Meinau
Capacity: 30,000

Le Havre
Stade Cavée Verte
Capacity: 16,400

Paris
Parc des Princes
Capacity: 60,000

Paris
Stade Olympique de Colombes
Capacity: 60,000

Bordeaux
Parc Lescure
Capacity: 34,000

Toulouse
Stade Chapou
Capacity: 35,000

Antibes
Stade du Fort Carré
Capacity: 7,000

Marseille
Stade Vélodrome
Capacity: 60,000

TOP GOAL SCORERS

LEÔNIDAS	Brazil	7 goals
Gyula ZSENGELLÉR	Hungary	6 goals
György SÁROSI	Hungary	5 goals
Silvio PIOLA	Italy	5 goals

GOLDEN BALL

LEÔNIDAS	Brazil

LEÔNIDAS
Known as "The Rubber Man," Leônidas was one of the pioneers of the bicycle kick and became a top scorer at the 1938 finals.

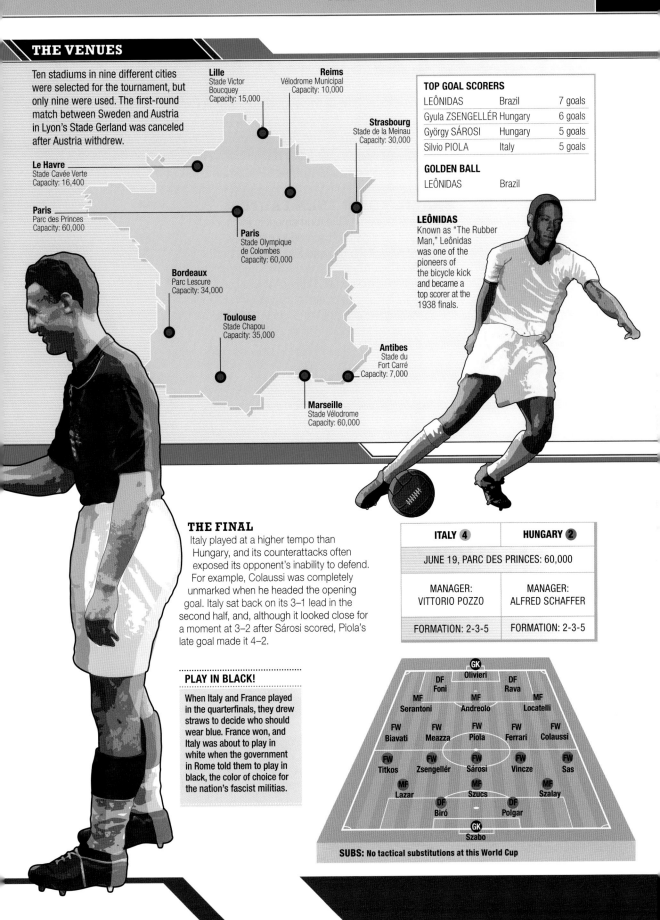

THE FINAL

Italy played at a higher tempo than Hungary, and its counterattacks often exposed its opponent's inability to defend. For example, Colaussi was completely unmarked when he headed the opening goal. Italy sat back on its 3–1 lead in the second half, and, although it looked close for a moment at 3–2 after Sárosi scored, Piola's late goal made it 4–2.

PLAY IN BLACK!

When Italy and France played in the quarterfinals, they drew straws to decide who should wear blue. France won, and Italy was about to play in white when the government in Rome told them to play in black, the color of choice for the nation's fascist militias.

ITALY 4	HUNGARY 2
JUNE 19, PARC DES PRINCES: 60,000	
MANAGER: VITTORIO POZZO	MANAGER: ALFRED SCHAFFER
FORMATION: 2-3-5	FORMATION: 2-3-5

GK Olivieri
DF Foni   **DF** Rava
MF Serantoni   **MF** Andreolo   **MF** Locatelli
FW Biavati   **FW** Meazza   **FW** Piola   **FW** Ferrari   **FW** Colaussi

FW Titkos   **FW** Zsengellér   **FW** Sárosi   **FW** Vincze   **FW** Sas
MF Lazar   **MF** Szucs   **MF** Szalay
DF Biró   **DF** Polgar
GK Szabo

SUBS: No tactical substitutions at this World Cup

BRAZIL 1950

Brazil was due to host the World Cup 1942, but World War II intervened. It wasn't until 1950 that the world was ready to resume. Domestic soccer was booming in Brazil. The Rio authorities built the world's biggest stadium—the Maracanã—and devoted the Rio Carnival to the World Cup. On the opening day, the Korean War broke out, but no one in Rio noticed.

BRAZIL ROMP THEN FALTER

Brazil was the team of the tournament in the opening stages. In its first game, it scored four goals to beat Mexico. It then scored two more against Switzerland and Yugoslavia. In the mini group of four that determined the winner, Brazil beat Sweden 7–1 and Spain 6–1. Uruguay, by contrast, had stuttered through the tournament. Against all odds, Uruguay managed to secure victory against Brazil in the final match of the tournament to win the World Cup.

JUAN SCHIAFFINO
Schiaffino, who was known as "Pepe," scored for Uruguay in the 1950 final. His Italian descent later allowed him to be capped for Italy, too.

ENGLAND EMBARRASSED

The big surprise of the group stages was the US's 1–0 victory over England, who had finally deigned to show up at the World Cup finals. Despite boasting players of the caliber of Tom Finney and Stanley Matthews, England was embarrassingly beaten by a goal from the Haitian-American Joe Gaetjens. Uruguay was in a group of two—due to Scotland and Turkey pulling out—and thrashed Bolivia 8–0 to progress to the final round.

ZIZINHO
Brazilian legend Pelé said Zizinho was the best player he ever saw. The attacker was lightning fast and very skillful and is remembered as the figurehead of an outstanding team.

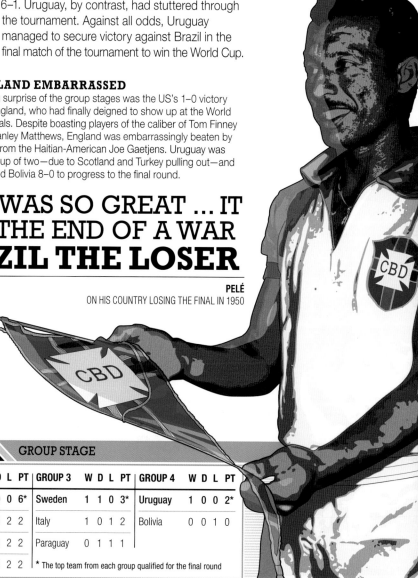

THE SADNESS WAS SO GREAT ... IT SEEMED LIKE THE END OF A WAR WITH BRAZIL THE LOSER

PELÉ
ON HIS COUNTRY LOSING THE FINAL IN 1950

THE MARACANÃ

The Maracanã was the largest and most elegant stadium in the world. With an official capacity of 160,000, it was a double-tiered ellipse with a flat, white, 360-degree roof. Its hidden cantilevers gave unobstructed views from every seat.

STAT ATTACK — GROUP STAGE

GROUP 1	W	D	L	PT	GROUP 2	W	D	L	PT	GROUP 3	W	D	L	PT	GROUP 4	W	D	L	PT
Brazil	2	1	0	5*	Spain	3	0	0	6*	Sweden	1	1	0	3*	Uruguay	1	0	0	2*
Yugoslavia	2	0	1	4	England	1	0	2	2	Italy	1	0	1	2	Bolivia	0	0	1	0
Switzerland	1	1	1	3	Chile	1	0	2	2	Paraguay	0	1	1	1					
Mexico	0	0	3	0	US	1	0	2	2										

* The top team from each group qualified for the final round

BARBOSA SHUNNED

Brazil's goalkeeper Barbosa and the other black players on the team were made the scapegoats of the great disaster by the press. In later life, Barbosa recalled going into a barber shop where a woman said to her son, "That's the man that made all Brazil cry," and he was shunned by the Brazilian team at its World Cup training camp in 1994.

THE FINAL

Brazil needed just a point from the final match of the final round to win the cup. Early in the second half, it was up 1–0 in front of the biggest-ever crowd at a soccer game. Uruguayan captain Obdulio Varela picked the ball out of his net and then, in a deliberate act of defiance, walked agonizingly slowly back to the center circle. The crowd turned from cheering to booing to silence. Something broke in Brazil, and two late goals from Uruguay made it the champion.

URUGUAY ②	BRAZIL 1
JULY 16, MARACANÃ: 199,954	
MANAGER: JUAN LÓPEZ FONTANA	MANAGER: FLÁVIO COSTA
FORMATION: 3-4-3	FORMATION: 3-4-3

SUBS: No tactical substitutions at this World Cup

THE VENUES

Six cities hosted matches in the tournament, all of them on or near the country's Atlantic coastline. Attendances varied wildly. A mere 3,500 spectators turned up to see Switzerland's victory over Mexico in Porto Alegre. Only 1,500 more watched Uruguay thrash Bolivia in Belo Horizonte, but the 199,954 crowd at the final in Rio was the biggest in history.

TOP GOAL SCORERS

ADEMIR	Brazil	8 goals
Estanislao BASORA	Spain	5 goals
Oscar MÍGUEZ	Uruguay	5 goals
CHICO	Brazil	4 goals
ZARRA	Spain	4 goals
Alcides GHIGGIA	Uruguay	4 goals

GOLDEN BALL
ZIZINHO	Brazil

ADEMIR
Nicknamed "Queixada" ("Jaw"), the Brazilian Ademir was the tournament's top scorer, but there is a controversy over whether he scored seven, eight, or nine goals.

Recife — Estádio Ilha do Retiro — Capacity: 35,000
Belo Horizonte — Estádio Sete de Setembro — Capacity: 18,000
Rio de Janeiro — Estádio do Maracanã — Capacity: 200,000
Sao Paulo — Estádio de Pacaembu — Capacity: 60,000
Curitiba — Estádio Durival de Britto — Capacity: 15,000
Porto Alegre — Estádio dos Eucaliptos — Capacity: 20,000

FINAL ROUND

FINAL ROUND	W	D	L	PT
Uruguay	2	1	0	5
Brazil	2	0	1	4
Sweden	1	0	2	2
Spain	0	1	2	1

AN UNCONVENTIONAL HEADER

Yugoslavia began its match against Brazil with only 10 men, since Mitic had gashed his head on an exposed girder in the underground passageways of the unfinished Maracanã stadium. By the time he had been patched up, Ademir had made it 1–0, and a late goal from Zizinho sealed Brazil's passage to the final round.

SWITZERLAND
1954

No team went to a World Cup as a bigger favorite than Hungary in 1954. As the reigning Olympic champion, it had lost just one game in 30 and had twice demolished England. The world waited to crown the kings of modern soccer. All its potential challengers—defending champions Uruguay, Brazil, Austria, and Yugoslavia—were in decline. West Germany, still barely a nation, had only recently been allowed back into FIFA and was considered rank outsiders.

THE BATTLE OF BERN

Hungary and Brazil's quarterfinal clash was marred by harsh fouls: Hidegkuti stamped on Indio's calves; Bózsik and Nilton Santos were sent off. The teams started fighting, and the police had to clear the field. As the game ended, a free-for-all broke out, continuing in the tunnel and into the changing rooms.

FERENC PUSKÁS
Puskás is widely regarded as the best finisher the game has ever seen—his lethal left foot claimed 84 goals in 85 appearances for Hungary.

FIRST TELEVISED WORLD CUP

Switzerland was chosen to host the 1954 World Cup because no other European country could. Europe was only just beginning to recover economically and psychologically from World War II. In a hint of the technological changes to come, the tournament was the first to be broadcast live on television to viewers across Europe—though few people anywhere had access to sets.

BIZARRE FORMATS

FIFA continued to experiment with bizarre, unfathomable formats in the group stage. This year in each group, two seeded teams played two unseeded teams but did not play each other. Playoffs separated teams that were level on points. Nevertheless, there were plenty of goals. The best action came in Group 2: including the playoff, this group yielded 39 goals in five games.

FRITZ WALTER
When he was a prisoner of war, Walter's life was spared by the Russians after a Hungarian guard recognized him as a soccer player and claimed Walter was Austrian. Later, he captained Germany in the 1954 final where they beat Hungary.

QUARTERFINALS		SEMIFINALS		FINAL	
BRAZIL	2			WEST GERMANY	3
HUNGARY	4	HUNGARY	4	HUNGARY	2
URUGUAY	4	URUGUAY	2		
ENGLAND	2			**3RD/4TH PLACE**	
YUGOSLAVIA	0				
WEST GERMANY	2	WEST GERMANY	6	AUSTRIA	3
AUSTRIA	7	AUSTRIA	1	URUGUAY	1
SWITZERLAND	5				

STAT ATTACK
GROUP STAGE

GROUP 1	W	D	L	PT	GROUP 2	W	D	L	PT	GROUP 3	W	D	L	PT	GROUP 4	W	D	L	PT
Brazil	1	1	0	3*	Hungary	2	0	0	4*	Uruguay	2	0	0	4*	England	1	1	0	3*
Yugoslavia	1	1	0	3*	West Germany	1	0	1	2*	Austria	2	0	0	4*	Switzerland	1	0	1	2*
France	1	0	1	2	Turkey	1	0	1	2	Czechoslovakia	0	0	2	0	Italy	1	0	1	2
Mexico	0	0	2	0	Korea	0	0	2	0	Scotland	0	0	2	0	Belgium	0	1	1	1

*The top two teams from each group qualified for the quarterfinals

THE FINAL

The game opened with a frantic exchange of goals. Hungary went two up in eight minutes, but soon West Germany drew level. The next hour saw a relentless Hungarian onslaught in the driving rain. Puskás had a goal disallowed before Rahn, unmarked on the edge of the box, scored the unlikely winner for West Germany with a long low shot.

SUBS: No tactical substitutions at this World Cup

WEST GERMANY ③	HUNGARY ②
JULY 4, WANKDORFSTADION: 64,000	
MANAGER: SEPP HERBERGER	MANAGER: GUSZTÁV SEBES
FORMATION: 3-2-5	FORMATION: 3-2-5

9 The biggest margin of victory in World Cup history achieved by Hungary against Korea. Later equaled when Yugoslavia beat Zaire 9–0 in 1974

12 The most goals scored in a single World Cup game—Austria 7 Switzerland 5

5.4 Average goals per game by Hungary at the 1954 World Cup—the highest in the competition's history

27 Number of goals scored by Hungary, the most by any team at a single World Cup tournament

THE VENUES

Several new stadiums were built for the occasion, and the six venues were evenly distributed between the German-, French-, and Italian-speaking parts of the nation. Despite Switzerland's small size, the average attendance was a healthy 34,211.

TOP GOAL SCORERS

Sándor KOCSIS	Hungary	11 goals
Erich PROBST	Austria	6 goals
Max MORLOCK	West Germany	6 goals
Josef HÜGI	Switzerland	6 goals

GOLDEN BALL

Ferenc PUSKÁS	Hungary

Basel
St. Jakob Stadium
Capacity: 65,000

Zurich
Hardturm Stadium
Capacity: 35,000

Lausanne
Stade Olympique
de la Pontaise
Capacity: 43,000

Bern
Wankdorfstadion
Capacity: 64,000

Geneva
Charmilles Stadium
Capacity: 20,000

Lugano
Cornaredo Stadium
Capacity: 26,000

SÁNDOR KOCSIS
A first-rate finisher, Kocsis was part of an incredible Hungarian team and was the top scorer in the 1954 finals, with a tally that included two hat tricks.

SWEDEN 1958

Before it started, Sweden 1958 seemed a very open World Cup. The host had a talented but aging squad. France, Argentina, and Brazil all promised much yet were untried. The great Hungarians were gone, but the Soviet Union looked strong, and, for the first and only time, all four British home nations qualified—England, Scotland, Northern Ireland, and Wales. In the end, however, there was just one team and one player—Brazil and the 17-year-old Pelé.

SCOUTS, SPIES, AND A DENTIST

Brazil was determined to win its first World Cup. The president's office underwrote the squad, which was supported by a team of experts, including a psychologist, a dentist, fitness trainers, and spies who checked up on other teams. The squad had more than 300 teeth extracted—most players had never been to a dentist. Twenty-five Swedish locations were scouted before a hotel was chosen and only then were the female staff replaced by men.

GUNNAR GREN
With Gunnar Nordahl and Nils Liedholm, Gren was one-third of Gre-No-Li, a deadly trio of Swedish strikers who scored many times at AC Milan (118 goals in 38 matches) and for their national side.

VARYING FORTUNES

Brazilian team's psychologist thought Pelé was "infantile" and considered Garrincha's IQ to be so low that he should not play. Fortunately, his advice was ignored, and, alongside Didi and Vavá, they cut a swathe through the tournament.

    The other teams enjoyed varying fortunes. The biggest surprise was the decimation of Argentina. Despite its considerable success in South America throughout the 1950s, the team looked slow and unsophisticated against European opponents. France went on a scoring spree (23 goals in the tournament) that began with seven against Paraguay and took it to the semifinals. Sweden looked comfortable, but Wales needed a playoff victory against Hungary to make the quarterfinals. West Germany won its group.

DANNY BLANCHFLOWER
One of the game's finest passers of the ball, the Tottenham Hotspur legend captained Northern Ireland to a quarterfinal against France.

QUARTERFINALS		SEMIFINALS		FINAL	
WEST GERMANY	1				
YUGOSLAVIA	0	WEST GERMANY	1	SWEDEN	2
		SWEDEN	3	BRAZIL	5
SWEDEN	2				
USSR	0			**3RD/4TH PLACE**	
FRANCE	4				
N. IRELAND	0	FRANCE	2	FRANCE	6
		BRAZIL	5	WEST GERMANY	3
BRAZIL	1				
WALES	0				

STAT ATTACK   GROUP STAGE

GROUP 1	W D L PT	GROUP 2	W D L PT	GROUP 3	W D L PT	GROUP 4	W D L PT
West Germany	1 2 0 4*	France	2 0 1 4*	Sweden	2 1 0 5*	Brazil	2 1 0 5*
Northern Ireland	1 1 1 3*	Yugoslavia	1 2 0 4*	Wales	0 3 0 3*	USSR	1 1 1 3*
Czechoslovakia	1 1 1 3	Paraguay	1 1 1 3	Hungary	1 1 1 3	England	0 3 0 3
Argentina	1 0 2 2	Scotland	0 1 2 1	Mexico	0 1 2 1	Austria	0 1 2 1

* The top two teams from each group qualified for the quarterfinals

THE FINAL

The host took an early lead when Liedholm scored in the fourth minute, but it didn't bode well. As its English coach George Raynor recalled, "Instead of looking dejected, the Brazilians called for the ball to restart the game." His fears were realized. Two goals from Vavá made it 2–1 to Brazil at halftime, and in the second half, three more goals followed, two from Pelé. When Pelé broke down in tears on the final whistle, his global stardom had begun.

BRAZIL 5	SWEDEN 2
JUNE 28, RÅSUNDA STADIUM: 51,800	
MANAGER: VICENTE FEOLA	MANAGER: GEORGE RAYNOR
FORMATION: 4-2-4	FORMATION: 2-4-4

WORLD CUP STREAKS

Brazil and Sweden hold the joint record—seven—for the number of games between two teams in the World Cup finals. When Mexico lost to Sweden, it completed the longest run of consecutive defeats at the World Cup finals—nine games.

Gilmar 3
4 Santos, D   2 Bellini   16 Orlando   12 Santos, N
6 Didi   19 Zito
11 Garrincha   20 Vavá   10 Pelé   7 Zagallo

11 Skoglund   9 Simonsson   8 Gren   7 Hamrin
6 Parling   4 Liedholm   14 Gustavsson   15 Börjesson
3 Axbom   2 Bergmark
Svensson 1

SUBS: No tactical substitutions at this World Cup

GARRINCHA WAS A PHENOMENAL PLAYER. WITHOUT HIM BY MY SIDE ... I WOULD NEVER HAVE WON THREE WORLD CUPS

PELÉ
GARRINCHA'S TEAMMATE AT THE 1958 AND 1962 FIFA WORLD CUPS

THE VENUES

The 12 venues used during the tournament were in the south of the country. They varied from the tiny Västerås stadium to the atmospheric Råsunda Stadium in Stockholm, which had been recently expanded.

Sandviken
Jernvallen
Capacity: 20,000

Västerås
Arosvallen
Capacity: 10,000

Eskilstuna
Tunavallen
Capacity: 20,000

Örebro
Eyravallen
Capacity: 13,000

Stockholm
Råsunda Stadium
Capacity: 50,000

Uddevalla
Rimnersvallen
Capacity: 12,000

Norrköping
Idrottsparken
Capacity: 20,000

Halmstad
Örjans Vall
Capacity: 15,000

Borås
Ryavallen
Capacity: 15,000

Helsingborg
Olympia
Capacity: 16,000

Gothenburg
Ullevi
Capacity: 43,200

Malmö
Malmö Stadion
Capacity: 26,500

JUST FONTAINE

The French striker holds the record for most goals scored at a single World Cup. Fontaine's total of 13 included four against the defending champion West Germany. He scored more goals for his country than he had caps.

TOP GOAL SCORERS

Just FONTAINE	France	13 goals
PELÉ	Brazil	6 goals
Helmut RAHN	Germany	6 goals
VAVÁ	Brazil	5 goals
Peter McPARLAND	Northern Ireland	5 goals

GOLDEN BALL

DIDI	Brazil

CHILE 1962

In 1960, an earthquake destroyed a third of Chile's buildings and made preparations for the World Cup very difficult. Carlos Dittborn, president of the Chilean Football Federation, called for a major national effort, and everything was ready just in time. Tragically, he died a month before the finals, but the tournament was enlivened by the host's best showing in a World Cup and by the magic of Brazil.

JOSEF MASOPUST
A tremendously skillful midfielder, Masopust was the linchpin of the Czech side and scored the opening goal of the 1962 final.

BRAZIL COMES ALIVE

Brazil approached this World Cup with the same organizational discipline it had shown in 1958, including high-altitude training and an inspection of local brothels by the Brazilian FA's technical commission. It had almost the same squad as well. It played within its capabilities during the opening rounds but lost Pelé to a groin strain. However, Brazil came alive in the quarter- and semifinals, with victories over England and Chile. No one else ever really looked likely to win.

BATTLE OF SANTIAGO

Chile versus Italy became a nasty battle. Bad feeling between the teams before the game were made worse by Ferrini's sending off for retaliating against Chile's Landu. The police had to escort Ferrini away. Then, after being punched by Sanchez, David kicked Sanchez in the neck and was sent off.

GARRINCHA
Manuel Francisco dos Santos—to give Garrincha his proper name—was a fantastic dribbler of the ball. If it wasn't for Pelé, he would probably have been regarded as the world's greatest player.

WE WILL DO EVERYTHING TO REBUILD AND HOST … THE WORLD CUP

CARLOS DITTBORN
PRESIDENT OF THE CHILEAN FOOTBALL FEDERATION, 1960

QUARTERFINALS		SEMIFINALS		FINAL	
CZECHOSLOVAKIA	1				
HUNGARY	0	CZECHOSLOVAKIA	3	CZECHOSLOVAKIA	1
		YUGOSLAVIA	1	BRAZIL	3
YUGOSLAVIA	1				
WEST GERMANY	0				
				3RD/4TH PLACE	
BRAZIL	3				
ENGLAND	1	BRAZIL	4	CHILE	1
		CHILE	2	YUGOSLAVIA	0
CHILE	2				
USSR	1				

GOALS DECIDE

In the group stage, teams even on points were separated by their goal average rather than playoffs, replays, or overtime. In the Arica group in the far north (see map opposite), tiny crowds saw the seeded Uruguayans knocked out by the USSR and Yugoslavia. Chile and West Germany also progressed, while Argentina were pushed out by Hungary and England. The eventual finalists, Brazil and Czechoslovakia, faced off in a 0–0 tie, when Pelé was injured.

STAT ATTACK

GROUP STAGE

GROUP 1	W	D	L	PT	GROUP 2	W	D	L	PT	GROUP 3	W	D	L	PT	GROUP 4	W	D	L	PT
USSR	2	1	0	5*	**West Germany**	2	1	0	5*	**Brazil**	2	1	0	5*	**Hungary**	2	1	0	5*
Yugoslavia	2	0	1	4*	**Chile**	2	0	1	4*	**Czechoslovakia**	1	1	1	3*	**England**	1	1	1	3*
Uruguay	1	0	2	2	Italy	1	1	1	3	Mexico	1	0	2	2	Argentina	1	1	1	3
Colombia	0	1	2	1	Switzerland	0	0	3	0	Spain	1	0	2	2	Bulgaria	0	1	2	1

* The top two teams from each group qualified for the quarterfinals

THE FINAL

The Czechs started their second appearance in a World Cup final brilliantly as Josef Masopust hit a low shot to make it 1–0 on 14 minutes. However, Brazil, looking better than ever, struck back. Amarildo made it 1–1 two minutes later and in the second half engineered a short cross to the unmarked Zito, who made it 2–1. Vavá killed off Czech hopes when he struck home the ball that Czech goalkeeper Schrojf had just let slip from his hands.

Gilmar ①

| 2 | 3 | 5 | 6 |
| Santos, D | Ramos | Zózimo | Santos, N |

4 Zito **8** Didi

| 7 | 19 | 20 | 21 |
| Garrincha | Vavá | Amarildo | Zagallo |

| 11 | 18 | 8 | 17 |
| Jelínek | Kadraba | Scherer | Pospíchal |

6 Masopust **19** Kvašnák

| 4 | 3 | 5 | 12 |
| Novák | Popluhár | Pluskal | Tichý |

Schrojf ①

SUBS: No tactical substitutions at this World Cup

BRAZIL 3	CZECHOSLOVAKIA ①
JUNE 17, ESTADIO NACIONAL: 68,679	
MANAGER: AYMORE MOREIRA	MANAGER: RUDOLF VYTLACIL
FORMATION: 4-2-4	FORMATION: 4-2-4

THE VENUES

As a result of the 1960 earthquake, only four venues were used, one in Arica in the north, the others around Santiago.

TOP GOAL SCORERS

GARRINCHA	Brazil	4 goals
VAVÁ	Brazil	4 goals
Leonel SANCHEZ	Chile	4 goals
Florian ALBERT	Hungary	4 goals
Valentin IVANOV	Soviet Union	4 goals
Drazan JERKOVIC	Yugoslavia	4 goals

GOLDEN BALL

GARRINCHA	Brazil

Arica
Estadio Carlos Dittborn
Capacity: 15,000

Viña del Mar
Estadio Sausalito
Capacity: 18,000

Santiago
Estadio Nacional
Capacity: 67,000

Rancagua
Estadio El Teniente
Capacity: 10,000

GARRINCHA'S BOOKING

Chilean defender Eladio Rojas spent 85 minutes of his team's semifinal clash with Brazil kicking Garrincha. The Brazilian finally snapped, kneeing Rojas from behind. Garrincha was sent off, ruling him out of the final. However, the Peruvian referee was persuaded to revoke his decision after discussions involving the Brazilian and Peruvian prime ministers and their ambassadors in Chile. Garrincha was allowed to play in the final.

VAVÁ

Brazilian striker Vavá was the first player to score in the final of two World Cups, netting twice in 1958 and again in 1962. The others to score in two finals are Pele, Paul Breitner, and Zinedine Zidane.

JULY 11 • JULY 30, 1966

ENGLAND 1966

Soccer returned to its birthplace for the 1966 finals, with FIFA selecting England as host nation to mark the codification of the laws of soccer there just over a century previously. Appropriately enough, Alf Ramsey's "wingless wonders" ended up winning the tournament in what remains the only major international triumph in England's history.

SOCCER GOES DEFENSIVE

In many ways, 1966 was a transition point between the old and new. Many matches were played in rickety old stadiums, and teams could still not make tactical substitutions. A new defensive spirit meant fear of losing often dominated the will to win. The number of goals scored in the group stages was sharply down, and cynical fouling was rife.

WORLD CUP WILLIE

The 1966 tournament was the first to feature an official mascot. World Cup Willie was a shaggy lion dressed in a Union Jack shirt. Willie featured on all kinds of merchandise and was the subject of a song by the skiffle star Lonnie Donegan.

BOBBY MOORE

Pelé claimed the West Ham and England captain was the greatest defender he ever played against. The pictures of Moore holding the trophy aloft are among the most iconic soccer images in the world.

QUARTERFINALS		SEMIFINALS		FINAL	
ENGLAND	1				
ARGENTINA	0	ENGLAND	2	ENGLAND	4•
		PORTUGAL	1	WEST GERMANY	2
PORTUGAL	5				
NORTH KOREA	3			3RD/4TH PLACE	
WEST GERMANY	4				
URUGUAY	0	WEST GERMANY	2	PORTUGAL	2
USSR	2	USSR	1	USSR	1
HUNGARY	1				

• After overtime

A DOG NAMED PICKLES

Four months before the start of the tournament in England in 1966, the World Cup Trophy went on display in London and promptly disappeared. After a week of national panic, a black-and-white mutt named Pickles found the Jules Rimet Trophy wrapped up in old newspaper at the end of a yard in South London. The dog quickly became an international celebrity.

THRILLS AND SPILLS

The Brazilians were effectively kicked into submission by their opponents and disappointingly went out during the group stage. The behavior of some of the Argentinian players in the quarterfinal against England caused England manager Alf Ramsey to brand them "animals." The biggest shock in the group stage came when the North Koreans condemned the mighty Italians to an early exit with a 1–0 victory. A glorious exception to the prevailing negativity was the thrilling quarterfinal in which Portugal recovered from a 3–0 deficit to beat North Korea 5–3.

STAT ATTACK — GROUP STAGE

GROUP 1	W	D	L	PT	GROUP 2	W	D	L	PT
England	2	1	0	5*	West Germany	2	1	0	5*
Uruguay	1	2	0	4*	Argentina	2	1	0	5*
Mexico	0	2	1	2	Spain	1	0	2	2
France	0	1	2	1	Switzerland	0	0	3	0

* The top two teams from each group qualified for the quarterfinals

THE VENUES

England's well-developed domestic game meant that the venues were bigger than those of previous World Cups. White City was used for one first-round match because Wembley Stadium's owner refused to rearrange a greyhound race meeting.

EUSEBIO
So impressed were the English by the tournament's top scorer, that Eusebio was honored with a figure at the famous Madame Tussauds waxworks in London.

Sunderland
Roker Park
Capacity: 60,000

Manchester
Old Trafford
Capacity: 80,000

Liverpool
Goodison Park
Capacity: 40,000

Sheffield
Hillsborough
Capacity: 40,000

Middlesbrough
Ayresome Park
Capacity: 54,000

Birmingham
Villa Park
Capacity: 43,000

London
Wembley Stadium
Capacity: 127,000

London
White City Stadium
Capacity: 68,000

TOP GOAL SCORERS

EUSEBIO	Portugal	9 goals
Helmut HALLER	West Germany	6 goals
Geoff HURST	England	4 goals
Franz BECKENBAUER	West Germany	4 goals
Ferenc BENE	Hungary	4 goals
Valeriy PORKUJAN	Soviet Union	4 goals

GOLDEN BALL

Bobby CHARLTON	England

THE FINAL

The defining moment came in the eighth minute of overtime. When Hurst struck a fierce shot against the underside of the crossbar, the Soviet linesman deemed that the rebound had crossed the line. With seconds to go, Hurst became the only player to score a hat trick in a World Cup final.

ENGLAND ④	WEST GERMANY ②
JULY 30, WEMBLEY STADIUM: 98,000	
MANAGER: ALF RAMSEY	MANAGER: HELMUT SCHÖN
FORMATION: 4-3-3	FORMATION: 4-4-2

SUBS: No tactical substitutions at this World Cup

GROUP STAGE

GROUP 3	W	D	L	PT	GROUP 4	W	D	L	PT
Portugal	3	0	0	6*	USSR	3	0	0	6*
Hungary	2	0	1	4*	Korea DPR	1	1	1	3*
Brazil	1	0	2	2	Italy	1	0	2	2
Bulgaria	0	0	3	0	Chile	0	1	2	1

* The top two teams from each group qualified for the quarterfinals

BOBBY CHARLTON
One of the game's greatest attacking midfielders and a player with the fiercest of finishes, Charlton was one of the stars of the 1966 World Cup. However, he was effectively marked out of the final by a young Franz Beckenbauer.

MEXICO 1970

Mexico 1970 is often regarded as the most exciting tournament in the history of the competition. Much credit for this goes to the Brazilians, who won with a dazzling, free-flowing brand of soccer that was the opposite of the cautious approach that had dominated the previous two finals.

NEW RULES UNDER THE SUN

The conditions in Mexico were tricky. Several matches kicked off at noon to suit European television schedules, exposing players to the intense heat. Three venues were more than 7,000 ft (2,130 m) above sea level in oxygen-thin conditions. Luckily, a new rule allowed each team two substitutions per match. Another new rule equipped referees with yellow and red cards to show to players who were booked or dismissed. The plan came from British referee Ken Aston, who got the idea while waiting at a set of stoplights in London.

JAIRZINHO
A huge star in a team of stars, Jairzinho was a fleet-footed winger who scored in every game Brazil played in the 1970 tournament.

BOBBY MOORE'S BRACELET

England's preparations for the tournament were disrupted by a bizarre incident in South America. Following a warm-up match in Colombia, the cup-holders' normally squeaky-clean captain Bobby Moore was arrested on suspicion of stealing a bracelet from a Bogotá jewelry store. The charges were eventually dropped.

THE VENUES

Five stadiums in the heart of the country were used for the finals of the Mexico 1970 World Cup. The jewel in the crown was the magnificent Estadio Azteca in Mexico City, which had been built as the centerpiece of the Summer Olympic Games in 1968.

Guadalajara
Estadio Jalisco
Capacity: 73,000

Mexico City
Estadio Azteca
Capacity: 105,000

Puebla
Estadio Cuauhtémoc
Capacity: 47,000

GERD MÜLLER
The tournament's top scorer, Müller scored 68 goals in 62 international outings, making him one of the most prolific marksmen of all time.

León
Estadio Nou Camp
Capacity: 34,000

Toluca
Estadio Luis Dosal
Capacity: 27,000

TOP GOAL SCORERS

Gerd MÜLLER	West Germany	10 goals
JAIRZINHO	Brazil	7 goals
Teófilo CUBILLAS	Peru	5 goals
PELÉ	Brazil	4 goals
Anatoliy BYSHOVETS	USSR	4 goals

GOLDEN BALL

PELÉ	Brazil

STAT ATTACK   GROUP STAGE

GROUP 1	W	D	L	PT	GROUP 2	W	D	L	PT	GROUP 3	W	D	L	PT	GROUP 4	W	D	L	PT
USSR	2	1	0	5*	Italy	1	2	0	4*	Brazil	3	0	0	6*	West Germany	3	0	0	6*
Mexico	2	1	0	5*	Uruguay	1	1	1	3*	England	2	0	1	4*	Peru	2	0	1	4*
Belgium	1	0	2	2	Sweden	1	1	1	3	Romania	1	0	2	2	Bulgaria	0	1	2	1
El Salvador	0	0	3	0	Israel	0	2	1	2	Czechoslovakia	0	0	3	0	Morocco	0	1	2	1

* The top two teams from each group qualified for the quarterfinals

REMARKABLE CLASSICS

In a memorable group match between England and Brazil, Gordon Banks denied a downward Pelé header with a seemingly impossible save, but Brazil prevailed with a goal from Jairzinho. The knockout stages saw some classics. West Germany came from two goals down to beat England, and in its semifinal against Italy, an astonishing five goals were scored in overtime.

In the other semifinal, Brazil finally exorcized the ghosts of its 1950 final defeat to Uruguay. Pelé was in exuberant form, almost scoring with a 50-yard volley and selling the Uruguayan keeper one of the most outrageous dummies of all time.

QUARTERFINALS		SEMIFINALS		FINAL	
USSR	0				
URUGUAY	1	URUGUAY	1	BRAZIL	4
		BRAZIL	3	ITALY	1
BRAZIL	4				
PERU	2			**3RD/4TH PLACE**	
ITALY	4				
MEXICO	1	ITALY	4•	WEST GERMANY	1
		WEST GERMANY	3	URUGUAY	0
WEST GERMANY	3				
ENGLAND	2				

• After overtime

THE FINAL

Italy reverted to defensive type in the final but was overwhelmed by Brazilian creativity in what is often called the greatest final. Player of the tournament Pelé opened the scoring, Gérson canceled out Boninsegna's equalizer, and Jairzinho scored for the sixth match in succession. Finally, Carlos Alberto rifled home a fourth after a sublime move involving eight outfield players in a classic World Cup encounter.

I TOLD MYSELF, HE'S MADE LIKE EVERYONE ELSE ... BUT I WAS WRONG

TARCISIO BURGNICH
ON MARKING PELÉ IN THE FINAL, 1970

PELÉ
Christened Edison Arantes do Nascimento, Pelé is regarded by many as the greatest player of all time. He is the only player to have three World Cup winners medals.

BRAZIL 4	ITALY 1
JUNE 21, ESTADIO AZTECA: 107,412	
MANAGER: MÁRIO ZAGALLO	MANAGER: FERRUCCIO VALCAREGGI
FORMATION: 4-3-3	FORMATION: 4-3-3

1 Félix
2 Brito   16 Everaldo   4 Alberto   3 Piazza
7 Jairzinho   8 Gérson   5 Clodoaldo
10 Pelé   9 Tostão   11 Rivellino

20 Boninsegna   15 Mazzola   13 Domenghini
11 Riva   16 De Sisti   10 Bertini
3 Facchetti   8 Rosato   5 Cera   2 Burgnich
1 Albertosi

SUBS: 14 Rivera   18 Juliano

WEST GERMANY

1974

As in the tournament in Switzerland 20 years earlier, when West Germany beat Hungary in the final, the 1974 World Cup is chiefly remembered for the skill and brilliance of the runner-up. The Netherlands, led by the magician Johan Cruyff, entranced spectators with its elegant "total soccer." Just as in 1954, however, West German grit and practicality triumphed and brought the host its second World Cup.

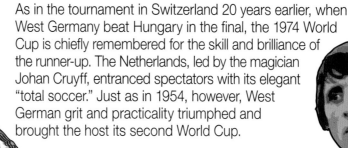

JOHAN CRUYFF
A true master of his art, Cruyff was instrumental in ensuring the Dutch cruised all the way to the final, knocking out the reigning champions Brazil on their way. That they didn't win the final is the eternal frustration of all Dutch fans.

GRZEGORZ LATO
Poland's most capped player, Lato was renowned for his blistering pace and lightning acceleration. The striker remains the only Pole to win a World Cup Golden Boot.

FINAL FLAP

Seconds before the final was due to kick off, English referee Jack Taylor suddenly noticed that something was wrong. There were no corner flags on the field. Amid the excitement of the pre-match ceremony, the official responsible had forgotten to set them up. It took five minutes for the situation to be rectified.

A NEW TOURNAMENT STRUCTURE

The tournament was structured in a new way, with a second group stage replacing the standard quarter- and semifinals. The idea was to minimize the lottery element of the old knockout system by forcing teams that had gotten through the first group stage to play three rather than two of their similarly successful rivals. Highlights of the first group stage included a politically charged clash between West and East Germany (the latter won 1–0). Yugoslavia trounced Zaire 9–0 and Haiti forced Italian keeper Dino Zoff to pick the ball out of his net for the first time in 1,147 minutes of international soccer.

TRICKY DECIDERS

The tournament may have lacked official semifinals, but the deciding matches in the second group stage amounted to much the same thing. The Netherlands defeated Brazil 2–0 in a strangely violent Group A decider, while the Group B equivalent was played on a field that was almost a swamp, with West Germany edging out Poland 1–0. Only in the 1978 World Cup finals would the pitfalls of a second group phase idea become apparent.

STAT ATTACK

FIRST GROUP STAGE

GROUP 1	W	D	L	PT	GROUP 2	W	D	L	PT	GROUP 3	W	D	L	PT	GROUP 4	W	D	L	PT
East Germany	2	1	0	5*	Yugoslavia	1	2	0	4*	Netherlands	2	1	0	5*	Poland	3	0	0	6*
West Germany	2	0	1	4*	Brazil	1	2	0	4*	Sweden	1	2	0	4*	Argentina	1	1	1	3*
Chile	0	2	1	2	Scotland	1	2	0	4	Bulgaria	0	2	1	2	Italy	1	1	1	3
Australia	0	1	2	1	Zaire	0	0	3	0	Uruguay	0	1	2	1	Haiti	0	0	3	0

* The top two teams from each group qualified for the second group stage

THE FINAL

Holland's Johan Neeskens converted a penalty, the first ever awarded in a World Cup final, before any West German player had even touched the ball. Twenty-five minutes later, the Germans scored a penalty of their own through Breitner. Their lethal striker Gerd Müller slotted home the winner just before halftime.

WEST GERMANY ②	NETHERLANDS ①
JULY 7, OLYMPIASTADION: 75,200	
MANAGER: HELMUT SCHÖN	MANAGER: RINUS MICHELS
FORMATION: 4-2-4	FORMATION: 3-4-3

THE VENUES

West Germany's economic strength furnished the finals with nine top-class venues. The Munich and Berlin stadiums had hosted past Olympic Games and the Parkstadion in Gelsenkirchen was built especially for the tournament. The average match attendance was 46,685.

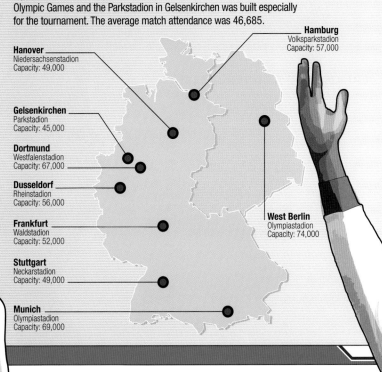

Hamburg
Volksparkstadion
Capacity: 57,000

Hanover
Niedersachsenstadion
Capacity: 49,000

Gelsenkirchen
Parkstadion
Capacity: 45,000

Dortmund
Westfalenstadion
Capacity: 67,000

Dusseldorf
Rheinstadion
Capacity: 56,000

Frankfurt
Waldstadion
Capacity: 52,000

Stuttgart
Neckarstadion
Capacity: 49,000

Munich
Olympiastadion
Capacity: 69,000

West Berlin
Olympiastadion
Capacity: 74,000

TOP GOAL SCORERS

Grzegorz LATO	Poland	7 goals
Johan NEESKENS	Netherlands	5 goals
Andrzej SZARMACH	Poland	5 goals
Gerd MÜLLER	West Germany	4 goals

GOLDEN BALL

Johan CRUYFF	Netherlands

FRANZ BECKENBAUER

Nicknamed "der Kaiser" (The Emperor) because of his dominance on the field, he was the first captain to lift the new World Cup trophy after Brazil retained the Jules Rimet Trophy four years before.

SECOND GROUP STAGE

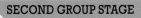

GROUP A	W	D	L	PT	GROUP B	W	D	L	PT
Netherlands	3	0	0	6*	West Germany	3	0	0	6*
Brazil	2	0	1	4	Poland	2	0	1	4
East Germany	0	1	2	1	Sweden	1	0	2	2
Argentina	0	1	2	1	Yugoslavia	0	0	3	0

* The top team from each group qualified for the final

ARGENTINA 1978

The staging of the 1978 World Cup in Argentina was highly controversial, because a military junta had recently seized power and the country was in political turmoil. Nevertheless, the tournament went ahead without major incident, and, to the delight of its beleaguered citizens, the host nation lifted the cup.

MARIO KEMPES
Despite his wiry exterior, Kempes was strong and skillful. Known as "El Matador," he was as lethal shooting from outside the box as many were in it. He was the only foreign-based player in the side, as he played for Valencia in Spain.

DRAWBACKS OF THE SYSTEM

As in 1974, there were no quarter- or semifinals. This time, however, the drawbacks of the system became glaringly obvious. When Peru lined up against Argentina in the final game of the second group stage, it had nothing to play for, having already been eliminated. This could not have happened under the knockout system. Moreover, the scheduling arrangements meant that Argentina's only rival to win the group, Brazil, had already played its last game, and so the host knew exactly how many goals it needed.

A SURPRISE AND A CONTROVERSY

In the first group stage, Tunisia was the surprise package, holding reigning champions West Germany to a 0–0 draw and beating Mexico to become the first African nation to win a game at a World Cup tournament. The eventual finalists both finished second in their groups, Argentina behind Italy and the Netherlands behind Peru.

In the second group stage, Group A became relatively straightforward. If either Holland or Italy won its clash, it would go through to the final. Group B was another matter. Argentina knew that it had to beat Peru by four goals to eliminate Brazil and duly won 6–0. The Brazilians, however, were convinced that the result had been rigged.

A BARBER'S PERSPECTIVE

The World Cup has witnessed many curious hairstyles, from the blond afro of Carlos Valderrama, captain of Colombia in 1990, 1994, and 1998, to Ronaldo's 2002 arrowhead. From a barber's perspective, however, the 1978 World Cup in Argentina was the greatest tournament of all. The Brazilians displayed some bubble perms, but they were all overshadowed by the flowing locks of top scorer Mario Kempes.

JOHAN NEESKENS
Replacing Johan Cruyff as the Dutch playmaker might seem like mission impossible, but Neeskens proved pivotal in the role as he guided the Dutch to their second World Cup final in a row.

STAT ATTACK — FIRST GROUP STAGE

GROUP 1	W	D	L	PT	GROUP 2	W	D	L	PT	GROUP 3	W	D	L	PT	GROUP 4	W	D	L	PT
Italy	3	0	0	6*	Poland	2	1	0	5*	Austria	2	0	1	4*	Peru	2	1	0	5*
Argentina	2	0	1	4*	West Germany	1	2	0	4*	Brazil	1	2	0	4*	Netherlands	1	1	1	3*
France	1	0	2	2	Tunisia	1	1	1	3	Spain	1	1	1	3	Scotland	1	1	1	3
Hungary	0	0	3	0	Mexico	0	0	3	0	Sweden	0	1	2	1	Iran	0	1	2	1

* The top two teams from each group qualified for the second group stage

STAT ATTACK

SECOND GROUP STAGE

GROUP A	W	D	L	PT
Netherlands	2	1	0	5*
Italy	1	1	1	3
West Germany	0	2	1	2
Austria	1	0	2	2

GROUP B	W	D	L	PT
Argentina	2	1	0	5*
Brazil	2	1	0	5
Poland	1	0	2	2
Peru	0	0	3	0

* The top two teams qualified for the final

PAPER SNOWSTORM

The crowd at the final produced one of the most spectacular displays seen at a soccer match. As the Argentina team ran onto the field, they were greeted by a "blizzard" of torn paper. Clearing it up was impossible, so the game was played on a carpet of the stuff.

THE VENUES

Six stadiums in five different cities were used for the finals in Argentina 1978. Three had been newly built: the Chateau Carreras in Córdoba, the Estadio Mar de Plata (later renamed the José María Minella), and the Malvinas Argentinas (later known as the Estadio Ciudad de Mendoza).

Córdoba
Estadio Chateau Carreras
Capacity: 46,000

Rosario
Estadio Gigante de Arroyito
Capacity: 42,000

Buenos Aires
Estadio Monumental
Capacity: 76,000

Buenos Aires
Estadio José Amalfitani
Capacity: 50,000

Mendoza
Estadio Ciudad de Mendoza
Capacity: 35,000

Mar del Plata
Estadio Jose Maria Minella
Capacity: 44,000

TOP GOAL SCORERS

Mario KEMPES	Argentina	6 goals
Rob RENSENBRINK	Netherlands	5 goals
Teofilo CUBILLAS	Peru	5 goals
Leopoldo LUQUE	Argentina	4 goals
Hans KRANKL	Austria	4 goals

GOLDEN BALL

Mario KEMPES	Argentina

DANIEL PASSARELLA

A natural leader, the Argentinian captain was one of the most complete defenders. He scored a number of goals, and many with his head, despite being 5ft 8in (1.73m) tall.

THE FINAL

Kickoff was delayed by Argentine protests about the hard bandaging on René van de Kerkhof's injured arm, which they claimed was dangerous. The match itself was dramatic. Holland had chances to win, but Argentina claimed the Cup through Kempes (two goals) and Bertoni who replied to Nanninga's strike for Holland.

ARGENTINA 3	NETHERLANDS 1
JUNE 25, ESTADIO MONUMENTAL: 71,483	
MANAGER: CÉSAR LUIS MENOTTI	MANAGER: ERNST HAPPEL
FORMATION: 4-3-3	FORMATION: 3-4-3

5 Fillol
15 Olguin **7** Galván **19** Passarella **20** Tarantini
6 Gallego **2** Ardiles **10** Kempes
4 Bertoni **14** Luque **16** Ortiz

12 Rensenbrink **16** Rep **10** van de Kerkhof, R
11 van de Kerkhof, W **13** Neeskens **9** Haan **6** Jansen
2 Poortvliet **5** Krol **22** Brandts
8 Jongbloed

SUBS: 12 Larrosa 9 Houseman 18 Nanninga 20 Suurbier

SPAIN 1982

This tournament was graced by the likes of France's Michel Platini, a young Diego Maradona, and a Brazilian team almost as good as its 1970 counterparts. But after overcoming a traditional slow start, it was the Italians who went on to claim their third World Cup.

A GAME OF NUMBERS

To ensure the participation of more African and Asian teams, FIFA had increased the number of finalists to 24, but whittling this down to four for the semifinals was a logistical challenge. The solution was a first stage consisting of six groups of four teams, followed by four randomly selected groups of three. Unfortunately, the draw for the second stage (see opposite) produced extremely unbalanced groups.

UNSPORTING PLAY

In a farcical first round, West Germany and Austria went into the final match of Group 2 knowing both would go through at Algeria's expense if the Germans won by two goals or fewer. After West Germany had scored, the teams kicked the ball around aimlessly. The crowd was furious; the Algerians livid.

FALCÃO
A sublimely gifted midfielder, Falcão was widely considered to be one of the best players of the tournament.

THE VENUES

The increased teams meant that 17 stadiums were used in Spain 1982. Three cities—Madrid, Barcelona, and Seville—had two venues each. Average attendance at the matches was the lowest since Chile 1962.

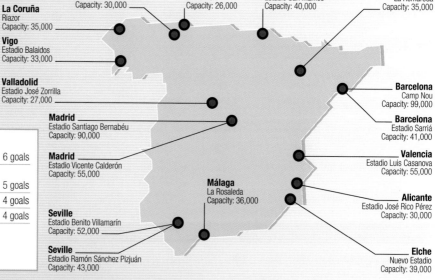

Oviedo
Estadio Carlos Tartiere
Capacity: 30,000

Gijón
El Molinón
Capacity: 26,000

Bilbao
Estadio San Mamés
Capacity: 40,000

Zaragoza
La Romareda
Capacity: 35,000

La Coruña
Riazor
Capacity: 35,000

Vigo
Estadio Balaídos
Capacity: 33,000

Valladolid
Estadio José Zorrilla
Capacity: 27,000

Barcelona
Camp Nou
Capacity: 99,000

Barcelona
Estadio Sarriá
Capacity: 41,000

Madrid
Estadio Santiago Bernabéu
Capacity: 90,000

Madrid
Estadio Vicente Calderón
Capacity: 55,000

Valencia
Estadio Luis Casanova
Capacity: 55,000

Málaga
La Rosaleda
Capacity: 36,000

Alicante
Estadio José Rico Pérez
Capacity: 30,000

Seville
Estadio Benito Villamarín
Capacity: 52,000

Seville
Estadio Ramón Sánchez Pizjuán
Capacity: 43,000

Elche
Nuevo Estadio
Capacity: 39,000

TOP GOAL SCORERS

Paolo ROSSI	Italy	6 goals
Karl-Heinz RUMMENIGGE	Germany	5 goals
ZICO	Brazil	4 goals
Zbigniew BONIEK	Poland	4 goals

GOLDEN BALL

Paolo ROSSI	Italy

STAT ATTACK

FIRST GROUP STAGE

GROUP 1	W	D	L	PT	GROUP 2	W	D	L	PT	GROUP 3	W	D	L	PT	GROUP 4	W	D	L	PT
Poland	1	2	0	4*	West Germany	2	0	1	4*	Belgium	2	1	0	5*	England	3	0	0	6*
Italy	0	3	0	3*	Austria	2	0	1	4*	Argentina	2	0	1	4*	France	1	1	1	3*
Cameroon	0	3	0	3	Algeria	2	0	1	4	Hungary	1	1	1	3	Czechoslovakia	0	2	1	2
Peru	0	2	1	2	Chile	0	0	3	0	El Salvador	0	0	3	0	Kuwait	0	1	2	1

* The top two teams from each group qualified for the second group stage

ROUTE TO THE FINAL

In the first group stage, highlights included Algeria beating West Germany and Northern Ireland defeating the host to win its group. Eventual winners Italy only just qualified. In the second stage, there were easy and difficult groups. The Germans won the first "group of death," and the other was decided by an Italy versus Brazil showdown.

The game of the tournament was the France versus West Germany semifinal. When the score was 1–1, the German goalkeeper Schumacher violently fouled Battiston but went unpunished. After overtime, the score was 3–3, and the Germans went on to win the first penalty shoot-out in World Cup finals history.

KARL-HEINZ RUMMENIGGE

Many said the striker was Germany's best player in the post-Beckenbauer era. In 1984, Rummenigge's move to Inter made him the world's most expensive player.

THE FINAL

Taking full advantage of West Germany's exhaustion after its epic semifinal victory against France, Italy's Rossi scored the crucial opener, Tardelli followed with a wonder strike, and Altobelli added a third. Breitner's late goal for West Germany didn't trouble the jubilant Italians.

SECOND GROUP STAGE

GROUP A	W	D	L	PT	GROUP B	W	D	L	PT
Poland	1	1	0	3*	West Germany	1	1	0	3*
USSR	1	1	0	3	England	0	2	0	2
Belgium	0	0	2	0	Spain	0	1	1	1

GROUP C	W	D	L	PT	GROUP D	W	D	L	PT
Italy	2	0	0	4*	France	2	0	0	4*
Brazil	1	0	1	2	Austria	0	1	1	1
Argentina	0	0	2	0	Northern Ireland	0	1	1	1

* The top team from each group qualified for the semifinals

SEMIFINALS

Italy	2	West Germany	3*
Poland	0	France	3

* West Germany won on penalties

ITALY ③	WEST GERMANY ①
JULY 11, BERNABÉU: 90,000	
MANAGER: ENZO BEARZOT	MANAGER: JUPP DERWALL
FORMATION: 5-3-2	FORMATION: 5-3-2

1 Zoff
4 Cabrini **7** Scirea **2** Bergomi **6** Gentile **5** Collovati
13 Oriali **16** Conti **14** Tardelli
20 Rossi **19** Graziani

8 Fischer **11** Rummenigge
6 Dremmler **7** Littbarski **3** Breitner
5 Förster, B **4** Förster, K-H **Briegel** **15** Stielike **20** Kaltz
1 Schumacher

SUBS: **15** Causio **18** Altobelli **10** Müller **9** Hrubesch

FIRST GROUP STAGE

GROUP 5	W	D	L	PT	GROUP 6	W	D	L	PT
Northern Ireland	1	2	0	4*	Brazil	3	0	0	6*
Spain	1	1	1	3*	USSR	1	1	1	3*
Yugoslavia	1	1	1	3	Scotland	1	1	1	3
Honduras	0	2	1	2	New Zealand	0	0	3	0

PAOLO ROSSI

The Juventus striker returned to action from a two-year domestic ban only months before the 1982 World Cup but ended up becoming the tournament's leading goal scorer.

MEXICO 1986

Originally scheduled to be held in Colombia, the finals were moved to Mexico when it became apparent that Colombia's stadiums were not up to FIFA standards. Despite a severe earthquake the previous September, the finals went ahead. They belonged to one man: Diego Maradona.

MEXICAN WAVE

During matches, dull passages of play were enlivened by the spectacle of the "Mexican wave." Sections of the crowd stood up, threw their arms in the air, then sat down again. This was the cue for the people on their left to repeat the action. The result was a human "wave" that took about 45 seconds to sweep around a stadium.

MICHEL PLATINI

A devastating midfielder who scored more goals than most strikers, Platini captained France, the reigning European champion, and led it to a second consecutive semifinal against the Germans.

WINNERS AND RUNNERS-UP

Mexico 1986 introduced an improved system in which the top two teams of each group, along with the four best runners-up, made it into the second round. Morocco won the least predictable group while Portugal was eliminated despite having beaten England.

ROUTE TO THE FINAL

Maradona decided the quarterfinal between Argentina and England, once with his hand and once with the greatest goal in World Cup history, as he dribbled from the center circle to finish a superb solo effort. He performed wonders again in the semifinal against Belgium. West Germany beat France 2–0 to reach the final.

2ND ROUND		QUARTERFINALS		SEMIFINALS		FINAL	
BRAZIL	4						
POLAND	0	BRAZIL	1				
FRANCE	2	FRANCE	1*				
ITALY	0			FRANCE	0		
MEXICO	2			WEST GERMANY	2		
BULGARIA	0	MEXICO	0				
MOROCCO	0	WEST GERMANY	0*				
WEST GERMANY	1					WEST GERMANY	2
ARGENTINA	1					ARGENTINA	3
URUGUAY	0	ARGENTINA	2				
ENGLAND	3	ENGLAND	1				
PARAGUAY	0			ARGENTINA	2		
USSR	3			BELGIUM	0		
BELGIUM	4•	BELGIUM	1*				
DENMARK	1	SPAIN	1				
SPAIN	5						

* Qualified by penalty shoot-out • After overtime

STAT ATTACK

GROUP STAGE

GROUP A	W	D	L	PT	GROUP B	W	D	L	PT	GROUP C	W	D	L	PT
Argentina	2	1	0	5*	Mexico	2	1	0	5*	USSR	2	1	0	5*
Italy	1	2	0	4*	Paraguay	1	2	0	4*	France	2	1	0	5*
Bulgaria	0	2	1	2*	Belgium	1	1	1	3*	Hungary	1	0	2	2
Korea Republic	0	1	2	1	Iraq	0	0	3	0	Canada	0	0	3	0

* The top two teams from each group qualified for the second round, along with the four best runners-up

THE FINAL

Argentina went into a 2–0 lead, but Germany was strong enough to fight back, scoring two goals through Karl-Heinz Rummenigge and Rudi Völler. However, Maradona sprang into life in the 83rd minute when, with a great pass, he set up Jorge Burruchaga for the winning goal.

ARGENTINA ③	WEST GERMANY ②
JUNE 29, ESTADIO AZTECA: 114,600	
MANAGER: CARLOS BILARDO	MANAGER: FRANZ BECKENBAUER
FORMATION: 4-5-1	FORMATION: 5-3-2

1 Pumpido
2 Batista **5** Ruggeri **5** Brown **9** Cuciuffo
14 Giusti **7** Burruchaga **10** Maradona **12** Enrique **16** Olarticoechea
11 Valdano
19 Allofs **11** Rummenigge
6 Eder **10** Magath **8** Matthaus
3 Brehme **4** Forster **17** Jakobs **14** Berthold **2** Briegel
1 Schumacher

SUBS: 21 Trobbiani 9 Völler 20 Hoeness

THE VENUES

As World Cup host only 16 years earlier, Mexico had no shortage of suitable stadiums. Seven others were added to the five that were used in the earlier tournament. Mexico City, Guadalajara, and Monterrey each had two stadiums.

Monterrey
Estadio Tecnologico
Capacity: 38,000

Irapuato
Estadio Sergio Leon Chavez
Capacity: 32,000

Monterrey
Estadio Universitario
Capacity: 44,000

Leon
Estadio Nou Camp
Capacity: 35,000

Mexico City
Estadio Azteca
Capacity: 115,000

Nezahualcoyotl
Estadio Neza 86
Capacity: 35,000

Puebla
Estadio Cuauhtemoc
Capacity: 46,000

Guadalajara
Estadio Tres de Marzo
Capacity: 30,000

Mexico City
Estadio Olímpico Universitario
Capacity: 72,000

Guadalajara
Estadio Jalisco
Capacity: 66,000

Toluca
Estadio Nemesio Diez
Capacity: 30,000

TOP GOAL SCORERS

Gary LINEKER	England	6 goals
Diego MARADONA	Argentina	5 goals
CARECA	Brazil	5 goals
Emilio BUTRAGUEÑO	Spain	5 goals

GOLDEN BALL

Diego MARADONA	Argentina

GARY LINEKER

A prolific goal scorer, Lineker was the first English player to win the Golden Boot at a World Cup finals with his six goals in 1986.

GROUP STAGE

DIEGO MARADONA

Thought by many to be the nearest rival to Pelé as the greatest-ever player, Diego Maradona's performances during the 1986 World Cup secured him global fame—especially the 2–1 win over England, when his dazzling 60-yard run beat six players before he scored the goal of the tournament.

GROUP D	W	D	L	PT
Brazil	3	0	0	6*
Spain	2	0	1	4*
N Ireland	0	1	2	1
Algeria	0	1	2	1

GROUP E	W	D	L	PT
Denmark	3	0	0	6*
West Germany	1	1	1	3*
Uruguay	0	2	1	2*
Scotland	0	1	2	1

GROUP F	W	D	L	PT
Morocco	1	2	0	4*
England	1	1	1	3*
Poland	1	1	1	3*
Portugal	1	0	2	2

* The top two teams from each group qualified for the second round, along with the four best runners-up

ITALY 1990

Italia 1990's theme tune was Puccini's "Nessun Dorma," but the tournament was short on operatic drama, with fewer goals per game than in any other World Cup. Still, it yielded some memorable images, including the bulging eyes of Italy's Schillaci and Cameroon's Milla dancing with the corner flag.

THE LUCK OF THE IRISH

Proceedings began with a shock win for nine-man Cameroon against Argentina, England won its group with a single goal difference, and Italy secured three cautious wins. Cameroon and Ireland reached the quarterfinals; the Africans with some style, the Irish without beating anybody, except Romania on penalties.

ROGER MILLA
The 38-year-old Cameroon striker was instrumental in his side's march to the quarterfinals. The way he danced around the corner flag as a way of celebrating goals also became popular.

ROUTE TO THE FINAL

Argentina, led by a half-fit Maradona, was a shadow of its 1986 self but progressed via a series of narrow victories, including a 1–0 defeat of Brazil. The eventual winner, West Germany, was one of the few teams to play attacking soccer, beating the Netherlands in a match marred by Rijkaard spitting at Völler. In an epic semifinal against England, the Germans took the lead when Shilton was beaten by a cruelly deflected free kick. Lineker equalized, Paul Gascoigne cried, and West Germany went through on penalties.

MARADONA'S MESSAGE
Before the semis, Maradona (then a Napoli player) said: "Neapolitans are not considered Italian by people up north. Why should they behave as Italians tomorrow?" The Napoli crowd refrained from booing Argentina's national anthem.

2ND ROUND		QUARTERFINALS		SEMIFINALS		FINAL	
BRAZIL	0						
ARGENTINA	1	ARGENTINA	3•				
		YUGOSLAVIA	2				
SPAIN	1			ARGENTINA	1*		
YUGOSLAVIA	2•			ITALY	1		
REP OF IRELAND	0*					WEST GERMANY	1
ROMANIA	0	ITALY	1			ARGENTINA	0
ITALY	2	REP OF IRELAND	0				
URUGUAY	0						
CZECHOSLOVAKIA	4						
COSTA RICA	1	WEST GERMANY	1				
		CZECHOSLOVAKIA	0				
WEST GERMANY	2					3RD/4TH PLACE	
NETHERLANDS	1			WEST GERMANY	1*		
CAMEROON	2•			ENGLAND	1	ITALY	2
COLOMBIA	1	ENGLAND	3•			ENGLAND	1
ENGLAND	1•	CAMEROON	2				
BELGIUM	0						

* Qualified by penalty shoot-out • After overtime

STAT ATTACK — GROUP STAGE

LOTHAR MATTHÄUS
The most capped German player of all time, Matthäus was the archetypal midfield general—a master of the pinpoint pass and the well-timed tackle. He captained Germany in its third consecutive final, against Argentina.

GROUP A	W	D	L	PT	GROUP B	W	D	L	PT
Italy	3	0	0	6*	Cameroon	2	0	1	4*
Czechoslovakia	2	0	1	4*	Romania	1	1	1	3*
Austria	1	0	2	2	Argentina	1	1	1	3*
US	0	0	3	0	USSR	1	0	2	2

* The top two teams plus the four best runners-up qualified for the second round.

THE VENUES

The distribution of the 12 tournament venues was remarkably evenhanded, given that power in Italian soccer is overwhelmingly concentrated in the North. A new stadium was built in Bari, and the country's two principal islands, Sicily and Sardinia, also hosted matches.

Milan Stadio San Siro Capacity: 86,000

Turin Stadio delle Alpi Capacity: 68,000

Genoa Stadio Luigi Ferraris Capacity: 36,000

Florence Stadio Artemio Franchi Capacity: 41,000

Rome Stadio Olimpico Capacity: 81,000

Naples Stadio San Paolo Capacity: 74,000

Cagliari Stadio Sant'Elia Capacity: 40,000

Palermo Stadio La Favorita Capacity: 36,000

Udine Stadio Friuli Capacity: 38,000

Verona Stadio Marcantonio Bentegodi Capacity: 42,000

Bologna Stadio Renato Dall'ara Capacity: 39,000

Bari Stadio San Nicola Capacity: 56,000

TOP GOAL SCORERS

Salvatore SCHILLACI	Italy	6 goals
Tomáš SKUHRAVÝ	Czechoslovakia	5 goals
Roger MILLA	Cameroon	4 goals
Gary LINEKER	England	4 goals
Lothar MATTHÄUS	West Germany	4 goals
MÍCHEL	Spain	4 goals

GOLDEN BALL

Salvatore SCHILLACI Italy

THE FINAL

In a match mainly memorable for its dullness, West Germany's Andy Brehme scored the only goal from a penalty, Pedro Monzon became the first player to be sent off in a World Cup final, and Franz Beckenbauer became the second man (after Brazil's Mário Zagallo) to win the World Cup Trophy as both a player and a manager.

WEST GERMANY ①	ARGENTINA ⓪
JULY 8, STADIO OLIMPICO: 73,603	
MANAGER: FRANZ BECKENBAUER	MANAGER: CARLOS BILARDO
FORMATION: 5-3-2	FORMATION: 5-4-1

SALVATORE SCHILLACI
Nicknamed "Toto," Schillaci made his debut at the 1990 finals. He landed the Golden Boot with six goals, each as vital to his side's third-place finish as the next.

SUBS: 2 Reuter 15 Monzon 6 Calderon

GROUP STAGE

GROUP C	W	D	L	PT	GROUP D	W	D	L	PT	GROUP E	W	D	L	PT	GROUP F	W	D	L	PT
Brazil	3	0	0	6*	West Germany	2	1	0	5*	Spain	2	1	0	5*	England	1	2	0	4*
Costa Rica	2	0	1	4*	Yugoslavia	2	0	1	4*	Belgium	2	0	1	4*	Rep of Ireland	0	3	0	3*
Scotland	1	0	2	2	Colombia	1	1	1	3*	Uruguay	1	1	1	3*	Netherlands	0	3	0	3*
Sweden	0	0	3	0	UAE	0	0	3	0	Korea Republic	0	0	3	0	Egypt	0	2	1	2

* The top two teams plus the four best runners-up qualified for the second round.

US 1994

OLEG SALENKO
The Russian striker scored six goals at US 1994, five against a weak team from Cameroon.

Held in the US as part of a concerted effort by FIFA to increase the profile of soccer in North America, this tournament was a mixed success. The majority of Americans were, and still are, lukewarm about the game, but the matches attracted enormous crowds.

A COLORFUL TOURNAMENT

To encourage more attractive play, teams were awarded three points for a win, rather than two, and goalkeepers were no longer permitted to handle back passes. Highlights included a record five goals in one match from Russia's Oleg Salenko, Ireland beating Italy, the first-ever indoor World Cup match, and Saudi Arabia qualifying for the second round. The biggest story, though, was the ejection of Maradona for taking a banned stimulant.

ROUTE TO THE FINAL

The quarterfinals produced two classics: Bulgaria, who had never won a World Cup finals match, beat reigning champion Germany 2–1, while Brazil beat the Netherlands in a five-goal thriller. In the semifinals, Italy overcame Bulgaria, and the ever-popular Brazil beat Sweden in the teams' second meeting of the tournament, going on to be the victor in the final.

ROMÁRIO
Striker Romário led Brazil's charge to a fourth World Cup crown with five goals in the tournament.

Bracket

2ND ROUND

NIGERIA	1
ITALY	2•
SPAIN	3
SWITZERLAND	0
MEXICO	1
BULGARIA	1*
GERMANY	3
BELGIUM	2
NETHERLANDS	2
REP OF IRELAND	0
BRAZIL	1
US	0
SAUDI ARABIA	1
SWEDEN	3
ROMANIA	3
ARGENTINA	2

QUARTERFINALS

ITALY	2
SPAIN	1
BULGARIA	2
GERMANY	1
NETHERLANDS	2
BRAZIL	3
SWEDEN	2*
ROMANIA	2

SEMIFINALS

ITALY	2
BULGARIA	1
BRAZIL	1
SWEDEN	0

FINAL

BRAZIL	0
ITALY	0

BRAZIL WON 3–2 ON PENALTIES

3RD/4TH PLACE

SWEDEN	4
BULGARIA	0

* Qualified by penalty shoot-out • After overtime

STAT ATTACK — GROUP STAGE

GROUP A	W	D	L	PT
Romania	2	0	1	6*
Switzerland	1	1	1	4*
US	1	1	1	4*
Colombia	1	0	2	3

GROUP B	W	D	L	PT
Brazil	2	1	0	7*
Sweden	1	2	0	5*
Russia	1	0	2	3
Cameroon	0	1	2	1

GROUP C	W	D	L	PT
Germany	2	1	0	7*
Spain	1	2	0	5*
Korea Republic	0	2	1	2
Bolivia	0	1	2	1

* The top two teams from each group qualified for the second round, along with the four best runners-up

THE FINAL

It may have been a disappointment for 120 scoreless minutes, but this final's penalty shoot-out was suitably dramatic. It began with two misses and ended with Roberto Baggio, Italy's star of the tournament, blasting the ball over the bar. Brazil had become world champion for a record fourth time.

BRAZIL 0	ITALY 0
BRAZIL WON 3–2 ON PENALTIES	
JULY 7, ROSE BOWL: 94,194	
MANAGER: CARLOS ALBERTO PARREIRA	MANAGER: ARRIGO SACCHI
FORMATION: 4-4-2	FORMATION: 4-4-2

SUBS: 14 Cafu 21 Viola 2 Apolloni 17 Evani

THE VENUES

The nine venues were mega-stadiums built for football. The average attendance was a record-breaking 68,991, despite fears that the matches would not capture local interest.

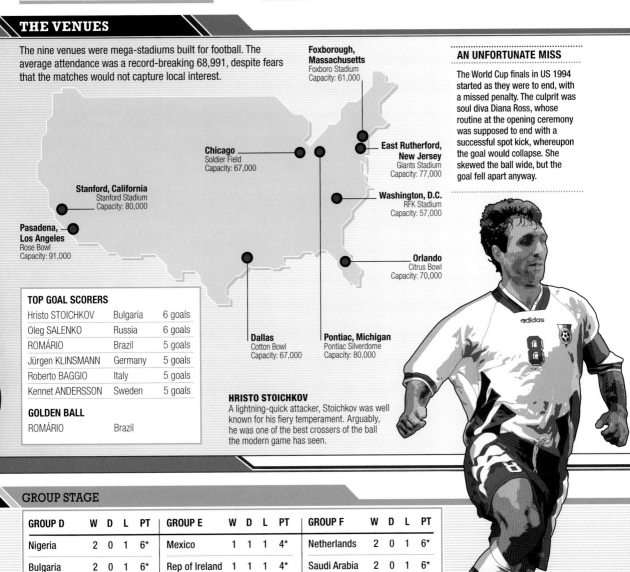

Foxborough, Massachusetts
Foxboro Stadium
Capacity: 61,000

Chicago
Soldier Field
Capacity: 67,000

East Rutherford, New Jersey
Giants Stadium
Capacity: 77,000

Stanford, California
Stanford Stadium
Capacity: 80,000

Washington, D.C.
RFK Stadium
Capacity: 57,000

Pasadena, Los Angeles
Rose Bowl
Capacity: 91,000

Orlando
Citrus Bowl
Capacity: 70,000

Dallas
Cotton Bowl
Capacity: 67,000

Pontiac, Michigan
Pontiac Silverdome
Capacity: 80,000

AN UNFORTUNATE MISS

The World Cup finals in US 1994 started as they were to end, with a missed penalty. The culprit was soul diva Diana Ross, whose routine at the opening ceremony was supposed to end with a successful spot kick, whereupon the goal would collapse. She skewed the ball wide, but the goal fell apart anyway.

TOP GOAL SCORERS		
Hristo STOICHKOV	Bulgaria	6 goals
Oleg SALENKO	Russia	6 goals
ROMÁRIO	Brazil	5 goals
Jürgen KLINSMANN	Germany	5 goals
Roberto BAGGIO	Italy	5 goals
Kennet ANDERSSON	Sweden	5 goals

GOLDEN BALL

ROMÁRIO	Brazil

HRISTO STOICHKOV

A lightning-quick attacker, Stoichkov was well known for his fiery temperament. Arguably, he was one of the best crossers of the ball the modern game has seen.

GROUP STAGE

GROUP D	W	D	L	PT	GROUP E	W	D	L	PT	GROUP F	W	D	L	PT
Nigeria	2	0	1	6*	Mexico	1	1	1	4*	Netherlands	2	0	1	6*
Bulgaria	2	0	1	6*	Rep of Ireland	1	1	1	4*	Saudi Arabia	2	0	1	6*
Argentina	2	0	1	6*	Italy	1	1	1	4*	Belgium	2	0	1	6*
Greece	0	0	3	0	Norway	1	1	1	4	Morocco	0	0	3	0

* The top two teams from each group qualified for the second round, along with the four best runners-up

FRANCE 1998

For the first time, 32 teams took part in the tournament and "golden goals" reduced the likelihood of penalty shoot-outs. The host won the cup without a seasoned striker; Thierry Henry, when he played, was deployed on the wing, and David Trezeguet had yet to flourish.

REVENGE MATCH

The highlight of the second round was England's first encounter with Argentina since the infamous "Hand of God" match in 1986 (see pp.308–309). Eighteen-year-old Michael Owen scored a wonder goal, but the Argentinians went through on penalties.

ROUTE TO THE FINAL

Three of the quarterfinals were high-quality matches. Croatia trounced Germany 3–0, Bergkamp scored an exquisite winner for the Netherlands against Argentina, and Brazil beat Denmark 3–2. The fourth match saw a disappointing 0–0 draw, with France going through on penalties. In the semifinals, Brazil beat the Netherlands on penalties, and France overcame Croatia with a 2–1 win.

DENNIS BERGKAMP

One of the finest poachers of the modern game, Bergkamp punished any team that gave him an inch. His winner for the Netherlands against Argentina in the final minute of their quarterfinal is regarded as one of the greatest-ever goals.

A REASON TO RETIRE

One year after the tournament, Argentina's Carlos Roa announced that he was retiring from soccer to devote himself to his religion. Lechuga ("lettuce"), as the vegetarian goalkeeper was known to his teammates, is a devout Seventh Day Adventist who reportedly believed the world was going to end in 2000.

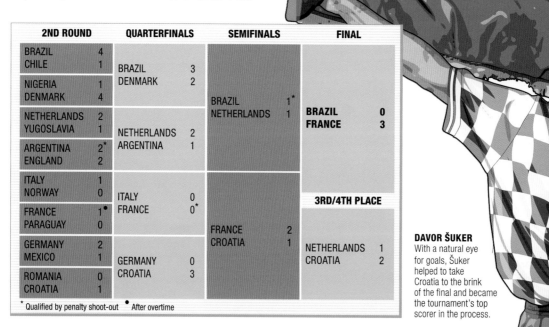

2ND ROUND		QUARTERFINALS		SEMIFINALS		FINAL	
BRAZIL	4						
CHILE	1	BRAZIL	3				
NIGERIA	1	DENMARK	2				
DENMARK	4			BRAZIL	1*	BRAZIL	0
NETHERLANDS	2			NETHERLANDS	1	FRANCE	3
YUGOSLAVIA	1	NETHERLANDS	2				
ARGENTINA	2*	ARGENTINA	1				
ENGLAND	2						
ITALY	1						
NORWAY	0	ITALY	0			**3RD/4TH PLACE**	
FRANCE	1•	FRANCE	0*				
PARAGUAY	0			FRANCE	2	NETHERLANDS	1
GERMANY	2			CROATIA	1	CROATIA	2
MEXICO	1	GERMANY	0				
ROMANIA	0	CROATIA	3				
CROATIA	1						

* Qualified by penalty shoot-out   • After overtime

DAVOR ŠUKER

With a natural eye for goals, Šuker helped to take Croatia to the brink of the final and became the tournament's top scorer in the process.

STAT ATTACK — GROUP STAGE

GROUP A	W	D	L	PT	GROUP B	W	D	L	PT	GROUP C	W	D	L	PT	GROUP D	W	D	L	PT
Brazil	2	0	1	6*	Italy	2	1	0	7*	France	3	0	0	9*	Nigeria	2	0	1	6*
Norway	1	2	0	5*	Chile	0	3	0	3*	Denmark	1	1	1	4*	Paraguay	1	2	0	5*
Morocco	1	1	1	4	Austria	0	2	1	2	South Africa	0	2	1	2	Spain	1	1	1	4
Scotland	0	1	2	1	Cameroon	0	2	1	2	Saudi Arabia	0	1	2	1	Bulgaria	0	1	2	1

* The top two teams from each group qualified for the second round

THE VENUES

Although the tournament had been expanded to include 32 teams, the organizers managed to fit all the matches into 10 stadiums scattered around the nation. Two were in Paris: the Parc des Princes and the brand new Stade de France.

Lens
Stade Félix Bollaert
Capacity: 42,000

Paris
Stade de France
Capacity: 80,000

Paris
Parc des Princes
Capacity: 49,000

Lyon
Stade de Gerland
Capacity: 41,000

Nantes
Stade de la Beaujoire
Capacity: 39,000

Bordeaux
Parc Lescure
Capacity: 33,000

Saint-Etienne
Stade Geoffroy-Guichard
Capacity: 36,000

Toulouse
Stadium de Toulouse
Capacity: 37,000

Marseille
Stade Vélodrome
Capacity: 60,000

Montpellier
Stade de la Mosson
Capacity: 34,000

TOP GOAL SCORERS

Davor ŠUKER	Croatia	6 goals
Gabriel BATISTUTA	Argentina	5 goals
Christian VIERI	Italy	5 goals
RONALDO	Brazil	4 goals
Marcelo SALAS	Chile	4 goals
Luis HERNÁNDEZ	Mexico	4 goals

GOLDEN BALL

RONALDO	Brazil

LILLIAN THURAM

The scorer of both goals that put France into the final, defender Thuram was at the heart of a defense that enabled France to win its first World Cup.

THE FINAL

Ronaldo reportedly suffered a seizure before the final but went on to play. Brazil looked completely shell-shocked by the drama and never really got going. Zinedine Zidane cemented his place as the planet's best player with two goals, and Emmanuel Petit added a third in stoppage time.

FRANCE 3	BRAZIL 0
JULY 12, STADE DE FRANCE: 75,000	
MANAGER: AIMÉ JACQUET	MANAGER: MARIO ZAGALLO
FORMATION: 4-1-3-2	FORMATION: 4-4-2

16 Barthez
15 Thuram   8 Desailly   7 Leboeuf   18   3 Lizarazu
Deschamps
19 Karembeu   6   10 Zidane   17 Petit
9 Djorkaeff   Guivarc'h
20 Bebeto   9 Ronaldo
10 Rivaldo   8 Dunga   5 Sampaio   18 Leonardo
6 Carlos   3 Aldair   4 Baiano   2 Cafu
1 Taffarel

SUBS: 14 Boghossian   21 Dugarry   4 Vieira   19 Denilson   21 Edmundo

GROUP STAGE

GROUP E	W	D	L	PT
Netherlands	1	2	0	5*
Mexico	1	2	0	5*
Belgium	0	3	0	3
Korea Republic	0	1	2	1

GROUP F	W	D	L	PT
Germany	2	1	0	7*
Yugoslavia	2	1	0	7*
Iran	1	0	2	3
US	0	0	3	0

GROUP G	W	D	L	PT
Romania	2	1	0	7*
England	2	0	1	6*
Colombia	1	0	2	3
Tunisia	0	1	2	1

GROUP H	W	D	L	PT
Argentina	3	0	0	9*
Croatia	2	0	1	6*
Jamaica	1	0	2	3
Japan	0	0	3	0

* The top two teams from each group qualified for the second round

SOUTH KOREA & JAPAN 2002

The first World Cup to be held in Asia, and the first to have joint hosts, exceeded expectations. Japan won its group, and South Korea reached the semifinal. Brazil won the tournament for a record fifth time and scarcely broke a sweat in the process.

OLIVER KAHN
Despite a costly error in the final, the big Bayern Munich man became the first goalkeeper to collect the Golden Ball for player of the tournament.

EARLY EXITS

Senegal sprung a surprise in the opening match, beating France 1–0. The champions failed to score in any of their three matches and departed. Argentina and Portugal also made embarrassingly early exits, but the real whipping boys were Saudi Arabia, conceding 12 goals without reply. The most eye-catching performances in the second round included the US's 2–0 defeat of Mexico, Senegal's narrow victory over Sweden, and South Korea's win over Italy.

TRIUMPH AND TROUBLE

Customs police detained the triumphant Brazilian team and its luggage on its return home to Rio airport— a call to the president's office was required to pay the huge import duties and get the bags moving.

ROUTE TO THE FINAL

In the quarterfinals, England scored first against Brazil, but saw its chances drain away when keeper David Seaman misjudged a speculative Ronaldinho free kick. Germany defeated a spirited US, South Korea beat Spain on penalties after a goalless stalemate, and Turkey looked ominously good in a 1–0 victory over Senegal. In the first semifinal, Michael Ballack sent Germany through, despite picking up a yellow card which ruled him out of the final. The Turks lost a closely contested match against Brazil, but they went home with their heads held high after beating the Koreans in the third-place playoff.

RONALDO
No one knew what to expect from the great Brazilian striker, but he finished the tournament as top scorer.

Bracket

2ND ROUND		QUARTERFINALS		SEMIFINALS		FINAL	
GERMANY	1						
PARAGUAY	0	GERMANY	1				
MEXICO	0	US	0				
US	2			GERMANY	1		
SPAIN	1*			S. KOREA	0		
IRELAND	1	SPAIN	0			GERMANY	0
S. KOREA	2•	S. KOREA	0*			BRAZIL	2
ITALY	1						
JAPAN	0						
TURKEY	1	TURKEY	1•				
SWEDEN	1	SENEGAL	0				
SENEGAL	2•			TURKEY	0		
DENMARK	0			BRAZIL	1	3RD/4TH PLACE	
ENGLAND	3	ENGLAND	1			TURKEY	3
BRAZIL	2	BRAZIL	2			S. KOREA	2
BELGIUM	0						

* Qualified by penalty shoot-out   • After overtime

STAT ATTACK

GROUP STAGE

GROUP A	W	D	L	PT	GROUP B	W	D	L	PT	GROUP C	W	D	L	PT	GROUP D	W	D	L	PT
Denmark	2	1	0	7*	Spain	3	0	0	9*	Brazil	3	0	0	9*	S. Korea	2	1	0	7*
Senegal	1	2	0	5*	Paraguay	1	1	1	4*	Turkey	1	1	1	4*	US	1	1	1	4*
Uruguay	0	2	1	2	South Africa	1	1	1	4	Costa Rica	1	1	1	4	Portugal	1	0	2	3
France	0	1	2	1	Slovenia	0	0	3	0	China	0	0	3	0	Poland	1	0	2	3

* The top two teams from each group qualified for the second round

THE VENUES

The number of participating teams was the same as France 1998, but twice as many stadiums were used. The host nations each provided 10, most specially built for the tournament. Many of the Korean venues would have been worthy for the final, but Yokohama was chosen for its superb media facilities.

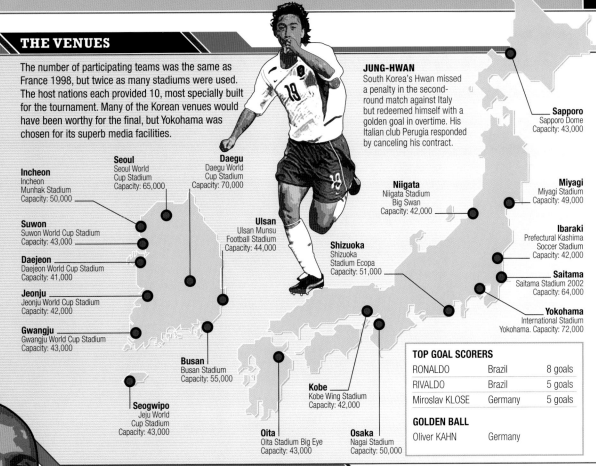

JUNG-HWAN
South Korea's Hwan missed a penalty in the second-round match against Italy but redeemed himself with a golden goal in overtime. His Italian club Perugia responded by canceling his contract.

Sapporo
Sapporo Dome
Capacity: 43,000

Incheon
Incheon
Munhak Stadium
Capacity: 50,000

Seoul
Seoul World
Cup Stadium
Capacity: 65,000

Daegu
Daegu World
Cup Stadium
Capacity: 70,000

Niigata
Niigata Stadium
Big Swan
Capacity: 42,000

Miyagi
Miyagi Stadium
Capacity: 49,000

Suwon
Suwon World Cup Stadium
Capacity: 43,000

Ulsan
Ulsan Munsu
Football Stadium
Capacity: 44,000

Ibaraki
Prefectural Kashima
Soccer Stadium
Capacity: 42,000

Daejeon
Daejeon World Cup Stadium
Capacity: 41,000

Shizuoka
Shizuoka
Stadium Ecopa
Capacity: 51,000

Saitama
Saitama Stadium 2002
Capacity: 64,000

Jeonju
Jeonju World Cup Stadium
Capacity: 42,000

Yokohama
International Stadium
Yokohama. Capacity: 72,000

Gwangju
Gwangju World Cup Stadium
Capacity: 43,000

Busan
Busan Stadium
Capacity: 55,000

Seogwipo
Jeju World
Cup Stadium
Capacity: 43,000

Kobe
Kobe Wing Stadium
Capacity: 42,000

Oita
Oita Stadium Big Eye
Capacity: 43,000

Osaka
Nagai Stadium
Capacity: 50,000

TOP GOAL SCORERS

RONALDO	Brazil	8 goals
RIVALDO	Brazil	5 goals
Miroslav KLOSE	Germany	5 goals

GOLDEN BALL

Oliver KAHN	Germany

THE FINAL

Amazingly, Brazil and Germany had never faced each other in the World Cup prior to the final. The South Americans won the contest with relative ease. Ronaldo scored both goals, the first after goalkeeper Oliver Kahn uncharacteristically spilled a long-range shot and the second after a fantastic dummy by Rivaldo.

BRAZIL 2	GERMANY ⓪
JUNE 30, INTERNATIONAL STADIUM: 69,029	
MANAGER: LUIZ FELIPE SCOLARI	MANAGER: RUDI VÖLLER
FORMATION: 3-5-2	FORMATION: 3-5-2

❶ Marcos
3 Lucio — **5 Edmilson** — **2 Linke**
2 Cafu — **11 Kleberson** — **11 Ronaldinho** — **8 Gilberto** — **6 Carlos**
9 Ronaldo — **10 Rivaldo**
11 Klose — **17 Bode**
7 Neuville — **16 Jeremies** — **8 Hamann** — **19 Schneider** — **22 Frings**
4 Junior — **5 Ramelow** — **21 Metzelder**
❶ Kahn

SUBS: 19 Juninho 17 Denilson 20 Bierhoff 21 Asamoah 6 Ziege

GROUP STAGE

GROUP E	W	D	L	PT	GROUP F	W	D	L	PT	GROUP G	W	D	L	PT	GROUP H	W	D	L	PT
Germany	2	1	0	7*	Sweden	1	2	0	5*	Mexico	2	1	0	7*	Japan	2	1	0	7*
Ireland	1	2	0	5*	England	1	2	0	5*	Italy	1	1	1	4*	Belgium	1	2	0	5*
Cameroon	1	1	1	4	Argentina	1	1	1	4	Croatia	1	0	2	3	Russia	1	0	2	3
Saudi Arabia	0	0	3	0	Nigeria	0	1	2	1	Ecuador	1	0	2	3	Tunisia	0	1	2	1

* The top two teams from each group qualified for the knockout stages.

GERMANY 2006

With an uncharacteristic display of patriotism, the Germans unfurled national flags throughout the country. Their underdog team played very well, ousting the excellent Argentinians and pushing the eventual winner Italy to overtime in its semifinal clash.

THREE STRIKES AND YOU'RE OUT

Referee Graham Poll mistakenly showed Croatia's Šimunic three yellow cards in one match. He remembered to dismiss the player after the last booking but by this stage had already blown for overtime. Luckily, the Australians still qualified.

PASSING PLAY

The group stage was fairly predictable, aside from Australia qualifying at the expense of Croatia and Ghana doing likewise to the Czech Republic. Argentina was hugely impressive, with Cambiasso scoring the goal of the tournament at the end of a 24-pass move in a 6–0 destruction of Serbia and Montenegro.

FABIO CANNAVARO

The mainstay of Italy's defense and captain of the team, Cannavaro lifted the coveted trophy on the occasion of his 100th cap. In 690 minutes, the Italians conceded just two goals.

ROUTE TO THE FINAL

In the second round, France beat perennial underachiever Spain 3–1, and Italy dispatched Australia in the dying seconds. Portugal knocked out the Netherlands in a match that saw the referee hand out a record 16 yellow and four red cards. England scraped through to the quarterfinals but was eliminated by Portugal on penalties. The Germans ran out of luck in their semifinal against the Italians. A Zidane penalty in the other semifinal was enough to get France past Portugal.

ZINEDINE ZIDANE

Like Cantona before him, Zidane was a flawed genius. This most sublime player picked up both the man of the tournament and a straight red card in the final for his headbutt on Marco Materazzi.

2ND ROUND		QUARTERFINALS		SEMIFINALS		FINAL	
GERMANY	2						
SWEDEN	0	GERMANY	1*				
ARGENTINA	2•	ARGENTINA	1				
MEXICO	1			GERMANY	0		
ITALY	1			ITALY	2•	ITALY	1
AUSTRALIA	0	ITALY	3			FRANCE	1
SWITZERLAND	0	UKRAINE	0			ITALY WON 5–3	
UKRAINE	0*					ON PENALTIES	
ENGLAND	1						
ECUADOR	0	ENGLAND	0				
PORTUGAL	1	PORTUGAL	0*				
NETHERLANDS	0			PORTUGAL	0	3RD/4TH PLACE	
BRAZIL	3			FRANCE	1		
GHANA	0	BRAZIL	0			GERMANY	3
SPAIN	1	FRANCE	1			PORTUGAL	1
FRANCE	3						

* Qualified by penalty shoot-out   • After overtime

STAT ATTACK

GROUP STAGE

GROUP A	W	D	L	PT	GROUP B	W	D	L	PT	GROUP C	W	D	L	PT	GROUP D	W	D	L	PT
Germany	3	0	0	9*	England	2	1	0	7*	Argentina	2	1	0	7*	Portugal	3	0	0	9*
Ecuador	2	0	1	6*	Sweden	1	2	0	5*	Netherlands	2	1	0	7*	Mexico	1	1	1	4*
Poland	1	0	2	3	Paraguay	1	0	2	3	Ivory Coast	1	0	2	3	Angola	0	2	1	2
Costa Rica	0	0	3	0	Trinidad & Tobago	0	1	2	1	Serbia & Montenegro	0	0	3	0	Iran	0	1	2	1

* The top two teams from each group qualified for the second round

MIROSLAV KLOSE

A clinical finisher renowned for his composure in front of goal, Klose was the tournament's top scorer. He was as good with his head as his feet—in the 2002 finals, he scored five headers.

THE VENUES

Many of the 12 top-class stadiums in Germany 2006 had to be temporarily renamed because FIFA regulations prohibited the sponsorship of stadiums during the tournament.

Hamburg
AOL Arena
Capacity: 51,000

Berlin
Olympiastadion
Capacity: 74,000

Hanover
AWD Arena
Capacity: 45,000

Leipzig
Zentralstadion
Capacity: 44,000

Gelsenkirchen
Veltins-Arena
Capacity: 54,000

Dortmund
Signal Iduna Park
Capacity: 67,000

Cologne
RheinEnergieStadion
Capacity: 46,000

Munich
Allianz Arena
Capacity: 66,016

Kaiserslautern
Fritz-Walter-Stadion
Capacity: 43,000

Frankfurt
Commerzbank-Arena
Capacity: 48,000

Nuremberg
EasyCredit-Stadion
Capacity: 42,000

Stuttgart
Mercedes Benz Arena
Capacity: 54,000

TOP GOAL SCORERS

Miroslav KLOSE	Germany	5 goals
Hernán CRESPO	Argentina	3 goals
Thierry HENRY	France	3 goals

GOLDEN BALL

Zinedine ZIDANE   France

ENTERTAINING THE CROWD

The Ivory Coast's training sessions included an unusual element: dance practice, in which they rehearsed a carefully choreographed goal celebration called the "Elephant Dance." The African team performed well enough in their group matches to treat the world to the ground-stomping routine on five occasions.

THE FINAL

The final revolved around the unlikely figure of Italian defender Marco Materazzi. He gave away an early penalty, which Zinedine Zidane converted via the crossbar, equalized with a powerful header, and provoked Zidane into headbutting him in overtime. The French genius was sent off, and Italy won the game on penalties.

ITALY ①	FRANCE ①
ITALY WON 5–3 ON PENALTIES	
JULY 9, OLYMPIASTADION: 69,000	
MANAGER: MARCELLO LIPPI	MANAGER: RAYMOND DOMENECH
FORMATION: 4-4-2	FORMATION: 4-5-1

Buffon ①

19 Zambrotta   **5** Cannavaro   **23** Materazzi   **3** Grosso

16 Camoranesi   **8** Gattuso   **21** Pirlo   **20** Perrotta

10 Totti   Toni

12 Henry

7 Malouda   **4** Vieira   **10** Zidane   **6** Makélélé   **22** Ribéry

3 Abidal   **5** Gallas   **15** Thuram   **19** Sagnol

Barthez ①

SUBS: 4 de Rossi   15 Iaquinta   7 Del Piero   18 Diarra   20 Trezeguet   11 Wiltord

GROUP STAGE

GROUP E	W	D	L	PT	GROUP F	W	D	L	PT	GROUP G	W	D	L	PT	GROUP H	W	D	L	PT
Italy	2	1	0	7*	Brazil	3	0	0	9*	Switzerland	2	1	0	7*	Spain	3	0	0	9*
Ghana	2	0	1	6	Australia	1	1	1	4*	France	1	2	0	5*	Ukraine	2	0	1	6*
Czech Republic	1	0	2	3	Croatia	0	2	1	2	Korea Republic	1	1	1	4	Tunisia	0	1	2	1
US	0	1	2	1	Japan	0	1	2	1	Togo	0	0	3	0	Saudi Arabia	0	1	2	1

* The top two teams from each group qualified for the second round

SOUTH AFRICA 2010

SOUND OF SOUTH AFRICA

Africa made a distinctive impression on the tournament in the shape of the vuvuzela. A modern plastic version of the traditional tribal horn was blown en masse by fans. The sound—like a swarm of angry bees—was ever present.

DAVID VILLA
Unlike many other strikers at the finals, Villa excelled on the big stage.

The legacy of the 2010 World Cup wasn't confined to the field of play—the competition went down in history as the first to be held on African soil. Despite concerns about safety, security, and transportation, South Africa hosted a successful and vibrant tournament.

SHOCKING DEPARTURES

South Africa hosted an unpredictable tournament, with two of the European superpowers failing to make it out of the group stages. Italy's wretched campaign saw its aging squad hit an all-time low when it was held to a draw by New Zealand, while infighting in the France camp led to the team eventually losing its final group game to South Africa.

ROUTE TO THE FINAL

It could have been a great year for African teams, but only Ghana escaped the group stages. At first it seemed like the South American sides would dominate, but the Europeans had other ideas. Special mentions go to the Netherlands, who beat Brazil in the quarterfinals, and the young German team, who shattered Maradona's dream of lifting the trophy as manager.

2ND ROUND		QUARTERFINALS		SEMIFINALS		FINAL	
URUGUAY	2						
SOUTH KOREA	1	URUGUAY	1				
US	1	GHANA*	1				
GHANA •	2			URUGUAY	2		
NETHERLANDS	2			NETHERLANDS	3		
SLOVAKIA	1	NETHERLANDS	2			NETHERLANDS	0
BRAZIL	3	BRAZIL	1			SPAIN	1 •
CHILE	0						
ARGENTINA	3						
MEXICO	1	ARGENTINA	0				
GERMANY	4	GERMANY	4	GERMANY	0		
ENGLAND	1			SPAIN	1	**3RD/4TH PLACE**	
PARAGUAY*	0					URUGUAY	2
JAPAN	0	PARAGUAY	0			GERMANY	3
SPAIN	1	SPAIN	1				
PORTUGAL	0						

* Qualified by penalty shoot-out • After overtime

DIEGO FORLÁN
Forlán guided Uruguay to the semifinals almost single-handedly and picked up the Golden Ball for the skill he showed throughout the competition.

REFEREEING RECORD

Howard Webb, the first English referee to oversee a World Cup final since Jack Taylor in 1974, made history by handing out a record number of cards during a final. By the end of the match, he had shown a total of 15 yellow cards and one red.

STAT ATTACK — GROUP STAGE

GROUP A	W	D	L	PT	GROUP B	W	D	L	PT	GROUP C	W	D	L	PT	GROUP D	W	D	L	PT
Uruguay	2	1	0	7*	Argentina	3	0	0	9*	US	1	2	0	5*	Germany	2	0	1	6*
Mexico	1	1	1	4*	South Korea	1	1	1	4*	England	1	2	0	5*	Ghana	1	1	1	4*
South Africa	1	1	1	4	Greece	1	0	2	3	Slovenia	1	1	1	4	Australia	1	1	1	4
France	0	1	2	1	Nigeria	0	1	2	1	Algeria	0	1	2	1	Serbia	1	0	2	3

* The top two teams from each group qualified for the second round

THE FINAL

As the underdogs, the Netherlands struggled to stifle the sleek passing of the Spanish. The first half saw the Dutch team put on a brutal display—they were lucky to keep 11 men on the field. While chances were squandered at both ends, the Spanish never lost their rhythm and were rewarded with Iniesta's winning goal in overtime.

SPAIN 1	NETHERLANDS 0
AFTER OVERTIME	
JULY 11, SOCCER CITY: 84,490	
MANAGER: VICENTE DEL BOSQUE	MANAGER: BERT VAN MARWIJK
FORMATION: 4-3-2-1	FORMATION: 4-3-2-1

GK Stekelenburg
2 van der Wiel · 3 Heitinga · 4 Mathijsen · 5 van Bronckhorst
6 van Bommel · 8 de Jong
11 Robben · 10 Sneijder · 7 Kuyt
9 van Persie
7 Villa
6 Iniesta · 8 Xavi · 18 Pedro
14 Alonso · 16 Busquets
11 Capdevila · 5 Puyol · 3 Piqué · 15 Ramos
GK Casillas

SUBS: 17 Elisa · 23 van der Vaart · 23 Braafheid · 22 Navas · 10 Fàbregas · 9 Torres

THE VENUES

Many of the stadiums were established sporting venues with spectacular settings. Sitting on the shore of the Atlantic Ocean and overlooked by Table Mountain, Green Point Stadium in Cape Town is one of the most breathtaking stadiums in the world. Soccer City in Johannesburg, Nelson Mandela Bay in Port Elizabeth, and Royal Bafokeng Stadium in Rustenburg made for a fine supporting cast.

Polokwane
Peter Mokaba Stadium
Capacity: 46,000

Pretoria
Loftus Versfeld Stadium
Capacity: 49,000

Nelspruit
Mbombela Stadium
Capacity: 46,000

Johannesburg
Soccer City
Capacity: 91,000

Rustenburg
Royal Bafokeng Stadium
Capacity: 42,000

Johannesburg
Ellis Park Stadium
Capacity: 62,567

Bloemfontein
Free State Stadium
Capacity: 48,000

Cape Town
Greenpoint Stadium
Capacity: 69,070

Port Elizabeth
Nelson Mandela Bay Stadium
Capacity: 48,000

Durban
Moses Mabhida Stadium
Capacity: 70,000

WESLEY SNEIJDER
Sneijder arrived in South Africa having won the Champions League with Inter. He led the Dutch to the final, scoring five goals along the way.

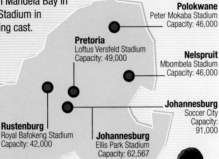

THOMAS MÜLLER
The 20-year-old finished the tournament with both the Golden Boot and Best Young Player awards.

TOP GOAL SCORERS		
Thomas MÜLLER	Germany	5 goals
David VILLA	Spain	5 goals
Diego FORLÁN	Uruguay	5 goals
Wesley SNEIJDER	Netherlands	5 goals
GOLDEN BALL		
Diego FORLÁN	Uruguay	

GROUP STAGE

GROUP E	W	D	L	PT
Netherlands	3	0	0	9*
Japan	2	0	1	6*
Denmark	1	0	2	3
Cameroon	0	0	3	0

GROUP F	W	D	L	PT
Paraguay	1	2	0	5*
Slovakia	1	1	1	4*
New Zealand	0	3	0	3
Italy	0	2	1	2

GROUP G	W	D	L	PT
Brazil	2	1	0	7*
Portugal	1	2	0	5*
Ivory Coast	1	1	1	4
North Korea	0	0	3	0

GROUP H	W	D	L	PT
Spain	2	0	1	6*
Chile	2	0	1	6*
Switzerland	1	1	1	4
Honduras	0	1	2	1

* The top two teams from each group qualified for the second round

BRAZIL 2014

PHILIPP LAHM
With two semifinal exits in the past due to injury, German captain Philipp Lahm finally won his World Cup winners' medal.

With the World Cup returning to Brazilian soil after 64 years, the country was at a carnivalesque fever pitch for the whole month, only to see their promising team go out in the semifinals.

SURPRISE ELIMINATIONS

Defending champion Spain crashed out in the group stages, having lost to both the Netherlands and Chile—the Dutch exacting revenge on the Spanish for its defeat in the 2010 final. England also disappointed, finishing last in its group, with Costa Rica topping the table as the unexpected winner.

ROUTE TO THE FINAL

Argentina dispatched Belgium and then eliminated the Netherlands on penalties to reach the final. Although Brazil beat Colombia, it then suffered its worst-ever World Cup defeat in the semifinal against Germany, with Neymar and captain Thiago Silva out due to injury and suspension, respectively. This loss was dubbed a "national humiliation" by media outlets and even led to rioting in some places.

JAMES RODRÍGUEZ
The Colombian made a name for himself at the 2014 World Cup, winning the Golden Boot for scoring six goals.

VANISHING SPRAYS

In a first, referees used a water-based spray to temporarily mark a 10-yard line for the defending team's position during a free kick and for the spot from where the kick should be taken.

Bracket

2ND ROUND		QUARTERFINALS		SEMIFINALS		FINAL	
BRAZIL	1*						
CHILE	1	BRAZIL	2				
COLOMBIA	2	COLOMBIA	1				
URUGUAY	0			BRAZIL	1		
FRANCE	2			GERMANY	7		
NIGERIA	0	FRANCE	0			ARGENTINA	0
GERMANY	2•	GERMANY	1			GERMANY	1•
ALGERIA	1						
NETHERLANDS	2						
MEXICO	1	NETHERLANDS	0*				
COSTA RICA	1*	COSTA RICA	0				
GREECE	1			NETHERLANDS	0	3RD/4TH PLACE	
ARGENTINA	1•			ARGENTINA	0*		
SWITZERLAND	0	ARGENTINA	1			NETHERLANDS	3
BELGIUM	2•	BELGIUM	0			BRAZIL	0
US	1						

* Qualified by penalty shoot-out   • After overtime

STAT ATTACK

GROUP STAGE

GROUP A	W	D	L	PT	GROUP B	W	D	L	PT	GROUP C	W	D	L	PT	GROUP D	W	D	L	PT
Brazil	2	1	0	7*	Netherlands	3	0	0	9*	Colombia	3	0	0	9*	Costa Rica	2	1	0	7*
Mexico	2	1	0	7*	Chile	2	0	1	6*	Greece	1	1	1	4*	Uruguay	2	0	1	6*
Croatia	1	0	2	3	Spain	1	0	2	3	Ivory Coast	1	0	2	3	Italy	1	0	2	3
Cameroon	0	0	3	0	Australia	0	0	3	0	Japan	0	1	2	1	England	0	1	2	1

* The top two teams from each group qualified for the second round

THE FINAL

In a repeat of the 2006 semifinal, the teams played out a goalless—but entertaining—90 minutes, with Higuaín having a goal disallowed for being offside and Messi firing wide of the German goal. The turning point hinged on Mario Götze's late substitution, the midfielder volleying in a goal worthy of the team's fourth title and its first ever as a unified nation.

GERMANY ①	ARGENTINA ⓪
AFTER OVERTIME	
JULY 13, ESTÁDIO DO MARACANÃ: 74,738	
MANAGER: JOACHIM LÖW	MANAGER: ALEJANDRO SABELLA
FORMATION: 4-3-3	FORMATION: 4-4-1-1

SUBS: 20 Agüero 18 Palacio 5 Gago 9 Schürrle 19 Götze 17 Mertesacker

THE VENUES

The 64 matches were held at 12 stadiums, across the major regions of Brazil. As a result, the 32 participating teams had to travel long distances from their base camps. The Estádio do Maracanã, which had hosted nearly 200,000 spectators for the 1950 World Cup Final, was renovated for the 2014 finals.

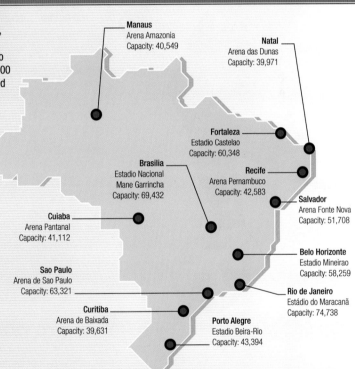

Manaus
Arena Amazonia
Capacity: 40,549

Natal
Arena das Dunas
Capacity: 39,971

Fortaleza
Estadio Castelao
Capacity: 60,348

Brasilia
Estadio Nacional
Mane Garrincha
Capacity: 69,432

Recife
Arena Pernambuco
Capacity: 42,583

Salvador
Arena Fonte Nova
Capacity: 51,708

Cuiaba
Arena Pantanal
Capacity: 41,112

Belo Horizonte
Estadio Mineirao
Capacity: 58,259

Sao Paulo
Arena de Sao Paulo
Capacity: 63,321

Rio de Janeiro
Estádio do Maracanã
Capacity: 74,738

Curitiba
Arena de Baixada
Capacity: 39,631

Porto Alegre
Estadio Beira-Rio
Capacity: 43,394

TOP GOAL SCORERS

James RODRÍGUEZ	Colombia	6 goals
Thomas MÜLLER	Germany	5 goals
NEYMAR	Brazil	4 goals
Lionel MESSI	Argentina	4 goals

GOLDEN BALL

Lionel MESSI	Argentina

EYES ON THE GOAL

FIFA introduced goal-line technology in the 2014 World Cup, opting for the German GoalControl-4D system (see pp.60–61), which used 14 high-speed cameras mounted around the goals. The technology came into its own during the group stages, confirming France's second goal against Honduras.

GROUP STAGE

GROUP E	W	D	L	PT
France	2	1	0	7*
Switzerland	2	0	1	6*
Ecuador	1	1	1	4
Honduras	0	0	3	0

GROUP F	W	D	L	PT
Argentina	1	2	0	5*
Nigeria	1	1	1	4*
Bosnia-Herzegovina	1	0	2	3
Iran	0	1	2	1

GROUP G	W	D	L	PT
Germany	2	1	0	7*
US	1	1	1	4*
Portugal	1	1	1	4
Ghana	0	1	2	1

GROUP H	W	D	L	PT
Belgium	3	0	0	9*
Algeria	1	1	1	4*
Russia	0	2	1	2
Korea Republic	0	1	2	1

* The top two teams from each group qualified for the second round

KYLIAN MBAPPÉ
The French teenager came of age in Russia. He scored four goals in the tournament and was voted the best young player.

RUSSIA 2018

There were surprises and goals aplenty in this hugely popular World Cup, but in the end, France lifted the trophy for the second time—following their triumph in 1998.

BOOTED OUT

Host Russia set the tone for the group stages in its opening game, thumping Saudi Arabia 3–0. Spain and Portugal played out the match of the round, a pulsating 3–3 draw, but the main talking point was defending champion Germany's failure to reach the knockout stages for the first time since 1934.

2ND ROUND		QUARTERFINALS		SEMIFINALS		FINAL	
FRANCE	4	FRANCE	2				
ARGENTINA	3	URUGUAY	0				
URUGUAY	2			FRANCE	1	FRANCE	4
PORTUGAL	1			BELGIUM	0	CROATIA	2
BRAZIL	2	BRAZIL	1				
MEXICO	0	BELGIUM	2				
BELGIUM	3•						
JAPAN	2						
SPAIN	1					3RD/4TH PLACE	
RUSSIA	1*	RUSSIA	2				
CROATIA	1*	CROATIA	2*				
DENMARK	1			CROATIA	2•	BELGIUM	2
SWEDEN	1			ENGLAND	1	ENGLAND	0
SWITZERLAND	0	SWEDEN	0				
ENGLAND	1*	ENGLAND	2				
COLOMBIA	1						

* Qualified by penalty shoot-out   • After overtime

VIDEO ASSISTANT REFEREES

VARs, or video assistant referees, were used for the first time at Russia 2018. Officials reviewing the action on screens advised the referee on the pitch on any decision involving goals, penalties, direct red card incidents, or cases of mistaken identity.

ROUTE TO THE FINAL

In the quarterfinals, France proved too strong for Uruguay, winning 2–0. Belgium beat Brazil 2–1, England eased past Sweden 2–0, and Croatia beat host Russia on penalties. In the semifinals, French pragmatism overcame Belgian flair (1–0), while Croatia came from behind to beat England 2–1 after overtime in the second semifinal.

STAT ATTACK   GROUP STAGE

GROUP A	W	D	L	PT	GROUP B	W	D	L	PT	GROUP C	W	D	L	PT	GROUP D	W	D	L	PT
Uruguay	3	0	0	9*	Spain	1	2	0	5*	France	2	1	0	7*	Croatia	3	0	0	9*
Russia	2	0	1	6*	Portugal	1	2	0	5*	Denmark	1	2	0	5*	Argentina	1	1	1	4*
Saudi Arabia	1	0	2	3	Iran	1	1	1	4	Peru	1	0	2	3	Nigeria	1	0	2	3
Egypt	0	0	3	0	Morocco	0	1	2	1	Australia	0	1	2	1	Iceland	0	1	2	1

* The top two teams from each group qualified for the second round

THE VENUES

FIFA chose 12 out of the 16 stadiums initially proposed by Russia for the 2018 World Cup. The venues spanned three different time zones and a distance of nearly 2,000 miles (3,200 km) from Kaliningrad in the west to Ekaterinburg in the east. Most of the matches were concentrated in the western half of the country, with the final at Moscow's Luzhniki Stadium.

TOP GOAL SCORERS		
Harry KANE	England	6 goals
Denis CHERYSHEV	Russia	4 goals
Romelu LUKAKU	Belgium	4 goals
Kylian MBAPPÉ	France	4 goals
GOLDEN BALL		
Luka MODRIĆ	Croatia	

Kaliningrad
Kaliningrad Stadium
Capacity: 35,212

St. Petersburg
St. Petersburg Stadium
Capacity: 68,134

Nizhny Novgorod
Nizhny Novgorod Stadium
Capacity: 45,331

Kazan
Kazan Arena
Capacity: 44,779

Ekaterinburg
Ekaterinburg Arena
Capacity: 35,696

Moscow
Spartak Stadium
Capacity: 43,298

Samara
Samara Arena
Capacity: 44,807

Moscow
Luzhniki Stadium
Capacity: 81,006

Volgograd
Volgograd Arena
Capacity: 45,568

Saransk
Mordovia Arena
Capacity: 44,442

Rostov-on-Don
Rostov Arena
Capacity: 45,145

Sochi
Fisht Stadium
Capacity: 47,700

HARRY KANE
The England captain scored six goals in the tournament to become only the second England player to win the Golden Boot.

THE FINAL

France and Croatia played out a thrilling final in Moscow's Luzhniki Stadium. France took the lead after 18 minutes and Croatia tied at 28 minutes before France regained the lead from the penalty spot 10 minutes later. Paul Pogba and Kylian Mbappé made it 4–1 to France, and although Croatia pulled one back, France hung on to win the World Cup for a second time, Deschamps triumphing as a manager, having won as a player in 1998.

FRANCE ④	CROATIA ②
JULY 15, LUZHNIKI STADIUM: 78,011	
MANAGER: DIDIER DESCHAMPS	MANAGER: ZLATKO DALIC
FORMATION: 4-2-3-1	FORMATION: 4-2-3-1

GROUP STAGE

GROUP E	W	D	L	PT	GROUP F	W	D	L	PT	GROUP G	W	D	L	PT	GROUP H	W	D	L	PT
Brazil	2	1	0	7*	Sweden	2	0	1	6*	Belgium	3	0	0	9*	Colombia	2	0	1	6*
Switzerland	1	2	0	5*	Mexico	2	0	1	6*	England	2	0	1	6*	Japan	1	1	1	4*
Serbia	1	0	2	3	South Korea	1	0	2	3	Tunisia	1	0	2	3	Senegal	1	1	1	4
Costa Rica	0	1	2	1	Germany	1	0	2	3	Panama	0	0	3	0	Poland	1	0	2	3

* The top two teams from each group qualified for the second round

QATAR 2022

With headlines around human rights, the treatment of foreign workers, and the tournament's carbon footprint, the 2022 World Cup was the subject of controversies before a ball was even kicked. Held late in the year to avoid the summer heat, it was an eventful World Cup both on and off the pitch. Argentina and France served up a classic in the final.

SHOCK SCORES

Argentina suffered a shock 2–1 defeat to Saudi Arabia in their opening group game. It seemed to set a path for other well-liked nations to stumble early on—Germany lost their opener to Japan, and Belgium were beaten by Morocco. Spain began with a comprehensive 7–0 victory against Costa Rica, but only scraped through in the subsequent group games. The four-time champions Germany made an early exit. Belgium's "golden generation" also failed to reach the knock-out stage.

QUARTER-FINALS		SEMI-FINALS		FINAL	
CROATIA	1*				
BRAZIL	1	ARGENTINA	3	ARGENTINA	3
NETHERLANDS	2	CROATIA	0	FRANCE	3
ARGENTINA	2*			ARGENTINA WON 4–2 ON PENALTIES	
MOROCCO	1				
PORTUGAL	0	FRANCE	2	3RD/4TH PLACE	
ENGLAND	1	MOROCCO	0	CROATIA	2
FRANCE	2			MOROCCO	1

* Qualified by penalty shoot-out   • After extra time

LIONEL MESSI
Perhaps playing in his last World Cup, Argentinian captain Messi got better with each game, eventually finishing with seven goals and three assists.

ROUTE TO THE FINAL

France's toughest test came in the quarter-finals, when England ran them close in a 2–1 victory. Morocco, resolute throughout the tournament, made history by becoming the first Arab and African nation to reach the semi-finals. They lost to France 2–0. Argentina defeated Australia and Netherlands to make it to the final four. Their 3–0 win over Croatia in the semi-finals highlighted their great form.

RECORD-BREAKING RONALDO

With an accurate penalty shot against Ghana in Portugal's opening group game, soccer legend Cristiano Ronaldo recorded another milestone: he became the first men's player to score at five World Cup tournaments. His first goal in the 2006 World Cup was also from the penalty spot. Ronaldo's tournament ended in tears, though, as Morocco knocked Portugal out with a stunning 1–0 win in the quarter-finals.

STAT ATTACK   GROUP STAGE

GROUP A	W	D	L	PT	GROUP B	W	D	L	PT	GROUP C	W	D	L	PT	GROUP D	W	D	L	PT
Netherlands	2	1	0	7*	England	2	1	0	7*	Argentina	2	0	1	6*	France	2	0	1	6*
Senegal	2	0	1	6*	US	1	2	0	5*	Poland	1	1	1	4*	Australia	2	0	1	6*
Ecuador	1	1	1	4	Iran	1	0	2	3	Mexico	1	1	1	4	Tunisia	1	1	1	4
Qatar	0	0	3	0	Wales	0	1	2	1	Saudi Arabia	1	0	2	3	Denmark	0	1	2	1

* The top two teams from each group qualified for the second round

THE FINAL

In one of the greatest World Cup finals, Argentina dominated the first half, leading 2–0 with Lionel Messi's penalty and Angel Di Maria's goal. France was struggling to make an impact when Kylian Mbappé netted twice in the last ten minutes. In a pulsating extra-time period, goals by both Messi and Mbappé took the tie to penalties. It was Gonzalo Montiel's winning shot that gave Argentina their first title in 36 years.

ARGENTINA ③	FRANCE ③
ARGENTINA WON 4–2 ON PENALTIES	
DECEMBER 18, LUSAIL STADIUM: 88,966	
MANAGER: LIONEL SCALONI	MANAGER: DIDIER DESCHAMPS
FORMATION: 4-3-3	FORMATION: 4-2-3-1

Lineup (France): 1 Lloris; 5 Kounde, 18 Upamecano, 4 Varane, 22 T.Hernandez; 14 Rabiot, 6 Tchouameni; 11 Dembele, 7 Griezmann, 10 Mbappé; 9 Giroud

Lineup (Argentina): 20 Di Maria, 12 Alvarez, 20 Messi; 7 Mac Allister, 10 Fernandez, 9 De Paul; 6 Tagliafico, 3 Romero, 19 Otamendi, 11 Molina; 23 Martinez

SUBS: 12 Kolo Muani, 26 Thuram, 20 Coman, 25 Camavinga, 13 Fofana, 24 Konate, 3 Disasi, 8 Acuna, 4 Montiel, 5 Paredes, 21 Dybala, 22 Martinez, 6 Pezzella

THE VENUES

Qatar lacked the sports infrastructure needed to stage an event of such scale. Seven of the eight stadiums for the 2022 World Cup were completely new. Only the Khalifa International Stadium in Doha—originally opened in 1976—was upgraded for the tournament. Nonetheless, many of the new grounds caught the eye: Al Bayt Stadium is designed to look like traditional Bedouin tents, and the Al Janoub Stadium's design reflects the wind-filled sails of Qatar's traditional dhow boats.

Al Khor
Al Bayt Stadium
Capacity: 68,895

Al Rayyan
Education City Stadium
Capacity: 44,667

Al Rayyan
Ahmad Bin Ali Stadium
Capacity: 45,032

Al Wakrah
Al Janoub
Capacity: 44,325

Lusail
Lusail Stadium
Capacity: 88,966

Doha
Khalifa International Stadium
Capacity: 45,857

Doha
Al Thumama Stadium
Capacity: 44,400

Doha
Stadium 974
Capacity: 44,089

KYLIAN MBAPPÉ
Despite losing the final, Mbappé finished as the competition's Golden Boot winner. He became just the second player to score a hat-trick in a men's World Cup final.

TOP SCORERS

Kylian MBAPPÉ	France	8 goals
Lionel MESSI	Argentina	7 goals
Julian ALVAREZ	Argentina	4 goals
Olivier GIROUD	France	4 goals

GOLDEN BALL

Lionel MESSI	Argentina

GROUP STAGE

GROUP E	W	D	L	PT	GROUP F	W	D	L	PT	GROUP G	W	D	L	PT	GROUP H	W	D	L	PT
Japan	2	0	1	6*	Morocco	2	1	0	7*	Brazil	2	0	1	6*	Portugal	2	0	1	6*
Spain	1	1	1	4*	Croatia	1	2	0	5*	Switzerland	2	0	1	6*	South Korea	1	1	1	4*
Germany	1	1	1	4	Belgium	1	1	1	4	Cameroon	1	1	1	4	Uruguay	1	1	1	4
Costa Rica	1	0	2	3	Canada	0	0	3	0	Serbia	0	1	2	1	Ghana	1	0	2	3

* The top two teams from each group qualified for the second round

CHINA 1991

The FIFA Women's World Cup finally began in November 1991, when the first tournament kicked off in China. With just 12 teams attending, there was obvious room for the women's showpiece competition to expand and improve. Strangely, the duration of games was fixed at 80 minutes and not 90, as FIFA thought that would be too tiring. Nevertheless, to have an official global tournament for the top nations was a significant step.

GROUP GAINS

World Cup 1991 produced no real shocks in the group rounds, with the US and Germany winning all three of their matches. Brazil failed to make it through and the hosts got off to a great start, outplaying the much-liked Norwegians 4–0. Denmark made it to the knockout stage as the highest-ranked third-placed team.

ROUTE TO THE FINAL

The Americans did not face a real test until they took on the Germans in the semi-final; however, it was a comfortable 5–2 victory. Their goal count stood at a staggering 23 in the five fixtures ahead of the final. Norway recovered from their opening loss to China to see off Italy in the last eight, then brushed aside Sweden to make the final on November 30 in Guangzhou.

TRIPLE THREAT

The US's prolific forward line of Carin Jennings, Michelle Akers, and April Heinrichs was dubbed the "Triple Edged Sword" during the tournament. Together they netted 20 of their team's 25 goals in China.

CARIN JENNINGS
The US's Carin Jennings was one of the standout stars in 1991, winning the Golden Ball for best player.

SEMI-FINALS		FINAL	
SWEDEN	1	NORWAY	1
NORWAY	4	US	2
		3RD/4TH PLACE	
GERMANY	2	SWEDEN	4
US	5	GERMANY	0

THE FINAL

More than 60,000 spectators filled Tianhe Stadium and were treated to an entertaining game. The US were clear favorites, and their confidence was telling as Michelle Akers gave them the lead at 20 minutes. Norway dug deep and levelled soon after and it took until the 78th minute for the Americans to net again, through Akers once more.

NORWAY ❶	US ❷
NOVEMBER 30, TIANHE STADIUM: 63,000	
MANAGER: EVEN PELLERUD	MANAGER: ANSON DORRANCE
FORMATION: 1-3-3-3	FORMATION: 3-4-3

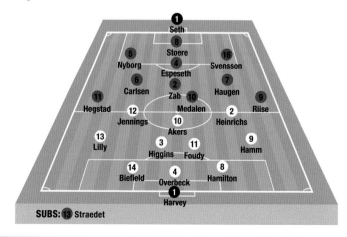

SUBS: ❸ Straedet

SWEDEN 1995

Sweden had hosted the men's World Cup in 1958, when Brazil swept all before them, and in 1995, it became the first country to hold both the men's and women's finals. The format remained the same as in 1991, with 12 teams from 6 confederations, but with 90-minute games this time. Another change involved awarding three points for a group stage win, instead of two. While the US were confident again, this event would be one for the Europeans.

GOAL FEST

Norway made their intentions clear from the start and opened their group fixtures with an 8–0 triumph over Nigeria. They won all three matches, scoring 17 goals and conceding none. No other nation went through to the last eight with a perfect record. The US suffered their first World Cup finals setback: a 3–3 draw with China. Germany came unstuck against a lively Sweden, going down 3–2 in their second game.

ROUTE TO THE FINAL

A Scandinavian quarter-final clash saw Norway cruise 3–1 past Denmark. They exacted revenge over the mighty US by settling a tight semi through Ann Aarønes' solitary goal. On the other side of the draw, Germany looked strong and resolute; they had a 3–0 quarter-final victory against England, followed by a 1–0 win over China.

THE FINAL

With plenty of firepower in attack, Norway was primed to shoot down the talented Germans. Two goals in the first half, including a fine solo effort from Hege Riise, was enough to capture the trophy in Sweden. The Norwegians were flying high—the squad's post-match flight home was escorted by two military aircraft as a sign of respect.

HEGE RIISE
The Norwegian midfielder played in the opening World Cup match in 1991. Four years later, she was very much the star player and leader for her successful team.

OLYMPIC PATHWAY

The 1995 World Cup was also a qualification route into the 1996 Olympics in Atlanta. Women's soccer would be part of the multi-sports event for the first time. The US qualified automatically as Olympic hosts, joined by China, Denmark, Germany, Norway, Sweden, and Japan. England were not an IOC member, so their Olympic spot instead went to Brazil.

GERMANY ⓪	NORWAY ②
JUNE 18, RASUNDA STADIUM: 17,158	
MANAGER: GERO BISANZ	MANAGER: EVEN PELLERUD
FORMATION: 3-5-2	FORMATION: 4-3-3

SEMI-FINALS		FINAL	
US	0	GERMANY	0
NORWAY	1	NORWAY	2
		3RD/4TH PLACE	
GERMANY	1	CHINA	0
CHINA	0	US	2

SUBS: **11** Brocker **18** Wunderlich **19** Smisek

US 1999

The women's World Cup in 1999 was a seminal tournament—an event that raised the status of the game to new heights. Backed by fantastic support across the US and crowds totaling more than 660,000, this World Cup was bigger than any other and was contested by 16 teams. The home nation were unstoppable as they clinched the trophy, although they did have to work hard in the knockout rounds.

EXTRA EXCITEMENT

With more teams involved, the group stage was more exciting than ever. The sight of Brazil—the most famous name in men's international soccer—finally making an impact was very welcoming. They topped their group ahead of the Germans, who strangely won only one group game. Nigeria also signaled their intentions by reaching the quarter-finals for the first time. The Americans were confident and cruising.

ROUTE TO THE FINAL

The US's quarter-final was on a knife edge for much of the 90 minutes. The Americans trailed Germany 2-1 at half-time, before eventually going through 3-2. Goals in the 5th and 80th minute put Brazil's great run to an end in the semi-finals. China were too strong for Russia in the last eight, and thrashed reigning champions Norway 5-0 to reach their first World Cup final.

SISSI
Brazil forward Sissi scored seven goals, including a sumptuous free-kick to win the quarter-final against Mexico.

RECORD CROWD

The 1999 final, at the Rose Bowl in Pasadena, was watched by 90,185 fans. It set a world record for a women's sporting event that stood until 2022, when 91,553 fans watched Barcelona women's team defeat Real Madrid in Spain.

QUARTER-FINALS		SEMI-FINALS		FINAL	
US	3			US	0
GERMANY	2	US	2	CHINA	0
		BRAZIL	0	US WON 5–4 ON PENALTIES	
BRAZIL	4•				
NIGERIA	3				
				3RD/4TH PLACE	
CHINA	2				
RUSSIA	0				
		NORWAY	0	BRAZIL	0*
		CHINA	5	NORWAY	0
NORWAY	3				
SWEDEN	1				

*Qualified by penalty shoot-out   • After extra time

STAT ATTACK — GROUP STAGE

GROUP A	W	D	L	PT	GROUP B	W	D	L	PT	GROUP C	W	D	L	PT	GROUP D	W	D	L	PT
US*	3	0	0	9	Brazil*	2	1	0	7	Norway*	3	0	0	9	China*	3	0	0	9
Nigeria*	2	0	1	6	Germany*	1	2	0	5	Russia*	2	0	1	6	Sweden*	2	0	1	6
North Korea	1	0	2	3	Italy	1	1	1	4	Canada	0	1	2	1	Australia	0	1	2	1
Denmark	0	0	3	0	Mexico	0	0	3	0	Japan	0	1	2	1	Ghana	0	1	2	1

*The top two teams from each group qualified for the quarter-finals

THE VENUES

FIFA's initial plan was to use small stadiums and for the tournament to be entirely played on the East Coast. That all changed after the 1996 Olympic final, when the US women won gold. The switch to huge stadiums, coast to coast, was still a risk. However, the success and attendance in 1999 prove it was the right decision.

Washington
Jack Kent Cooke Stadium
Capacity: 80,116

Chicago
Soldier Field
Capacity: 65,080

Boston
Foxboro Stadium
Capacity: 58,868

Portland
Civic Stadium
Capacity: 27,396

San Jose
Spartan Stadium
Capacity: 26,000

Stanford
Stanford Stadium
Capacity: 85,429

New Jersey
Giants Stadium
Capacity: 77,716

Pasadena
Rose Bowl
Capacity: 95,542

TOP SCORERS

SISSI	Brazil	7 goals
Sun WEN	China	7 goals
Ann AARØNES	Norway	4 goals
Nine players tied on three goals		

GOLDEN BALL

Sun WEN	China

MIA HAMM
American striker Hamm was the face of the 1999 World Cup. She scored twice and a penalty in the shoot-out win against China to claim her second title.

THE FINAL

The US and China had notched 37 goals between them to reach the final. The showpiece game in California—a repeat of the 1996 Olympic final, which the US won 2-1—was a much more cagey and defensive affair. With the game still locked at 0-0 after 120 minutes, spot kicks would decide the winner. Brandi Chastain had the pressure of converting the home team's fifth penalty, which she did to capture the trophy in front of a joyous stadium and with tens of millions watching across the States.

SUBS: **5** Xie Huilin **7** Zhang Ouying **15** Qiu Haiyan **7** Whalen **8** MacMillan **15** Venturini

US ⓞ	CHINA ⓞ
US WON 5–4 ON PENALTIES	
JULY 10, ROSE BOWL: 90,185	
MANAGER: TONY DICICCO	MANAGER: MA YUANAN
FORMATION: 4-3-3	FORMATION: 4-4-2

US 2003

The 2003 FIFA Women's World Cup was originally planned to be in China. A severe outbreak of SARS in the country had FIFA concerned and, on May 26, it was announced that the US would once again stage the event. Group games began on September 20. The Americans staged another successful competition despite the rush to get everything ready, albeit on a smaller scale than the 1999 extravaganza.

FAMILIAR AND NEW FACES

Many of the stars of 1999 returned—Mia Hamm (US), Hege Riise (Norway), and Sun Wen (China)—but it was also encouraging to see France, Argentina, and South Korea make their debut at the World Cup. As a sign of what was to come, Germany went through their group undefeated, as did the hosts. China and Brazil topped out and were joined by Sweden, Norway, Canada, and Russia in the last eight.

BIRGIT PRINZ
A natural striker, Prinz was the top-scorer at the 2003 Women's World Cup. She was voted Germany's player of the year consecutively from 2001 to 2007.

QUARTER-FINALS		SEMI-FINALS		FINAL	
US	1				
NORWAY	0				
		US	0		
		GERMANY	3		
GERMANY	7			GERMANY	2•
RUSSIA	1			SWEDEN	1
BRAZIL	1				
SWEDEN	2				
		SWEDEN	2	3RD/4TH PLACE	
		CANADA	1	US	3
CHINA	0			CANADA	1
CANADA	1				

* After extra time

ROUTE TO THE FINAL

Germany put on a stunning show in the quarter-finals to blitz Russia 7–1, with Kerstin Garefrekes and Birgit Prinz scoring a brace. To the disappointment of the host nation, they then breezed past the US to reach their second final. Sweden dug deep to beat the talented Brazilians in the quarter-final and sneaked past Canada with a late winner to meet the Germans.

STAT ATTACK — FIRST GROUP STAGE

GROUP A	W	D	L	PT	GROUP B	W	D	L	PT	GROUP C	W	D	L	PT	GROUP D	W	D	L	PT
US	3	0	0	9*	Brazil	2	1	0	7*	Germany	3	0	0	9*	China	2	1	0	7*
Sweden	2	0	1	6*	Norway	2	0	1	6*	Canada	2	0	1	6*	Russia	2	0	1	6*
North Korea	1	0	2	3	France	1	1	1	4	Japan	1	0	2	3	Ghana	1	0	2	3
Nigeria	0	0	3	0	South Korea	0	0	3	0	Argentina	0	0	3	0	Australia	0	1	2	1

* The top two teams from each group qualified for the quarter-finals

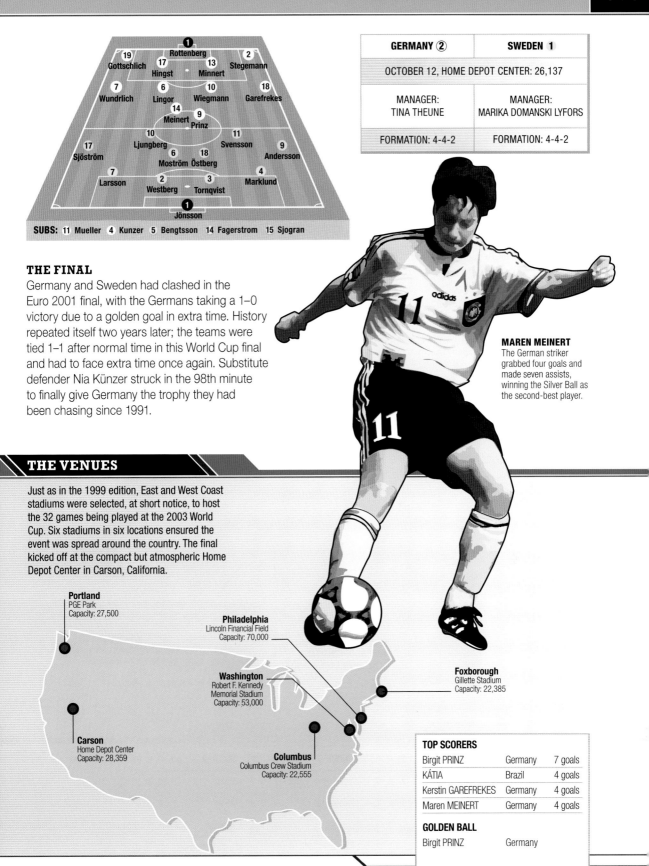

GERMANY ②	**SWEDEN 1**
OCTOBER 12, HOME DEPOT CENTER: 26,137 ||
MANAGER: TINA THEUNE	MANAGER: MARIKA DOMANSKI LYFORS
FORMATION: 4-4-2	FORMATION: 4-4-2

Lineup (Germany):
19 Gottschlich, 17 Hingst, 13 Minnert, 2 Stegemann (Rottenberg 1)
7 Wundrlich, 6 Lingor, 10 Wiegmann, 18 Garefrekes
14 Meinert, 9 Prinz

Lineup (Sweden):
10 Ljungberg, 11 Svensson
17 Sjöström, 6 Moström, 18 Östberg, 9 Andersson
7 Larsson, 2 Westberg, 3 Tornqvist, 4 Marklund
1 Jönsson

SUBS: 11 Mueller 4 Kunzer 5 Bengtsson 14 Fagerstrom 15 Sjogran

THE FINAL

Germany and Sweden had clashed in the Euro 2001 final, with the Germans taking a 1–0 victory due to a golden goal in extra time. History repeated itself two years later; the teams were tied 1–1 after normal time in this World Cup final and had to face extra time once again. Substitute defender Nia Künzer struck in the 98th minute to finally give Germany the trophy they had been chasing since 1991.

MAREN MEINERT
The German striker grabbed four goals and made seven assists, winning the Silver Ball as the second-best player.

THE VENUES

Just as in the 1999 edition, East and West Coast stadiums were selected, at short notice, to host the 32 games being played at the 2003 World Cup. Six stadiums in six locations ensured the event was spread around the country. The final kicked off at the compact but atmospheric Home Depot Center in Carson, California.

Portland
PGE Park
Capacity: 27,500

Philadelphia
Lincoln Financial Field
Capacity: 70,000

Washington
Robert F. Kennedy
Memorial Stadium
Capacity: 53,000

Foxborough
Gillette Stadium
Capacity: 22,385

Carson
Home Depot Center
Capacity: 28,359

Columbus
Columbus Crew Stadium
Capacity: 22,555

TOP SCORERS

Birgit PRINZ	Germany	7 goals
KÁTIA	Brazil	4 goals
Kerstin GAREFREKES	Germany	4 goals
Maren MEINERT	Germany	4 goals

GOLDEN BALL

Birgit PRINZ	Germany

SEPTEMBER 10 • SEPTEMBER 30, 2007

CHINA 2007

China staged the fifth women's World Cup in 2007, 16 years after they hosted the very first tournament. This edition would be the first time the trophy was retained, with the all-conquering Germany cementing their reputation as the best national team. Brazil also showed what a fantastic force they had become.

ELEVEN HEAVEN

Defending champions Germany kicked off the competition in superb style, registering a then-tournament record win of 11–0 against Argentina in the curtain raiser. Germany did not win all their group games, though; a 0–0 draw with England came before a 2–0 victory over Japan. Brazil was the only team to go through their group with three wins from three games.

ROUTE TO THE FINAL

Germany made very light work of making the final. Their quarter-final was an easy 3–0 win over North Korea, followed by the same score against Norway in the semi-final in Tianjin. They were yet to concede a goal in the tournament. Brazil let in their first goals during a tight 3–2 win against Australia but improved in the semi-final with a surprise 4–0 win over the US. There was no doubt that the two best teams were left standing.

MARTA
Brazil's #10 had a wonderful tournament in front of goal. Her solo effort in the semi-final against the US was the tournament's best strike.

QUARTER-FINALS		SEMI-FINALS		FINAL	
GERMANY	3				
NORTH KOREA	0	GERMANY	3	GERMANY	2
NORWAY	1	NORWAY	0	BRAZIL	0
CHINA	0				
US	3			3RD/4TH PLACE	
ENGLAND	0	US	0	NORWAY	1
BRAZIL	3	BRAZIL	4	US	4
AUSTRALIA	2				

GOLDEN GONE

For this women's World Cup, the "golden goal" rule in extra time no longer applied. In the past, such as with Germany's winner in the 2003 final, the first team to score in extra time would instantly be awarded the victory. Despite this rule change to align the women's tournament with the men's, World Cup 2007 did not have any matches that needed extra time.

STAT ATTACK — GROUP STAGE

GROUP A	W	D	L	PT	GROUP B	W	D	L	PT	GROUP C	W	D	L	PT	GROUP D	W	D	L	PT
Germany	2	1	0	7*	US	2	1	0	7*	Norway	2	1	0	7*	Brazil	3	0	0	9*
England	1	2	0	5*	North Korea	1	1	1	4*	Australia	1	2	0	5*	China	2	0	1	6*
Japan	1	1	1	4	Sweden	1	1	1	4	Canada	1	1	1	4	Denmark	1	0	2	3
Argentina	0	0	3	0	Nigeria	0	1	2	1	Ghana	0	0	3	0	New Zealand	0	0	3	0

*The top two teams from each group qualified for the quarter-finals

THE FINAL

The first ever women's World Cup between South American and European nations went Germany's way. The in-form Marta barely had an effort in front of goal. In the end, Brazil, with their attacking flair and South American skill, were defeated by the confident and defensive power of the Germans. Nadine Angerer, the German goalkeeper, achieved her target of going through the whole campaign without conceding a single goal.

GERMANY ②	BRAZIL 0
SEPTEMBER 30, HONGKOU STADIUM: 31,000	
MANAGER: SILVIA NEID	MANAGER: JORGE BARCELLOS
FORMATION: 4-4-1-1	FORMATION: 3-4-1-2

SUBS: 16 Müller   19 Bajramaj   6 Rosana   15 Katia   18 Pretinha

THE VENUES

None of the venues used in the 1991 World Cup were selected to stage games 16 years later. The five stadiums in use were spread around the vast country, unlike the opener that was based in Guangdong province in southern China. The smallest venue was Hongkou Stadium, Shanghai, but it still boasted a capacity of more than 30,000 spectators. This was preferred for the venue, rather than larger arenas in Wuhan, Hangzhou, and Tianjin.

CHENGDU SPORTS CENTER
Capacity: 40,000, Chengdu

HONGKOU STADIUM
Capacity: 33,000, Shanghai

TIANJIN OLYMPIC CENTRE STADIUM
Capacity: 60,000, Tianjin

WUHAN STADIUM
Capacity: 60,000, Wuhan

YELLOW DRAGON SPORTS CENTER
Capacity: 51,000, Hangzhou

AWESOME ANGERER
Germany's Nadine Angerer had nothing to do with scoring goals. Her focus, as goalkeeper, was in keeping them out, something she did in all six games. Marta beat her to the Golden Ball best player award.

TOP SCORERS

MARTA	Brazil	7 goals
Ragnhild GULBRANDSEN	Norway	6 goals
Abby WAMBACH	US	6 goals
CRISTIANE	Brazil	5 goals
Birgit PRINZ	Germany	5 goals

GOLDEN BALL

MARTA	Brazil

GERMANY 2011

After failing to clear the group stage four years earlier, Japan were aiming to do much better in 2011. Not only did Japan perform well—they went on to make history for their country and for Asia. On their home patch, reigning champions Germany were confident ahead of kick-off on June 26.

GROUP GLORY

Germany, Brazil, and Sweden scored three wins from three games in their groups to set the early pace. With average group game attendance of over 24,000, the tournament was taking shape nicely. Germany's 4–2 win over France was the pick of the games at this stage, while England beat Japan 2–0 to emerge as Group B winners.

ROUTE TO THE FINAL

The quarter-finals signaled the end of Germany's pursuit of a third consecutive triumph. It took a nervy, 1–0 extra-time win for Japan to put them out. They followed this with a classy semi-final win over Sweden. The US scraped through on penalties against Brazil, after Abby Wambach's injury-time leveller in extra-time, but then comfortably defeated France in the other semi-final.

HOMARE SAWA
Japan's surprise success simply would not have been possible without Homare Sawa, their midfield maestro. She netted five goals and was named the Golden Ball winner.

QUARTER-FINALS		SEMI-FINALS		FINAL	
ENGLAND	1*				
FRANCE	1	FRANCE	1	JAPAN	2
BRAZIL	2	US	3	US	2
US	2*			JAPAN WON 3–1 ON	
SWEDEN	3			PENALTIES	
AUSTRALIA	1	JAPAN	3	3RD/4TH PLACE	
GERMANY	0	SWEDEN	1	SWEDEN	2
JAPAN	1•			FRANCE	1

* Qualified by penalty shoot-out   • After extra time

DEVASTATING TIME

In March 2011, a huge earthquake off the east coast of Japan triggered a devastating tsunami for the country. Thousands of lives were lost, with damage estimated at $300 billion. Japan's victory at the 2011 World Cup came at a time when the nation needed a sporting lift. "We felt we had the support of the world," said goalkeeper Ayumi Kaihori many years later.

STAT ATTACK — GROUP STAGE

GROUP A	W	D	L	PT	GROUP B	W	D	L	PT	GROUP C	W	D	L	PT	GROUP D	W	D	L	PT
Germany	3	0	0	9*	England	2	1	0	7*	Sweden	3	0	0	9*	Brazil	3	0	0	9*
France	2	0	1	6*	Japan	2	0	1	6*	US	2	0	1	6*	Australia	2	0	1	6*
Nigeria	1	0	2	3	Mexico	0	2	1	2	North Korea	0	1	2	1	Norway	1	0	2	3
Canada	0	0	3	0	New Zealand	0	1	2	1	Columbia	0	1	2	1	Equatorial Guinea	0	0	3	0

*The top two teams from each group qualified for the quarter-finals

ABBY WAMBACH
Wambach spearheaded the American attack, scoring four goals. She scored in the final penalty shoot-out as well.

THE FINAL

Both Japan and the US scored late, taking the game into extra-time with a 1–1 score line. Abby Wambach edged the Americans ahead, before the in-form Homare Sawa made it 2–2, leading to penalties. Only Wambach scored her spot kick for the US, leaving Saki Kumagai to convert and see Japan take the trophy. Ahead of this tournament, the Nadeshiko—the nickname for Japan Women's National Team—had won just 3 of their 16 World Cup matches.

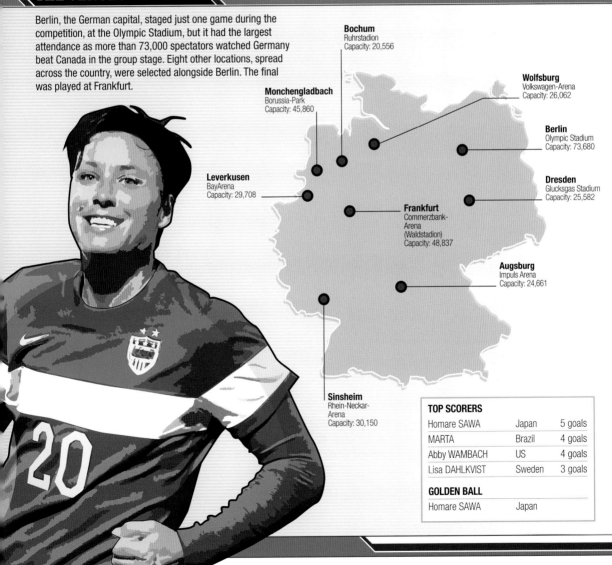

JAPAN ②	US ②
JAPAN WON 3–1 ON PENALTIES	
JULY 17, WALDSTADION: 48,817	
MANAGER: NORIO SASAKI	MANAGER: PIA MARIANE SUNDHAGE
FORMATION: 4-4-2	FORMATION: 4-4-2

1 Kaihori

| 15 Sameshima | 3 Iwashimizu | 4 Kumagai | 2 Kinga |

| 8 Miyama | 6 Sakaguchi | 10 Sawa | 11 Ohno |

| 9 Kawasumi | 7 Ando |

| 20 Wambach | 12 Cheney |

| 15 Rapinoe | 10 Lloyd | 7 Boxx | 9 O'Reilly |

| 6 LePeilbet | 3 Rampone | 19 Buehler | 11 Krieger |

1 Solo

SUBS: **18** Maruyama　**17** Nagasato　**20** Iwabuchi　**13** Morgan　**17** Heath

THE VENUES

Berlin, the German capital, staged just one game during the competition, at the Olympic Stadium, but it had the largest attendance as more than 73,000 spectators watched Germany beat Canada in the group stage. Eight other locations, spread across the country, were selected alongside Berlin. The final was played at Frankfurt.

Bochum
Ruhrstadion
Capacity: 20,556

Wolfsburg
Volkswagen-Arena
Capacity: 26,062

Monchengladbach
Borussia-Park
Capacity: 45,860

Berlin
Olympic Stadium
Capacity: 73,680

Leverkusen
BayArena
Capacity: 29,708

Dresden
Glucksgas Stadium
Capacity: 25,582

Frankfurt
Commerzbank-Arena
(Waldstadion)
Capacity: 48,837

Augsburg
Impuls Arena
Capacity: 24,661

Sinsheim
Rhein-Neckar-Arena
Capacity: 30,150

TOP SCORERS

Homare SAWA	Japan	5 goals
MARTA	Brazil	4 goals
Abby WAMBACH	US	4 goals
Lisa DAHLKVIST	Sweden	3 goals

GOLDEN BALL

Homare SAWA	Japan

CANADA 2015

With 24 teams competing, this was the biggest women's World Cup so far. The event was spread from the east to west coast of Canada, and across five time zones. Several teams featured for the first time, such as Ecuador, Ivory Coast, and Switzerland. The US were determined to capture the trophy once again.

GOAL FEST

The 36 group games produced 107 goals, giving the tournament a fantastic start, and gripping the Canadian public and the wider soccer world. The US negotiated a tricky group by only dropping two points—due to a 0–0 draw with Sweden—and the defending champions Japan got three wins from three games. Both Germany and Switzerland scored 10 goals in a single game against Ivory Coast and Ecuador, respectively.

CARLI LLOYD
American Lloyd played both as midfielder and forward. She enjoyed a memorable campaign in Canada: she was joint top scorer, Golden Ball winner, and a champion by the final whistle on July 5.

2ND ROUND		QUARTER-FINALS		SEMI-FINALS		FINAL	
GERMANY	4						
SWEDEN	1	GERMANY	1*				
FRANCE	3	FRANCE	1				
SOUTH KOREA	0			US	2		
CHINA	1			GERMANY	0		
CAMEROON	0	CHINA	0			US	5
US	2	US	1			JAPAN	2
COLOMBIA	0						
BRAZIL	0						
AUSTRALIA	1	AUSTRALIA	0				
JAPAN	2	JAPAN	1				
NETHERLANDS	1			JAPAN	2	3RD/4TH PLACE	
NORWAY	1			ENGLAND	1		
ENGLAND	2	ENGLAND	2			GERMANY	0
CANADA	1	CANADA	1			ENGLAND	1•
SWITZERLAND	0						

* Qualified by penalty shoot-out   • After extra time

ARTIFICIAL PITCHES

While various records were broken on the pitch, the pitches were also record breaking. This was the first World Cup—men's and women's—where all the games took place on artificial turf. Fears of the surface causing an increased injury risk and poorer quality games were not borne out.

ROUTE TO THE FINAL

With 24 nations involved, the knock-out stage was played after the group games. The US defeated Colombia, then China in the quarters, and Germany in the semi-final, letting in just one goal in their three games. Japan's knock-out route included wins over the Netherlands, Australia, and England.

STAT ATTACK   GROUP STAGE

GROUP A	W	D	L	PT	GROUP B	W	D	L	PT	GROUP C	W	D	L	PT	GROUP D	W	D	L	PT
Canada	1	2	0	5*	Germany	2	1	0	7*	Japan	3	0	0	9*	US	2	1	0	7*
China	1	1	1	4*	Norway	2	1	0	7*	Cameroon	2	0	1	6*	Australia	1	1	1	4*
Netherlands	1	1	1	4*	Thailand	1	0	2	3	Switzerland	1	0	2	3*	Sweden	0	3	0	3*
New Zealand	0	2	1	2	Ivory Coast	0	0	3	0	Ecuador	0	0	3	0	Nigeria	0	1	2	1

* The top two teams from each group qualified for the quarter-finals, along with the four best third-placed teams

THE VENUES

FIFA chose six cities to stage the action: Ottawa, Moncton, Winnipeg, Vancouver, Montreal, and Edmonton. The Commonwealth Stadium kicked off the tournament in style as 53,000 spectators watched the hosts defeat China 1–0. The highest attendance, 54,027, was in Vancouver, during England's 1–0 defeat of Canada in the quarter-finals.

TOP SCORERS

Carli LLOYD	US	6 goals
Celia SASIC	Germany	6 goals
Anja MITTAG	Germany	5 goals
Eight players tied on three goals		

GOLDEN BALL

Carli LLOYD	US

Moncton
Moncton Stadium
Capacity: 13,000

Montreal
Olympic Stadium
Capacity: 56,040

Vancouver
BC Place
Capacity:
54,320

Ottawa
Lansdowne Stadium
Capacity: 24,000

Edmonton
Commonwealth
Stadium
Capacity: 56,300

Winnipeg
Winnipeg Stadium
Capacity: 33,422

CELIA SASIC
Sasic opened her account for Germany with a hat-trick against Ivory Coast. She added three goals in the knock-out phase, including two important penalties.

THE FINAL

In a repeat of the 2011 final, the US faced off against Japan once again. It couldn't afford another loss and effectively won the game inside 16 minutes. By that mark they led 3–0, with a hat-trick from Carli Lloyd. It became 4–0, before Japan pulled two goals back. Tobin Heath's strike early in the second half settled the score at 5–2. This match redeemed Lloyd after she missed her penalty kick in the final shoot-out in 2011.

US ⑤	JAPAN ②
SEPTEMBER 30, BP BLACE STADIUM: 53,341	
MANAGER: JILL ELLIS	MANAGER: NORIO SASAKI
FORMATION: 4-4-1-1	FORMATION: 4-4-2

GROUP STAGE

GROUP E	W	D	L	PT	GROUP F	W	D	L	PT
Brazil	3	0	0	9*	France	2	0	1	6*
South Korea	1	1	1	4*	England	2	0	1	6*
Costa Rica	0	2	1	2	Colombia	1	1	1	4*
Spain	0	1	2	1	Mexico	0	1	2	1

US
1 Solo
22 Klingenberg   4 Sauerbrunn   19 Ertz   11 Krieger
17 Heath   14 Gautrat   12 Holiday   15 Rapinoe
10 Lloyd   13 Morgan

Japan
11 Ohno   17 Ogimi
8 Miyama   6 Sakaguchi   13 Utsugi   9 Kawasumi
5 Sameshima   3 Iwashimizu   4 Kumagai   19 Ariyoshi
1 Kaihoro

SUBS: 3 Rampone 5 O'Hara 20 Wambach 10 Sawa 15 Sugasawa 16 Iwabuchi

FRANCE 2019

The World Cup 2019 was another spectacular tournament. FIFA proudly boasted about the viewing figures it achieved. Across TV and digital channels, 1.12 billion viewers witnessed the action in cities such as Paris, Lyon, Nice, and Rennes. Many talented teams qualified, with Chile, Scotland, and Jamaica making their debuts. The US once again emerged as the best of the best.

RECORD MAKERS

The US had to wait until match day five to make their entrance. It was well worth the wait, as they defeated Thailand by a record score of 13–0. Alex Morgan scored five goals in this historical win. In just their second World Cup, the Netherlands also breezed through, qualifying with three wins. Other teams that reached the knock-out stage included England, Germany, and the hosts, France.

ROUTE TO THE FINAL

The Netherlands, the reigning UEFA Euros champions, looked set for another shot at international glory. They beat Japan 2–1 in the second round with a last-minute penalty, before seeing off Italy and Sweden to reach their first World Cup final. The US needed two penalties to beat Spain with the score at 2–1. They moved through to the final after wins against France and England.

MEGAN RAPINOE
Not only did American forward Rapinoe score six goals, she also won the Golden Ball. She scooped the Best FIFA Women's Player and Ballon d'Or Féminin awards later in the year.

AWESOME ELLIS

The US's triumph in France made them the second team to retain the women's World Cup, after Germany's success in 2003 and 2007. The American double was achieved with the same coach, Jill Ellis. The only other coach to accomplish this feat was Vittorio Pozzo, with the men's side in 1934 and 1938.

2ND ROUND		QUARTER-FINALS		SEMI-FINALS		FINAL	
NORWAY	1*						
AUSTRALIA	1	NORWAY	0				
ENGLAND	3	ENGLAND	3				
CAMEROON	0			ENGLAND	1		
FRANCE	2•			US	2		
BRAZIL	1	FRANCE	1			US	2
SPAIN	1	US	2			NETHERLANDS	0
US	2						
ITALY	2						
CHINA	0	ITALY	0				
NETHERLANDS	2	NETHERLANDS	2				
JAPAN	1			NETHERLANDS	1•	**3RD/4TH PLACE**	
GERMANY	3			SWEDEN	0		
NIGERIA	0	GERMANY	1			ENGLAND	1
SWEDEN	1	SWEDEN	2			SWEDEN	2
CANADA	0						

* Qualified by penalty shoot-out   • After extra time

STAT ATTACK   GROUP STAGE

GROUP A	W	D	L	PT	GROUP B	W	D	L	PT	GROUP C	W	D	L	PT	GROUP D	W	D	L	PT
France	3	0	0	9*	Germany	3	0	0	9*	Italy	2	0	1	6*	England	3	0	0	9*
Norway	2	0	1	6*	Spain	1	1	1	4*	Australia	2	0	1	6*	Japan	1	1	1	4*
Nigeria	1	0	2	3*	China	1	1	1	4*	Brazil	2	0	1	6*	Argentina	0	2	1	2
South Korea	0	0	3	0	South Africa	0	0	3	0	Jamaica	0	0	3	0	Scotland	0	1	2	1

* The top two teams from each group qualified for the quarter-finals, along with the four best third-placed teams

THE FINAL

The determined Dutch team held the US until the 61st minute, when captain Megan Rapinoe netted a penalty. The breakout star Rose Lavelle doubled the lead eight minutes later. However, it wasn't to be a Euro-World Cup double for the Dutch as the mighty US went the distance yet again.

US ②	NETHERLANDS ⓪
JULY 7, STADE DE LYON: 57,900	
MANAGER: JILL ELLIS	MANAGER: SARINA WIEGMAN
FORMATION: 4-3-3	FORMATION: 4-3-3

SUBS: 10 Lloyd 11 Krieger 23 Press 7 Van de Sanden 19 Roord

THE VENUES

Lyon seemed to be an obvious choice to stage the final. It is home to the French giants Olympique Lyonnais Féminini, who, by the summer of 2019, had won the women's Champions League six times. The stadium was only three years old, and such was its appeal, both semi-finals were also played here.

Reims
Stade Auguste-Delaune
Capacity: 20,500

Valenciennes
Stade du Hainaut
Capacity: 22,600

Le Havre
Stade Océane
Capacity: 24,000

...nnes
...zhon Park
...acity: 28,600

Paris
Parc des Princes
Capacity: 45,600

Lyon
Stade de Lyon
Capacity: 57,900

Grenoble
Stade des Alpes
Capacity: 18,000

Nice
Stade de Nice
Capacity: 35,100

Montpellier
Stade de la Mosson
Capacity: 19,300

TOP SCORERS

Alex MORGAN	US	6 goals
Megan RAPINOE	US	6 goals
Ellen WHITE	England	6 goals
Sam KERR	Australia	5 goals
CRISTIANE	Brazil	4 goals
Wendie RENARD	France	4 goals

GOLDEN BALL

Megan RAPINOE	US

GROUP STAGE

GROUP E	W	D	L	PT	GROUP F	W	D	L	PT
Netherlands	3	0	0	9*	US	3	0	0	9*
Canada	2	0	1	6*	Sweden	2	0	1	6*
Cameroon	1	0	2	3*	Chile	1	0	2	3
New Zealand	0	0	3	0	Thailand	0	0	3	0

ELLEN WHITE
England striker White scored against Scotland, Japan, Cameroon, Norway, and the US. Her "goggles" celebration—where she would create goggles around her eyes with fingers—followed many of her memorable goals.

AUSTRALIA & NEW ZEALAND 2023

Spain became world champions for the first-time with a thrilling victory over England in Sydney, Australia. They joined Germany as the only nations to have won both men's and women's FIFA World Cups. The 2023 tournament was the first women's World Cup to be cohosted by two countries. It proved to be a landmark event for women's soccer, boasting record-breaking match attendances and a worldwide TV audience of 2 billion people.

MATCHES LEADING UP TO THE FINAL

African teams, often considered underdogs, impressed at the tournament, with South Africa, Nigeria, and Morocco challenging the heavyweights. Legends of the women's game, Marta Vieira da Silva (Brazil) and Megan Rapinoe (US), bid farewell as Brazil suffered a shock exit in the group stages, and Rapinoe missed a crucial penalty when the US crashed out to Sweden. The quarter-final between Australia and France featured a record-breaking 120-minute goalless match, resolved with a dramatic 7-6 penalty shoot-out.

2ND ROUND		QUARTER-FINALS		SEMIFINALS		FINAL	
SWITZERLAND	1						
SPAIN	5	SPAIN	2•				
NETHERLANDS	2	NETHERLANDS	1				
SOUTH AFRICA	0			SPAIN	2		
JAPAN	3			SWEDEN	1		
NORWAY	1	JAPAN	1			SPAIN	1
SWEDEN	0*	SWEDEN	2			ENGLAND	0
US	0						
AUSTRALIA	2						
DENMARK	0	AUSTRALIA	0*				
FRANCE	4	FRANCE	0				
MOROCCO	0			AUSTRALIA	1	3RD/4TH PLACE	
ENGLAND	0*			ENGLAND	3		
NIGERIA	0	ENGLAND	2			SWEDEN	1
COLOMBIA	1	COLOMBIA	1			AUSTRALIA	2
JAMAICA	0						

* Qualified by penalty shoot-out   • After extra time

SAM KERR
The face of the tournament, Kerr faced injury setbacks in the World Cup, missing the early matches. But in the semifinal, she scored a remarkable equalizer against England, earning a nomination for FIFA's goal of the year.

STAT ATTACK — GROUP STAGE

GROUP A	W	D	L	PT	GROUP B	W	D	L	PT	GROUP C	W	D	L	PT	GROUP D	W	D	L	PT
Switzerland	1	2	0	5*	Australia	2	0	1	6*	Japan	3	0	0	9*	England	3	0	0	9*
Norway	1	1	1	4*	Nigeria	1	2	0	5*	Spain	2	0	1	6*	Denmark	2	0	1	6*
New Zealand	1	1	1	4	Canada	1	1	1	4	Zambia	1	0	2	3	China	1	0	2	3
Philippines	1	0	2	3	Rep. of Ireland	0	1	2	1	Costa Rica	0	0	3	0	Haiti	0	0	3	0

* The top two teams from each group qualified for the second round

THE TOURNAMENTS

Ten stadiums in nine locations hosted the tournament. The rebuilt Sydney Football Stadium was the only new venue, hosting six group games and the Netherlands vs South Africa in the round of 16. Eden Park in Auckland hosted eight fixtures along with a breathtaking semifinal that saw Spain beat Sweden 2-1, while the other semifinal and final were held at Stadium Australia in Sydney.

TOP SCORERS

Miyazawa HINATA	Japan	5 goals
Kadidiatou DIANI	France	4 goals
Amanda ILESTEDT	Sweden	4 goals
Alexandra POPP	Germany	4 goals
Jill ROORD	Netherlands	4 goals
Lauren JAMES	England	3 goals
Aitana BONMATÍ	Spain	3 goals
Jenni HERMOSO	Spain	3 goals

Brisbane
Lang Park
Capacity: 52,500

Perth
Perth Rectangular Stadium
Capacity: 22,500

Adelaide
Hindmarsh Stadium
Capacity: 16,500

Sydney
Stadium Australia
Capacity: 82,000

Sydney
Sydney Football Stadium
Capacity: 42,500

Auckland
Eden Park
Capacity: 50,000

Hamilton
Waikato Stadium
Capacity: 25,800

Wellington
Wellington Regional Stadium
Capacity: 34,500

Dunedin
Dunedin Stadium
Capacity: 30,748

Melbourne
Melbourne Rectangular Stadium
Capacity: 30,050

CONTROVERSIAL KISS

Spain's victory was marred when the Spanish FA President, Luis Rubiales, kissed Jenni Hermoso during the award ceremony. Rubiales claimed it was consensual, while Hermoso disagreed. The incident led to more than 80 players refusing to play for the national team until Rubiales was removed. He eventually resigned and was banned from soccer by FIFA for three years.

THE FINAL

Olga Carmona's left-foot strike in the 29th minute secured Spain's 1-0 victory over England in the final at Stadium Australia. Spain dominated possession in a tight game with few goal scoring opportunities for either side. Jenni Hermoso had a penalty saved by England goalkeeper Mary Earps, but Spain held on to clinch their first senior women's title.

ENGLAND 0	SPAIN ①
AUGUST 20, STADIUM AUSTRALIA: 82,000	
MANAGER: SARINA WIEGMAN	MANAGER: MONTSE TOME
FORMATION: 3-4-3	FORMATION: 4-3-3

SUBS: ⑫ Hernandez ⑤ Andres ⑪ Putellas 7 James 18 Kelly 19 England

GROUP STAGE

GROUP E	W	D	L	PT
Netherlands	2	1	0	7*
United States	1	2	0	5*
Portugal	1	1	1	4
Vietnam	0	0	3	0

GROUP F	W	D	L	PT
France	2	1	0	7*
Jamaica	1	2	0	5*
Brazil	1	1	1	4
Panama	0	0	3	0

GROUP G	W	D	L	PT
Sweden	3	0	0	9*
South Africa	1	1	1	4*
Italy	1	0	2	3
Argentina	0	1	2	1

GROUP H	W	D	L	PT
Colombia	2	0	1	6*
Morocco	2	0	1	6*
Germany	1	1	1	4
South Korea	0	1	2	1

* The top two teams from each group qualified for the second round

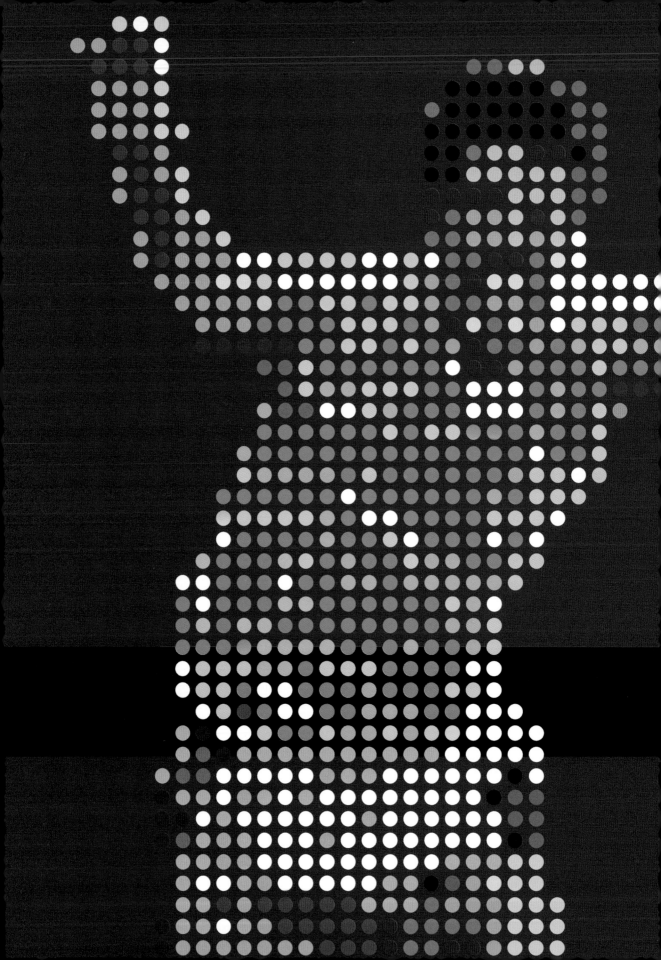

CONTINENTAL COMPETITIONS

EUROPE

EUROPEAN CHAMPIONSHIP

COMPETITION:
UEFA EUROPEAN FOOTBALL CHAMPIONSHIP
FOUNDED: 1960
CONFEDERATION: UEFA

A European soccer championship was first proposed in the 1920s, but it took until 1960 for the first tournament to be played. The championship has been held every four years since and has grown from just four to 24 teams. As the tournament has grown, fans have come in increasing numbers—although the COVID-19 pandemic led to the 2020 tournament being postponed to 2021, with 11 venues used for matches, and reduced crowds.

OTTO REHHAGEL
The German coach of the victorious Greek team at Euro 2004, Rehhagel pulled off the impossible and gave the Greek squad tactical nous and a Germanic work rate.

BIRTH OF A DREAM

Henri Delaunay, head of the French FA, first proposed a European nations' tournament in 1927, but at the time, there was no European soccer federation to administer such a contest. It was not until the creation of UEFA in 1954 that Delaunay was able to revive the idea. Delaunay himself died in 1955, but the qualifying rounds of the tournament he had imagined were first played in 1958. In 1960, the USSR won the first final and claimed the Henri Delaunay Trophy.

EURO 2020

UEFA Euro 2020 was to be a celebration of the 60th anniversary of the European tournament, but it was delayed for a year due to the COVID-19 outbreak. It would, however, still be called Euro 2020 and not 2021. Starting on June 11 in Rome, the games took place in 11 different cities in a unique setup. Italy were finally crowned champions at Wembley Stadium, London, on July 11.

STAT ATTACK

MOST WINS

	1	2	3
Germany			
Spain			
France			
Italy			

MARCO VAN BASTEN
Dutch striker van Basten scored the tournament's greatest goal—a flying volley from close to the byline on the edge of the penalty area—in the 1988 final, sealing the Netherlands' 2–0 win over the USSR.

MOST APPEARANCES

Name	Country	Games
Cristiano RONALDO	Portugal	25
Joao MOUTINHO	Portugal	19
PEPE	Portugal	19
Bastian SCHWEINSTEIGER	Germany	18
Leonardo BONUCCI	Italy	18
Gianluigi BUFFON	Italy	17

TOP GOAL SCORERS

Name	Country	Goals
Cristiano RONALDO	Portugal	14
Michel PLATINI	France	9
Alan SHEARER	England	7
Antoine GRIEZMANN	France	7
Thierry HENRY	France	6
Patrick KLUIVERT	Netherlands	6

THE COMPETITORS

Western European countries, notably Germany, Spain, and France have dominated the competition even after the championship expanded to include other nations. Teams from 24 countries now compete in the finals tournament. Moreover, cohosting allows smaller nations to pool resources and become hosts.

Sweden
Years hosted: 1992
(8) participants

England
Years hosted: 1996
(16) participants

Denmark
Winners:
1992

Netherlands
Years hosted:
Cohosted with Belgium
2000 (16) participants
Winners: 1988

Russia (USSR)
Winners: 1960

Czechoslovakia
Winners: 1976

Germany
Years hosted:
1988 (8) participants
Winners: 1972,
1980, 1996

**Poland and
Ukraine**
Years hosted:
2012 (16) participants

France
Years hosted:
1960 (4) participants
1984 (8) participants
2016 (24) participants
Winners:
1984, 2000

**Austria and
Switzerland**
Years hosted:
2008 (16) participants

Belgium
Years hosted:
1972 (4) participants
Cohosted with
Netherlands 2000
(16) participants

Greece
Winners:
2004

Portugal
Years hosted:
2004 (16) participants
Winners: 2016

Spain
Years hosted:
1964 (4) participants
Winners:
1964, 2008,
2012

Italy
Years hosted:
1968 (4) participants
1980 (8) participants
Winners:
1968,
2020

Yugoslavia
Years hosted:
1976 (4) participants

FROM STRENGTH TO STRENGTH

The tournament began as a series of two-leg knockout games, the winners of which progressed to the semifinals, followed by a single-leg final. For the 1980 tournament in Italy, UEFA expanded the competition to eight teams in two groups, playing in a fixed location. The contest doubled in size again for Euro 1996 in England, with 16 teams competing. Alongside the leading powers—Germany, Italy, the Netherlands, Spain, and France—there has been room for smaller champions: Czechoslovakia in 1976, Denmark in 1992, and Greece in 2004. France hosted a 24-team finals tournament in 2016, with Portugal turning out the winners.

OLIVER BIERHOFF
The German striker scored both goals in his country's 2–1 victory over the Czech Republic in the 1996 final.

SOVIET CHAMPIONS, EURO 1960

The Soviet team that won the first European Championship received a bye through the quarterfinals, when Spanish dictator General Franco refused to allow his team to travel to Moscow. Once at the finals, the USSR proved its worth, led by goalkeeping legend Lev Yashin and consisting of the best talent drawn—for once—from more than just the Moscow clubs. Its winner against Yugoslavia in the final in Paris was scored by SKA Rostov-on-Don's Viktor Ponedelnik. Fewer than 18,000 people attended.

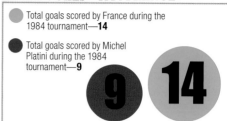

TOTAL GOALS—1984 FRANCE

Total goals scored by France during the 1984 tournament—**14**

Total goals scored by Michel Platini during the 1984 tournament—**9**

9   **14**

BRIAN LAUDRUP
One of two soccer-playing brothers, Brian Laudrup was the linchpin of the Denmark team that won Euro 1992. Laudrup brought thoughtful passing and an attacking threat to a team set up to defend.

SPANISH REVENGE, EURO 1964

The Soviet Union was fated to defend its title in Spain, who had refused to travel to Moscow in 1960. It met the host in the final at the Bernabeu in front of 105,000 people and the entire Spanish political elite. It was 1–1 until the 86th minute, when Marcelino headed home from near the penalty spot. There was no ambiguity about the meaning of the event for the government. Newspaper headlines the following day described the game as a "victory over communism and its fellow travelers."

SOCCER IS NOT ABOUT JUSTICE; WHEN THE REFEREE DECIDES, IT IS LIKE HE IS GOD

FORMER AUSTRIA COACH **JOSEF HICKERSBERGER** ON AUSTRIA'S LAST-MINUTE PENALTY AGAINST POLAND

SEMIFINAL SHOCK, EURO 1984

The home team was fearsome at France 1984 and led for much of the semifinal until Portugal's Rui Jordão scored to take the game into overtime. He then went one better and scored again to give the Portuguese a shock lead in the 98th minute, but France was up to the challenge, and two late goals in a flurry of magnificent attacking play saw it through to the final, which it won against Spain.

DANISH MIRACLE, EURO 1992

Denmark failed to qualify for the 1992 European Championship, having trailed to Yugoslavia in its qualifying group. But as the Yugoslav civil war raged, international sanctions saw the Balkan side excluded from the tournament and its place given to the Danes. A solid defense backed by the huge presence of goalkeeper Peter Schmeichel saw Denmark claw its way into the knockout stages, before Brian Laudrup's sparky play helped it beat the Netherlands and then Germany in the final. Celebrations in Copenhagen closely followed Denmark's "no" vote in a referendum on the reforming of the European Union. The crowds were the largest to have gathered in the country since the end of World War II.

FRENCH DOUBLE, EURO 2000

The final of Euro 2000 was notable for its open play. Delvecchio gave Italy a 1–0 lead 10 minutes into the second half; rather than putting down the defensive shutters, the Italians took the game to France in a torrid exchange of chances in the second half. France was on the brink of defeat until Sylvain Wiltord squeezed the ball past Italy's Toldo deep into injury time. The momentum switched to France, and in the 103rd minute, France's Robert Pirès's sharp cut back from the Italian goal found David Trezeguet, who scored. France became the second team (after Germany) to hold the World Cup and European Championships at the same time.

YUGOSLAVIA VS. SPAIN, 2000

The group match between Yugoslavia and Spain was a pulsating, relentless game in which the Yugoslavs took the lead three times, but each time, Spain found an equalizer. Komljenovic made it 3–2 with just 15 minutes to go, but Mendieta equalized from the spot in the final minute. Deep into injury time, Alfonso fired a searing volley to make it 4–3 to the Spaniards.

SPANISH DELIGHT, EURO 2008

Euro 2008 was cohosted by Austria and Switzerland, neither of whom performed well. Italy was below par, and even the Dutch and Portuguese fell before the final. Germany, solid as ever, reached the final to meet Spain. The Spaniards played with uncommon aplomb and confidence—a close-fought match saw a single, brilliant goal from Fernando Torres give Spain its first international title since 1964.

DAVID TREZEGUET
France striker Trezeguet scored the Golden Goal in the Euro 2000 final that broke the deadlock and gave the French victory over Italy.

ANDRÉS INIESTA
A clever midfielder, Iniesta added trickery to Spain's metronomic passing. He won the man of the match award in all three of his country's successive major tournament victories.

RECORD BREAKERS, EURO 2012

Spain entered the 2012 tournament in Poland and Ukraine knowing that victory would make it the first team in the modern era to win three major trophies consecutively. It conceded only one goal en route to the final against Italy, who it overwhelmed with its precision passing. Spain cruised into the record books with a 4–0 victory, the biggest winning margin in the history of the competition. Vicente del Bosque—or The Most Illustrious The Marquis of Del Bosque, to give him his official title—became the first manager to have won the Champions League, the World Cup, and the European Championship.

18 Time (in minutes) taken for France's Michel Platini to score a hat trick against Yugoslavia in 1984

2 Number of countries to win the tournament three times—Germany and Spain

6 Most goals scored by a single player in Euro 2016—Antoine Griezmann, France

ICE-COOL ITALY, EURO 2020

Euro 2016 was the first to have 24 teams involved, with Portugal battling through to the final after surprisingly finishing third in their group. Once there, they caused another surprise by beating hosts France 1–0 in Paris. Euro 2020 was actually played in 2021, a year later than planned, because of the COVID-19 pandemic. The format for the 24 nations involved saw the games played around 11 host cities as part of the competition's 60th anniversary. Italy kept their nerve and beat England on penalties in the final match held in London, which gave them their second triumph in the tournament.

TROPHY CABINET

Pots, mugs, jugs, silverware, and brass—every soccer culture has its own slang for trophies, which reflects the importance of these objects in the professional game. The oldest national cup—the FA Cup—started a trend when the original trophy was stolen and reportedly melted down to make counterfeit coins. The same fate befell the first World Cup Trophy, too.

1.

2.

3.

4.

5.

6.

7.

8. **9.** **10.**

1. FIFA WORLD CUP TROPHY

The trophy for this world international competition depicts two human figures holding up the Earth.

2. WOMEN'S WORLD CUP

This world international competition was first played in 1991, but the current trophy was first presented to the US in 1999.

3. ASIA CUP TROPHY

When the trophy for this Asian international competition was won by Iraq in 2007, it was taken on a nationwide celebratory tour.

4. COPA AMÉRICA

This South American international competition boasts the oldest international soccer trophy in the world.

5. UEFA EUROPEAN CHAMPIONSHIPS TROPHY

This European international competition trophy was named after Henri Delaunay, the first General Secretary of UEFA.

6. GOLD CUP

This international competition is contested by Caribbean and Central and North American countries in the CONCACAF federation.

7. AFRICA CUP OF NATIONS

This is the trophy for the African international competition, which was first held in 1957 and has been held every two years since 1968.

8. FIFA CONFEDERATIONS CUP

This competition was contested by the winners of the six FIFA championship confederations and the Word Cup winner and host.

9. THE FIFA CLUB WORLD CUP

The trophy for this competition for champion clubs around the world was designed by family-run designers Thomas Fattorini Ltd.

10. UEFA CUP/EUROPA LEAGUE

This trophy is awarded to the winner of the competition held between European clubs and was first contested in 1971.

11. EUROPEAN CHAMPIONS CUP

Contested by elite European clubs, this trophy is nicknamed La Orejona (big ears) in Spanish because of the shape of the handles.

12. COPA LIBERTADORES

Contested by South American clubs, this competition pays homage to the main leaders of independence in South America.

11. **12.**

EUROPE

UEFA CHAMPIONS LEAGUE

COMPETITION:
UEFA CHAMPIONS
LEAGUE

TROPHY NAME:
EUROPEAN
CHAMPION
CLUBS' CUP

FOUNDED: 1955

CONFEDERATION:
UEFA

Although some in South America might disagree, the Champions League is the world's most important club competition. It is contested by the biggest teams, showcases the best players in the world, and attracts TV and sponsorship revenues that dwarf those of the Copa Libertadores. The financial and psychological rewards of victory are enormous—the winning team can expect to get more than $61.5 million (£50 million), and no great player feels complete until he has lifted "Old Big Ears."

CLARENCE SEEDORF is the only
player to win the men's Champions
League with three different clubs—
Ajax, Real Madrid, and AC Milan.

EUROPEAN IDEALS

Although European club contests were first played as far back as 1897, it was not until 1954 and a proposal by Gabriel Hanot, editor of French magazine *L'Équipe*, that a regular tournament was taken seriously. UEFA adopted the proposal, creating the European Cup for the 1955–1956 season. Entry was restricted to national champions and the previous year's winners.

LEAGUES APART

The European Cup became the UEFA Champions League in 1992 but its transformation came in 1995. UEFA, following the commercial lines of the FIFA World Cup, reorganized and rebranded the contest, centralizing sponsorship and TV sales, stadium standards, and match officiation. The UEFA Women's Champion League began in 2001–2002 as the Women's Cup, and was rebranded in 2009–2010.

UNLIKELY BEGINNINGS

The Champions League owes much to Wolverhampton Wanderers. Wolves beat Hungarian champions Honvéd 3–2 in December 1954, leading manager Stan Cullis to declare them "Champions of the World." Gabriel Hanot disagreed and persuaded UEFA to introduce a competition to settle the issue.

SIR MATT BUSBY
Manchester United
manager Sir Matt Busby
assembled a team bound
for European glory in
the 1950s, only to lose
seven players in the
Munich air disaster. He
recovered to build a side
that became the first
English club to win
the European
Cup in 1968.

STAT ATTACK

MOST APPEARANCES

Name	Club	Played
Cristiano RONALDO	Man Utd, R Madrid, Juventus	183
Iker CASILLAS	R Madrid, Porto	177
XAVI	Barcelona	151
Karim BENZEMA	Lyon, R Madrid	142
RAÚL	R Madrid, Schalke 04	142
Ryan GIGGS	Man Utd	141
Paolo MALDINI	Milan	139
Lionel MESSI	Barcelona	136

TOP GOAL SCORERS

Name	Club	Goals
Cristiano RONALDO	Man Utd, R Madrid, Juventus	140
Lionel MESSI	Barcelona, PSG	129
Robert LEWANDOWSKI	B Dortmund, Bayern Munich, Barcelona	91
Karim BENZEMA	Lyon, R Madrid	86
RAÚL	R Madrid, Schalke 04	71
Ruud VAN NISTELROOY	PSV, Man Utd, R Madrid	56

THE WINNERS

The European Cup has been won by Eastern European clubs just twice—Steaua Bucharest of Romania and Red Star Belgrade of Serbia. In the west, the nations who have won it comprise an exclusive club. All but two winners (Celtic and Marseilles) have come from just six nations: England, Germany, Holland, Italy, Portugal, and Spain.

PSV Eindhoven
Country: Netherlands
Winners: 1988

Celtic
Country: Scotland
Winners: 1967

Manchester United
Country: England
Winners: 1968, 1999, 2008

Nottingham Forest
Country: England
Winners: 1979, 1980

Liverpool
Country: England
Winners: 1977, 1978, 1981, 1984, 2005, 2019

Ajax
Country: Netherlands
Winners: 1971, 1972, 1973, 1995

Hamburg
Country: Germany
Winners: 1983

Aston Villa
Country: England
Winners: 1982

Borussia Dortmund
Country: Germany
Winners: 1997

Chelsea
Country: England
Winners: 2012, 2021

Feyenoord
Country: Netherlands
Winners: 1970

Steaua Bucharest
Country: Romania
Winners: 1986

Bayern Munich
Country: Germany
Winners: 1974, 1975, 1976, 2001, 2013, 2020

Olympique Marseille
Country: France
Winners: 1993

Porto
Country: Portugal
Winners: 1987, 2004

Juventus
Country: Italy
Winners: 1985, 1996

Red Star Belgrade
Country: Serbia and Montenegro (Yugoslavia)
Winners: 1991

Benfica
Country: Portugal
Winners: 1961, 1962

Real Madrid
Country: Spain
1956, 1957, 1958, 1959, 1960, 1966, 1998, 2000, 2002, 2014, 2016, 2017, 2018, 2022

Barcelona
Country: Spain
Winners: 1992, 2006, 2009, 2011, 2015

AC Milan
Country: Italy
Winners: 1963, 1969, 1989, 1990, 1994, 2003, 2007

Inter
Country: Italy
Winners: 1964, 1965, 2010

EUROPEAN EVOLUTION

Before any other side had a look in, Real Madrid had earned the right to keep the original trophy. It won five straight European Cups before being eliminated by archrival Barcelona in the first round of the 1960–1961 tournament. Since then, more than 20 teams have won the competition or its successor the Champions League, five of them on five or more occasions.

The knockout format of the European Cup remained unchanged until 1992, when a group stage was introduced and the competition was renamed the Champions League. Five years later, the rules were amended to admit teams finishing immediately behind the champions of their respective leagues. The highest ranking UEFA nations now receive up to four places in the competition each year.

ALESSANDRO MAZZOLA
A cross between a striker and a playmaker, the mustachioed Mazzola was a key member of the great Inter Milan side that won back-to-back European Cups in the mid-1960s.

REAL MADRID

Propelled by the sublime talents of Alfredo di Stéfano and Ferenc Puskás, Real Madrid had a monopoly on the first five European Cups. Although it won the trophy again in 1966, it had to wait another 32 years for its next success—defeating Juventus 1–0 in the 1998 final. Two years later, Madrid beat Valencia in the final, and in 2002, it collected its third Champions League title in five years with a superb Zinedine Zidane volley. Madrid has dominated the tournament in recent years, winning in 2014, 2016, 2017, 2018, and 2022.

10 Seconds it took Bayern Munich's Roy Makaay to score against Real Madrid in a 2007 tie

20 Unbeaten games in the competition, held by Ajax

136,505 Record attendance at a European Cup match—Celtic vs. Leeds United in 1970

40 Romanian fans who defected to the west after Steaua Bucharest won the 1986 final

11 Division One position of Aston Villa the year it won the European Cup

AC MILAN

With four European Cup and three Champions League titles, AC Milan has won the contest more times than any other club except Real Madrid. Its victories have also been more evenly spread out than those of its rivals, making AC Milan arguably the most consistent side in the history of the competition. The "Rossoneri" have a tradition of electing to wear their all-white away uniform for Champions League finals, having won six out of eight in those colors but only one out of three in their regular red-and-black uniform.

BENFICA 5, REAL MADRID 3

The two Iberian teams who lined up for the 1962 Final had won all the previous European Cups between them. The Spanish champions went into the interval 3–2 ahead, courtesy of a hat trick from Ferenc Puskás, but Benfica coach Béla Guttmann transformed the game at halftime by placing a man marker on the deep-lying Alfredo di Stéfano. This cut off Puskás' supply line and allowed Benfica to take control. The Portuguese equalized through a long-range strike from Coluna and clinched the contest with two goals from a 20-year-old Eusébio.

CRISTIANO RONALDO
Arguably the best player ever to don the Real Madrid jersey, Ronaldo was key to a string of the club's recent successes, including in the Champions League. His tally of 140 European goals, five Champions League trophies, and five Ballon d'Ors is nothing short of phenomenal.

AC MILAN 4, BARCELONA 0

Barcelona went into the 1994 final as favorites, having just won La Liga and boasting an awesome strike force of Hristo Stoichkov and Romário. Milan, by contrast, was in disarray, with defenders Franco Baresi and Alessandro Costacurta suspended and striker Marco Van Basten out with the ankle injury that ultimately ended his career. Nevertheless, Fabio Capello's team annihilated the Catalans 4–0 in a performance many regard as the greatest in the history of the competition.

FILIPPO INZAGHI
A forward with an uncanny ability to play off the shoulder of the last defender, "Pippo" Inzaghi scored both AC Milan goals in the club's victory over Liverpool in the 2007 final.

LIVERPOOL

The "Reds" won four European Cups between 1977 and 1984, three of them under slipper-wearing manager Bob Paisley. They would almost certainly have won more had their period of domination not ended in tragedy—rioting Liverpool fans caused 39 deaths ahead of the 1985 European Cup Final against Juventus at the Heysel Stadium in Brussels, leading UEFA to ban English clubs from its competitions for seven years. In 2005, Liverpool reached the summit of European soccer once more, overcoming a three-goal deficit to beat AC Milan in "The Miracle of Istanbul" (see pp.208–209).

LIVERPOOL WITHOUT EUROPEAN FOOTBALL IS LIKE
... A BANQUET WITHOUT WINE

ROY EVANS
LIVERPOOL DEFENDER (1965–1974) AND MANAGER (1994–1998)

THE MIRACLE OF ISTANBUL

The comeback of all time, the miracle of belief transmuted into victory; Liverpool's win in the 2005 final offered up every religious and magical metaphor. Utterly outplayed by AC Milan and down 3–0 at halftime, Liverpool appeared shattered but, in an extraordinary 15 minutes, clawed its way back to 3–3, held on in overtime, and won a nerve-jangling penalty shoot-out to claim its fifth European Cup (see pp.208–209).

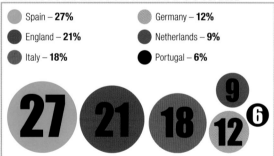

GRAEME SOUNESS
A fiercely competitive midfielder, Souness won three European Cups with Liverpool between 1978 and 1984. A superb passer, he was tough and elegant at the same time.

BAYERN MUNICH

The Bavarian giants swept all before them in the mid-1970s, winning three European Cups in succession. Spearheaded by goal-poacher extraordinaire Gerd Müller, they had quality all over the field and a peerless captain in sweeper Franz Beckenbauer. Bayern fans have had to endure final defeats in 1982, 1987, 1999, 2010, and 2012. However, they managed to win Europe's premier club trophy three times more in 2001, 2013, and 2020.

CHAMPIONS LEAGUE WINS BY COUNTRY

- Spain – **27%**
- Germany – **12%**
- England – **21%**
- Netherlands – **9%**
- Italy – **18%**
- Portugal – **6%**

27 **21** **18** **12** **9** **6**

MOST WINS BY CLUB

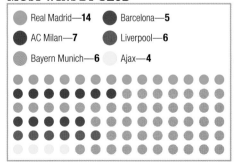

- Real Madrid—**14**
- Barcelona—**5**
- AC Milan—**7**
- Liverpool—**6**
- Bayern Munich—**6**
- Ajax—**4**

BARCELONA

Ronald Koeman's free kick, which clinched Barcelona's first European Cup victory in 1992, marked a euphoric end to the club's spell of weak performances. In 2009, under rookie coach Pep Guardiola, Barcelona won the treble of La Liga, Copa del Rey, and Champions League—the first Spanish club to do so. Barcelona was known for its unique style—called tiki-taka—which combined high-speed movement with fluid passing. The club made a record 993 passes against German side Borussia Mönchengladbach in a 2011 Champions League match, a game it went on to win. Barcelona has never been relegated from La Liga so far, a record it shares with rival Real Madrid.

EINTRACHT FRANKFURT
VS. REAL MADRID

Between 1956 and 1960, Real Madrid won the first five European cups, setting a standard of excellence and achievement, a pinnacle of sporting glamour and class, against which all future European triumphs would be measured. Real Madrid was not a tactical innovator nor possessed of a charismatic coach (it went through four in this period), but its squad was peerless, and its fight was legendary. The 1960 European Cup Final was its peak.

EINTRACHT FRANKFURT 3	REAL MADRID 7
FORMATION: 3-2-5	FORMATION: 3-2-5
MANAGER: PAUL OSSWALD	MANAGER: MIGUEL MUNOZ

HAMPDEN PARK, GLASGOW, SCOTLAND, MAY 18, 1960

ATTENDANCE: 134,000

REFEREE: JOHN MOWAT (SCOTLAND)

1 Loy
2 Lutz 5 Eigenbrodt 3 Höfer
4 Weilbächer 6 Stinka
7 Kress 8 Lindner 9 Stein 10 Pfaff 11 Meier

11 Gento 8 Del Sol 9 Di Stefano 10 Puskás 7 Canario
6 Zarraga 4 Vidal
3 Pachin 5 Santamaria 2 Marquitos
1 Dominguez

SUBS: None permitted

18 M

Eintracht Frankfurt (who had scored 12 goals in the semifinals) opens the scoring with a goal from striker Richard Kress, but it merely serves to rouse Real: 1–0.

In front of 134,000 supporters, Real Madrid's captain Zarraga (right) exchanges pennants with Eintracht Frankfurt captain Pfaff before the game.

0 M

Real takes the game straight back to Frankfurt, and after half an hour, Real center forward Di Stefano ties from short range at the far post after some good work down the right-hand side by Canario: 1–1.

30 M

Three minutes later, Real is ahead. Canario's shot, struck with the outside of his foot, spins from the grasp of the Frankfurt keeper Egon Loy, and Di Stefano pounces to fire the ball into the roof of the net: 2–1.

33 M

71 M

Real is now in control, and Puskás embarks on 40 minutes of brilliant play that brings four goals. The first of the four comes from a shot fired at a seemingly impossible angle, the second as a result of a controversial penalty. The third is a stooping header after a cross from Gento. Then, in the 71st minute, Puskás sends a rocket of a shot, struck on the turn, inside the post and just under the bar: 6–1.

72 M

Center forward Erwin Stein pulls a goal back for Frankfurt, but Di Stefano responds immediately: a pass from Puskás sees him head straight for goal, and he sends the ball flying past Loy: 7–2. A careless back pass by the Real defense lets Stein in again, but by now it is far too late, and Real claims the cup: 7–3.

EUROPE

UEFA EUROPA LEAGUE

COMPETITION:
UEFA EUROPA LEAGUE

NAME OF TROPHY:
THE BERTONI TROPHY

FOUNDED:
1955 (FAIRS CUP),
1971 (UEFA CUP),
2009 (EUROPA LEAGUE)

CONFEDERATION: UEFA

Formerly known as the UEFA Cup, Europe's second-most-important cup contest lacks the glamor of the Champions League but provides vital income for clubs involved. It gives "lesser" teams a shot at European glory and provides a safety net for clubs eliminated from the Champions League. To give the competition greater importance, the winner now qualifies for the following year's Champions League.

DINO BAGGIO
Midfielder Dino Baggio scored in two UEFA Cup finals for two different teams—for Juventus in 1993 and Parma in 1995, against his old club.

EXHIBITIONIST ORIGINS

The UEFA Cup grew out of the esoteric-sounding Inter-City Fairs Cup, a competition first played in the 1950s. It was devised by the Swiss magnate Ernst Thommen and was open to teams from cities that hosted international trade fairs. League position was irrelevant and a one-team-per-city rule applied, leading to the entry of artificial sides, such as a London XI.

THE 2001 FINAL

In a roller-coaster classic, Liverpool was two up against Alavés within 16 minutes and ahead 3–1 at halftime. The Spanish team pulled the score back to 4–4 but had two men sent off in overtime and conceded a "golden" own goal with penalties just four minutes away.

ONE CUP, MANY NAMES

The first Fairs Cup (1955–1958), which was won by Barcelona, was renamed the Runner's Up Cup in 1968, before UEFA took over the tournament in 1971–1972. Further changes have included the amalgamation of the contest with the UEFA Cup Winners' Cup in 1999 and the introduction of a group stage in 2004–2005.

THE NEW ERA—THE EUROPA LEAGUE

The UEFA Cup was renamed the UEFA Europa League from the 2009–2010 season. The qualification criteria also changed, with a range of methods of gaining entry. Teams finishing immediately below the qualifiers for the Champions League in their domestic divisions are awarded a place, as are the winners of the main, and in some countries the secondary, domestic cup competition. Three teams that top their domestic Fair Play leagues also gain a place, while clubs eliminated from the Champions League enter later. Four qualifying rounds precede a group stage in which teams play each other twice, followed by four knockout rounds and a final. The Europa Conference League, which is a level below the main competition, started in the 2021–2022 season.

JUANDE RAMOS
In 2007, Sevilla's manager Juande Ramos became only the second manager to lead his club to a second successive UEFA Cup win.

STAT ATTACK

COUNTRIES WITH MOST WINS

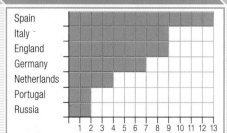

Spain, Italy, England, Germany, Netherlands, Portugal, Russia — 1 2 3 4 5 6 7 8 9 10 11 12 13

TOP GOAL SCORERS

Name	Club	Goals
Henrik LARSSON	Feyenoord, Helsingborg, Celtic	31
Klass Jan HUNTELAAR	Heerenveen Ajax, Schalke 04	30
Dietmar MULLER	FC Koln, VfB Stuttgart, Bordeaux	29
Aritz ADURIZ	Athletic Bilbao	26

THE WINNERS

During the 1980s and 1990s, the UEFA Cup seemed to belong to Italy—its clubs won it eight times between 1988 and 1999. Since then, Spain's second-tier clubs and the big teams from new powers Russia and Turkey have become champions.

IFK Göteborg
Country: Sweden
Winners: 1982, 1987

Zenit St. Petersburg
Country: Russia
Winners: 2008

Chelsea
Country: England
Winners: 2013, 2019

Ipswich Town
Country: England
Winners: 1981

Tottenham Hotspur
Country: England
Winners: 1972, 1984

Ajax
Country: Netherlands
Winners: 1992

Liverpool
Country: England
Winners: 1973, 1976, 2001

Schalke 04
Country: Germany
Winners: 1997

CSKA Moscow
Country: Russia
Winners: 2005

Manchester United
Country: England
Winners: 2017

Borussia Mönchengladbach
Country: Germany
Winners: 1975, 1979

Eintracht Frankfurt
Country: Germany
Winners: 1980, 2022

Shakhtar Donetsk
Country: Ukraine
Winners: 2009

Feyenoord
Country: Netherlands
Winners: 1974, 2002

PSV Eindhoven
Country: Netherlands
Winners: 1978

Bayern Munich
Country: Germany
Winners: 1996

RSC Anderlecht
Country: Belgium
Winners: 1983

Internazionale
Country: Italy
Winners: 1991, 1994, 1998

Porto
Country: Portugal
Winners: 2003, 2011

Atlético Madrid
Country: Spain
Winners: 2010, 2012, 2018

Villarreal
Country: Spain
Winners: 2021

Parma
Country: Italy
Winners: 1999, 1995

Valencia
Country: Spain
Winners: 2004

Bayer Leverkusen
Country: Germany
Winners: 1988

Sevilla
Country: Spain
Winners: 2006, 2007, 2014, 2015, 2016, 2020

Real Madrid
Country: Spain
Winners: 1985, 1986

Juventus
Country: Italy
Winners: 1977, 1990, 1993

Napoli
Country: Italy
Winners: 1989

Galatasaray
Country: Turkey
Winners: 2000

TEAMS WITH MOST WINS

Sevilla
Juventus
Internazionale
Liverpool
Atlético Madrid
Borussia Mönchengladbach
Tottenham

1 2 3 4 5 6

PAVEL POGREBNYAK
The Zenit St. Petersburg striker was top scorer in the 2007–2008 UEFA Cup, with 10 goals. He unfortunately missed his team's victory in the final.

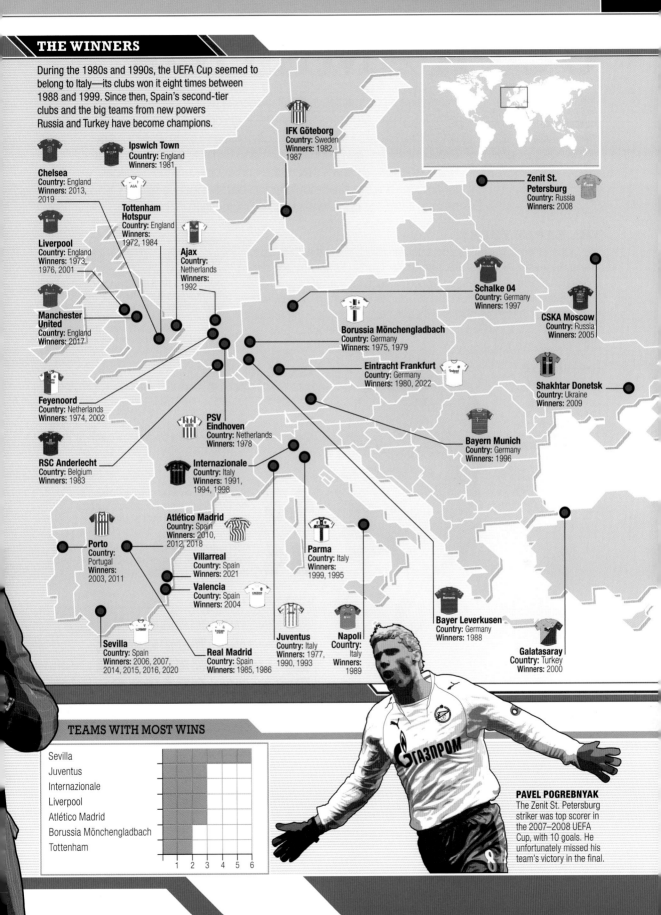

SOUTH AMERICA

COPA AMÉRICA

COMPETITION:
COPA AMÉRICA
FOUNDED: 1910
CONFEDERATION:
CONMEBOL

International competition in South America was under way as early as 1905, when Argentina and Uruguay competed for the Lipton Cup, donated by English tea merchant Sir Thomas Lipton. In 1910, the Argentine FA invited Uruguay, Chile, and Brazil to the first unofficial Copa América, six years before the continent even had a soccer federation. The first official outing was held in Buenos Aires in 1916, making it the first continental soccer competition in the world.

THE EARLY YEARS

The Copa América was playcd on a near-annual basis in the 1920s but took a six-year break in the 1930s while the sport in South America turned professional. The tournament continued throughout the 1950s and 1960s but took an eight-year break from 1967 due to Brazil and Argentina taking less interest in the tournament and their domestic clubs exerting pressure to retain players for the Copa Libertadores. It recommenced in 1975 as a finals-only tournament.

COPA 2007

Venezuela is one of the weaker South American soccer nations but finally hosted its first Copa América in 2007. Hugo Chávez, the country's former president, indulged in a spot of grandstanding, including an on-field kickaround with Diego Maradona and President Morales of Bolivia. But it was steely Brazil, flattening Argentina 3–0 in the final, who stole the limelight.

ALEXIS SANCHEZ
Sanchez has appeared for huge clubs such as Barcelona, Arsenal, Manchester United, and Inter Milan. He has made the most appearances for Chile and is also their record scorer. He netted the winning penalty in the 2015 Copa América, and then grabbed the Golden Ball at the 2016 event as Chile finished top again.

THE MODERN ERA

From 1987, the Copa was relaunched with TV broadcasting deals, sponsorship money, and a single host country every four years. Ten South American teams and two wild-card teams—such as Mexico or Japan—make up three groups of four. Group winners, runners-up, and the two best third-place teams qualify for the quarterfinals. Only ten teams took part in the 2021 Copa América in Brazil, which was rescheduled from 2020 due to COVID-19.

43 Number of minutes of overtime played in the 1919 final before Friedenreich scored the winner for Brazil against Uruguay

34 Most appearances in the Copa América, held jointly by Sergio Livingstone of Chile (1941–1953) and Zizinho of Brazil (1942–1957)

HOST NATIONS

Argentina—**9 times**
Uruguay—**7 times**
Chile—**7 times**
Peru, Brazil—**6 times**

STAT ATTACK

MOST TOURNAMENTS WON

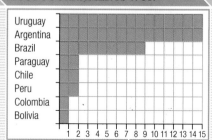

Uruguay
Argentina
Brazil
Paraguay
Chile
Peru
Colombia
Bolivia

1 2 3 4 5 6 7 8 9 10 11 12 13 14 15

TOP GOAL SCORERS

Name	Country	Goals
Norberto MÉNDEZ	Argentina	17
ZIZINHO	Brazil	17
Severino VARELA	Uruguay	15
Teodoro FERNÁNDEZ	Peru	15
Paolo GUERRERO	Peru	14
Eduardo VARGAS	Chile	14
Lionel MESSI	Argentina	13

THE COMPETITORS

Since the Copa América was relaunched as a tournament in 1987, the trophy has been well distributed throughout the continent—every CONMEBOL member has either hosted or won the tournament. Brazil, Argentina, and Uruguay are multiple winners, and Colombia took a single title, as host, in 2001.

THE SPREAD OF COPA AMÉRICA

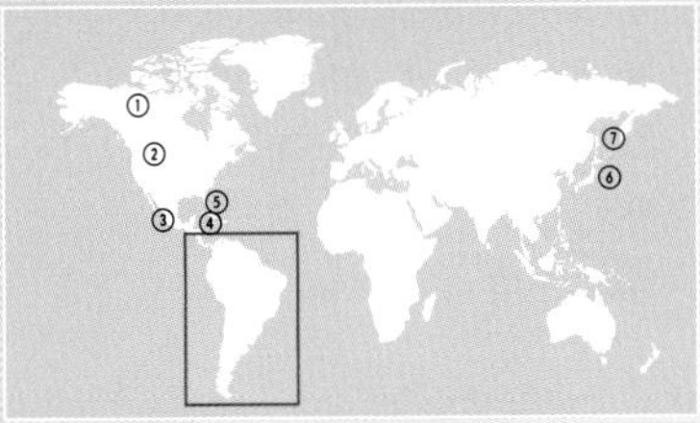

① Canada

② US
Year hosted: 2016

③ Mexico

④ Honduras

⑤ Costa Rica

⑥ Japan

⑦ South Korea

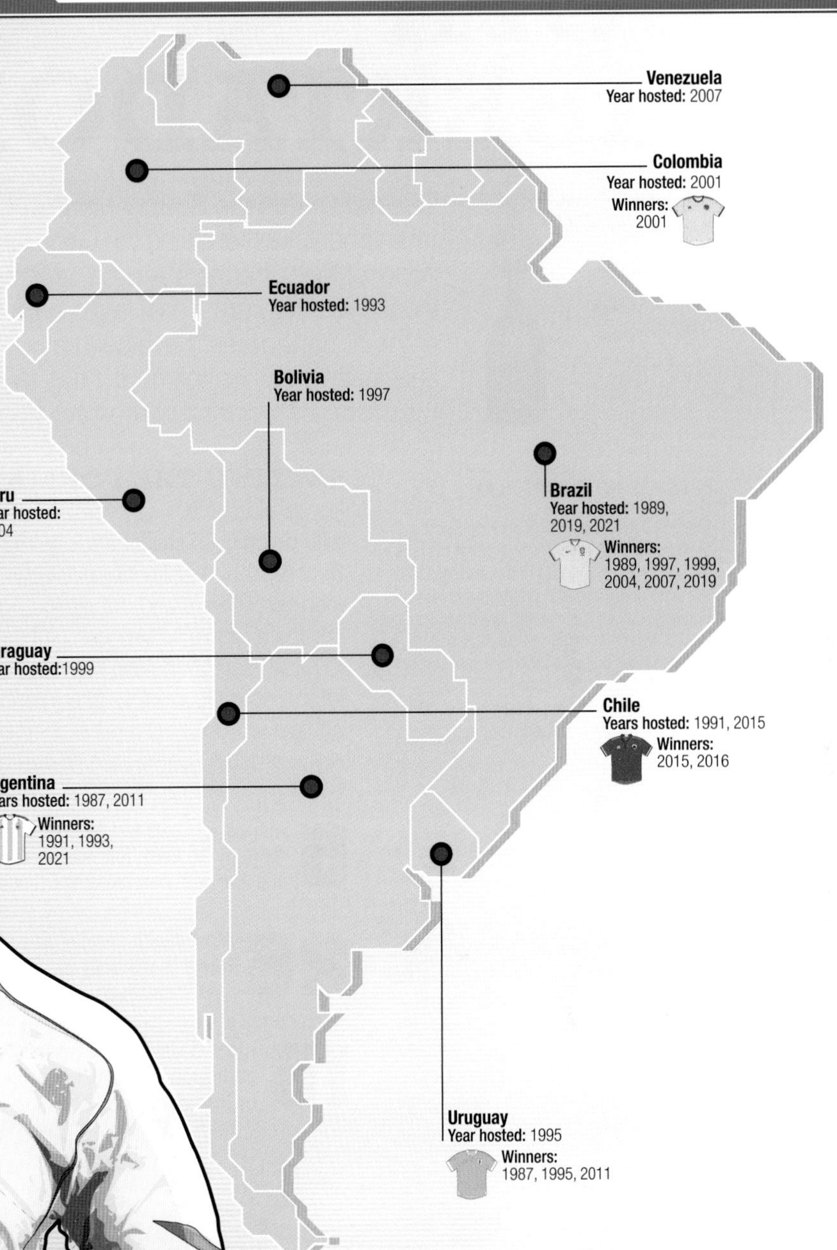

Venezuela
Year hosted: 2007

Colombia
Year hosted: 2001
Winners: 2001

Ecuador
Year hosted: 1993

Bolivia
Year hosted: 1997

Brazil
Year hosted: 1989, 2019, 2021
Winners: 1989, 1997, 1999, 2004, 2007, 2019

Peru
Year hosted: 2004

Paraguay
Year hosted:1999

Chile
Years hosted: 1991, 2015
Winners: 2015, 2016

Argentina
Years hosted: 1987, 2011
Winners: 1991, 1993, 2021

Uruguay
Year hosted: 1995
Winners: 1987, 1995, 2011

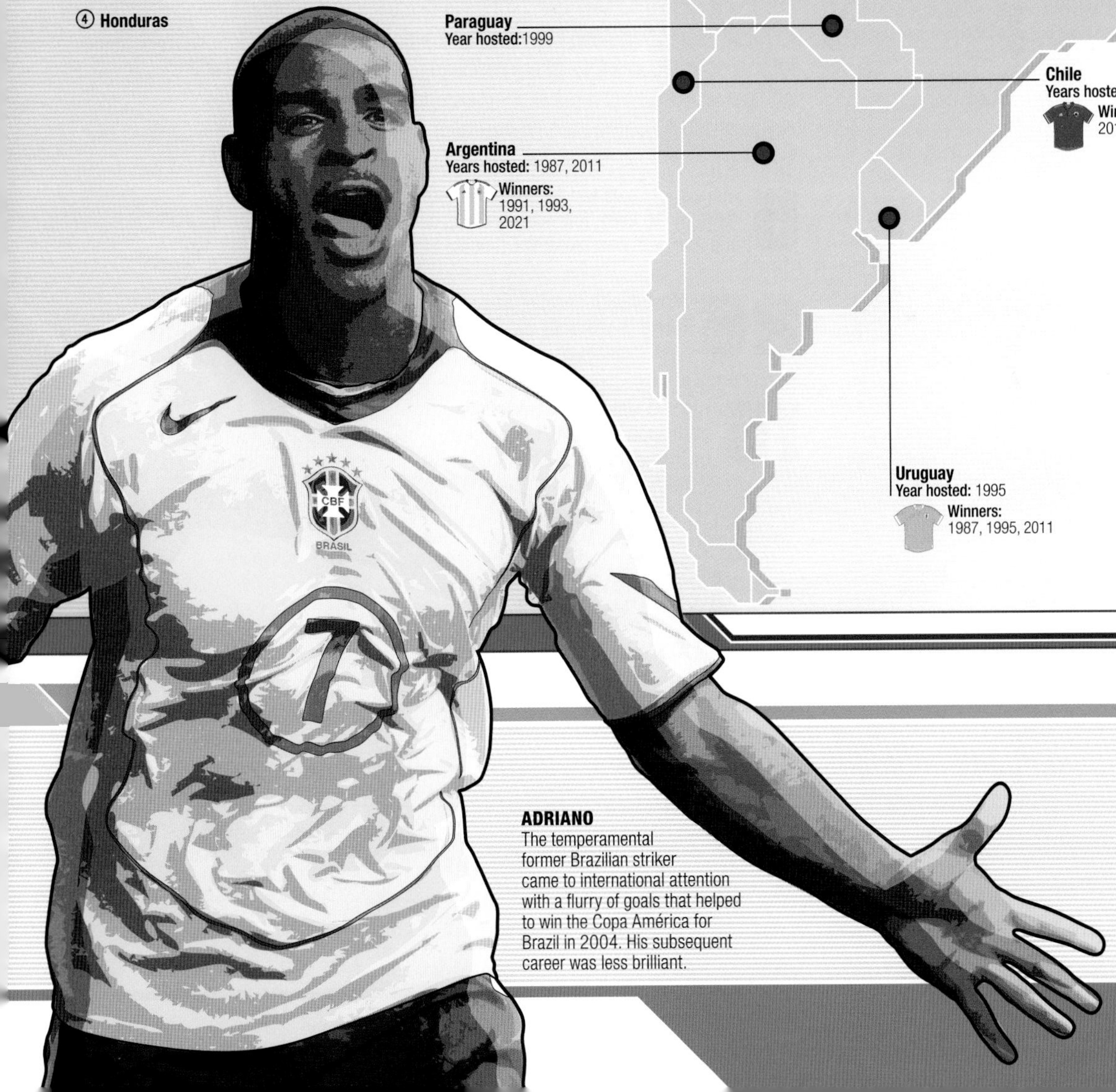

ADRIANO

The temperamental former Brazilian striker came to international attention with a flurry of goals that helped to win the Copa América for Brazil in 2004. His subsequent career was less brilliant.

SOUTH AMERICA

COPA LIBERTADORES

COMPETITION:
TAÇA LIBERTADORES
DA AMÉRICA
FOUNDED: 1960
CONFEDERATION:
CONMEBOL

Originally called the South American Championships, the tournament was renamed the Copa Libertadores in 1960 in honor of the "Liberators"—such as Simón Bolívar—who fought for independence from Spain in the early 19th century. Just as the ideas of the "Libertadores" have been a huge symbol for the pan-American imagination, so has the cup. It has also proved to be a field on which the continent's bitter rivalries have been staged and fought.

MISSILES INTERRUPT PLAY

The 1962 final saw Brazilian side Santos beat Peñarol of Uruguay 2–1 in the first leg. Peñarol was up 3–2 late in the second half of the second leg when the referee was knocked unconscious by a stone thrown from the crowd. He resumed the game after waking 40 minutes later, but when the assistant referee was hit by a second stone after a Santos equalizer, the goal was disallowed and the game abandoned. Santos won the playoff.

AN OPEN CONTEST

For most of the Libertadores' history, the cup has been dominated by teams from Brazil and Argentina. The Uruguayan teams—Peñarol and Nacional—were powers in the 1960s and 1970s but have not lifted the trophy since 1988. However, there remains room for smaller teams— Paraguayan champions Olimpia won its third Libertadores title in 2002; Once Caldas, a tiny Colombian provincial club, won in 2004; and LDU Quito from Ecuador triumphed in 2008.

SETTING THE FORMAT

It took almost 30 years for the format of the tournament to be established, with clubs from several nations regularly prevaricating on whether to enter. Brazilian teams asked for extra gate money, while Venezuelan sides were in, then out, then in and out again and have only recently begun to compete regularly. Mexican clubs were added in the 1990s to raise interest and the standard of the competition. The tournament is currently—after qualifying rounds—a 32-team contest with eight groups of four leading to a knockout stage of 16. All games are played over two legs.

5 Number of finals lost by Colombian player Anthony De Ávila, four with América di Cali and one with Barcelona of Ecuador

26 Most penalties taken in a shoot-out— Newell's Old Boys vs. América in the 1992 semifinals

15 Highest number of consecutive participations in the tournament, by Peñarol (1965–1979)

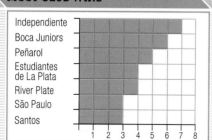

STAT ATTACK

MOST CLUB WINS

Independiente
Boca Juniors
Peñarol
Estudiantes de La Plata
River Plate
São Paulo
Santos

1 2 3 4 5 6 7 8

TOP GOAL SCORERS

Name	Club	Goals
Alberto SPENCER	Peñarol, Barcelona	54
Fernando MORENA	Peñarol	37
Pedro VIRGILIO ROCHA	Peñarol, São Paulo, Palmeiras	36
Daniel ONEGA	River Plate	31
Julio MORALES	Nacional	30

CARLOS TEVEZ
An explosive striker, Tevez hails from the poor barrio of Buenos Aires in Argentina. He made his mark on the soccer world as a teenager, winning the Copa Libertadores with Boca Juniors in 2003.

THE COMPETITORS

Unlike the UEFA Champions League, there still seems to be room for small clubs to win the Copa Libertadores, with Ecuador's LDU winning its first title in 2008, and Paraguay's Olimpia winning for a third time in 2002. However, clubs from the cities—Rio, São Paulo, Montevideo, and Buenos Aires—are the most frequent winners.

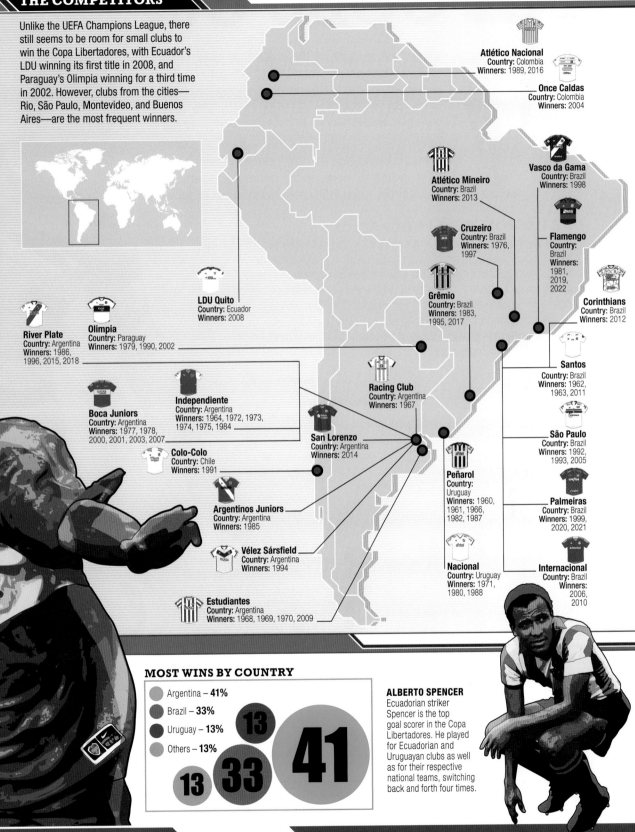

Atlético Nacional
Country: Colombia
Winners: 1989, 2016

Once Caldas
Country: Colombia
Winners: 2004

Vasco da Gama
Country: Brazil
Winners: 1998

Atlético Mineiro
Country: Brazil
Winners: 2013

Cruzeiro
Country: Brazil
Winners: 1976, 1997

Flamengo
Country: Brazil
Winners: 1981, 2019, 2022

Grêmio
Country: Brazil
Winners: 1983, 1995, 2017

Corinthians
Country: Brazil
Winners: 2012

Santos
Country: Brazil
Winners: 1962, 1963, 2011

São Paulo
Country: Brazil
Winners: 1992, 1993, 2005

Palmeiras
Country: Brazil
Winners: 1999, 2020, 2021

Internacional
Country: Brazil
Winners: 2006, 2010

LDU Quito
Country: Ecuador
Winners: 2008

Olimpia
Country: Paraguay
Winners: 1979, 1990, 2002

River Plate
Country: Argentina
Winners: 1986, 1996, 2015, 2018

Independiente
Country: Argentina
Winners: 1964, 1972, 1973, 1974, 1975, 1984

Boca Juniors
Country: Argentina
Winners: 1977, 1978, 2000, 2001, 2003, 2007

San Lorenzo
Country: Argentina
Winners: 2014

Racing Club
Country: Argentina
Winners: 1967

Colo-Colo
Country: Chile
Winners: 1991

Argentinos Juniors
Country: Argentina
Winners: 1985

Vélez Sársfield
Country: Argentina
Winners: 1994

Estudiantes
Country: Argentina
Winners: 1968, 1969, 1970, 2009

Peñarol
Country: Uruguay
Winners: 1960, 1961, 1966, 1982, 1987

Nacional
Country: Uruguay
Winners: 1971, 1980, 1988

MOST WINS BY COUNTRY

- Argentina – **41%**
- Brazil – **33%**
- Uruguay – **13%**
- Others – **13%**

13 13 33 41

ALBERTO SPENCER
Ecuadorian striker Spencer is the top goal scorer in the Copa Libertadores. He played for Ecuadorian and Uruguayan clubs as well as for their respective national teams, switching back and forth four times.

CONCACAF

THE GOLD CUP

COMPETITION: GOLD CUP
FOUNDED: 1963
CONFEDERATION: CONCACAF

Launched by CONCACAF in 1991 as its first truly pan-regional tournament, the Gold Cup has been hosted exclusively by the US, although contests have been cohosted with Mexico, Canada, Costa Rica, and Jamaica. It has grown from 8 to 16 teams, media coverage and crowds have been good, and since 2003, teams from outside the confederation have no longer been invited to make up the numbers. However, the tournament gains little recognition in the wider world.

ONE REGION, TWO FEDERATIONS

The first international soccer tournament held in the northern half of the Americas was a round of Olympic qualifiers in Havana, Cuba, in 1930. The organizers became the Confederación Centroamericana y del Caribe de Fútbol (CCCF) in 1938 and held their first official tournament in Costa Rica in 1941. It remained a Central American affair—few Caribbean nations could afford to travel, and Mexico, Canada, and the US played each other irregularly under the North Mexican Football Confederation.

BEGINNER'S LUCK

The tiny Caribbean island of Guadeloupe—a French province with a population of just 450,000—debuted at the 2007 Gold Cup. It got past the group stage by beating Canada, beat Honduras in the quarterfinal, and lost to Mexico in the semifinal by a single goal. Had it won the trophy, it would have forfeited the winner's place at the Confederations Cup, since it's not actually a member of FIFA.

LANDON DONOVAN

With 18 goals, Donovan is the US's leading scorer at the Gold Cup. Four of them came in a single game, when the US beat Cuba 5–0 in 2003. He scored another two against the Cubans in the 2005 tournament, too.

0 Number of minutes of live English-language soccer from the Gold Cup broadcast on US television in 2005

2 Times that the Netherlands Antilles reached the CONCACAF Championship semifinals

1991 Year the first Gold Cup final was settled on penalties—the US beat Honduras 4–3

3 Number of times Brazil has played in the Gold Cup

STAT ATTACK

COUNTRIES WITH MOST WINS

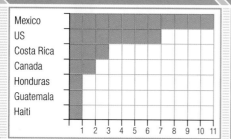

Mexico
US
Costa Rica
Canada
Honduras
Guatemala
Haiti

1 2 3 4 5 6 7 8 9 10 11

TOP GOAL SCORERS

Name	Country	Goals
Landon DONOVAN	US	18
Clint DEMPSEY	US	13
Andrés GUARDADO	Mexico	13
Luis Roberto ALVES	Mexico	12
Blas PÉREZ	Panama	11
Luis TEJADA	Panama	10

EARLY STAGES

With the creation of CONCACAF in 1963, a regular CONCACAF championship was staged. However, participation and enthusiasm was low, even when the competition was turned into the qualifying rounds for the region's World Cup places between 1973 and 1989.

PAULO WANCHOPE

The gangly, flaying legs of Paulo Wanchope may not have been elegant, but they helped him score 45 goals for Costa Rica and become a key figure in every World Cup and Gold Cup campaign in which he played.

HOME DISADVANTAGE

Playing at home is normally an advantage, but that wasn't the case for the US in the 1998 Gold Cup Final against Mexico in Los Angeles. The city's Latino community turned out in force to make the final more of a home game for Mexico. Uncharacteristically for games held in the US, the national anthem was booed, and a torrent of bottles and other debris was thrown onto the field. Buoyed by this support, Mexico won its third title in a row.

THE COMPETITORS

CONCACAF's early international competitions were small enough to be held in Central America and even on the larger Caribbean islands, but the advent of the Gold Cup has meant the US and Mexico have a stranglehold on hosting rights.

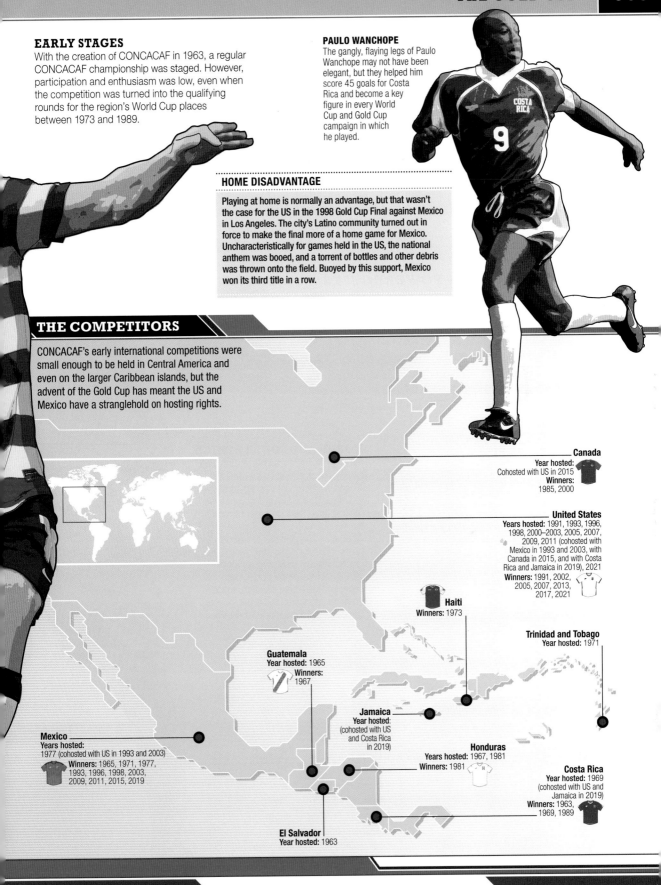

Canada
Year hosted:
Cohosted with US in 2015
Winners:
1985, 2000

United States
Years hosted: 1991, 1993, 1996, 1998, 2000–2003, 2005, 2007, 2009, 2011 (cohosted with Mexico in 1993 and 2003, with Canada in 2015, and with Costa Rica and Jamaica in 2019), 2021
Winners: 1991, 2002, 2005, 2007, 2013, 2017, 2021

Haiti
Winners: 1973

Trinidad and Tobago
Year hosted: 1971

Guatemala
Year hosted: 1965
Winners: 1967

Jamaica
Year hosted:
(cohosted with US and Costa Rica in 2019)

Honduras
Years hosted: 1967, 1981
Winners: 1981

Costa Rica
Year hosted: 1969
(cohosted with US and Jamaica in 2019)
Winners: 1963, 1969, 1989

Mexico
Years hosted:
1977 (cohosted with US in 1993 and 2003)
Winners: 1965, 1971, 1977, 1993, 1996, 1998, 2003, 2009, 2011, 2015, 2019

El Salvador
Year hosted: 1963

AFRICA CUP OF NATIONS

COMPETITION:
AFRICA CUP OF NATIONS
FOUNDED: 1957
CONFEDERATION: CAF

The Africa Cup of Nations is the continent's most celebrated and closely followed sports event. First contested in 1957 by just three teams, it now comprises 24 countries and is played every two years. It has acquired a high standing in global soccer and offers a window on Africa's extraordinary pool of talent, which European clubs are increasingly exploiting.

THE WEST AFRICAN POWERHOUSES

Although the first three Cup of Nations were won by founding members Egypt and Ethiopia, a change of guard occurred in 1963 when Ghana hosted the tournament and won in some style. Ghana went on to win one and lose two more finals in the 1960s and 1970s, first to Zaire and then to Brazzaville-Congo, before winning again in 1982. Nigeria soon rose to the fore, winning the trophy in 1980 and 1994, while Cameroon won in 1984, 1988, 2000, and 2002. The Ivory Coast completed the success for West Africa in 1992.

YAYA TOURÉ
A commanding presence in the Ivory Coast's midfield, Yaya Touré featured in three squads that made it to the final of the Africa Cup of Nations. His country was defeated in the first two finals by Egypt and then by Zambia before he finally won a winner's medal in 2015.

CROSSING THE DESERT

The biggest away crowd at the Africa Cup of Nations was at the 2004 Algeria vs. Egypt game in Sousse, Tunisia, when around 20,000 Algerians crossed the Sahara. Algeria went 1–0 up in the opening minutes only for Egypt to equalize, before Algeria had a player sent off. After holding on for most of the game, the Algerians sneaked a last-minute winner, which must have made the long road home a lot shorter.

NORTH AND SOUTH AFRICA

Although North African nations have not been quite as strong as they have in African club tournaments, Egypt has won the Africa Cup of Nations seven times, making them the tournament's most successful nation. Egypt, Tunisia, Algeria, and Nigeria have all won as hosts, in 2006, 2004, 1990, and 1980 respectively, while Morocco won in 1976. Southern Africa's only victory came in 1996 when, on short notice, South Africa hosted the event, beating Tunisia 2–0 in the Johannesburg final.

1970
Year that the tournament—held in Sudan—was first broadcast on television

21
Number of penalties required to separate the Ivory Coast and Ghana in the 1992 final, which the Ivory Coast won 11–10

STAT ATTACK

COUNTRIES WITH MOST WINS

Egypt
Cameroon
Ghana
Nigeria
DR Congo
Ivory Coast
Algeria

1 2 3 4 5 6 7

TOP GOAL SCORERS

Player	Country	Goals
Samuel ETO'O	Cameroon	18
Laurent POKOU	Ivory Coast	14
Rashidi YEKINI	Nigeria	13
Hassan EL-SHAZLY	Egypt	12
Hossam HASSAN	Egypt	11
Patrick MBOMA	Cameroon	11
Didier DROGBA	Ivory Coast	11

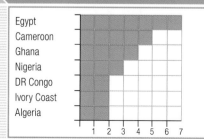

THE COMPETITORS

Winners and hosts have tended to come from West and North Africa, although the tournaments held in Mali and Burkina Faso have shown that CAF is ready to award hosting rights to less-developed nations. The 2010 contest in Angola was the first Southern African tournament since South Africa in 1996.

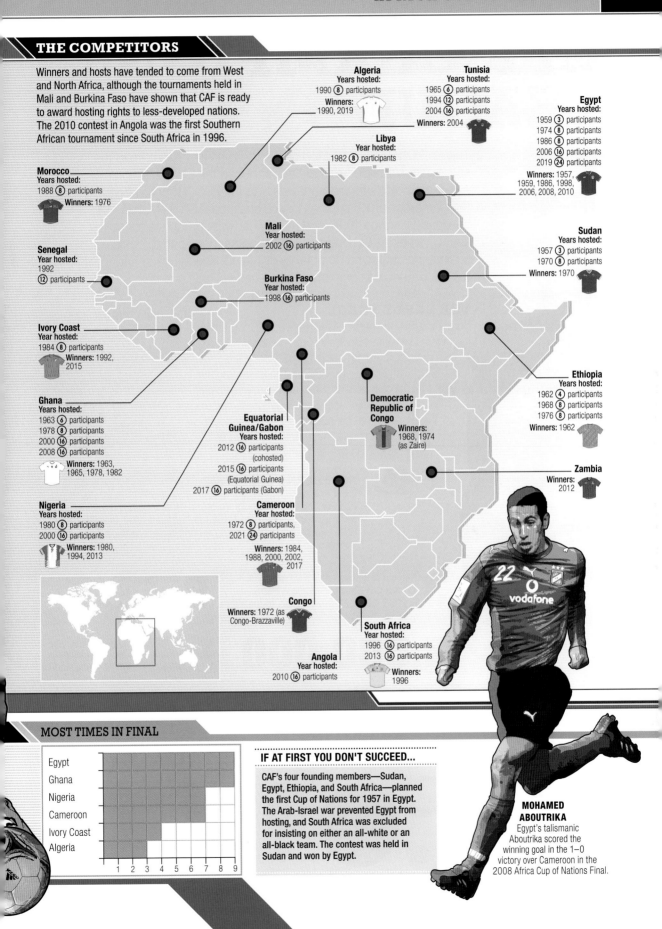

Algeria
Years hosted:
1990 (8) participants
Winners:
1990, 2019

Tunisia
Years hosted:
1965 (6) participants
1994 (12) participants
2004 (16) participants
Winners: 2004

Egypt
Years hosted:
1959 (3) participants
1974 (8) participants
1986 (8) participants
2006 (16) participants
2019 (24) participants
Winners: 1957, 1959, 1986, 1998, 2006, 2008, 2010

Libya
Year hosted:
1982 (8) participants

Morocco
Years hosted:
1988 (8) participants
Winners: 1976

Mali
Year hosted:
2002 (16) participants

Sudan
Years hosted:
1957 (3) participants
1970 (8) participants
Winners: 1970

Senegal
Year hosted:
1992
(12) participants

Burkina Faso
Year hosted:
1998 (16) participants

Ivory Coast
Year hosted:
1984 (8) participants
Winners: 1992, 2015

Ghana
Years hosted:
1963 (6) participants
1978 (8) participants
2000 (16) participants
2008 (16) participants
Winners: 1963, 1965, 1978, 1982

Equatorial Guinea/Gabon
Years hosted:
2012 (16) participants (cohosted)
2015 (16) participants (Equatorial Guinea)
2017 (16) participants (Gabon)

Democratic Republic of Congo
Winners: 1968, 1974 (as Zaire)

Ethiopia
Years hosted:
1962 (4) participants
1968 (8) participants
1976 (8) participants
Winners: 1962

Zambia
Winners: 2012

Nigeria
Years hosted:
1980 (8) participants
2000 (16) participants
Winners: 1980, 1994, 2013

Cameroon
Year hosted:
1972 (8) participants,
2021 (24) participants
Winners: 1984, 1988, 2000, 2002, 2017

Congo
Winners: 1972 (as Congo-Brazzaville)

South Africa
Year hosted:
1996 (16) participants
2013 (16) participants
Winners: 1996

Angola
Year hosted:
2010 (16) participants

MOST TIMES IN FINAL

	1	2	3	4	5	6	7	8	9
Egypt									
Ghana									
Nigeria									
Cameroon									
Ivory Coast									
Algeria									

IF AT FIRST YOU DON'T SUCCEED...

CAF's four founding members—Sudan, Egypt, Ethiopia, and South Africa—planned the first Cup of Nations for 1957 in Egypt. The Arab-Israel war prevented Egypt from hosting, and South Africa was excluded for insisting on either an all-white or an all-black team. The contest was held in Sudan and won by Egypt.

MOHAMED ABOUTRIKA
Egypt's talismanic Aboutrika scored the winning goal in the 1–0 victory over Cameroon in the 2008 Africa Cup of Nations Final.

AFRICA

CAF CHAMPIONS LEAGUE

COMPETITION: CAF CHAMPIONS LEAGUE
FOUNDED: 1964
CONFEDERATION: CAF

The CAF Champions League was first played in 1964, born of the same pan-African ideals that had produced the Cup of Nations. A four-team finals tournament was held in Accra, Ghana, where the Cameroonian champions Oryx Douala beat Stade Malian. Held continuously since 1996, and relaunched with group stages as the CAF Champions League in 1997, the contest has had to battle against the costs and complexity of intercontinental travel and the poor resources of many clubs—even national champions.

THE EARLY YEARS

During the first 15 years of its existence, the tournament was a West and Central African preserve, with victorious teams hailing from Ghana, Zaire, Cameroon, and Guinea. The first victory for a club outside these regions came in 1981, when JS Kabylie, the Algerian Berber side, swept aside AS Vita of Zaire to announce the arrival of the full force of North African soccer in the tournament.

THIRD TIME UNLUCKY

The 1967 final was played between Asante Kotoko of Ghana and TP Mazembe of Zaire. Drawn after two games and with no provision for penalties, a third match was required. However, the message did not reach Asante Kotoko, who did not show up for the final game. TP Mazembe did, and won the title.

NORTHERN DOMINANCE

Every final—except for Asante Kotoko's victory in 1983—was won by a side from the northern half of Africa until Orlando Pirates, the giants of a newly post-apartheid South Africa, took the title in 1995. South African clubs have generally struggled in the competition ever since. One exception was Mamelodi Sundowns' 3–0 victory over Zamalek in the 2016 final.

3 Number of times Al-Ahly have won back to back CAF Champions League titles—in 2005–2006, 2012–2013, and 2020–2021

8 Number of times Ghanaian clubs have lost a CAF Champions League final

2,500,000 Amount of prize money received in US dollars, by the CAF Champions League winner Espérance Sportive de Tunis, in 2019

HOSSAM HASSAN
Former Egyptian striker Hassan, uniquely, won the CAF Champions League with both of the mighty Cairo rivals, Al Ahly in 1987 and Zamalek in 2002.

STAT ATTACK

PRIZE MONEY

Prize money compared to winners of the 2009 Champions League.

● ES Tunis—
US $2.5 million

● Liverpool—
US $61.5 million

61.5

2.5

COUNTRIES WITH MOST WINS

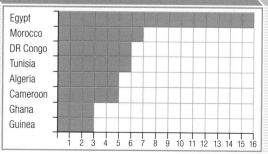

	1	2	3	4	5	6	7	8	9	10	11	12	13	14	15	16
Egypt																
Morocco																
DR Congo																
Tunisia																
Algeria																
Cameroon																
Ghana																
Guinea																

THE MODERN ERA

Since the contest was rebranded the CAF Champions League in 1997, there have been wins for West African teams ASEC Abidjan of the Ivory Coast and two for Nigeria's Enyimba. North African and, above all, Egyptian teams remain the dominating force. Al Ahly made it 9 in 2020 and, along with Zamalek and Ismaily's victories, took the total for Egyptian sides to 15. The competition has increased its levels of prize money, sponsorship, and television coverage but suffers in the latter from competition with the UEFA Champions League, where many leading African players are playing, as well as with the Copa Libertadores.

PRESIDENTIAL SELECTION

Hafia Conakry, from the Guinean capital, won the cup three times (1972, 1975, and 1977). The team was effectively the club of Guinea's populist president Sékou Touré, who ensured that the best players stayed with the club. On their return from the 1976 final, which they had lost to Mouloudia d'Alger, a number of the team members were sent to the infamous Camp Boiro for "political reeducation." When they lost the 1978 final to Canon Yaoundé, the increasingly erratic Sékou Touré issued a decree that seven of the players should be put in irons.

THE WINNERS

Nearly all of the winners of the CAF Champions League are located on the coast of Africa or on the continent's navigable rivers; even the inland teams are not far from the coast. Only TP Mazembe in the Democratic Republic of Congo is truly from the interior of Africa.

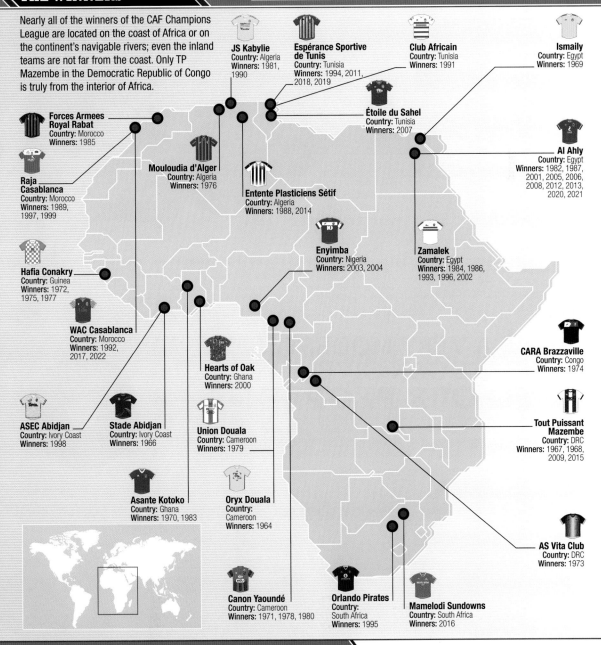

JS Kabylie
Country: Algeria
Winners: 1981, 1990

Espérance Sportive de Tunis
Country: Tunisia
Winners: 1994, 2011, 2018, 2019

Club Africain
Country: Tunisia
Winners: 1991

Ismaily
Country: Egypt
Winners: 1969

Étoile du Sahel
Country: Tunisia
Winners: 2007

Al Ahly
Country: Egypt
Winners: 1982, 1987, 2001, 2005, 2006, 2008, 2012, 2013, 2020, 2021

Forces Armees Royal Rabat
Country: Morocco
Winners: 1985

Mouloudia d'Alger
Country: Algeria
Winners: 1976

Raja Casablanca
Country: Morocco
Winners: 1989, 1997, 1999

Entente Plasticiens Sétif
Country: Algeria
Winners: 1988, 2014

Enyimba
Country: Nigeria
Winners: 2003, 2004

Zamalek
Country: Egypt
Winners: 1984, 1986, 1993, 1996, 2002

Hafia Conakry
Country: Guinea
Winners: 1972, 1975, 1977

WAC Casablanca
Country: Morocco
Winners: 1992, 2017, 2022

Hearts of Oak
Country: Ghana
Winners: 2000

CARA Brazzaville
Country: Congo
Winners: 1974

ASEC Abidjan
Country: Ivory Coast
Winners: 1998

Stade Abidjan
Country: Ivory Coast
Winners: 1966

Union Douala
Country: Cameroon
Winners: 1979

Tout Puissant Mazembe
Country: DRC
Winners: 1967, 1968, 2009, 2015

Asante Kotoko
Country: Ghana
Winners: 1970, 1983

Oryx Douala
Country: Cameroon
Winners: 1964

AS Vita Club
Country: DRC
Winners: 1973

Canon Yaoundé
Country: Cameroon
Winners: 1971, 1978, 1980

Orlando Pirates
Country: South Africa
Winners: 1995

Mamelodi Sundowns
Country: South Africa
Winners: 2016

ASIA

AFC ASIAN CUP

COMPETITION: AFC ASIAN CUP
FOUNDED: 1956
CONFEDERATION: AFC

First held in 1956 as a mini-league of just four teams, the AFC Asian Cup has grown into a 24-team tournament held every four years that attracts ever-bigger Asian TV audiences and sponsorship packages. The tournament has further grabbed the limelight by rescheduling into odd years and has benefitted hugely from avoiding a clash with the major Olympic, FIFA, and UEFA tournaments.

THE EARLY YEARS

The crown of Asian soccer has been passed around the continent for more than a decade. In the late 1950s and early 1960s, South Korea and Israel shared the laurels, but Iran came on the scene in the late 1960s, winning every game on the way to three tournaments in a row. With Iran consumed by the 1979 Islamic Revolution and Israel expelled from the AFC, Arab nations came to dominate—Saudi Arabia went on to win three titles.

ALI DAEI
Known simply as "The King" in Iran, Daei is the all-time top scorer in the AFC Asian Cup. However, in three Asian Cups, Daei's Iran made it only as far as the semifinals.

LEBANON 2000

Showing grace under fire, Lebanon managed to host the AFC Asian Cup during a brief interlude between the country's civil wars. Despite the fighting in nearby Gaza and the West Bank, and the kidnapping of Israeli soldiers by Hezbollah on the Israel-Lebanon border, the games went on. The home team departed after the first round while Japan, scoring an amazing 21 goals, romped to victory.

JAPAN

The steady progress of domestic soccer in Japan in the 1990s bore fruit with victories in the AFC Asian Cup in 1992, 2000, 2004, and 2011. The victory at the 2004 tournament, which was held in China, was all the more remarkable for the anti-Japanese vitriol that came from the bleachers in every city in which Japan played. The final was played against China in a hostile Workers Stadium in Beijing, and after Japan triumphed 3–1, the Chinese fans went on an anti-Japanese riot in the aftermath of the defeat.

THIS IS A VERY MODEST THING WE CAN GIVE TO OUR PEOPLE

NOOR SABRI
IRAQI GOALKEEPER ON MAKING IT TO THE FINAL OF THE 2007 AFC ASIAN CUP

MOST WINS BY COUNTRY

- Japan—**25%**
- Iran—**19%**
- Saudi Arabia—**19%**
- South Korea—**13%**
- Others—**25%**

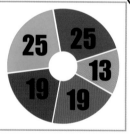

25 25 13 19 19

STAT ATTACK

COUNTRIES WITH MOST WINS

Japan
Saudi Arabia
Iran
South Korea
Israel
Kuwait
Iraq
Australia

1 2 3 4

TOP GOAL SCORERS

Player	Country	Goals
Ali DAEI	Iran	14
Lee DONG-GOOK	South Korea	10
Ali MABKHOUT	UAE	9
Almoez ALI	Qatar	9
Naohiro TAKAHARA	Japan	9
Jasem AL-HUWAIDI	Kuwait	8
Younis MAHMOUD	Iraq	8

THE TOURNAMENTS

The cohosting of the 2007 AFC Asian Cup by Vietnam, Thailand, Malaysia, and Indonesia greatly enlarged the pool of tournament winners and hosts. Israel is no longer a member of the AFC, having joined UEFA in 2002, while Australia joined the AFC in 2006 and hosted the tournament in 2015.

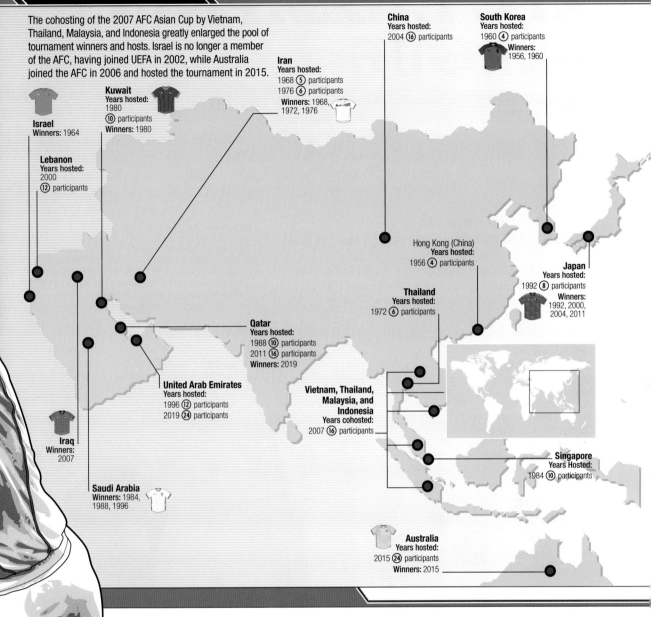

China
Years hosted:
2004 ⑯ participants

South Korea
Years hosted:
1960 ④ participants
Winners:
1956, 1960

Iran
Years hosted:
1968 ⑤ participants
1976 ⑥ participants
Winners: 1968, 1972, 1976

Kuwait
Years hosted:
1980
⑩ participants
Winners: 1980

Israel
Winners: 1964

Lebanon
Years hosted:
2000
⑫ participants

Hong Kong (China)
Years hosted:
1956 ④ participants

Japan
Years hosted:
1992 ⑧ participants
Winners:
1992, 2000, 2004, 2011

Thailand
Years hosted:
1972 ⑥ participants

Qatar
Years hosted:
1988 ⑩ participants
2011 ⑯ participants
Winners: 2019

United Arab Emirates
Years hosted:
1996 ⑫ participants
2019 ㉔ participants

Vietnam, Thailand, Malaysia, and Indonesia
Years cohosted:
2007 ⑯ participants

Singapore
Years Hosted:
1984 ⑩ participants

Iraq
Winners: 2007

Saudi Arabia
Winners: 1984, 1988, 1996

Australia
Years hosted:
2015 ㉔ participants
Winners: 2015

ASIAN MINNOWS
The expansion of the AFC Asian Cup to 24 teams has ushered in a host of smaller nations. First-timer nations include Guam, Kazakhstan, Turkmenistan, Uzbekistan, Tajikistan, Kyrgyzstan, Vietnam, Yemen, and the Maldives in 1996; Palestine, Laos, Bhutan, and Mongolia in 2000; and Timor-Leste in 2004.

BITTERSWEET VICTORY
Iraq was the surprise team at the 2007 AFC Asian Cup, beating Australia and South Korea then Saudi Arabia in the final. Tragically, two bombs exploded in Baghdad during celebrations for the semifinal victory, killing more than 50 people and injuring 150.

500 Number of spectators at Iraq vs. Oman in Bangkok at the 2007 tournament

3 Number of Brazilians who have won the AFC Asian Cup as coach—Carlos Alberto Parreira (twice), Zico, and Jorvan Vieira

1,020,050 Total attendance at the 2004 Asian Cup in China—a tournament record, with an average attendance of 31,877 per game

1 Number of Asian Cup appearances by Burma (in 1968)

ASIA

AFC CHAMPIONS LEAGUE

COMPETITION:
AFC CHAMPIONS LEAGUE
FOUNDED: 1967
REGION: AFC

The Asian Champions League, which was relaunched and reformatted by the AFC in 2002, is the leading competition for club sides in Asia. It has since grown from 16 to 40 clubs and has been dominated by South Korean, Japanese, and Saudi Arabian clubs, who have won six titles. In recent times, however, the rise of Chinese teams and the inclusion of Australian teams has made the tournament more competitive.

TEETHING PROBLEMS

Gathering together the leading clubs from a continent as vast as Asia proved to be an economic and logistical challenge. The AFC launched the Asian Champion Club Tournament in 1967 with mini-leagues at a single location, but the competition folded four years later after just two contests in Tehran and Bangkok. The 1970 final was abandoned when the Iraqi police team, Al-Shorta, refused to play Israel's Maccabi Tel Aviv.

THIRD TIME LUCKY

The tournament was relaunched as the Asian Club Championship in 1985 with qualifying rounds and a finals tournament. The first outing was held in Jeddah, Saudi Arabia, and was won by South Korea's Daewoo Royals, but the contest still faced two problems—high transportation costs and a gulf in quality between the clubs. Both were addressed when the third incarnation of the competition was launched—the AFC Champions League—in 2002. Higher sponsorship allowed transportation subsidies, and the bulk of the places in the tournament were allocated to the strongest nations.

HIGHLY ORGANIZED FANS' ORGANIZATION

Urawa Red Diamonds of Japan have some of the noisiest—and best-organized—supporters in Asia. The choreography for the second leg of the 2007 AFC Champions League Final against Sepahan of Iran was extraordinary, with the entire stadium decked out in red and white stripes and stars—an effect created from the plastic squares left on every seat. Urawa went on to win 2–0 and take the title.

KIM DO-HOON
One of South Korea's most famous players, Kim Do-Hoon was the top scorer in the 2004 AFC Champions League, playing for Seongnam Ilhwa Chunma, and was the competition's top scorer during its Club Championship phase.

MOST WINS BY COUNTRY

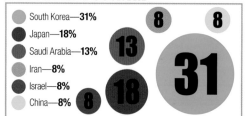

- South Korea—**31%**
- Japan—**18%**
- Saudi Arabia—**13%**
- Iran—**8%**
- Israel—**8%**
- China—**8%**

8 8 13 31 8 18

STAT ATTACK

TOP GOAL SCORERS

Player	Club	Goals
Dejan DAMJANOVIĆ	FC Seoul, Beijing Guoan, Suwon Samsung Bluewings, Kitchee SC	42
L. DONG-GOOK	Jeonbuk Hyundai Motors	37
Nasser AL-SHAMRANI	Al-Shabab, Al-Hilal, Al-Ain, Al-Ittihad	32
ELKESON	Guangzhou Evergrande, Shanghai SIPG	29

MOST MATCHES WON

Club	Country	Wins
Al-Hilal	Saudi Arabia	69
Jeonbuk Hyundai Motors	South Korea	64
Al-Ittihad	Saudi Arabia	49
Al-Ain	UAE	45
Pakhtakor	Uzbekistan	43
Guangzhou Evergrande	China	40

RINGING THE CASH REGISTERS

The AFC Champions League has become an increasingly businesslike affair. The AFC has secured elite corporate sponsorship and increased the annual prize money to $14.5 million (£9.8 million), more than three times the prize pot of the African equivalent—though still small compared to Europe and Latin America. Television coverage across the region is also growing since broadcasting is a condition of participation, with major networks carrying the tournament from Beirut to Tokyo and in Adelaide to Melbourne.

AL-HILAL 3, JÚBILO IWATA 2

Saudi Arabian champions Al-Hilal declined the chance to play in the final against Japanese side Yomiuri in the 1988 AFC Champions Cup. In 2000, however, they did show up to play a final against Japan's Júbilo Iwata. The Saudis were down 2–1 for nearly the whole game until their Brazilian striker Ricardo scored a second goal in the final minute of the game, forcing overtime. He made it a hat trick in overtime to secure the title for Al-Hilal.

2003 Year the tournament was canceled due to the SARS virus in Asia and the Iraq War

2,250,000 Prize money, in dollars, for winning the 2012 AFC Champions League

6 Number of Asian soccer associations that don't participate in the AFC Champions League—Laos, Timor-Leste, Afghanistan, Bhutan, Mongolia, and Chinese Taipei

3 Number of back-to-back defenses of the title: Al-Ittihad (2004–2005), Thai Farmers Bank (1994–1995), and Suwon Samsung Bluewings (2001–2002)

THE WINNERS

The AFC Champions League pits western against eastern Asia. South Asia, where cricket is king, has yet to produce any serious challenger in the tournament. With Israel now in Europe, the western challenge has come from the Gulf and Iran; in the east from Japan, South Korea, and China.

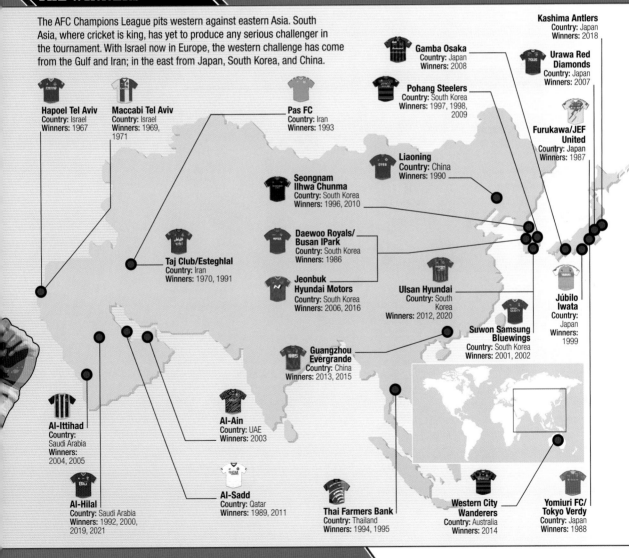

Kashima Antlers
Country: Japan
Winners: 2018

Urawa Red Diamonds
Country: Japan
Winners: 2007

Gamba Osaka
Country: Japan
Winners: 2008

Pohang Steelers
Country: South Korea
Winners: 1997, 1998, 2009

Furukawa/JEF United
Country: Japan
Winners: 1987

Hapoel Tel Aviv
Country: Israel
Winners: 1967

Maccabi Tel Aviv
Country: Israel
Winners: 1969, 1971

Pas FC
Country: Iran
Winners: 1993

Liaoning
Country: China
Winners: 1990

Seongnam Ilhwa Chunma
Country: South Korea
Winners: 1996, 2010

Taj Club/Esteghlal
Country: Iran
Winners: 1970, 1991

Daewoo Royals/Busan IPark
Country: South Korea
Winners: 1986

Jeonbuk Hyundai Motors
Country: South Korea
Winners: 2006, 2016

Ulsan Hyundai
Country: South Korea
Winners: 2012, 2020

Júbilo Iwata
Country: Japan
Winners: 1999

Suwon Samsung Bluewings
Country: South Korea
Winners: 2001, 2002

Guangzhou Evergrande
Country: China
Winners: 2013, 2015

Al-Ittihad
Country: Saudi Arabia
Winners: 2004, 2005

Al-Ain
Country: UAE
Winners: 2003

Al-Hilal
Country: Saudi Arabia
Winners: 1992, 2000, 2019, 2021

Al-Sadd
Country: Qatar
Winners: 1989, 2011

Thai Farmers Bank
Country: Thailand
Winners: 1994, 1995

Western City Wanderers
Country: Australia
Winners: 2014

Yomiuri FC/Tokyo Verdy
Country: Japan
Winners: 1988

CLUB WORLD CUP

COMPETITION:
CLUB WORLD CUP
FOUNDED: 1960
REGION: GLOBAL

The FIFA Club World Cup is now an annual seven-team competition between the winners of each of the Champions Leagues plus the host nation's champion team. It grew out of the Intercontinental Cup, created in 1960 as a two-leg tie between the winners of the European Cup and the Copa Libertadores.

GOING INTERCONTINENTAL

Henri Delaunay, first general secretary of UEFA, proposed an annual contest in 1958 between the winner of the European Cup and the champions of South America. The Copa Libertadores commenced in 1960, providing a South American champion, and Real Madrid beat Peñarol in the first Intercontinental Cup that year.

TONI KROOS
All-action midfielder Kroos has picked up the Club World Cup a record five times—four times with Real Madrid, in 2014, 2016, 2017, and 2018, and once with Bayern Munich in 2013.

EUROPEAN WINNERS

Italian clubs have proved the best at following European success with World Championship glory—the big three having won nine titles between them. Guile, patience, and steel was often required to win the title. English clubs, by contrast, have been far less successful.

*Club World Championship winners

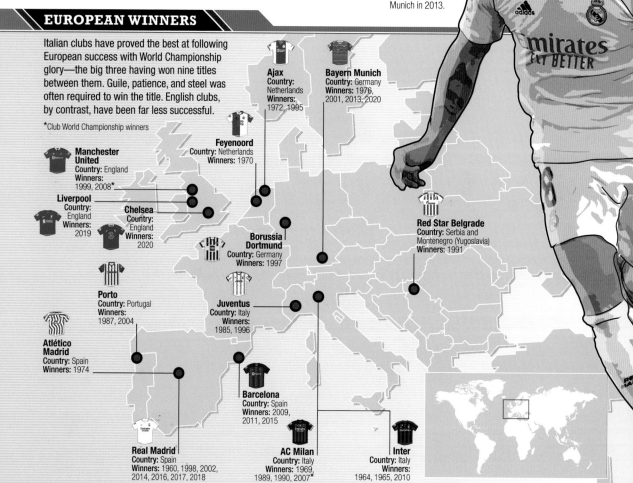

Ajax
Country: Netherlands
Winners: 1972, 1995

Bayern Munich
Country: Germany
Winners: 1976, 2001, 2013, 2020

Feyenoord
Country: Netherlands
Winners: 1970

Manchester United
Country: England
Winners: 1999, 2008*

Liverpool
Country: England
Winners: 2019

Chelsea
Country: England
Winners: 2020

Borussia Dortmund
Country: Germany
Winners: 1997

Red Star Belgrade
Country: Serbia and Montenegro (Yugoslavia)
Winners: 1991

Porto
Country: Portugal
Winners: 1987, 2004

Juventus
Country: Italy
Winners: 1985, 1996

Atlético Madrid
Country: Spain
Winners: 1974

Barcelona
Country: Spain
Winners: 2009, 2011, 2015

Real Madrid
Country: Spain
Winners: 1960, 1998, 2002, 2014, 2016, 2017, 2018

AC Milan
Country: Italy
Winners: 1969, 1989, 1990, 2007*

Inter
Country: Italy
Winners: 1964, 1965, 2010

2009
The first year that Dubai, UAE hosted the tournament

6
Number of contests played in by Paolo Maldini for AC Milan

3
Record number of wins as a coach—Carlos Bianchi with Vélez Sársfield in 1994, and Boca Juniors in 2000 and 2003

1
Hat trick in a final, scored by Pelé for Santos

2
Number of Uruguayans who have won the cup as both player and coach—Luis Cubilla (Peñarol in 1961 and Nacional in 1971 as player then Olimpia Asunción in 1979 as coach) and Juan Mujica (Nacional as player in 1971 and coach in 1980)

INTERCONTINENTAL CUP FINAL, 1967

In the 1967 final, Celtic took a 1–0 lead from the home leg in Scotland to Racing in Buenos Aires. The Argentines denied Celtic a warm-up ball, the Celtic goalkeeper was hit by a stone and substituted, and the referee was cowed by a fanatical crowd. Racing won 2–1, and the subsequent decider in Montevideo, Uruguay, saw five players being sent off. Racing scored once and won.

A TOURNAMENT FOR THE WORLD

The Intercontinental Cup became increasingly fractious in the 1960s and 1970s, leading to a number of European teams declining the invite. In 1980 the fixture, now a single game known as the Club World Championship, was transferred to Japan and sponsored by Toyota.

To accommodate the rising power of world soccer, FIFA initiated an expanded tournament in Brazil in 2000 with other regional champions. The FIFA Club World Cup replaced each of these contests in 2006, creating a six-team tournament. The top clubs from the weaker federations—CAF, CONCACAF, AFC, and OFC—play against each other for a place in the semifinals against the South American or European champions. In 2010, Congo's TP Mazembe became the first club from outside CONMEBOL or UEFA to reach the final.

WINNERS BY CONTINENT

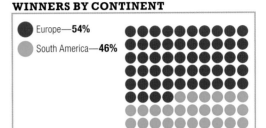

- Europe—**54%**
- South America—**46%**

SOUTH AMERICAN WINNERS

The Intercontinental Cup was accorded a much higher status in South America than in Europe for most of its history. In a rare opportunity to test their domestic soccer against the "Old World" of Europe, South America's leading clubs proved themselves more than a match. Some of the top sides of Argentina and Brazil have been crowned World Champions since 2000.

GUERILLA SOCCER

Estudiantes built a reputation for anti-soccer across South America, winning three Copa Libertadores. Notoriously rough, cynical, sharp, and tricky, they reached their apogee in the second leg of the 1969 Intercontinental Cup, hosting AC Milan in Buenos Aires. By the time they had lost the tie, they were down to nine men, had broken the collarbone of Milan's Combin, and kicked Rivera to the ground. El Grafico, the sports newspaper, reported that "TV took the deformed image of the match and transformed it into urban guerrilla warfare all over the world."

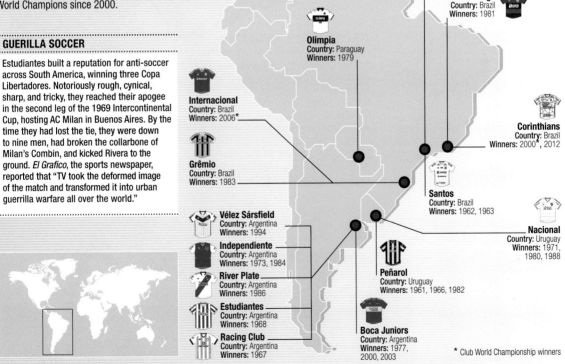

São Paulo
Country: Brazil
Winners: 1992, 1993, 2005*

Flamengo
Country: Brazil
Winners: 1981

Olimpia
Country: Paraguay
Winners: 1979

Corinthians
Country: Brazil
Winners: 2000*, 2012

Internacional
Country: Brazil
Winners: 2006*

Grêmio
Country: Brazil
Winners: 1983

Santos
Country: Brazil
Winners: 1962, 1963

Nacional
Country: Uruguay
Winners: 1971, 1980, 1988

Vélez Sársfield
Country: Argentina
Winners: 1994

Independiente
Country: Argentina
Winners: 1973, 1984

River Plate
Country: Argentina
Winners: 1986

Estudiantes
Country: Argentina
Winners: 1968

Racing Club
Country: Argentina
Winners: 1967

Peñarol
Country: Uruguay
Winners: 1961, 1966, 1982

Boca Juniors
Country: Argentina
Winners: 1977, 2000, 2003

* Club World Championship winners

OLYMPIC GAMES

COMPETITION: OLYMPIC GAMES—MEN'S SOCCER
FOUNDED: 1900
CONFEDERATION: FIFA/IOC

COMPETITION: OLYMPIC GAMES—WOMEN'S SOCCER
FOUNDED: 1996
CONFEDERATION: FIFA/IOC

Soccer at the Olympic Games has taken on many forms, from an informal kickaround in the early days to effectively being the championship of the world in the 1920s. With the arrival of the World Cup in 1930, it was demoted to a tournament for the amateurs and state-sponsored athletes of Scandinavia and the Communist Bloc. With the addition of a women's tournament in 1996, and the running of the men's competition as a FIFA-administered Under-23 tournament since 1992, interest is rising once again.

HAZY BEGINNINGS

Soccer was an exhibition sport at the earliest Olympic Games. In Athens in 1896, the tournament was contested by teams from Denmark, Athens, and Izmir (a Greek-speaking part of Turkey). The records of the Athenian team have been lost, but the Danes thrashed Izmir 15–0. Upton Park FC of East London took on a Paris XI at the 1900 Paris Olympics and won 4–0, and records also mention a match against a team of Belgian students in the Bois de Boulogne, Paris. The first official tournament, held in London in 1908, was won by a Great Britain side against Denmark.

JAVIER MASCHERANO
The former captain of Argentina was the first male soccer player to win back-to-back Olympic golds (2004 and 2008) since the Uruguay team of 1928.

105,000
Highest attendance for an Olympic game, recorded at the Mexico vs. Japan third-place playoff at Estadio Azteca, Mexico City, 1968

0
Attendance at both the men's and women's final in 2020, because of the pandemic

THE 1920 OLYMPICS

When Czech defender Karel Steiner was sent off by English referee John Lewis in the 40th minute of the 1920 Olympic final in Belgium, it was the last straw for the Czech team, who followed him off the field. Belgium was awarded the game by default. The Czechs didn't like the refereeing by 65-year-old Mr. Lewis, especially his awarding of a second Belgian goal, nor the menacing presence of Belgian soldiers in the crowd and the field invasion they led later on. All of the Czech complaints were dismissed.

GROWTH OF THE GAMES

Olympic soccer in the 1920s belonged to Latin America, but with the arrival of professionalism all over the world, the tournament was fought out by the Swedes, Danes, and Eastern Europeans until the 1980s. Since 1992, the men's contest has been an Under-23 tournament with each side permitted to field three older players. Two African gold medals—Nigeria in 1996 and Cameroon in 2000—have boosted TV audiences and crowds.

STAT ATTACK

MEN'S TOP SCORERS

Player	Country	Goals
Ferenc BENE	Hungary	12
Sophus NIELSEN	Denmark	11
Gottfried FUCHS	Germany	10
Domingo TARASCONI	Argentina	9
Kazimierz DEYNA	Poland	9

WOMEN'S TOP SCORERS

Player	Country	Goals
CRISTIANE	Brazil	14
Christine SINCLAIR	Canada	6
Birgit PRINZ	Germany	5
Ann Kristin AARØNES	Denmark	4
Linda MEDALEN	Denmark	4
PRETINHA	Brazil	4

HERE COME THE LADIES

The women's game was finally added to the Olympics in Atlanta in 1996, when the US beat China in the final. Unlike the men's contest, the women's tournament is for full international teams. The US has reached five finals so far, winning four of them, and losing to Norway once at Sydney 2000. Germany took the gold medal for the first time at Rio 2016. Canada were 2020 champions (held in 2021).

THE 1928 OLYMPICS

The Amsterdam Games of 1928 was the peak of Olympic soccer's importance. It was effectively the world championships, and Argentina and Uruguay met in the final. After a 1–1 draw, the rematch saw more than a quarter of a million people apply for tickets. Uruguay won the match 2–1 but has failed to qualify for the competition ever since.

THE MEN'S TOURNAMENTS

More democratic than the World Cup, the map of Olympic soccer reveals hosts or winners on every soccer continent. It is also the only soccer map that shows Great Britain rather than the four home nations—England, Scotland, Wales, and Northern Ireland.

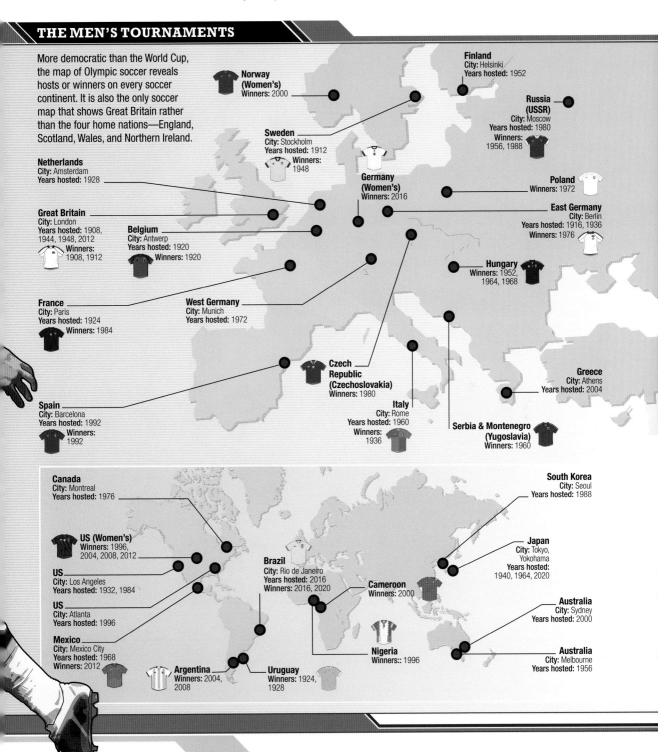

Norway (Women's)
Winners: 2000

Finland
City: Helsinki
Years hosted: 1952

Russia (USSR)
City: Moscow
Years hosted: 1980
Winners: 1956, 1988

Sweden
City: Stockholm
Years hosted: 1912
Winners: 1948

Germany (Women's)
Winners: 2016

Poland
Winners: 1972

Netherlands
City: Amsterdam
Years hosted: 1928

East Germany
City: Berlin
Years hosted: 1916, 1936
Winners: 1976

Great Britain
City: London
Years hosted: 1908, 1944, 1948, 2012
Winners: 1908, 1912

Belgium
City: Antwerp
Years hosted: 1920
Winners: 1920

Hungary
Winners: 1952, 1964, 1968

France
City: Paris
Years hosted: 1924
Winners: 1984

West Germany
City: Munich
Years hosted: 1972

Czech Republic (Czechoslovakia)
Winners: 1980

Greece
City: Athens
Years hosted: 2004

Spain
City: Barcelona
Years hosted: 1992
Winners: 1992

Italy
City: Rome
Years hosted: 1960
Winners: 1936

Serbia & Montenegro (Yugoslavia)
Winners: 1960

Canada
City: Montreal
Years hosted: 1976

South Korea
City: Seoul
Years hosted: 1988

US (Women's)
Winners: 1996, 2004, 2008, 2012

US
City: Los Angeles
Years hosted: 1932, 1984

Brazil
City: Rio de Janeiro
Years hosted: 2016
Winners: 2016, 2020

Japan
City: Tokyo, Yokohama
Years hosted: 1940, 1964, 2020

US
City: Atlanta
Years hosted: 1996

Cameroon
Winners: 2000

Australia
City: Sydney
Years hosted: 2000

Mexico
City: Mexico City
Years hosted: 1968
Winners: 2012

Nigeria
Winners: 1996

Australia
City: Melbourne
Years hosted: 1956

Argentina
Winners: 2004, 2008

Uruguay
Winners: 1924, 1928

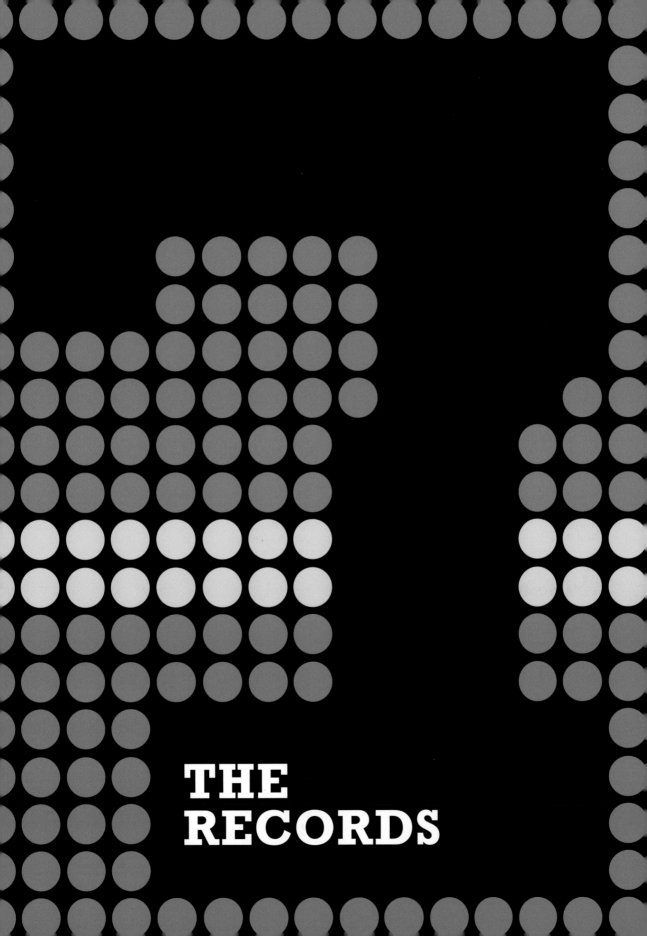

THE
RECORDS

WORLD

INTERNATIONAL AWARDS

FIFA MEN'S WORLD CUP WINNERS

YEAR	VENUE	WINNER	SCORE	RUNNER-UP
1930	Uruguay	**Uruguay**	4–2	Argentina
1934	Italy	**Italy**	2–1	Czechoslovakia*
1938	France	**Italy**	4–2	Hungary
1950	Brazil	**Uruguay**	2–1	Brazil
1954	Switzerland	**West Germany**	3–2	Hungary
1958	Sweden	**Brazil**	5–2	Sweden
1962	Chile	**Brazil**	3–1	Czechoslovakia
1966	England	**England**	4–2*	West Germany
1970	Mexico	**Brazil**	4–1	Italy
1974	West Germany	**West Germany**	2–1	Netherlands
1978	Argentina	**Argentina**	3–1*	Netherlands
1982	Spain	**Italy**	3–1	West Germany
1986	Mexico	**Argentina**	3–2	West Germany
1990	Italy	**West Germany**	1–0	Argentina
1994	US	**Brazil**	0–0	Italy* (3–2)●
1998	France	**France**	3–0	Brazil
2002	South Korea & Japan	**Brazil**	2–0	Germany
2006	Germany	**Italy**	1–1	France* (5–3)●
2010	South Africa	**Spain**	1–0*	Netherlands
2014	Brazil	**Germany**	1–0	Argentina
2018	Russia	**France**	4–2	Croatia
2022	Qatar	**Argentina**	3–3	France* (4–2)●

FIFA MEN'S WORLD CUP TOP SCORERS

NAME	GOALS	COUNTRY		NAME	GOALS	COUNTRY
Miroslav Klose	16	Germany		**Pelé**	12	Brazil
Ronaldo	15	Brazil		**Kylian Mbappé**	12	France
Gerd Müller	14	Germany		**Jurgen Klinsmann**	11	Germany
Just Fontaine	13	France		**Sandor Kocsis**	11	Hungary
Lionel Messi	13	Argentina		**Thomas Müller**	10	Germany

FIFA WOMEN'S WORLD CUP WINNERS

YEAR	VENUE	WINNER	SCORE	RUNNER-UP
1991	China	**US**	2–1	Norway
1995	Sweden	**Norway**	2–0	Germany
1999	US	**US**	0–0	China*(5–4)●
2003	US	**Germany**	2–1	Sweden°
2007	China	**Germany**	2–0	Brazil
2011	Germany	**Japan**	2–2	US*(3–1)●
2015	Canada	**US**	5–2	Japan
2019	France	**US**	2–0	Netherlands

FIFA WOMEN'S WORLD CUP TOP SCORERS

NAME	GOALS	COUNTRY		NAME	GOALS	COUNTRY
Marta	15	Brazil		**Ann Kristin Aarønes**	10	Norway
Birgit Prinz	14	Germany		**Carli Lloyd**	10	US
Abby Wambach	14	US		**Christine Sinclair**	10	Canada
Michelle Akers	12	US		**Heidi Mohr**	10	Germany
Sun Wen	11	China		**Linda Medalen**	9	Norway
Bettina Wiegmann	11	Germany		**Hege Riise**	9	Norway

*After overtime   ●After penalty shoot-out   °Match decided on golden goal

CLUB AWARDS

INTERNATIONAL CLUB CUP

YEAR	WINNER
1960	Real Madrid
1961	Peñarol
1962	Santos
1963	Santos
1964	Inter
1965	Inter
1966	Peñarol
1967	Racing Club
1968	Estudiantes
1969	Milan
1970	Feyenoord
1971	Nacional
1972	Ajax
1973	Independiente
1974	Atlético Madrid
1975	not held
1976	Bayern Munich
1977	Boca Juniors
1978	not held
1979	Olimpia

TOYOTA CUP

YEAR	WINNER
1980	Nacional
1981	Flamengo
1982	Peñarol
1983	Grêmio
1984	Independiente
1985	Juventus
1986	River Plate
1987	Porto
1988	Nacional
1989	AC Milan
1990	AC Milan
1991	Red Star Belgrade
1992	São Paulo
1993	São Paulo
1994	Vélez Sarsfield
1995	Ajax
1996	Juventus
1997	Borussia Dortmund
1998	Real Madrid
1999	Manchester United
2000	Boca Juniors
2001	Bayern Munich
2002	Real Madrid
2003	Boca Juniors
2004	Porto

CLUB WORLD CUP

YEAR	WINNER	YEAR	WINNER
2000	Corinthians	2019	Liverpool
2001–04	NO COMPETITION	2020	Bayern Munich
2005	São Paulo	2021	Chelsea
2006	Internacional		
2007	AC Milan		
2008	Manchester United		
2009	Barcelona		
2010	Inter		
2011	Barcelona		
2012	Corinthians		
2013	Bayern Munich		
2014	Real Madrid		
2015	Barcelona		
2016	Real Madrid		
2017	Real Madrid		
2018	Real Madrid		

FIFA MEN'S WORLD PLAYER OF THE YEAR

YEAR	WINNER	COUNTRY	CLUB	YEAR	WINNER	COUNTRY	CLUB
1991	Lothar Matthäus	Germany	Inter	2006	Fabio Cannavaro	Italy	Juventus & Real Madrid
1992	Marco van Basten	Netherlands	AC Milan	2007	Kaká	Brazil	AC Milan
1993	Roberto Baggio	Italy	Juventus	2008	Cristiano Ronaldo	Portugal	Manchester United
1994	Romário	Brazil	Barcelona	2009	Lionel Messi	Argentina	Barcelona
1995	George Weah	Liberia	AC Milan	2010	Lionel Messi	Argentina	Barcelona
1996	Ronaldo	Brazil	PSV Eindhoven & Barcelona	2011	Lionel Messi	Argentina	Barcelona
1997	Ronaldo	Brazil	Barcelona & Inter	2012	Lionel Messi	Argentina	Barcelona
1998	Zinedine Zidane	France	Juventus	2013	Cristiano Ronaldo	Portugal	Real Madrid
1999	Rivaldo	Brazil	Barcelona	2014	Cristiano Ronaldo	Portugal	Real Madrid
2000	Zinedine Zidane	France	Juventus	2015	Lionel Messi	Argentina	Barcelona
2001	Luis Figo	Portugal	Real Madrid	2016	Cristiano Ronaldo	Portugal	Real Madrid
2002	Ronaldo	Brazil	Inter & Real Madrid	2017	Cristiano Ronaldo	Portugal	Real Madrid
2003	Zinedine Zidane	France	Real Madrid	2018	Luka Modrić	Croatia	Real Madrid
2004	Ronaldinho	Brazil	Barcelona	2019	Lionel Messi	Argentina	Barcelona
2005	Ronaldinho	Brazil	Barcelona	2020	Robert Lewandowski	Poland	Bayern Munich
				2021	Robert Lewandowski	Poland	Bayern Munich

FIFA WOMEN'S WORLD PLAYER OF THE YEAR

YEAR	WINNER	COUNTRY	CLUB	YEAR	WINNER	COUNTRY	CLUB
2001	Mia Hamm	US	Washington Freedom	2011	Homare Sawa	Japan	INAC Kobe Leonessa
2002	Mia Hamm	US	Washington Freedom	2012	Abby Wambach	US	Western New York Flash
2003	Birgit Prinz	Germany	Carolina Courage	2013	Nadine Angerer	Germany	FFC Frankfurt
2004	Birgit Prinz	Germany	1.FFC Frankfurt	2014	Nadine Kessler	Germany	VfL Wolfsburg
2005	Birgit Prinz	Germany	1.FFC Frankfurt	2015	Carli Lloyd	US	Houston Dash
2006	Marta	Brazil	Umeå IK	2016	Carli Lloyd	US	Houston Dash
2007	Marta	Brazil	Umeå IK	2017	Lieke Martens	Netherlands	Barcelona
2008	Marta	Brazil	Umeå IK	2018	Marta	Brazil	Orlando Pride
2009	Marta	Brazil	Los Angeles Sol & Santos	2019	Megan Rapinoe	US	Reign FC
2010	Marta	Brazil	Los Angeles Sol, FC Gold Pride, & Santos	2020	Lucy Bronze	England	Lyon and Manchester City
				2021	Alexia Putellas	Spain	Barcelona

*After overtime •After penalty shoot-out

EUROPE: UEFA

INTERNATIONAL AWARDS

UEFA EUROPEAN CHAMPIONSHIP WINNERS

YEAR	WINNER	SCORE	RUNNER-UP
1960	**Soviet Union**	2–1	Yugoslavia*
1964	**Spain**	2–1	Soviet Union
1968	**Italy**	1–1	Yugoslavia* (replay 2–0)
1972	**West Germany**	3–0	Soviet Union
1976	**Czechoslovakia**	2–2	West Germany* (5–3)•
1980	**West Germany**	2–1	Belgium
1984	**France**	2–0	Spain
1988	**Netherlands**	2–0	Soviet Union
1992	**Denmark**	2–0	Germany
1996	**Germany**	2–1	Czech Republic**
2000	**France**	2–1	Italy**
2004	**Greece**	1–0	Portugal
2008	**Spain**	1–0	Germany
2012	**Spain**	4–0	Italy
2016	**Portugal**	1–0	France*
2020***	**Italy**	1–1	England* (3–2)•

UEFA EUROPEAN CHAMPIONSHIP TOP SCORERS

NAME	GOALS	COUNTRY
Cristiano Ronaldo	14	Portugal
Michel Platini	9	France
Antoine Griezmann	7	France
Alan Shearer	7	England
Romelu Lukaku	6	Belgiuml
Patrick Kluivert	6	Netherlands
Nuno Gomes	6	Portugal
Thierry Henry	6	France
Zlatan Ibrahimovic	6	Sweden
Ruud van Nistelrooy	6	Netherlands
Wayne Rooney	6	England
Fernando Torres	5	Spain
Milan Baroš	5	Czech Republic
Marco van Basten	5	Netherlands
Jürgen Klinsmann	5	Germany
Savo Milosevic	5	Serbia
Zinedine Zidane	5	France
Mario Gómez	5	Germany

CLUB AWARDS

UEFA CHAMPIONS LEAGUE/EUROPEAN CUP WINNERS

YEAR	WINNER	SCORE	RUNNER-UP	YEAR	WINNER	SCORE	RUNNER-UP
1956	**Real Madrid**	4–3	Stade Reims	1988	**PSV Eindhoven**	0–0	Benfica* (6–5)•
1957	**Real Madrid**	2–0	Fiorentina	1989	**AC Milan**	4–0	Steaua Bucharest
1958	**Real Madrid**	3–2	AC Milan*	1990	**AC Milan**	1–0	Benfica
1959	**Real Madrid**	2–0	Stade Reims	1991	**Red Star Belgrade**	0–0	Olympique Marseille* (5–3)•
1960	**Real Madrid**	7–3	Eintracht Frankfurt	1992	**Barcelona**	1–0	Sampdoria*
1961	**Benfica**	3–2	Barcelona	1993	**Olympique Marseille**	1–0	AC Milan
1962	**Benfica**	5–3	Real Madrid	1994	**AC Milan**	4–0	Barcelona
1963	**AC Milan**	2–1	Benfica	1995	**Ajax**	1–0	AC Milan
1964	**Inter**	3–1	Real Madrid	1996	**Juventus**	1–1	Ajax* (4–2)•
1965	**Inter**	1–0	Benfica	1997	**Borussia Dortmund**	3–1	Juventus
1966	**Real Madrid**	2–1	Partizan Belgrade	1998	**Real Madrid**	1–0	Juventus
1967	**Celtic**	2–1	Inter	1999	**Manchester United**	2–1	Bayern Munich
1968	**Manchester United**	4–1	Benfica*	2000	**Real Madrid**	3–0	Valencia
1969	**AC Milan**	4–1	Ajax	2001	**Bayern Munich**	1–1	Valencia* (5–4)•
1970	**Feyenoord**	2–1	Celtic*	2002	**Real Madrid**	2–1	Bayer Leverkusen
1972	**Ajax**	2–0	Panathinaikos	2003	**AC Milan**	0–0	Juventus* (3–2)•
1973	**Ajax**	2–0	Inter	2004	**Porto**	3–0	Monaco
1974	**Ajax**	1–0	Juventus	2005	**Liverpool**	3–3	AC Milan* (3–2)•
1975	**Bayern Munich**	1–1	Atlético Madrid* (4–0 Replay)	2006	**Barcelona**	2–1	Arsenal
1975	**Bayern Munich**	2–0	Leeds United	2007	**AC Milan**	2–1	Liverpool
1976	**Bayern Munich**	1–0	Saint-Etienne	2008	**Manchester United**	1–1	Chelsea* (6–5)•
1977	**Liverpool**	3–1	Borussia Mönchengladbach	2009	**Barcelona**	2–0	Manchester United
1978	**Liverpool**	1–0	FC Brugge	2010	**Inter**	2–0	Bayern Munich
1979	**Nottingham Forest**	1–0	Malmö FF	2011	**Barcelona**	3–1	Manchester United
1980	**Nottingham Forest**	1–0	Hamburg	2012	**Chelsea**	1–1	Bayern Munich* (4–3)•
1981	**Liverpool**	1–0	Real Madrid	2013	**Bayern Munich**	2–1	Borussia Dortmund
1982	**Aston Villa**	1–0	Bayern Munich	2014	**Real Madrid**	4–1	Atlético Madrid*
1983	**Hamburg**	1–0	Juventus	2015	**Barcelona**	3–1	Juventus
1985	**Juventus**	1–0	Liverpool	2016	**Real Madrid**	1–1	Atlético Madrid* (5–3)•
1986	**Steaua Bucharest**	0–0	Barcelona* (2–0)•	2017	**Real Madrid**	4–1	Juventus
1987	**Porto**	2–1	Bayern Munich	2018	**Real Madrid**	3–1	Liverpool
				2019	**Liverpool**	2–0	Tottenham Hotspur
				2020	**Bayern Munich**	1–0	Paris Saint Germain
				2021	**Chelsea**	1–0	Manchester City
				2022	**Real Madrid**	1–0	Liverpool

*After extra time   •After penalty shoot-out   **Match decided on golden goal   *** Staged in 2021 because of COVID-19 pandemic

UEFA CHAMPIONS LEAGUE/EUROPEAN CUP TOP SCORERS

NAME	GOALS	COUNTRY	CLUBS
Cristiano Ronaldo	140	Portugal	Manchester United, Real Madrid, Juventus
Lionel Messi	129	Argentina	Barcelona, Paris Saint-Germain
Robert Lewandowski	91	Poland	Borussia Dortmund, Bayern Munich, Barcelona
Karim Benzema	86	France	Lyon, Real Madrid
Raúl	71	Spain	Real Madrid, Schalke 04
Ruud van Nistelrooy	56	Netherlands	PSV Eindhoven, Manchester United, Real Madrid
Thomas Muller	53	Germany	Bayern Munich
Thierry Henry	50	France	Monaco, Arsenal, Barcelona
Andriy Shevchenko	48	Ukraine	Dynamo Kiev, AC Milan, Chelsea
Zlatan Ibrahimovic	48	Sweden	Ajax, Juventus, Inter, Barcelona, Milan, Paris Saint-Germain
Eusébio	47	Portugal	Benfica

EUROPA LEAGUE (FORMERLY UEFA CUP) (AGGREGATE SCORES)

YEAR	WINNER	SCORE	RUNNER-UP
1972	Tottenham Hotspur	3–2	Wolverhampton Wanderers
1973	Liverpool	3–2	Borussia Mönchengladbach
1974	Feyenoord	4–2	Tottenham Hotspur
1975	Borussia Mönchengladbach	5–1	FC Twente
1976	Liverpool	4–3	FC Brugge
1977	Juventus	2–2	Athletic Bilbao (Juventus win on away goals)
1978	PSV Eindhoven	3–0	Bastia
1979	Borussia Mönchengladbach	2–1	Red Star Belgrade
1980	Eintracht Frankfurt	3–3	Borussia Mönchengladbach (Eintracht Frankfurt win on away goals)
1981	Ipswich Town	5–4	AZ Alkmaar '67
1982	IFK Göteborg	4–0	Hamburg
1983	Anderlecht	2–1	Benfica
1984	Tottenham Hotspur	2–2	Anderlecht* (4–3)•
1985	Real Madrid	3–1	Videoton
1986	Real Madrid	5–3	1.FC Köln
1987	IFK Göteborg	2–1	Dundee United
1988	Bayer Leverkusen	3–3	Español* (3–2)•
1989	Napoli	5–4	VfB Stuttgart
1990	Juventus	3–1	Fiorentina
1991	Inter	2–1	Roma
1992	Ajax	2–2	Torino (Ajax win on away goals)
1993	Juventus	6–1	Borussia Dortmund
1994	Inter	2–0	Austria Salzburg
1995	Parma	2–1	Juventus
1996	Bayern Munich	5–1	Girondins Bordeaux
1997	Schalke 04	1–1	Internazionale* (4–1)•
1998	Inter	3–0	Lazio
1999	Parma	3–0	Olympique Marseille
2000	Galatasaray	0–0	Arsenal* (4–1)•
2001	Liverpool	5–4	Alavés*
2002	Feyenoord	3–2	Borussia Dortmund
2003	Porto	3–2	Celtic*
2004	Valencia	2–0	Olympique Marseille
2005	CSKA Moscow	3–1	Sporting CP
2006	Sevilla	4–0	Middlesbrough
2007	Sevilla	2–2	Espanyol* (3–1)•
2008	Zenit St. Petersburg	2–0	Rangers
2009	Shakhtar Donetsk	2–1	Werder Bremen*
2010	Atlético Madrid	2–1	Fulham*
2011	Porto	1–0	Braga
2012	Atlético Madrid	3–0	Athletic Bilbao
2013	Chelsea	2–1	Benfica
2014	Sevilla	0–0	Benfica* (4–2)•
2015	Sevilla	3–2	Dnipro Dnipropetrovsk
2016	Sevilla	3–1	Liverpool
2017	Manchester United	2–0	Ajax
2018	Atlético Madrid	3–0	Marseille
2019	Chelsea	4–1	Arsenal
2020	Sevilla	3–2	Inter Milan
2021	Villarreal	1–1	Manchester United* (11–10)
2022	Eintracht Frankfurt	1–1	Rangers (5-4)•

*After sudden death extra time   •After penalty shoot-out

THE RECORDS

UEFA CUP WINNERS' CUP WINNERS

YEAR	WINNER	SCORE	RUNNER-UP
1961	**Fiorentina**	4–1	Rangers (Final played over two legs)
1962	**Atletico Madrid**	1–1	Fiorentina (Atletico won the replay 3–0)
1963	**Tottenham Hotspur**	5–1	Atletico Madrid
1964	**Sporting CP**	3–3	MTK Budapest* (Sporting CP won the replay 1–0)
1965	**West Ham**	2–0	1860 Munich
1966	**Borussia Dortmund**	2–1	Liverpool*
1967	**Bayern Munich**	1–0	Rangers*
1968	**AC Milan**	2–0	Hamburg
1969	**Slovan Bratislava**	3–2	Barcelona
1970	**Manchester City**	2–1	Gornik Zabrze
1971	**Chelsea**	1–1	Real Madrid* (Chelsea won the replay 2–1)
1972	**Rangers**	3–2	Dynamo Moscow
1973	**AC Milan**	1–0	Leeds United
1974	**Magdeburg**	2–0	AC Milan
1975	**Dynamo Kiev**	3–0	Ferencváros
1976	**Anderlecht**	4–2	West Ham
1977	**Hamburg**	2–0	Anderlecht
1978	**Anderlecht**	4–0	Austria Wien
1979	**Barcelona**	4–3	Fortuna Dusseldorf*
1980	**Valencia**	0–0	Arsenal* (5–4)•
1981	**Dinamo Tbilisi**	2–1	Carl Zeiss Jena
1982	**Barcelona**	2–1	Standard Liege
1983	**Aberdeen**	2–1	Real Madrid*
1984	**Juventus**	2–1	Porto
1985	**Everton**	3–1	Rapid Vienna
1986	**Dynamo Kiev**	3–0	Atletico Madrid
1987	**Ajax**	1–0	Lokomotive Leipzig
1988	**KV Mechelen**	1–0	Ajax
1989	**Barcelona**	2–0	Sampdoria
1990	**Sampdoria**	2–0	Anderlecht*
1991	**Manchester United**	2–1	Barcelona
1992	**Werder Bremen**	2–0	AS Monaco
1993	**Parma**	3–1	Royal Antwerp
1994	**Arsenal**	1–0	Parma
1995	**Real Zaragoza**	2–1	Arsenal*
1996	**Paris Saint-Germain**	1–0	Rapid Vienna
1997	**Barcelona**	1–0	Paris Saint-Germain
1998	**Chelsea**	1–0	Stuttgart
1999	**Lazio**	2–1	Mallorca

*After overtime   •After penalty shoot-out

UEFA BEST PLAYER IN EUROPE AWARD (FORMERLY "BALLON D'OR")

YEAR	NAME	CLUB
1956	**Stanley Matthews** (England)	Blackpool
1957	**Alfredo Di Stéfano*** (Spain)	Real Madrid
1958	**Raymond Kopa** (France)	Real Madrid
1959	**Alfredo Di Stéfano*** (Spain)	Real Madrid
1960	**Luis Suárez** (Spain)	Barcelona
1961	**Omar Sivori*** (Italy)	Juventus
1962	**Josef Masopust** (Czechoslovakia)	Dukla Praha
1963	**Lev Yashin** (Soviet Union)	Dynamo Moscow
1964	**Denis Law** (Scotland)	Manchester United
1965	**Eusébio** (Portugal)	Benfica
1966	**Bobby Charlton** (England)	Manchester United
1967	**Flórián Albert** (Hungary)	Ferencváros
1968	**George Best** (Northern Ireland)	Manchester United
1969	**Gianni Rivera** (Italy)	AC Milan
1970	**Gerd Müller** (West Germany)	Bayern Munich
1971	**Johan Cruyff** (Netherlands)	Ajax
1972	**Franz Beckenbauer** (West Germany)	Bayern Munich
1973	**Johan Cruyff** (Netherlands)	Barcelona
1974	**Johan Cruyff** (Netherlands)	Barcelona
1975	**Oleg Blokhin** (Soviet Union)	Dynamo Kiev
1976	**Franz Beckenbauer** (West Germany)	Bayern Munich
1977	**Allan Simonsen** (Denmark)	Borussia Mönchengladbach
1978	**Kevin Keegan** (England)	Hamburg
1979	**Kevin Keegan** (England)	Hamburg
1980	**Karl-Heinz Rummenigge** (West Germany)	Bayern Munich
1981	**Karl-Heinz Rummenigge** (West Germany)	Bayern Munich
1982	**Paolo Rossi** (Italy)	Juventus
1983	**Michel Platini** (France)	Juventus
1984	**Michel Platini** (France)	Juventus
1985	**Michel Platini** (France)	Juventus
1986	**Igor Belanov** (Soviet Union)	Dynamo Kiev
1987	**Ruud Gullit** (Netherlands)	AC Milan
1988	**Marco van Basten** (Netherlands)	AC Milan
1989	**Marco van Basten** (Netherlands)	AC Milan
1990	**Lothar Matthäus** (Germany)	Inter
1991	**Jean-Pierre Papin** (France)	Olympique Marseille
1992	**Marco van Basten** (Netherlands)	AC Milan
1993	**Roberto Baggio** (Italy)	Juventus
1994	**Hristo Stoitchkov** (Bulgaria)	Barcelona
1995	**George Weah** (Liberia)	AC Milan
1996	**Matthias Sammer** (Germany)	Borussia Dortmund
1997	**Ronaldo** (Brazil)	Inter

YEAR	NAME	CLUB
1998	**Zinedine Zidane** (France)	Juventus
1999	**Rivaldo** (Brazil)	Barcelona
2000	**Luis Figo** (Portugal)	Real Madrid
2001	**Michael Owen** (England)	Liverpool
2002	**Ronaldo** (Brazil)	Real Madrid
2003	**Pavel Nedved** (Czech Republic)	Juventus
2004	**Andriy Shevchenko** (Ukraine)	AC Milan
2005	**Ronaldinho** (Brazil)	Barcelona
2006	**Fabio Cannavaro** (Italy)	Real Madrid
2007	**Kaká** (Brazil)	AC Milan
2008	**Cristiano Ronaldo** (Portugal)	Manchester United
2009	**Lionel Messi** (Argentina)	Barcelona
2010–11	**Lionel Messi** (Argentina)	Barcelona
2011–12	**Lionel Messi** (Argentina)	Barcelona
2012–13	**Franck Ribéry** (France)	Bayern Munich
2013–14	**Cristiano Ronaldo** (Portugal)	Real Madrid
2014–15	**Lionel Messi** (Argentina)	Barcelona
2016–17	**Cristiano Ronaldo** (Portugal)	Real Madrid
2017–18	**Luka Modrić** (Croatia)	Real Madrid
2018–19	**Virgil van Dijk** (Netherlands)	Liverpool
2019–20	**Robert Lewandowski** (Poland)	Bayern Munich
2020–21	**Jorginho** (Italy)	Chelsea
2021–22	**Karim Benzema** (France)	Real Madrid

* Di Stéfano and Sivori were born in Argentina and first played for that country.

SOUTH AMERICA: CONMEBOL

INTERNATIONAL AWARDS

COPA AMÉRICA WINNERS

(No final match was played until 1979)

YEAR	VENUE	WINNER	RUNNER-UP
1916	Argentina	**Uruguay**	Argentina
1917	Uruguay	**Uruguay**	Argentina
1919	Brazil	**Brazil**	Uruguay
1920	Chile	**Uruguay**	Argentina
1921	Argentina	**Argentina**	Brazil
1922	Brazil	**Brazil**	Paraguay
1923	Uruguay	**Uruguay**	Argentina
1924	Uruguay	**Uruguay**	Argentina
1925	Argentina	**Argentina**	Brazil
1926	Chile	**Uruguay**	Argentina
1927	Peru	**Argentina**	Uruguay
1929	Argentina	**Argentina**	Paraguay
1935	Peru	**Uruguay**	Argentina
1937	Argentina	**Argentina**	Brazil
1939	Peru	**Peru**	Uruguay
1941	Chile	**Argentina**	Uruguay
1942	Uruguay	**Uruguay**	Argentina
1945	Chile	**Argentina**	Brazil
1946	Argentina	**Argentina**	Brazil
1947	Ecuador	**Argentina**	Paraguay
1949	Brazil	**Brazil**	Paraguay
1953	Peru	**Paraguay**	Brazil
1955	Chile	**Argentina**	Chile
1956	Uruguay	**Uruguay**	Chile
1957	Peru	**Argentina**	Brazil

YEAR	VENUE	WINNER	RUNNER-UP
1959	Argentina	Argentina	Brazil
1959	Ecuador	Uruguay	Argentina
1963	Bolivia	Bolivia	Paraguay
1967	Uruguay	Uruguay	Argentina

YEAR	VENUE	WINNER	SCORE	RUNNER-UP
1975	Venezuela	Peru	2–0/0–1	Peru win playoff 1–0
1979	Argentina	Paraguay	3–0/0–1	Chile
	Paraguay win on aggregate			
1983	no fixed venue	Uruguay	2–0/1–1	Brazil
1987	Argentina	Uruguay	1–0	Chile
1989	Brazil	Brazil	1–0	Uruguay
1991	Chile	Argentina	3–2	Brazil
1993	Ecuador	Argentina	2–1	Mexico
1995	Uruguay	Uruguay	1–1	Brazil (5–3)•
1997	Bolivia	Brazil	3–1	Bolivia
1999	Paraguay	Brazil	3–0	Uruguay
2001	Colombia	Colombia	1–0	Mexico
2004	Peru	Brazil	2–2	Argentina (4–2)•
2007	Venezuela	Brazil	3–0	Argentina
2011	Argentina	Uruguay	3–0	Paraguay
2015	Chile	Chile	0–0	Argentina (4–1)•
2016	US	Chile	0–0	Argentina (4–2)•
2019	Brazil	Brazil	3–1	Peru
2020***	Brazil	Argentina	1–0	Brazil

COPA AMÉRICA TOP SCORERS

NAME	GOALS	COUNTRY
Norberto Méndez	17	Argentina
Zizinho	17	Brazil
Severino Varela	15	Uruguay
Teodoro Fernández	15	Peru
Paolo Guerrero	14	Peru
Eduardo Vargas	14	Chile
Lionel Messi	13	Argentina
Gabriel Batistuta	13	Argentina
Ademir	13	Brazil
Jairzinho	13	Brazil

NAME	GOALS	COUNTRY
Héctor Scarone	13	Uruguay
Jose Manuel Moreno	13	Argentina
Angel Romano	12	Uruguay
Roberto Porta	12	Uruguay
Herminio Masantonio	11	Argentina
Victor Ugarte	11	Bolivia

CLUB AWARDS
COPA LIBERTADORES WINNERS

(The final was contested over two legs until 2018.)

YEAR	WINNER	SCORE	RUNNER-UP
1960	**Peñarol**	1–0/1–1	Olimpia
1961	**Peñarol**	1–0/0–1	Palmeiras
1962	**Santos**	2–1/2–3 Santos win play-off 3–0	Peñarol
1963	**Santos**	3–2/2–1	Boca Juniors
1964	**Independiente**	0–0/1–0	Nacional

•After penalty shoot-out   *** Staged in 2021 because of COVID-19 pandemic

YEAR	WINNER	SCORE	RUNNER-UP
1965	**Independiente**	1–0/0–1 Independiente win playoff 4–1	Peñarol
1966	**Peñarol**	2–0/2–3 Peñarol win playoff 4–2	River Plate
1967	**Racing Club**	0–0/0–0 Racing Club win playoff 2–1	Nacional
1968	**Estudiantes**	2–1/1–3 Estudiantes win playoff 2–0	Palmeiras
1969	**Estudiantes**	1–0/2–0	Nacional
1970	**Estudiantes**	1–0/0–0	Peñarol
1971	**Nacional**	0–1/1–0 Nacional win playoff 2–0	Estudiantes
1972	**Independiente**	0–0/2–1	Universitario
1973	**Independiente**	1–1/0–0 Independiente win playoff 2-1	Colo-Colo
1974	**Independiente**	1–2/2–0 Independiente win playoff 1–0	São Paulo
1975	**Independiente**	0–1/3–1 Independiente win playoff 2–0	Unión Española
1976	**Cruzeiro**	4–1/1–2 Cruzeiro win playoff 3–2	River Plate
1977	**Boca Juniors**	1–0/0–1 playoff 0–0, (5–4)•	Cruzeiro
1978	**Boca Juniors**	0–0/4–0	Deportivo Cali
1979	**Olimpia**	2–0/0–0	Boca Juniors
1980	**Nacional**	0–0/1–0	Internacional
1981	**Flamengo**	2–1/0–1 Flamengo win playoff 2–0	Cobreloa
1982	**Peñarol**	0–0/1–0	Cobreloa
1983	**Grêmio**	1–1/2–1	Peñarol
1984	**Independiente**	1–0/0–0	Grêmio
1985	**Argentinos Juniors**	1–0/0–1 playoff 1–1, Argentinos win 5–4 on penalties	América de Cali
1986	**River Plate**	2–1/1–0	América de Cali
1987	**Peñarol**	0–2/2–1 Peñarol win playoff 1–0	América de Cali
1988	**Atlético Nacional**	0–1/3–0	Newell's Old Boys
1989	**Atlético Nacional**	0–2/2–0	Olimpia (5–4)•
1990	**Olimpia**	2–0/1–1	Barcelona
1991	**Colo Colo**	0–0/3–0	Olimpia
1992	**São Paulo**	0–1/1–0	Newell's Old Boys (3–2)•
1993	**São Paulo**	5–1/0–2	Universidad Católica
1994	**Vélez Sarsfield**	1–0/0–1	São Paulo (5–3)•
1995	**Grêmio**	3–1/1–1	Atlético Nacional
1996	**River Plate**	0–1/2–0	América de Cali
1997	**Cruzeiro**	0–0/1–0	Sporting Cristal
1998	**Vasco da Gama**	2–0/2–1	Barcelona
1999	**Palmeiras**	0–1/2–1	Deportivo Cali (4–3)•
2000	**Boca Juniors**	2–2/0–0	Palmeiras (4–2)•
2001	**Boca Juniors**	1–0/0–1	Cruz Azul (3–1)•
2002	**Olimpia**	0–1/2–1	São Caetano (4–2)•
2003	**Boca Juniors**	2–0/3–1	Santos
2004	**Once Caldas**	0–0/1–1	Boca Juniors (2–0)•
2005	**São Paulo**	1–1/4–0	Atlético Paranaense
2006	**Internacional**	2–1/2–2	São Paulo
2007	**Boca Juniors**	3–0/2–0	Grêmio
2008	**LDU Quito**	4–2/1–3	Fluminense (3–1)•
2009	**Estudiantes**	0–0/2–1	Cruzeiro
2010	**Internacional**	2–1/3–2	Guadalajara
2011	**Santos**	0–0/2–1	Peñarol
2012	**Corinthians**	1–1/2–0	Boca Juniors
2013	**Atlético Mineiro**	0–2/2–0	Olimpia (4–3)•
2014	**San Lorenzo**	1–1/1–0	Nacional
2015	**River Plate**	0–0/3–0	UANL
2016	**Atlético Nacional**	1–1/1–0	Independiente del Valle
2017	**Grêmio**	1–0/1–2	Lanus
2018	**River Plate**	2–2/3–1	Boca Juniors
2019	**Flamengo**	2–1	River Plate
2020	**Palmeiras**	1–0	Santos
2021	**Palmeiras**	2–1	Flamengo
2022	**Flamengo**	1–0	Athletico Paranaense

•After penalty shoot-out

THE RECORDS

COPA MERCONORTE WINNERS

YEAR	WINNER	SCORE	RUNNER-UP
1998	**Atlético Nacional**	4–1	Deportivo Cali
1999	**América de Cali**	2–2	Independiente Santa Fe (5–3)•
2000	**Atlético Nacional**	2–1	Millonarios
2001	**Millonarios**	2–2	Emelec (3–1)•

COPA MERCOSUR WINNERS

(Aggregate scores where applicable)

YEAR	WINNER	SCORE	RUNNER-UP
1998	**Palmeiras**	1–2/3–1 playoff 1–0	Cruzeiro Palmeiras win
1999	**Flamengo**	7–6	Palmeiras
2000	**Vasco da Gama**	2–0/0–1 playoff 4–3	Palmeiras Vasco da Gama win
2001	**San Lorenzo**	1–1	Flamengo (3–4)•

COPA SUDAMERICANA WINNERS

(Aggregate scores)

YEAR	WINNER	SCORE	RUNNER-UP
2002	**San Lorenzo**	4–0	Atlético Nacional
2003	**Cienciano**	4–3	River Plate
2004	**Boca Juniors**	2–1	Bolívar
2005	**Boca Juniors**	2–2	Pumas UNAM (4–3)•
2006	**Pachuca**	3–2	Colo Colo
2007	**Arsenal de Sarandi**	4–4	CF América Arsenal de Sarandi win on away goals
2008	**Internacional (PA)**	2–1*	Estudiantes (LP)
2009	**LDU Quito**	5–4	Fluminense
2010	**Independiente**	3–3	Goiás (5–3)•
2011	**Universidad de Chile**	4–0	LDU Quito
2012	**Sao Paolo**	2–0	Tigre
2013	**Lanús**	3–1	Ponte Preta
2014	**River Plate**	3–1	Atlético Nacional
2015	**Santa Fe**	0–0	Huracán (3–1)•
2016	**Chapecoense**		Atlético Nacional#
2017	**Independiente**	3–2	Flamengo
2018	**Atletico Paranaense**	1–1	Junior (4–3)*
2019	**Independiente del Valle**	3–1	Colon
2020	**Defensa y Justicia**	3–0	Lanus
2021	**Athletico Paranaense**	1-0	Red Bull Bragantino
2022	**Independiente del Valle**	2-0	Sao Paulo

SOUTH AMERICAN PLAYER OF THE YEAR

By *El Mundo* (Caracas, Venezuela)

YEAR	WINNER	CLUB
1971	**Tostão** (Brazil)	Cruzeiro
1972	**Teófilo** Cubillas (Peru)	Alianza Lima
1973	**Pelé** (Brazil)	Santos
1974	**Elías Figueroa** (Chile)	Internacional
1975	**Elías Figueroa** (Chile)	Internacional
1976	**Elías Figueroa** (Chile)	Internacional
1977	**Zico** (Brazil)	Flamengo
1978	**Mario Kempes** (Argentina)	Valencia
1979	**Diego Maradona** (Argentina)	Argentinos Juniors
1980	**Diego Maradona** (Argentina)	Argentinos Juniors
1981	**Zico** (Brazil)	Flamengo
1982	**Zico** (Brazil)	Flamengo
1983	**Socrates** (Brazil)	Corinthians
1984	**Enzo Francescoli** (Uruguay)	River Plate
1985	**Julio César Romero** (Brazil)	Fluminense
1986	**Diego Maradona** (Argentina)	Napoli
1987	**Carlos Valderrama** (Columbia)	Deportivo Cali
1988	**Rubén Paz** (Uruguay)	Racing Club
1989	**Diego Maradona** (Argentina)	Napoli
1990	**Diego Maradona** (Argentina)	Napoli
1991	**Gabriel Batistuta** (Argentina)	Boca Juniors
1992	**Diego Maradona** (Argentina)	Sevilla

By *El País* (Montevideo, Uruguay)

YEAR	WINNER	CLUB
1986	**Antonio Alzamendi** (Uruguay)	River Plate
1987	**Carlos Valderrama** (Colombia)	Deportivo Cali
1988	**Rubén Paz** (Uruguay)	Racing Club
1989	**Bebeto** (Brazil)	Vasco da Gama

YEAR	WINNER	CLUB
1990	**Raúl Amarilla** (Paraguay)	Olimpia
1991	**Oscar Ruggeri** (Argentina)	Vélez Sarsfield
1992	**Raí** (Brazil)	São Paulo
1993	**Carlos Valderrama** (Colombia)	Atlético Junior
1994	**Cafú** (Brazil)	São Paulo
1995	**Enzo Francescoli** (Uruguay)	River Plate
1996	**José Luis Chilavert** (Paraguay)	Vélez Sarsfield
1997	**Marcelo Salas** (Chile)	River Plate
1998	**Martín Palermo** (Argentina)	Boca Juniors
1999	**Javier Saviola** (Argentina)	River Plate
2000	**Romário** (Brazil)	Vasco da Gama
2001	**Juan Román Riquelme** (Argentina)	Boca Juniors
2002	**José Saturnino** Cardozo (Paraguay)	Club Deportivo Toluca
2003	**Carlos Tevez** (Argentina)	Boca Juniors
2004	**Carlos Tevez** (Argentina)	Boca Juniors
2005	**Carlos Tevez** (Argentina)	Corinthians
2006	**Matías Fernández** (Chile)	Colo Colo
2007	**Salvador Cabañas** (Paraguay)	CF América
2008	**Juan Sebastián Verón** (Argentina)	Estudiantes de La Plata
2009	**Juan Sebastián Verón** (Argentina)	Estudiantes de La Plata
2010	**Andrés d'Alessandro** (Argentina)	Internacional
2011	**Neymar** (Brazil)	Santos
2012	**Neymar** (Brazil)	Santos
2013	**Ronaldinho** (Brazil)	Atlético Mineiro
2014	**Teófilo Gutiérrez** (Colombia)	River Plate
2015	**Carlos Sánchez** (Uruguay)	River Plate
2016	**Miguel Borja** (Colombia)	Atlético Nacional
2017	**Luan** (Brazil)	Grêmio
2018	**Pity Martinez** (Argentina)	River Plate
2019	**Gabriel Barbosa** (Brazil)	Flamengo
2020	**Marinho** (Brazil)	Santos
2021	**Julian Alvarez** (Argentina)	River Plate

*After extra time   •After penalty shoot-out
#Final cancelled after plane carrying the Chapecoense players crashed. Title awarded to Chapecoense at the request of Atlético Nacional

AFRICA: CAF
INTERNATIONAL AWARDS
AFRICA CUP OF NATIONS WINNERS

YEAR	VENUE	WINNER	SCORE	RUNNER-UP
1957	Sudan	**Egypt**	4–0	Ethiopia
1959	United Arab Republic	**United Arab Republic**	2–1	Sudan
1962	Ethiopia	**Ethiopia**	4–2	United Arab* Republic
1963	Ghana	**Ghana**	3–0	Sudan
1965	Tunisia	**Ghana**	3–2	Tunisia*
1968	Ethiopia	**DR Congo**	1–0	Ghana
1970	Sudan	**Sudan**	1–0	Ghana
1972	Cameroon	**Republic of Congo**	3–2	Mali
1974	Egypt	**DR Congo**	2–2 (Replay 2–0)	Zambia*
1976	Ethiopia	**Morocco**	1–1 (group format)	Guinea
1978	Ghana	**Ghana**	2–0	Uganda
1980	Nigeria	**Nigeria**	3–0	Algeria
1982	Libya	**Ghana**	1–1 (7–6)•	Libya*
1984	Ivory Coast	**Cameroon**	3–1	Nigeria
1986	Egypt	**Egypt**	0–0 (5–4)•	Cameroon*

YEAR	VENUE	WINNER	SCORE	RUNNER-UP
1988	Morocco	**Cameroon**	1–0	Nigeria
1990	Algeria	**Algeria**	1–0	Nigeria
1992	Senegal	**Ivory Coast**	0–0 (11–10)•	Ghana*
1994	Tunisia	**Nigeria**	2–1	Zambia
1996	South Africa	**South Africa**	2–0	Tunisia
1998	Burkina Faso	**Egypt**	2–0	South Africa
2000	Nigeria and Ghana	**Cameroon**	2–2 (4–3)•	Nigeria*
2002	Mali	**Cameroon**	0–0 (3–2)•	Senegal*
2004	Tunisia	**Tunisia**	2–1	Morocco
2006	Egypt	**Egypt**	0–0 (4–2)•	Ivory Coast*
2008	Ghana	**Egypt**	1–0	Cameroon
2010	Angola	**Egypt**	1–0	Ghana
2012	Gabon Equatorial Guinea	**Zambia**	0–0 (8–7)•	Ivory Coast*
2013	South Africa	**Nigeria**	1–0	Burkina Faso
2015	Equatorial Guinea	**Ivory Coast**	0–0 (9–8)•	Ghana*
2017	Gabon	**Cameroon**	2–1	Egypt
2019	Egypt	**Algeria**	1–0	Senegal
2021	Cameroon	**Senegal**	0–0 (4–2)•	Egypt

AFRICA CUP OF NATIONS TOP SCORERS

NAME	GOALS	COUNTRY
Samuel Eto'o	18	Cameroon
Laurent Pokou	14	Côte d'Ivoire
Rashidi Yekini	13	Nigeria
Hassan El-Shazly	12	Egypt
Didier Drogba	11	Côte d'Ivoire
Hossam Hassan	11	Egypt
Patrick Mboma	11	Cameroon
Andre Ayew	10	Ghana
Kalusha Bwalya	10	Zambia
Ndaye Mulamba	10	DR Congo
Francileudo Santos	10	Tunisia
Joel Tiéhi	10	Côte d'Ivoire
Mengistu Worku	10	Ethiopia
Abdoulaye Traoré	9	Côte d'Ivoire
Manucho	9	Angola

NAME	GOALS	COUNTRY
Ahmed Hassan	8	Egypt
Asamoah Gyan	8	Ghana
Sadio Mane	8	Senegal
Seydou Keita	8	Mali
Taher Abouzaid	7	Egypt
Flávio	7	Angola
Frédéric Kanouté	7	Mali
Benni McCarthy	7	South Africa
Roger Milla	7	Cameroon
Jay-Jay Okocha	7	Nigeria
Ali Abo Gresha	7	Egypt
Osei Kofi	7	Ghana
Christopher Katongo	7	Zambia
Riyad Mahrez	7	Algeria

*After overtime   •After penalty shoot-out

THE RECORDS

CLUB AWARDS

AFRICAN CHAMPIONS LEAGUE WINNERS (Aggregate scores)

YEAR	WINNER	SCORE	RUNNER-UP
1964	**Oryx Douala**	2–1	Stade Malien
1966	**Stade Abidjan**	5–4	AS Real Bamako
1967	**Tout Puissant Englebert**	3–3	Asante Kotoko Ghana
	(Cup awarded to Tout Puissant Englebert)		
1968	**Tout Puissant Englebert**	6–4	Etoile Filante
1969	**Ismaily**	5–3	Tout Puissant Englebert
1970	**Asante Kotoko**	3–2	Tout Puissant Englebert
1971	**Asante Kotoko**	3–0	Canon Yaoundé
	Canon Yaoundé	2–0	Asante Kotoko
	Canon Yaoundé	1–0	Asante Kotoko
			(match abandoned Canon Yaoundé win)
1972	**Hafia (Conakry)**	7–4	Simba FC
1973	**AS Vita Club**	5–4	Asante Kotoko
1974	**CARA Brazzaville**	6–3	Mahalla Al–Kubra
1975	**Hafia (Conakry)**	3–1	Enugu Rangers
1976	**MC Algiers**	3–3	Hafia (Conakry)* (4–1)●
1977	**Hafia (Conakry)**	4–2	Hearts of Oak
1978	**Canon Yaoundé**	2–0	Hafia (Conakry)
1979	**Union Douala**	1–1	Hearts of Oak* (5–3)●
1980	**Canon Yaoundé**	5–2	AS Bilima
1981	**JE Tizi-Ouzou**	5–0	AS Vita Club
1982	**Al Ahly (Cairo)**	4–1	Asante Kotoko
1983	**Asante Kotoko**	1–0	Al Ahly (Cairo)
1984	**Zamalek**	3–0	Shooting Stars
1985	**FAR Rabat**	6–3	AS Bilima
1986	**Zamalek**	2–2	Africa Sports* (4–2)●
1987	**Al Ahly (Cairo)**	2–0	Al-Hilal
1988	**EP Setif**	4–1	Iwuanyanwu Owerri
1989	**Raja CA Casablanca**	1–1	Mouloudia Petroliers Oran* (4–2)●
1990	**JS Kabylie**	1–1	Nkana Red Devils* (5–3)●
1991	**Club Africain**	7–3	Nakivubo Villa SC
1992	**Wydad AC Casablanca**	2–0	Al-Hilal
1993	**Zamalek**	0–0	Asante Kotoko* (7–6)●
1994	**Espérance Tunis**	3–1	Zamalek
1995	**Orlando Pirates**	3–2	ASEC (Abidjan)
1996	**Zamalek**	3–3	Shooting Stars* (5–4)●
1997	**Raja CA Casablanca**	1–1	Obuasi Goldfields* (5–4)●
1998	**ASEC (Abidjan)**	4–2	Dynamos
1999	**Raja CA Casablanca**	0–0	Espérance Tunis* (4–3)●
2000	**Hearts of Oak**	5–2	Espérance Tunis
2001	**Al Ahly (Cairo)**	4–1	Mamelodi Sundowns

*After overtime   ●After penalty shoot-out

AFRICAN CHAMPIONS LEAGUE WINNERS (CONTINUED)

YEAR	WINNER	SCORE	RUNNER-UP	YEAR	WINNER	SCORE	RUNNER-UP
2002	**Zamalek**	1–0	Raja CA Casablanca	2012	**A Ahly**	3–2	ES Tunis
2003	**Enyimba**	2–1	Ismaily	2013	**Al Ahly**	3–1	Orlando Pirates
2004	**Enyimba**	3–3	Etoile du Sahel	2014	**ES Sétif**	3–3	AS Vita Club[+]
2005	**Al Ahly** (Cairo)	3–0	Etoile du Sahel	2015	**TP Mazembe**	4–1	USM Alger
2006	**Al Ahly** (Cairo)	2–1	CS Sfaxien	2016	**Mamelodi Sundowns**	3–1	Zamalek
2007	**Etoile du Sahel**	3–1	Al Ahly (Cairo)	2017	**Wydad Casablanca**	2–1	Al-Ahly
2008	**Al Ahly** (Cairo)	4–2	Coton Sport Garoua	2018	**Espérance de Tunis**	4–3	Al-Ahly
2009	**TP Mazembe**	2–2	Heartland	2019	**Espérance de Tunis**	1–1	Wydad Casablanca
2010	**TP Mazembe**	6–1	ES Tunis	2020	**Al Ahly**	2–1	Zamalek
2011	**ES Tunis**	1–0	Wydad Casablanca	2021	**Al-Ahly**	3–0	Kaizer Chiefs
				2022	**Wydad AC**	2–0	Al-Ahly

AFRICAN CUP WINNERS' CUP WINNERS

YEAR	WINNER	YEAR	WINNER	YEAR	WINNER
1975	**Tonnerre Yaoundé**	1985	**Al Ahly** (Cairo)	1995	**Jeunesse Sportive Kabylie**
1976	**Shooting Stars**	1986	**Al Ahly** (Cairo)	1996	**Al-Mokawloon**
1977	**Enugu Rangers**	1987	**Gor Mahia**	1997	**Etoile du Sahel**
1978	**Horoya AC** (Conakry)	1988	**Club Athlétique Bizerte**	1998	**Espérance Tunis**
1979	**Canon Yaoundé**	1989	**Al-Merreikh**	1999	**Africa Sports**
1980	**Tout Puissant Mazembe**	1990	**BCC Lions**	2000	**Zamalek**
1981	**Union Douala**	1991	**Power Dynamos**	2001	**Kaizer Chiefs**
1982	**Al-Mokawloon**	1992	**Africa Sports**	2002	**Wydad AC Casablanca**
1983	**Al-Mokawloon**	1993	**Al Ahly** (Cairo)	2003	**Etoile du Sahel**
1984	**Al Ahly** (Cairo)	1994	**Daring Club Motema Pemba**		

CAF CUP WINNERS

The CAF Cup merged with the Cup Winners' Cup in 2004 and was renamed the Confederation Cup.

YEAR	CLUB	COUNTRY	YEAR	CLUB	COUNTRY
1992	**Shooting Stars**	Nigeria	1998	**CS Sfaxien**	Tunisia
1993	**Stella Abidjan**	Ivory Coast	1999	**Etoile du Sahel**	Tunisia
1994	**Bendel Insurance**	Nigeria	2000	**JS Kabylie**	Algeria
1995	**Etoile du Sahel**	Tunisia	2001	**JS Kabylie**	Algeria
1996	**Kawkab AC Marrakech**	Morocco	2002	**JS Kabylie**	Algeria
1997	**Espérance de Tunis**	Tunisia	2003	**Raja CA Casablanca**	Morocco

CONFEDERATION CUP WINNERS

YEAR	CLUB	COUNTRY	YEAR	CLUB	COUNTRY
2004	**Hearts of Oak**	Ghana	2021	Raja Casablanca	Morocco
2005	**FAR Rabat**	Morocco	2022	RS Berkane	Morocco
2006	**Etoile du Sahel**	Tunisia			
2007	**CS Sfaxien**	Tunisia			
2008	**CS Sfaxien**	Tunisia			
2009	**Stade Malien**	Mali			
2010	**FUS Rabat**	Morocco			
2011	**MAS Fez**	Morocco			
2012	**AC Leopards**	DR Congo			
2013	**CS Sfaxien**	Tunisia			
2014	**Al Ahly**	Egypt			
2015	**Etoile du Sahel**	Tunisia			
2016	**TP Mazembe**	DR Congo			
2017	**TP Mazembe**	DR Congo			
2018	**Raja Casablanca**	Morocco			
2019	**Zamalek**	Egypt			
2020	**RS Berkane**	Morocco			

[+]Away goals

AFRICAN PLAYER OF THE YEAR 1970–1994

YEAR	PLAYER	CLUB	YEAR	PLAYER	CLUB
1970	**Salif Keita** (Mali)	Saint-Etienne	1982	**Thomas N'kono** (Cameroon)	RCD Español
1971	**Ibrahim Sunday** (Ghana)	Asante Kotoko	1983	**Mahmoud Al-Khatib** (Egypt)	Al Ahly
1972	**Chérif Souleymane** (Guinea)	Hafia Conakry	1984	**Théophile Abega** (Cameroon)	Toulouse
1973	**Tshimimu Bwanga** (DR Congo)	TP Mazembe	1985	**Mohamed Timoumi** (Morocco)	FAR Rabat
1974	**Paul Moukila** (Congo)	CARA Brazzaville	1986	**Zaki Badou** (Morocco)	RCD Mallorca
1975	**Ahmed Faras** (Morocco)	SC Chabab Mohammedia	1987	**Rabah Madjer** (Algeria)	Porto
			1988	**Kalusha Bwalya** (Zambia)	Cercle Brugge
1976	**Roger Milla** (Cameroon)	Canon Yaoundé	1989	**George Weah** (Liberia)	Monaco
1977	**Tarak Dhiab** (Tunisia)	Espérance de Tunis	1990	**Roger Milla** (Cameroon)	JS Saint-Pierroise
1978	**Abdul Razak** (Ghana)	Asante Kotoko	1991	**Abedi Pelé** (Ghana)	Olympique Marseille
1979	**Thomas N'kono** (Cameroon)	Canon Yaoundé	1992	**Abedi Pelé** (Ghana)	Olympique Marseille
1980	**Jean Manga Onguene** (Cameroon)	Canon Yaoundé	1993	**Abedi Pelé** (Ghana)	Olympique Marseille
1981	**Lakhdar Belloumi** (Algeria)	GCR Mascara	1994	**George Weah** (Liberia)	Paris Saint-Germain

CAF AFRICAN PLAYER OF THE YEAR 1992–PRESENT

YEAR	PLAYER	CLUB
1992	**Abedi Ayew Pelé** (Ghana)	Olympique Marseille
1993	**Rashidi Yekini** (Nigeria)	Vitória FC Setúbal
1994	**Emmanuel Amunike** (Nigeria)	Sporting CP / El Zamalek
1995	**George Weah** (Liberia)	Paris Saint-Germain / AC Milan
1996	**Nwankwo Kanu** (Nigeria)	Ajax / Inter
1997	**Victor Ikpeba** (Nigeria)	Monaco
1998	**Mustapha Hadji** (Morocco)	Deportivo La Coruña
1999	**Nwankwo Kanu** (Nigeria)	Arsenal
2000	**Patrick Mboma** (Cameroon)	Parma / Cagliari
2001	**El-Hadji Diouf** (Senegal)	Lens
2002	**El-Hadji Diouf** (Senegal)	Lens / Liverpool FC
2003	**Samuel Eto'o** (Cameroon)	Real Mallorca
2004	**Samuel Eto'o** (Cameroon)	Real Mallorca / Barcelona
2005	**Samuel Eto'o** (Cameroon)	Barcelona
2006	**Didier Drogba** (Côte d'Ivoire)	Chelsea
2007	**Frederic Kanouté** (Mali)	Sevilla
2008	**Emmanuel Adebayor** (Togo)	Arsenal
2009	**Didier Drogba** (Côte d'Ivoire)	Chelsea
2010	**Samuel Eto'o** (Cameroon)	Inter
2011	**Yaya Touré** (Côte d'Ivoire)	Manchester City
2012	**Yaya Touré** (Côte d'Ivoire)	Manchester City
2013	**Yaya Touré** (Côte d'Ivoire)	Manchester City
2014	**Yaya Touré** (Côte d'Ivoire)	Manchester City
2015	**Pierre-Emerick Aubameyang** (Gabon)	Borussia Dortmund
2016	**Riyad Mahrez** (Algeria)	Leicester City
2017	**Mohamed Salah** (Egypt)	Liverpool
2018	**Mohamed Salah** (Egypt)	Liverpool
2019	**Sadio Mane** (Senegal)	Liverpool
2022	**Sadio Mane** (Senegal)	Bayern Munich

Note: No CAF African Player of the Year award in 2020 and 2021

NORTH AND CENTRAL AMERICA AND THE CARIBBEAN: CONCACAF

CCCF AND CONCACAF CHAMPIONSHIPS

The CCCF (Confederación Centroamericana y del Caribe de Fútbol) was founded in 1938 and is the precursor of CONCACAF, which was formed in 1961. The precursors of the current Gold Cup tournament were held under the auspices of the CCCF, then CONCACAF. The last CCCF/CONCACAF Championship was held in 1971; afterward, the winner of the CONCACAF World Cup qualifying zone was considered CCCF champions. Since 1991, the tournament has been revitalized as the Gold Cup.

CCCF WINNERS

YEAR	WINNER
1941	**Costa Rica**
1943	**El Salvador**
1946	**Costa Rica**
1948	**Costa Rica**
1951	**Panama**
1953	**Costa Rica**
1955	**Costa Rica**
1957	**Haiti**
1960	**Costa Rica**
1961	**Costa Rica**

CONCACAF WINNERS

YEAR	WINNER
1963	**Costa Rica**
1965	**Mexico**
1967	**Guatemala**
1969	**Costa Rica**
1971	**Mexico**

WORLD CUP QUALIFYING CONCACAF WINNERS

YEAR	WINNER
1973	**Haiti**
1977	**Mexico**
1981	**Honduras**
1985	**Canada**
1989	**Costa Rica**

GOLD CUP

YEAR	VENUE	WINNER	SCORE	RUNNER-UP
1991	US	**US**	0–0	Honduras* (4–3)•
1993	Mexico and US	**Mexico**	4–0	US
1996	US	**Mexico**	2–0	Brazil U–23
1998	US	**Mexico**	1–0	US
2000	US	**Canada**	2–0	Colombia
2002	US	**US**	2–0	Costa Rica
2003	Mexico and US	**Mexico**	1–0	Brazil
2005	US	**US**	0–0	Panama* (3–1)•
2007	US	**US**	2–1	Mexico
2009	US	**Mexico**	5–0	US
2011	US	**Mexico**	4–2	US
2013	US	**US**	1–0	Panama
2015	US and Canada	**Mexico**	3–1	Jamaica
2017	US	**US**	2–1	Jamaica
2019	US/Costa Rica/Jamaica	**Mexico**	1–0	US
2021	US	**US**	1–0	Mexico*

*After overtime   •After penalty shoot-out

THE RECORDS

CONCACAF CHAMPIONS LEAGUE WINNERS

YEAR	WINNER
1962	**Guadalajara** (Mexico)
1963	**RC Haïtien** (Haiti)
1964	TOURNAMENT ABANDONED
1965	TOURNAMENT ABANDONED
1966	TOURNAMENT ABANDONED
1967	**Alianza** (El Salvador)
1968	**Deportivo** Toluca (Mexico)
1969	**Cruz Azul** (Mexico)
1970	**Cruz Azul** (Mexico)
1971	**Cruz Azul** (Mexico)
1972	**Olimpia** (Honduras)
1973	**Transvaal** (Suriname)
1974	**Municipal** (Guatemala)
1975	**Atlético Español** (Mexico)
1976	**CD Águila** (El Salvador)
1977	**Club América** (Mexico)
1978	**Universidad de Guadalajara** (Mexico)
	Comunicaciones (Guatemala)
	Defence Force * (Trinidad & Tobago)
1979	**FAS** (El Salvador)
1980	**UNAM** (Mexico)
1981	**Transvaal** (Suriname)
1982	**UNAM** (Mexico)
1983	**Atlante** (Mexico)
1984	**Violette** (Haiti)
1985	**Defence Force** (Trinidad & Tobago)
1986	**Alajuelense** (Costa Rica)
1987	**Club América** (Mexico)
1988	**Olimpia** (Honduras)
1989	**UNAM** (Mexico)
1990	**Club América** (Mexico)

YEAR	WINNER
1991	**Puebla** (Mexico)
1992	**Club América** (Mexico)
1993	**Saprissa** (Costa Rica)
1994	**Cartaginés** (Costa Rica)
1995	**Saprissa** (Costa Rica)
1996	**Cruz Azul** (Mexico)
1997	**Cruz Azul** (Mexico)
1998	**DC United** (US)
1999	**Necaxa** (Mexico)
2000	**Los Angeles Galaxy** (US)
2001	TOURNAMENT ABANDONED
2002	**Pachuca** (Mexico)
2003	**Deportivo Toluca** (Mexico)
2004	**Alajuelense** (Costa Rica)
2005	**Saprissa** (Costa Rica)
2006	**Club América** (Mexico)
2007	**Pachuca** (Mexico)
2008	**Pachuca** (Mexico)
2009	**Atlante** (Mexico)
2010	**Pachuca** (Mexico)
2011	**Monterrey** (Mexico)
2012	**Monterrey** (Mexico)
2013	**Monterrey** (Mexico)
2014	**Cruz Azul** (Mexico)
2015	**Club América** (Mexico)
2016	**Club América** (Mexico)
2017	**Pachuca** (Mexico)
2018	**Guadalajara** (Mexico)
2019	**Monterrey** (Mexico)
2020	**UANL** (Mexico)
2021	Monterrey (Mexico)
2022	Seattle Sounders (US)

CARIBBEAN NATIONS CUP / CARIBBEAN CHAMPIONSHIP WINNERS

Currently serving biannually as qualifying for the Gold Cup. From 1999 called the Caribbean Nations Cup.
From 2008, called the Caribbean Championship.

DATE	WINNER
1989	**Trinidad and Tobago**
1990	TOURNAMENT ABANDONED
1991	**Jamaica**
1992	**Trinidad and Tobago**
1993	**Martinique**
1994	**Trinidad and Tobago**
1995	**Trinidad and Tobago**
1996	**Trinidad and Tobago**
1997	**Trinidad and Tobago**
1998	**Jamaica**

DATE	WINNER
1999	**Trinidad and Tobago**
2000	NOT HELD
2001	**Trinidad and Tobago**
2002–2004	NOT HELD
2005	**Jamaica**
2006	NOT HELD
2007	**Haiti**
2008	**Jamaica**
2010	**Jamaica**
2012	**Cuba**
2014	**Jamaica**
2017	**Curaçao**

* Announced joint winners after tournament was canceled

ASIA: AFC
INTERNATIONAL AWARDS

ASIAN CUP WINNERS
(Until 1972, no final match was played)

YEAR	WINNERS	SCORE	RUNNER-UP
1956	South Korea	N/A	Israel
1960	South Korea	N/A	Israel
1964	Israel	N/A	India
1968	Iran	N/A	Burma
1972	Iran	2–1	South Korea
1976	Iran	1–0	Kuwait
1980	Kuwait	3–0	South Korea
1984	Saudi Arabia	2–0	China
1988	Saudi Arabia	0–0	South Korea* (4–3)•
1992	Japan	1–0	Saudi Arabia
1996	Saudi Arabia	0–0	UAE* (4–2)•
2000	Japan	3–1	China
2004	Japan	1–0	Saudi Arabia
2007	Iraq	1–0*	Australia
2011	Japan	1–0*	Australia
2015	Australia	2–1*	South Korea
2019	Qatar	3–1	Japan

ASIAN PLAYER OF THE YEAR

YEAR	PLAYER	COUNTRY
1988	Ahmed Radhi	Iraq
1989	Kim Joo-Sung	South Korea
1990	Kim Joo-Sung	South Korea
1991	KimJoo-Sung	South Korea
1992	NO AWARD	
1993	Kazuyoshi Miura	Japan
1994	Saeed Al-Owairan	Saudi Arabia
1995	Masami Ihara	Japan
1996	Khodadad Azizi	Iran
1997	Hidetoshi Nakata	Japan
1998	Hidetoshi Nakata	Japan
1999	Ali Daei	Iran
2000	Nawaf Al–Temyat	Saudi Arabia
2001	Fan Zhiyi	China
2002	Shinji Ono	Japan
2003	Mehdi Mahdavikia	Iran
2004	Ali Karimi	Iran
2005	Hamad Al–Montashari	Saudi Arabia
2006	Khalfan Ibrahim	Qatar
2007	Yasser Al-Qahtani	Saudi Arabia
2008	Server Djeparov	Uzbekistan
2009	Yasuhito End	Japan
2010	Saša Ognenovski	Australia
2011	Server Djeparov	Uzbekistan
2012	Lee Keun-Ho	South Korea
2013	Zheng Zhi	Guangzhou Evergrande
2014	Nasser Al-Shamrani	Al-Hilal
2015	Ahmed Khalil	Al-Hilal
2016	Omar Abdulrahman	Al-Ain
2017	Omar Kharbin	Syria
2018	Abdelkarim Hassan	Qatar
2019	Akram Afif	Qatar

ASIAN CUP TOP SCORERS

NAME	GOALS	COUNTRY
Ali Daei	14	Iran
Lee Dong-Gook	10	South Korea
Almoez Ali	9	Qatar
Ali Mabkhout	9	UAE
Naohiro Takahara	9	Japan
Jasem Al-Huwaidi	8	Kuwait
Younis Mahmoud	8	Iraq
Behtash Fariba	7	Iran
Hossein Kalani	7	Iran
Choi Soon-Ho	7	South Korea
Faisal Al-Dakhil	7	Kuwait
Alexander Geynrikh	6	Uzbekistan
Sardar Azmoun	6	Iran
Ahmed Khalil	6	UAE

NAME	GOALS	COUNTRY
Yasser Al-Qahtani	6	Saudi Arabia
Tim Cahill	6	Australia
A'ala Hubail	5	Bahrain
Ali Karimi	5	Iran
Ali Jabbari	5	Iran
Akinori Nishizawa	5	Japan
Woo Sang-Kwon	5	South Korea
Hwang Sun-Hong	5	South Korea
Nahum Stelmach	5	Israel
Ismail Abdullatif	5	Bahrain
Chung Hae-Won	5	South Korea
Koo Ja-Cheol	5	South Korea
Shao Jiayi	5	China
Ali Mabkhout	5	UAE

*After overtime   •After penalty shoot-out

CLUB AWARDS

AFC CHAMPIONS LEAGUE WINNERS

(The final has been played over two legs between 2003 and 2008 and from 2013 to 2019.)

YEAR	WINNER	SCORE	RUNNER-UP
1967	**Hapoel**	2–1	Selangor
1969	**Maccabi**	1–0	Yangzee
1970	**Esteghlal**	2–1	Hapoel
1971	**Maccabi**	walkover	Al-Shorta
1986	**Daewoo Royals**	3–1	Al-Ahly
1987	**Furukawa**	group stage win	Al-Hilal
1988	**Yomiuri**	walkover	Al-Hilal
1989	**Al-Saad**	3–3	Al-Rasheed
		Al-Saad win on away goals	
1990	**Liaoning**	3–2	Nissan
1991	**Esteghlal**	2–1	Liaoning
1991	**Al-Hilal**	1–1	Esteghlal* (4–3)●
1993	**PAS**	1–0	Al-Shabab
1994	**Thai Farmers Bank**	2–1	Omani Club
1995	**Thai Farmers Bank**	1–0	Al-Arabi
1995	**Cheonan Ilhwa Chunma**	1–0	Al-Nasr
1997	**Pohang Steelers**	2–1	Cheonan Ilhwa Chunma** (4–3)●
1998	**Pohang Steelers**	0–0	Dalian Wanda
1999	**Jubilo**	2–1	Esteghlal
2000	**Al-Hilal**	3–2	Jubilo Iwata
2001	**Suwon Samsung Bluewings**	1–0	Jubilo Iwata
2002	**Suwon Samsung Bluewings**	0–0	Anyang LG Cheetahs** (4–2)●
2003	**Al-Ain**	2–1	BEC Tero Sasana
2004	**Al-Ittihad**	6–3	Seongnam Ilhwa Chunma
2005	**Al-Ittihad**	5–3	Al-Ain
2006	**Jeonbuk Hyundai Motors**	3–2	Al-Karama
2007	**Urawa Red Diamonds**	3–1	Sepahan
2008	**Gamba**	5–0	Adelaide
2009	**Pohang Steelers**	2–1	Al-Ittihad
2010	**Seongnam Ilhwa Chunma**	3–1	Zob Ahan
2011	**Al-Saad**	2–2	Jeonbuk Hyundai Motors* (4–2)●
2012	**Ulsan Hyundai**	3–0	Al-Ahli SC
2013	**Guangzhou Evergrande**	3–3	FC Seoul+
2014	**Western Sydney Wanderers**	1–0	Al-Hilal
2015	**Guangzhou Evergrande**	1–0	Al-Hilal
2016	**Jeonbuk Hyundai Motors**	3–2	Al-Ain
2017	**Urawa Red Diamonds**	2–1	Al-Hilal
2018	**Kashima Antlers**	2–0	Persepolis
2019	**Al-Hilal**	3–0	Urawa Red Diamonds
2020	**Ulsan Hyundai**	2–1	Persepolis
2021	**Al-Hilal**	2–0	Pohang Steelers

** After sudden-death overtime   *After overtime   ●After penalty shoot-out   +Away goals

OCEANIA: OFC

INTERNATIONAL AWARDS

OFC NATIONS CUP WINNERS

YEAR	WINNER	SCORE	RUNNER-UP
1973	New Zealand	2–0	Tahiti
1980	Australia	4–2	Tahiti
1996	Australia	11–0	Tahiti
1998	New Zealand	1–0	Australia
2000	Australia	2–0	New Zealand
2002	New Zealand	1–0	Australia
2004	Australia	11–1	Solomon Islands
2008	New Zealand	win	New Caledonia
2012	Tahiti	1–0	New Caledonia
2016	New Zealand	0–0	Papua New Guinea* (4–2)•

CLUB AWARDS

OFC CHAMPIONS LEAGUE WINNERS

YEAR	WINNER	SCORE	RUNNER-UP
1987	Adelaide City	1–1	Mount Wellington* (4–1)•
1999	South Melbourne	5–1	Nadi
2001	Wollongong City Wolves	1–0	Tafea
2005	Sydney FC	2–0	AS Magenta
2006	Auckland City	3–1	AS Piraé
2007	Waitakere United	2–2	4R Electrical Ba (Waitakere United win on away goals)
2008	Waitakere United	6–3	Kossa FC
2009	Auckland City	9–4	Koloale FC Honiara
2010	PRK Hekari United	4–2	Waitakere United
2011	Auckland City	6–1	Amicale FC
2012	Auckland City	3–1	Tefana
2013	Auckland City	2–1	Waitakere United
2014	Auckland City	3–2	Amicale FC
2015	Auckland City	1–1	Team Wellington* (4–3)•
2016	Auckland City	3–0	Team Wellington
2018	Team Wellington	10–3	Lautoka
2019	Hienghene Sport	1-0	AS Magenta
2022	Auckland City	3-0	Venus

OCEANIA PLAYER OF THE YEAR

YEAR	PLAYER	COUNTRY	YEAR	PLAYER	COUNTRY
1988	Frank Farina	Australia	2000	Mark Viduka	Australia
1989	Wynton Rufer	New Zealand	2001	Harry Kewell	Australia
1990	Wynton Rufer	New Zealand	2002	Brett Emerton	Australia
1991	Robert Slater	Australia	2003	Harry Kewell	Australia
1992	Wynton Rufer	New Zealand	2004	Tim Cahill	Australia
1993	Robert Slater	Australia	2005	Marama Vahirua	Tahiti
1994	Aurelio Vidmar	Australia	2006	Ryan Nelsen	New Zealand
1995	Christian Karembeu	New Caledonia	2007	Shane Smeltz	New Zealand
1996	Paul Okon	Australia	2008	Shane Smeltz	New Zealand
1997	Mark Bosnich	Australia	2009	Ivan Vicelich	New Zealand
1998	Christian Karembeu	New Caledonia	2010	Ryan Nelsen	New Zealand
1999	Harry Kewell	Australia	2011	Bertrand Kai	New Caledonia
			2012	Marco Rojas	New Zealand
			2013–2014	NO AWARD	
			2015	Ryan Thomas	New Zealand

*After overtime   •After penalty shoot-out

INDEX

INDEX

FURTHER READING

YEARBOOKS AND ENCYCLOPEDIAS

Ballard, J. and Suff, P., **The Dictionary of Football**, Boxtree, Basingstoke, 1999.

Creswell, P. and Evans, S., **European Football: A Fan's Handbook**, Rough Guides, London 2000.

Deloitte and Touche Annual Review of Football Finance, Manchester, annual.

Il Calcio Italiano Analisi Economico, Deloitte and Touche, Milan, annual

Hammond M. (ed.), **The European Football Yearbook**, Sports Projects, Birmingham, annual.

Jelinek, R., and Tomes, J., **Prvni Fotbalovy Atlas Sveta**, Infokart, Prague, 2002.

Mantz, G., **The Asian Football Yearbook**, Cleethorpes, Soccer Books Ltd, annual.

Mantz, G., **The South American Football Yearbook**, Cleethorpes, Soccer Books Ltd, annual.

Oliver, G., **Almanack of World Football**, Harpastum Publishing, London, annual.

Oliver, G., **The Guinness Book of World Soccer**, 2nd Edition, Guinness, Enfield, 1995.

Radnedge, K., **The Complete Encyclopedia of Soccer**, Carlton Books, London, 2012.

Rollin, J., **Sky Sports Football Yearbook**, Headline Books, London, annual.

FA Premier League National Fan Survey, Sir Norman Chester Centre for Football Research, Leicester, annual survey.

Van Hoof, S., Parr, M., and Yamenetti, C., **The North and Latin American Football Guide**, Heart Books, Rijmenam, annual.

MAGAZINES AND NEWSPAPERS

African Football, AS, A Bola, Calcio 2000, Champions, L'Equipe, FourFourTwo, France Football, La Gazzetta dello Sport, Kicker, Lance, Marca, Placar, Voetbal International, When Saturday Comes, World Soccer, Soccer America

OVERVIEWS, GLOBAL HISTORIES, COLLECTIONS

Armstrong, G. and Giulianotti, R. (eds.), **Entering the Field: New Perspectives on World Football**, Berg, Oxford, 1997.

Armstrong, G. and Giulianotti, R. (eds.), **Football Culture and Identities**, Macmillan, Basingstoke, 1998.

Armstrong, G. and Giulianotti, R. (eds.), **Fear and Loathing in World Football**, Berg, Oxford, 2001.

Finn, G. and Giulianotti, R. (eds.), **Football Cultures: Local Conflicts, Global Visions**, Cass, London, 2000.

Giulianotti, R., **Football: A Sociology of the Global Game**, Polity Press, Cambridge, 1999.

Glanville, B., **The Story of the World Cup**, Faber, London, 2014.

Inglis, S., **The Football Grounds of England and Wales**, Willow, London, 1983.

Inglis, S., **The Football Grounds of Europe**, Willow, London, 1990.

Inglis, S., **Sightlines: A Stadium Odyssey**, Yellow Jersey, London, 2001.

Kuper, S., **Soccer against the Enemy**, Nation Books, New York, 2010.

Murray, B., **The World's Game: A History of Soccer**, University of Illinois Press, Urbana, 1998.

Sugden, J. and Tomlinson, A., **Hosts and Champions: Soccer Cultures, National Identities and the USA World Cup**, Arena, Aldershot, 1994.

Walvin, J., **The People's Game: The History of Football Revisited**, Mainstream, London, 2014.

Wilson, Jonathan, **Inverting the Pyramid**, Weidenfeld and Nicolson, 2018.

Goldblatt, David, **The Ball is Round**, Penguin, 2007

BRAZIL

Bellos, A., **Futbol: The Brazilian Way of Life**, Bloomsbury, London, 2014.

Lever, J., **Soccer Madness**, Waveland Press, Illinois, 1995.

FRANCE

Ruhn, C. (ed.), **Le Foot: The Legends of French Football**, Abacus, London, 2000.

Holt, R., **Sport and Society in Modern France**, Macmillan, Basingstoke, 1981.

ITALY

Manna, A. and Gibbs, M., **The Day Italian Football Died**, Breedon Books, Derby, 2000.

Parks, T., **A Season with Verona**, Vintage, London, 2003.

JAPAN

Birchall, J., **Ultra Nippon: How Japan Reinvented Football**, Headline, London 2001.

Moffet, S., **Japanese Rules: Why Japan Needed Football and How It Got It**, Yellow Jersey, London, 2002.

LATIN AMERICA

Mason, T., **Passion of the People? Football in South America**, Verso, London, 1995.

Taylor, C., **The Beautiful Game: A Journey Through Latin American Football**, Phoenix, London, 1999.

NETHERLANDS

Winner, D., **Brilliant Orange: The Neurotic Genius of Dutch Soccer**, The Overlook Press, New York, 2008.

SPAIN

Ball, P., **Morbo: The Story of Spanish Football**, WSC Books Ltd, London, 2011.

Burns, J., **Barça: A People's Passion**, Bloomsbury, London, 2016.

USSR

Edleman, R., **Serious Fun: a History of Spectator Sports in the USSR**, Oxford University Press, Oxford, 1993.

WEBSITES

Women, USA
www.ussoccer.com/teams/uswnt

Women, England
www.thefa.com/womens-girls-football

UEFA
www.uefa.com

FIFA
www.fifa.com

MLSsoccer.com - The Official Site of Major League Soccer
www.mlssoccer.com

ACKNOWLEDGMENTS

Dorling Kindersley would like to thank the following organizations and people for their help in the preparation of this book:
Kevin Pettman, consultant

Marc Staples, for additional production editorial work; Chris Stone, for additional editorial work; Foster + Partners Ltd, Hiroshi Hara + ATELIER Ø, and Souto Moura Arq. S.A. (Porto); Shumina Begum, Matt Robbins, Sarah Arnold, Bobby Birchall, Adam Clifton, and Mark Lloyd, for design assistance; Mikhail Sipovich at Colours Of Football and Paul Wootton, for input on the artworks; Ian D. Crane, for the index; Ishita Jha, Tina Jindal, and Suefa Lee, for editorial assistance; Yashashvi Choudhary, for additional assistance; Rabia Ahmad, Nobina Chakravorty, Arshti Narang, and Anjali Sachar, for design assistance; Jenny Baskaya, for ordering agency images and compiling the picture credits; Harish Agarwal, for pre-production assistance; Mohammad Rizwan, for production assistance; Surya Sankash Sarangi, for picture research.

For Cooling Brown Ltd
Creative director: Arthur Brown
Design: Tish Jones, Alistair Plumb, Jon Morgan
Editorial: Richard Gilbert, Philip Morgan, Phil Hunt, Jemima Dunne, Dawn Bates
Production: Peter Cooling

For eighth edition
DK DELHI: Senior Editor Dharini Ganesh; Project Art Editor Anjali Sachar; Art Editor Nobina Chakravorty; DTP Designer Jaypal Chauhan; Pre-production Manager Balwant Singh; Senior Managing Editor Rohan Sinha; Managing Art Editor Sudakshina Basu; Editorial Head Glenda Fernandes; Design Head Malavika Talukder.

DK LONDON: Senior Art Editor Gadi Farfour; Production Editor Kavita Varma; Senior US Editor Megan Douglass; Senior Production Controller Rachel Ng; Jacket Designer Akiko Kato; Jacket Design Development Manager Sophia MTT; Managing Editor Gareth Jones; Senior Managing Art Editor Lee Griffiths; Art Director Karen Self; Design Director Phil Ormerod; Associate Publishing Director Liz Wheeler; Publishing Director Jonathan Metcalf.

For this revised edition, DK India would like to thank Anita Kakar for editorial assistance, Anjali Sachar for design assistance, and Deepak Negi for picture research assistance.

PICTURE CREDITS